Six Ideas That Shaped Physics

Unit E: Electric and Magnetic Fields Are Unified

Third Edition (Draft)

Thomas A. Moore

Boston Burr Ridge, IL Dubuque, IA New York San Francisco St. Louis
Bangkok Bogotá Caracas Lisbon London Madrid
Mexico City Milan New Delhi Seoul Singapore Sydney Taipei Toronto

The McGraw·Hill Companies

SIX IDEAS THAT SHAPED PHYSICS
UNIT E: ELECTRIC AND MAGNETIC FIELDS ARE UNIFIED

3 4 5 6 7 8 9 0 DIG DIG 0 9 8 7 6

ISBN-13: 978-0-07-354099-3
ISBN-10: 0-07-354099-4

Editor: Shirley Grall
Production Editor: Carrie Braun
Printer/Binder: Digital Impressions

Electromagnetic Constants

Coulomb constant	k	$8.99 \times 10^9\ \text{N}\cdot\text{m}^2/\text{C}^2$
	$4\pi k/c$	$377\ \Omega = 377\ \text{N}\cdot\text{m}\cdot\text{s}/\text{C}^2$
Permittivity constant	ε_0	$8.85 \times 10^{-12}\ \text{C}^2\cdot\text{N}^{-1}\cdot\text{m}^{-2} = (4\pi k)^{-1}$
Permeability constant	μ_0	$1.26 \times 10^{-6}\ \text{N}\cdot\text{s}^2/\text{C}^2 = 4\pi k/c^2 = 1/\varepsilon_0 c^2$
Conductivity:		
Silver		$6.3 \times 10^7\ (\Omega\cdot\text{m})^{-1}$
Copper		$5.9 \times 10^7\ (\Omega\cdot\text{m})^{-1}$
Nichrome		$6.7 \times 10^5\ (\Omega\cdot\text{m})^{-1}$

Electromagnetic Units and Conversion Factors

$1\ \text{C} = 1$ coulomb = total charge of 6.242×10^{18} protons
$1\ \text{N/C}$ = units for the electric and magnetic fields = V/m
$1\ \text{T} = 1$ tesla $= 1\ \text{N}\cdot\text{s}\cdot\text{C}^{-1}\cdot\text{m}^{-1}$, a magnetic field unit equivalent to 299.792458 MN/C
$1\ \text{G} = 1$ gauss = another unit for the magnetic field, equivalent to 10^{-4} T or about 30 kN/C
$1\ \text{V} = 1\ \text{volt} = 1\ \text{J/C} = 1\ \text{N}\cdot\text{m/C} = 1\ \text{kg}\cdot\text{m}^2\cdot\text{s}^{-2}\cdot\text{C}^{-1}$ = unit of energy per unit charge
$1\ \text{A} = 1$ ampere $= 1\ \text{C/s}$ = unit of current
$1\ \Omega = 1\ \text{ohm} = 1\ \text{V/A} = 1\ \text{J}\cdot\text{s/C}^2 = 1\ \text{N}\cdot\text{m}\cdot\text{s/C}^2 = 1\ \text{kg}\cdot\text{m}^2\cdot\text{s}^{-1}\cdot\text{C}^{-2}$ = unit of resistance
$1\ \text{W} = 1\ \text{watt} = 1\ \text{J/s} = 1\ \text{V}\cdot\text{A} = 1\ \text{kg}\cdot\text{m}^2/\text{s}^3$ = unit of power
$1\ \text{F} = 1\ \text{farad} = 1\ \text{C/V} = 1\ \text{C}^2/\text{J} = \text{C}^2\cdot\text{s}^2\cdot\text{m}^{-1}\cdot\text{kg}^{-1}$ = unit of capacitance
$1\ \text{H} = 1\ \text{henry} = 1\ \Omega\cdot\text{s} = \text{kg}\cdot\text{m}^2/\text{C}^2$ = unit of inductance
Units of conductivity = $\text{C}^2\cdot\text{s}\cdot\text{m}^{-3}\cdot\text{kg}^{-1} = \text{A}\cdot\text{m}^2\cdot(\text{N/C})^{-1} = (\Omega\cdot\text{m})^{-1}$
Units of current density = $\text{A/m}^2 = \text{C/m}^3\cdot(\text{m/s})$
$\vec{B}$ is the magnetic field measured in teslas
$\vec{\mathbb{B}} = c\vec{B}$ is magnetic field measured in newtons per coulomb

Useful Integrals

$$\int \frac{dx}{(x^2+a^2)^{1/2}} = \ln[x + (x^2+a^2)^{1/2}]$$

$$\int \frac{dx}{x^2+a^2} = \frac{1}{a}\tan^{-1}\left(\frac{x}{a}\right)$$

$$\int \frac{dx}{(x^2+a^2)^{3/2}} = \frac{1}{a^2}\frac{x}{(x^2+a^2)^{1/2}}$$

$$\int \frac{x\,dx}{(x^2+a^2)^{1/2}} = (x^2+a^2)^{1/2}$$

$$\int \frac{x\,dx}{(x^2+a^2)^{3/2}} = -\frac{1}{(x^2+a^2)^{1/2}}$$

$$\int \frac{x^2\,dx}{(x^2+a^2)^{3/2}} = -\frac{x}{(x^2+a^2)^{1/2}} + \ln[x + (x^2+a^2)^{1/2}]$$

Maxwell's Equations (differential form)

$$\text{div}(\vec{E}) = \frac{\rho}{\varepsilon_0}$$

$$\text{div}(\vec{\mathbb{B}}) = 0$$

$$\vec{\text{curl}}(\vec{\mathbb{B}}) - \frac{1}{c}\frac{\partial \vec{E}}{\partial t} = \frac{1}{\varepsilon_0}\left(\frac{\vec{J}}{c}\right)$$

$$\vec{\text{curl}}(\vec{E}) + \frac{1}{c}\frac{\partial \vec{\mathbb{B}}}{\partial t} = 0$$

(integral form)

$$\oint \vec{E}\cdot d\vec{A} = \frac{Q_{enc}}{\varepsilon_0}$$

$$\oint \vec{\mathbb{B}}\cdot d\vec{A} = 0$$

$$\oint \vec{\mathbb{B}}\cdot d\vec{S} - \frac{1}{c}\frac{\partial}{\partial t}\int \vec{E}\cdot d\vec{A} = \frac{1}{\varepsilon_0}\left(\frac{i_{enc}}{c}\right)$$

$$\oint \vec{E}\cdot d\vec{S} + \frac{1}{c}\frac{\partial}{\partial t}\int \vec{\mathbb{B}}\cdot d\vec{A} = 0$$

Contents: Unit E

Electric and Magnetic Fields Are Unified

Chapter E12

Chapter E13

Chapter E14

Chapter E15

Chapter E16

Dedication

To Joyce
The light of my life

Photo credits:

Cover, Title page		**NASA photo***
Chapter E1:	E1.3	© McGraw-Hill Higher Education / Photo by Chris Hammond
	E1.10	© McGraw-Hill Higher Education / Photo by Chris Hammond
Chapter E2:	E2.7	© McGraw-Hill Higher Education / Photo by Chris Hammond
	E2.10	Photo by David Haley and Tom Moore
Chapter E5:	E5.3	© McGraw-Hill Higher Education / Photo by Chris Hammond
	p. 99	© McGraw-Hill Higher Education / Photo by Chris Hammond
Chapter E6:	E6.2	Courtesy PASCO Scientific
	p.3	© McGraw-Hill Higher Education / Photo by Chris Hammond
Chapter E7:	E7.3	Photo by David Haley and Tom Moore
	E7.11	Courtesy PASCO Scientific
	E7.13	Courtesy Stanford Linear Accelerator Center, Stanford University
	E7.14a	Photo by Lee Snyder, Geophysical Institute, University of Alaska, Fairbanks
	E7.14b	NASA photo*
Chapter E8:	E8.4	Photo by David Haley and Tom Moore
Chapter E9:	E9.1	Photo by David Haley and Tom Moore
	E9.8	Courtesy of Dr. R. D. Gomez
	E9.12	Courtesy PASCO Scientific
Chapter E11:	E11.9	NASA photo*
Chapter E12:	E12.7	Courtesy of Gepco Wire and Cable
Chapter E14:	E14.1	Photo by David Haley and Tom Moore
	E14.6	© McGraw-Hill Higher Education / Photo by Chris Hammond
	E14.8	© McGraw-Hill Higher Education / Photo by Chris Hammond
	p. 293	Courtesy Sargent-Welch / Central Scientific Company
Chapter E15:	E15.1a	NOAA photo*
	E15.1b	NASA Dryden Flight Research Center, photo by Dr. Leonard Weinstein*
	E15.1b	NASA, Kirk Borne (ST Sci)*
	E15.8	Courtesy PASCO Scientific
Chapter E16:	E16.4a	Photo by David Haley
	E16.4b	Photo by David Haley
	E16.4c	© McGraw-Hill Higher Education / Photo by Chris Hammond
	E16.4d	NASA photo*

*NASA and NOAA photos are all public domain

Preface

Introduction

Opening comments about *Six Ideas That Shaped Physics*

This volume is one of six that together comprise the text materials for *Six Ideas That Shaped Physics*, a fundamentally new approach to the two- or three semester calculus-based introductory physics course. *Six Ideas That Shaped Physics* was created in response to a call for innovative curricula offered by the Introductory University Physics Project (IUPP), which subsequently supported its early development. In its present form, the course represents the culmination of more than a decade of development, testing, and evaluation at a number of colleges and universities nationwide.

This course is based on the premise that innovative approaches to the presentation of topics and to classroom activities can help students learn more effectively. I have completely rethought from the ground up the presentation of every topic, taking advantage of research into physics education wherever possible, and have done nothing just because "that is the way it has always been done." Recognizing that physics education research has consistently underlined the importance of active learning, I have also provided tools supporting multiple opportunities for active learning both inside and outside the classroom. This text also strongly emphasizes the process of building and critiquing physical models and using them in realistic settings. Finally, I have sought to emphasize contemporary physics and view even classical topics from a thoroughly contemporary perspective.

I have not sought to "dumb down" the course to make it more accessible. Rather, my goal has been to help students become *smarter*. I intentionally set higher-than-usual standards for sophistication in physical thinking, and have then used a range of innovative approaches and classroom structures to help even average students reach this standard. I don't believe that the mathematical level required by these books is significantly different from that in most university physics texts, but I do ask students to step beyond rote thinking patterns to develop flexible, powerful conceptual reasoning and model-building skills. My experience and that of other users are that normal students in a wide range of institutional settings can, with appropriate support and practice, meet these standards.

The six volumes of the *Six Ideas* text

The six volumes that comprise the complete *Six Ideas* course are:

Unit C (**C**onservation Laws):	Conservation Laws Constrain Interactions
Unit N (**N**ewtonian Mechanics):	The Laws of Physics Are Universal
Unit R (**R**elativity):	The Laws of Physics Are Frame-Independent
Unit E (**E**lectricity and Magnetism):	Electricity and Magnetism Are Unified
Unit Q (**Q**uantum Physics):	Matter Behaves Like Waves
Unit T (**T**hermal Physics):	Some Processes Are Irreversible

I have listed these units in the order that I recommend they be taught, though other orderings are possible. At Pomona, we teach the first three units during the first semester and the last three during the second semester of a yearlong course, but one can easily teach the six units in three quarters or even over three semesters if one wants a slower pace. The chapters of all these texts have been designed to correspond to what one might realistically discuss in a single 50-minute class session at the *highest possible pace:* while one might design a syllabus that covers chapters at a slower rate, one should *not* try to discuss more than one chapter in a 50-minute class.

For more information than I can include in this short preface about the goals of the *Six Ideas* course, its organizational structure (and the rationale behind that structure), the evidence for its success, and information about how to cut and/or rearrange material, as well as many other resources for both teachers and students, please visit the *Six Ideas* web site (see the next section).

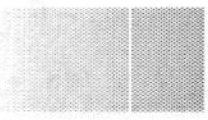

Important Resources

Instructions about how to use this text

I have summarized important information about how to read and use this text in an *Introduction for Students* immediately preceding chapter E1. Please look this over, particularly if you have not seen other volumes of this text. The *Six Ideas* web site contains a wealth of up-to-date information about the course that I think both instructors and students will find very useful. The URL is

The *Six Ideas* website

www.physics.pomona.edu/sixideas/

Essential computer programs

One of the most important resources available at this site are a number of computer applets that illustrate important concepts and aid in difficult calculations. In several places, this unit draws on some of these programs, and past experience indicates that students learn the ideas much more effectively when these programs are used both in the classroom and for homework. These applets are freeware and are available for both the Mac (OS X) and Windows operating systems.

Some Notes Specifically About Unit E

The goal of this unit

The fundamental goal of unit E is to provide a compact and modern introduction to electromagnetic field theory that takes students from Coulomb's law to electromagnetic waves in as short a time as possible. I have written this unit partly because I have been profoundly dissatisfied with most traditional treatments of this material, which tend to treat topics as essentially unrelated bits of "stuff to know" instead of helping students perceive the underlying shape and beauty of the theory. Therefore, I have sought to provide a carefully logical and sequential development of this material whose ultimate goal is to have students appreciate why electricity and magnetism *must be unified* if their field theories are to make sense in the context of the principle of relativity. The climax of the unit is therefore in chapters E12 and E13, where we see how relativity and logical necessity link the electric and magnetic fields and constrain the form of Maxwell's equations. This is an admittedly 21st-century perspective on the topic, not a development that parallels the historical development of the discipline. However, I consider this a strength: I strongly believe that 21st-century hindsight in this case makes the structure of electromagnetic field theory much clearer and easier for students to grasp. Moreover, I think that it provides a more interesting and exciting story line than history does.

Because time in this unit is so tight (to make room for contemporary physics in other units), I have tried to streamline it as much as possible, keeping the focus on what moves the main argument forward rather than on interesting but tangential material. Someone comparing this unit to a traditional text may find it somewhat sparse: I intentionally ignore topics such as dielectrics, AC circuits, *LRC* circuits, mutual induction, diamagnetism, paramagnetism, superconductivity, and so on. Rather than "cover" such a laundry list of (admittedly fascinating) topics, I have tried to focus on the logic and interconnectedness of the material I do present as well as to take the time to explicitly teach important problem-solving skills in circuit analysis and field calculations. Some of these topics are treated in homework problems for instructors and students who are interested. At Pomona, we also flesh out the brief treatment of electric circuits by using a sequence of laboratory exercises designed to challenge misconceptions and help students practice circuit analysis skills.

This unit is a perennially difficult one for students. In this revision particularly, my goal has also been to make the mathematics as simple and as straightforward as possible, and to make liberal use of concrete visual and mechanical models to make the abstractions easier to understand. Even so, it is probably inevitable that students will find this unit to be the most difficult of the six.

Nontraditional aspects of this unit

Instructors will note several nontraditional aspects about the way that I approach the material. First, I avoid the use of field line diagrams. Published articles have recently discussed why two-dimensional field line diagrams can be inaccurate and misleading and how students routinely misunderstand these diagrams (for example, by assuming that charges will move along the field lines). I have been convinced by my colleagues Bruce Sherwood and Ruth Chabay that these diagrams are not really helpful to students, and that it is more important to spend time developing the field arrow representation of electric and magnetic fields. This representation can be awkward to draw, but its interpretation is straightforward and less prone to misunderstanding. Moreover, it focuses students on, rather than distracting them from, the basic mathematical model of the fields.

In this edition, I have expressed most of equations using the traditional constants ε_0 and μ_0 , partly because I saw that majors at Pomona were having trouble linking their work in the introductory class with later treatments of the subject. However, I do strive keep the link between these constants and the Coulomb constant k in view throughout. There are multiple reasons for doing this. The Coulomb constant has an easily remembered magnitude in SI units, and it is easier to understand its conceptual role (especially if one is not spending much time with dielectrics or magnetic materials). However, the most important reason is that using keeping the Coulomb constant in view helps clarify the links between electric fields, magnetic fields, and gravitational fields, and so it serves the goal of enabling students to develop a more powerful understanding of the field concept.

Starting in chapter E7, I use the symbol $\bar{\boldsymbol{B}} = c\boldsymbol{B}$ (read "B-bar") to stand for the magnetic field expressed in newtons per coulomb (N/C). This notation gives one all the advantages of gaussian units in simplifying equations and clearly displaying the link between electric and magnetic fields *without* abandoning any of the more familiar and useful SI electrical units. I still describe B as being measured in teslas and describe the definition of that unit (along with the gauss), but my premise here is that the tesla is the electromagnetic unit that is both least familiar and least useful to students, so if it is effectively replaced by the newton per coulomb, the cost is more than made up by the gain.

Instructors may also find that I take unconventional approaches to the use of symmetry in magnetic fields, to developing the time-dependent terms in Maxwell's equations, and to explaining the wave equation and how electromagnetic fields satisfy the wave equation. I hope that these approaches make these perennially difficult topics more straightforward for students.

Changes in this edition

symmetry into the chapters on electric field and magnetic field calculations, partly to make room for the other expansions but also so that students can become used to symmetry arguments *before* facing Gauss's law and Ampere's law (instead of dealing with all these difficult topics simultaneously).

I also compressed the chapters on current and circuits to two chapters instead of three, to make room for other more important expansions. The material I regret losing most was that on electrical safety: I hope that instructors will spend some class time dealing with this topic (perhaps in the form of active-learning exercises that use circuit concepts to explore this issue).

In this edition, I have also returned to highlighting the *differential* form of Maxwell's equations. However, I have *greatly* simplified the treatment of these equations compared to their previous appearance in the first edition, and (by rearranging material and cutting the chapter devoted to the relativistic field transformation) have made room for an entire new chapter on the integral form of the equations and their use. I think that this compromise recognizes the strengths of both forms of the equations, and (even better) helps students understand the connection between the forms. I have also greatly simplified the development of the time-dependent terms in Maxwell's equations, drawing on more realistic examples. Finally, I have also improved and made more rigorous the treatment of the wave equation in chapter E15.

The instructor can play an important and positive role in helping all these approaches succeed pedagogically by spending the time required to get used to them and embracing them (and the value of their pedagogical goals) in front of the class.

How this unit is related to the other units

This unit is based on the foundation of newtonian mechanics constructed in units C and N, and so must follow these units in any projected course sequence. However, this unit does not depend on these particular units in any detailed way, so any calculus-based introduction to mechanics would be suitable preparation for this unit.

In the recommended unit sequence, this unit also follows unit R, which discusses the theory of relativity. This unit, because it looks at electricity and magnetism from a 21st-century perspective, does make use of some relativity. Indeed, the unit's main point is to show that the principle of relativity *requires* that electric and magnetic fields be linked! However, I have been deliberate about arranging things so that students need to know only three simple things about relativity: (1) the principle of relativity, which states that the laws of physics are the same in all inertial reference frames, (2) the idea that the speed of light is the ultimate speed limit, and (3) the fact that moving objects are Lorentz-contracted. No other knowledge about relativity is required. Therefore, if it is impossible at your institution to discuss unit R in full before getting into this unit, you can prepare students adequately by spending a single class day exploring these three ideas. I strongly believe that using these simple relativistic ideas pays off handsomely in terms of helping students understand the deep link between electricity and magnetism.

The material in this unit is not needed for any of the other units, except for chapter E15, which helps prepare students for unit Q.

How to make cuts if necessary

The unit's stated goal is essentially achieved by chapter E13, so chapters E14 through E16 could be dropped if necessary. Of the three, I think that chapter E14, which introduces an important implication of Faraday's law, is most valuable in supporting the main goal of the unit. However, omitting even chapters E15 and E16 means that students would miss out on seeing how electromagnetic waves emerge from Maxwell's field theory, an important secondary goal for this unit. Moreover, chapter E15 really is required for unit Q, if that unit follows this one.

The integral form of the equations presented in chapter E12 is used only in the beginning of chapter E14, so one could cut these chapters. One could cut just E12 if one provides an alternative introduction to chapter E14.

If more severe cuts are absolutely necessary, chapters E1 through E9 provide an essentially irreducible basic introduction to electric and magnetic fields. Such a truncation would essentially lobotomize the unit, putting its basic goal (and stated "great idea") out of reach, but would still have some value as an first treatment of electromagnetic fields. Adding chapters E10 through E11 (and maybe E12) would also provide a basic introduction to Gauss's and Ampere's laws.

Please see the Instructor's Manual for more detailed comments about this unit and suggestions about how to teach it effectively.

Appreciation

Thanks!

A project of this magnitude cannot be accomplished alone. I would first like to thank the others who served on the IUPP development team for this project: Edwin Taylor, Dan Schroeder, Randy Knight, John Mallinckrodt, Alma Zook, Bob Hilborn, and Don Holcomb. I'd like to thank John Rigden and other members of the IUPP steering committee for their support of the project in its early stages, which came ultimately from an NSF grant and the special efforts of Duncan McBride. Users of the texts, especially Bill Titus, Richard Noer, Woods Halley, Paul Ellis, Doreen Weinberger, Nalini Easwar, Brian Watson, Jon Eggert, Catherine Mader, Paul De Young, Alma Zook, Dan Schroeder, David Tanenbaum, Alfred Kwok, Dave Dobson, Michael Kaurin-Burns, and Tom Bernatowicz, have offered invaluable feedback and encouragement. I'd also like to thank Alan Macdonald, Roseanne Di Stefano, Ruth Chabay, Bruce Sherwood, and Tony French for ideas, support, and useful suggestions. Thanks also to Robs Muir for helping with several of the indexes. My editors Jim Smith, Denise Schanck, Jack Shira, Karen Allanson, Lloyd Black, J. P. Lenney, and Daryl Bruflodt as well as Spencer Cotkin, Donata Dettbarn, David Dietz, Larry Goldberg, Sheila Frank, Jonathan Alpert, Zanae Roderigo, Mary Haas, Janice Hancock, Lisa Gottschalk, Debra Hash, David Hash, Patti Scott, Chris Hammond, Rick Hecker, and Susan Brusch have all worked very hard to make this text happen, and I deeply appreciate their efforts. I'd like to thank all the reviewers, including Edwin Carlson, David Dobson, Irene Nunes, Miles Dressler, O. Romulo Ochoa, Qichang Su, Brian Watson, and Laurent Hodges, for taking the time to do a careful reading of various units and offering valuable suggestions.

I also wish to thank the following panel of reviewers for providing carefuland insightful comments on Unit E:

Soumya Chakravarti	*Cal State University-Pomona*
Nathanael Fortune	*Smith College*
Hugh Gallagher	*State University of New York-Oneonta*
Doug Harper	*Western Kentucky University*
Andrzej Herczynski	*Boston College*
Paul Lee	*California State University-Northridge*
David Lynch	*Iowa State University*
Allen Miller	*Syracuse University*
Kimberly Shaw	*Southern Illinois University-Edwardsville*
William Smith	*Boise State University*
Shubha Tewari	*Mount Holyoke College*
Joel Weisberg	*Carleton College*

Thanks to Connie Wilson, Hilda Dinolfo, Connie Inman, and special student assistants Michael Wanke, Paul Feng, and Mara Harrell, Jennifer Lauer, Tony Galuhn, Eric Pan, and all the Physics 51 mentors for supporting (in various ways) the development and teaching of this course at Pomona College. David Haley has also been very valuable in helping to develop a number of unique demonstrations and labs for the class, and I also appreciate is help in taking a number of pictures for this edition.

Thanks also to my Physics 51 students, and especially Win Yin, Peter Leth, Eddie Abarca, Boyer Naito, Arvin Tseng, Rebecca Washenfelder, Mary Donovan, Austin Ferris, Laura Siegfried, and Miriam Krause, who have offered many suggestions and have together found many hundreds of typos and other errors. A number of students in my class last spring, especially, Erin Kahle, Nora Becker, Alex Palmerton, Rachel Zeno, Michael Bayley, and John Baxter, helped me find typos and errors in this edition. Onaolapo Wali Akande of Washington University also put in many hours tracking down errors in a draft of this edition. Eric and Brian Daub and Ryan McLaughlin were indispensable in helping me put the second edition together. Finally, very special thanks to my wife, Joyce, and to my daughters, Brittany and Allison, who contributed with their support and patience during this long and demanding project. Heartfelt thanks to all!

Thomas A. Moore
Claremont, California
November 2005

About the Author

Thomas A. Moore graduated from Carleton College (magna cum laude with Distinction in Physics) in 1976. He won a Danforth Fellowship that year that supported his graduate education at Yale University, where he earned a Ph.D. in 1981. He taught at Carleton College and Luther College before taking his current position at Pomona College in 1987, where he won a Wig Award for Distinguished Teaching in 1991. He served as an active member of the steering committee for the national Introductory University Physics Project (IUPP) from 1987 through 1995. This textbook grew out of a model curriculum that he developed for that project in 1989, which was one of only four selected for further development and testing by IUPP.

He has published a number of articles about astrophysical sources of gravitational waves, detection of gravitational waves, and new approaches to teaching physics, as well as a book on special relativity entitled *A Traveler's Guide to Spacetime* (McGraw-Hill, 1995). He has also served as a reviewer and an associate editor for *American Journal of Physics*. He currently lives in Claremont, California, with his wife Joyce and two college-aged daughters. When he is not teaching, doing research in relativistic astrophysics, or writing, he enjoys reading, hiking, scuba diving, teaching adult church-school classes on the Hebrew Bible, calling contradances, and playing traditional Irish fiddle music.

Introduction for Students

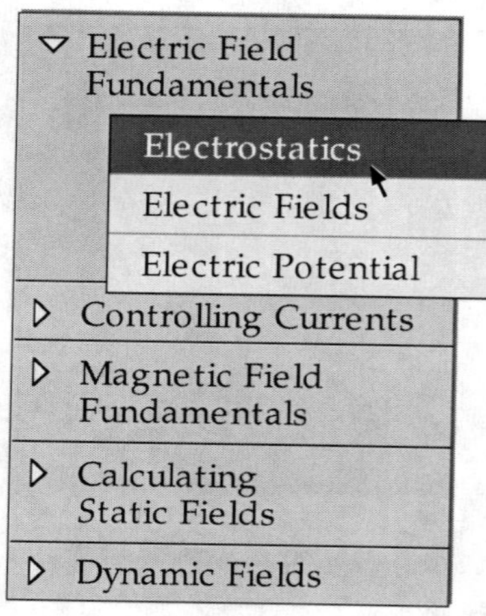

Introduction

Welcome to *Six Ideas That Shaped Physics!* This text has been designed using insights from recent research into physics learning to help you learn physics as effectively as possible. It thus has many features that may be different from science texts you have probably encountered. This section discusses these features and how to use them effectively.

Why Is This Text Different?

Research consistently shows that people learn physics most effectively if they participate in activities that help them practice applying physical reasoning in realistic situations. This is so because physics is not a collection of facts to absorb, but rather is a set of thinking skills requiring practice to master. You cannot learn such skills by going to factual lectures any more than you can learn to play the piano by going to concerts!

This text is designed, therefore, to support active learning both inside and outside the classroom by providing (1) resources for various kinds of learning activities, (2) features that encourage active reading, and (3) features that make it easier for the text (as opposed to lectures) to serve as the primary source of information, so that more class time is available for active learning.

The Text as Primary Source

Features that help the text serve as the primary source of information

To serve the last goal, I have adopted a conversational style that I hope will be easy to read, and I tried to be concise without being so terse that you need a lecture to fill in the gaps. There are also many text features designed to help you keep track of the big picture. The unit's central idea is summarized on the front cover where you can see it daily. Each chapter is designed to correspond to one 50-minute class session, so that each session is a logically complete unit. The two-page chapter overview at the beginning of each chapter provides a compact summary of that chapter's contents to consider before you are submerged by the details (it also provides a useful summary when you review for exams). An accompanying chapter-location diagram uses a computer menu metaphor to display how the current chapter fits into the unit (see the example at the upper left). Major unit subdivisions appear as gray boxes, with the current subdivision highlighted in color. Chapters in the current subdivision appear in a submenu with the current chapter highlighted in black and indicated by an arrow.

All technical terms are highlighted using a bold type when they first appear, and a Glossary at the end of the text summarizes their definitions. Please also note the tables of useful information, including definitions of common symbols, that appear inside the front cover.

A physics formula is both a mathematical equation and a context that gives the equation meaning. Every important formula in this text appears in a formula box. Each contains the equation, a purpose (describing the formula's meaning and utility), a definition of the symbols used in the equation, a description of any limitations on the formula's applicability, and possibly some other useful notes. Treat everything in such a box as an indivisible unit to be remembered and used together.

Active Reading

What it means to be an active reader

Like passively listening to a lecture, passively scanning a text does not really help you learn. Active reading is a crucial study skill for effectively learning from this text (and other types of technical literature as well). An active reader stops frequently to pose internal questions such as these: Does this make sense? Is this consistent with my experience? Am I following the logic here? Do I see how I might use this idea in realistic situations? This text provides two important tools to make this easier.

Tools to help you become an active reader

Use the wide margins to (1) record questions that occur to you as you read (so that you can remember to get them answered), (2) record answers when you receive them, (3) flag important passages, (4) fill in missing mathematics steps, and (5) record insights. Doing these things helps keep you actively engaged as you read, and your marginal comments are also generally helpful as you review. Note that I have provided some marginal notes that summarize the points of crucial paragraphs and help you find things quickly.

The single most important thing you can do

The in-text exercises help you develop the habits of (1) filling in missing mathematics steps and (2) posing questions that help you practice using the chapter's ideas. Also, though this text has many examples of worked problems similar to homework or exam problems, some of these appear in the form of in-text exercises (as you are more likely to learn from an example if you work on it some yourself instead of just scanning someone else's solution). Answers to all exercises appear at the end of each chapter so you can get immediate feedback on how you are doing. Doing at least some of the exercises as you read is probably the single most important thing you can do to become an active reader.

Active reading does take effort. Scanning the 5200 words of a typical chapter might take 45 minutes, but active reading could take several times as long. I personally tend to "blow a fuse" in my head after about 20 minutes of active reading, so I take short breaks to do something else to keep alert. Pausing to fill in missing math also helps me to stay focused longer.

Class Activities and Homework

End-of-chapter problems support active learning

The problems appearing at the end of each chapter are organized into categories that reflect somewhat different active-learning purposes. Two-minute problems are short, concept-oriented, multiple-choice problems that are primarily meant to be used in class as a way of practicing the ideas and/or exposing conceptual problems for further discussion. (The letters on the back cover make it possible to display responses to your instructor.) The other types of problems are primarily meant for use as homework outside class. Basic problems are simple, drill-type problems that help you practice in straightforward applications of a single formula or technique. Synthetic problems are more challenging and realistic questions that require you to bring together multiple formulas and/or techniques (maybe from different chapters) and to think carefully about physical principles. These problems define the level of sophistication that you should strive to achieve. Rich-context problems are yet more challenging problems that are often written in a narrative format and ask you to answer a practical, real-life question rather than explicitly asking for a numerical result. Like situations you will encounter in real life, many provide too little information and/or too much information, requiring you to make estimates and/or discard irrelevant data (this is true of some synthetic problems as well). Rich-context problems are generally too difficult for most students to solve alone; they are designed for group problem-solving sessions. Advanced problems are very sophisticated problems that provide supplemental discussion of subtle or advanced issues related to the material discussed in the chapter. These problems are for instructors and truly exceptional students.

Read the Text *Before* Class!

Class time works best if you are prepared

You will be able to participate in the kinds of activities that promote real learning only if you come to each class having already read and thought about the assigned chapter. This is likely to be much more important in a class using this text than in science courses you may have taken before! Class time can also (if you are prepared) provide a great opportunity to get your particular questions about the material answered.

E1 Basic Electrostatics

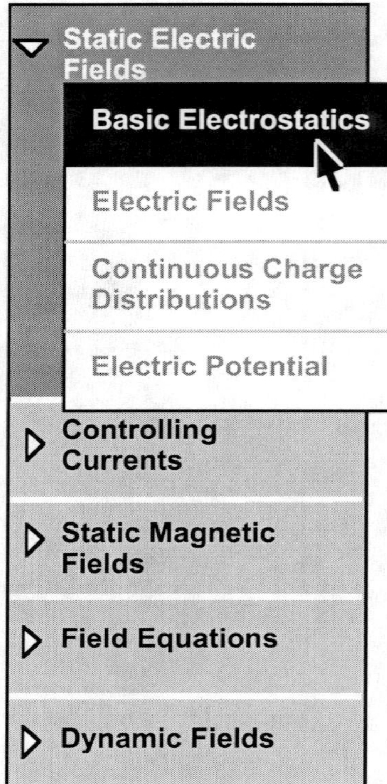

Chapter Overview

Introduction

This chapter begins our study of the rich and fascinating topic of electricity and magnetism. Historically, the work done by a handful of 19th-century physicists not only set the tone and agenda for contemporary physics but also ignited a technological revolution that has utterly changed our lives. Much of what is distinctive about 20th-century civilization (electric power, telecommunications, computers, television, movies, and so on) would not exist if not for their efforts.

Section E1.1: Introduction to the Unit

To physicists before the 19th century, **electricity**, **magnetism**, and **light** seemed like entirely distinct phenomena. Perhaps the greatest triumph of 19th-century physics was James Clerk Maxwell's beautiful and comprehensive theory linking these phenomena. In this theory, electricity and magnetism are two different manifestations of an **electromagnetic field** whose structure and time-evolution is described by **Maxwell's equations**. Light consists of ripples flowing through an electromagnetic field as it flexes as described by these equations.

This unit explores the great idea that *electricity and magnetism are unified* in five subdivisions. The first three explore the fundamentals of electric fields, creating and controlling electric currents, and using currents to create magnetic fields. The fourth introduces Maxwell's equations as powerful tools for calculating static (time-independent) electric and magnetic fields. The last shows that special relativity *requires* that electric and magnetic fields be parts of a unified electromagnetic field, and shows how we have to modify Maxwell's equations to handle **dynamic** (time-dependent) fields.

This chapter launches the first subdivision by exploring the nature of electric charge and the forces that charged particles at rest exert on each other.

Section E1.2: What is the Nature of Charge?

Elementary particles can interact electromagnetically only if they have nonzero charge. Experiments show that there are exactly two types of charge, which we call *positive* and *negative* because we can model them using positive and negative numbers. We observe that the interaction between two charged particles is repulsive if the particle charges have like signs and attractive if they have opposite signs. However, which of the charge types we identify as *negative* is purely a matter of convention.

Section E1.3: How Objects Become Charged

Rubbing surfaces can become charged because rubbing causes the electron clouds of molecules on the surfaces to become intermingled, and some molecules are more prone than others to snatch an extra electron when the clouds separate. If only one molecule in a million captures such an extra electron, the surface can become noticeably charged.

The SI unit of charge is the **coulomb** (abbreviation: C), which we will define to be a charge equivalent to that on 6.242×10^{18} protons. This means that the charge of a proton is 1.602×10^{-19} C $\equiv +e$, and that of an electron is $-e$.

Section E1.4: Conservation of Charge

The electric charge of an isolated system is *always* conserved. Most physical processes merely shuffle around protons and electrons without creating or destroying them (and thus trivially conserve charge), but even exotic nuclear interactions that *can* create or destroy protons or electrons conserve charge.

Section E1.5: Coulomb's Law

We find experimentally that the electromagnetic interaction between two charged particles essentially at rest exerts on each particle a force whose magnitude depends on its charge and separation from the other as follows:

$$F_e = \frac{k\,|q_1 q_2|}{r^2} = \frac{1}{4\pi\varepsilon_0}\frac{|q_1 q_2|}{r^2} \qquad \text{(E1.3a)}$$

$$\text{where } k \equiv \frac{1}{4\pi\varepsilon_0} = 8.99\times10^9\ \frac{\text{N}\cdot\text{m}^2}{\text{C}^2} \qquad \text{(E1.3b)}$$

Purpose: This equation specifies the magnitude F_e of the electrostatic force exerted on each of two interacting charged particles separated by a distance r.

Symbols: q_1 and q_2 are the charges of the two particles, k is a constant of proportionality called the **Coulomb constant**, and $\varepsilon_0 \equiv 8.85\times10^{-12}\ \text{C}^2\text{N}^{-1}\text{m}^{-2}$ is a constant called the "permittivity of free space."

Limitations: This equation applies only to *point particles* essentially at *rest*.

Notes: The absolute value signs are necessary because q_1 and q_2 might be negative but F_e must be positive.

The force on each particle points *away from* the other if the two charges have the same sign, or *toward* that particle if the charges have opposite signs. **Coulomb's law** is analogous to Newton's law of universal gravitation $F_g = Gm_1m_2/r^2$ (note that in the gravitational equation, m_1 and m_2 play the roles analogous to q_1 and q_2, and the constant G plays the role analogous to $k = (4\pi\varepsilon_0)^{-1}$.

The **superposition principle** states that the force on any point charge q_1 due to its interactions with a *set* of point charges $q_2, q_3, \ldots$ is simply the *vector sum* of the forces that $q_2, q_3, \ldots$ would exert if each interacted with q_1 alone. Even though Coulomb's law applies only to point particles, the superposition principle implies that we can simply sum over all the pairs of interacting charges in a pair of macroscopic objects to find the net force that each exerts on the other.

Section E1.6: Conductors and Insulators

We call a substance a **conductor** if charges can readily move through it and an **insulator** if they cannot. Metals and salty water are good conductors; glass, rubber, and most plastics are good insulators. We will define these terms quantitatively in chapter E4.

Rubbing a conducting object can deposit charge on the conductor's surface, but these charges usually disperse (since they repel each other and are free to move) by flowing through the conductor and out through the person holding it. Therefore it is usually easier to charge insulators.

Section E1.7: The Mystery du Jour

Coulomb's law explains how charged objects attract or repel each other. But we notice that charged objects can attract (but never repel) neutral objects. Moreover, this attraction seems to decrease much more rapidly with separation than $1/r^2$. How is this possible?

E1.1 Introduction to the Unit

Electricity and magnetism and light are linked

Since the beginning of history, humanity has pondered three great mysteries that no one originally imagined were related. Our ancestors experienced **electricity** in the form of lightning and the tiny sparks that amber produces when rubbed with cloth. Certain rocks (including those from the region called Magnesia by the ancient Greeks) exhibited an attractive effect that came to be called **magnetism**. The greatest mystery of all was that of **light**, essential to life and sight, which according to the ancient Hebrews was the first thing created by God, and which in many times and places has served as a metaphor for divinity and knowledge.

One of the greatest intellectual triumphs of the late 19th century was the recognition that electricity, magnetism, and light were not separate and distinct phenomena, but instead are but different aspects of an **electromagnetic field**. The creators of this model were surprised to find that the model required electromagnetic fields to have a reality somewhat apart from the electric charges that create them. The model also required that **dynamic** (time-dependent) fields obey "equations of motion" (called **Maxwell's equations**) in much the same way that material objects obey Newton's second law. The final surprise was that light turns out to be comprised of ripples that flow through a dynamic electromagnetic field as it flexes as required by Maxwell's equations. All of these conclusions spring from this unit's fundamental idea: *electricity and magnetism are unified*.

Our technological civilization is founded on this great idea. The generation and transportation of electric power, radio, electronics, radar, television, and computers are all progeny of this idea, and these technologies have changed the direction of history. The power of this idea also opened the floodgates of science, not only providing scientists with a host of new ways to probe and measure the universe, but also uncovering perplexing new mysteries that rapidly led to the development of relativity and quantum mechanics in the early 20th century.

Our purpose in this unit is to explore the concept of the electromagnetic field and the meaning of its equations of motion, so as to better understand the consequences of the idea that *electricity and magnetism are unified*. Rather than follow the historical path of this idea's development, which is full of twists and blind alleys, we will take a retrospective look from a contemporary perspective, since we now understand the full power and breadth of this idea.

The first of this unit's five subdivisions introduces the concept of a *field* and explores electric fields created by stationary charged particles. The second discusses how we can use electric fields to create and control *electric currents*. The third explores how such currents both react to and create magnetic fields. The fourth introduces Maxwell's equations as powerful tools for calculating **static** (time-independent) electric and magnetic fields.

The final subdivision builds on the background provided by the first four to explore the unit's core idea and its consequences. That subdivision's first chapter argues that special relativity *requires* that electric and magnetic fields be inseparable aspects of a more general electromagnetic field. In the next chapter, we will use these ideas to discover the missing terms in Maxwell's equations that allow them to handle dynamic fields. The remaining chapters explore important applications and implications of these equations. *Induction* is a time-dependent electromagnetic phenomenon predicted by Maxwell's equations that makes it possible to *create* currents with time-dependent magnetic fields. This phenomenon has abundant applications in modern technology. The final two chapters discuss electromagnetic waves and their relationship to light. The structure of the entire unit is summarized in Figure E1.1.

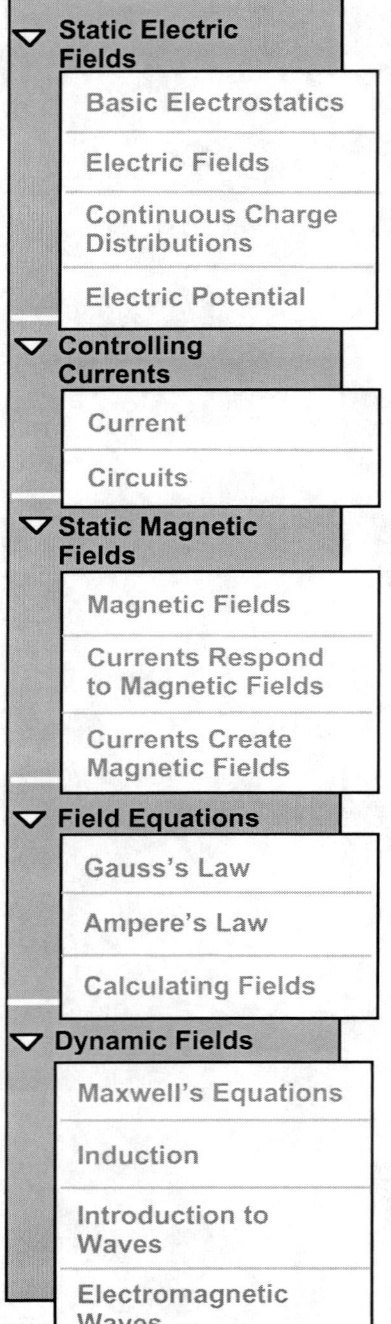

Figure E1.1
An overview of the structure of this unit.

In this subdivision, we will focus on **electrostatics**, the aspect of the electromagnetic interaction that acts between charges at rest. We begin in this chapter by exploring the most basic questions about such interactions: What is the nature of electric charge? Why do we describe charge as being "positive" or "negative"? How can we describe electrostatic forces mathematically?

E1.2 What is the Nature of Charge?

Historical Notes

At least 2500 years ago, Greek scholars knew that rubbing amber (which they called *elektron*) changed it in a way that enabled it to attract light objects such as straw or feathers, and that sometimes little sparks could be seen jumping between the amber and other objects. The Greeks thought that this was a unique property of amber, but in 1600 William Gilbert showed that many objects could be similarly **electrically charged**. (This was not easy to show, because few *natural* substances other than amber are easily charged.)

Objects made of plastic, rubber, or synthetic fibers make the phenomenon of "static electricity" a common experience nowadays (particularly on days when the humidity is low). Nearly everyone has experienced delivering an electric spark to something after rubbing one's shoes on a rug. After running a rubber or plastic comb through your hair, you will find that the comb attracts dust and bits of paper, and you may even hear the crackle of sparks jumping if you bring it near to something. When you pull clothes out of the dryer (particularly clothes made of synthetic fibers) you can feel how they attract each other and hear the crackle of sparks as you pull them apart (you can actually see the sparks in the dark).

Learning about charge with sticky tape experiment

We can learn much about the nature of electric charge by doing some simple experiments with ordinary transparent adhesive ("Scotch") tape. The characteristics of the adhesive make it easy to electrify a piece of such tape (as you may already know from experience!) and the cellophane or plastic used as a backing holds charges well. Find a dispenser of transparent tape: cheap shiny cellophane tape is fine (maybe actually better than some brands of expensive "magic" tape, which are actually treated to reduce electrification). Tear off two pieces of tape about 20 cm (8 inches) long. Fold about a half inch of the tape over on itself to make a non-sticky handle, as shown in Figure E1.2a. Label the handle of one tape *T* and the handle of the other *U*. Then (this is important!) apply the tacky side of the *T* tape to the non-tacky side of the *U* tape along the length of both, as shown in Figure E1.2b (the *T* and *U* labels refers to whether it is "tacky" or "untacky" side of the tape in each case that is in contact with the other). Grip the handles, and then quickly pull the two tapes apart. Hang one piece of tape handle down from the edge of a table or chair and bring the other

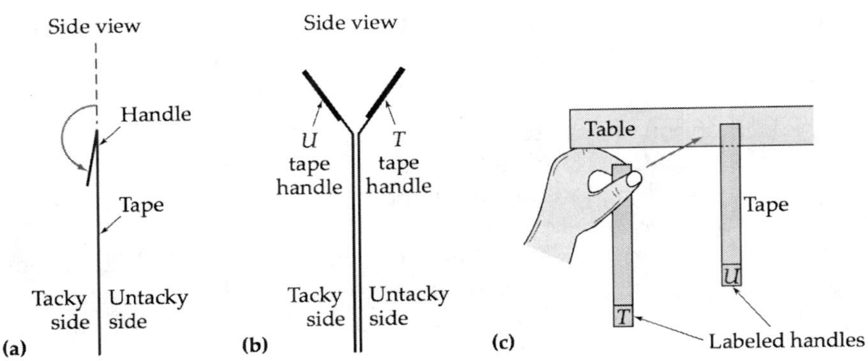

Figure E1.2
(a) Give a piece of tape a non-sticky handle by folding about a half-inch of the tape down on itself. **(b)** To electrify the tapes, place the tacky side of the *T* tape in contact with the untacky side of the *U* tape, and pull the tapes apart suddenly. **(c)** Hang one tape from the edge of a table with its handle down and bring the other near it. What happens?

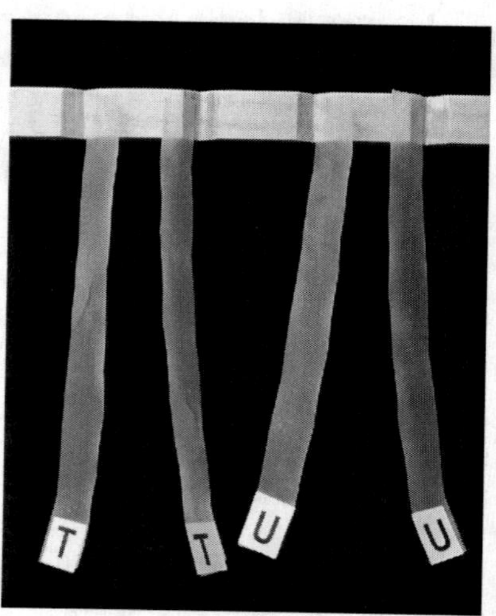

Figure E1.3
A photograph of charged tapes interacting.

tape near to it, as shown in Figure E1.2c. You should find that the two pieces of tape strongly attract each other. Tearing the tapes apart therefore somehow charges both.

The way that electrically charged objects attract each other is similar to the way that massive objects attract each other gravitationally. From this point of view, the surprising thing is that electrically charged objects can also *repel* each other. This was first documented in 1733 by the King of France's gardener, Charles François de Cisternay Dufay. You can demonstrate this as follows. Prepare and label *another* two pieces of tape as shown in Figure E1.2. You should find that the new *U* tape *repels* the first *U* tape, the new *T* tape repels the first *T* tape and the *T* and *U* tapes attract each other (see Figure E1.3).

There are exactly *two* kinds of electric charge

These observations imply that the *T* and *U* tapes must have different kinds of electric charge: if there were only one kind of electric charge, all of the charged tapes would either attract or repel each other, not attract some tapes and repel others. In a series of papers published in the late 1740s and early 1750s Benjamin Franklin and several collaborators proposed a simple model for understanding electrostatic phenomena. Franklin proposed that there were exactly two kinds of charge, which he called **positive** and **negative**. Franklin also asserted that objects having *like* charges repel each other, while objects having *unlike* charges always attract.

Self-Test E1X.1

How are we sure that it is *like* charges that repel each other? Explain how the tape experiments described above support Franklin's conclusion. (What makes us think that the two *U* tapes have the same type of charge?)

Charges combine like positive and negative numbers

Why did Franklin choose to describe these two types of charges as being "positive" and "negative" (and not, for example, *U* and *T*, or "Type A" and "Type B")? These designations are a metaphorical way of saying that in certain ways, *electric charges behave like positive and negative numbers*.

For example, consider the experiment illustrated in Figure E1.2b, where we stripped apart two originally uncharged pieces of tape. The act of stripping the two tapes apart must give them *unlike* charges, as they attract each other afterwards. One can also show that these tapes have about the same *magnitude* of charge (for example, by showing that the magnitude of the attractive or repulsive force exerted by each on a third tape is the same). When the tapes are brought together again, they behave as if they were again uncharged. This suggests, as Franklin first argued, that the charges on these objects can be described by positive and negative numbers. The net charge on the uncharged tapes is originally zero. When the tapes are separated, they are found to have unlike charges with the same magnitudes, just like positive and negative numbers that have the same absolute value. When the tapes are brought together, they become uncharged again, just as a positive and a negative number having the same absolute value add up to zero. The behavior of signed numbers is thus a good metaphor for the behavior of charges.

The choice of which kind of charge is positive and which is negative, however, is completely arbitrary. The accepted convention is based on Franklin's historical choice: a glass rod rubbed with silk cloth becomes *positively* charged. A more modern way of describing the same convention is to say that if you comb your hair with a plastic comb, the comb becomes *negatively* charged.

Which of the two types of charge we call *positive* is a matter of convention

---

Self-Test E1X.2

According to this convention, what is the sign of the charge on a *U* tape? What is the sign of the charge on a *T* tape? Describe and perform an experiment that answers this question.

E1.3 How Objects Become Charged

Neither Gilbert nor Franklin were able to offer anything more than speculation about *how* objects such as amber, glass, and rubber could become electrically charged (Franklin speculated that electric charge was some kind of continuous fluid, and that a surplus of this fluid gave an object a positive charge while a deficit of the fluid gave it a negative charge). Since the early decades of the 20th century, scientists have known with certainty that material objects are made up of *atoms*, and we now know a great deal about the internal structure of the atoms themselves. This atomic model of matter enables us to offer a better explanation of how macroscopic objects can become electrically charged.

The atomic model of matter explains how objects can become charged

A macroscopic object is constructed from a huge number (on the order of magnitude of 10^{23}) of tiny atoms (roughly 0.2 nm in diameter). Each atom in turn consists of a *very* tiny central nucleus (comprised of protons and neutrons) surrounded by a cloud of electrons. The number of electrons in a normal atom is the same as the number of protons in its nucleus, and the number of neutrons in the nucleus is usually a bit larger than the number of protons. A schematic diagram of a copper atom is shown in Figure E1.4.

Avogadro's number (6.02×10^{23}) of either protons or neutrons has a mass of very nearly 1.0 g (this is essentially how Avogadro's number was defined). The mass of an electron is more than 1800 times smaller than the mass of either. This means that the mass of an atom is essentially determined by the number of protons and neutrons it has: the total mass of the electrons in the atom is negligible in comparison. On the other hand, the size of this massive nucleus is tiny compared to the atom as a whole (the radius of the nucleus is roughly 20,000 times smaller than the atom's radius): most of the *volume* of an atom is occupied by the electron clouds.

Avogadro's number of protons or neutrons has a mass of very nearly 1 g

Protons are always observed to have *positive* charge (according to Franklin's convention), while electrons are always negatively charged and neutrons are always uncharged. It is precisely the strong electrostatic attraction between

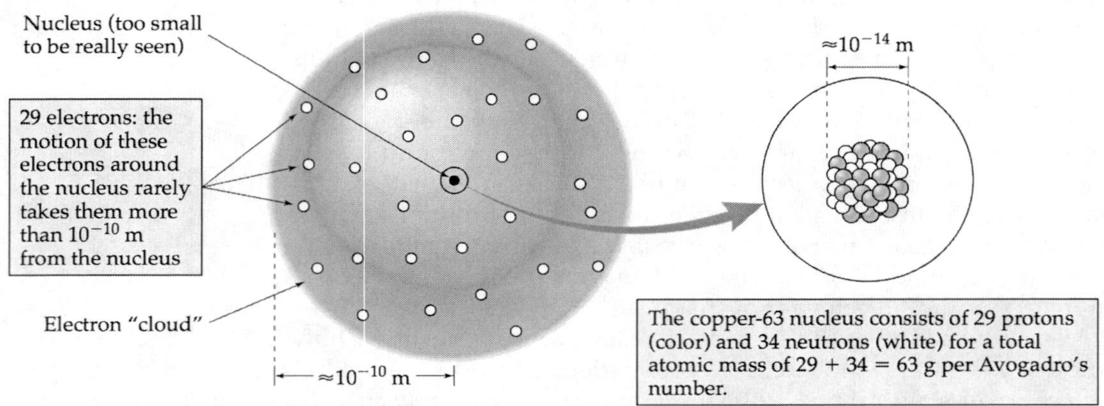

Figure E1.4
A schematic representation of a copper-63 atom. (Quantum mechanics implies that the charge of the 29 electrons behaves as if it were distributed smoothly throughout the gray "cloud" instead of being concentrated at 29 points.

the electrons and protons that keeps the electrons attached to the atom's nucleus. Experiments also show that an atom with an equal number of protons and electrons behaves as if it were exactly uncharged (to many decimal places), implying that a proton and electron must have electric charges that are exactly equal in magnitude and opposite in sign. The numerical magnitude of this basic atomic unit of charge is designated by the letter e: an electron is said to have a charge of $-e$ and the proton a charge of $+e$.

The SI unit of charge

The unit of electric charge in the SI system is the **coulomb** (abbreviation: C), after Charles-Augustin de Coulomb, who quantitatively investigated the forces between charged objects in the late 1780s. This unit was defined long before the structure of the atom was understood, and so is not related to the fundamental unit of charge e in any simple manner. We will define the coulomb as follows (though its *technical* definition in the SI system is somewhat different):

$$1\text{ C} \equiv \text{charge of } 6.242 \times 10^{18} \text{ protons} = (6.242 \times 10^{18})e \qquad \text{(E1.1a)}$$

$$\Rightarrow \quad e = 1.602 \times 10^{-19}\text{ C} \qquad \text{(E1.1b)}$$

Any uncharged macroscopic object therefore contains an enormous amount of positive charge (in the form of protons) exactly balanced by an enormous amount of negative charge (in the form of electrons). If we define the net charge of an object to be the sum of the total positive and total negative charges on the object, an uncharged object has a net charge of zero, since the positive charges exactly cancel the negative charges. When two originally uncharged objects come into close physical contact (as when rubbed, or when two pieces of tape are stuck together), the electron clouds of the atoms on the surfaces of the two objects become somewhat intermingled. When the surfaces are separated, the atoms on one surface may by chance pull away some extra electrons, leaving the other with a deficit of electrons. The surface with the excess of electrons will thus have a small negative net charge, while the other has a small positive net charge.

Rubbing objects together can transfer electrons

Certain kinds of materials are more prone to lose electrons while other materials are more prone to capture extra electrons. For example, rubber molecules are slightly more able to capture and hold electrons than fur or cloth molecules are, so when a rubber balloon is rubbed on with cloth or fur, the balloon ends up with a net negative charge. The imbalance between these materials does not have to be very large: even if only about one in every million surface molecules gets an extra electron, the balloon will accumulate an obvious net charge.

Table E1.1 lists a number of common substances in decreasing order of their empirically measured tendency to lose electrons when rubbed by another substance. When two substances are rubbed, whichever is higher on the list will lose electrons to the one lower on the list: the higher substance will therefore become positive and the lower negative. Physicists call such a list a **triboelectric series** (*tribein* is a Greek verb meaning "to rub"). One has to be careful in taking this list too literally, however, because surface finishes or contamination can substantially influence where a specific example of a substance appears in the series.

Table E1.1 A triboelectric series

Air
Human skin (if very dry)
Rabbit Fur
Glass
Human Hair
Nylon
Wool
Lead
Silk
Aluminum
Paper
Cotton
Steel
Wood
Amber
Hard rubber
Nickel, Copper
Brass, Silver
Synthetic rubber
Gold, Platinum
Polyester
Styrene (Styrofoam)
Saran Wrap
Polyethylene (used in Scotch tape)
Polypropylene
Vinyl (used in PVC pipes)
Silicon
Teflon
Silicone Rubber

(Adapted from J. M. Zavista, *Understanding Static Electricity* [on www.howstuffworks.com] and other sources.)

Self-Test E1X.3

A copper penny has a mass of about 5 grams. The protons in this penny represent roughly how much total positive charge, in Coulombs? (For comparison, a typical charged comb or balloon has a net charge on the order of 10 nC to 100 nC, that is, 10^{-8} C to 10^{-7} C.)

E1.4 Conservation of Charge

One of the most important assertions made by Franklin and his collaborators was that *electric charge is conserved*: that is, the net charge of any isolated system of objects remains constant in time. We now can see that this follows from the atomic model considered in the previous section. Everyday physical processes do not destroy or create either protons or electrons, so an isolated system has a fixed number of protons, a fixed number of electrons, and thus a fixed net charge. Protons or (more usually) electrons can be shuffled around between objects in the system, but the net number of protons and electrons will not change. Therefore the net charge of any isolated system will remain constant.

Since about the 1930s, physicists have known of physical processes that *do* destroy and/or create electrons and protons. What happens to charge conservation in this case? In all physical processes known to date, the net charge in an isolated system is conserved even when the particles carrying that charge are created or destroyed. For example, an isolated neutron (zero charge) spontaneously decays after about 10 minutes, creating a proton (charge $+e$), an electron (charge $-e$), and a third particle called an antineutrino (zero charge): the net charge of the system is zero both before and after the decay. No physical process has *ever* been discovered that violates charge conservation at either the macroscopic or microscopic level.

An isolated system's total charge is conserved, even when internal processes create or destroy particles

Self-Test E1X.4

Electrons have the smallest mass of any known *charged* particle, though a variety of less massive *neutral* particles (such as photons and neutrinos) exist. Argue that the principles of conservation of relativistic energy and charge imply that an electron *cannot* decay into something else.

E1.5 Coulomb's Law

How can we mathematically describe the forces that motionless charged objects exert on each other? The force exerted by a charged *point* particle on another charged *point* particle is described by **Coulomb's law**, a law very similar in form to Newton's law of universal gravitation (which was discussed in Unit N). Newton's law of universal gravitation asserts that the gravitational force exerted by a point particle of mass m_1 on a point particle of mass m_2 has a magnitude given by the expression:

$$F_g = \frac{Gm_1m_2}{r^2} \quad \text{(where } G = 6.67 \times 10^{-11}\ \text{N·m}^2/\text{kg}^2\text{)} \tag{E1.2}$$

In this equation, r is the distance between the two particles and G is a constant of proportionality having the stated value. The force acting on either particle is directed *toward* the other particle along the line connecting them. Note that the force acting on either particle is equal in magnitude and opposite in direction to the force acting on the other particle, so the law of universal gravitation is consistent with Newton's third law.

Similarly, Coulomb's law asserts that the electrostatic force of attraction or repulsion exerted by two point particles on each other has the magnitude

Coulomb's Law

$$F_e = \frac{k\,|q_1q_2|}{r^2} = \frac{1}{4\pi\varepsilon_0}\frac{|q_1q_2|}{r^2} \tag{E1.3a}$$

$$\text{where } k \equiv \frac{1}{4\pi\varepsilon_0} = 8.99\times10^9\ \frac{\text{N}\cdot\text{m}^2}{\text{C}^2} \tag{E1.3b}$$

Purpose: This equation specifies the magnitude F_e of the electrostatic force exerted on each of two interacting charged particles separated by a distance r.

Symbols: q_1 and q_2 are the charges of the two particles; k is a constant called the **Coulomb constant**, and $\varepsilon_0 \equiv 8.85\times10^{-12}\ \text{C}^2\text{N}^{-1}\text{m}^{-2}$ is a constant called the "permittivity of free space."

Limitation: This equation technically only applies to *point* particles that are essentially at rest.

Notes: The absolute value signs are necessary because q_1 and q_2 might be negative but F_e must be positive.

The force acting on one particle points either *toward* the other particle (if the particles have opposite signs) or *away from* the other particle (if the particles have like signs). In either case (see figure E1.5) the forces exerted by the particles on each other have equal and opposite directions, consistent with Newton's third law.

In the form of the law written with the constant k, the similarity between Coulomb's law and the law of universal gravitation is most obvious: k in the former corresponds to G in the latter and q_1 and q_2 in the former correspond to m_1 and m_2 in the latter. The Coulomb constant k specifies the intrinsic strength of the electrostatic interaction between two particles in the same way that G characterizes the intrinsic strength of the gravitational interaction.

Because it makes certain other equations easier, Coulomb's law is most often written in the form involving the constant ε_0, a practice I will subsequently follow. This constant appears so commonly in electromagnetic equations that you should memorize its value and units. (Note that $[4\pi\varepsilon_0]^{-1} \approx 9\times10^9$ and $1/\varepsilon_0 = 1.13\times10^{11}$ in SI units: both are easily-remembered numbers.)

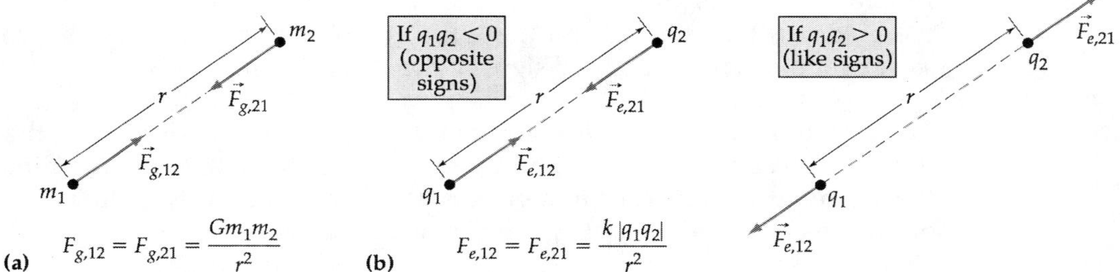

Figure E1.5
(a) The gravitational force exerted by one point particle on another points directly toward the other particle.
(b) The electrostatic force exerted by one particle on the other either points directly *toward* or directly *away* from the other particle.

Limitations of Coulomb's law

Coulomb's law has two important limitations that you must understand to use it properly (the same restrictions actually apply to the law of universal gravitation). First, it strictly applies only to point particles (like electrons, for example). It gives the *approximate* force between two macroscopic objects if the sizes of both objects are very small compared to their separation. Second, Coulomb's law technically only applies to particles *at rest*. In practice, this law is a good approximation as long as the particles are not *accelerating* relative to each other. We'll see later how we have to generalize this law in dynamic cases.

Self-Test E1X.5

Consider the copper penny discussed in self-test E1X.3. Imagine that we were miraculously able to remove one out of every 1000 electrons on two such coins. If we were to hold the coins 1.0 m apart, what would be the magnitude of the force that each coin exerts on the other? Compare to your weight. (Pennies are small enough so that at a separation of 1.0 m they can be considered to be approximately point-like.)

How to compute electrostatic forces on macroscopic objects

How can we compute the electrostatic force exerted by one macroscopic object on another if the objects are not small enough to be considered "point-like"? While a macroscopic object may not itself be point-like, it is constructed of charged particles (quarks and electrons) that *are*. Moreover, it turns out that experimentally, the *net* force exerted on any particle of charge q_1 by a *set* of particles with charge $q_2, q_3, \ldots$ is simply the *vector sum* of the forces exerted by each individual particle $q_2, q_3, \ldots$ on the first particle q_1. This is one way to state what is called the **superposition principle** for the electrostatic interaction. This principle does not *have* to be true: the effects of two charges *could* reinforce each other in such a way that the net force they exert on the third could be different than the sum of the forces each would exert individually. But experiments strongly support the superposition principle as an accurate model of electrostatic interactions.

The superposition principle

Therefore (at least theoretically), we can calculate the net force exerted on a macroscopic charged object A by another such object B by determining the net force on *each* particle in A due to *all* of the particles in B (using the superposition principle) and then summing over all of the particles in A.

Example E1.1

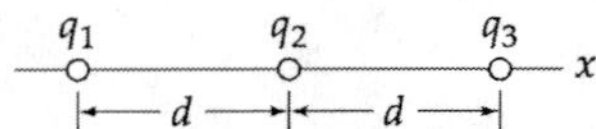

Figure E1.6
Three point charges equally spaced along the x axis.

Problem Consider three point charges q_1, q_2, and q_3 equally spaced along the x axis as shown in figure E1.6. If the net force on q_3 is zero, what can we say about the magnitudes and signs of the other charges?

Model Since all three charges lie along x axis, the vectors describing the electrostatic forces exerted by q_1 and q_2 on q_3 must be parallel to the x direction. According to the superposition principle, the net force on q_3 is the vector sum of the forces exerted on it by q_1 and q_2 individually.

Solution The only way that these force vectors can add to zero is for the vectors to be equal in magnitude but opposite in direction. Therefore, q_1 and q_2 must have opposite signs to exert opposite forces on q_3. For the forces to have the same *magnitude*, we must have

$$\frac{|q_1 q_3|}{4\pi\varepsilon_0(2d)^2} = \frac{|q_2 q_3|}{4\pi\varepsilon_0 d^2} \quad \text{(according to Coulomb's law)} \tag{E1.4}$$

since q_1 is a distance $2d$ from q_3, while q_2 is a distance d from q_3. Dividing both sides of this equation by $|q_3|/4\pi\varepsilon_0 d^2$, we find that $\frac{1}{4}|q_1| = |q_2|$. So from the information given, we can determine that q_1 and q_2 must have opposite signs and that the magnitude of q_1 must be 4 times that of q_2.

Evaluation We cannot determine anything more about the signs of the charges, and since $|q_3|$ divides out of equation E1.4, we can say nothing about the sign or magnitude of q_3.

Example E1.2

Problem Point charges q_1, q_2, and q_3 are arranged in an equilateral triangle whose sides have length d, as shown in figure E1.7a. All three charges have the same magnitude, and q_2 is negative and the other two charges are positive. Qualitatively, what is the direction of the force on charge q_1?

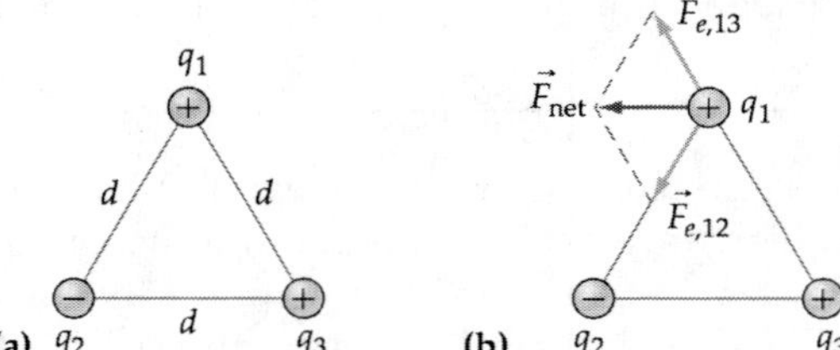

Figure E1.7
(a) Three charges arranged in the form of an equilateral triangle.
(b) The net force on q_1 is the vector sum of the forces exerted on that charge by q_2 and q_3 individually.

Solution Since $|q_2| = |q_3|$, the magnitudes of the forces that q_2 and q_3 exert on q_1 will be the same. But because q_1 and q_2 have opposite signs, the force that q_2 exerts on q_1 points *toward* q_2, but since q_1 and q_3 have the same sign the force that q_3 exerts on q_1 points *away* from q_3, as shown in figure E1.7b. The vector sum of these two vectors points leftward in the diagram.

Self-Test E1X.6

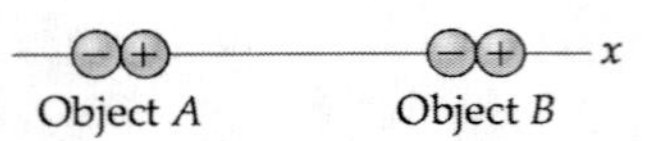

Figure E1.8
Interaction of two neutral objects.

Consider an object constructed of two point charges separated by a small distance. Assume that the charges have equal magnitudes but opposite signs: the net charge on the object is thus zero. Imagine that we place two such objects on the x axis, with the positive side of each object oriented in the $+x$ direction, as shown in Figure E1.8. Will the objects, attract each other, repel each other, or have no effect on each other? Explain.

Example E1.3

Problem In the situation shown in figure E1.7, calculate the magnitude and direction of $\vec{F}_{\text{net}}$ in terms of $q \equiv |q_1| = |q_2| = |q_3|$ and d.

Translation Let us define a coordinate system for this problem as shown in figure E1.9. Since the triangle is equilateral, the $\theta = 60°$. Note that this means that both $\vec{F}_{e,13}$ and $\vec{F}_{e,12}$ make an angle of θ with respect to the x axis.

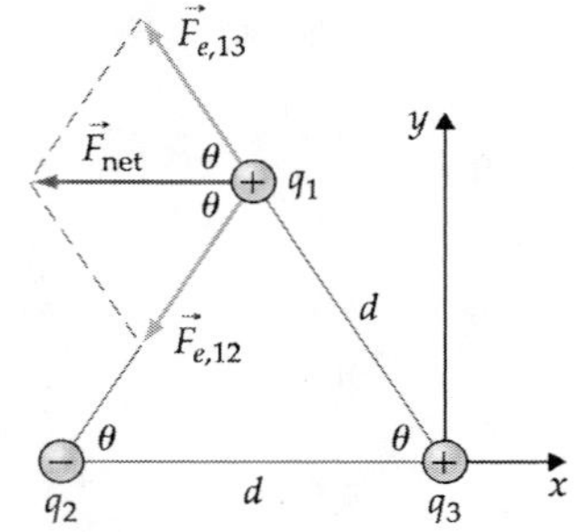

Figure E1.9
A diagram of the situation shown in example E1.3

Model Assuming that these charges are small enough to be point-like, we can use Coulomb's law to calculate the forces $\vec{F}_{e,13}$ and $\vec{F}_{e,12}$ separately. The superposition principle implies that the net force $\vec{F}_{\text{net}}$ on q_1 is the vector sum of these forces.

Solution Since charges q_1 and q_3 are separated by the distance d, the magnitude of the force on q_1 will be

$$F_{e,13} \equiv \text{mag}(\vec{F}_{e,13}) = \frac{1}{4\pi\varepsilon_0}\frac{|q_1 q_3|}{r^2} = \frac{1}{4\pi\varepsilon_0}\frac{q^2}{d^2} \tag{E1.5}$$

The magnitude of $\vec{F}_{e,12}$ will be the same. Looking at the diagram, we see that the components of these two force *vectors* are:

$$\vec{F}_{e,13} = \begin{bmatrix} -F_{e,13}\cos\theta \\ F_{e,13}\sin\theta \\ 0 \end{bmatrix} = \frac{q^2}{4\pi\varepsilon_0 d^2}\begin{bmatrix} -\cos\theta \\ \sin\theta \\ 0 \end{bmatrix} \tag{E1.6a}$$

$$\vec{F}_{e,12} = \begin{bmatrix} -F_{e,12}\cos\theta \\ -F_{e,12}\sin\theta \\ 0 \end{bmatrix} = \frac{q^2}{4\pi\varepsilon_0 d^2}\begin{bmatrix} -\cos\theta \\ -\sin\theta \\ 0 \end{bmatrix} \tag{E1.6b}$$

Adding, we find that

$$\vec{F}_{\text{net}} = \vec{F}_{e,13} + \vec{F}_{e,12} = \frac{q^2}{4\pi\varepsilon_0 d^2}\begin{bmatrix} -\cos\theta \\ \sin\theta \\ 0 \end{bmatrix} + \frac{q^2}{4\pi\varepsilon_0 d^2}\begin{bmatrix} -\cos\theta \\ -\sin\theta \\ 0 \end{bmatrix}$$

$$= \frac{q^2}{4\pi\varepsilon_0 d^2}\begin{bmatrix} -2\cos\theta \\ 0 \\ 0 \end{bmatrix} = \frac{q^2}{4\pi\varepsilon_0 d^2}\begin{bmatrix} -1 \\ 0 \\ 0 \end{bmatrix} \tag{E1.7}$$

since $\cos 60° = 1/2$. We see that $\vec{F}_{\text{net}}$ points entirely in the $-x$ direction and has a magnitude of $q^2/(4\pi\varepsilon_0 d^2)$.

Evaluation: This direction is consistent with the result of the previous exercise.

E1.6 Conductors and Insulators

Why do materials like amber, plastic, rubber and glass become easily charged when rubbed, while most other materials do not? For example, you can easily charge a plastic cup by rubbing it with a towel, but you do not become appreciably charged when you dry yourself after a shower. While it is easy to charge a rubber balloon by rubbing it on your sweater, you can rub a piece of silverware on your sweater all day, and it will never gain a discernible charge. Is it just because materials like amber, plastic and rubber are that much more prone than flesh or metal to gain or lose electrons in the rubbing process?

Charges are not free to move in an insulator

It is true that some materials more effectively lose or gain electrons than others, but this is not the most important effect. Materials like amber, plastic, and so on are easy to charge mostly because electrons in these substances (even the extra electrons created by rubbing) cannot move around on the surface of the substance or into its interior. So if rubbing a plastic comb through your hair (for example) deposits extra electrons on the surface of the comb, those extra electrons *stay* on the comb where they were deposited. A material whose protons and electrons are both essentially immobile is called an **insulator**. Glass, amber, most plastics, rubber, and dry cloth are all reasonably good insulators.

Charges *are* free to move in a conductor

At the other extreme are materials in which charges move very easily from place to place: such materials are called **conductors**. Salty water is a fairly good conductor and most metals are excellent conductors. Copper and silver are especially good conductors: electrons move through either of these metals about 10^{27} times more easily than they move through polystyrene (a common plastic). In a metal, the outermost electron in each atom essentially becomes detached from its atom and becomes free to roam around the metal (though such electrons cannot easily *leave* the metal). Charge can flow through salty water because the salt disassociates into ions that are free to move through the water (chemically pure water with no dissolved ions is an excellent insulator).

Why insulators are relatively easy to charge

Materials that are exceptionally good insulators are easy to charge: any charges deposited on an insulator's surface remain fixed in place even though these charges strongly repel each other. On the other hand, extra electrons (for example) deposited on the surface of a conductor almost immediately disperse in response to the repulsive forces that they exert on each other. For example, if you rub a spoon on your sweater, any excess electrons deposited on the spoon, in their rush to get away from each other, disperse themselves by moving through the spoon into your hand and then through your body (which is mostly salt water) to the ground, where they can disperse themselves very widely. So it is not so much that rubbing a spoon does not create excess charge as it is that this excess charge is almost instantly dissipated because the electrons are free to move away from each other.

Because rubbing typically moves only a tiny amount of charge (on the order of 10^{-8} C) from one object to another, a material must be an exceptionally good insulator if this tiny charge is not to escape. Most natural materials (even such things as wood or rock) are pretty bad conductors, but they are not terrific insulators either. Almost anything that is the least bit moist will conduct electrons well enough to quickly dissipate the small amount of charge deposited by rubbing: this is why it is difficult to do experiments involving static electricity on a humid day.

How to charge a conducting object

It is possible to charge a conducting object if that object is separated from any other conductor by an exceptionally good insulator. A metal sphere on an insulating plastic or glass stand can retain an electric charge very well. A piece of silverware can become nicely charged if you hold it with plastic gloves. Even a human body can become highly charged if it is well-insulated from its

Figure E1.10
These pieces of plastic wrap have been charged by the Van de Graaff generator and therefore are strongly repelled by it.

surroundings. A classic demonstration of static electricity involves a person who holds on to one end of a Van de Graaff generator (a device that mechanically creates a substantial excess charge) while standing on an insulating stool. Assuming the generator produces a negative charge, then electrons from the generator will disperse themselves through the person's body, including in the person's hair. Eventually the person's hair begins to stand up as the electrons in the hair strain to get as far away from each other as possible!

Figure E1.10 illustrates a version of this demonstration where thin colored sheets of plastic create a nice "flower" above the Van de Graaff generator.

E1.7 The Mystery du Jour

Coulomb's law clearly explains why electrically charged objects attract or repel each other. However, if one brings a charged object close to an electrically *neutral* object, one will usually find that they attract each other as well (and never repel!). For example, a charged comb will easily attract electrically neutral bits of paper. This does not seem to be consistent with Coulomb's law, which states that a charged object should exert *zero* force on a neutral object!

Moreover, if one investigates in more detail the force exerted by the interaction between a small charged object and a small neutral object, one finds that the force falls off as $1/r^5$, where r is the separation between the objects. (This is why one has to get a charged object pretty close to a neutral object before one can observe much effect, but once the separation becomes sufficiently small, the force suddenly seems to increase dramatically.) Again, this is nothing like the $1/r^2$-behavior we would expect from Coulomb's law.

In the next chapter, we will explore the crucial concept of an *electric field*. This concept is one of the most important and powerful ideas in the unit, and comprises the foundation on which we will construct the remainder of the edifice of electromagnetism. Our first small illustration of the power of this idea will be to resolve the small mystery of how a charged object attracts a neutral object and why that attraction should fall off as $1/r^5$. (Self-test E1X.6 provides a hint as to the answer.)

TWO-MINUTE PROBLEMS

E1T.1 All uncharged macroscopic objects contain a large amount of positive charge exactly balanced by a large amount of negative charge. The positive charge in a cubic centimeter of water (mass = 1 g) is closest to what value?

A. 10^{-19} C
B. 10^{-4} C
C. 1 C
D. 10^{4} C
E. 10^{23} C

E1T.2 If you rub Saran Wrap on your cotton shirt, which becomes positively charged?

A. The cotton shirt
B. The Saran Wrap
C. Neither: both are insulators and so the charges remain where they are

E1T.3 Two nickels are each given a charge of +1 nC. If these nickels are placed 0.1 m apart, the magnitude of the force that each exerts on the other is closest to

A. zero
B. 10^{-16} N
C. 10^{-8} N
D. 1 μN
E. 10^{12} N
F. It is hard to calculate, because Coulomb's law doesn't apply (even approximately)

E1T.4 Consider two point charges q_1 and q_2 lying on the x axis. Consider a third charge q_3 located somewhere near q_1 and q_2. Assume that the net force exerted by these charges on q_3 is zero. This implies that q_3 *must* lie somewhere along the x axis, true (T) or false (F)?

E1T.5 Consider two point particles lying along the x axis separated by a distance d. These particles have charges that are equal in magnitude but opposite in sign. Where can a third point charge be placed so the net force on it is zero?

A. Halfway between the two charges
B. A distance d from both charges (so the three charges form an equilateral triangle)
C. Some point on the x axis but not between the two charges (I could compute the exact location given enough time)
D. There is *no* point where the force would be zero
E. Depends on the charges' signs and/or magnitudes
F. Other (explain)

E1T.6 Three identical charged particles are arranged in an equilateral triangle. If the force that each *individual* particle exerts on another is 1.0 N, the magnitude of the net force F_e exerted on any one of the three particles is

A. $F_e = 0$
B. $0 < F_e < 1.0$ N
C. $F_e = 1.0$ N
D. $1.0 \text{ N} < F_e < 2.0$ N
E. $F_e = 2.0$ N
F. $F_e > 2.0$ N

E1T.7 A friend claims that rubbing a rubber balloon with the friend's specially designed cloth gives the balloon a negative charge, but the cloth remains uncharged. Is this possible?

A. Yes
B. Yes, but only if the cloth is a conductor and the person using it is not insulated from the ground
C. No, this is not possible.

E1T.8 An inventor claims to have invented a device that, when activated, becomes strongly charged, even if the device is suspended by an insulating thread in a vacuum. This is physically possible (T or F).

E1T.9 We can certify that an object is definitely positively charged using which of the following tests by

A. Showing the object is attracted by a negative charge
B. Showing the object is repelled by a positive charge
C. Doing either of the tests above

HOMEWORK PROBLEMS

Basic Skills

E1B.1 Two point particles separated by 8.0 cm have charges $q_1 = +12$ nC and $q_2 = -42$ nC respectively. Find the magnitude of the force that each exerts on the other.

E1B.2 What is the magnitude of the force exerted by a proton on an electron when the two are 0.05 nm apart? (This is roughly the typical separation of these particles in a hydrogen atom).

E1B.3 What is the total charge (in coulombs) of the protons in a gram of hydrogen gas?

E1B.4 Avogadro's number of water molecules has a mass of 18 g. If we were somehow able to remove an electron from one out of every 10^9 molecules in a gram of water, what would be its charge?

E1B.5 Two point charges ($q_1 = +20$ nC and $q_2 = -40$ nC are placed 10.0 cm apart along the x axis. Where can a third charge ($q_3 = +20$ nC) be placed so that the net electrical force on that charge is zero?

E1B.6 Two point charges ($q_1 = +25$ nC and $q_2 = +100$ nC are placed 12 cm apart along the x axis. Where can a third charge ($q_3 = -15$ nC) be placed so that the net electrical force on that charge is zero?

E1B.7 Two point particles (with charges $q_1 = +30$ nC and $q_2 = -30$ nC) are placed on the x axis 20 cm apart, with the negative particle to the left of the positive particle. A third point particle (with charge $q_3 =$ +20 nC) is placed on the x axis halfway between the first two. What is the force (magnitude and direction) on the third particle?

E1B.8 Two point particles (with charges $q_1 = +120$ nC and $q_2 = +30$ nC) are placed on the x axis 20 cm apart, with the second to the left of the first. A third particle (with $q_3 = -60$ nC) is placed on the x axis halfway between the first two. What is the force (magnitude and direction) on the third particle?

E1B.9 Compute the ratio between the magnitudes of the gravitational force and the electrical force between two electrons separated by 1.0 m. How does this ratio change if we bring the electrons closer?

Synthetic

E1S.1 Two small steel balls (mass ≈ 5.6 g each) are separated by a distance of 5.0 cm. If one in every billion electrons could be removed from each ball, what would be the approximate magnitude of the electrostatic force exerted by each ball on the other? (*Hint:* Steel is essentially iron, and an iron nucleus contains 26 protons and 30 neutrons).

E1S.2 Two small steel balls (mass ≈ 5.6 g each) separated by 10 cm are given the same positive charge and are found to repel each other with a force of 0.1 N (somewhat less than an ounce). What fraction of the electrons in each steel ball have been removed? (*Hint:* Steel is essentially iron, and iron nucleus contains 26 protons and 30 neutrons).

E1S.3 If the density of charge on a surface exceeds about 5×10^{-5} C/m^2, the electrical forces exerted by the charge will be strong enough to ionize air near the surface, making the air a conductor and thus draining the charge away from the surface. What is the maximum charge that can be put on the surface of a sphere 1.0 cm in diameter? (This effect is what in practice defines the upper limit of the charge that can be put on an object by rubbing.)

E1S.4 Three particles, each having a charge of +10 nC, are arranged in an equilateral triangle 10 cm on a side. What is the magnitude of the force on any one of the particles?

E1S.5 Four identical particles, each having a charge of +120 nC, are arranged in a square 6.0 cm on a side. Find the magnitude of the force acting on any one of the charges, and describe the direction of this force in words.

E1S.6 Four particles are arranged in a square 5.0 cm on a side. The magnitude of each of the charges is 33 nC, but the signs of the charges alternate as you go around the square. Find the magnitude of the force acting on any one of the particles, and describe in words the direction of the force vector. Does your description of the direction of the force depend on the sign of the charge you chose?

E1S.7 A particle with charge $q_1 = +30$ nC is placed on the x axis of a certain coordinate system at $x = 10$ cm. A particle with charge $q_2 = -60$ nC is placed on the y axis at $y = 15$ cm. Determine the magnitude and direction of the force on a particle with charge $q_3 =$ +10 nC placed at the origin.

E1S.8 A particle with charge $q_1 = +1.0$ nC is placed on the x axis of a certain coordinate system at $x = 10$ cm. A particle with charge $q_2 = -0.50$ μC is placed on the

y axis at $y = -20$ cm. Determine the magnitude and direction of the force on a particle with charge $q_3 = +0.10$ nC at the origin.

E1S.9 Two point charges, one with charge $+q$ and one with charge $+9q$ are placed a distance d apart. It is possible to place a third charge so that the net electrical force on *all three* charges is zero. What is the sign, magnitude, and position of this third charge (in terms of q and d)?

E1S.10 Two small spheres with mass m are suspended with insulating threads of length L from a common point. When the spheres are uncharged, they hang so they touch each other, but when they are both given the same charge q, they repel each other and hang a distance d apart, as shown in figure E1.11. Assume that d is pretty small compared to L but large compared to the diameter of the balls.

(a) Explain using a net-force diagram why the magnitude of the electrostatic force $\vec{F}_e$ acting on either ball must be

$$F_e = mg\tan\theta \tag{E1.8}$$

(b) Explain why in this situation we can approximate

$$\tan\theta \approx \frac{d}{2L} \tag{E1.9}$$

By what percent is this expression in error if $d = L/10$?

(c) Combine the answers to parts (a) and (b) with Coulomb's law to show that

$$|q| = \sqrt{\frac{mgd^3}{2kL}} \tag{E1.10}$$

(d) If this situation is demonstrated in your class, use the measured values of L, m, and d to estimate q. Otherwise, calculate q assuming that $L = 70$ cm, $d = 4.0$ cm, and $m = 0.4$ g.

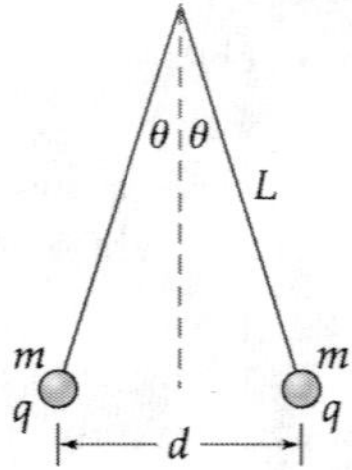

Figure E1.11 The situation discussed in problem E1S.10.

Rich-Context

E1R.1 Two small 0.1-g Styrofoam balls are strung like beads on a vertical insulating thread. The lower ball is glued to the thread but the upper ball is free to move. Imagine that both are given an equal amount of negative charge such that the upper ball is suspended above the lower with their centers 4.0 cm apart. (Assume that each ball repels the other as if it were a point charge located at its center.) Roughly how many electrons have have been added to each ball? Express your result as a fraction of the total number of electrons initially inside each ball. [*Hint*: Styrofoam is made mostly of low-mass atoms having roughly equal numbers of protons and neutrons.]

E1R.2 Imagine that you rub about a 10-cm length of a rubber rod 1.0 cm in diameter with fur, giving it a charge of −100 nC (this is close to the maximum charge one can put on such a rod). Rubber (which has a density about equal to water) can be considered to be made of building blocks of C_5H_8. Using this information, very roughly estimate what fraction of these building blocks on the surface of the rubber have gained an electron from the rubbing.

Advanced

E1A.1 Imagine that we place two particles, both with charge $+q$, on the y axis at $y = +d$ and $y = -d$ respectively. Imagine further that we have a particle with charge $-q$ constrained to move along the x axis.

(a) Argue that for small displacements from the origin such that $x \ll d$, the net x-force on the negative particle has the form of Hooke's law:

$$F_x = -k_s x \tag{E1.11}$$

where k_s is some constant.

(b) Find an expression for the frequency of small oscillations in terms of ε_0, q, d and the mass m of the negative charge. (*Hint:* See chapter N11.)

(c) Say that the particles are actually small Styrofoam balls. Reasonable values of q, d, and m in such a case might be $q = 5$ nC, $d = 10$ cm, and $m = 0.05$ g. Compute the frequency of small oscillations of the negative ball.

ANSWERS TO SELF-TESTS

E1X.1 Both *U* tapes were prepared in the same way, so they really *should* have like charges. It is *conceivable* that they might get charges of random signs from the preparation process, but this would mean that sometimes the *U* tapes would attract and sometimes repel. Since we consistently observe *U* tapes to behave the same way, the model that they get the *same* charges from the process makes more sense. Assuming that this is true, it must be like charges that repel.

E1X.2 See which tape is repelled by a charged comb (which is negatively charged). You should find that the *T* tape is negative (for most brands of tape).

E1X.3 *Model* Avogadro's number of *nucleons* (protons and/or neutrons) has a mass of about 1 g. Copper has 29 protons per 63 nucleons (see figure E1.2). *Solution* The number of protons in the penny is about

$$5\,\cancel{g}\left(\frac{6.02\times10^{23}\ \text{nu}\cancel{\text{cle}}\text{ons}}{1\ \cancel{g}}\right)\left(\frac{29\ \text{protons}}{63\ \text{nu}\cancel{\text{cle}}\text{ons}}\right)$$

$$= 1.4\times10^{24}\ \text{protons} \tag{E1.12}$$

The total charge of these protons is

$$1.4\times10^{24}\ \text{pro}\cancel{\text{to}}\text{ns}\left(\frac{1.60\times10^{-19}\ \text{C}}{1\ \text{pr}\cancel{\text{ot}}\text{on}}\right)$$

$$= 220{,}000\ \text{C}. \tag{E1.13}$$

Evaluation This is an *enormous* amount of charge, about 10^{13} times the charge that one can put on an object that size in practice.

E1X.4 A decay process involves the disintegration of a particle into fragments. Conservation of relativistic energy implies that the fragments must have smaller total rest mass than the electron. But if there is no lighter charged particle than the electron, then any decay process that is consistent with conservation of relativistic energy will violate conservation of charge.

E1X.5 *Model* We can calculate the force using Coulomb's law (approximating the pennies by point objects) *Solution* According to the results of self-test E1X.3, if we remove one electron out of every thousand, each penny will end up with a positive charge of about 220 C. If we separate two such pennies by 1.0 m, the magnitude of the electrostatic force acting on either will be

$$F_e = \frac{|q_1 q_2|}{4\pi\varepsilon_0 r^2} = 8.99\times10^9\,\frac{\text{N}\cdot\text{m}^2}{\text{C}^2}\,\frac{(220\ \text{C})^2}{(1.0\ \text{m})^2}$$

$$= 4.4\times10^{14}\ \text{N} \tag{E1.14}$$

Evaluation My weight is about 550 N, so this would be the weight of roughly a trillion people!

E1X.6 Consider the forces acting on the charges in object *A*. The positive charge in *A* is slightly closer to the negative charge in object *B* than to the positive charge in *B*, so the positive charge in *A* will be somewhat attracted to *B*. On the other hand, the negative charge in *A*, will be somewhat repelled by *B*, because the negative charge in *B* is closer. However, the negative charge in *A* is a bit further from *B* as a whole than the positive charge in *A* is, so the repulsion it feels will be slightly weaker than the attraction that the positive charge in A feels. Therefore, these objects will very weakly attract each other.

E2 Electric Fields

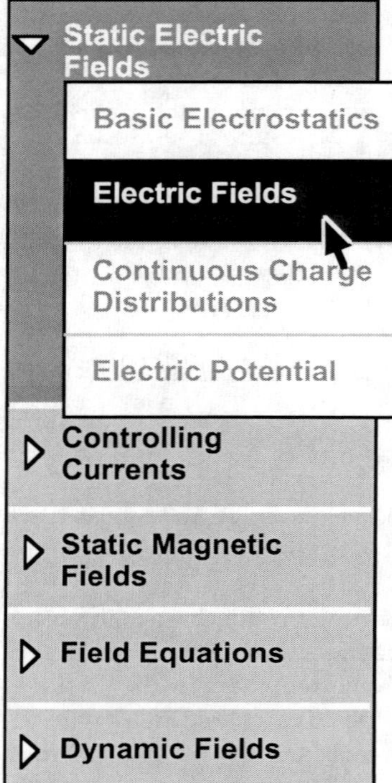

Chapter Overview

Introduction

Coulomb's law provides a straightforward model of how charged particles interact. However, this chapter introduces an alternative *field model* of electrostatic interactions that proves more useful in the long run.

Section E2.1: The Field Concept

Taken literally, Coulomb's law describes an **action-at-a-distance** model of electrostatic interactions where charged particles exert forces directly and instantaneously on one another across the distance separating them. A **field model** instead imagines that a charged particle creates a **field** in the space around it, and another particle responds to the field at its own location, not to the first particle directly:

$$\text{charge} \leftrightarrow \text{field} \leftrightarrow \text{charge} \quad (\text{instead of} \quad \text{charge} \leftrightarrow \text{charge}) \tag{E2.1}$$

We need a field model because the instantaneous action-at-a-distance implied by Coulomb's law violates the relativistic principle that no effect can travel faster than the speed of light c. A field can carry effects between particles at a speed $\leq c$.

Note that a field (*unlike* a particle) exists not at a specific location but throughout space. Even so, we will see subsequent chapters that a field is a physical object that (*like* a particle) has energy, carries momentum and obeys equations of motion.

Section E2.2: An Operational Definition of the Electric Field

We describe an electric field by attaching to every point in space an **electric field vector** $\vec{E}$ such that

$$\vec{E} \equiv \frac{\vec{F}_e}{q} \quad \Leftrightarrow \quad \vec{F}_e = q\vec{E} \qquad \text{(E2.2 and E2.3)}$$

Purpose: The first version of this equation *defines* the electric field vector $\vec{E}$ at a point in space and time in terms of the electrostatic force $\vec{F}_e$ experienced by a particle with charge q at rest at that point and time. When the field vector $\vec{E}$ at a given point and time is known, the second (inverted) version allows one to calculate the electrostatic force $\vec{F}_e$ acting on a particle with charge q at that point.

Limitation: The charge q on the particle must be small enough so that *it* does not significantly push around the charges in the distribution creating $\vec{E}$.

Note: $\vec{E}$ points in the same direction as $\vec{F}_e$ if q is positive.

Performing the measurement $\vec{E} \equiv \vec{F}_e / q$ at all points in space at a given time determines the entire field at that time as a **vector function** $\vec{E}(x, y, z)$ of position.

The electric field vector $\vec{E}$ is for electrostatics what the gravitational field vector $\vec{g}$ for gravity: $\vec{g}$ is defined analogously as being $\vec{g} \equiv \vec{F}_e / m$.

Section E2.3: The Electric Field of a Single Charged Particle

Coulomb's law and the definition of $\vec{E}$ imply that the electric field of a point particle is

$$\vec{E} = \frac{1}{4\pi\varepsilon_0}\frac{q}{r_{PC}^2}\hat{r}_{PC} = \frac{1}{4\pi\varepsilon_0}\frac{q}{r_{PC}^3}\vec{r}_{PC} \qquad \text{(E2.9)}$$

Purpose: This equation describes the electric field vector $\vec{E}$ at an arbitrary point P created by a point charge q located at point C.

Symbols: $\vec{r}_{PC} \equiv \vec{r}_P - \vec{r}_C$ is the position of point P relative to C, $r_{PC} = \text{mag}(\vec{r}_{PC})$, and $\hat{r}_{PC} \equiv \vec{r}_{PC}/r_{PC}$ is a directional (unit vector) standing for the direction at P that is "away from the charge q." ε_0 is the permittivity constant.

Limitations: The charge q must be a point particle at rest.

Note: The field vector $\vec{E}$ points away from q if $q > 0$, and *toward* q if $q < 0$.

Section E2.4: The Superposition Principle

The **superposition principle** implies that the net electric field $\vec{E}$ created at a given point P by a *set* of charged particles is simply

$$\vec{E} = \vec{E}_1 + \vec{E}_2 + \vec{E}_3 + \ldots \qquad \text{(E2.12)}$$

Purpose: This equation describes how electric fields combine.

Symbols: $\vec{E}$ is the total electric field at point P, $\vec{E}_1$ is the electric field vector produced at P by particle q_1 alone, $\vec{E}_2$ same for q_2 alone, and so on.

Limitations: None are known!

We can therefore (in principle) calculate the field created by any charged object simply by summing the fields created by each charged particle in the object.

Section E2.5: The Electric Field of a Dipole

An **electric dipole,** which is a pair of charges $+q$ and $-q$ separated by a small distance d, creates an electric field (see figure E2.4) whose magnitude at points a distance r from the dipole along a given line going through the dipole $\propto qd/r^3$ when $r >> d$. Note that this field falls off more rapidly with increasing r than that of a point charge.

Section E2.6: Electrostatic Polarization

The electric field created by an external point charge can distort an atom's electron cloud, making the atom an electric dipole. Alternatively, a molecule that has a natural permanent dipole will experience a torque $\vec{\tau}$ in an external electric field that seeks to twist the dipole so that it is aligned with the field:

$$\vec{\tau}_{\text{dp}} = \vec{p}_e \times \vec{E} \qquad \text{(E2.18)}$$

Purpose: This equation describes the torque $\vec{\tau}_{\text{dp}}$ that a dipole with **dipole moment** $\vec{p}_e$ experiences in an external electric field $\vec{E}$.

Symbols: $\vec{p}_e = q\vec{d}$ where $\vec{d}$ is the displacement from the dipole's negative charge $-q$ to its positive charge $+q$. Note that $\text{mag}(\vec{p}) = qd$.

Limitations: In practice, equation E2.18 defines the dipole moment vector $\vec{p}_e$.

In either case, a charged object's electric field creates oriented dipoles in a neutral object that in turn attract the charged object. This process of **electrostatic polarization** explains how a charged object can attract an electrically neutral object. The net dipole moment produced by an external field $\vec{E}$ in a small object is typically $\propto \text{mag}(\vec{E})$ at that object, which is $\propto 1/r^2$ if the external field is created by a charged particle. Since the field created by the resulting net dipole is $\propto 1/r^3$, the attractive force between a charged particle and a small neutral object will be roughly $\propto 1/r^5$.

Section E2.7: The Mystery du Jour

Section E2.1 claims that an electric field is a form of energy. What is the evidence for this? We will develop the tools we need to answer this question in chapter E3.

E2.1 The Field Concept

As we saw in the last chapter, Coulomb's law provides a simple model for understanding how charged particles interact. Physicists in the mid 1800s took a crucial step toward a better understanding of the electromagnetic phenomena by developing a more sophisticated *field model* of the electromagnetic interaction. In this section, we will see why such a model is needed.

Coulomb's law expresses action at a distance

Coulomb's law presents a straightforward picture of how two point charges q_1 and q_2 interact: each exerts *directly* on the other a force parallel to the line connecting them. This model of the electrostatic interaction is called an **action-at-a-distance** model, since each charge is imagined to act *directly* on another charge across the distance between them. (Newton's law of universal gravitation implies the same kind of model for the gravitational interaction.)

Coulomb's law is accurate as long as the charged objects in question are essentially at rest, but problems arise if they are not. Taken literally, Coulomb's law implies that the force exerted by one charge on the other at a given instant of time depends on the distance between those charges *at that instant* and acts along the line connecting those charges *at that instant*. If this were really true, then we could make a device that would allow us to communicate instantaneously over large distances. For example, imagine that at point P, I suddenly wiggle a point charge. If you measure the electrical force acting on another charge at point Q, you will see the direction of that force wiggle a bit at exactly the same time I wiggle the charge. We could use this effect to send a message instantaneously between points P and Q, even over very large distances.

But this is inconsistent with the theory of relativity, which asserts that *no* signal can travel between two points faster than the speed of light. So if the theory of relativity is true, then Coulomb's law *cannot* be literally correct.†

The field model presents an alternative to an action-at-a-distance model

The **field model** provides an alternative that avoids this problem. In the field model, we imagine that the space around a charged particle is filled with something called an **electric field**. Unlike a particle, a field does not occupy a single point but rather exists at *all* points in space simultaneously. We in fact describe a field mathematically by assigning some kind of numerical quantity to every point in the space. Like a particle, though, a field (as we will see) is a real thing that has energy, carries momentum, and obeys equations of motion that describe how it evolves with time in response to its surroundings.

In a field model, the field *mediates* the interaction

In the field model, charges do not *directly* exert forces on each other but each rather responds to the *field* that the other creates in its vicinity. The field thus *mediates* the interaction between the two charges. If we represent the action-at-a-distance model schematically by

$$\text{charge} \leftrightarrow \text{charge} \qquad \text{(action-at-a-distance model)} \tag{E2.1a}$$

(expressing the idea that in this model, the charges interact *directly* with each other), then we can represent the field model schematically by:

$$\text{charge} \leftrightarrow \text{field} \leftrightarrow \text{charge} \qquad \text{(field model)} \tag{E2.1b}$$

expressing the idea each charge sets up a field to which the other responds.

This makes consistency with relativity possible

How does this resolve the problem with regard to the instantaneous communication implied by Coulomb's law? In the field model, if one charged particle is wiggled, it does not *directly* affect a distant particle. Rather, the wiggling particle wiggles the values of the field in its immediate vicinity, and these wiggles in turn affect the field values at slightly more distant locations, and so

†If Coulomb's law were literally true, then (according to chapter R8) it would be possible to find an inertial reference frame in which the force on the point charge at point Q changes before the charge at point P is wiggled, which is absurd!

on. The net effect is that ripples in the field move away from the wiggling particle at a finite speed like ripples on the surface of a pond. Only when these ripples reach the distant charged particle will it feel a wiggling electrical force. As long as these ripples move at a speed less than or equal to that of light, then the field model will be consistent with relativity. Maxwell's theory of the electromagnetic field, which we will develop throughout this unit, provides a complete and relativistically consistent picture of how this all works.

This argument was not the historical path to the field model

While this argument makes it clear why we need a field model, I also want to make it clear that the physics community did not *historically* arrive at the model this way. It rather arose slowly as the community struggled (through an involved process of trial and error) to understand electromagnetic phenomena. Einstein invented the theory of relativity, decades after Maxwell's field theory was complete, to explain how that theory was consistent with the principle of relativity. Thus the historical process was actually the *reverse* of the argument I have presented! Even so, our present understanding of relativity helps us see why we need an electromagnetic field theory more clearly and immediately than following the historical path would.

General relativity is the analogous field theory for gravitation

By the way, the same problem arises with Newton's law of universal gravitation. General relativity solves the problem by providing a field theory for gravity analogous to Maxwell's field theory for the electromagnetic interaction. Both theories have surprising and exciting consequences unanticipated by the newtonian action-at-a-distance models.

E2.2 An Operational Definition of the Electric Field

Even in the absence of wiggling charges, the field concept is very useful when we consider the combined effects of a *set* of charges distributed in space. A distribution of charges also fills the space around it with a total electric field that is in some sense a combination of the fields of the individual point charges in the set. Our most important task in this chapter and the next will be to learn how to represent and calculate the electric field created by such distributions.

How can we quantitatively describe the electric field filling the space around a distribution of charges? *We define the field in terms of what it does.* If the basic action of a field is to exert a force on a charged particle, why not *define* the field in terms of the force that it exerts?

So, to evaluate the electric field at a given point in space and time, imagine taking a test particle with some known test charge q, holding it *at rest* at that point, and measuring the electrical force $\vec{F}_e$ exerted on the charge at that time. (Note that if we hold the charge at rest, the *net* force on the charge will be zero, so the magnitude of the electrostatic force will be equal to that of the measurable opposing force we need to apply to the charge to keep it at rest.) Define the **electric field vector** $\vec{E}$ at that point and at that time to be

The operational definition of the electric field vector at a point in space at a given time

$$\vec{E} \equiv \frac{\vec{F}_e}{q} \qquad \text{(E2.2)}$$

Purpose: This equation defines the electric field vector $\vec{E}$ at a point in space and time.

Symbols: $\vec{F}_e$ is the electromagnetic force experienced at that time by a small test particle with charge q placed *at rest* at that point in space.

Limitation: The charge q must be small enough so that it does not significantly push around the charges in the distribution creating $\vec{E}$.

Note: $\vec{E}$ points in the same direction as $\vec{F}_e$ if q is positive, but opposite to $\vec{F}_e$ if q is negative.

Self-Test E2X.1

What are the SI units of the electric field vector?

Why divide the force by the test particle's charge q? We find experimentally (and will shortly see theoretically) that for *any* charge distribution, the force a test charge experiences at a given location is *proportional* to q. Dividing by q thus produces a quantity $\vec{E}$ that depends *only* on the character of the distribution creating the field and one's position in space relative to that distribution, and has nothing to do with the particular test charge we use.

Note we want q to be small enough so that the electrical forces that *it* exerts do not significantly push around the set of charges creating $\vec{E}$, thus *changing* the spatial distribution of the charges whose field we are trying to measure! (Technically, we should take the limit of equation E2.2 as $q \to 0$.) The reason that the test charge must be at *rest* will become clearer in chapter E7.

The concept of a *vector function*

The definition in equation E2.2 implies that the numerical quantity that we assign to every point in space to describe an electric field is in fact a *vector* $\vec{E}$. It is essential to understand, however, that a charged object's electric field is not a single vector in the same way that a moving particle has a single velocity vector. An object's electric field is rather an infinite *set* of vectors, with (potentially) a different vector for every point in space. One has to specify the field vectors at *all* points to describe the field fully. However, literally listing field vectors for *all* points in space impossible. Whenever possible, physicists instead describe an object's total electric field at a given instant of time using a **vector function** $\vec{E}(x,y,z)$. Just as an ordinary function $f(x)$ implicitly attaches a number to every point x on the number line by describing how to *calculate* that number in terms of x, so a vector function $\vec{E}(x,y,z)$ implicitly assigns a vector to every point in space by describing how to calculate $\vec{E}$ for every possible choice of that point's position coordinates x, y, and z. Such a function, when available, provides a compact and useful way to describe a field. (In practice, one can do this quite easily by describing the vector's components E_x, E_y, and E_z as ordinary scalar functions of x, y, and z.)

How to calculate the force on a charge given the field vector at the charge's location

If we know the electric field vector $\vec{E}$ at a given point, we can invert the definition given by equation E2.2 to determine the force exerted by that field on any charge q at that location location using

$$\vec{F}_e = q\vec{E} \tag{E2.3}$$

A field having a magnitude of 1 N/C at a point thus exerts a force of 1 N on a 1-C charge placed at that point. Again, this equation will only be accurate if q is small enough that it does not significantly push around the charges that are creating the electric field $\vec{E}$.

Field strength benchmarks

The magnitude of the electric field outdoors on a sunny day (due to various processes that separate atmospheric charges) is about 100 to 150 N/C. During a thunderstorm, atmospheric fields may exceed 10,000 N/C. Charges separated by moving water in your morning shower can create a 800-N/C field. If the field strength in air anywhere exceeds 3×10^6 N/C, air breaks down and becomes a conductor, and sparks fly.

Comparing the electric and gravitational field vectors

You are already familiar with the analogous *gravitational* field vector $\vec{g}$, the vector whose value near the earth's surface is 9.8 m/s^2 toward the earth's center. We define $\vec{g}$ at a given point near a massive object in a way very similar to equations E2.2 and E2.3: we measure the gravitational force exerted on a test particle placed at the point in question and then divide by the mass m of that test particle.

$$\vec{F}_g \equiv m\vec{g} \quad \Rightarrow \quad \vec{g}\text{ (at a point } P) \equiv \frac{\vec{F}_g(\text{on mass } m \text{ at } P)}{m} \tag{E2.4}$$

Just as $\vec{E}$ is measured in N/C, so $\vec{g}$ is measured in N/kg, which happens to be the same as m/s^2. Thus $\vec{g}$ is to the gravitational field what $\vec{E}$ is to the electric field. This analogy may help you become more comfortable with what the electric field vector $\vec{E}$ represents.

E2.3 The Electric Field of a Single Charged Particle

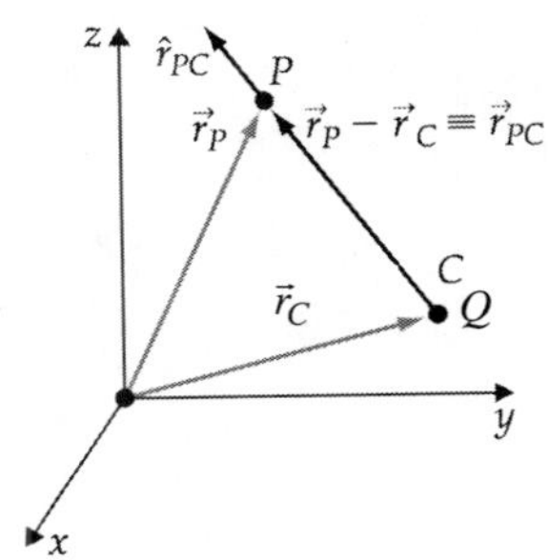

Figure E2.1
A diagram illustrating the definition of the vector $\vec{r}_{PC} \equiv \vec{r}_P - \vec{r}_C$ and the unit vector $\hat{r}_{PC}$.

Let us now apply this definition to determine the electric field of the simplest possible charge distribution: an isolated charged particle. Consider a a particle with charge Q placed at a point C whose position is $\vec{r}_C = [x_C, y_C, z_C]$. What is the electric field produced by this particle at an arbitrary point P whose position is $\vec{r}_P = [x, y, z]$? Coulomb's law tells us that the electrostatic force on a test particle of charge q at P is

$$F_e = \frac{1}{4\pi\varepsilon_0}\frac{|Qq|}{r_{PC}^2}, \quad \text{where} \quad \begin{array}{l}\vec{F}_e \text{ points } \textit{away} \text{ from charge } Q \text{ if } Qq > 0 \\ \vec{F}_e \text{ points } \textit{toward} \text{ charge } Q \text{ if } Qq < 0\end{array} \tag{E2.5}$$

where $\vec{r}_{PC} \equiv \vec{r}_P - \vec{r}_C$ is the position of point P relative to the charged particle's position at point C, and r_{PC} is the distance between the two points: $r_{PC} \equiv \text{mag}(\vec{r}_P - \vec{r}_C)$ (see figure E2.1). Now, the indication of the direction in equation E2.5 is more awkward than necessary. We can make this simpler if we note that the vector $\vec{r}_{PC} \equiv \vec{r}_P - \vec{r}_C$ points directly *away* from the particle with charge Q at point C. Therefore, the directional

Definition of the useful directional $\hat{r}_{PC}$.

$$\hat{r}_{PC} \equiv \frac{\vec{r}_{PC}}{r_{PC}} = \frac{\vec{r}_P - \vec{r}_C}{\text{mag}(\vec{r}_P - \vec{r}_C)} \tag{E2.6}$$

is a vector of unit magnitude that points in the direction "away from C."

Self-Test E2X.2

Take the magnitude of both sides of equation E2.6 and verify that $\hat{r}_{PC}$ has a magnitude of 1 (with no units).

Using this directional, we can express equation E2.5 in the compact form:

$$\vec{F}_e = \frac{1}{4\pi\varepsilon_0}\frac{Qq}{r_{PC}^2}\hat{r}_{PC} \tag{E2.7}$$

Note that if $Qq > 0$, this vector points in the direction $\hat{r}_{PC}$ = "away from C" and if $Qq < 0$, it points in the direction $-\hat{r}_{PC}$ = "toward C."

Equation E2.2 then implies the electric field vector at point P due to Q is

$$\vec{E}(\text{at } P) \equiv \frac{\vec{F}_e}{q} = \frac{1}{q}\left(\frac{1}{4\pi\varepsilon_0}\frac{Qq}{r_{PC}^2}\hat{r}_{PC}\right) = \frac{1}{4\pi\varepsilon_0}\frac{Q}{r_{PC}^2}\hat{r}_{PC} \tag{E2.8}$$

Note how dividing by q has erased all references to the test particle's charge q! The electric field vector produced at a given point P by an isolated particle of charge Q at point C therefore depends *only* on Q and the position of point P relative to point C.

To summarize, the formula that describes the electric field of a single isolated particle with charge Q is

The formula describing the electric field of an isolated charged particle

$$\vec{E} = \frac{1}{4\pi\varepsilon_0}\frac{Q}{r_{PC}^2}\hat{r}_{PC} \tag{E2.9a}$$

Purpose: This equation describes the electric field vector $\vec{E}$ at an arbitrary point P created by a particle with charge Q located at point C.

Symbols: $\vec{r}_{PC} \equiv \vec{r}_P - \vec{r}_C$ is the position of point P relative to C, $r_{PC} = \text{mag}(\vec{r}_{PC})$, $\hat{r}_{PC} \equiv \vec{r}_{PC}/r_{PC}$ is a directional (unit vector) standing for the direction at P that is "away from the charged particle," and $(4\pi\varepsilon_0)^{-1}$ is the Coulomb constant $8.99\times10^9\ \text{N·m}^2/\text{C}^2$.

Limitations: This equation technically applies only to a charged particle at rest.

Note: $\vec{E}$ points away from Q if $Q > 0$, *toward* Q if $Q < 0$.

A *field diagram*

Equation E2.9 describes a vector *function* for the electric field in the sense that either tells us how to compute the field vector at an *arbitrary* point P. Figure E2.2 illustrates the total field created by positive and negative point charges by showing what the field vectors look like at a sampling of points surrounding the point charge. We call such a picture a **field diagram**.

Displaying explicitly how this vector function depends on x, y, and z

If we want to display $\vec{E}(x, y, z)$ *explicitly* as a vector *function* of the point P's position coordinates x, y, and z, it helps to use the definition of $\hat{r}_{PC}$ to write equation E2.9a in the form

$$\vec{E} = \frac{1}{4\pi\varepsilon_0}\frac{Q}{r_{PQ}^2}\hat{r}_{PQ} = \frac{1}{4\pi\varepsilon_0}\frac{Q}{r_{PQ}^2}\frac{\vec{r}_{PQ}}{r_{PQ}} = \frac{1}{4\pi\varepsilon_0}\frac{Q}{r_{PQ}^3}\vec{r}_{PQ} \tag{E2.9b}$$

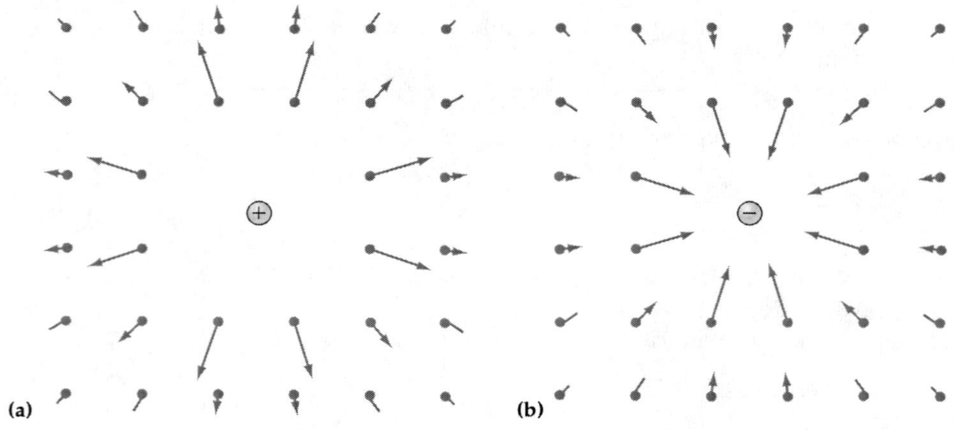

Figure E2.2
These drawings illustrate the electric fields of a positive charged particle and a negative charged particle respectively. The arrow at a point represents the magnitude and direction of the electric field at that point (the arrow head is omitted if the vector is too short). Note that the vectors are longest near the charge; the magnitudes of the field vectors fall off as the inverse square of the distance from the charge.

Equation E2.9a has the advantage of clearly displaying that the magnitude of $\vec{E}$ at P depends on $1/r_{PC}^2$, but equation E2.9b is often more practical when we actually want to calculate $\vec{E}$. Since $\vec{r}_{PC} = \vec{r}_P - \vec{r}_C = [x - x_C,\ y - y_C,\ z - z_C]$,

$$\vec{E}(x,y,z) = \frac{1}{4\pi\varepsilon_0}\frac{Q}{r_{PQ}^3}\vec{r}_{PQ}$$

$$= \frac{1}{4\pi\varepsilon_0}\frac{Q}{[(x-x_C)^2+(y-y_C)^2+(z-z_C)^2]^{3/2}}\begin{bmatrix} x-x_C \\ y-y_C \\ z-z_C \end{bmatrix} \qquad \text{(E2.9c)}$$

This makes it clear that equation E2.9 does indeed specify a vector *function* that implicitly defines the charged particle's entire electric field.

E2.4 The Superposition Principle

According to the *superposition principle* discussed in chapter E1, the net electric *force* $\vec{F}_e$ exerted on a test particle of charge q at an arbitrary point P by a set of other particles with charges $q_1, q_2, q_3, \ldots$ is the *sum* of the forces that each individually exerts on the test charge:

$$\vec{F}_e = \vec{F}_1 + \vec{F}_2 + \vec{F}_3 + \ldots = \frac{1}{4\pi\varepsilon_0}\frac{qq_1}{r_{P1}^2}\hat{r}_{P1} + \frac{1}{4\pi\varepsilon_0}\frac{qq_2}{r_{P2}^2}\hat{r}_{P2} + \frac{1}{4\pi\varepsilon_0}\frac{qq_3}{r_{P3}^2}\hat{r}_{P3} + \ldots$$

$$= q\left[\frac{1}{4\pi\varepsilon_0}\frac{q_1}{r_{P1}^2}\hat{r}_{P1} + \frac{1}{4\pi\varepsilon_0}\frac{q_2}{r_{P2}^2}\hat{r}_{P2} + \frac{1}{4\pi\varepsilon_0}\frac{q_3}{r_{P3}^2}\hat{r}_{P3} + \ldots\right] \qquad \text{(E2.10)}$$

Note that this $\vec{F}_e$ is always proportional to the charge of the test particle (as I asserted in section E2.1). According to our definition of electric field, the net electric field vector $\vec{E}$ at an arbitrary point P is thus

$$\vec{E} \equiv \frac{\vec{F}_e}{q} = \frac{1}{4\pi\varepsilon_0}\frac{q_1}{r_{P1}^2}\hat{r}_{P1} + \frac{1}{4\pi\varepsilon_0}\frac{q_2}{r_{P2}^2}\hat{r}_{P2} + \frac{1}{4\pi\varepsilon_0}\frac{q_3}{r_{P3}^2}\hat{r}_{P3} + \ldots \qquad \text{(E2.11)}$$

But this is just the vector sum of the electric field vectors that the particles with charges $q_1, q_2, q_3, \ldots$ would individually produce at point P. Therefore

$$\vec{E} = \vec{E}_1 + \vec{E}_2 + \ldots \qquad \text{(E2.12)}$$

Purpose: This equation describes how electric fields combine.
Symbols: $\vec{E}$ is the total electric field at an arbitrary point P, $\vec{E}_1$ is the electric field vector produced at P by particle with charge q_1 alone, $\vec{E}_2$ is the same for the particle with charge q_2 alone, and so on.
Limitations: None are known!

The superposition principle

Since all charge distributions are ultimately collections of charged particles, this equation applies quite generally to any charged object or set of objects.

Note that if we place a point charge q_0 at point P, the force it experiences is $\vec{F}_e = q_0\vec{E}$, where $\vec{E}$ is the total electric field created at P by charged particles *other* than the one with charge q_0. No matter how a charged particle's field might contribute to the total electric field *elsewhere*, that particle's field *never* exerts a force on the particle *itself*. This is a very important to understand!

A charged particle does not exert an electrostatic force on itself

Example E2.1

Problem Calculate the magnitude and directions of the field vectors at points A and B in figure E2.3, expressing your results in terms of ε_0, q, and d. (Note that q in this problem does not refer to the charge of a test particle, but simply represents a certain positive quantity of charge.)

Model Assume that the charged objects in this diagram are point-like particles. We can then use equation E2.9b to compute the electric field created by each particle at the point in question, and add the field vectors (as *vectors*) to find the total field vector at that point.

Solution In the given coordinate system, point A is a distance d in the $-x$ direction from q_1 and $2d$ in the same direction from q_2, so $\vec{r}_{A1} = [-d, 0, 0]$ and $\vec{r}_{A2} = [-2d, 0, 0]$. (We could have *calculated* $\vec{r}_{A1}$ using $\vec{r}_{A1} = \vec{r}_A - \vec{r}_1$, but this is actually more work in this case.) So

$$\vec{E}_A = \frac{kq_1}{r_{A1}^3}\vec{r}_{A1} + \frac{kq_2}{r_{A2}^3}\vec{r}_{A2} = \frac{kq}{d^3}\begin{bmatrix}-d\\0\\0\end{bmatrix} + \frac{k(-q)}{(2d)^3}\begin{bmatrix}-2d\\0\\0\end{bmatrix}$$

$$= \frac{kq}{d^2}\begin{bmatrix}-1\\0\\0\end{bmatrix} + \frac{kq}{4d^2}\begin{bmatrix}1\\0\\0\end{bmatrix} = \frac{kq}{4d^2}\begin{bmatrix}-4+1\\0\\0\end{bmatrix} = \frac{3kq}{4d^2}\begin{bmatrix}-1\\0\\0\end{bmatrix} \tag{E2.13}$$

(Note that I am using the symbol $k \equiv 1/4\pi\varepsilon_0$ in these equations to save a lot of writing. Feel free to do this in your problem solutions as well.) So $\vec{E}_A$ points in the $-x$ direction and has a magnitude of $E_A = 3kq/4d^2 = 3q/16\pi\varepsilon_0 d^2$.

Similarly, point B is a distance d in the $+y$ direction and a displacement of $\pm\frac{1}{2}d$ in the $+x$ direction from points 1 and 2 respectively, so $\vec{r}_{B1} = [+\frac{1}{2}d, d, 0]$ and $\vec{r}_{B2} = [-\frac{1}{2}d, d, 0]$. As $r_{B1} = r_{B2} = [(\pm\frac{1}{2}d)^2 + d^2 + 0]^{1/2} = [\frac{5}{4}d^2]^{1/2} = [\frac{5}{4}]^{1/2}d$. we have,

$$\vec{E}_B = \frac{kq_1}{r_{B1}^3}\vec{r}_{B1} + \frac{kq_2}{r_{B2}^3}\vec{r}_{B2} = \frac{kq}{[\frac{5}{4}]^{3/2}d^3}\begin{bmatrix}+\frac{1}{2}d\\d\\0\end{bmatrix} + \frac{k(-q)}{[\frac{5}{4}]^{3/2}d^3}\begin{bmatrix}-\frac{1}{2}d\\d\\0\end{bmatrix}$$

$$= \frac{kq}{[\frac{5}{4}]^{3/2}d^3}\begin{bmatrix}\frac{1}{2}d+\frac{1}{2}d\\d-d\\0\end{bmatrix} = [\tfrac{4}{5}]^{3/2}\frac{kq}{d^2}\begin{bmatrix}1\\0\\0\end{bmatrix} = 0.72\frac{kq}{d^2}\begin{bmatrix}1\\0\\0\end{bmatrix} \tag{E2.14}$$

So $\vec{E}_B = 0.72kq/d^2 = 0.72q/4\pi\varepsilon_0 d^2$ in the $+x$ direction.

Evaluation Both results have directions consistent with those obtained by *qualitatively sketching* the sum of the field vectors, as shown in figure E2.3.

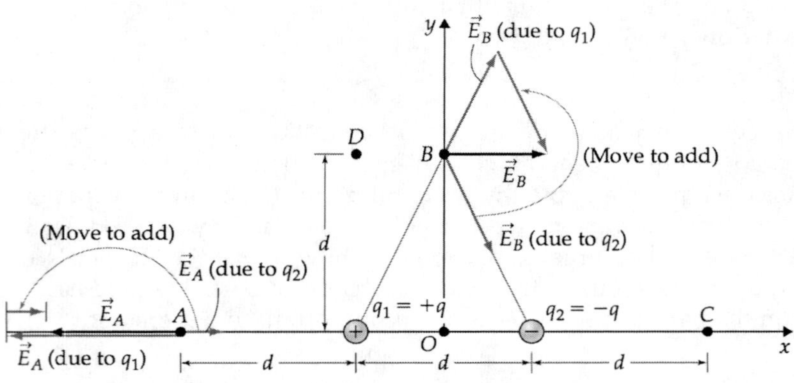

Figure E2.3
This drawing illustrates ho we can apply the superposition principle to sketch the electric field vectors at points near a simple pair of charged particles. To do the sketch, we have to estimate the relative magnitudes of the electric field vectors created at the point in question by each individual charged particle in the pair, then add them as vectors to get the total electric field.

Self-Test E2X.3

Calculate the electric field vectors at points C and D on figure E2.3 and check your calculation by sketching arrows on the diagram.

Self-Test E2X.4

Consider two point charges of arbitrary sign and (nonzero) magnitude. Explain why it is *impossible* for $\vec{E}$ to be zero at any point (not at infinity) that does not lie somewhere on the line connecting the two charges.

E2.5 The Electric Field of a Dipole

Definition of an *electric dipole*

An **electric dipole** is a pair of particles separated by a small distance d whose charges have equal magnitudes and opposite signs. The particles shown in figure E2.3 comprise a dipole, and in example E2.1 we evaluated this dipole's electric field at a few selected points. Figure E2.4 shows a more complete field diagram of a dipole's electric field. (The computer program that drew this figure calculated each field arrow basically as we did in example E2.1.) Note how the electric field vectors point generally away from the positive charge and toward the negative charge, and at points on the plane midway between the charges, the field vectors point parallel to the line connecting the charges.

A dipole's field decreases with distance more rapidly than that of an isolated charge

Since a dipole *as a whole* is electrically neutral, it may be surprising that it has an electric field at all, but it clearly does. Even so, the magnitude of a dipole's electric field does decrease with distance much more rapidly than that of a charged particle.

We can demonstrate this most easily at an arbitrary point P lying along a line going through the dipole's particles, as shown in figure E2.5. The net elec-

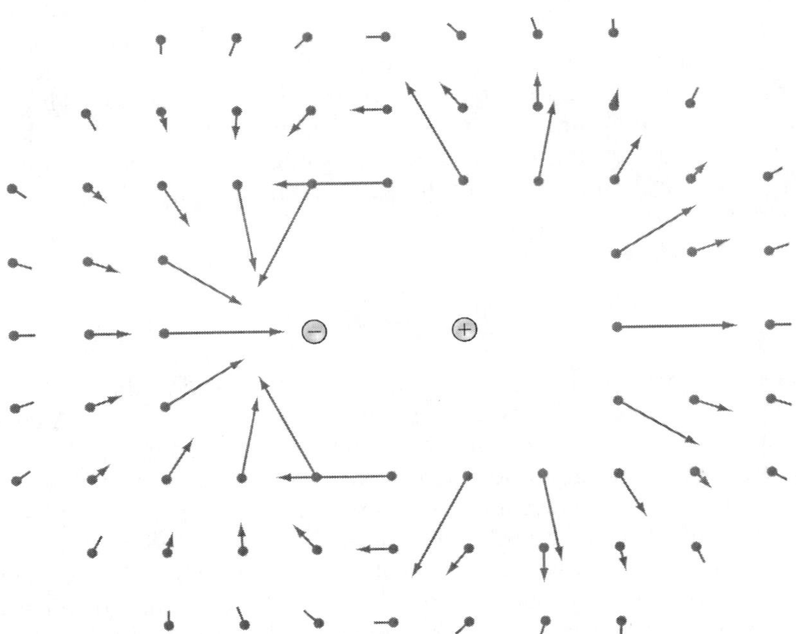

Figure E2.4
A field diagram of the electric field of a dipole. (As usual, the arrowhead on an electric field vector is not shown if that vector is too short.)

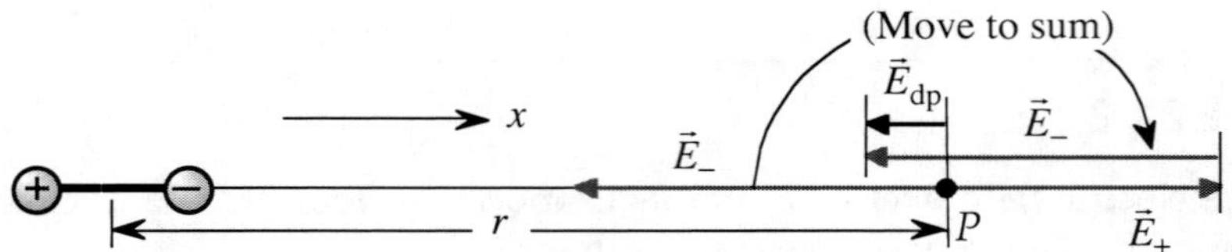

Figure E2.5
This diagram illustrates how we can calculate the electric field of a dipole at a point P along a line going through the dipole's charged particles.

tric field $\vec{E}_{dp}$ at P is the vector sum of the field vectors $\vec{E}_+$ and $\vec{E}_-$ created at point P by the dipole's positive and negative particles respectively. In this particular case, $\vec{E}_{dp}$ is nonzero because the field vector due to the more distant charge is not quite as long as that due to the nearer charge. Specifically, if we take the x direction to be the direction of point P relative to either charge and and define r to be the distance between P and the dipole's midpoint, then

$$\vec{E}_{dp}(r,0,0) = \frac{1}{4\pi\varepsilon_0}\frac{q}{(r+\frac{1}{2}d)^2}\hat{x} + \frac{1}{4\pi\varepsilon_0}\frac{-q}{(r-\frac{1}{2}d)^2}\hat{x}$$

$$= \frac{1}{4\pi\varepsilon_0}\frac{q}{r^2}\left[\frac{1}{\left(1+\frac{d}{2r}\right)^2} - \frac{1}{\left(1-\frac{d}{2r}\right)^2}\right]\begin{bmatrix}1\\0\\0\end{bmatrix} \qquad \text{(E2.15)}$$

Now, in the limit that $r >> d$ (that is, the limit that point P is very far from the dipole compared to the separation of the dipole's charges), $d/r << 1$, so we can use the binomial approximation to simplify the quantity in brackets. Since $(1+x)^{-2} \approx 1-2x$ when $x << 1$, we see that

A dipole's electric field strength at points along a line connecting the charges

$$\vec{E}_{dp}(r,0,0) \approx \frac{1}{4\pi\varepsilon_0}\frac{q}{r^2}\left[\left(\cancel{1}-\frac{2d}{2r}\right)-\left(\cancel{1}+\frac{2d}{2r}\right)\right]\begin{bmatrix}1\\0\\0\end{bmatrix} = \frac{1}{4\pi\varepsilon_0}\frac{2qd}{r^3}\begin{bmatrix}-1\\0\\0\end{bmatrix} \qquad \text{(E2.16)}$$

We see that in this case the dipole's net electric field at P points toward the nearer negative charge, consistent with figures E2.4 and E2.5. While calculating $\vec{E}_{dp}$ at an arbitrary point P is more difficult, a general calculation (see problem E2A.1) shows that along *any* line going through the dipole's center, the magnitude of $\vec{E}_{dp}$ is proportional to qd/r^3 (in the limit that $r >> d$), just as it is along the x axis. Thus the magnitude of a dipole's electric field does indeed decrease *more rapidly* with increasing r than that of a single particle does (as the latter only falls off as $1/r^2$). Since $\vec{F}_e = q\vec{E}$, this also means that the electric *force* that a dipole exerts on a charged particle decreases as $1/r^3$.

E2.6 Electrostatic Polarization

We are now in a position to resolve the mystery raised at the end of chapter E1. A charged comb will pick up small bits of uncharged paper. A charged balloon will be attracted to a neutral wall. How is this possible? Moreover, why is the force between charged and uncharged objects always attractive, and (if the objects are small) why does it decreases with increasing distance as $1/r^5$?

The charge of a normal atom's positive nucleus is exactly canceled by that of its negative electrons. Now, an *isolated* atom's electron cloud is normally exactly centered on its nucleus (see figure E2.6a). If an atom were to remain this way, it could neither attract nor be attracted by an external charged particle.

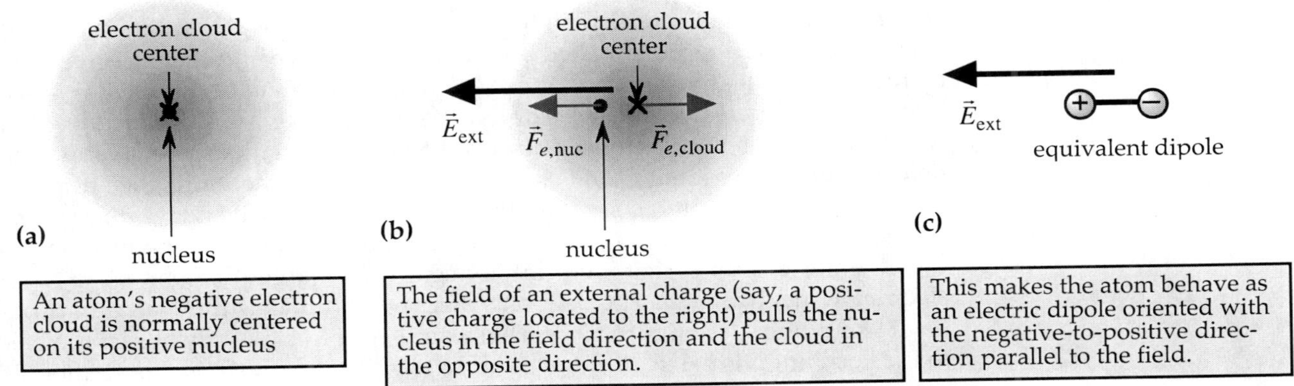

Figure E2.6
(a) An atom far from any charged object. (b) The same atom immersed in an external electric field. (c) Such an atom behaves as if it were an electric dipole.

A neutral atom responds to an external electric field by becoming an electric dipole

However, if we place an atom in an external electric field whose field vector at the atom's location is $\vec{E}_{ext}$, equation E2.3 implies that the field will pull the atom's positively charged nucleus in the direction of $\vec{E}_{ext}$ while pushing the negatively charged electron cloud in the opposite direction, displacing the center of the electron cloud a small amount relative to the nucleus, as shown in figure E2.6b. As we will discuss in the chapter E3, the essentially spherical electron cloud will behave as if all its charge were located at its center. Therefore, we can (as an excellent approximation) treat the atom's nucleus and displaced electron cloud as if they were two particles separated by a small distance and having charges of equal magnitude but opposite sign, that is, as an *electric dipole* (see figure E2.6c). The separation between the charges is typically along the direction of the external field and proportional to the magnitude of that field.

Why the force an induced dipole exerts on an external particle decreases as $1/r^5$

Now consider the interaction of such an "induced" dipole with an external charged particle. Assume that the field whose field vector is $\vec{E}_{ext}$ at the atom in figure E2.6b was created by a particle with positive charge Q located at a point P a large distance r to the atom's right. As shown in figure E2.5, the atom's equivalent dipole will create a weak *leftward* electric field at the particle's position P. Therefore, the external charge will be weakly attracted to the atom and, by Newton's third law, the atom will be weakly attracted to the external charge. Since the displacement d between the atom's electron cloud relative to the nucleus is proportional to the magnitude of $\vec{E}_{ext}$ at the atom created by the external charge ($d = bE_{ext}$ for some constant b) and since that field vector has a magnitude $E_{ext} = Q/4\pi\varepsilon_0 r^2$, equation E2.16 implies that the magnitude of the electrostatic force exerted on the external charge is

$$F_e = QE_{dp} = Q\frac{qd}{2\pi\varepsilon_0 r^3} = Q\frac{q}{2\pi\varepsilon_0 r^3}\frac{bQ}{4\pi\varepsilon_0 r^2} \propto \frac{Q^2 q}{r^5} \qquad \text{(E2.17)}$$

Therefore, an external positive charge will attract a neutral atom (and vice versa) with a force whose magnitude is indeed proportional to $1/r^5$. This calculation also shows that the force is quadrupled when the external charge is doubled!

Why the force an induced dipole exerts on an external particle is always attractive

One can see that the force will *always* be attractive as follows. We have already seen that the force will be attractive if the external particle is positively charged. A negatively charged particle to the right in figure E2.6b would create a rightward electric field at the atom, which will pull its nucleus rightward and the electron cloud leftward. The atom's equivalent dipole will therefore be reversed, with its positive end toward the negative charge. Since its positive end is slightly closer to the external charge than the negative end, the negative external particle will be slightly more attracted by the nearer positive end then it is repelled by the farther negative end, so the external charge will *still* be attracted. We see that the dipole created by the external field will *always* be oriented so that whichever end is more strongly attracted to the external particle creating the field also ends up being the end closest to that particle. Therefore, the attractive part of the dipole's interaction with the external charge will always dominate.

So we now understand how a charged object can attract a neutral object. Imagine, for example, that we bring a negatively charged balloon close to an electrically neutral wall. The balloon's electric field makes the wall atoms behave like dipoles (see figure E2.7). These dipoles in turn weakly attract the balloon. Each individual wall atom is only *slightly* polarized by the balloon's charge, and attractive forces between each atom and the balloon is correspondingly tiny. But because there are a huge number of atoms in the wall, the sum of these tiny attractive forces can be enough to hold the balloon to the wall. The same effect explains why bits of paper are attracted to a charged comb, etc.

The definition of *electrostatic polarization*

We call the phenomenon of an external electric field turning a neutral substance into a collection of oriented dipoles **electrostatic polarization**, and we say that the external field **polarizes** the atoms. This polarization is stronger in some substances than others, but almost all substances are polarized to some extent by an external electric field.

Some molecules have natural permanent dipoles

There is a second way that some electrically neutral substances can become polarized. Certain kinds of molecules have permanent natural dipoles even when there is no charged object nearby. For example, the oxygen atom in a water molecule grips the molecule's electrons more tightly than the two hydrogen atoms do: this makes the oxygen atom somewhat negatively charged and the

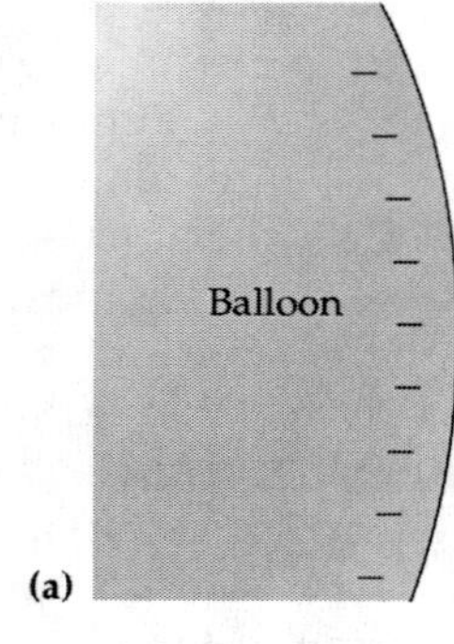

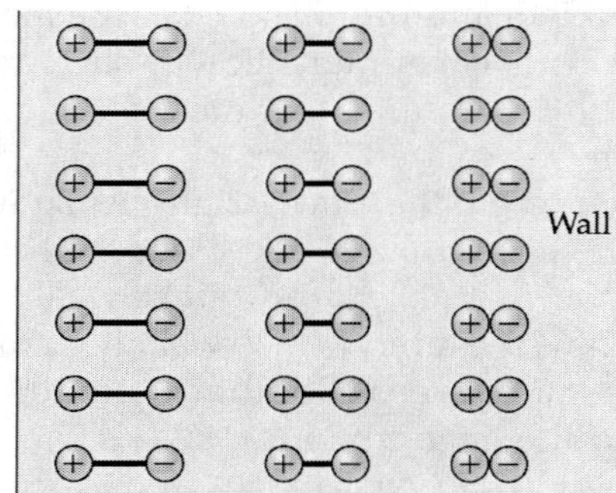

Figure E2.7
(a) A charged balloon polarizes the atoms in a nearby wall. (Note that because the electric field strength decreases with distance from the balloon, wall atoms closer to the balloon will be more strongly polarized than those farther from it.) Each atomic dipole exerts a small attractive force on the balloon, since the dipole's positive end is closer to the negative balloon than the negative end is. (b) The net effect is that the balloon is attracted to the wall.

hydrogen atoms positively charged, as shown in figure E2.8. (This is part of the reason that water is such a good solvent: the charged ends of the water molecule grab onto the oppositely charged ends of the solute molecules, enabling the water molecules to pull the solute molecules into solution.)

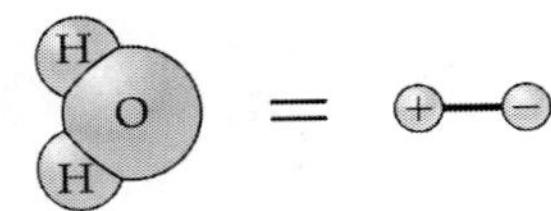

Figure E2.8
Because oxygen atoms tend to grab electrons more strongly than hydrogen atoms do, a water molecule has a permanent natural dipole.

Under normal circumstances, any permanent dipoles in a substance will be randomly oriented in space, so that the net electric field produced by a sample of that substance will be zero. However, if we put such a substance in an external electric field, the positive end of any given molecule will be pulled in the field direction while the negative end will be pushed the other way. The molecule will thus try to twist to align itself with the field.

Indeed, figure E2.9 illustrates how we can quantify the torque that a permanent dipole experiences in an electric field. Let the displacement from the dipole's negative end to its positive end be $\vec{d}$. Consider the torque exerted on the dipole's positive end first. According to equation E2.3, the electrostatic force on the positive end will be $\vec{F}_e = q\vec{E}$, where q is the charge of the positive end. The position vector of the place where this force is exerted relative to the dipole's center is $\vec{r} = \frac{1}{2}\vec{d}$, so (according to chapter C13) the torque exerted by this force about the dipole's center is $\vec{\tau}_+ = \vec{r} \times \vec{F}_e = \frac{1}{2}\vec{d} \times q\vec{E}$. The force acting on the negative end has the same magnitude qE and seeks to twist the dipole the same direction around the same axis, so the total torque on the dipole is simply double that contributed by the positive end:

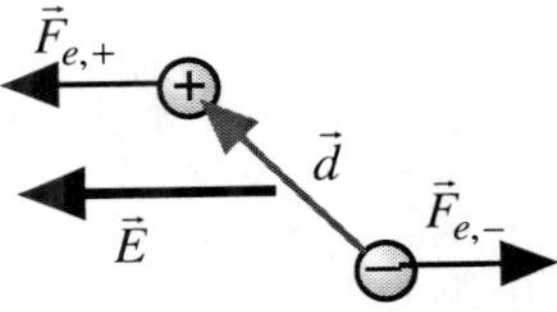

Figure E2.9
An external electric field will exert a torque on the dipole that seeks to align the dipole with the direction of the field.

The torque a dipole feels in an external electric field

$$\vec{\tau}_{\text{dp}} = \vec{d} \times q\vec{E} = q\vec{d} \times \vec{E} \equiv \vec{p}_e \times \vec{E} \qquad \text{(E2.18)}$$

Purpose: This equation describes the torque $\vec{\tau}_{\text{dp}}$ that a dipole having a **dipole moment** $\vec{p}_e$ experiences in an external electric field $\vec{E}$.

Symbols: $\vec{p}_e \equiv q\vec{d}$ where $\vec{d}$ is the displacement from the dipole's negative charge $-q$ to its positive charge $+q$. If the charge separation is d, then $\text{mag}(\vec{p}_e) = qd$.

Limitations: In practice, equation E2.18 defines the vector $\vec{p}_e$.

The *dipole moment* vector $\vec{p}_e$

Note that the *dipole moment* vector $\vec{p}_e$ is a convenient way of quantifying both the orientation and magnitude of a dipole. Its direction specifies the position of the dipole's positive end relative to its negative end, and its magnitude $p_e = qd$ specifies the crucial factor qd that appears in both the expression for the torque and that for the dipole's own electric field (see equation E2.16).

I have introduced the expression for $\vec{\tau}_{\text{dp}}$ mostly for comparison to a similar magnetic quantity that I will introduce in chapter E8. The point here is that an external electric field will exert a torque on a natural dipole that seeks to twist it so that its dipole moment becomes more parallel to the external electric field, and that the strength of this twisting effect is both proportional to the external field strength and the product qd that specifies the magnitude and separation of the dipole charges. If the permanent dipoles in a substance are free to rotate, they will end up aligned in the same orientation as the induced dipoles we considered earlier, so they will also attract whatever charged objects are creating the external electric field.

This twisting effect means that a free permanent dipole large enough to see will align itself with the external electric field direction at its location and thus indicate that direction like a compass! Some techniques for visually displaying electric fields depend on this effect.

The polarization of water

Let us return to the specific case of water. If a sample of water is put in the electric field created by an external charged object, the water molecules will experience a torque that attempts to twist them to the orientation that will be attractive to the external charged object. Because water is a liquid, the molecules

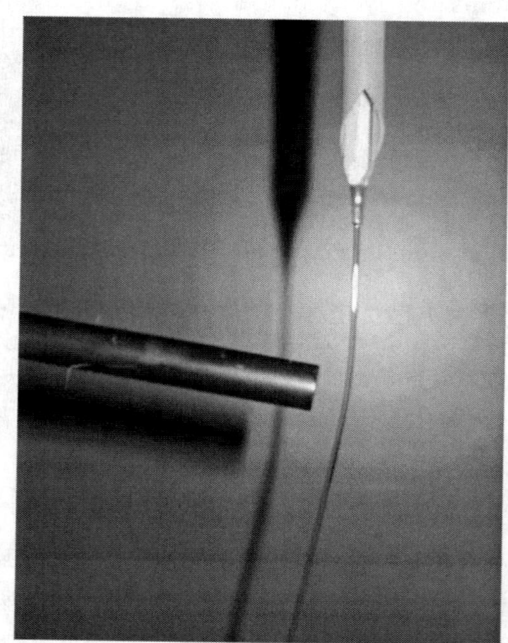

Figure E2.10
A charged rubber rod attracts an electrically neutral stream of water.

are free to rotate. However, the molecules are also in ceaseless thermal motion, so collisions between water molecules tend to knock the molecular dipoles out of alignment. Even so, the torque exerted by the electric field causes a molecule's average orientation to be slightly weighted toward the attractive orientation. Therefore, water can be polarized at the macroscopic scale by an external electric field.

The permanent dipole moment of a water molecule is about 100,000 times larger than the dipole moment a typical atom gets even in the strongest electric fields one can maintain in air. So though dealigning thermal collisions substantially reduce the average polarization of water molecules, empirically, water still responds to an external charge between 10 to 50 times as strongly as an equivalent volume of a typical solid (see figure E2.10).

E2.7 The Mystery du Jour

The definition of the electric field and superposition principle provide a means (in principle) for calculating the electric field produced by any distribution of charged particles. In practical cases, charged objects may involve trillions of excess charged particles arranged in complicated ways. We have so far only considered the electric fields of single particles and pairs of particles; obviously, we are going to have to do better than that. Our goal in the next chapter is to develop mathematical techniques capable of handling larger numbers of charges in more complicated arrangements.

What is an electric field?

This will open a path to answering a more fundamental question that my students ask me year after year: what *is* an electric field, really? At the moment, it might seem as if it were simply a theoretical construct representing an alternative way of thinking about Coulomb's law. However, part of the importance of the field concept is that it describes a physical entity as real and dynamic as a particle. What makes us think this? The next chapter will provide the first step toward an answer.

TWO-MINUTE PROBLEMS

E2T.1 The electric field created by a negative point charge at any given position points in what direction?
A. Toward the charge
B. Away from the charge
C. The direction depends on how close you are
D. The direction depends on the sign of ε_0.

E2T.2 A negative point charge placed at point P experiences an electrostatic force in the $+x$ direction. The electric field $\vec{E}$ at P must point in the $-x$ direction, true (T) or false (F).

E2T.3 Imagine that we place two particles a certain distance apart. The electric field at some point on the line *between* the particles is zero. What is the most general thing we can say about the (otherwise unknown) signs and magnitudes of the particles' charges? The charges have
A. the same sign and magnitude
B. opposite signs but the same magnitude
C. the same sign, but may have different magnitudes
D. opposite signs, but may have different magnitudes
E. zero magnitude necessarily (both of them)
F. other (specify)
T. we can say nothing about the signs or magnitudes

E2T.4 Imagine that we place two particles a certain distance apart. The electric field is zero at some point that is *not* on the line connecting them. What is the most general thing we can say about the signs and magnitudes of the particles' charges? The charges have ... (choose an answer from the list for problem E2T.3).

E2T.5 Imagine that we place two particles a certain distance apart. The electric field at some point on a line connecting the particles (but *not* between them) is zero. What is the most general thing we can say about the signs and magnitudes of the particles' charges? The charges have
A. the same sign and magnitude
B. opposite signs but the same magnitude
C. the same sign, but *must* have different magnitudes
D. opposite signs, but *must* have different magnitudes
E. zero magnitude necessarily (both of them)
F. other (specify)
T. we can say nothing about the signs or magnitudes

E2T.6 The electric field vector created by a dipole at an arbitrary point near the dipole is parallel to that dipole's dipole moment vector, T or F?

E2T.7 The charges in an electrostatically polarized atom separate along an axis parallel to the electric field $\vec{E}$ that polarizes it, T or F?

E2T.8 The magnitude of the electrostatic torque exerted on a permanent dipole by an external electric field is zero when the dipole moment is aligned with the field, T or F? It is also zero when it is opposite to the field, T or F?

E2T.9 Imagine two dipoles oriented as shown below. These dipoles will

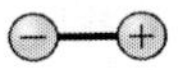

A. attract each other
B. repel each other
C. exert zero force on each other.

E2T.10 Imagine two dipoles oriented as shown below. These dipoles will

A. attract each other
B. repel each other
C. exert zero force on each other

HOMEWORK PROBLEMS

Basic Skills

E2B.1 Imagine that you place a particle with a charge of 1.0 nC at a certain point in space and find that it experiences a net force of 5.0 μN. What is the magnitude of the electric field at this point?

E2B.2 Imagine that you place a particle with a charge of 120 nC at a certain point in space and find that it experiences a net force of 0.3 mN. What is the magnitude of the electric field at this point?

E2B.3 Imagine that at a certain time during a thunderstorm, the electric field near the earth's surface is measured to be 5200 N/C upward. If you place a small Styrofoam ball with a charge of –10 nC in this field, what is the magnitude and direction of the electrostatic force on the ball?

E2B.4 The maximum electric field that a Van de Graaff generator can produce at the surface of its upper sphere is about 3×10^6 N/C outward. If you place a Styrofoam ball with a charge of +11 nC very near the surface of the upper sphere, what will be the magnitude and direction of the electric force on the ball?

E2B.5 If the absolute value of the charge of both particles in figure E2.3 is 15 nC and d = 2.0 cm, what is the magnitude of the electric field at point A?

E2B.6 What is the direction and magnitude of the electric field vector at the point marked A in figure E2.12 if q = +11 nC and d = 1.0 cm?

E2B.7 What is the direction and magnitude of the electric field vector at the point marked B in Figure E2.12 if q = +11 nC and d = 1.0 cm?

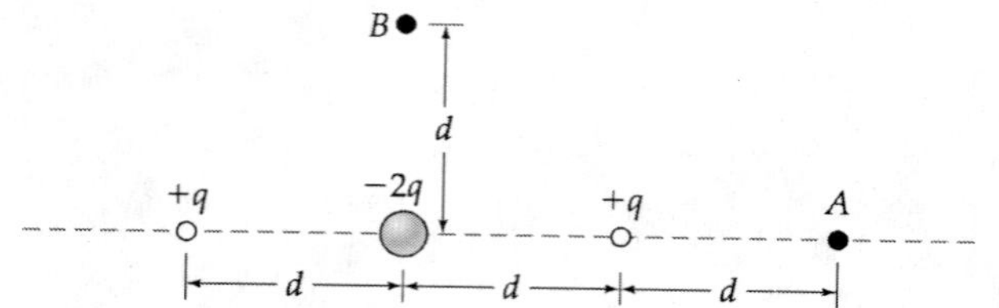

Figure E2.12
The charge arrangement discussed in problems E2B.6 and E2B.7.

E2B.8 A stream of water can be noticeably deflected by a charged object. Imagine that a friend, upon seeing the demonstration, exclaims, "But this cannot be! The water molecules in the stream are certainly randomly oriented, so as many will be repelled by the object as attracted to it. Therefore, the net force exerted on the stream *must* be zero". Courteously correct the error in your friend's reasoning.

Synthetic

E2S.1 If the absolute value of the charge of both particles in figure E2.3 is 15 nC and d = 2.0 cm, what is the magnitude and direction of the electric field at the point D, if D is a distance d from the nearest charged particle? (*Hint:* break down the electric field vectors into components.)

E2S.2 A square with sides d has particles with charges q, $2q$, $3q$ and $4q$ arranged clockwise around the corners of the square. What is the magnitude and direction of the electric field at the square's center? [*Hints*: Consider *pairs* of particles on opposite sides of the square. Choose a coordinate system that makes finding the field vectors' components easy.]

E2S.3 Consider three charged particles arranged in an equilateral triangle with sides of length d. Two of the particles have positive charge $+q$, and the other has negative charge $-q$. Find the electric field vector at the triangle's center. Express your answer as a unitless multiple of kq/d^2, where $k \equiv 1/4\pi\varepsilon_0$.

E2S.4 A particle with charge $-3q$ (where q = 12 nC) is located at the origin of a coordinate system. Another point particle with charge $+q$ is located at x = 2.0 cm. Find the location of any point or points along the x axis where the electric field is zero.

E2S.5 Two particles with charges q are located at $y = \pm d$ along the y axis, and two particles with charges $-q$ are located at $x = \pm d$ along the x axis. Find an expression for the magnitude and direction of the electric field at $y = 2d$, $x = 0$. (Express your result as a unitless multiple of kq/d^2, where $k \equiv 1/4\pi\varepsilon_0$.

E2S.6 A point particle with charge $-q$ is located at the origin of a coordinate system. Another point particle with charge $+q$ is located a distance d away along the x axis. Argue (in words, but possibly with the help of a diagram) that the electric field of two point charges along the x axis could only possibly be zero at some point along the x axis. Then prove that the electric field *cannot* be zero anywhere along the x axis either in this particular case.

E2S.7 Consider a dipole whose dipole moment vector $\vec{p}_e$ lies on the x axis and whose center is at the origin. Find an expression for the electric field at a point P along the y axis a distance r from the dipole's center, assuming that $r >> d$. [*Hints:* The calculation in this problem is a bit different from the one in section E2.5. There the vectors had exactly opposite directions and almost equal lengths. Here the vectors have exactly equal length but almost opposite directions. Use equation E2.9b and similar triangles to find component expressions for the electric field vectors that each charged particle contributes at point P. If you end up with several terms, keep only the term that is largest when $r >> d$. You should find that the magnitude of the electric field at P is proportional to p_e/r^3.]

E2S.8 Consider a pair of dipoles oriented as shown below. Will they attract, repel, or exert zero force each other? If they do exert a force on each other, find an expression that specifies how the magnitude of this force depends on r when $r >> d$. (Your expression should depend on q, d, r, and $k \equiv 1/4\pi\varepsilon_0$.)

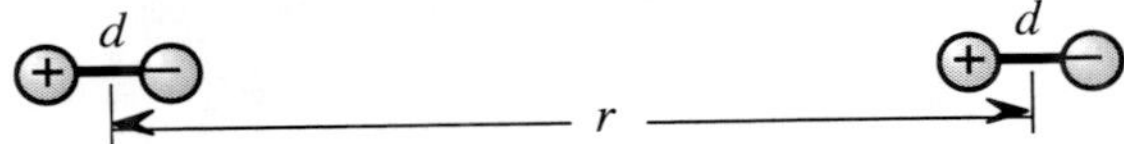

E2S.9 Consider a pair of dipoles oriented as shown below. Will they attract, repel, or exert zero force each other? If they do exert a force on each other, find an expression that specifies how the magnitude of this force depends on r when $r >> d$. (Your expression should depend on q, d, r, and $k \equiv 1/4\pi\varepsilon_0$.)

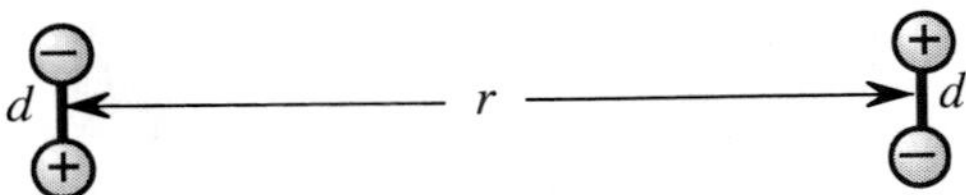

Rich-Context

E2R.1 We can very roughly estimate the strength of the polarization effect as follows. Consider an atom consisting of a negative electron cloud with charge $-Q$ and approximate radius a bound to a positive, point-like nucleus with charge $+Q$. The strength of the nucleus' electric field at the edge of the electron cloud is $E_0 \approx kQ/a^2$, where $k \equiv 1/4\pi\varepsilon_0$. Now imagine that we apply external electric field that at the atom has some magnitude E_A. Let us *assume* that this field shifts the electron cloud by a distance d that is to the cloud radius a what the imposed field strength E_A is to the nucleus' field strength E_0 at the cloud's outer edge.

(a) Show that this means that

$$d \approx \frac{3V_{\text{atom}}}{4\pi kQ} E_A \tag{E2.19}$$

where $V_{\text{atom}} = \frac{4}{3}\pi a^3$ is the atom's volume.

(b) Now, note from equation E2.16 that the electric field *created* by this polarized atom at a point a distance r from the atom along its polarization axis has a magnitude of $2kQd/r^3$. Use this and equation E2.19 to show that the total electric field $\vec{E}_P$ created by the polarized atoms in a small solid object of volume V at a point along a line through that object's center and parallel to the atoms' common polarization direction will have a magnitude of

$$E_P = \frac{3V}{2\pi r^3} E_A \tag{E2.20}$$

assuming that the object is small enough so that $\vec{E}_A$ is approximately constant in magnitude and direction throughout its volume. (*Hint:* The number of atoms in a solid object is $\approx V/V_{\text{atom}}$.)

Comment: The crude model discussed in this problem is better than it has any right to be: experiments show that the actual field is within a factor of 3 of that predicted by this model for a wide variety of solid substances. However, one has to be careful when using this result to, say, calculate the electric force between a point charge and a small polarizable object, because the external electric field $\vec{E}_A$ that each atom in the object experiences is not just the electric field created by charged particles *outside* the object but also the fields of nearby dipoles *inside* the object. This makes it trickier to calculate $\vec{E}_A$ in many circumstances.)

E2R.2 As we will see in unit Q, light striking a metal plate can eject electrons from the plate's surface (this is called the *photoelectric effect*). Imagine that we place the plate in a vacuum and set up an electric field in the plate's vicinity that is uniform in magnitude and direction such that the electric field vector $\vec{E}$ at any point near the plate has a magnitude of 1000 N/C and points directly away from the plate, perpendicular to its surface. Electrons ejected by the photoelectric effect will have initial kinetic energies of no more than about 3 eV, where 1 eV $\equiv$ 1.6×10^{-19} J. Roughly estimate the maximum distance that an ejected electron can get from the plate under these circumstances. [*Hint:* Consider an analogy to the behavior of a thrown ball in a uniform gravitational field.]

Advanced

E2A.1 Our task in this problem is to evaluate the electric field vector $\vec{E}$ of a dipole at an arbitrary point P far from the dipole compared to its charge separation d. Imagine that line drawn from the dipole's center to P makes an angle of θ with respect to a line drawn through the dipole charges in the direction from the negative charge to the positive charge. The situation is shown in figure E2.13. We assume that r is so large that $\phi \approx 0$, the lines from P to both charges are almost parallel, and the angles those lines make with the dipole's axis are both $\approx \theta$. We will describe the field vector $\vec{E}$ by stating its component E_r in the radial direction (that is, directly away from the dipole) and its component $E_\perp$ perpendicular to the radial direction to the left as we look toward P from the dipole. In this case, $\vec{E} \neq 0$ both because the contributions $\vec{E}_+$ and $\vec{E}_-$ do not point in the same direction and because they have different lengths.

(a) Argue that $E_\perp \approx kqd\sin\theta/r^3$, given our assumptions, where $k \equiv 1/4\pi\varepsilon_0$. (Be sure to check that this has the right sign for all θ.)

(b) Argue that $E_r \approx 2kqd\cos\theta/r^3$, given our assumptions. (Be sure to check that this has the right sign for all θ.)

(c) Find the magnitude of $\vec{E}$ in this limit, and argue that it is always proportional to kqd/r^3 for a given θ.

(d) Argue that these results are consistent with equation E2.16 and qualitatively consistent with figure E2.4.

(e) Argue that these results are enough to specify $\vec{E}$ at *any* point P (in 3 dimensions!) sufficiently far from the dipole.

E2A.2 Consider a dipole lying along the x axis with its positive charge at $x = +\frac{1}{2}d$ and its negative charge at $x = -\frac{1}{2}d$. Write down an exact expression for the dipole's field components $[E_x, E_y]$ in the xy plane as a function of position components x and y. Then take the dot product of $\vec{E}$ with the radial unit vector $\hat{r} = [x/r, y/r]$ and the unit vector $\hat{e}_\perp = [-y/r, x/r]$ perpendicular to it to find the components E_r and $E_\perp$. Compare with the results of problem E2A.1 in the limit that $r >> d$.

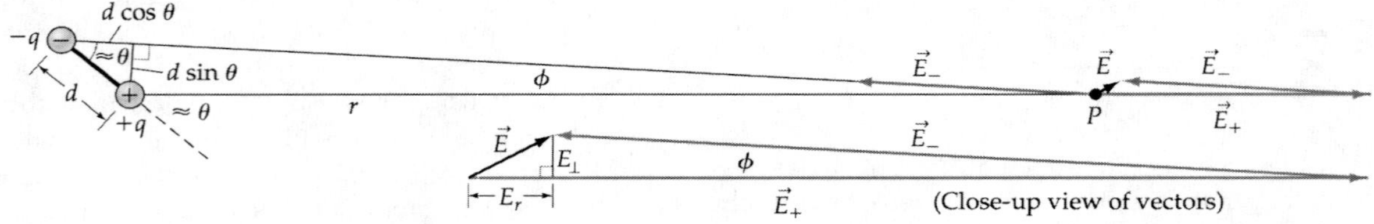

Figure E2.13
(See problem E2A.1.)

ANSWERS TO SELF-TESTS

E2X.1 For the units to be consistent on the right and left sides of equation E2.2, the electric field vector must have units of force over charge or N/C in SI units.

E2X.2 We have

$$\text{mag}(\hat{r}_{P1}) = \text{mag}\left(\frac{\vec{r}_{P1}}{r_{P1}}\right) = \frac{\text{mag}(\vec{r}_{P1})}{r_{P1}} = \frac{r_{P1}}{r_{P1}} = 1 \qquad \text{(E2.21)}$$

E2X.3 $\vec{E}_C$ has the same magnitude and direction as $\vec{E}_A$. $\vec{E}_D = [0.35kq/d^2, 0.64kq/d^2, 0]$, which is a vector about as long as $\vec{E}_A$ but oriented at an angle of about 30° to the right of vertical.

E2X.4 $\vec{E}$ can be zero at a point P if and only if the two electric field vectors contributed by the two charges happen to cancel. If the two vectors are to cancel, they must lie on the same line. But since each of the two vectors lies on a line connecting P to the corresponding charge, it follows that the line connecting the first charge with P must be the same line as the line connecting the second charge with P. So the two charges and P must all lie on the same line.

E3 Continuous Charge Distributions

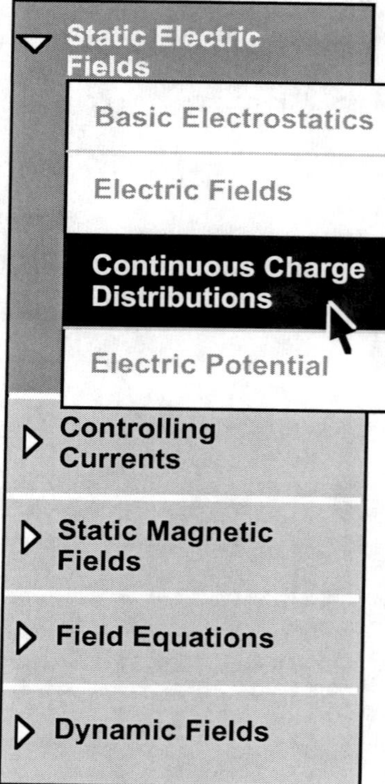

Chapter Overview

Introduction

In chapter E2, we learned how to calculate the electric field produced by of a countable number of charged particles. In this chapter, we learn how to calculate the electric field created by essentially continuous charge distributions, and examine closely a couple of practical special cases that we will find useful in future chapters

Section E3.1: Handling Charge Distributions

We can most easily calculate the electric field of a continuous distribution of charge at a certain point P by dividing the distribution into tiny bits (each small enough to be modeled accurately as a point charge, and using the following five-step process (which examples in the section illustrate) to evaluate the sum of the fields contributed by all the bits:

1. Find a variable that you can use to locate each bit in the distribution.
2. Express each bit's charge in terms of an infinitesimal change in that variable.
3. Express the distance between the bit and the point P in terms of the variable.
4. Use the equation for the field of a point charge to find the field vector E_b created at P by the bit.
5. Convert the sum of $d\vec{E}$ over all bits to an integral and evaluate.

One of the interesting results derived in this section is that the magnitude of the electric field at points near a very long wire decreases approximately as $1/r$ (where r is the distance to the wire), instead of as $1/r^2$ like a point charge.

Section E3.2: Symmetry Arguments

A **symmetry argument** is a logical argument that uses the following principle to determine the characteristics of the field of a symmetric charge distribution:

> If a charge distribution is unchanged by a certain transformation (such as a rotation around an axis or sliding along an axis) then the distribution's *field* is also unchanged by that same transformation.

If a charge distribution exhibits a high degree of symmetry, such arguments can be used to determine a great deal about the field created by that distribution without doing any calculations. For example, one of the examples in the section proves that the electric field of *any* spherically symmetric charge distribution must (1) point radially toward or away from the distribution's center, (2) must have a magnitude that depends at most on the distance r that one is from the center, and (3) must be exactly zero at the distribution's center.

Section E3.3: The Electric Field of a Spherical Shell

This section discusses the important practical case of the electric field created by a thin uniform shell of charge (e.g. the charge distribution on the surface of a charged conducting sphere). We find that in such a case

1. The electric field at any point outside the shell is the same as for a point particle with the same total charge located at the shell's center.

2. The electric field at all points inside the shell is zero.

Physicists refer to these results collectively as the **shell theorem**.

Section E3.4: The Electric Field of a Circular Plate

This section discusses the electric field created by an uniformly charged, flat, circular plate. It turns out that the component of the electric field *perpendicular* to the plate has a nearly constant magnitude of $E = \frac{1}{2}|\sigma| / \varepsilon_0$ at points sufficiently close to the plate, where σ is the surface charge density (charge per unit area) on the plate. The component of the field *parallel* to the plate at points near to the plate is zero at the plate's center but grows as one goes toward the edges.

Section E3.5: The Electric Field of Parallel Flat Plates

If two oppositely charged flat plates are placed so that they are parallel and separated by a distance that is small compared to the plates' size, it turns out that the the fields created by the plates add in such a way that the components parallel to the plates almost completely cancel, leaving an electric field having the following characteristics:

$$\vec{E} \approx \begin{cases} |\sigma|\hat{n} / \varepsilon_0 & \text{at points between the plates} \\ 0 & \text{at points not between the plates} \end{cases} \qquad \text{(E3.21)}$$

Purpose: This equation describes the electric field created by closely spaced parallel plates with uniform and opposite charges.

Symbols: $\varepsilon_0 \equiv (4\pi k)^{-1}$ is the permittivity constant, σ is the surface charge density (charge per unit area) on either plate, and $\hat{n}$ is a directional away from and perpendicular to the positive plate.

Limitations: The plates must be identical, parallel and have a separation small compared to their size. Their charges must be equal in magnitude and opposite in sign. The approximation is not accurate for points that are closer than several plate-separations from plate edges.

Note: The electric field in the region between the plates is very nearly uniform in magnitude and direction.

These results are important because setting up oppositely charged parallel plates is the most practical way to create a uniform electric field in a region of space.

Section E3.6: The Electric Field Is a Form of Energy

By considering the energy required to pull oppositely charged parallel plates apart, one can deduce that the density of energy in a region of space filled with an electric field is given by

$$u_E = \tfrac{1}{2}\varepsilon_0 E^2 \qquad \text{(E3.26)}$$

Purpose: This equation expresses the energy density u_E of an electric field in a region where the electric field has a magnitude E.

Symbols: $\varepsilon_0 = (4\pi k)^{-1}$ is the permittivity constant.

Limitations: There are no known limitations (this expression even works for nonstatic fields).

This result turns out to apply in all circumstances: an electric field is a dispersed form of energy just as a particle with mass is a concentrated form of energy.

Section E3.7: The Mystery du Jour

How does charge distribute itself on a conducting object?

E3.1 Handling Charge Distributions

A technique for computing the field of macroscopic charge distributions

In chapter E2, we learned how to calculate the electric field created by a handful of charged particles. However, any macroscopic charged object involves a vast number of charged particles (usually electrons) distributed in some way over the object's surface or through its volume. We can *in principle* calculate the electric field vector such a **charge distribution** creates at a given point P by summing the field vectors that each of its charged particles creates at P. *In practice*, though, the huge number of particles in any macroscopic object makes doing this sum hopelessly impractical.

A more practical way to do the sum is to divide the charge distribution into a large number of tiny "bits", each of which may contain a large number of actual charged particles but is still small enough to model as a point particle. We can then calculate the tiny vector $d\vec{E}$ contributed by a given bit with tiny charge dQ using the equation for the field of a single particle

$$d\vec{E} = \frac{1}{4\pi\varepsilon_0}\frac{dQ}{r_{Pb}^2}\hat{r}_{Pb} = \frac{1}{4\pi\varepsilon_0}\frac{dQ}{r_{Pb}^3}\vec{r}_{Pb} \tag{E3.1}$$

(where $\vec{r}_{Pb}$ is the vector from the bit in question to point P) and sum the contributions $d\vec{E}$ over all bits.

In general, a computer program might be necessary to perform the summation, but we can learn even more in the special cases where we can convert the sum over the bits into a tractable *integral*. When it can be done, this process yields a much more informative *symbolic* result for the total electric field vector. Examples E3.1 and E3.2 illustrate the process.

Example E3.1 The Field Along the Axis of a Thin Charged Ring

Problem Consider a very thin ring of radius r carrying a uniformly distributed positive total charge Q. What is the electric field at a point P a given distance z from the center of the ring along the ring's central axis?

Translation Figure E3.1 defines an appropriate coordinate system and defines some useful symbols.

Model We can describe the position of each bit of the ring in terms of the angle ϕ that a line connecting the ring's center with that bit makes with the x axis. The infinitesimal length of each bit is then $dL = r\,d\phi$.

Solution If the charge Q on the ring is uniformly distributed, then the charge dQ of a bit of ring of length dL will be to the total charge Q as the bit's length dL is to ring's total circumference $2\pi r$. Therefore

$$\frac{dQ}{Q} = \frac{dL}{2\pi r} = \frac{r\,d\phi}{2\pi r} = \frac{d\phi}{2\pi} \quad\Rightarrow\quad dQ = Q\frac{d\phi}{2\pi} \tag{E3.2}$$

Now, the distance between every bit on our ring and the point P has the fixed value $R \equiv [r^2 + z^2]^{1/2}$. Equation E3.1 and the geometry of figure E3.1 imply that the field vector $d\vec{E}$ contributed by the bit located at angle ϕ is

$$d\vec{E} = dE\begin{bmatrix} -\sin\theta\cos\phi \\ -\sin\theta\sin\phi \\ \cos\theta \end{bmatrix} \quad \text{where } dE = \frac{kdQ}{R^2} = \frac{kQ}{R^2}\frac{d\phi}{2\pi} = \frac{kQ}{2\pi R^2}d\phi \tag{E3.3}$$

where $k \equiv 1/4\pi\varepsilon_0$. In this case, $\sin\theta$ and $\cos\theta$ have the fixed values $\sin\theta = r/R$ and $\cos\theta = z/R$. Plugging these results into equation E3.3, summing $d\vec{E}$ over all bits, and converting the sum to an integral over ϕ from 0 to 2π, we get

$$\vec{E} = \sum_{\text{all bits}} d\vec{E} = \begin{bmatrix} \sum_{\text{all bits}} -\frac{kQr}{2\pi R^3}\cos\phi\, d\phi \\ \sum_{\text{all bits}} -\frac{kQr}{2\pi R^3}\sin\phi\, d\phi \\ \sum_{\text{all bits}} \frac{kQz}{2\pi R^3} d\phi \end{bmatrix} \rightarrow \begin{bmatrix} -\frac{kQr}{2\pi R^3}\int_0^{2\pi}\cos\phi\, d\phi \\ -\frac{kQr}{2\pi R^3}\int_0^{2\pi}\sin\phi\, d\phi \\ \frac{kQz}{2\pi R^3}\int_0^{2\pi} d\phi \end{bmatrix} \quad \text{(E3.4)}$$

These integrals are actually pretty easy:

$$\int_0^{2\pi}\cos\phi\, d\phi = \sin\phi\,\Big|_0^{2\pi} = \sin 2\pi - \sin 0 = 0 - 0 = 0 \quad \text{(E3.5a)}$$

$$\int_0^{2\pi}\sin\phi\, d\phi = -\cos\phi\,\Big|_0^{2\pi} = -\cos 2\pi + \cos 0 = -1 + 1 = 0 \quad \text{(E3.5b)}$$

$$\int_0^{2\pi} d\phi = \phi\Big|_0^{2\pi} = 2\pi - 0 = 2\pi \quad \text{(E3.5c)}$$

So the total electric field at point P a distance z from the center of the ring along its central axis is simply:

$$\vec{E}(0,0,z) = \frac{kQz}{2\pi R^3}\begin{bmatrix} 0 \\ 0 \\ 2\pi \end{bmatrix} = \frac{kQz}{R^3}\begin{bmatrix} 0 \\ 0 \\ 1 \end{bmatrix} = \frac{kQz}{[r^2+z^2]^{3/2}}\begin{bmatrix} 0 \\ 0 \\ 1 \end{bmatrix} \quad \text{(E3.6)}$$

Evaluation It also makes sense that the horizontal components should add up to zero: for every bit one side of the ring that contributes a rightward component (say) to the sum, there is a bit on the opposite side that contributes an equal leftward component. You can easily check that the units of $\vec{E}$ in equation E3.6 are correct as well. (see Problem E3S.1 for some other checks.)

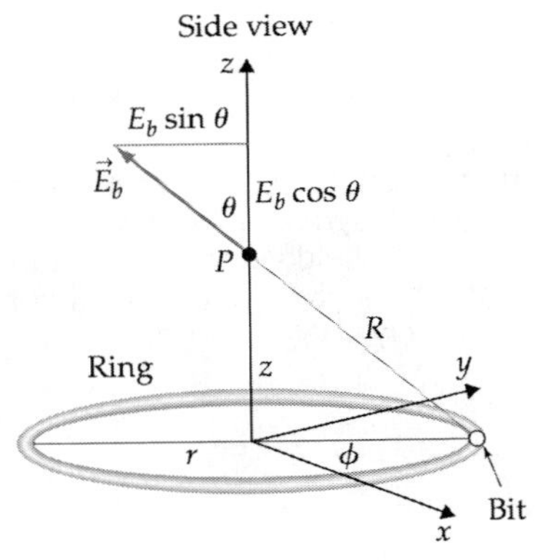

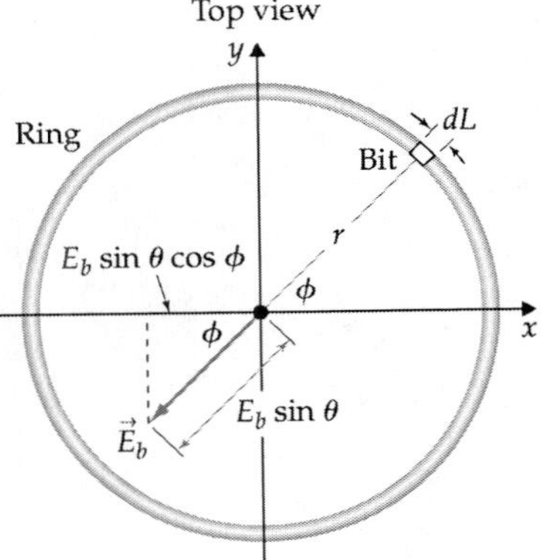

Figure E3.1
A side view and a top view of a uniformly charged circular ring.

Example E3.2 The Field a Distance *r* from a Thin Charged Wire

Problem Imagine a straight, very thin wire of length L that has a uniformly-distributed charge Q. What is the electric field vector produced by this wire at an arbitrary point P a distance r from the center of the wire?

Translation The first step is to set up a useful reference frame. Let us choose the x axis to coincide with the wire and set $x = 0$ to be the point on the axis closest to P. Let us also take advantage of our freedom to choose coordinates to choose our y axis so that it goes through the point P. Figure E3.2 illustrates the situation and defines some appropriate symbols.

Model We can express each bit's position in terms of its coordinate x on the x-axis and its size in terms of the increment dx in that variable.

Solution If charge is uniformly distributed on the wire, then a given bit's charge dQ is to the wire's charge Q what the bit's length dx is to the wire's length L. Therefore

$$\frac{dQ}{Q} = \frac{dx}{L} \quad \Rightarrow \quad dQ = \frac{Q}{L}dx \quad \text{(E3.7)}$$

The vector that specifies the position of point P relative to the bit of charge at position x is

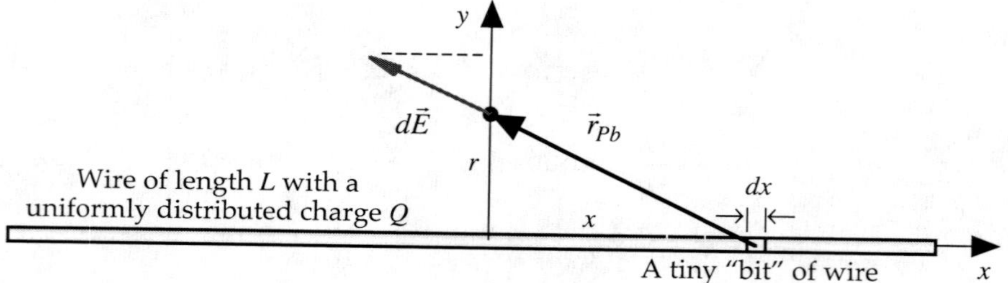

Figure E3.2
An appropriate coordinate system and useful symbols for evaluating the electric field vector produced at point P by a given tiny segment of a uniformly charged wire.

$$\vec{r}_{Pb} = \vec{r}_P - \vec{r}_b = \begin{bmatrix} 0 \\ r \\ 0 \end{bmatrix} - \begin{bmatrix} x \\ 0 \\ 0 \end{bmatrix} = \begin{bmatrix} -x \\ r \\ 0 \end{bmatrix} \tag{E3.8}$$

Therefore, if we use the second version of equation E3.9 to compute the electric field created by each bit and sum over all bits, we get

$$\vec{E}(0,r,0) = \sum_{\text{all bits}} d\vec{E} = \sum_{\text{all bits}} \frac{k\,dQ}{r_{Pb}^3}\vec{r}_{Pb} = \sum_{\text{all bits}} \frac{k(Q/L)dx}{(r^2+x_b^2)^{3/2}} \begin{bmatrix} -x_b \\ r \\ 0 \end{bmatrix}$$

$$= \frac{kQ}{L} \begin{bmatrix} \sum\limits_{\text{all bits}} \dfrac{-x\,dx}{(r^2+x^2)^{3/2}} \\ \sum\limits_{\text{all bits}} \dfrac{r\,dx}{(r^2+x^2)^{3/2}} \\ 0 \end{bmatrix} \rightarrow \frac{kQ}{L} \begin{bmatrix} \displaystyle\int_{-\frac{1}{2}L}^{+\frac{1}{2}L} \frac{-x\,dx}{(r^2+x^2)^{3/2}} \\ r\displaystyle\int_{-\frac{1}{2}L}^{+\frac{1}{2}L} \frac{dx}{(r^2+x^2)^{3/2}} \\ 0 \end{bmatrix} \tag{E3.9}$$

These integrals are *not* simple to do by hand, but they are easy to look up in a table of integrals (see also the inside front cover). The results are

$$\int_{-\frac{1}{2}L}^{+\frac{1}{2}L} \frac{-x\,dx}{(r^2+x^2)^{3/2}} = \frac{1}{(r^2+x^2)^{1/2}}\Bigg|_{-\frac{1}{2}L}^{+\frac{1}{2}L} = \frac{1-1}{(r^2+\frac{1}{4}L^2)^{1/2}} = 0 \tag{E3.10a}$$

$$\int_{-\frac{1}{2}L}^{+\frac{1}{2}L} \frac{dx}{(r^2+x^2)^{3/2}} = \frac{x}{r^2(r^2+x^2)^{1/2}}\Bigg|_{-\frac{1}{2}L}^{+\frac{1}{2}L}$$

$$= \frac{\frac{1}{2}L-(-\frac{1}{2}L)}{r^2(r^2+\frac{1}{4}L^2)^{1/2}} = \frac{L}{r^2(r^2+\frac{1}{4}L^2)^{1/2}} \tag{E3.10b}$$

Therefore

$$\vec{E}(0,r,0) = \frac{kQ}{L}\frac{rL}{r^2(r^2+\frac{1}{4}L^2)^{1/2}} \begin{bmatrix} 0 \\ 1 \\ 0 \end{bmatrix} = \frac{kQ}{r\sqrt{r^2+\frac{1}{4}L^2}} \begin{bmatrix} 0 \\ 1 \\ 0 \end{bmatrix} \tag{E3.11}$$

Evaluation The square root in this expression has SI units of $(\text{m}^2)^{1/2} = \text{m}$, so the entire quantity has SI units of $(\text{N}\cdot\text{m}^2\text{C}^{-2})\text{C}/\text{m}^2 = \text{N}/\text{C}$, the correct SI units for an electric field. It also makes intuitive sense that the electric field would point directly away from the wire's center.

The limiting case for an extremely long wire

Note that if $r \ll L$, we can ignore the r in the square root, and we get

$$\vec{E}(0,r,0) \approx \frac{kQ}{r(\frac{1}{2}L)} = \frac{2k\lambda}{r} = \frac{\lambda}{2\pi\varepsilon_0 r} \tag{E3.12}$$

where $\lambda \equiv Q/L$ is the charge per unit length on the wire. The electric field magnitude therefore decreases as $1/r$, not $1/r^2$, as one moves away from a very long wire's center. This is a result we will find useful later.

The point of these examples is not the *results* we get (the fields of uniformly charged rings and wires are rarely of practical interest) but rather the *method*. A summary of the crucial steps might look like this:

Summary of the crucial steps in the technique

1. Choose a variable (ϕ in Example E3.1, x in example E3.2) you can use to describe everything you need to know about the position and size of each bit.
2. Express the bit's charge dQ in terms of the variable and the infinitesimal change in that variable (see equations E3.2 and E3.7).
3. Express the position $\vec{r}_{Pb}$ of the point P relative to the bit in terms of that variable (see equation E3.8).
4. Use either form of equation E3.1 to find the components of the electric field $d\vec{E}$ created by each bit at point P (see equations E3.4 and E3.9).
5. Convert the sum over all bits to an integral over the variable and evaluate to find the total electric field $\vec{E}$ (see equations E3.5 and E3.9).

Problems E3S.3 and E3S.4 will give you some practice using this technique, which is valuable in a number of areas of physics.

E3.2 Symmetry Arguments

In example E3.1, (as discussed in the *Evaluation* section) we might have intuited from the ring's symmetry that the horizontal component of $\vec{E}$ at point P would be zero. Similarly, we might have guessed from the right-left symmetry of the wire that E at point P in example E3.2 would have no x or z component.

A **symmetry argument** is a general technique for placing such intuitive guesses on a firmer logical foundation. Symmetry arguments concerning electric fields are based on the following principle:

What is a symmetry argument?

> If a charge distribution is unchanged by a certain transformation (such as a rotation around an axis or sliding along an axis) then the distribution's *field* is also unchanged by that same transformation.

For example, if a ring's final charge distribution after it is rotated around its central axis is indistinguishable from its initial charge distribution, then it makes sense that the electric fields created by the ball in its initial and final orientations will likewise be indistinguishable.

A careful logical argument based on this principle can determine an astonishing amount about the field created by a suitably symmetric object in advance of doing any calculations. This can greatly reduce the remaining work we must do to determine the field completely.

When I construct symmetry arguments, I visualize the field vectors created by an object to be rigidly attached to it like bristles are attached to the body of a brush. Thus if we rotate or slide a charge distribution, its field vectors rotate or slide along with it, just as a brush's bristles would rotate or slide along with a brush.

Visualizing what a transformation does to a field

The easiest way to illustrate how a symmetry argument works is to work some concrete examples. In this section, we will use symmetry arguments to determine the characteristics of the electric fields of three important types of symmetric charge distributions.

Example E3.3 A Spherical Charge Distribution

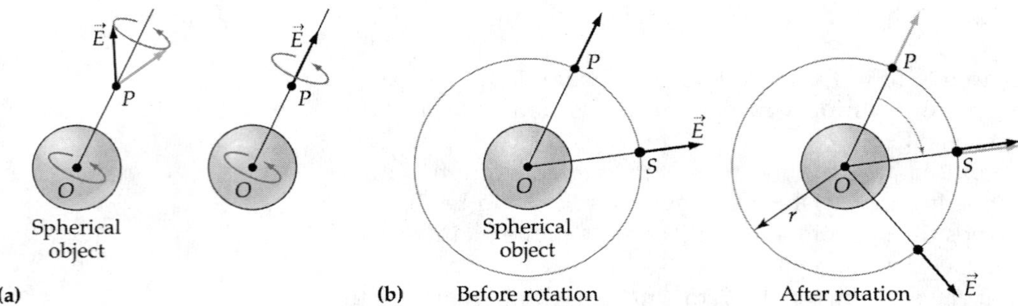

Figure E3.3
A rotation about the axis *OP* changes the direction of the field vector at *P* unless it points directly away from or toward *O*. (b) Rotation around an axis perpendicular to *OP* moves the field vector at *P* to a new position *S* the same distance *r* from *O*. If the field is to remain unchanged by this rotation, the vectors originally at *P* and *S* must have the same magnitude.

Problem Use symmetry arguments to show that an electric field vector created by *any* **spherically symmetric** charge distribution at a point *P* inside or outside that distribution (1) must point radially toward or away from the distribution's center, (2) have a magnitude that depends at most on the distance that *P* is from that center, and (3) must be zero at the distribution's center.

Solution A distribution is *spherically symmetric* if can rotate it around *any* axis through its center without changing it. A spherical object (like a ball or shell) whose charge density is either uniform or depends at most on the radial distance *r* from its center is such a distribution. The symmetry principle strongly constrains the electric field of such a distribution.

For example, imagine that the electric field vector $\vec{E}$ at a given point *P* near the charge distribution does *not* point along the line connecting the object's center *O* to *P*. Then rotating the object around this axis rotates the field vector $\vec{E}$ at *P* to point in a new direction, as shown in figure E3.3a. But this rotation is not supposed to change the vector! We can avoid this logical contradiction only if $\vec{E}$ at *P* points either directly toward or away from *O* (see the right drawing in figure E3.3a): a vector pointing in either of these directions will be unchanged by the rotation. This proves the claim made by statement (1). (Note that while figure E3.3 illustrates the idea for a point *outside* the charge distribution, the argument applies just as well to a point *inside* .)

Now consider rotating the object around any axis perpendicular to the line connecting *O* and *P*. This rotates the field vector that was at point *P* to a new position *S* that is the same distance *r* from point *O* (see figure E3.3b). Because this rotation does not affect the charge distribution, it cannot affect the field. If the field is not to change, then the length of the vector that was at *P* and is now at *S* must have the same length as the vector *originally* at *S* so that the replacement exactly matches the original. Since both the magnitude and the axis of the rotation are completely arbitrary, it follows that the electric field vectors at *all* points that are the same distance *r* from the object's center *O* *must* have the same magnitude. This means that mag($\vec{E}$) can at most depend on the distance *r*. This proves the claim made by statement (2).

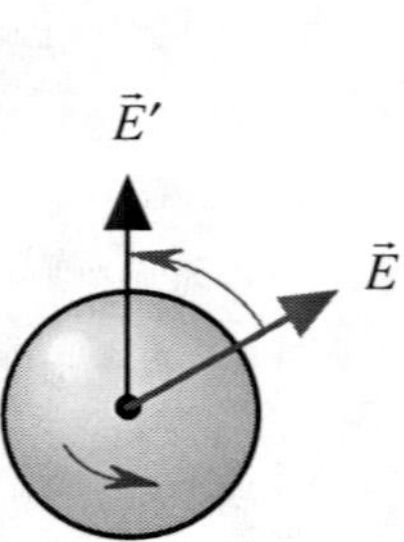

Figure E3.4
A rotation about a spherical distribution's central point *O* will rotate any nonzero field vector at *O* to point in a new direction.

Finally, *assume* for the sake of argument that the field vector $\vec{E}$ at the distribution's center *O* has a nonzero magnitude, as shown in figure E3.4. If we rotate the spherical distribution around any axis that is not parallel to the original direction of $\vec{E}$, the direction of $\vec{E}$ will change to some new direction $\vec{E}'$, as shown. But this rotation does not change the spherical distribution and so should not change the field vector at O, contrary to what is shown in the diagram. The only way to avoid this contradiction is to assume that the field vector at O is zero: only a zero vector at O is unchanged by an arbitrary rotation around O. This proves the claim made by statement (3).

Evaluation Note that these assertions would have been *very* hard to prove if we had to construct the mathematical sum of the field vectors that all bits of charge contribute to the total electric field at point P!

Example E3.4 An Infinite Cylindrical Charge Distribution

Problem An infinite **cylindrically symmetric** charge distribution is unchanged by rotating it *around* some central axis or sliding it any distance *along* that axis. (An infinite straight cylinder, pipe, or wire would be cylindrically symmetric.) Use symmetry arguments to show that an electric field vector created by such a distribution at an arbitrary point P inside or outside the distribution (1) must point radially toward or away from the nearest point on the distribution's central axis, and (2) must have a magnitude that depends at most on the radial distance r that P is away from that axis.

Solution Let O be the point on the axis closest to our arbitrary point P. If the distribution is really infinite in length, it is unchanged by flipping it end-for-end around the OP axis, so this flip should also not change the field vector at point P. As figure E3.5 illustrates, the field vector at P is unchanged by this transformation only if it points directly toward or away from the nearest point O on the central axis, as statement (1) claims.

This infinite distribution is also unchanged by either sliding it along the central axis or rotating it around that axis. Either transformation moves the vector at point P to a different point S the same distance r from the central axis (see figure E3.6). Since the vector originally at P must be identical to the one originally at S if this transformation is not to change the field, the magnitude of the electric field must be the same at P and S. Indeed, a combination of a slide and a rotation can move the vector at P to *any* other arbitrary point the same distance r from the axis, so the vectors at *all* points a given distance r from the axis must have the same magnitude. Therefore, this magnitude can at most depend on r, as statement (2) claims.

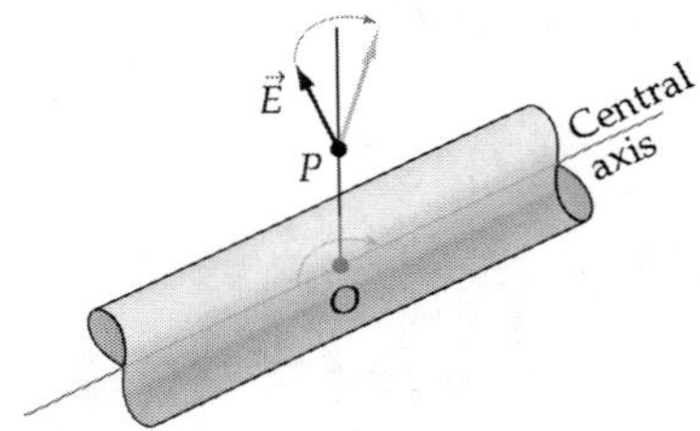

Figure E3.5
A 180° flip around the axis OP does not change a cylindrical charge distribution but does change the field vector at P unless it points directly toward or away from O.

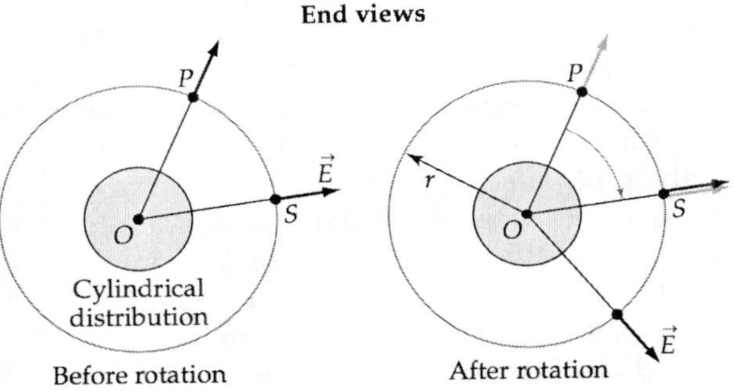

Figure E3.6
Rotation around the central axis moves the field vector at P to a new position S the same distance r from O. If the field is to remain unchanged by this rotation, the vectors originally at P and S must have the same magnitude.

The two kinds of symmetry arguments

Each of these examples illustrates two *different* kinds of symmetry arguments. When we make an argument determining the field's *direction* (or determining that it is zero) at a given point P, we usually consider a transformation that potentially changes the direction of the field vector at P but does not move it *away* from point P. On the other hand, when making an argument determining how the field vector's magnitude depends on position, we consider transformations that *do* transport vectors from one place to another (in the examples, a rotation that moved the vector at point P to point S), so that vectors at different positions can be compared. This is generally the case in such symmetry arguments.

Note how much we can determine about the electric fields of the simple symmetric cases discussed in examples E3.3 and E3.4. Symmetry arguments are enormously powerful and useful tools in many areas of physics. In particular, we will find symmetry arguments useful in many places in this unit, especially in chapter E12.

Self-Test E3X.1

Argue that the electric field at any point along the central axis of an infinite cylindrically symmetric charge distribution must be zero.

Self-Test E3X.2

Consider an infinite, uniformly charged flat plane. Argue that the electric field vectors at all points must point perpendicular to the plane.

E3.3 The Electric Field of a Spherical Shell

Let us turn our attention now to some practical applications of the tools we have just developed. If one places some excess charge on a conducting sphere, the charged particles (in an effort to get as far away from each other as possible) will rapidly distribute themselves uniformly on the sphere's outer surface. The resulting charge distribution is therefore an extremely thin uniformly distributed spherical shell. What can we say about the electric field created by the charge distribution in this very practical situation?

Since the charge distribution in this case is spherically symmetric, the arguments presented in example E3.3 apply. Therefore, we know immediately that the electric field inside and outside the shell will point radially inward or outward, that the magnitude of the field vector at a point can depend at most on the distance r that point is from the shell's center, and that the electric field at the shell's center must be zero.

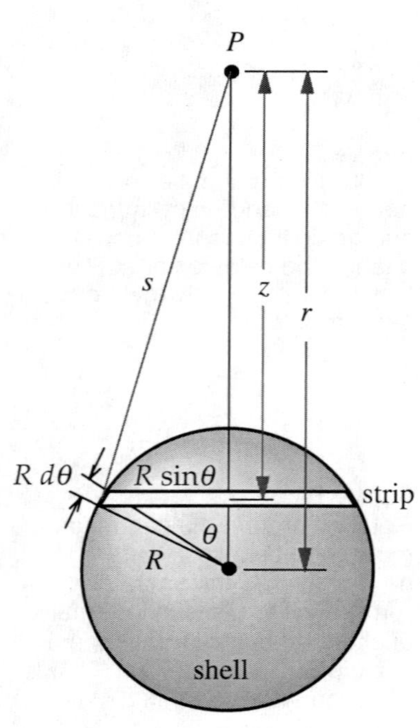

Figure E3.7
How to calculate the electric field outside a spherical shell of charge.

The only thing that remains to determine is exactly how the magnitude of the electric field depends on r. One can calculate this using the methods discussed in section E3.1. Let us orient our coordinate system so the z axis goes through the point P where we would like to evaluate the field. We can then divide the shell into a series of thin, ring-like strips, one of which is shown in figure E3.5. It is most convenient in this case to choose the variable θ to describe the position and width of the rings. The ratio of the charge dQ on a given a strip to the sphere's total charge Q will be equal to the ratio of the strip's area (which is equal to its width $R\,d\theta$ times its circumference $2\pi R\sin\theta$) to the sphere's total surface area $4\pi R^2$:

$$\frac{dQ}{Q} = \frac{2\pi R^2 \sin\theta\, d\theta}{4\pi R^2} = \tfrac{1}{2}\sin\theta\, d\theta \qquad \text{(E3.13)}$$

We can then use equation E3.6, which in this case becomes

$$dE_z = \frac{k\,dQ\,z}{[R^2\sin^2\theta + z^2]^{3/2}} \tag{E3.14}$$

to calculate the outward component of the electric field at point P contributed by each ring. Using equation E3.13 and expressing z as a function of r, R, and θ, we get:

$$dE_z = \frac{kQ(r - R\cos\theta)\sin\theta\,d\theta}{2[R^2\sin^2\theta + (r - R\cos\theta)^2]^{3/2}} \tag{E3.15}$$

To compute the total outward component of the electric field at point P, we only need to sum over all strips and convert the sum to an integral over θ.

Self-Test E3X.3

Make sure that you can fill in the missing steps between equations E3.13 and E3.14 and equation E3.15.

The only difficulty in this case is that the integral in this case is really pretty nasty. There is a clever trick that makes the integral more tractable, but the calculation is still sufficiently difficult that I will simply tell you the surprisingly simple results:

1. If P is outside the shell, then $\vec{E} = (kQ/r^2)\hat{r}$.
2. If P is inside the shell, then $\vec{E} = 0$.

The shell theorem

In words, the first statement says *that the electric field outside a uniform spherical shell of charge is exactly as if the shell's total charge Q were concentrated to a point at its center.* The second statement asserts that not only is the electric field zero at the shell's center, *it is zero everywhere in the shell's interior.* Together, these simple results are called the **shell theorem.**

If you are curious to see how this works out, look at problem E3S.7. We will also prove this result very simply using a totally different approach in chapter E12. For now, however, you should memorize these important and useful results.

E3.4 The Electric Field of a Circular Plate

Another case of great practical interest is the electric field produced by a uniformly charged flat plate. We can actually quite easily calculate the electric field at points along the central axis of a flat circular disk. Let us divide the disk's surface into thin rings of varying radii r and width dr. In this case, the radial variable r specifies all that we need to know about the placement and size of the rings. Since the ratio of the charge dQ on a given ring to the disk's total charge must be the same as the ratio of the ring's area to the disk's total area, the charge on a given ring of radius r must be

$$dQ = Q\frac{2r\,dr}{R^2} \tag{E3.16}$$

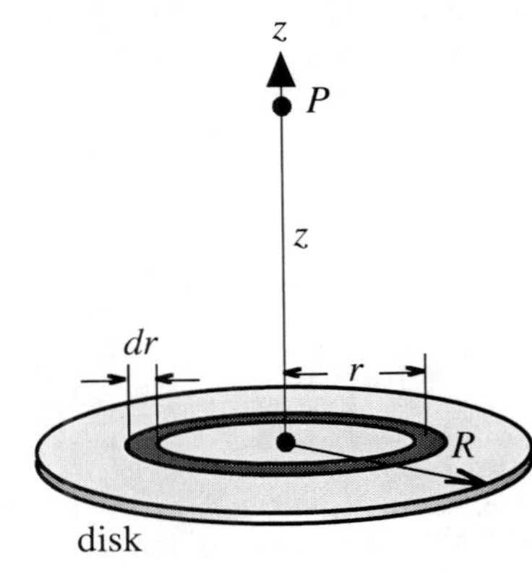

Figure E3.8
How to calculate the electric field at points along the axis of a uniformly charged circular plate.

Self-Test E3X.4

Verify equation E3.16.

Equation E3.6 then implies that at point P, a ring of radius r contributes an electric field of

$$d\vec{E} = \frac{k\,dQ\,z}{[r^2+z^2]^{3/2}}\begin{bmatrix}0\\0\\1\end{bmatrix} = \frac{2kQzr\,dr}{R^2[r^2+z^2]^{3/2}}\,\hat{z} \tag{E3.17}$$

To calculate the total electric field at point P we sum over all rings, and convert the sum to an integral over r. Here, thankfully, the integral is not so bad: according to one of the integrals listed on the inside front cover

$$E_z = \frac{2kQz}{R^2}\int_0^R \frac{r\,dr}{[r^2+z^2]^{3/2}} = -\frac{2kQz}{R^2}\left[\frac{1}{\sqrt{r^2+z^2}}\right]_0^R \tag{E3.18}$$

From here, a few steps of algebra show that the electric field is given by:

$$E_z = \frac{\sigma}{2\varepsilon_0}\left[1-\frac{1}{\sqrt{1+(R/z)^2}}\right]\mathrm{sgn}(z) \tag{E3.19}$$

where $\sigma = Q/\pi R^2$ = the charge per unit area on the plate, $\varepsilon_0 = (4\pi k)^{-1}$, and $\mathrm{sgn}(z)$ is the sign of z. This means that if Q is positive, the electric field points upward (away from the plate) when $z > 0$, and downward (also away from the plate) when $z < 0$. The easy way to remember this is that the electric field points away from a positively charge plate and toward a negatively charged plate.

Self-Test E3X.5

Verify equation E3.19.

An approximation useful for points close to the disk's center

Note that if $z << R$ (meaning that the point P of interest is very close to the plate compared to its radius), the second quantity in the brackets is very small, meaning that the electric field is very nearly independent of z:

$$E_z \approx \frac{\sigma}{2\varepsilon_0}\,\mathrm{sgn}(z) \quad \text{if } |z| << R \tag{E3.20}$$

This is an interesting and (as we will see) useful result.

A qualitative look at the electric field at points close to the plate but not on the central axis

The electric field is much harder to calculate at points that are not along the disk's central axis. However, we can qualitatively guess what the field must look like at least at points very close to the plate. Figure E3.9 illustrates that the electric field vectors contributed by charges closest to P point mostly in the vertical direction and are pretty large, while vectors contributed by distant charges are more nearly horizontal. (It is important to keep in mind, however, that there are many more distant charges than there are close charges.)

This means the z component of the field at P is primarily determined by the charges that are close to P. This is *not* primarily because the far

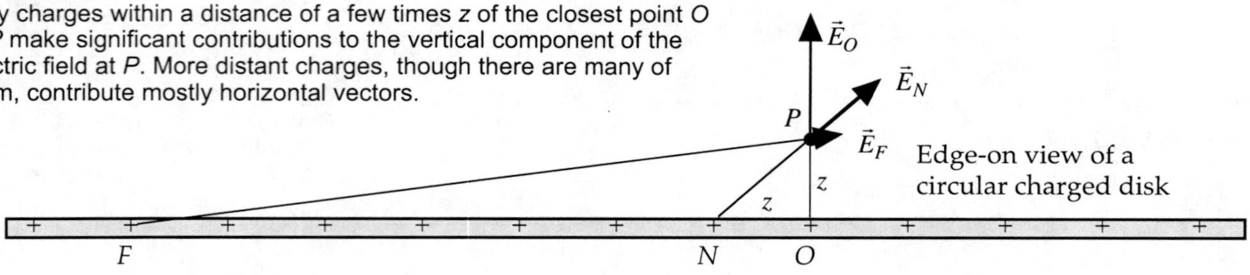

Figure E3.9
Only charges within a distance of a few times z of the closest point O to P make significant contributions to the vertical component of the electric field at P. More distant charges, though there are many of them, contribute mostly horizontal vectors.

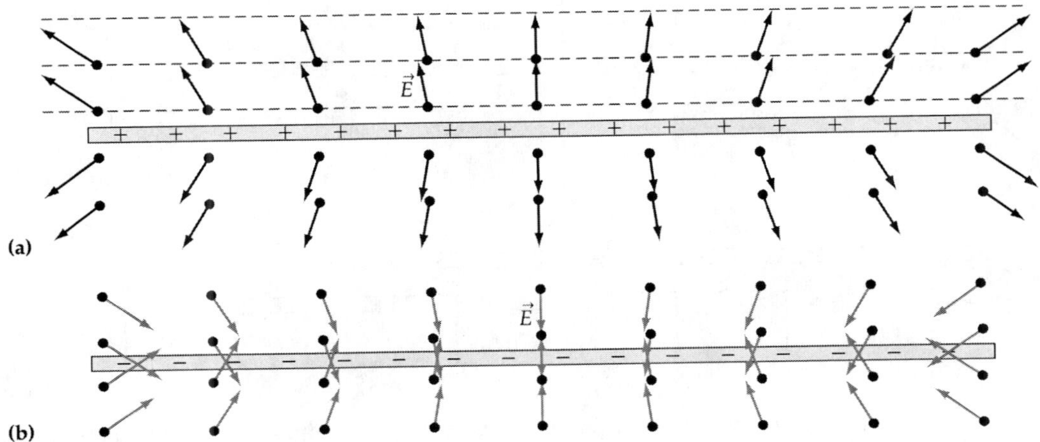

Figure E3.10
(a) Electric field vectors at points near a positively charged plate. The dashed lines help one see that the vertical components of these field vectors are very nearly the same at all points. (b) The field vectors at corresponding points near a negatively charged plate.

charges contribute weaker vectors than the near charges (it turns out that since there are many more far charges, the contributions of near and far charges have comparable total magnitudes), but rather that the far charges contribute vectors having very small z components. Since the z component pretty much ignores the contributions of distant charges, that component should be essentially the same at all points P close to the plate. Therefore, equation E3.20 should apply to all points near the plate as long as $|z| <<$ the distance to the nearest edge.

However, close charges contribute relatively weak horizontal components, so we would expect any horizontal component to the electric field to be determined primarily by the more numerous far charges. Because our point P in figure E3.9 is somewhat off-center to the right, there are more distant charges to the left of P than the right, so the sum of the contributed horizontal components will be toward the right. Therefore, we would expect the total field vector to have essentially the same vertical component as at the center but a horizontal component that grows larger as we move away from the center. Figure E3.10 illustrates the electric fields at points near a positively charged plate and a negatively charged plate.

E3.5 The Electric Field of Parallel Flat Plates

A qualitative look at the electric field created by oppositely charged parallel plates

Imagine now that we arrange two flat plates so that they are parallel and separated by a distance that is small compared to the diameter of the plates. Moreover, imagine that we give these plates uniform charge distributions that are equal in magnitude but opposite in sign (for the sake of concreteness, assume that the upper plate has a positive charge and the lower has a negative charge). Figure E3.10 implies that at a given point in the region between the plates, the two plates contribute electric field vectors that both have downward vertical components but opposite horizontal components. The horizontal components will thus essentially cancel out, but the vertical components will add, yielding a field that essentially everywhere between the plates points vertically downward. Moreover, since the vertical component contributed by each plate is very nearly independent of distance from that plate (assuming that distance is small compared to the plate's diameter), the electric field between closely separated

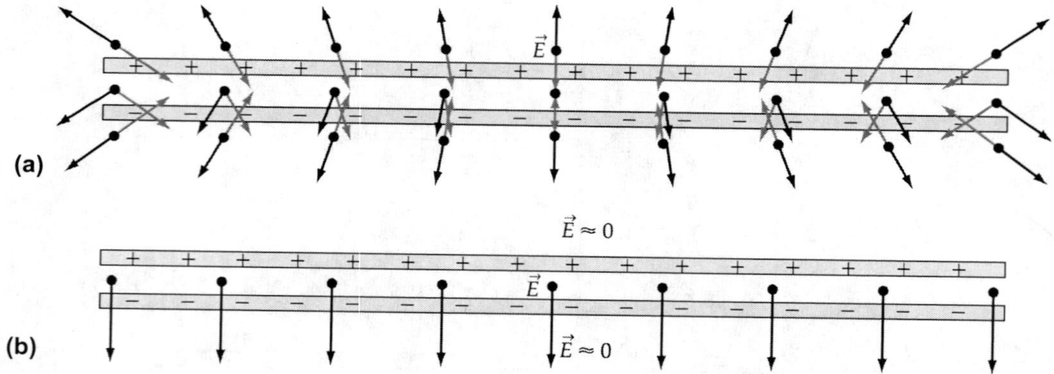

Figure E3.11
(a) When oppositely charged but otherwise identical plates are close together, the field vectors contributed by the plates at a point between them add to a vertical vector whose magnitude is roughly twice the vertical component of each (the horizontal components cancel). At a point outside plates, the contributed vectors essentially cancel. (b) The result is a strong and nearly uniform vertical field in the region between the plates, but essentially no electric field outside the plates.

parallel plates will be very nearly uniform in both direction and magnitude. This is illustrated in Figure E3.11.

The figure also shows that at a given point that is *not* between the plates, the electric field vectors contributed by each plate very nearly cancel. Therefore the electric field outside the region between the plates is very nearly zero. Therefore the electric field at almost all points near such parallel plates is approximately described as follows:

The electric field created by closely spaced and oppositely charged parallel plates

$$\vec{E} \approx \begin{cases} |\sigma|\hat{n}\,/\,\varepsilon_0 & \text{at points between the plates} \\ 0 & \text{at points not between the plates} \end{cases} \tag{E3.21}$$

Purpose: This equation describes the electric field created by closely spaced parallel plates with uniform and opposite charges.

Symbols: $\varepsilon_0 = (4\pi k)^{-1}$ is the permittivity constant, σ is the surface charge density (charge per unit area) on either plate, and $\hat{n}$ is a directional away from and perpendicular to the positive plate.

Limitations: The plates must be identical and parallel. Their separation must be small compared to their size. The charges on the plates must be equal in magnitude and opposite in sign. The approximation is not accurate for points that are closer than several plate-separations from plate edges.

Note: The electric field in the region between the plates is very nearly uniform in magnitude and direction.

The magnitude of the electric field between the plates is $|\sigma|/\varepsilon_0$ because the magnitude of the vertical component contributed by each of the two plates is $\frac{1}{2}|\sigma|/\varepsilon_0$ according to equation E3.20.

This represents a practical way to create a uniform electric field

This result described in the box is of great practical interest because setting up parallel and oppositely charged plates represents the the most practical way to create a nearly uniform electric field in a region of space.

For finite plates separated by a nonzero distance, the electric field outside the region between plates is not *exactly* zero, because the field created by the more distant plate will be slightly smaller in magnitude than that created by the nearer plate (see problem E3S.10 for a discussion of this). However, the magnitude of the external field in practical situations can be many orders of magnitude smaller than that between the plates. The approximation becomes better and better as the ratio of the plate separation to plate diameter or side length goes to zero.

E3.6 The Electric Field Is a Form of Energy

Overview

In unit R, we saw that a particle's mass is a form of energy, meaning that a massive particle is energy in a compacted form. In this section, we will use the result we have just found for the field between parallel flat plates to show that an electric field is a *dispersed* form of energy, and we will derive an expression for the density of energy stored in an electric field.

The argument

The most straightforward way to determine this energy is to determine the electrostatic force that two closely spaced parallel charged plates exert on each other and from that infer the energy required to separate the plates by a certain vertical distance dz. Consider two parallel plates having the same area A and uniformly distributed charges Q and $-Q$ respectively, as shown in figure E3.11. Assume that the negative plate is anchored to the ground but the positive plate is free to move.

Let us focus for the moment on a single one of the positively charged atoms (ions) on the positive plate that have been stripped of an electron in the process of charging the plate. The plate's other ions will exert purely horizontal forces on the ion in question, so the vertical component of the net electrostatic force on our ion will be due solely to the vertical component of the negative plate's electric field at the ion's position. According to equation E3.20, this component is $E_z = -\frac{1}{2}\sigma/\varepsilon_0 = -\frac{1}{2}(Q/A)/\varepsilon_0$ (negative because the electric field points downward toward the negative plate). If the separation between the plates is very small, this vertical component is approximately the same at the positions of *all* ions on the positive plate, so if we denote the charge of the ith ion by q_i, the net vertical force component on the positive plate is

$$F_z = \sum_{\text{all ions}} q_i E_z = -\frac{1}{2\varepsilon_0}\left(\frac{Q}{A}\right)\sum_{\text{all ions}} q_i = -\frac{Q^2}{2\varepsilon_0 A} \tag{E3.23}$$

since the total charge of all the positive plate's ions is Q. To keep the plates at their current separation, therefore, we have to exert an external force on the positive plate whose vertical component is $F_{\text{ex},z} = +\frac{1}{2}Q^2/(\varepsilon_0 A)$.

Now imagine that we slowly displace the upper plate by an infinitesimal vertical displacement $d\vec{r} = [0, 0, dz]$. Doing this will require doing a certain amount of k-work on the upper plate:

$$[dK] = \vec{F}_{\text{ex}} \cdot d\vec{r} = F_{\text{ex},x}dx + F_{\text{ex},y}dy + F_{\text{ex},z}dz = 0 + 0 + \frac{Q^2}{2\varepsilon_0 A}dz \tag{E3.24}$$

This k-work is positive, meaning that we are putting this amount of energy into the positive plate. But at the end of the displacement, the plate is at rest and the charges are distributed in the same way on the plate and the plate has not increased in temperature or changed its chemical composition, so where has the energy gone? The only difference between the initial and final situations is that the volume of the region between the plates has increased by a tiny amount $dV = A\,dz$, and that volume has been filled with an electric field of magnitude $E = Q/(\varepsilon_0 A)$ according to equation E3.21. The k-work that we have done to separate the plates, therefore, must have gone to creating this amount of electric field!

We can calculate the density of energy stored in this electric field by dividing the increase in the internal energy $dU = dK$ of the electric field between the plates by increase in the volume dV. We find that the energy density u_E of the electric field in the region between two plates is

$$u_E \equiv \frac{dU}{dV} = \frac{Q^2 dz}{2\varepsilon_0 A(A\,dz)} = \frac{\varepsilon_0}{2}\left(\frac{Q}{\varepsilon_0 A}\right)^2 = \frac{\varepsilon_0}{2}E^2 \qquad \text{(E3.25)}$$

Self-Test E3X.6

Fill in the missing steps in equation E3.25.

Self-Test E3X.7

Does equation E3.25 have the right units to be an energy density?

We have shown this to be true only in the special case where the electric field is uniform, but it turns out that the same result applies even in cases where the field is not uniform (see problem E3R.2). One indeed finds that quite generally, we model the electric field as being a dispersed form of energy whose energy density at a particular point is

The density of energy in an electric field

$$u_E = \tfrac{1}{2}\varepsilon_0 E^2 \qquad \text{(E3.26)}$$

Purpose: This equation expresses the energy density u_E of an electric field in a region where the electric field has a magnitude E.
Symbols: $\varepsilon_0 = (4\pi k)^{-1}$ is the permittivity constant.
Limitations: There are no known limitations (this expression even works for nonstatic fields).

If E is uniform in a region of volume V, the total field energy U contained in that region is simply $U = u_E V = \frac{1}{2}\varepsilon_0 E^2 V$. To compute the total energy in a region of space filled by a *nonuniform* electric field, we need only divide the space into bits of volume small enough so that E is essentially the same throughout the bit, compute the energy contained in the bit of volume using $dU = u_E dV = \frac{1}{2}\varepsilon_0 E^2 dV$, and sum over all bits. This can be tedious in practice but it is conceptually simple.

We can interpret this result as meaning that an electric field in space, just like matter, is ultimately a form of energy. The only difference is that the energy in an electric field is dispersed smoothly over a volume instead of being concentrated into particles. That equation E3.26 usefully describes the energy contained by an electric field in a wide variety of contexts makes it clear that an electric field is a real physical object, like matter, not some mathematical abstraction.

E3.7 The Mystery du Jour

We have imagined the charge distributions in this chapter to be fixed. We can set up a fixed charge distribution on or inside an insulator, but charged particles can move in a conductor. If we put some excess charge on a conductor, how does it distribute itself on that conductor and why? We need to know this if we are to calculate the fields of such distributions!

TWO-MINUTE PROBLEMS

E3T.1 Consider the finite piece of wire with a uniformly distributed *negative* charge shown below. What is the field direction at the point P? Point S? (Pick the vector you think will be closest.)

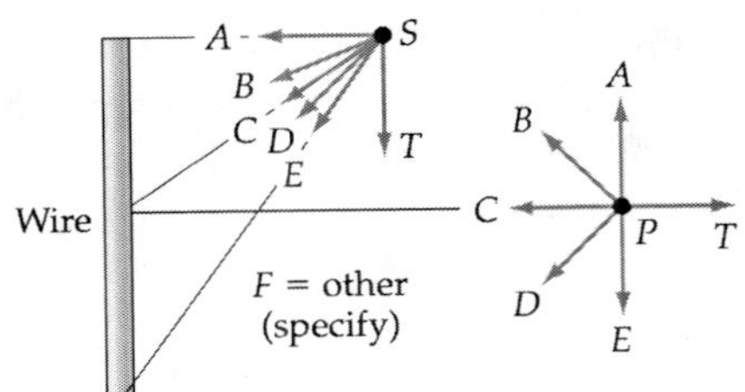

E3T.2 Consider the wire shown in figure E3.12. This wire is part of a circle with radius r. Imagine that we want to calculate the electric field at point P. Which of the symbols shown do you think would make the best variable for step one of the five-step process discussed in section E3.1?

A. x
B. y
C. r
D. θ
E. either x or θ
F. some other variable (specify)

E3T.3 Consider the wire shown in figure E3.12. This wire is a portion of a circle with radius r. Assume that the wire has a uniformly distributed charge. Imagine that we would like to calculate the electric field at point P. What is the *most* that symmetry alone (and symmetry *alone*) can tell us about the direction of the field vector at point P?

A. It must point parallel to the $\pm x$ direction.
B. It must point in the $\pm y$ direction.
C. It must point in the $+y$ direction.
D. It must point in the $-y$ direction.
E. Symmetry alone tells us nothing here.

E3T.4 Consider a uniformly charged circular ring. Which of the following transformations leave the charge distribution unchanged?

A. A rotation about the ring's central axis
B. A rotation about an axis in the ring's plane
C. A reflection across any plane containing the ring's central axis
D. Sliding the ring parallel to its central axis
E. All of the above
F. A, B, and C
T. A and C

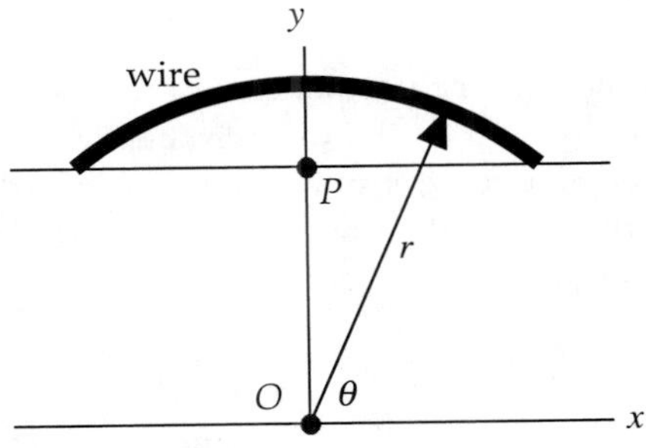

Figure E3.12
The charged wire discussed in problems E3T.3 and E3T.4.

E3T.5 Imagine a plastic disk whose surface contains a uniformly distributed charge. What does symmetry alone tell us about the electric field vector $\vec{E}_P$ at a point P sitting *on* the disk's surface?

A. $\vec{E}_P = 0$.
B. $\vec{E}_P$ points radially away from or toward the disk's center.
C. $\vec{E}_P$ is perpendicular to the disk's surface
D. $\vec{E}_P$ has components both parallel and perpendicular to the disk's surface.
E. Symmetry alone tells us nothing here.

E3T.6 Consider two concentric spherical shells, one with radius R and one with radius $2R$. Both have the same charge Q. At a point just inside the outer shell, the magnitude of the electric field is

A. zero
B. $kQ/R \quad (k \equiv 1/4\pi\varepsilon_0)$
C. $kQ/2R$
D. $2kQ/R^2$
E. kQ/R^2
F. $kQ/2R^2$
T. $kQ/4R^2$

E3T.7 Imagine a plastic ball of radius R that has been given a total positive charge of Q that has somehow been uniformly distributed throughout its interior. The magnitude of the electric field at at a distance of $\frac{1}{2}R$ from the ball's center is

A. zero
B. $kQ/8R^2 \quad (k \equiv 1/4\pi\varepsilon_0)$
C. $kQ/4R^2$
D. $kQ/2R^2$
E. kQ/R^2
F. $4kQ/R^2$
T. some other result (specify)

(*Hint:* Consider the ball to be constructed of a nested set of thin spherical shells. What proportion of the charge is within the radius $\frac{1}{2}R$?)

HOMEWORK PROBLEMS

Basic Skills

E3B.1 Calculate the components of the electric field at the point P in the diagram below. Assume that the charge Q is uniformly distributed over the wire. (*Hint:* What would the limits of integration in equation E3.10 be?)

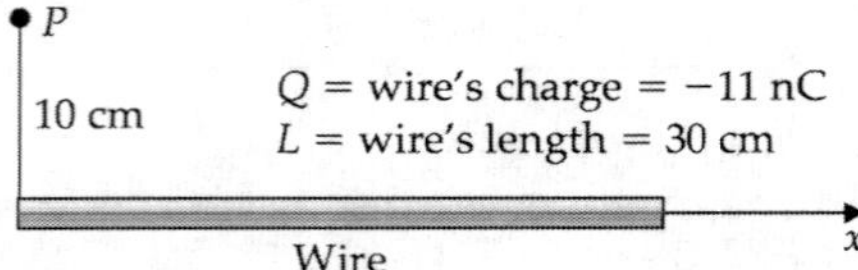

E3B.2 Consider a uniformly charged circular thin ring. Use a rotation symmetry argument to prove that the electric field vector created by this ring at any point along its central axis must point parallel to that axis.

E3B.3 Consider a uniformly charged circular thin ring. Use a rotation symmetry argument to prove that the electric field vector at any point in the plane of the ring must point directly toward or away from the ring's center.

E3B.4 Consider a uniformly charged circular thin ring. Use a rotation symmetry argument to prove that the magnitude of the electric field at any point in the plane of the ring can depend at most on the distance r the point is from the ring's center.

E3B.5 Consider a sphere 4 cm in diameter with a uniformly distributed charge of 33 nC. What is the magnitude of the electric field 5 cm from its center? 3 cm from its center?

E3B.6 Imagine that we have two nested spherical metal shells, one with a radius of R and the other with a radius of $2R$. Assume that the inner sphere has a charge of Q uniformly distributed on its surface and the outer sphere has a charge of $-Q$ uniformly distributed on its surface (where Q is some positive quantity). Draw a qualitatively accurate graph of the electric field magnitude as a function of radius r for $0 \le r \le 3R$.

E3B.7 Imagine that a horizontal disk of radius 10 cm has a uniformly-distributed charge of 33 nC on its surface. What is approximate the strength of the electric field at a point just above its center?

E3B.8 Two parallel plates 30 cm in diameter are separated by 0.5 cm and have uniformly distributed charges of +22 nC and −22 nC respectively. What is the approximate strength of the electric field at an arbitrary point between the plates?

E3B.9 If typical atmospheric electric fields are roughly 200 N/C on a cloudless day, roughly how much electric field energy is contained in a cubic meter of atmosphere?

Synthetic

E3S.1 Consider equation E3.6, which specifies the electric field vector produced by a uniformly charged ring at any point along the z axis.

(a) Verify that this equation has the correct units for an electric field vector.

(b) Intuitively, what do you think that the electric field ought to be at the exact center of a uniformly charged ring, and why? Check that equation E3.6 evaluated at this point yields the result you expect.

(c) When z becomes extremely large, the ring's electric field ought to become approximately the same as that of a point charge, since the ring will become a tiny speck compared to z. Show that equation E3.6 is consistent with this expectation in the limit that $z >> r$.

E3S.2 Consider equation E3.11, which specifies the electric field at points along the y axis produced by a uniformly charged thin wire lying along the x axis and centered on $x = 0$.

(a) Verify that this equation has the correct units for an electric field.

(b) When the distance r between the point and the wire's center becomes extremely large, the wire's electric field ought to become approximately the same as that of a point charge, since the wire will become a tiny speck compared to r. Show that equation E3.11 is consistent with this expectation in the limit that $r >> L$.

E3S.3 Consider the half-ring shown below. Assume that it carries a positive charge Q uniformly distributed along its length. Use the five-step plan discussed in section E3.1 to calculate the electric field vector at the point P.

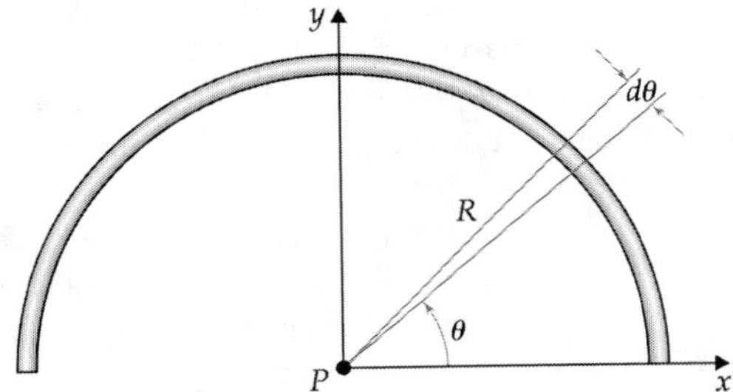

E3S.4 Use the five-step plan of section E3.1 to calculate the electric field at the point P in the figure below. (*Hint:* Think about changing the variable from x to $u \equiv r + x$ when you do the integral.)

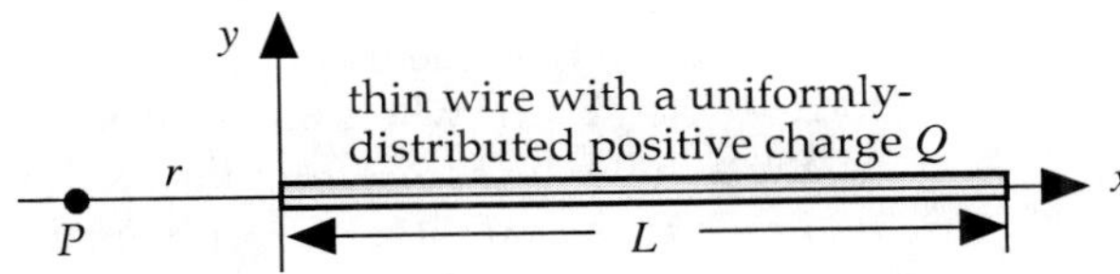

E3S.5 Consider an infinite flat plate whose surface has a uniformly distributed charge. Use symmetry to prove the following claims about the electric field $\vec{E}$ at the given point P.

(a) $\vec{E} = 0$ for any point P on the plate's surface
(b) $\vec{E}$ points perpendicular to the plate at any point not on the surface.
(c) $\vec{E}$ depends at most on the distance that P is from the nearest point on the plate.

E3S.6 Consider a finite cylindrical can shape that has charge uniformly distributed on its surface. Symmetry does allow us to say some things about the electric field of this distribution (a) at points along the can's central axis, (b) at points lying on the plane that cuts the can in half perpendicular to its central axis, and (c) at the can's exact center. What does symmetry tell us in these three cases? (*Hint:* Be sure to consider both the direction of the electric field and on what variables it might or might not depend.)

E3S.7 In this problem, we will prove the shell theorem. (I recommend that you keep a finger on figure E3.7 as you read the problem.) Note that symmetry requires that the electric field of a spherical shell must point radially toward or away from the shell's center, so if we use our freedom to choose coordinates to define the z axis with its origin at the shell's center and so that it goes through point P, then only the z component of the electric field will be nonzero.

(a) We will begin with a clever (but non-obvious) trick that makes the integral much easier. Note in figure E3.7 that the distance s between point P and any point on the ring is

$$s^2 = z^2 + R^2\sin^2\theta = (r - R\cos\theta)^2 + R^2\sin^2\theta$$

$$= r^2 - 2rR\cos\theta + R^2 \qquad \text{(E3.26a)}$$

$$\text{since} \quad z = r - R\cos\theta \qquad \text{(E3.26b)}$$

(Note that equations E3.26 are true even if P is inside the shell.) In our problem, r and R are constants and θ is our master variable. By taking the θ-derivative of both sides of equation E3.26a show that

$$\frac{s\,ds}{rR} = \sin\theta\, d\theta \qquad \text{(E3.27)}$$

(b) Show that equations E3.26 also imply that

$$z = \frac{s^2 + r^2 - R^2}{2r} \qquad \text{(E3.28)}$$

(c) Show that plugging eqs. E3.26a, E3.27, and E3.28 into equation E3.15 yields

$$dE_z = \frac{kQ(s^2 + r^2 - R^2)\,ds}{4Rr^2s^2} \qquad \text{(E3.29)}$$

where $k = (4\pi\varepsilon_0)^{-1}$. This gives the outward component of the electric field at P that is contributed by the strip whose charges are a distance s from P. Note that I have implicitly switched the master variable from θ to s.

(d) To find the total outward field component at P, we need to sum over all strips. If P is outside the shell, then s varies from $r - R$ to $r + R$, so doing the sum and converting the sum to an integral over s, we get

$$E_z = \frac{kQ}{4Rr^2}\int_{r-R}^{r+R}\frac{(s^2 + r^2 - R^2)\,ds}{s^2} \qquad \text{(E3.30)}$$

$$= \frac{kQ}{4Rr^2}\left[\int_{r-R}^{r+R} ds + (r^2 - R^2)\int_{r-R}^{r+R}\frac{ds}{s^2}\right]$$

Do the two integrals in the last expression and show that in this case that $E_z = kQ/r^2$, exactly as if the shell's charge was concentrated at its center.

(e) If P is inside the shell, everything is the same except that s now varies from $R - r$ to $R + r$. Do the integrals with these new limits and show that now we get $E_z = 0$ as required by the shell theorem.

E3S.8 Imagine we have a solid plastic ball of radius R with a positive charge Q distributed uniformly throughout its interior. Use the shell theorem draw a quantitatively accurate graph of the magnitude of the electric field as a function of radius r from $r = 0$ at the ball's center to $r = 3R$. Calibrate your graph's vertical scale in units of kQ/R^2. (*Hint:* Think of the ball's interior as consisting of a nested set of thin spherical shells. How much charge is enclosed by any given radius r?)

E3S.9 If the magnitude of the electric field at a point in air exceeds about 3×10^6 N/C, air (which is normally an excellent insulator) will begin to conduct electricity. This is because a field this strong accelerates any free electrons that happen to be around so violently that they crash into nearby air molecules with enough energy to ionize them, which creates more free electrons, and so on. This creates an avalanche of ionization that frees a huge number of electrons for conduction. What is the maximum charge that you could put on the surface of a plastic sphere 1 cm in diameter without causing the air to conduct electricity (thus dissipating the charge)? [This will give an estimate of the maximum charge a typical small object can hold.]

E3S.10 In section E3.5, I claimed that the electric field is approximately zero at a point outside a set of oppositely charged parallel plates. The field is not *exactly* zero, because whichever plate is more distant will contribute a *slightly* smaller field vector than the closer plate will at a point outside the plates. Let's explore this more quantitatively for points on the plates' central axis, which we will take to be the z axis (as in figure E3.8). Assume that the positive plate is at $z = 0$, and the negative plate is slightly farther away, at $z = -s$. According to equation E3.19, the z component of the field vector contributed by the nearer plate at a position z above the plate on the z axis is

$$E_{z+} = +\frac{\sigma}{2\varepsilon_0}\left(1 - \frac{1}{\sqrt{1+(R/z)^2}}\right) \qquad \text{(E3.31a)}$$

while that contributed by the negative plate is

$$E_{z-} = -\frac{\sigma}{2\varepsilon_0}\left(1 - \frac{1}{\sqrt{1+[R/(z+s)]^2}}\right) \qquad \text{(E3.32)}$$

Assuming that $R >> z$ and $R >> (z+s)$, find the approximate electric field magnitude outside the plates as a fraction of that between the plates. (*Hint:* The fraction will depend on s and R. Check that your fraction has the correct units and goes to a plausible value as s goes to zero.)

Rich-Context

E3R.1 The shell theorem also applies to the gravitational field of a thin spherical shell of mass M if we change $\vec{E} \to \vec{g}$, , $1/4\pi\varepsilon_0 \to G$, and $Q \to M$, because Newton's law of universal gravitation has the same mathematical form as Coulomb's law but for these substitutions. We can apply this to a simple newtonian model of the universe as follows. Observations have shown that the universe is expanding in such a way that a galaxy a distance r from us moves away from us with a speed $v \approx Hr$, where H is a constant quantity called the *Hubble constant.* Model the universe as an infinite distribution of pointlike galaxies with an uniform average density of ρ.

(a) Divide the universe into an infinite set of thin nested shells centered on the earth. Use the shell theorem to argue that the gravitational force exerted by the whole universe on given galaxy a finite distance r from the earth (see figure E3.13 is as if there were a point particle of mass $M = \frac{4}{3}\pi r^3 \rho$ located at the earth.

(b) The universe will thus expand forever if and only if each galaxy's speed exceeds that mass' escape speed at that galaxy's location (see chapter C7 for a discussion of escape speed). Show that this will be true for every galaxy if and only if ρ is smaller than a critical density ρ_{crit} whose value depends on G and H. (Surprisingly, the best general relativistic models yield the same result!)

(c) The currently accepted value of the Hubble constant is $H = 2.3 \times 10^{-18}$ s^{-1} and the total density of visible matter and dark matter is $\rho \approx 2.6 \times 10^{-30}$ g/cm^3. Assuming our model is correct, what is the fate of the universe?

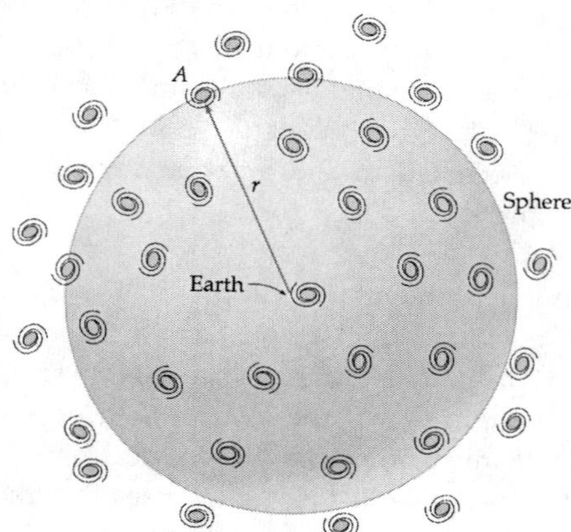

Figure E3.13
The gravitational field at the galaxy marked A is as if the mass of the galaxies within the gray sphere were concentrated at the sphere's center.

E3R.2 Imagine two concentric nested conducting shells with uniformly distributed surface charges. The inner shell has charge $+Q$ and radius R while the other has charge $-Q$ and radius $2R$.

(a) Use the shell theorem to show that the electric field is zero inside the inner shell and outside the outer shell.

(b) How much k-work would one have to supply to expand the outer shell to a radius of $3R$ (ignoring the energy needed to stretch the conducting material of the shell itself)?

(c) Show that this is equal to the total energy of the newly created electric field in the region between $r = 2R$ and $r = 3R$.

(Remember that the electric field depends on radius r between the shells.)

ANSWERS TO SELF-TESTS

E3X.1 Assume for the sake of argument that the electric field at a certain point P along the central axis is not zero. If we rotate the distribution about the central axis, it does not change either the charge distribution or the location of P, so the electric field vector at P must be unchanged by this rotation. This will only be true if the electric field lies along central axis. Now imagine flipping the distribution 180° end-for-end around any axis that is perpendicular to the central axis and goes through P. This rotation will also not change the distribution, but if the electric field at P is nonzero and lies along the central axis, then it would be flipped by this rotation. Only the zero vector at P is unchanged by both a rotation around the central axis *and* a flip around an axis perpendicular to the central axis, so $\vec{E}$ must be zero at P.

E3X.2 Imagine that we would like to evaluate the field at some specific but arbitrary point P. Consider rotating the plane around an axis that goes from P to the plate perpendicular to the plate. If we rotate the plate around this axis, neither the location of P nor the charge distribution changes (assuming that the plate really is infinite). Therefore, the electric field vector at P should not change. But that field vector will be unaffected by the rotation only if it lies along the axis of rotation, that is, perpendicular to the plane.

E3X.3 We get equation E3.14 if we simply substitute $R\sin\theta$ for the radius r of the ring in equation E3.6. Note that figure E3.7 implies that $z = r - R\cos\theta$. Plugging this and equation E3.13 into equation E3.14 yields equation E3.15.

E3X.4 The area of a given ring is simply its width dr times its length $2\pi r$. The total area of the disk is πR^2. The ratio of the ring charge is to the total charge as the ring area is to the total area, so

$$\frac{dQ}{Q} = \frac{2\pi r\,dr}{\pi R^2} = \frac{2r\,dr}{R^2} \tag{E3.31}$$

Multiplying both sides of this equation by Q yields equation E3.16.

E3X.5 Equation E3.18 reads

$$E_z = -\frac{2kQz}{R^2}\left[\frac{1}{\sqrt{r^2+z^2}}\right]_0^R \tag{E3.32}$$

Evaluating this at the limits yields

$$E_z = -\frac{2kQz}{R^2}\left[\frac{1}{\sqrt{R^2+z^2}} - \frac{1}{\sqrt{z^2}}\right]$$

$$= -\frac{2kQz}{R^2\sqrt{z^2}}\left[\frac{1}{\sqrt{(R/z)^2+1}} - 1\right]$$

$$= +\frac{2kQz}{R^2\sqrt{z^2}}\left[1 - \frac{1}{\sqrt{(R/z)^2+1}}\right] \tag{E3.33}$$

Note that $z/(z^2)^{1/2}$ is equal to +1 if z is positive and −1 if z is negative, which is the definition of $\text{sgn}(z)$. Note also that σ is the charge per unit area on the disk, which in this case is $Q/\pi R^2$. If we plug these things into equation E3.33 and use $k = (4\pi\varepsilon_0)^{-1}$, we get equation E3.19.

E3X.6 According to equation E3.21, the electric field strength between the plates is $E = |\sigma|/\varepsilon_0$, where $|\sigma| = |Q/A|$ in this case. Therefore

$$\left|\frac{Q}{A}\right| = \varepsilon_0 E \quad\Rightarrow\quad \frac{Q^2}{A^2} = \varepsilon_0^2 E^2 \tag{E3.34}$$

If we plug this into the next-to-last item in equation E3.25, we get

$$\frac{1}{2\varepsilon_0}\left(\frac{Q}{A}\right)^2 = \frac{1}{2\varepsilon_0}\varepsilon_0^2 E^2 = \tfrac{1}{2}\varepsilon_0 E^2 \tag{E3.35}$$

E3X.7 The units of ε_0 are $\text{C}^2/(\text{N}\cdot\text{m}^2)$ (from the inside front cover) and the units of E are N/C, so the units of equation E3.25 are

$$\left(\frac{\text{N}}{\cancel{\text{C}}}\right)^2\left(\frac{\cancel{\text{C}^2}}{\text{N}\cdot\text{m}^2}\right) = \frac{\cancel{\text{N}}}{\text{m}^2}\left(\frac{1\text{ J}}{1\cancel{\text{N}}\cdot\text{m}}\right) = \frac{\text{J}}{\text{m}^3} \tag{E3.36}$$

which are indeed the units of energy density.

E4 Electric Potential

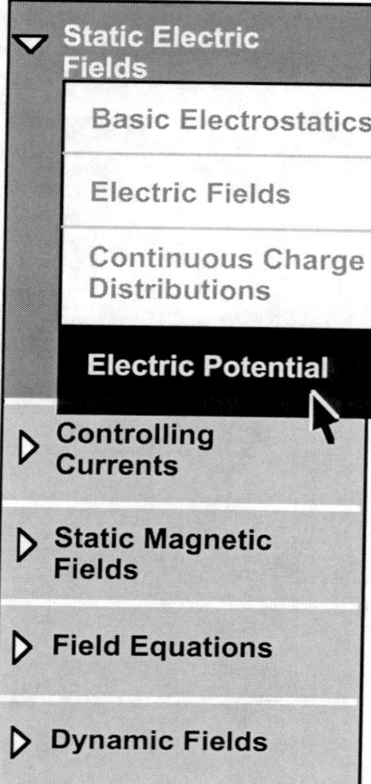

Chapter Overview

Introduction

We close the subdivision on static electric fields with a discussion of the *electric potential,* which provides an alternative way of describing the electric field created by a charge distribution. This is essential background for the next subdivision.

Section E4.1: Electric Potential

The electric potential ϕ at a point in space near a charge distribution is defined to be the *change in electrostatic potential energy per unit charge* that results when we move a charged test particle to that point from some reference point.

$$\phi(x,y,z) \equiv \frac{V_e(x,y,z)}{q} \tag{E4.2}$$

Purpose: This equation defines the electric potential ϕ at a point in space.
Symbols: $V_e(x,y,z)$ is the electrostatic potential energy, relative to some reference point, of a test particle with charge q placed at point $[x, y, z]$.
Limitations: The test particle's charge must be small enough so that it does not significantly disturb the charge distribution creating the field.
Note: The SI unit of electric potential is the **volt:** $1\text{ V} \equiv 1\text{ J/C}$. Note also that $\phi(x,y,z)$ is a *scalar* function of position: it has no direction.

This and the potential energy formula for charged particles imply that

$$\phi = \frac{1}{4\pi\varepsilon_0}\frac{q}{r_{PC}} \tag{E4.6}$$

Purpose: This equation describes the potential field of a charged particle.
Symbols: ϕ is the potential at point P, q is the charge of a particle at point C; r_{PC} is the distance between P and C; and ε_0 is the permittivity constant.
Limitations: This equation assumes that the reference point where we define $\phi \equiv 0$ is infinity, and technically it applies only to charges at rest.

Potentials obey the **superposition principle:** the total potential at a point due to a set of charges is the sum of each charge's contribution to the potential at that point.

We can represent the potential field $\phi(x,y)$ on any given two-dimensional plane using an **equipotential diagram** analogous to a topographical map. **Equipotential curves** on such a diagram connect points having the same potential.

Section E4.2: Calculating ϕ from $\vec{E}$

The definition of the potential implies that

$$d\phi = -\vec{E}\cdot d\vec{r} \tag{E4.11}$$

Purpose: This equation allows us to find the change $d\phi$ in the electric potential ϕ as we move a small displacement $d\vec{r}$ in a *static* electric field $\vec{E}$.
Limitations: The displacement $d\vec{r}$ must be so small that $\vec{E}$ is approximately constant during the displacement.

Section E4.3: Calculating $\vec{E}$ from ϕ

Conversely, if we know $\phi(x,y,z)$, we can calculate $\vec{E}(x,y,z)$ as follows

$$\vec{E}(x,y,z) = \begin{bmatrix} E_x(x,y,z) \\ E_y(x,y,z) \\ E_z(x,y,z) \end{bmatrix} = \begin{bmatrix} -\partial\phi/\partial x \\ -\partial\phi/\partial y \\ -\partial\phi/\partial z \end{bmatrix} \tag{E4.18}$$

Purpose: This equation describes how to calculate the components E_x, E_y, E_z of the electric field as a function of position *x, y, z* knowing the electric potential $\phi(x,y,z)$ as a function of position.

Symbols: $\partial\phi/\partial x$, $\partial\phi/\partial y$ and $\partial\phi/\partial y$ are **partial derivatives** of ϕ (which are just like ordinary derivatives except that one treats the two variables not involved in the derivative as constants).

Limitations: Applies to static electromagnetic fields only.

Note: $\vec{E}$ at a point *P* points "downhill" perpendicular to the equipotential going through *P*; $\text{mag}(\vec{E})$ is proportional to the uphill slope of ϕ.

Section E4.4: Static Charges on Conductors

Any excess charge placed on a conducting object will rapidly redistribute itself into a **static equilibrium** distribution such that $\vec{E} = 0$ everywhere in the object's conducting interior. This statement has the following corollaries: in static equilibrium

1. The potential is constant throughout the object's conducting interior.
2. The object's electric field will be perpendicular to its surface.
3. The object's conducting interior will be electrically neutral.

Excess charge on a conducting sphere will be uniformly distributed on its surface.

Section E4.5: Capacitance

A **capacitor** consists of two isolated conductors (or a single conductor with infinity serving as an implicit second conductor) and has **capacitance**

$$C \equiv \left| \frac{Q}{\Delta\phi} \right| \tag{E4.22}$$

Purpose: This equation defines the capacitance *C* of a capacitor.

Symbols: *Q* is the charge we have moved from one initially neutral conductor to the other and $\Delta\phi$ is their resulting potential difference.

Limitations: This equation assumes that the conductors are isolated.

Note: The SI unit of capacitance is the **farad**, where $1\text{ F} \equiv 1\text{ C/V}$.

Section E4.6: The Parallel-Plate Capacitor

The static equilibrium distribution of charges on closely spaced parallel flat conducting plates with opposite charges is a uniform distribution on the inside surface of each plate. The results of section E4.5 then imply that the potential difference $\Delta\phi$ between plates separated by a distance *s* is

$$|\Delta\phi| = Es \tag{E4.25}$$

and that the capacitance of a parallel-plate capacitor with plates of area *A* is

$$C = \varepsilon_0 \frac{A}{s}. \tag{E4.26}$$

Section E4.7: The Mystery du Jour

We have assumed that charges on conductors are "free" to move, but what does this mean? What if anything limits the flow of charge through a conductor?

E4.1 The Electric Potential

Definition of the electric potential $\phi(x,y,z)$

In chapter E2, we defined the *electric field vector* $\vec{E}(x,y,z)$ at a point to be the electrostatic *force per unit charge* a particle at rest experiences at that point:

$$\vec{E}(x,y,z) \equiv \frac{\vec{F}_e}{q}, \quad \text{where } q \text{ is the test particle's (small) charge} \tag{E4.1}$$

This is a straightforward way of describing the electrostatic field around a charge distribution because force is a fairly intuitive concept and the force experienced by a test charge is something easy to measure and imagine.

However, we can also describe the field created by a charge distribution at a point in space in terms of the *change in electrostatic potential energy per unit charge* required to move a charged particle from some reference point to that point. We in fact define the **electric potential** ϕ (usually called simply the **potential**) at a point as follows:

$$\phi(x,y,z) \equiv \frac{V_e(x,y,z)}{q} \tag{E4.2}$$

Purpose: This equation defines the electric potential ϕ at a point in space.

Symbols: $V_e(x,y,z)$ is the electrostatic potential energy, relative to some reference point (usually infinity), of a test particle with charge q placed at the point $[x, y, z]$.

Limitations: The test particle charge q must be small enough so that forces exerted by the test particle do not significantly disturb the charge distribution whose potential field we are trying to measure.

Note: The SI unit of the electric potential is the **volt**: $1 \text{ V} \equiv 1 \text{ J/C}$. Note that $\phi(x,y,z)$ is a *scalar* function of position: it has no direction.

Knowing the electric potential ϕ at all points around a charged object is completely equivalent to knowing the electric field $\vec{E}$ around the object. Indeed, in sections E4.2 and E4.3, we will learn how to calculate $\phi(x,y,z)$ around a charged object knowing $\vec{E}(x,y,z)$ and vice versa.

Advantages of using the potential field approach

Though using ϕ to describe an electric field is somewhat more abstract than using $\vec{E}$ (because potential energy is less intuitive than force), it does have some offsetting advantages. First of all, ϕ is a *scalar* quantity instead of a vector quantity, which makes it quite a bit easier to calculate than $\vec{E}$ in most circumstances. Secondly, energy is an important concept that is useful in many situations, and describing the field in terms of ϕ makes it easy to calculate the energy implications of electric fields.

The similarity in terminology makes it easy to confuse electric *potential* ϕ with electrostatic *potential energy* V_e: keep in mind that potential ϕ is potential energy *per unit charge*, and is measured in volts, not joules.

The analogy to gravitational potential

Note that we can we can define a **gravitational potential** ϕ_g in a directly analogous way: the gravitational potential at a certain point in space is

$$\phi_g = \frac{V_g}{m} \tag{E4.3}$$

where V_g is the gravitational potential energy of a test object of mass m at that point. At points near the surface of the earth where $V_g = mgh$, the gravitational potential (relative to whatever position we define to have $h = 0$) is simply

$$\phi_g = gh \tag{E4.4}$$

So electrostatic potential is to an electric field what gh is to the earth's gravitational field: $\Delta\phi$ describes the electrostatic energy per unit charge and $\Delta\phi_g$ describes the gravitational potential energy per unit mass released if the object changes position in the field. Note that just as *electric potential* (which is measured in J/C) is not the same as *electrostatic potential energy* (which is measured in J), so *gravitational potential* (which is measured in $\text{J/kg} = \text{m}^2/\text{s}^2$) is not the same as *gravitational potential energy*. Both potential *energies* depend on characteristics of the test particle we use, but that information has been stripped out of the potentials: they depend only on the fields.

Let's see how we can compute the potential field at a given point P near a single particle with charge Q. As we saw in unit C, the potential energy associated with the interaction between a test particle with charge q and a particle with charge Q at point C is (when we take V_e to be zero at infinity) simply

$$V_e = \frac{kQq}{r_{PC}} = \frac{1}{4\pi\varepsilon_0}\frac{Qq}{r_{PC}} \tag{E4.5}$$

where r_{PC} is the distance between the point P and the charge q at C. According to equation E4.2, this means that the electrical potential at point P due to Q is

$$\phi = \frac{1}{4\pi\varepsilon_0}\frac{Q}{r_{PC}} \tag{E4.6}$$

Purpose: This equation describes the electric potential field created at point P by a single pointlike particle with charge Q at point C.
Symbols: ϕ is the potential at point P, r_{PC} is the distance between P and C, and $\varepsilon_0 \equiv 1/4\pi k$ is the permittivity constant.
Limitations: This equation strictly applies only to *particles at rest*. It also assumes that the reference point (where $\phi = 0$) is at infinity.

The potential field of a single charged particle

Potentials also obey the superposition principle, so the total potential ϕ at a point due to a *set* of charged objects is simply

$$\phi = \phi_1 + \phi_2 + \ldots + \phi_N \tag{E4.7}$$

Purpose: Describes the superposition principle for potentials.
Symbols: $\phi_1, \phi_2, \ldots$ are the potentials due to objects 1, 2, ... alone.
Limitations: This equation has no known limitations (this equation even applies to time-dependent fields)!

The potential field of a set of charged objects

For example, the total potential ϕ at point P due to N point charges $q_1, q_2, \ldots$ is

$$\phi = \frac{1}{4\pi\varepsilon_0}\frac{q_1}{r_{P1}} + \frac{1}{4\pi\varepsilon_0}\frac{q_2}{r_{P2}} + \ldots + \frac{1}{4\pi\varepsilon_0}\frac{q_N}{r_{PN}} = \frac{1}{4\pi\varepsilon_0}\sum_{i=1}^{N}\frac{q_i}{r_{Pi}} \tag{E4.8}$$

These quantities are all scalars, so we do not have to worry about directions or vector components! This is why ϕ is generally much easier to calculate than $\vec{E}$.

Self-Test E4X.1

Consider two positive point charges with equal charges Q that sit along the x axis at points $x = \pm a$. Find the total electric potential ϕ for these point charges as a function of y at all points along the y axis.

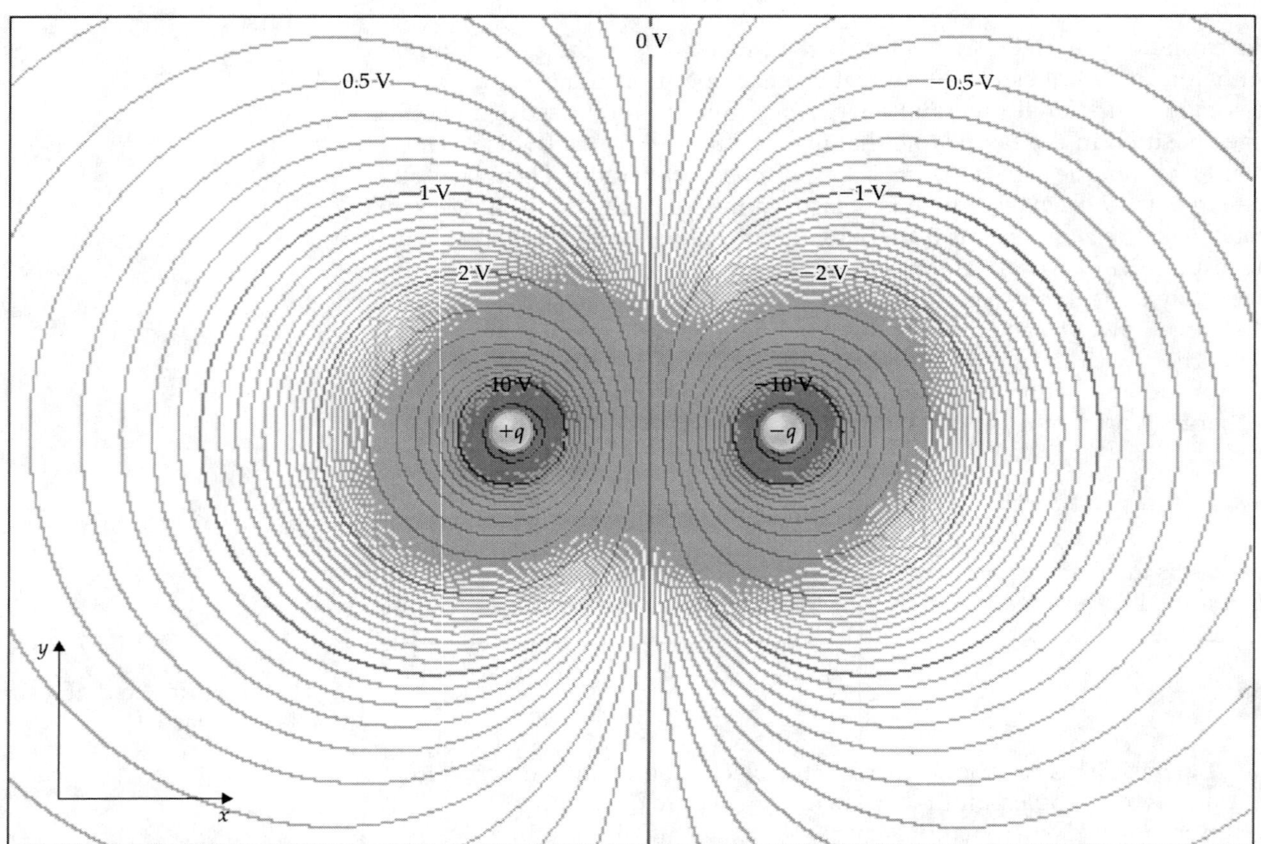

Figure E4.1
An equipotential diagram for a dipole. Each contour connects points that have the same electric potential.

Using an equipotential diagram to display a potential field

Since the electrical potential at any given point is simply a number, we can conveniently depict the potential field around a charge distribution using a contour map, much like a topographical map that describes the altitude of various points on the earth's surface. Figure E4.1 shows such a map for a dipole in the $z = 0$ plane. Each curve on the map connects points having the same electrical potential. These curves are thus called **equipotential curves** or just **equipotentials**, and the diagram is called an **equipotential diagram**.

(Figure E4.1 ignores the fact that the potential can depend on z as well as x and y. Thus the equipotential curves shown in the diagram are really just two-dimensional slices through balloon-like **equipotential surfaces** that connect all points in *three*-dimensional space that have the same potential.)

An equipotential map for a gravitational field is essentially same as a topographical map displaying height above some arbitrary reference altitude. An equipotential curve on a topographical map is simply the contour line that connect points having a given elevation. The only thing that we technically need to do to convert a topographical map to a gravitational equipotential map is to relabel the contours to display the value of gh instead of just h.

E4.2 Calculating ϕ from $\vec{E}$

Knowing the potential field $\phi(x, y, z)$ created by a set of charges is equivalent to knowing the electric field $\vec{E}(x, y, z)$ around those charges: one can compute either representation of the field knowing the other. My goal in this section is to show you how to compute $\phi(x, y, z)$ from $\vec{E}(x, y, z)$.

Consider a point particle with charge q that experiences an electrostatic force $\vec{F}_e = q\vec{E}$ at a certain point in space. Now imagine we move this particle through an infinitesimal displacement $d\vec{r}$ that is so small that $\vec{E}$ is essentially constant during the displacement. Under these circumstances, according to chapter C8, the electrostatic interaction contributes a k-work

$$[dK] = \vec{F}_e \cdot d\vec{r} = q\vec{E} \cdot d\vec{r} \tag{E4.9}$$

to the particle during this displacement. (Note that this equation involves a *dot product* of the vectors $\vec{E}$ and $d\vec{r}$. If you don't remember much about the dot product, see section C8.2.) This energy transfer to the particle's kinetic energy must come at the expense of electrostatic potential energy, so the particle's electrostatic potential energy V_e must change by

$$dV_e = -[dK] = -q\vec{E} \cdot d\vec{r} \tag{E4.10}$$

during this displacement. According to the definition of the potential, though, this means that the change in the electric potential between the endpoints of the displacement is

$$d\phi = \frac{dV_e}{q} = \frac{-q\vec{E} \cdot d\vec{r}}{q} \quad \Rightarrow \quad d\phi = -\vec{E} \cdot d\vec{r} \tag{E4.11}$$

Purpose: This equation tells us how to calculate the change $d\phi$ in the electric potential ϕ as we move a small displacement $d\vec{r}$ in a *static* electric field $\vec{E}$.

Limitations: The displacement $d\vec{r}$ must be so small that changes in $\vec{E}$ are negligible during the displacement.

The change in potential along an infinitesimal displacement

Therefore, if we know the electric field $\vec{E}(x, y, z)$ and value of the potential ϕ at any specific point A, we can (in principle) find the potential at any other point B as follows: we

A plan for calculating the potential at any point in an electric field

1. Define a convenient path through space connecting A to B.
2. Divide the path up into steps small enough that $\vec{E} \approx$ constant for each step
3. Compute $-\vec{E} \cdot d\vec{r}$ for each step along the path
4. Add the results to find the total change in potential $\Delta\phi$
5. Use the known value of the potential at A to find the value at B.

Doing this for all possible points B determines the entire potential field $\phi(x, y, z)$ from the electric field $\vec{E}(x, y, z)$. Example E4.1 illustrates the process.

Example E4.1 Calculating the Potential Field of a Point Particle

Problem Using equation E2.9 for the electric field $\vec{E}$ of a point particle, find the potential ϕ at an arbitrary point P near a particle with positive charge Q.

Translation Let r_P be the distance between point P and the charged particle.

Model We know that the electric potential is zero at infinity, so let us choose our path to be a radial line going from $r = r_P$ to $r = \infty$. We can divide this path into an infinite number of inward infinitesimal steps $d\vec{r}$. The displacement $d\vec{r}$ for any step of this path points directly away from the particle and $\vec{E}$ also points in this direction, so the dot product becomes

$$\vec{E} \cdot d\vec{r} = [\text{mag}(\vec{E})][\text{mag}(d\vec{r})]\cos 0° = +E\,dr \tag{E4.12}$$

But equation E2.9 tells us that $E = \text{mag}(\vec{E}) = kQ/r^2$ for a point particle, where $k = (4\pi\varepsilon_0)^{-1}$. If we plug this into equation E4.11 and sum over all steps along the path we get

$$\phi(\infty) - \phi(r_P) = \Delta\phi_{\text{path}} = \sum_{\text{all steps}} -\vec{E}\cdot d\vec{r} = \sum_{\text{all steps}} -\frac{kQ}{r^2}dr \tag{E4.13}$$

If we make the steps infinitesimal, we can convert this sum to an integral:

$$\phi(\infty) - \phi(r_P) = \int_{r_P}^{\infty} -\frac{kQ}{r^2}dr = +\frac{kQ}{r}\bigg|_{r_P}^{\infty} = 0 - \frac{kQ}{r_P} = -\frac{kQ}{r_P} \tag{E4.14}$$

Finally, since $\phi(\infty) = 0$ by definition, the electric potential at point P due to a charged point particle is

$$0 - \phi(r_P) = -\frac{kQ}{r_P} \quad \Rightarrow \quad \phi(r_P) = \frac{kQ}{r_P} = \frac{1}{4\pi\varepsilon_0}\frac{Q}{r} \tag{E4.15}$$

Since P is arbitrary, this expression specifies the particle's entire potential field.

Evaluation This is the result given by equation E4.6, which is comforting.

Self-Test E4X.2

Go through the argument again assuming that Q is negative and prove that the result is the same.

Self-Test E4X.3

Consider a line that is perpendicular to the axis of a dipole and goes through that axis halfway between the dipole's charges (this is the vertical straight line in figure E4.1). Figure E2.4 implies that the electric field at all points along such a line is perpendicular to the line. Argue that the potential at all points along this line must be 0 V, as shown in figure E4.1.

The potential difference for a static field is path-independent

If this process is to yield a well-defined value for ϕ at a point B given $\phi(A)$, the potential difference $\Delta\phi$ that we compute between two points *cannot* depend on the path we choose to go from one point to the other. Why can we assume this? For a static electric field, conservation of energy *requires* that $\Delta\phi$ be path-independent. To see this, pretend for the sake of argument that the potential difference from A to B along the one path is *smaller* than the difference from A to B along a second path. If we transport the particle in a loop from A up the first path and then down the second, the particle will have a lower potential (and thus a lower potential energy) when it returns to A than it did initially. But this means it must have more kinetic energy than it did originally. If we continue to transport it around the loop, we can give it as much kinetic energy as we like! But where is this energy coming from? In a static electric field nothing *else* is changing, so there is nowhere that this energy can come from!

(The gravitational analogy would be like going down a spiral staircase and finding that after making one complete turn, you end up on the same floor at which you started! You could generate endless amounts of energy by rolling objects down such a staircase without changing anything external, in violation of the law of conservation of energy.)

If, however, the potential difference is the *same* for both paths, then the particle will return to point A with exactly the same potential, and thus neither gains nor loses energy in the cycle, preserving conservation of energy. Thus conservation of energy demands that the potential difference $\Delta\phi$ between two points in a *static* electric field be *independent* of the path we use to compute it. (We will see in chapter E14 that this is *not* true in a time-dependent field.)

E4.3 Calculating $\vec{E}$ from ϕ

There is also a straightforward way to calculate the components of the electric field vector $\vec{E}$ at any point P if we know $\phi(x, y, z)$ in a given xyz coordinate system. Consider first a small displacement $d\vec{r} = [dx, 0, 0]$ purely in the x direction away from P. Equation E4.11 and the component definition of the dot product imply that

$$d\phi = -\vec{E} \cdot d\vec{r} = -E_x dx - E_y \cdot 0 - E_z \cdot 0 = -E_x dx$$

$$\Rightarrow E_x = -\frac{d\phi}{dx} \quad \text{for a step purely in the } x \text{ direction} \tag{E4.16}$$

A step purely in the x direction does not change the value of y or z, so in equation E4.16, we are computing the derivative of $\phi(x, y, z)$ with respect to x while holding y and z constant. We call such a derivative a **partial derivative** and denote it using "curly d's" in the numerator and denominator:

$$\frac{\partial\phi}{\partial x} \equiv \lim_{\Delta x \to 0}\left[\frac{\phi(x+\Delta x, y, z) - \phi(x, y, z)}{\Delta x}\right] = \left[\frac{d\phi}{dx}\right]_{\text{holding } y,\, z \text{ constant}} \tag{E4.17}$$

So the formally correct way to write equation E4.16 is $E_x = -\partial\phi/\partial x$. The analysis is the same for the y and z components of $\vec{E}$, so

$$\vec{E}(x, y, z) = \begin{bmatrix} E_x(x, y, z) \\ E_y(x, y, z) \\ E_z(x, y, z) \end{bmatrix} = \begin{bmatrix} -\dfrac{\partial\phi}{\partial x} \\ -\dfrac{\partial\phi}{\partial y} \\ -\dfrac{\partial\phi}{\partial z} \end{bmatrix} \quad \text{evaluated at } x, y, z \tag{E4.18}$$

How to find the components of $\vec{E}$ at any point given the potential field $\phi(x, y, z)$

Purpose: This equation describes how to calculate the electric field vector $\vec{E}(x, y, z)$ at a point whose coordinates are x, y, z if we know the electric potential $\phi(x, y, z)$ as a function of position.

Symbols: E_x, E_y, and E_z are the components of $\vec{E}$ and $\partial\phi/\partial x$, $\partial\phi/\partial y$ and $\partial\phi/\partial z$ are partial derivatives of ϕ (evaluated by treating the variables not involved in the derivative as constants).

Limitations: Applies to static electromagnetic fields only.

Mathematicians call the vector $[\partial\phi/\partial x, \partial\phi/\partial y, \partial\phi/\partial z]$ the **gradient** of $\phi(x, y, z)$, so $\vec{E}$ at a given point in space is the *negative gradient of* ϕ at that point.

Calculating partial derivatives is easy!

Please do not be put off by the terminology or the strange partial derivative symbol: evaluating a partial derivative is not at all different from evaluating an ordinary derivative, something you already know how to do! The *only* point of the "partial" derivative name and "curly" symbols are to remind us that when we evaluate the derivative of ϕ with respect to one of the three variables, we are to treat the other two as if they were constants. For example, if $\phi(x,y,z) = ax^2\sin(yz)$ (where a is truly constant), then

$$\frac{\partial\phi}{\partial x} = \frac{\partial}{\partial x}\left[ax^2\sin(yz)\right] = a\sin(yz)\frac{d(x^2)}{dx} = 2ax\sin(yz) \tag{E4.19a}$$

$$\frac{\partial\phi}{\partial y} = \frac{\partial}{\partial y}\left[ax^2\sin(yz)\right] = ax^2\frac{\partial}{\partial y}[\sin(yz)] = ax^2z\cos(yz) \tag{E4.19b}$$

Note that in evaluating $\partial\phi/\partial x$, I treated y and z exactly as if they were constant, pulling the constant $\sin(yz)$ out in front of the derivative. I similarly treated x and z as constants (the latter as a constant inside the sine function) when evaluating $\partial\phi/\partial y$. Evaluating these partial derivatives is no more difficult than evaluating an ordinary derivative!

Self-Test E4X.4

What is $\partial\phi/\partial z$ in the example considered above?

It may not seem so, but equation E4.18 has a simple and intuitive interpretation. Imagine that we want to find the electric field vector $\vec{E}$ at a certain point P. Let's take advantage of our freedom to choose coordinate axes to orient the yz plane so that it is tangent to the equipotential surface that goes through point P. This means that for a small step in either the y or z direction, the potential ϕ does not change. But if ϕ does not change during such steps, then $\partial\phi/\partial y = 0$ and $\partial\phi/\partial z = 0$, so $\vec{E}$ (if nonzero) must point in the $\pm x$ direction, the direction perpendicular to the equipotential surface. Since $E_x = -\partial\phi/\partial x$, if ϕ increases with x, then $\vec{E}$ points in the $-x$ direction, and if ϕ decreases with x, $\vec{E}$ points in the $+x$ direction. Removing references to our arbitrary coordinate system, we can say quite generally that *the electric field vector $\vec{E}$ at a point P must point perpendicular to whatever equipotential curve or surface goes through that point in the direction that ϕ decreases* (the "downhill" direction, if you like). The magnitude of $\vec{E}$ is simply equal to the slope of ϕ in this downhill direction. One can easily use this intuitive interpretation to sketch the electric field vectors at various points on an equipotential diagram, as illustrated in figure E4.2.

The intuitive interpretation of the gradient expression for $\vec{E}$

Self-Test E4X.5

Draw electric field arrows at various points on the equipotential diagram shown in figure E4.1, and compare your resulting picture of the electric field with that shown in figure E2.4.

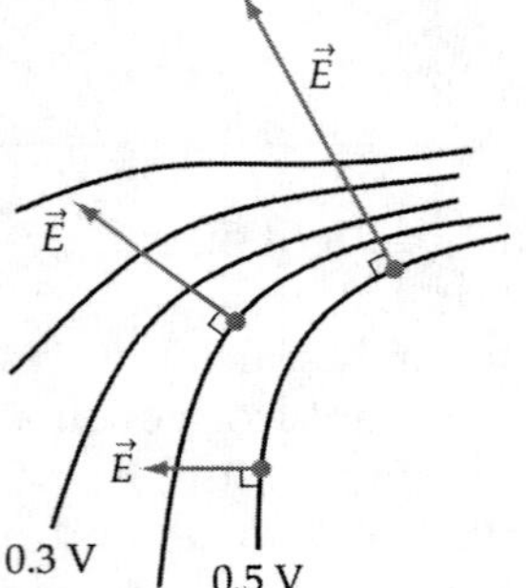

Figure E4.2
The electric field vector at a point on an equipotential diagram is perpendicular to the equipotential through that point and has a magnitude proportional to the slope of the potential function in that direction (and thus *inversely* proportional to the distance between the equally spaced equipotential curves at that point).

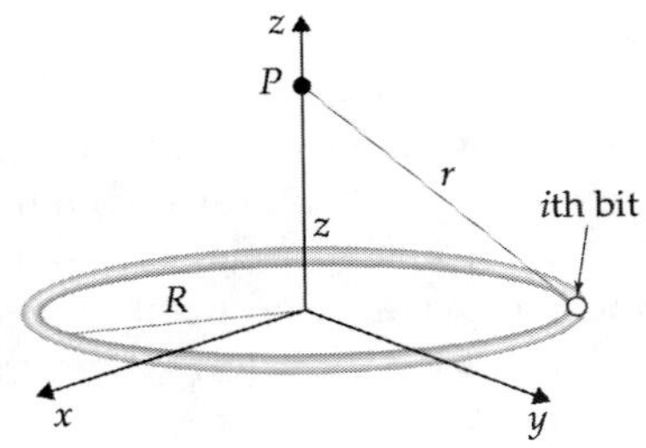

Figure E4.3
This diagram illustrates how we can calculate the electric potential at point P along the ring's central axis. Note that I have set up the coordinate system so that the ring's center is at the origin and its central axis coincides with the z axis.

Using the potential as a first step to calculating electric field vectors

It is often easier to calculate $\phi(x,y,z)$ than $\vec{E}(x,y,z)$ for a complicated charge distribution because we can add the *potential* fields contributed by bits of the distribution as scalars whereas we have to add the contributed electric fields as vectors. Example E4.2 illustrates how much simpler a a calculation involving potentials can be (compare with example E3.1).

Example E4.2 The Field Along the Axis of a Thin Charged Ring

Problem Consider a thin ring of radius R with a uniformly distributed total charge Q. What is **(a)** the potential and **(b)** the electric field at a point P a distance z from the ring's center along the ring's central axis (see figure E4.3)?

(a) *Model* The first step, as usual, is to subdivide the ring into a set of bits that are sufficiently small to model as point charges. If the ring is very thin compared to its radius R, all the ring's bits are essentially the same distance $r = (z^2 + R^2)^{1/2}$ from the point P. Let the charge of the ith bit be q_i.

Solution This means that the total potential at P is simply

$$\phi(0,0,z) = \sum_{\text{all } i} \frac{kq_i}{r} = \frac{k}{r}\sum_{\text{all } i} q_i = \frac{kQ}{r} = \frac{kQ}{\sqrt{z^2+R^2}} = \frac{1}{4\pi\varepsilon_0}\frac{Q}{\sqrt{z^2+R^2}} \quad \text{(E4.20)}$$

Evaluation That was easy!

(b) *Model* Equation E4.20 only gives the potential along the z axis, so we cannot tell exactly how ϕ might depend on x and y. But we know from symmetry that the electric field must point directly along the ring's central axis (otherwise a rotation around that axis would change the field vector even though there is no change in the charge distribution). So only the z component of $\vec{E}$ is nonzero, and since we do know the value of ϕ at all values of z (holding x and y constant and equal to zero) we can evaluate the partial derivative needed to determine this component.

Solution Therefore, we must have $E_x = E_y = 0$ and

$$E_z(\text{at } P) = -\frac{\partial\phi}{\partial z}(\text{at } P) = -\left[\frac{d\phi}{dz}\right]_{x=y=0} = -\frac{d}{dz}\left[kQ(z^2+R^2)^{-1/2}\right]$$

$$= -(-\tfrac{1}{2})kQ(z^2+R^2)^{-3/2}\frac{d}{dz}(z^2+R^2) \quad \text{(by the chain rule)}$$

$$= \tfrac{1}{2}kQ(z^2+R^2)^{-3/2}\,2z = \frac{kQz}{(z^2+R^2)^{3/2}} = \frac{Qz}{4\pi\varepsilon_0(z^2+R^2)^{3/2}} \quad \text{(E4.21)}$$

Evaluation This is the same result we found in example E3.1.

E4.4 Static Charges on Conductors

Static charge distributions

Chapter E1 claimed that charges inside conductors are free to move in response to electric fields. Indeed, as we will see in detail in chapter E5, charges in a conducting region *must* move if there is a nonzero electric field in that region. Charges placed on a conductor will therefore move around until they settle (typically within a fraction of a microsecond) into a distribution where they can remain at rest (usually trapped against the conductor's boundaries). We call such a distribution a **static equilibrium** charge distribution.

The fundamental characteristic of such a distribution is the following:

The fundamental criterion for a static distribution

> In static equilibrium, any excess charges placed on a conducting object will be arranged so that $\vec{E} = 0$ at all points within the object's conducting interior.

This must be so, because if the $\vec{E} \neq 0$ in *any* conducting region, then charges in that region would be free to move in response to the field, meaning that the charges had not yet settled into their final static configuration.

Useful corollaries of the fundamental criterion

This statement has some interesting corollaries: in static equilibrium,

1. The potential ϕ is the same at all points inside an isolated conducting region. (*Proof:* According to equation E4.11, $d\phi = -\vec{E} \cdot d\vec{r} = 0 \cdot d\vec{r} = 0$ for any displacement $d\vec{r}$ between two points inside a conductor.) The conductor's surface must therefore be an equipotential surface for whatever field the conductor creates.
2. The electric field at points on a conductor's surface must point perpendicular to that surface. (*Proof:* We just saw in the last section that the electric field points perpendicular to any equipotential surface.)
3. The conducting interior of a conducting object must be electrically neutral in static equilibrium: any excess charge must be located on the object's *surface*. (We will see the proof in chapter E12.)

These statements only apply to charge distributions in static equilibrium

Please note that these statements only apply to the *static* equilibrium that obtains after the charges have finished moving around. In the next chapter, we will discuss *dynamic* equilibrium in electrical circuits, where current flows are maintained for a significant amount of time. In such a case $\vec{E} \neq 0$ in the circuit's conducting wires, and so the corollaries do not apply (except, as it happens, for corollary 3, which still does work.)

Any excess charge on an isolated metal sphere is distributed uniformly on its surface

As an example of a static equilibrium distribution, imagine that we give an isolated solid metal sphere an excess charge Q. All our conditions for static equilibrium are met if this excess charge ends up uniformly distributed on the sphere's *outer* surface (consistent with corollary 3). According to the shell theorem (see section E3. 3) such a surface charge distribution creates an electric field that is zero *inside* that surface and thus inside the ball (satisfying our fundamental criterion for a static distribution). The shell theorem also implies that the electric field at points just *outside* the surface points radially away from the sphere's center, and thus perpendicular to its surface, consistent with corollary 2. Finally, the shell theorem also states that the electric field outside any uniformly charged spherical distribution is the same as if its charge were concentrated at its center. Since we can calculate ϕ from $\vec{E}$, the potential field ϕ outside the sphere must *also* be the same as that for a point charge Q located at its center.* This potential is $\phi = kq/r$ and this will indeed be the same at all points

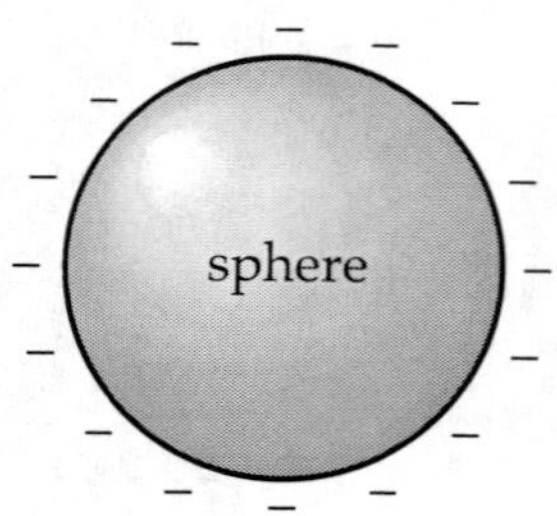

Figure E4.4
In static equilibrium, excess charge placed on a metal sphere will end up uniformly distributed on the sphere's surface.

*Technically, we can only calculate the potential up to an overall constant. But the presence of such a constant does not change the argument in the next sentence.

on the sphere's surface (consistent with corollary 1) because all these points are the same distance from the center. This uniform surface charge distribution (illustrated in figure E4.4) indeed turns out to be the *only* distribution satisfying our criteria for an isolated spherical conductor.†

A static distribution shields a conducting object's interior from external fields

However, this distribution is not correct if the sphere is *not* isolated, that is, if there are charges outside the sphere that create an external electric field. For example, imagine bringing a positive point charge close to our charged sphere. If the charge distribution on the sphere were to remain uniform, it would contribute nothing to the field in the sphere's interior, but by the superposition principle, the field in the interior would then be that of the external charge, which is not zero, which is impossible for a static charge distribution.

We can intuit what will happen: because of their attraction to the positive external charge, the excess negative charges on the sphere's surface will crowd toward the side of the sphere nearest to the charge, perhaps even leaving the far side a bit positive (see figure E4.5). Note that this unbalanced distribution will create an electric field that tends to cancel the external charge's field in the sphere's interior. Indeed, the fundamental criterion for static distribution implies that the final surface charge distribution must be whatever distribution *exactly* cancels the external charge's *everywhere* in the sphere's interior.

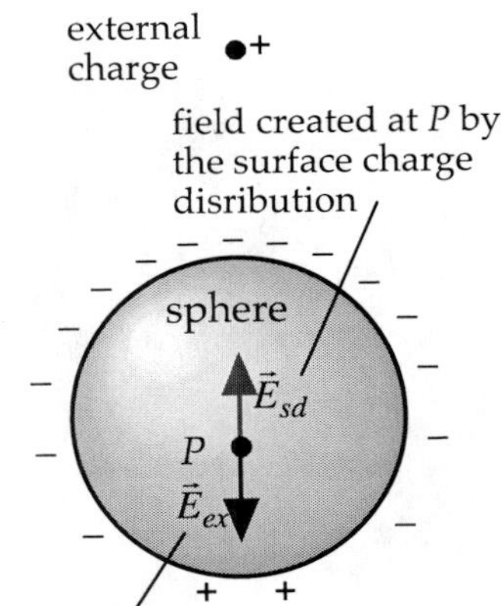

Figure E4.5
Negative charges on the sphere will be attracted by an external point charge. The final surface charge distribution will completely cancel the external charge's field at any arbitrary point *P* inside the sphere's conducting interior.

Indeed, the fundamental criterion implies that the static equilibrium surface charge distribution on *any* conducting object must be exactly that distribution that shields its interior from any external electric fields. This will be true even if the conducting object is *hollow*! Since the charge distribution that ensures that $\vec{E} = 0$ in the object's interior is located on the object's surface (by corollary 3), removing the interior does not change the distribution, so $\vec{E}$ is still zero in the newly created cavity.

Even time-dependent external fields are screened as long as they vary slowly compared to the time it takes the charges to redistribute themselves on the conductor (which is typically a fraction of a microsecond). You may have noticed that when your car crosses a metal-framed bridge, your radio may cut out, particularly if you are tuned to the (relatively low-frequency) AM band. Charges on the bridge's metal frame are able to move quickly enough to cancel out the varying electromagnetic field that comprises the radio signal.

What you need to know

Calculating the correct surface charge distributions for nonspherical charged conductors (or for spherical conductors in an external field) is generally pretty difficult. We will not do any such calculations in this class. It will be enough if you know the fundamental criterion for static equilibrium and its corollaries and have some qualitative sense of what the appropriate distribution might look like (as in figure E4.5).

E4.5 Capacitance

Definition of a *capacitor*

Consider two initially neutral conductors A and B that are isolated from other charged objects. Imagine that we move a certain amount of charge Q from A to B, and we allow everything to come into static equilibrium. Since each object has a certain fixed potential throughout its conducting interior, the potential difference $\Delta\phi = \phi_B - \phi_A$ between the two objects is precisely defined. We call such a pair of objects a **capacitor**. We call the two conductors that comprise the capacitor the capacitor's **plates** (even if they are not shaped like plates.). We define a capacitor's **capacitance** C to be

†One *can* prove mathematically that the fundamental criterion *uniquely* determines the charge distribution for an isolated conducting object.

The definition of *capacitance*

$$C \equiv \left| \frac{Q}{\Delta\phi} \right| \tag{E4.22}$$

Purpose: This equation defines the capacitance C of a two-conductor capacitor.

Symbols: Q is the charge that we have moved from one conducting object to the other (both are assumed to be initially neutral) and $\Delta\phi$ is the resulting potential difference between the conductors.

Limitations: This equation assumes that the conductors are isolated from other charged objects.

Note: The SI unit of capacitance is the **farad**, where $1\text{ F} \equiv 1\text{ C/V}$.

A capacitor with a larger capacitance thus holds more charge on its plates for a given potential difference than one with smaller capacitance. This is the root idea behind the terms *capacitor* and *capacitance*. Capacitors are commonly used in electronic circuits to temporarily store electric charge.

Self-Test E4X.6

What is the farad in terms of the more basic units of coulomb, kilogram, meter, and second?

A capacitor's capacitance C turns out to depend only on the size, shape, and arrangement of its plates (and the material in which these plates are embedded), not on the magnitude of the potential difference between those plates. Generally, C is hard to calculate for a given arrangement of conductors, but section E4.6 and problem E4S.8 illustrate the calculation of C in simple cases.

The capacitance of a single object

One can also talk about the capacitance of a *single* isolated conductor if we assume that the other conductor is essentially a spherical shell whose radius is infinite. The following example illustrates this idea.

Example E4.3 The Capacitance of an Isolated Sphere

Problem Calculate the capacitance of an isolated spherical conductor of radius R relative to infinity.

Model According to section E4.4, any charge Q on an isolated spherical conductor will be uniformly distributed on its surface. According to the shell theorem, the electric field (and thus the potential field) of such a distribution will be as if the charge Q is concentrated at the sphere's center. The potential ϕ of the sphere's surface relative to infinity (and thus the potential difference $\Delta\phi$ between that surface and the imaginary shell at infinity) is therefore the same as the potential of a point charge Q evaluated at the sphere's surface radius R:

$$\Delta\phi = \phi(\text{at } R) = \frac{1}{4\pi\varepsilon_0}\frac{Q}{R} \tag{E4.23}$$

Solution Plugging this into equation E4.22 yields

$$C = 4\pi\varepsilon_0 R \tag{E4.24}$$

Evaluation It makes some intuitive sense that as a sphere grows, it would have greater capacitance (that is, a greater ability to hold charge for a given potential difference relative to infinity).

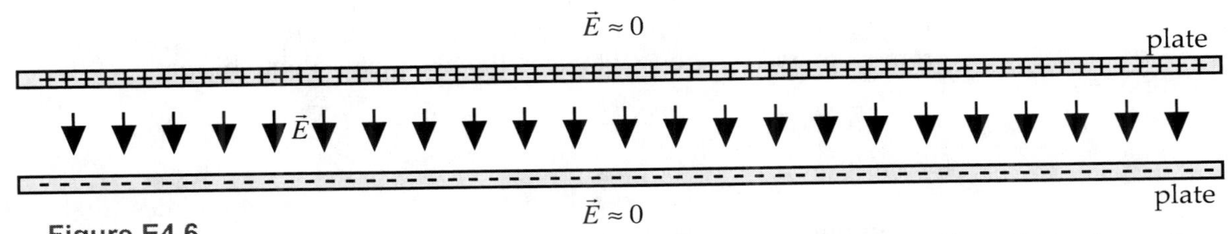

Figure E4.6
On a parallel-plate capacitor, the excess charges on each metal plate form a uniform distribution on the surface closest to the other plate. The electric field will be strictly zero throughout the conducting interior of each plate, but will be only approximately zero in the space beyond. The electric field between the plates is approximately uniform. These approximations become better as the distance between the plates decreases.

E4.6 The Parallel-Plate Capacitor

Description of a parallel-plate capacitor

The most straightforward (and conceptually important) kind of two-conductor capacitor is the **parallel-plate capacitor**, which consists of two parallel flat conducting plates separated by a small distance. This section will discuss this type of capacitor in some detail.

The static equilibrium distribution of excess charge on a isolated conducting plate is *not* uniform

In static equilibrium, excess charge on a single isolated flat metal plate will *not* be uniformly distributed, because as figure E3.10 shows, the electric field of a *uniform* distribution on a plate has an electric-field component parallel to the plate at most locations, so charge on the surface of the plate will be driven outward if the distribution is initially uniform. Therefore a single plate will settle down to a distribution where more charge is located at the plate's periphery compared to its center.

However, it *is* uniform on a pair of parallel, oppositely charged conducting plates

However, two oppositely-charged flat plates placed parallel to each other a small distance apart influence each other in such a way that the excess charge on each *does* distribute itself uniformly in static equilibrium. We can see that such a distribution satisfies our criteria for static equilibrium in this situation as follows. According to section E3.5, the electric field created by two uniformly and oppositely charged planes will be uniform in magnitude and perpendicular to the planes in the region between the planes and essentially zero outside that region. So if the charge on each of our capacitor plates distributes itself uniformly on the surface closest to the other plate (see figure E4.6), the electric field in the conducting interior of each plate will indeed be zero (since it is outside the region between the two planes of surface charge). This satisfies the fundamental criterion for static equilibrium. Note also that the electric field between the plates is perpendicular to the plates, as required by criterion 2, and the charge is on each plate's inner surface, satisfying criterion 3.

The surface charge distribution is actually only approximately uniform

Of course, the electric field created by closely spaced uniformly distributed planes of charge is not *exactly* zero outside the plates (as discussed in section E3.5), but the fundamental criterion for static equilibrium requires it to be *exactly* zero in the conducting interior of each plate. This means that the charge distribution on each plate will not be *exactly* uniform, nor will it be solely on the inner surface, but will tweak itself a bit away from this idealized distribution to make the electric field in the metal *exactly* zero. However, as long as the plates' separation is *very* small compared to their size, a uniform distribution represents an excellent approximation to the actual distribution.

Granting this, we can calculate the potential difference between two such plates of area A carrying charges $\pm Q$ respectively as follows. E3.21 implies that the electric field in the region between the plates has a uniform magnitude of $E = |\sigma| / \varepsilon_0 = |Q| / \varepsilon_0 A$ and points perpendicular to the plates. Imagine now a path going from one plate to the other perpendicular to the plates and parallel to $\vec{E}$, and imagine dividing this path into a sequence of tiny displacements. Let the ith displacement in the sequence be $d\vec{r}_i$. According to equation E4.11, the total potential difference between the two plates along this path will be

The potential difference between the plates of a parallel-plate capacitor

$$\Delta\phi = \sum_{\text{all } i} -\vec{E}\cdot d\vec{r}_i = \sum_{\text{all } i} -E\,dr_i \cos 0° = -E\sum_{\text{all } i} dr_i = -Es \qquad \text{(E4.25)}$$

where s is the total perpendicular distance between the plates (that is, their separation).

Self-Test E4X.7

Can you explain why $\Delta\phi$ is negative in equation E4.25?

If we plug equation E4.25 and $E = |Q|/\varepsilon_0 A$ into equation E4.28, we find that the capacitance of a parallel-plate capacitor is

The capacitance of a parallel-plate capacitor

$$C = \left|\frac{Q}{\Delta\phi}\right| = \left|\frac{Q}{(Q/\varepsilon_0 A)s}\right| = \frac{\varepsilon_0 A}{s} \qquad \text{(E4.26)}$$

We see that the capacitance of a parallel-plate capacitor increases as the plates' area A increases and as their separation s decreases.

Qualitatively, the same general results apply to more general capacitors. A capacitor's capacitance generally increases as the area of each plate increases and/or their separation decreases (though the dependence is generally not as simple as it is in this case). Therefore, the parallel-plate capacitor serves as a good qualitative model for more general capacitors.

E4.7 The Mystery du Jour

In section E4.5, I claimed that excess charge will typically arrange itself in the static equilibrium distribution within a fraction of a microsecond. What determines this characteristic time of arrangement? Is it different for different kinds of objects? Can we set up a situation where this time is very long, so that we can observe the rearrangement in process? During the rearrangement process, electrons will pick up energy from the yet nonzero electric fields. Where does this energy go when the electrons stop moving?

In order to answer questions like these, we need to understand more about how charges move through a conductor. In the next chapter, we will develop a simple model of a conductor that will allow us to answer these questions.

TWO-MINUTE PROBLEMS

E4T.1 The electric field is normally measured in units of newtons per coulomb. It could also be expressed in units of volts per meter, true or false (T or F)?

E4T.2 Consider two charged particles, one with charge q and one with charge $-q$, separated by a distance d. The potential at a point halfway between the two particles is
A. $kq/d \quad (k \equiv 1/4\pi\varepsilon_0)$
B. $2kq/d$
C. $4kq/d$
D. zero
E. $-4kq/d$
F. Other (specify)

E4T.3 The electric potential at a point can have a negative value, T or F?

E4T.4 The equipotential curves in a certain region of an equipotential diagram for the xy plane are parallel to the y axis and are equally spaced, with the potential increasing in the $+x$ direction. An electric field in this region would point in the
A. In the $+x$ direction
B. In the $-x$ direction
C. In the $+x$ direction
D. In the $-y$ direction
E. Other (specify)

E4T.5 Suppose that we drew the electric field vector $\vec{E}$ to be 1 cm long in the situation mentioned in problem E4T.4. If in a different region of the same equipotential diagram, the equipotentials are twice as widely spaced as they were in the first region, we should draw the electric field in this second region with a length of
A. 4 cm
B. 2 cm
C. 1 cm
D. 0.5 cm
E. 0.25 cm
F. Other (specify)
T. A length we can't determine from the information given

E4T.6 If the potential is constant in a region of space, the electric field in that region must be zero, true or false (T or F)?

E4T.7 Due to electrostatic polarization, a sufficiently charged rubber balloon will attract a neutral horizontal insulating plate strongly enough so that it sticks firmly to the plate's bottom. If this neutral horizontal plate is a conductor instead of an insulator, the charged balloon will
A. Still stick
B. Stick only if the plate is connected to the earth
C. Stick only if the plate is insulated from the earth
D. Not stick at all
E. not one little bit.

E4T.8 Imagine that you have two oppositely charged metal spheres on insulating supports. If you slowly bring the spheres closer and closer together, the surface charge density σ on each sphere will
A. Remain uniform over the sphere's surface
B. Be largest at the point nearest the other sphere
C. Be smallest at the point nearest the other sphere
D. Eventually no longer shield the sphere's interior from the other sphere's electric field
E. not one little bit.

E4T.9 Imagine that we suspend a negatively charged balloon from the upper inside surface of a closed metal box. The balloon is entirely enclosed by the box. Assume that the balloon hangs a few inches from one of the box's vertical faces. Imagine that we now bring a very strongly charged object a few inches away from the balloon but on the opposite side of the face (that is, outside the box). The balloon in this case will be deflected
A. strongly toward the external charge
B. strongly away from the external charge
C. weakly toward the external charge.
D. weakly away from the external charge
E. not one little bit.

HOMEWORK PROBLEMS

Basic Skills

E4B.1 Imagine that a particle with positive charge $+q$ is placed on the x axis at $x = +a$, and a particle with negative charge $-q$ is placed on the x axis at $x = -a$. Find the potential at all points along the y axis.

E4B.2 Imagine that a particle with positive charge $+q$ is placed on the x axis at $x = +a$, and a particle with negative charge $-2q$ is placed on the x axis at $x = -a$. Find the potential at all points along the y axis.

E4B.3 Use equation E4.11 and equation E2.16 for the electric field of a dipole at points along its axis to find the dipole's potential field points along that axis.

E4B.4 Use the *Equipotential* computer program (available from the *Six Ideas* web site) to construct an equipotential diagram for two equally charged particles spaced some distance apart. On a printout of this diagram draw at least 20 electric field vectors at various positions.

E4B.5 Imagine that in a certain region of an equipotential diagram, the equipotentials are spaced 2 mm apart, and the potential increases by 0.1 V per equipotential curve as one moves toward the left. What is the magnitude and direction of the electric field at that point?

E4B.6 Imagine that you have a ring 10 cm in diameter that has a uniformly distributed charge of 11 nC. What is the potential at the center of the ring (in volts)? What is the potential at a point on the central axis of the ring that is 10 cm from its center?

E4B.7 Imagine that you have a sphere 4 cm in diameter with a uniformly distributed charge of 33 nC. What is the potential (in volts) 5 cm from its center? What is E there?

E4B.8 Assume that the electric potential field in a certain region of space is $\phi(x,y,z) = Axyz + B$, where A and B are constants. Compute the electric field $\vec{E}(x,y,z)$ in this region of space.

E4B.9 Assume that the potential field in a certain region of space is $\phi(x,y,z) = A(x^2+y^2+z^2)$, where A is a constant. Compute the electric field $E(x,y,z)$ in this region of space.

E4B.10 Imagine that two parallel plates having an area of 0.2 m^2 and separated by 0.5 cm are given charges of +2 μC and −2 μC respectively. What is the potential difference between the plates?

E4B.11 A parallel-plate capacitor holds 0.10 μC of charge on its positive plate (and −0.10 μC on its negative plate) when the potential difference between the plates is 10 V. If the plates are separated by 1.0 mm, what is their area?

E4B.12 What is the capacitance of two parallel plates that each have an area of 1 m^2 and that are separated by 1 mm? Would be easy to make a capacitor having a capacitance of 1 F?

Synthetic

E4S.1 Consider a dipole consisting of two charged particles on the x axis, one with positive charge $+q$ located at $x = +\frac{1}{2}d$ and one with negative charge $-q$ located at $x = -\frac{1}{2}d$.

(a) Derive an exact expression for the three-dimensional potential field created by this dipole at a point P whose coordinates are $[x, y, z]$.

(b) Use the binomial approximation to show that for points whose distance r from the origin is very large compared to d, the electric potential is approximately given by

$$\phi(x,y,z) = \frac{kqd}{r^2}\frac{x}{r} = \frac{kqd}{r^2}\cos\theta \qquad \text{(E4.27)}$$

where $k = 1/4\pi\varepsilon_0$ and θ is the angle that point P's position vector makes with the x axis (so $\cos\theta = x/r$. Note that the potential of a dipole falls off as $1/r^2$ compared to $1/r$ for a charged particle. Note also that it is a lot easier to compute the electric field of a dipole using this formula than it is to calculate the field directly! [*Hints:* You should have an expression in the denominator of your answer for (a) that involves $(x \pm \frac{1}{2}d)^2 + y^2 + z^2$. Write out the square involving d and drop the d^2 term because it is very small compared to the other two terms. Then factor out a factor of r^2 to make the expression look like $r^2(1 \pm \text{something small})$. Then apply the binomial approximation.]

E4S.2 Consider the expression for the potential field of a dipole given by equation E4.27.

(a) Use this to find an expression for the electric field $\vec{E}$ of a dipole at a point P along the x axis a distance r from the dipole. (Your result should be consistent with equation E2.16.)

(b) At all points along the y axis, $\theta = 90°$, so the potential is zero. This means that the y axis is an equipotential line. Use this information and equation E4.27 to determine the electric field vector $\vec{E}$ (magnitude and direction!) at a point P along the y axis that is a distance r from the dipole.

E4S.3 Consider a circular disk with radius R that has a uniformly distributed surface charge of Q.

(a) Calculate the electric potential ϕ at various points along the central axis of this disk. (*Hints:* The diagram below shows how you can break the disk up into thin rings of infinitesimal thickness dr. We know from the chapter how to compute the potential of each ring if we can determine the charge of each ring. The ratio of the charge q on the ring with a given radius r to the disk's total charge is the same as ratio of the ring's surface area, which is $2\pi r\,dr$, to the area of the entire disk, which is πR^2. Express q in terms of Q, R, and dr, sum up the potentials contributed by each disk, and convert the sum to an integral. According to my integral table,

$$\int \frac{x\,dx}{\sqrt{x^2 + a^2}} = \sqrt{x^2 + a^2} \qquad \text{(E4.28)}$$

You may find this integral helpful.)

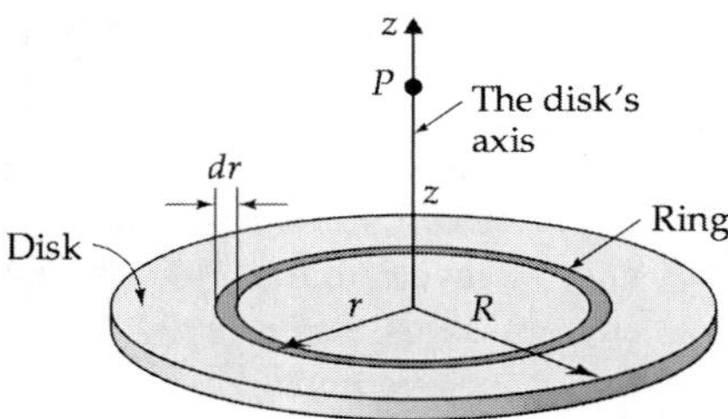

(b) Use the result of part (a) to determine the electric field at points along the axis. (*Hints*: Argue that the field vectors at such points should point along the axis. You should then be able to show that the magnitude of the electric field at such points is

$$E = \frac{\sigma}{2\varepsilon_0}\left[1 - \frac{1}{\sqrt{1 + (R/z)^2}}\right] \qquad \text{(E4.29)}$$

where $\sigma \equiv Q/\pi R^2$ is the charge per unit area on the disk.

E4S.4 Consider a thin wire of length L with a uniformly distributed charge Q. Assume that the wire lies on the x axis with the wire's center at $x = 0$. (See figure E3.2 for a drawing.)

(a) Find the potential as a function of y along the y axis [that is, find $\phi(0, y, 0)$].

(b) Use symmetry and the result you get for part (a) to calculate $\vec{E}(0,y,0)$, the electric field along the y axis. Verify that your result is consistent with equation E3.11.

E4S.5 Imagine that you have two identical neutral metal spheres on insulating stands and a charged rubber rod. Using diagrams, carefully describe a step-by-step process that uses the rod to give the two spheres *exactly* opposite charges (all without touching either sphere with the rod). Take care to construct your procedure so that it ensures that the charges each sphere will be *exactly* equal in magnitude, not just approximately equal.(*Hint:* Start with the spheres touching each other. If you then bring the rod close to one sphere, what happens?)

E4S.6 Consider two initially neutral metal spheres on insulating stands. Imagine that we give one a fairly strong positive charge and then bring it slowly closer and closer to the other sphere. Experimentally, we find that at a certain separation distance, a spark jumps from one sphere to the other, carrying some of the excess charge from the charged sphere to the other. Draw a set of diagrams showing the charge distribution on each sphere as they approach each other and explain why the spark jumps only when they are a certain distance apart. (*Hint*: The electric field just outside a conductor is strongest where the surface charge density is highest.)

E4S.7 Imagine a small, initially neutral metal ball hanging as a pendulum bob between two oppositely charged metal spheres on insulating stands. It happens that if the spheres have enough charges, the ball will begin to swing rapidly back and forth, hitting first one sphere and then the other. After a certain time (typically a few seconds) the ball stops. Carefully explain (with the help of appropriate diagrams) both what drives the ball's swinging initially and why the ball eventually stops.

E4S.8 Calculate the capacitance of a pair of concentric nested spherical metal shells. Assume that the inner shell has an outside radius of R_1 and the outer shell has an inner radius of R_2.

E4S.9 Imagine we want to build a 100 μF parallel-plate capacitor whose metal plates have an area of 1 m^2.

(a) What should the plate separation be? Does this seem practical?

(b) If the potential difference between the two plates is only 1 V, what is the magnitude of the electric field between the plates? Air breaks down and conducts electricity at field strengths above 3 MN/C. Is this a problem?

E4S.11 Show that the total energy U stored in the electric field of a charged parallel-plate capacitor with capacitance C is given by

$$U = \tfrac{1}{2}C(\Delta\phi)^2 \qquad \text{(E4.31)}$$

where $\Delta\phi$ is the potential difference between the plates.

E4S.12 Imagine that we place a slab of polarizable insulating material between the two plates of a parallel plate capacitor. If we charge the plates, the uniform electric field between the plates will polarize the material, turning its atoms into dipoles.

(a) Let us model the positive and negative charges in the slab's atoms as being two rigid blocks of charge. Before the slab is unpolarized, these blocks of charge completely overlap, so the slab is neutral. When the slab's atoms are polarized by an external electric field, it is as if the entire positive block moves a bit in the field direction and the negative block moves a bit opposite the field. In the slab's interior, these blocks still overlap, so the slab's interior remains neutral after polarization. But as the blocks move in opposite directions, the slab faces perpendicular to the field end up with an uncancelled surface charge. This is illustrated in figure E4.7. Use the superposition principle to argue that the net effect of these induced surface charges is to *reduce* the strength of the electric field in the slab by a certain amount.

(b) The strength of this effect depends on the degree to which the insulating material is polarized by the original field between the plates. Let's define the **permittivity** ε of an insulating substance so that

$$\vec{E} = \frac{\varepsilon_0}{\varepsilon}\vec{E}_{\text{vac}} \qquad \text{(E4.32)}$$

where ε_0 is the permittivity of the vacuum, $\vec{E}$ is the electric field inside the insulator and $\vec{E}_{\text{vac}}$ is the electric field that would exist at the same point if the entire insulator were replaced by a vacuum. It turns out that this formula applies very generally, not just when we have an insulating slab between flat plates. The ratio $\varepsilon/\varepsilon_0$ is sometimes called the insulator's **dielectric constant**: note that since $E < E_{\text{vac}}$ this ratio is always greater than 1. Use equation E4.32 to carefully argue that when the plates of a capacitor are separated by an insulating material with permittivity ε instead of a vacuum, the capacitor's capacitance becomes

$$C = \frac{\varepsilon}{\varepsilon_0}C_{\text{vac}} \qquad \text{(E4.33)}$$

Since $\varepsilon/\varepsilon_0$ can be quite a bit greater than 1 for some materials, this presents a way of dramatically increasing the capacitance represented by a given configuration of plates.

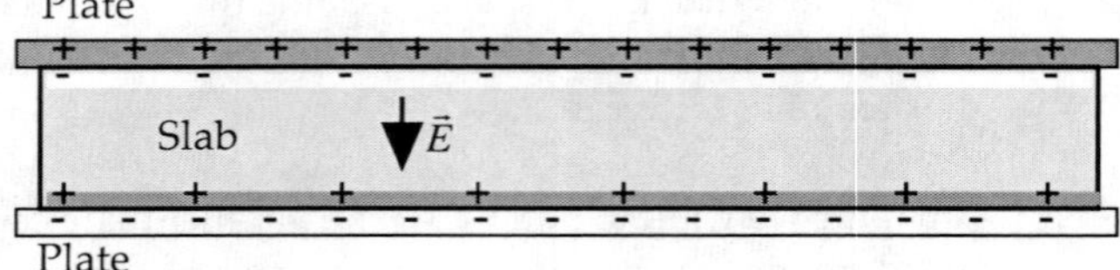

Figure E4.7
Think of the positive charges in the slab's atoms as comprising a rigid, dark gray block and the negative charges as comprising a rigid white block. In response to the field created by the plates, the positive charges move down and the negative charges up, leaving the slab's interior neutral (light gray) but uncancelled surface charges on the slab's top and bottom faces.

Rich-Context

E4R.1 The following problem was adapted from E. F. Purcell, *Electricity and Magnetism*, 2nd ed. McGraw-Hill, New York, 1985.

(a) *Estimate* the capacitance C of a human being relative to infinity. (*Hint:* Section E4.5 taught us how to compute the capacitance of only one kind of isolated object. Use this to set some limits on C.)

(b) When one shuffles one's feet on a rug on a dry day, one can get charged to a potential difference of several thousand volts relative to one's surroundings. *Estimate* the the person's charge under the circumstances.

(c) About how much energy is released when the person touches something and a spark jumps? (*Hint:* See problem E4S.11.)

E4R.2 Imagine two circular flat plates of radius R that are separated by a small distance s. Imagine that we somehow charge the plates until the potential difference $\Delta\phi$ between them reaches a certain value.

(a) Show that the magnitude of the force that each plate exerts on the other is given by

$$F = \frac{\pi\varepsilon_0}{2}\left(\frac{R\Delta\phi}{s}\right)^2 \qquad \text{(E4.34)}$$

(*Hint:* See section E3.6.)

(b) If you have an actual setup of this experiment, calculate the force for measured values of R, $\Delta\phi$, and s, and check your result experimentally. (Otherwise, simply calculate F when $R =$

10 cm, $\Delta\phi = 1000$ V, and $s = 2.0$ mm.

Advanced

E4A.1 (a) Using Coulomb's law and the superposition principle argue that if the total electric field created by any charge distribution is zero at any point P, it will still be zero at P if the distribution's total charge is multiplied by some factor without changing the distribution of charge.

(b) Use this result to argue that if a certain charge distribution on a pair of conductors produces an electric field that is zero inside both conductors, then multiplying all charges in the distribution by some factor without changing the distribution of charge will also produce an electric field that is zero inside both conductors.

(c) There is a mathematical theorem asserting that if we move a given amount of charge Q from one conductor to another, there is a *unique* static charge distribution that will yield zero electric field inside both conductors. Argue, then, that if we pump *more* charge from one conductor to the other, the charge *distribution* on the conductors will *not* change (the charge density at each point on each conductor's surface is simply multiplied by a common factor).

(d) Argue, therefore, that the potential difference $\Delta\phi$ between two conductors in static equilibrium must always be directly proportional to Q.

(e) Finally, argue from this that the capacitance C of any arbitrary pair of conductors must be independent of $\Delta\phi$.

ANSWERS TO SELF-TESTS

E4X.1 Both charges are a distance $r = [a^2 + y^2]^{1/2}$ from a point at coordinate y on the y axis. The total potential at such a point is therefore

$$\phi = \frac{kQ_1}{r_{P1}} + \frac{kQ_2}{r_{P1}} = \frac{2kQ}{r} = \frac{2kQ}{\sqrt{a^2+y^2}} \tag{E4.35}$$

Note that this potential is maximum at the origin.

E4X.2 If the charge is negative, its electric field points toward the charge and opposite to the displacement $d\vec{r}$. Therefore $\vec{E}\cdot d\vec{r} = [\text{mag}(\vec{E})][\text{mag}(d\vec{r})]\cos 180° = -E\,dr$ in this case. We also have $E \equiv \text{mag}(\vec{E}) = k|Q|/r^2 = -kQ/r^2$ when Θ is negative, because the magnitude of $\vec{E}$ must be positive. Therefore,

$$-\vec{E}\cdot d\vec{r} = -(-E\,dr) = +E\,dr = \left(-\frac{kQ}{r}\right)dr \tag{E4.36}$$

This means that

$$\phi(\infty) - \phi(r_P) = \sum_{\text{all steps}} -\vec{E}\cdot d\vec{r} = \sum_{\text{all steps}} -\frac{kQ}{r}dr \tag{E4.37}$$

which is the same as equation E4.13. The rest of the steps follow as before.

E4X.3 The distances to the two charged particles from any point P on this line will have equal values r_P, so the total potential at P will be

$$\phi = \frac{kQ_1}{r_{P1}} + \frac{kQ_2}{r_{P2}} = \frac{k(Q_1+Q_2)}{r_P} = 0 \tag{E4.38}$$

E4X.4 In this case, we have

$$\frac{\partial\phi}{\partial z} = \frac{\partial}{\partial z}\left[ax^2\sin(yz)\right] = ax^2\frac{\partial}{\partial z}[\sin(yz)]$$
$$= ax^2 y\cos(yz) \tag{E4.39}$$

E4X.5 The arrows you draw *should* look qualitatively like the arrows shown in figure E2.4.

E4X.6 We can convert to basic units as follows:

$$1\text{ F} = 1\,\frac{\text{C}}{\cancel{\text{V}}}\left(\frac{1\,\cancel{\text{V}}}{1\,\cancel{\text{J}}/\text{C}}\right)\left(\frac{1\,\cancel{\text{J}}}{1\text{ kg}\cdot\text{m}^2/\text{s}^2}\right) = \frac{1}{\text{kg}}\left(\frac{\text{C}\cdot\text{s}}{\text{m}}\right)^2 \tag{E4.35}$$

E4X.7 According to section E4.3, the electric field $\vec{E}$ points in the direction of *decreasing* ϕ. If we choose our displacements $d\vec{r}_i$ to be parallel to $\vec{E}$, then our path will take us from the plate that was at the highest potential to the plate at the lowest potential. Therefore, the change in potential should be negative for the path we have chosen.

E5 Currents

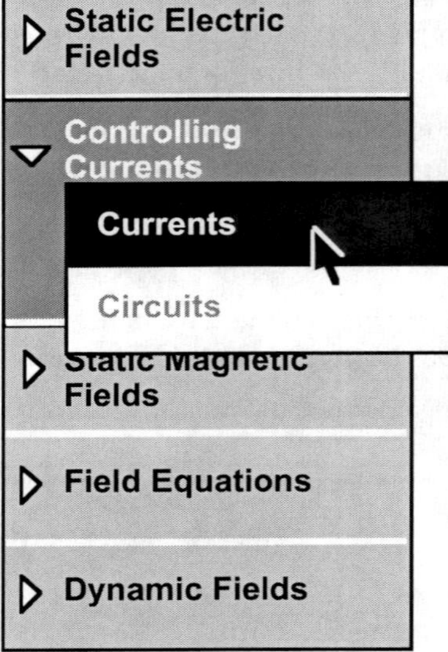

Chapter Overview

Introduction

This chapter is the first of a two-chapter subdivision that explores how we can create and control electric currents. This subdivision is essential background for the subdivisions on magnetic fields and Maxwell's equations. This chapter provides an introduction to the qualitative and quantitative description of current.

Section E5.1: A Model of Current Flow

In many metals, at least one electron per atom is free to roam through the conductor. According to the **Drude model**, these electrons move with large, random thermal velocities between collisions with atoms, but an applied electric field $\vec{E}$ gives an electron a average **drift velocity** $\vec{v}_d$ opposite to $\vec{E}$ before the next collision re-randomizes its velocity. Collisions between electrons and atoms transfer energy that electrons gain from the field to thermal energy in the wire. In some conductors, the mobile charged particles are not electrons: we call the mobile charged particles in a conductor its **charge carriers**.

Section E5.2: Quantifying Current Flow

The **current density** $\vec{J}$ describes how rapidly charge is moving past a given point:

$$\vec{J} \equiv \rho\vec{v}_d \equiv nq\vec{v}_d \tag{E5.4}$$

Purpose: This equation defines the current density $\vec{J}$ in the neighborhood of a given point in a conductor.

Symbols: $\vec{v}_d$ is the charge carriers' drift velocity in that neighborhood, $\rho = nq$ is the charge density (in C/m^3) and n is the **number density** (in particles /m^3) of carriers in that neighborhood, and q is the charge of a single carrier.

Limitations: This expression assumes the conductor has only one type of charge carrier: otherwise, $\vec{J} = \rho_1\vec{v}_{d1} + \rho_2\vec{v}_{d2} + \ldots$, with a term for each carrier type.

Note: The units of current density are C·m^{-2}s^{-1} = A/m^2.

We define a conductor's *conductivity* as follows

$$\vec{J} = \sigma_c\vec{E} \tag{E5.6}$$

Purpose: This equation defines a conductor's **conductivity** σ_c. This equation also expresses the idea that the current density $\vec{J}$ at a given point in a conductor is proportional to the electric field $\vec{E}$ at that point.

Limitations: This expression assumes that charge carriers drift either along or opposite to $\vec{E}$ (which is only rarely untrue). The conductivity may not be independent of $\vec{E}$ if mag($\vec{E}$) is very large.

Notes: In this text, σ_c is the symbol for *conductivity*, but σ is the symbol for *charge per unit area*. The units of σ_c are C^{2}s·m^{-3}kg^{-1} = (Ω·m)$^{-1}$.

The magnitude of the total **electric current** flowing across a boundary is defined to be

$$I \equiv \left|\frac{dQ}{dt}\right| \tag{E5.7}$$

Purpose: This equation defines the magnitude of the *electric current* I flowing through a specified boundary surface in a conductor.

Symbols: dQ is the net amount of charge that crosses the specified boundary during the infinitesimal time interval dt.

Limitations: The interval dt must be short enough so that the current I is approximately constant during the interval.

Note: The SI unit of current is the **ampere**, where $1\text{ A} \equiv 1\text{ C/s}$.

In the fairly common case where the flow of current density is uniform across the cross-section of a thin wire, we can define a total current vector such that

$$\vec{I} = \vec{J}A = \rho\vec{v}_d A = nqA\vec{v}_d \tag{E5.9}$$

where A is the wire's cross-sectional area and the other symbols are defined as in equation E5.4. We will find this equation very useful in chapter E9.

Section E5.3: Surface Charges Direct the Flow

This section discusses how an initially nonuniform current flowing in a wire rapidly sets up surface charges that ensure that the electric field inside the wire has the same strength at all points and points directly along the wire.

Section E5.4: Resistance

This result implies that for a uniform, thin wire of length L, the potential difference $|\Delta\phi_{\text{wire}}|$ between the wire's ends is related to the field strength E in the wire by

$$|\Delta\phi_{\text{wire}}| = EL \tag{E5.15}$$

We define a conductor's resistance to be

$$R \equiv \frac{|\Delta\phi|}{I} \tag{E5.17}$$

Purpose: This equation defines a conducting object's resistance R.

Symbols: I is the magnitude of the current the object conducts when the potential difference between its ends is $|\Delta\phi|$.

Limitations: The object must have well-defined "ends"!

Note: The SI unit of resistance is the **ohm**, where $1\ \Omega \equiv 1\text{ V/A}$.

Ohm's Law asserts that R is independent of V and I for many conductors. We say that conductors obeying Ohm's law are **ohmic**.

Section E5.5: The Power Dissipated in a Conductor

In an ohmic conductor whose resistance is R, which carries current I, and which has a potential difference $|\Delta\phi|$ between its ends, electrostatic potential energy is converted to thermal energy at a rate of

$$P = I|\Delta\phi| = I^2R = |\Delta\phi|^2/R \tag{E5.20}$$

Section E5.6: Discharging a Capacitor

If we connect the plates of a capacitor of capacitance C with a thin wire of resistance R, the potential difference V_C across the plates decreases exponentially with time:

$$V_C(t) = V_0 e^{-t/RC} \quad (\text{where } V_0 \equiv V_C \text{ at } t = 0) \tag{E5.28}$$

Section E5.7: The Mystery du Jour

How can we create and control currents that last for more than a few seconds?

E5.1 A Model of Current Flow

As we have discussed in previous chapters, charge can move through a conductor if driven by an electric field. In the last chapter, we explored the distribution of charges *after* charges had moved into static equilibrium. The purpose of this chapter is to explore in more depth the physics of the movement of charge itself. This will help us understand the *dynamic* equilibrium that characterizes working electric circuits.

The Drude model is a simple microscopic model of current flow in metals

The kind of charge flow that we will most commonly encounter in the daily life (and in this course) is the flow of electrons through metals. In this section, we will explore the **Drude model** for this kind of charge flow, first proposed by P. K. Drude in 1900 shortly after the electron was discovered.

In a typical metal, at least one electron per atom becomes detached from its parent atom and is free to roam around the metal. The Drude model imagines a metal to consist of a lattice of positively charged atoms surrounded by a "gas" of mobile electrons. As we saw in unit C, the particles of any substance with a nonzero absolute temperature T move randomly with an average kinetic energy proportional to T. The atoms the lattice are thus constantly vibrating, while the (very light) free electrons bounce around the lattice at very high speeds (roughly 10^6 m/s!) like balls in a pinball game. The Drude model assumes that electrons only interact with the lattice during short-duration collisions with individual atoms, and otherwise move as free particles.

An electric field causes the bouncing electrons to drift slowly opposite to the field

If there is no electric field, the bouncing electrons bounce around randomly as shown in figure E5.1a, so (on the average) there is no net movement of charge. However, any electric field $\vec{E}$ in the metal causes an electron (which has charge $-e$ and mass m_e) to accelerate at the rate $\vec{a} = \vec{F}_e/m_e = -e\vec{E}/m_e$ during the interval between collisions. This acceleration allows it to accumulate a tiny velocity component opposite to $\vec{E}$ before the next collision randomizes its velocity, causing it to "forget" its direction of motion and starting the process over. This small extra velocity component causes the electrons to slowly drift in the direction opposite to $\vec{E}$ (see figure E5.1b) like balls in a tilted pinball game.

How is the magnitude of this drift velocity related to $\vec{E}$? Consider an electron that at time $t = 0$ collides with a lattice atom and acquires an initial velocity $\vec{v}_0$. Assuming that the electric field $\vec{E}$ the electron experiences is constant during that (very short) time interval, the electron's velocity after time t will be

$$\vec{v}(t) = \vec{v}_0 + \vec{a}t = \vec{v}_0 - \frac{e\vec{E}}{m_e}t \tag{E5.1}$$

Now let's average this expression at a given instant over the huge number of electrons in even a tiny volume of the metal. Since the electrons' initial velocities $\vec{v}_0$ are completely random, all directions for $\vec{v}_0$ are equally probable, so the average value of $\vec{v}_0$ will be zero. Assuming that the electric field is uniform over the tiny volume, the electrons' average velocity at that instant will be

$$\vec{v}_{avg} = 0 - \left(\frac{e}{m_e}\right)\vec{E}[t_{last}]_{avg} \tag{E5.2}$$

where $[t_{last}]_{avg}$ is the average time that has elapsed since the last collision. Now in this case, the average time that has elapsed since the last collision is actually the same as the average time τ *between* collisions. This is because in a strictly random sequence of collisions, the past looks statistically just like the future, so at any particular instant in the sequence, the time since the last collision must (on the average) be the same that to the *next* collision $[t_{next}]_{avg}$. But in a strictly random sequence, it is also true that no instant in the sequence is statistically different than any other, so $[t_{next}]_{avg}$ must be the same even if I choose my instant to be the instant of a collision. Therefore $[t_{last}]_{avg} = [t_{next}]_{avg}$

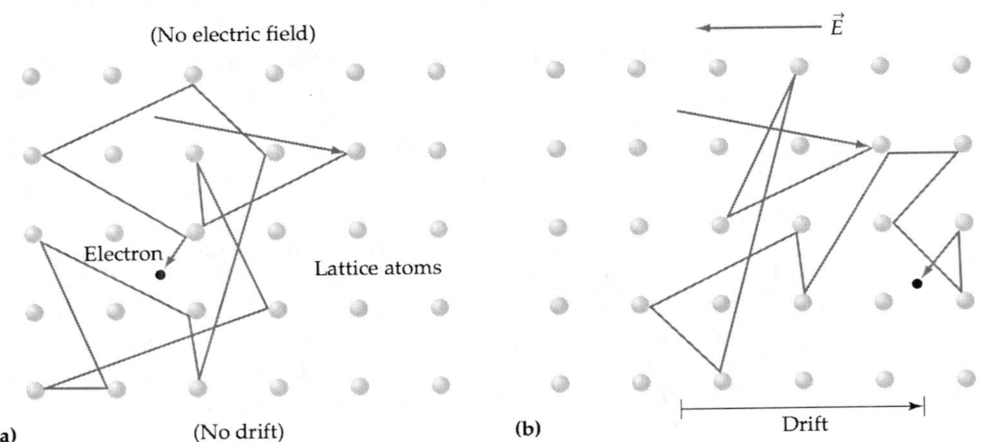

Figure E5.1
(a) When there is no applied external electric field, an electron in a metal bounces randomly from atom to atom in the lattice, getting nowhere on the average. **(b)** When an external electric field is applied to the metal, an electron will accelerate between collisions in the direction of the electric force on the electron. This causes the electron's average position to drift in that direction as time passes.

$= \tau$. (If you still need more convincing, see problem E5S.1). The average electron **drift velocity** in any reasonably small volume of the metal is therefore

The electron drift speed in a microscopic volume of metal

$$\vec{v}_d = -\frac{e}{m_e}\vec{E}\tau \qquad \text{(E5.3)}$$

This result is very interesting. We see that the electron's drift speed depends on properties of the electron (e/m_e), the applied field strength, and the average time between collisions τ, which in turn depends on characteristics of the metal (the electrons' random thermal speed, the average distance between lattice atoms, and how large a target an atom represents to a passing electron). Copper is an excellent conductor partly because its atoms represent smaller effective targets than those in poorer conductors.

The drift speed is constant and proportional to mag($\vec{E}$)

Notice that this model predicts that the electrons' average drift *speed* (not their acceleration) is proportional to the magnitude E of the applied electric field. If the electrons in a metal were genuinely free, they would experience a constant *acceleration* due to the electric field, and their average velocity would increase with time, like objects freely falling in a gravitational field. The fact that the electrons move at a *constant* average drift velocity in the presence of a constant electric field means that they behave more like particles falling at their terminal speeds through a viscous fluid.

Collisions transfer energy to thermal energy in the conductor, making it hot

Electrons do accelerate in response to the applied field *between* collisions, and as they do so, they gain kinetic energy at the expense of electrostatic potential energy. However, subsequent collisions with lattice atoms convert this energy to the kinetic energy of random electron motion and random atomic vibrations, the kind of energy that at the macroscopic level we call thermal energy. The Drude model therefore predicts that *a conductor carrying an electric current will become warmer*. This is again analogous to the physics of particles falling in a viscous fluid: the drag interactions between the falling particles and the fluid converts the gravitational potential energy released as the particles descend to thermal energy in both the particles and the fluid.

The validity of the Drude model

Both of these crucial predictions are consistent with experimental results. Charge does indeed flow through a metal object placed in a fixed electric field at a constant rate proportional to $\text{mag}(\vec{E})$, and metals conducting significant currents do indeed get warmer. The Drude model has its limitations. Because it does not take quantum effects into account, it incorrectly predicts how the drift velocity depends on temperature unless the metal is quite hot (see problem E5R.2). The assumption that the average time between collisions τ is independent of $\text{mag}(\vec{E})$ can be violated when $\text{mag}(\vec{E})$ is very large. Even so, for our purposes, this model provides a reasonably useful model for visualizing electron transport in metals under typical conditions.

The Drude model was designed to explain electron flow in metals, but the same principles apply to current flow through other kinds of conductors. A conducting fluid, for example, contains ions that randomly collide with neutral fluid molecules, so they drift in response to an applied electric field in much the same way that electrons colliding with metal atoms drift through the lattice. Charged particles in an ionized gas behave in a qualitatively similar way.

The definition of a *charge carrier*

Note in this context that while electrons transport charge from place to place in a metal, other kinds of charged particles may transport charge in other conductors. We call the moveable charged particles in a specific conductor (whether they are positive or negative) the **charge carriers** for that conductor.

E5.2 Quantifying Current Flow

Just as water can flow at different rates at different points across or along a river, so charge can flow at different rates at different points in a conductor. The **current density** $\vec{J}$ provides a natural way to quantify how rapidly charge is flowing in the neighborhood of a certain point in a conductor:

The definition of *current density*

$$\vec{J} \equiv \rho \vec{v}_d \equiv nq\vec{v}_d \tag{E5.4}$$

Purpose: This equation defines the current density $\vec{J}$ in the neighborhood of a given point in a conductor.

Symbols: $\vec{v}_d$ is the drift velocity of charge carriers in the neighborhood of the point in question, $\rho = nq$ is the density of the charge (in C/m^3) transported by charge carriers in that neighborhood, n is the **number density** (in particles/m^3) of charge carriers in that neighborhood, and q is the charge of a single carrier.

Limitations: This expression assumes that the conductor has only one type of charge carrier. If the conductor has more than one type of carrier, then $\vec{J} = \rho_1\vec{v}_{d1} + \rho_2\vec{v}_{d2} + \ldots$, with a term for each carrier type.

Note: The units of current density are C·m^{-2}s^{-1}.

Note that the direction of $\vec{J}$ is the same as the charge carriers' drift velocity $\vec{v}_d$ if those carriers are positively charged but opposite to $\vec{v}_d$ if the carriers are negatively charged (as in the case of metals). Since charge carriers will drift in the direction of $\vec{E}$ if they are positive and opposite to $\vec{E}$ if negative, $q\vec{v}_d$ and thus $\vec{J}$ will have the same direction as $\vec{E}$ in all but the most unusual cases.

Indeed, for any conductor accurately described by the Drude model, equations E5.4 and E5.3 imply that

$$\vec{J} = nq\left(\frac{q\vec{E}}{m_e}\right)\tau = \left(\frac{nq^2\tau}{m_e}\right)\vec{E} \tag{E5.5}$$

This means that $\vec{J}$ has the same direction as $\vec{E}$ in such a conductor, independent of the sign of the charge carriers, and that the constant of proportionality depends only on characteristics of the conducting material and its carriers. These ideas are compactly expressed by the following equation

$$\vec{J} = \sigma_c \vec{E} \qquad \text{(E5.6)}$$

The definition of *conductivity*

Purpose: This equation defines a conductor's **conductivity** σ_c. This equation also expresses the idea that the current density $\vec{J}$ at a given point in a conductor is proportional to the electric field $\vec{E}$ at that point.

Limitations: This expression assumes that charge carriers drift either in the direction of or opposite to $\vec{E}$ (which is only rarely untrue). The conductivity may not be independent of $\vec{E}$ if mag($\vec{E}$) is very large.

Notes: In this text, σ_c is the symbol for *conductivity*, but σ is the symbol for *charge per unit area*. The SI units of σ_c are $C^2 \cdot s \cdot m^{-3} kg^{-1}$ (see equation E5.5) or $(\Omega \cdot m)^{-1}$, where 1 **ohm** $\equiv 1\ \Omega \equiv 1\ kg \cdot m^2 C^{-2} s^{-1}$.

A material's conductivity is *typically* a constant independent of the field strength

For conductors accurately described by the Drude model, the conductivity σ_c depends on properties of the conductor but not on $\vec{E}$. *Sometimes* this is not true. For example, σ_c increases sharply when $E = \text{mag}(\vec{E})$ exceeds roughly 3.0×10^6 N/C, because processes that ionize air molecules then become possible. Many other insulators similarly "break down" when E becomes sufficiently large. Semiconductors have conductivities that typically vary smoothly with E. Even so, we can *usually* treat σ_c as being independent of E. Table E5.1 lists the conductivities of various substances at room temperature.

The current density $\vec{J}$ provides the most powerful method of quantifying the motion of charge, and is crucial in any situation where $\vec{E}$ varies from point to point in a conductor. However, we are often only interested in the total rate at which charge moves across a specified boundary surface in a conductor. We define the magnitude I of the **electric current** crossing a boundary surface to be

$$I \equiv \left| \frac{dQ}{dt} \right| \qquad \text{(E5.7)}$$

The quantitative definition of *electric current*

Purpose: This equation defines the magnitude of the *electric current* I flowing through a specified boundary surface in a conductor.

Symbols: dQ is the net amount of charge that crosses the specified boundary during the infinitesimal time interval dt.

Limitations: The interval dt must be short enough so that the current I is approximately constant during the interval.

Note: The SI unit of current is the **ampere**, where $1\ A \equiv 1\ C/s$.

Table E5.1 Conductivities of various substance at room temperature [in $(\Omega \cdot m)^{-1}$]

Substance	Conductivity	Note
Silver	6.3×10^7	Note that metals have conductivities on the order of magnitude of $10^7\ (\Omega \cdot m)^{-1}$.
Copper	5.7×10^7	
Gold	4.1×10^7	
Aluminum	3.6×10^7	
Iron	1.0×10^7	
Lead	4.6×10^6	
Nichrome	6.7×10^5	"Nichrome" is a nickle-chromium alloy used in electric heating elements because of its low conductivity.
Carbon	4.9×10^4	
Sea water	4	The conductivity of water depends significantly on the number and types of ions dissolved in it.
Pure water	4.0×10^{-8}	
Glass	$\approx 10^{-12}$	Note the stark difference between the conductivity of metals and these typical insulators. This is mostly so because there are very few free charge carriers in insulators.
Rubber	$\approx 10^{-13}$	

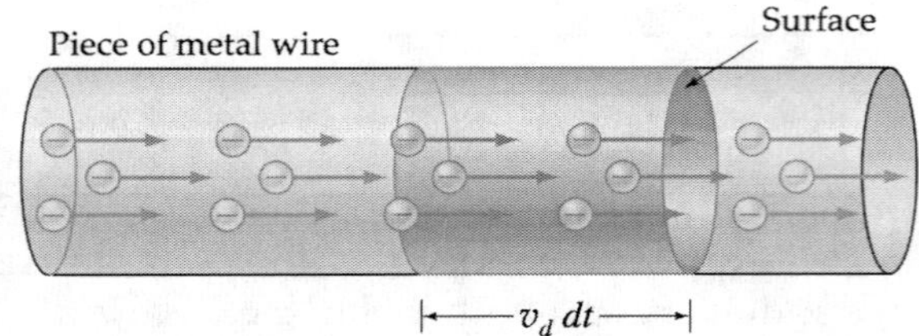

Figure E5.2
If we assume that all electrons in a certain region of a conducting wire have the same drift velocity $\vec{v}_d$ along the wire, then every electron in the shaded volume will pass through the surface in a time Δt.

How is the total current I linked to the current density $\vec{J}$? As a simple example consider the (very common) case of current flowing through a thin cylindrical wire. Assume for simplicity's sake that the wire's composition is uniform and the applied electric field within a certain region is uniform and directed along the wire. This implies that all electrons in this region will move with the same drift velocity $\vec{v}_d$ parallel to the wire (see figure E5.2). Consider an imaginary surface spanning the wire's cross section perpendicular to the wire's axis: this will serve as our boundary for calculating the current flowing in the wire. During an infinitesimal time interval dt, all charge carriers within a distance $v_d\,dt$ upstream of the surface will pass through that surface. If the wire's cross-sectional area is A, the volume occupied by these carriers is $Av_d\,dt$, and the total charge of carriers in that region is $dQ = \rho A v_d dt$, where ρ is the charge density of carriers in the region. Therefore the current flowing in the wire is

$$I = \left|\frac{\rho A v_d dt}{dt}\right| = |\rho v_d|A = \text{mag}(\vec{J})A \qquad \text{(E5.8)}$$

In this simple case, where the current density $\vec{J}$ is uniform throughout the cylindrical volume of interest, we can define a **current vector** $\vec{I}$ as follows:

The definition of the *current vector* in a wire segment

$$\vec{I} = \vec{J}A = \rho\vec{v}_d A = nqA\vec{v}_d \qquad \text{(E5.9)}$$

Purpose: This defines the current vector $\vec{I}$ for a segment of wire in which the current density $\vec{J}$ is uniform in magnitude and direction.

Symbols: A is the wire's cross-sectional area, ρ is the charge density (in C/m^3) and n the number density (in particles $/\text{m}^3$) of carriers in the segment, respectively, $\vec{v}_d$ is the carriers' common drift velocity, and q is the charge of a single carrier.

Limitations: This equation *only* applies to conductors having a uniform composition and constant $\vec{J}$ within the region of interest.

Notes: This equation makes it clear that we can express the units of $\vec{J}$ as being A/m^2 as well as being $\text{C}\cdot\text{m}^{-2}\text{s}^{-1}$.

As we will see in the next section, this expression is more useful than the stringent limitations might suggest.

The *conventional current* direction is the direction that positive carriers would move

Now, $\vec{I}$ and $\vec{J}$ as defined by equations E5.4 and E5.9 point in the direction of the drift velocity $\vec{v}_d$ if the charge carriers are positive and are opposite to $\vec{v}_d$ if the carriers are negative, but in either case, $\vec{I}$ and $\vec{J}$ have the same direction as the driving electric field $\vec{E}$. Now in virtually all macroscopic circumstances, the sign of the charge carriers is physically irrelevant: whether positive charges move from point A to point B or negative particles move from point B to point A, the only macroscopically observable result is that point A becomes more negatively charged and point B becomes more positively charged. It turns out to be more convenient to define the directions of the current vectors $\vec{I}$ and $\vec{J}$ to be the same as that of $\vec{E}$ (which is the direction that positive charge carriers would move in response to the field) than it is to have these vectors correspond to the actual direction of the motion of charges. We call the direction of $\vec{I}$ and $\vec{J}$ the direction of the **conventional current**.

How to calculate the number density of charge carriers

Actually using equations E5.4 or E5.9 requires knowing the density of charge carriers in a conductor. In many metals, including copper, silver, and gold, roughly one electron per atom is free to serve as a charge carrier. On the other hand, each aluminum atom contributes 3. Let's call this number j. This means that the number density n of carriers in a metal is j times the number of *atoms* per cubic meter. Say that we know the metal's mass density ρ_m (in kilograms per cubic meter). Since the atomic weight M_A of a metal is defined to be the mass of Avogadro's number N_A of its atoms, the value of n is

$$n = \frac{\text{carriers}}{\text{volume}} = j\left(\frac{\text{atoms}}{\text{volume}}\right) = j\left(\frac{\text{mass}}{\text{volume}}\right)\Big/\left(\frac{\text{mass}}{\text{atom}}\right) = \rho_m \frac{N_A}{M_A} j \qquad \text{(E5.10)}$$

Example E5.1 A Typical Drift Speed

Problem Consider a household copper wire (see figure E5.3) with a diameter of 1.0 mm carrying a current of 1.0 A (typical values in such a case). What is the electron drift speed in this wire? (The mass density of copper is 8900 kg/m^3.)

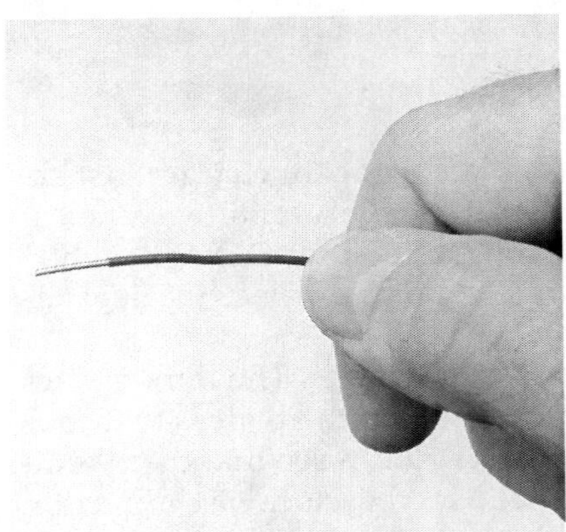

Figure E5.3
How fast do electrons typically move through a wire like this?

Translation Let $r = 0.0005$ m be the wire's radius.

Model We know from the previous paragraph that that there is roughly one mobile electron per copper atom, and we can look up copper's atomic weight on the periodic table on the inside back cover, so we can use equation E5.10 to calculate the number density of electrons in the wire. The wire's cross-sectional area A is $\pi r^2 = \pi(0.0005\ \text{m})^2 = 7.9 \times 10^{-7}\ \text{m}^2$. We also know $\text{mag}(\vec{I})$ and the electron's charge, so we can solve equation E5.9 for $\text{mag}(\vec{v}_d)$.

Solution: The periodic table tells us that copper's atomic weight is 63.5 g per Avogadro's number of atoms, so equation E5.10 tells us that:

$$n = \left(\frac{1\ \text{electron}}{\cancel{\text{atom}}}\right)\left(\frac{8900\ \cancel{\text{kg}}}{\text{m}^3}\right)\left(\frac{6.02 \times 10^{23}\ \cancel{\text{atoms}}}{0.0635\ \cancel{\text{kg}}}\right) = \frac{8.4 \times 10^{28}}{\text{m}^3} \qquad \text{(E5.11)}$$

If we take the magnitude of both sides of equation E5.9 and solve for $\text{mag}(\vec{v}_d)$, we get

$$v_d = \text{mag}(\vec{v}_d) = \frac{\text{mag}(\vec{I})}{n|-e|A} = \frac{1.0\ \cancel{\text{C}}/\text{s}}{(8.4 \times 10^{28}\ \text{m}^{-\cancel{3}1})(1.6 \times 10^{-19}\ \cancel{\text{C}})(7.9 \times 10^{-7}\ \cancel{\text{m}^2})}$$

$$= 9.4 \times 10^{-5}\ \text{m/s} \approx 8.2\ \text{m/day (!)} \qquad \text{(E5.12)}$$

Evaluation The units are right, but the drift speed is astonishingly slow!

Why the average time between collisions does not depend on the electric field

The average thermal speed of electrons in a metal is very roughly 10^6 m/s. We see that the drift speed of the electrons in the wire is about a factor of 10^{10} smaller than the typical speed of the electrons due to their thermal motion! This is why we can get away with assuming that the electric field in the wire has no significant effect on the average time between an electron's collisions with the lattice: the field's effect on the electron's motion is just too small!

The fundamental reason that the wire conducts a significant current even when the drift speed is so small is that a wire contains a *huge* number of electrons: they don't have to move very fast to transport a substantial amount of charge past any given boundary in the wire.

Self-Test E5X.1

An aluminum wire 1.5 mm in diameter carries a current of 5.2 A = 5.2 C/s. The density of aluminum is 2700 kg/m^3 and its atomic mass is 26.98 g per Avogadro's number of atoms. What is the drift speed of the electrons in this wire?

E5.3 Surface Charges Direct the Flow

Imagine that we give the plates of a parallel-plate capacitor charges that are equal in magnitude but opposite in sign. If the plates have a finite size, then at a point outside the plates, the nearest plate's contribution to the field slightly dominates that of the farther plate, so the plates will create a very weak external electric field, as illustrated in figure E5.4.

A technique for computing the field of macroscopic charge distributions

Now imagine that we connect the two plates with a wire. The dark arrows in figure E5.4 show the electric field vectors produced by the plates at various points along the wire at the instant of connection. You can see that there is always a nonzero component of the electric field in the clockwise direction around the wire, so current will begin to flow in that direction. (Note that I am talking about *conventional current* here: the electrons actually flow counterclockwise along the wire. In what follows, I will pretend that the charge carriers in the wire are positive: it makes it clearer to describe what is going on and the fact that the carriers are actually negative is physically irrelevant.)

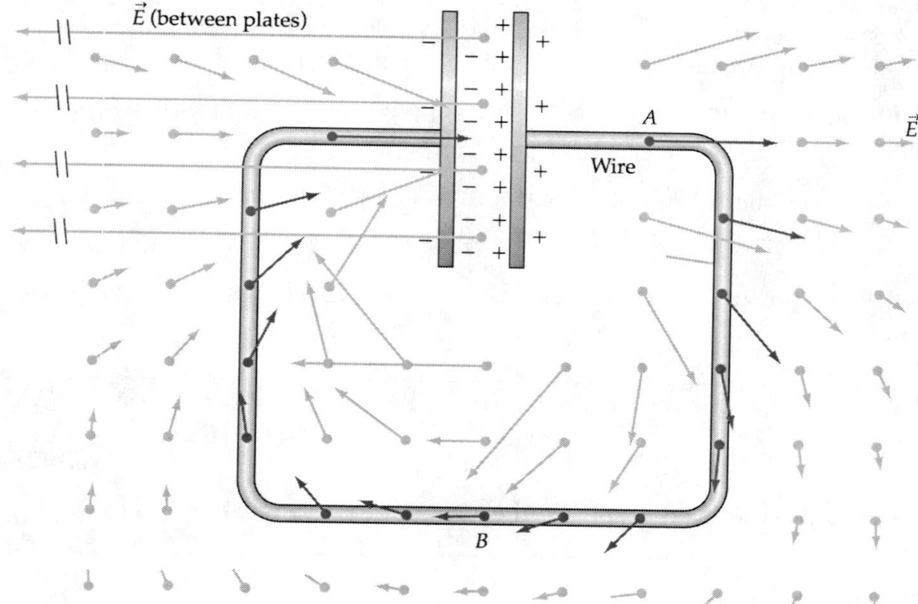

Figure E5.4
The electric field of a parallel-plate capacitor at the instant its plates are connected by the wire shown (before any significant amount of current flows). The darker arrows indicate the electric field at selected points inside the wire at that instant.

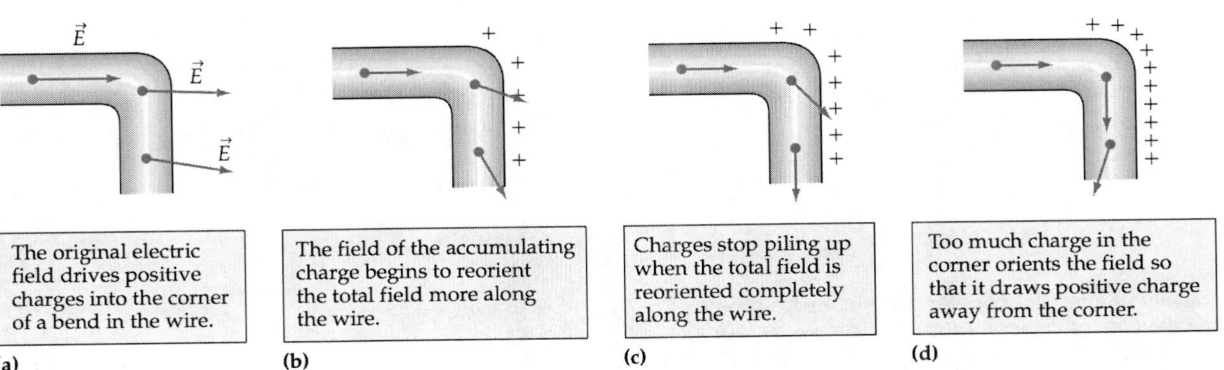

Figure E5.5
How accumulating surface charge reorients the electric field on a wire to point directly along the wire.

How surface charges reorient the electric field so that it points directly along the wire

Let's think in some detail about what happens as the current begins to flow. In particular, let's focus on what happens at upper right hand bend of the wire shown in figure E5.4. At the instant the wire is connected, conventional current starts to flow in the direction of $\vec{E}$. But near the corner, this field drives positive charges toward the wire's outer right edge. But charges cannot move beyond the wire's surface, so they begin to pile up there, as shown in figure E5.5. The accumulation of positive charge on the wire's outer edge ceases only when the electric field at all points inside the wire is directed *parallel* to the wire's surface, that is, directly along the wire's axis. As illustrated in figure E5.5d, feedback effects keep the electric field pointing along the wire's axis even if the system is perturbed or the external field changes.

How surface charges also ensure that the field has a uniform magnitude in the wire

Similar feedback effects quickly ensure that the electric field also has the same *magnitude* at all points in the wire. If it does *not* have the same magnitude everywhere, then charge carriers will move faster where the electric field is stronger and slower where it is weaker. This causes charge carriers to be depleted in any region where they move out faster than they come in and accumulate in any region where the opposite is true. Do self-test E5X.2 to see if *you* can figure out how the accumulation of excess charge (which will end up on the wire's surface) works to even out the electric field (and thus the current flow) in the wire.

Self-Test E5X.2

Imagine that an external electric field causes (conventional) current to flow faster in the left part of a wire segment than in the right, as shown below. What happens to the surface charge on the wire as a result? How does this help even out the current flow?

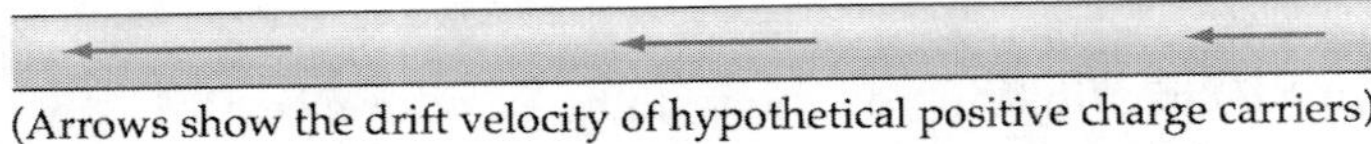

(Arrows show the drift velocity of hypothetical positive charge carriers)

The bottom line: $\vec{E}$ everywhere inside a uniform wire has the same magnitude and points directly along the wire

The point is that when current flows in a wire, charges will rapidly distribute themselves on the wire's surface in such a way as to ensure that *the electric field in a uniform wire's interior has the same magnitude everywhere and always points parallel to the wire.* We will use this idea extensively in what follows.

This rearrangement of surface charge occurs very rapidly (typically within a few tens of nanoseconds). Even though the drift velocity of charge carriers is very small, the density of charge carriers in even a microscopic volume of wire is so large that the carriers need only move a tiny bit to establish the required surface charges. If the capacitor plates have a significant charge, it will take

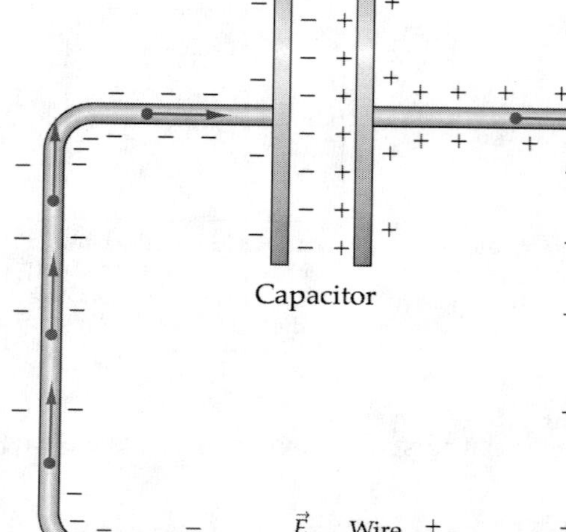

Figure E5.6
The initially uneven flow of electrons in a wire creates quasistatic charge concentrations on the wire's surface that redirect the current until it flows uniformly along the wire. The arrows show the direction of the electric field and thus the direction of conventional current flow. Note that hypothetical positive carriers will be drawn forward in all parts of the wire because they see less positive charge ahead than behind. Note also that excess charge at the corners help the current change direction.

much longer (up to a billion times longer) for enough positive charge to move out of the positive plate and into the negative plate to significantly discharge the capacitor. Therefore connecting the plates with a wire will almost instantly create a quasistatic surface charge distribution which establishes an electric field in the wire that is uniform in magnitude and directed along the wire, an electric field that weakens only very slowly as the capacitor discharges.

Figure E5.6 schematically illustrates the surface charge distribution on a wire connecting two capacitor plates and the resulting uniform-magnitude electric field established in the wire once the quasistatic distribution has been established. Note that at every point in the wire the surface charge is increasingly positive behind and increasingly negative ahead: this is what creates the forward electric field and what draws (assumedly positive) carriers forward.

Note also that since the surface charge distribution is established within nanoseconds, charge almost *immediately* begins begins draining out of the positive plate into the part of the wire adjacent to that plate and flowing into the negative plate from the part of the wire adjacent to *that* plate at the same rate. It is not necessary for charge carriers to move all the way from one plate to the other to discharge the capacitor. Indeed, there is so much movable charge in the wire that charge carriers may only have to move a tiny fraction of a millimeter into or out of each plate to make both plates electrically neutral.

E5.4 Resistance

The fact that the surface charge distribution on the wire almost instantly ensures that the electric field inside the wire points directly along the wire and has the same magnitude everywhere means that we can easily link the electric field's magnitude inside the wire to the potential difference between the wire's ends. According to equation E4.11, the potential difference $d\phi$ between two points in the wire separated by a small displacement $d\vec{r}$ is given by $d\phi = -\vec{E} \cdot d\vec{r}$. To find the potential difference between the wire's two ends, we can divide the wire (no matter how it bends or loops) into a set of small displacements $d\vec{r}_i$, each of which points along the wire in the direction that conventional current flows (see figure E5.7). Since $\vec{E}$ *also* points parallel to the wire in this direction, the angle between $\vec{E}$ and $d\vec{r}_i$ is zero for each such displacement. The change in the potential due to the ith displacement is thus

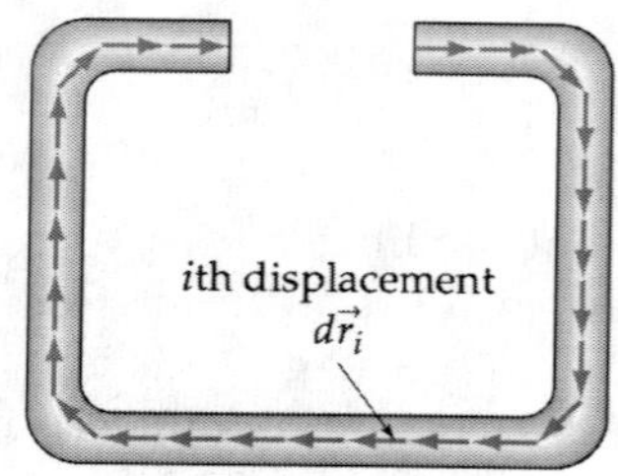

Figure E5.7
This figure illustrates how we can divide a wire into a set of small displacements.

$$d\phi_i = -\vec{E}\cdot d\vec{r}_i = -E\,dr_i \cos 0° = -E\,dr_i \tag{E5.13}$$

(The sign here simply says that if we define the displacement $d\vec{r}_i$ to be in the direction the current flows, then the potential *decreases* as we traverse the displacement. This is because current flows in the direction of decreasing potential, just as a river flows downhill.) Now, since $E \equiv \text{mag}(\vec{E})$ is the same at all points in the wire, the total potential difference between the wire's ends is

$$\Delta\phi = \sum_{\text{all } i} d\phi_i = \sum_{\text{all } i} -E\,dr_i = -E\sum_{\text{all } i} dr_i \tag{E5.14}$$

But the sum over the lengths dr_i of all the displacements is simply the wire's total length L, so for all thin wires (no matter how they bend), we have

How the potential difference between a wire's ends is related to the field in the wire

$$|\Delta\phi_{\text{wire}}| = EL \tag{E5.15}$$

Purpose and Symbols: This equation links the electric field magnitude E inside a thin wire to its length L and the absolute value of the potential difference $|\Delta\phi|$ between its ends.

Limitations: This equation assumes that the wire is uniform and thin, and that surface charges have had time to rearrange themselves into the appropriate quasistatic distribution.

Self-Test E5X.3

Imagine that the potential difference is 1.5 V between the ends of a wire that is 0.5 m long and has a diameter of 0.2 mm. What is the magnitude of the electric field in the wire? Does it depend on the wire's diameter?

Now, we saw in section E5.2 that $J = \sigma_c E$. For reasons we will understand better in chapter E12, the fact that the electric field has the same magnitude at all points along the wire means that it must also have the same magnitude at all points across the wire as well, so $I = JA$, where A is the wire's cross-sectional area. If you combine these equations with equation E5.15, you will get

$$|\Delta\phi_{\text{wire}}| = I\left(\frac{L}{\sigma_c A}\right) \tag{E5.16}$$

Self-Test E5X.4

Verify equation E5.16.

Now, we define the electrical **resistance** R of any conducting object to be

The definition of a conducting object's *resistance*

$$R \equiv \frac{|\Delta\phi|}{I} \tag{E5.17}$$

Purpose: This equation defines a conducting object's resistance R.

Symbols: I is the magnitude of the current the object conducts when the potential difference between its ends is $|\Delta\phi|$.

Limitations: The object must have well-defined "ends"!

Note: The SI unit of resistance is the **ohm**, where $1\,\Omega \equiv 1$ V/A $= 1\,(\text{J/C})/(\text{C/s}) = 1\,\text{kg·m}^2\text{C}^{-2}\text{s}^{-1}$ (see equation E5.6).

Equations E5.17 and E5.16 together imply that that

The resistance of a wire

$$R_{\text{wire}} = \frac{L}{\sigma_c A} \tag{E5.18}$$

for a uniform wire. As long as σ_c is independent of the electric field strength, we see that a wire of a given length and cross-sectional area has a fixed resistance independent of the field inside it and therefore the current it carries.

Many other objects also have a fixed resistance. We call the statement that

Ohm's law

$$R \equiv \frac{|\Delta\phi|}{I} \approx \text{constant} \quad \Rightarrow \quad I \propto |\Delta\phi| \tag{E5.19}$$

Ohm's law, and any object obeying this law **ohmic**. *The current flowing through an ohmic object is proportional to the potential difference between its ends.*

Self-Test E5X.5

A piece of copper wire 1.0 m long and 0.2 mm in diameter has what resistance?

E5.5 The Power Dissipated in a Conductor

Assume that the potential difference between a conducting object's two ends is $|\Delta\phi|$. The definition of the potential difference implies that a charge carrier's electrostatic potential energy *decreases* by $|q\Delta\phi|$ as it flows through the object. As we discussed in section E5.1, the lost potential energy shows up as increased thermal energy in the conductor.

Imagine now that the object is carrying a total current $I = |dQ/dt|$. The rate at which carriers in the conductor convert electrostatic potential energy to thermal energy (that is, the power P associated with the energy conversion) is

The power dissipated in a current-carrying object

$$P = \frac{|(dQ)\Delta\phi|}{dt} = I|\Delta\phi| \tag{E5.20a}$$

Purpose: This equation allows one to calculate the power P (the rate at which electrostatic potential energy is converted to thermal energy) for a conducting object carrying a total current I when the potential difference between the object's ends is $|\Delta\phi|$.

Limitations: The object must have well-defined ends!

You can use equation E5.17 to express either $|\Delta\phi|$ or I in terms of the other variable and the conducting object's resistance R: the results are

$$P = I^2 R = \frac{|\Delta\phi|^2}{R} \tag{E5.20b}$$

Self-Test E5X.6

Verify both equalities in equation E5.20*b*.

The power in these equations comes out in watts

The SI unit for current is the ampere and the SI unit of potential difference is the volt, so the units of $P = I|\Delta\phi|$ should be *watts*, the SI unit of power:

$$\cancel{V}\cdot\cancel{A}\left(\frac{1\ \text{J}/\cancel{\text{C}}}{1\ \cancel{V}}\right)\left(\frac{1\ \cancel{\text{C}}/\text{s}}{1\ \cancel{A}}\right) = \frac{\text{J}}{\text{s}} \equiv \text{W} \tag{E5.21}$$

A 100-W light bulb therefore converts electrical energy to thermal energy at a rate of 100 J/s, a 2000-W toaster converts energy at a rate of 2000 J/s, and so on.

Power companies measure electrical energy in **kilowatt-hours**, where

The *kilowatt-hour* as a unit of energy

$$1\ \text{kW}\cdot\text{h} = \left(\frac{1000\ \text{J}}{\cancel{\text{s}}}\right)(1\ \cancel{\text{h}})\left(\frac{3600\ \cancel{\text{s}}}{1\ \cancel{\text{h}}}\right) = 3.6\times 10^{6}\ \text{J} \tag{E5.22}$$

In southern California in 2005, 1 kW·h of electrical energy costs about $0.15.

E5.6 Discharging a Capacitor

What happens if we discharge a capacitor through a wire?

Consider again what happens if we connect the charged plates of a capacitor with a piece of wire. Qualitatively, we know that current will flow through the wire until the capacitor discharges. But how long will this take?

Assume that the time is long compared to the few tens of nanoseconds required to establish a uniform current flow through the wire. Assume that the capacitor's capacitance is C and the wire's resistance is R. To save writing, let's define $V_C \equiv |\Delta\phi_C|$ = the potential difference between the capacitor's plates. (Do not confuse V_C with potential energy: I am sorry that this traditional notation is "potentially" confusing). If we connect the wire directly to the capacitor plates, then V_C is also the potential difference across the wire's ends.

The definition of capacitance tells us that

$$C = \frac{Q}{|\Delta\phi_C|} = \frac{Q}{V_C} \quad\Rightarrow\quad V_C = \frac{Q}{C} \tag{E5.23}$$

where Q is the charge on the capacitor's positive plate. Note that V_C decreases with time as the capacitor discharges. The definition of resistance tells us that

$$R = \frac{|\Delta\phi_{\text{wire}}|}{I} \quad\Rightarrow\quad I = \frac{|\Delta\phi_{\text{wire}}|}{R} = \frac{V_C}{R} \tag{E5.24}$$

where I is the current flowing through the wire. Since this current comes entirely at the expense of charge on the capacitor's plates, and the current is simply the rate at which charge moves past a certain boundary (say the junction between the wire and the capacitor's positive plate), we have

$$I = -\frac{dQ}{dt} \tag{E5.25}$$

The minus sign is necessary because we need I to be positive in equation E5.24, but Q is decreasing with time (and so dQ/dt is negative) as the capacitor discharges. Now, if we take the time derivative of both sides of equation E5.23, substitute $-I$ for dQ/dt, and then use equation E5.24 to get rid of the I, we get

The differential equation for the potential difference across the capacitor's plates

$$\frac{dV_C}{dt} = -\frac{1}{RC}V_C \tag{E5.26}$$

where V_C is a function of time. By taking the time derivative of both sides of

$$V_C(t) = Ae^{-t/RC} \tag{E5.27}$$

(where A is some unknown constant, and e = 2.7183... is the base of the natural logarithms, not the charge of the proton), you can check that this function satisfies equation E5.26. Equation E5.27 is therefore the solution to equation E5.26 (see problem ES5.10 for another approach to solving equation E5.26).

Self-Test E5X.7

Verify that the function given in equation E5.27 satisfies equation E5.26.

Now, at time $t = 0$, equation E5.27 implies that $V_C(0) = Ae^{-0/RC} = A$. If we define V_0 to be the initial potential difference between the plates, then $A = V_0$, and our final equation for the potential difference between the capacitor's plates as it discharges through the wire is therefore

How the potential difference between a discharging capacitor's plates varies with time

$$V_C(t) = V_0 e^{-t/RC} \tag{E5.28}$$

Purpose: This equation describes how the potential difference V_C between a capacitor's plates decreases exponentially with time t as it discharges through a wire with resistance R.

Symbols: C is the capacitor's capacitance, and V_0 is the potential difference between its plates at time $t = 0$.

Limitations: This solution assumes that the wire is ohmic and that RC is much greater than the time required for the surface charges on the wire to arrange themselves in their quasistatic configuration.

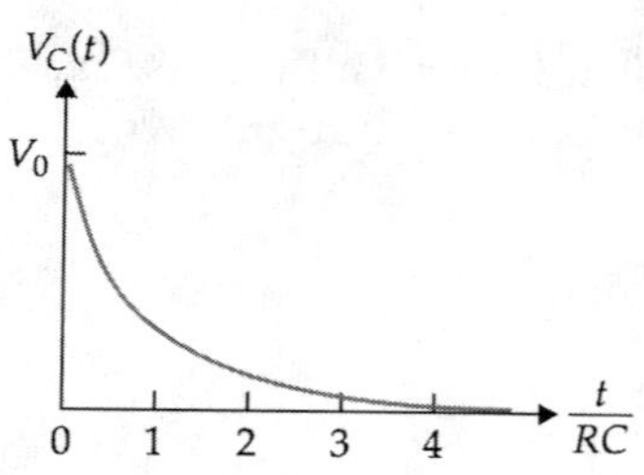

Figure E5.8
A graph of the potential difference between a discharging capacitor's plates plotted as a function of time.

We see that the potential difference between the capacitor's plates decreases exponentially with time, decreasing by a factor of $e = 2.7183$ during each time interval of duration RC (see figure E5.8). It is possible to set up situations where RC has a value of several seconds, meaning that time required to discharge the capacitor can be millions or even billions of times larger than the time required for the surface charges to attain the quasistatic configuration required to drive the current.

Note also that the capacitor never quite becomes fully discharged: the potential difference between its plates only approaches zero asymptotically. However, after a time equal to about 4 or 5 times RC has passed, the potential difference is zero for all practical purposes.

Self-Test E5X.8

Verify RC has units of time. (It had better have these units: the power to which we raise e in the exponential function must be a unitless number.)

Energy is conserved during the discharge process

One can show that the total thermal energy dissipated in the wire during the discharge process is the same initially stored in the capacitor's electric field (see problem E5S.11), which is another piece of evidence supporting the idea that the electric field is a form of energy.

Because the potential difference between a discharging capacitor's plates varies so predictably with time, one can use a discharging capacitor as a clock. This is a common role for capacitors in electronic circuits.

E5.7 The Mystery du Jour

We have seen how a discharging capacitor can push a current through a wire for a short period of time. However, current can flow through the lights in your room indefinitely. How can we create such persistent currents and manipulate them to do useful things? Our focus in the next chapter will be answering such questions.

TWO-MINUTE PROBLEMS

E5T.1 Consider two wires with the same length. Wire A has a diameter half that of B but is otherwise identical. Both have the same electric field acting in them. How do the *currents* in these wires compare?
A. $I_A = 4I_B$
B. $I_A = 2I_B$
C. $I_A = I_B$
D. $I_B = 2I_A$
E. $I_B = 4I_A$
F. Other (specify)
T. It is impossible to know

E5T.2 Consider two wires with the same diameter. Wire A is twice as long as wire B but is otherwise identical Both have the same electric field acting in them. How do the *currents* in these wires compare? (Select your response from the answers to problem E5T.1.)

E5T.3 Consider two wires that are identical except that wire A is twice as long as wire B. Both have the same potential difference between their ends. How do the currents in these wires compare? (Select your response from the answers to problem E5T.1.)

E5T.4 If you increase the temperature of a metal, what happens to its conductivity, assuming the Drude model is accurate? Its conductivity should
A. Increase
B. Decrease
C. Remain the same
D. It is impossible to tell

E5T.5 Imagine that we have two isolated metal spheres. The one on the left has a negative charge, while the one on the right has a positive charge. If these spheres are connected with a straight *metal* wire, what direction do we conventionally consider the current to flow?
A. Left to right
B. Right to left
C. Because there is no complete circuit, no current flows
D. Because there is no electric field, no current flows

E5T.6 If each copper atom in a wire were to contribute *two* conduction electrons instead of just one, the wire's resistance would
A. quadruple
B. double
C. remain the same
D. decrease by a factor of 2
E. decrease by a factor of 4

E5T.7 Wire 1 is 25 cm long and has a diameter of 0.6 mm, and wire 2 has double that length and diameter. Both wires are made of copper. How do their resistances compare?
A. $R_1 \approx 4R_2$
B. $R_1 \approx 2R_2$
C. $R_1 \approx R_2$
D. $R_2 \approx 2R_1$
E. $R_2 \approx 4R_1$
F. Some other relationship (specify)

E5T.8 A light-emitting diode (LED) of the type shown below has the property that the potential difference between its ends is approximately 1.5 V when it conducts currents ranging from 1 mA to 50 mA. This device is ohmic, T or F?

E5T.9 When it is conducting 10 mA of current, the LED described in problem E5T.8 has a resistance of
A. 0.015 Ω
B. 0.15 Ω
C. 150 Ω
D. 1500 Ω
E. We cannot calculate R: the LED is not ohmic

E5T.10 Assume that the brightness of an ohmic light bulb with resistance R is proportional to the power it dissipates. If we connect it to the plates of a capacitor with capacitance at time $t = 0$, by what factor is it dimmer than its initial brightness at time $t = 2RC$?
A. $1/2$
B. $1/4$
C. $1/e$
D. $1/2e$
E. $1/e^2$
F. some other factor (specify)

HOMEWORK PROBLEMS

Basic Skills

E5B.1 A lightning flash during a thunderstorm (see the cover picture) can consist of one to tens of strokes, each with a duration between 0.01 s and 0.1 s. Peak currents in a stroke can be as high as 20 kA. If a certain lightning flash has 10 separate strokes, each lasting 0.05 s and carrying an average current of 8 kA, about how much charge gets transferred from the earth to the sky (or vice versa)?

E5B.2 Imagine a spark leaping between two electrically charged spheres.
(a) If the spark transfers a charge of 200 μC from one sphere to the other and lasts about 0.1 ms, what is the average current the spark carries?
(b) If the leftmost sphere was initially positive relative to the other, which way did electrons flow in the spark, left to right or right to left? Which way did conventional current flow? Explain.

E5B.3 What is the drift speed of electrons in a 22-cm length of silver wire that carries a current of 5.0 A and has a cross-sectional area of 0.2×10^{-6} m^2? (Silver has an atomic mass of 107.9 g/mole, a density of 10,500 kg/m^3, and a conductivity of about 6.3×10^7 Ω^{-1}m^{-1}.)

E5B.4 What is the drift speed of electrons in a 1.0-m length of copper wire that carries a current of 50 mA and has a cross-sectional area of 0.4×10^{-6} m^2? About how long will it take an electron to travel the wire's length?

E5B.5 A 10.0-cm length of copper wire has a uniform cross-sectional area of 1.0 mm^2. If the drift speed of electrons in this wire is 2.0×10^{-4} m/s and the electrons all move directly along the wire, what is the magnitude of the current density in the wire? What is the total current carried by the wire?

E5B.6 A 2.0-m length of silver wire has a uniform cross-sectional area of 0.6 mm^2. If the drift speed of electrons in this wire is 5.0×10^{-5} m/s and the electrons all move in the same direction along the wire, what is the magnitude of the current density in the wire? What is the total current carried by the wire? (Silver has an atomic mass of 107.9 g/mole, a density of 10,500 kg/m^3, and a conductivity at room temperature of about 6.3×10^7 Ω^{-1}m^{-1}.)

E5B.7 The electric field inside a wire is 36 N/C when the potential difference between its ends is 9 V. How long is the wire? What else would we need to know to determine the current in the wire?

E5B.8 Imagine that if the potential difference between the ends of a 5.0-m length of an unknown type of wire with a diameter of 0.75 mm is 1.5 V, we find that it conducts 3.0 A. What is this wire's resistance? What is the magnitude of the electric field in the wire?

E5B.9 Power cords for lamps and the like are often made of #18 copper wire, which has a diameter of 1.01 mm. What is the resistance of 50 feet of such wire?

E5B.10 Imagine that you need to create a circuit element having a resistance of 12 Ω. You have some nichrome wire whose diameter is 0.82 mm. How long would a piece of such wire have to be to have a resistance of 12 Ω?

E5B.11 Imagine that a certain light bulb has a tungsten filament with a length of 8.0 mm and a cross-sectional area of 1.2×10^{-7} m^2. This bulb conducts 0.24 A of current when connected to a 2.0-V battery. What is the magnitude of the electric field in the filament?

E5B.12 One of the many expenses associated with a home swimming pool is the electrical power required to run the pool filter. The motor that pumps pool water through the filter typically draws about 1.5 hp of power and has to run about 8 hours a day during the swim season. About how much would this add one's electric bill in Southern California?

Synthetic

E5S.1 In section E5.1, I claimed that the average time τ between successive collisions of an electron with the lattice is equal to both the average time $[t_{\text{last}}]_{\text{avg}}$ since the last collision and the average $[t_{\text{next}}]_{\text{avg}}$ to the next collision. Argue that this must be true using the following analogy. Consider throwing a coin repeatedly, generating a lengthy list of heads and tails, e.g. THHTTHTHHHT...
(a) Use a coin to generate a list 100 throws long.
(b) Arbitrarily pick at least 20 different starting positions on the list, and show experimentally that the average number of throws between an arbitrary starting point and the previous H or to the next H is roughly equal to 2 throws (with only 20 starting points, you are likely to find an average value between about 1.3 and 2.7).
(c) Now pick 20 different starting points in the sequence where H was displayed. Experimen-

tally, what is the average number of throws to the next H? While you will not get exactly the same result as in the previous case, is it plausible that the result for this case is twice as large as the result for part b? Why or why not?

(d) Would you get the same result if you started with a T? Why or why not?

(e) Explain how this situation is analogous to a sequence of electron collisions, and therefore why $[t_{\text{last}}]_{\text{avg}} = \tau$.

E5S.2 Imagine that in a certain proton accelerator, roughly 10^{11} protons at a time go around a ring having a radius of 1.0 km. The speed of the protons is essentially the same as the speed of light. What is the current flowing in the ring in amperes?

E5S.3 (a) Compute the average time between collisions τ for conduction electrons in copper, using the information available in example E5.1.

(b) Show that electrons traveling at a typical thermal speed of 10^6 m/s will cover an average distance of about 25 nm between collisions.

E5S.4 Compute the average time between collisions τ for silver, assuming that each atom contributes one conduction electron per atom. (Pure silver metal has an atomic mass of 107.9 g/mole, a density of 10,500 kg/m^3, and a room-temperature conductivity of about $6.3\times10^7\ \Omega^{-1}\text{m}^{-1}$.)

E5S.5 A silver wire that has a length of 28 cm and a diameter of 0.20 mm is carrying a current of 230 mA. The electrons in the wire are moving to the left. What is the magnitude and direction of the electric field in that wire?

E5S.6 A nichrome wire that has a length of 2.4 m and a diameter of 0.40 mm is carrying a current of 2.5 A. The electrons in the wire are moving to the right. What is the magnitude and direction of the electric field in that wire?

E5S.7 Imagine that you have a wire made of an unknown metal. The wire is 1.0 m long and has a diameter of 1.0 mm, and it conducts 1.0 A when the potential difference between its ends is 2.0 V. What would you guess the metal to be? (*Hints*: Can you determine mag($\vec{E}$) in this wire? The current density? How might knowing these quantities help?)

E5S.8 Consider a capacitor connected to a wire bent in the shape shown below. Just before the wire is connected, the electric field of the plates will tend to push positive charges at points *A*, *B*, and C toward the *left*. Explain in detail how connecting the wire to the capacitor produces surface charges that redirect the current at point *B* so that it flows "uphill" against the field produced by the capacitor's plates. Sketch these charges on a copy of the drawing.

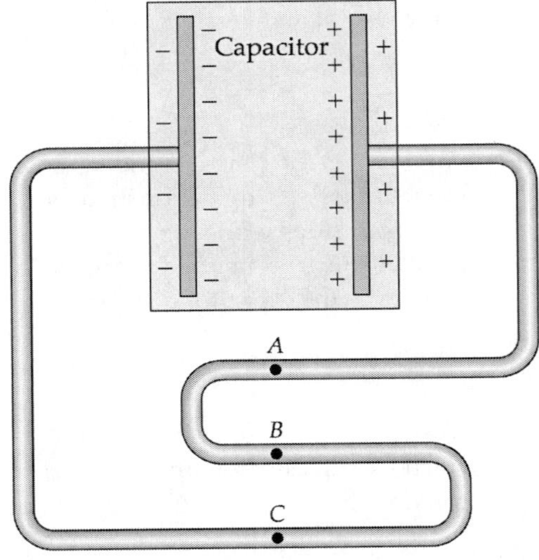

E5S.9 Imagine that you have a light-bulb that has a resistance of about 10 Ω and that can tolerate a maximum voltage of 3 V. Imagine that you want to connect this to a charged capacitor large enough to keep the bulb glowing reasonably brightly for more than 10 s. Roughly what should the capacitor's capacitance be?

E5S.10 If you are uncomfortable with the way that we guessed the solution for equation E5.26, perhaps you will be happier with the following method. Divide both sides of equation E5.26 by $-RCV_C$ and multiply both sides by *dt*. you should get:

$$\frac{-dt}{RC} = \frac{dV_C}{V_C} \tag{E5.29}$$

If you integrate this expression with appropriate limits on both sides, you should get an expression that with a little more manipulation can be shown to be equal to equation E5.27. Do this.

E5S.11 Consider a parallel-plate capacitor whose plates have an area *A* and are separated by a distance *d* such that $d \ll [A]^{1/2}$.

(a) Argue that the energy stored in the electric field of such a capacitor is $U_{\text{field}} = \frac{1}{2}CV_0^2$, if V_0 is the potential difference between the capacitor's plates. (*Hint*: Argue that between the plates, the field strength is $E \approx V_0/d$, where *d* is the distance between the plates. Use the equation for the capacitance of a parallel-plate capacitor given in section E4.6 to eliminate *d* in the equation for E in favor of C. Roughly how much volume does this field occupy?)

(b) Imagine we discharge this capacitor by connecting its plates with a wire of resistance R. The rate at which thermal energy is produced in the wire at any given instant of time is

$$\frac{dU^{\text{th}}}{dt} = P = \frac{V_R^2}{R} = \frac{V_C^2}{R} \quad \text{(E5.30)}$$

where V_C is the time-dependent potential difference across the capacitor's plates. If we integrate both sides with respect to t, we find that the total energy converted to thermal energy in the wire as the capacitor discharges is

$$U^{\text{th}} = \frac{1}{R}\int_0^{\infty} V_C^2\, dt = \frac{1}{R}\int_0^{\infty} [V_0 e^{-t/RC}]^2\, dt \quad \text{(E5.31)}$$

Do this integral, and show that $U^{\text{th}} = \frac{1}{2}CV_0^2$, which is consistent with the energy initially stored in the field according to part (a).

E5S.12 Nerve cells in the human body have long extensions called axons that connect to other cells. An axon typically maintains a resting potential difference of about 80 mV across its membrane (with the inside negative) by actively excluding positive sodium ions and retaining negatively charged protein ions. This builds up opposite concentrations of charge on either side of the membrane, making the membrane like a capacitor whose plates are the conducting fluid inside and outside the membrane.

We can model how a signal moves down an axon by imagining the axon to be divided into short segments. When the nerve cell "fires", it makes the membrane on the axon segment closest to the cell porous to sodium ions. This allows a current to flow across the membrane, effectively discharging this segment's capacitor (the technical term is "depolarizing the membrane"). The discharge instigates chemical changes that make the next segment's membrane porous, causing it to discharge even as the first segment recovers by actively pumping potassium ions out of its interior (thus making the interior negative again). The second segment's depolarization makes the next segment's membrane porous, and so on. The depolarization thus moves segment by segment down the axon.

The speed with which a signal moves down the axon depends on how rapidly a segment's capacitor can be discharged. The membranes of some axons are covered with a fatty insulator called *myelin* that effectively makes the membrane thicker (thus increasing the distance between the "plates" of each segment's capacitor). Will this increase or decrease the speed at which signals move down the axon? Present an argument for your conclusion. Also support your conclusion by a footnote or URL to some document that contrasts the speeds of signals traveling along myelinated and unmyelinated axons. (This problem is based on information in Cameron, et. al., *Physics of the Body*, 2/e, Medical Physics Publishing, Madison, WI, 1999.)

Rich-Context

E5R.1 It is not clear that the Drude model should describe the movement of ions through a liquid with any accuracy, but it is interesting to see whether the average time between collisions τ that we calculate assuming that the Drude model does apply to such systems is physically reasonable. Pure water has about 6×10^{19} H^+ ions (or more technically H_3O^+ ions) and the same number of OH^- ions in a cubic meter. What is τ? If the ions have an average thermal speed of about 500 m/s at room temperature, about how far would an ion travel on the average between collisions? How does this compare to the size of a water molecule (which is on the order of magnitude of 0.1 nm)? Is your answer physically reasonable?

E5R.2 The Drude model predicts that a metal's conductivity should depend on the metal's absolute temperature T according to the power-law relationship $\sigma_c \propto T^a$, where a is an integer or simple fraction. Determine a and explain why. (*Hint*: The conductivity depends on the mean time between collisions, which depends on the temperature. Why?)

Comment: Metal conductivities at room temperature and colder do *not* depend on temperature in the manner predicted by the Drude model. This is one of the major inadequacies of the model, which fails because the behavior of electrons in metals is dominated by quantum effects (not considered in the Drude model) until the metal's temperature is significantly larger than room temperature.

E5R.3 Assume that the top globe of a Van de Graaff generator (which we can model as a sphere 30 cm in diameter) is charged to the maximum potential it can have relative to infinity without causing the air surrounding it to break down. A person whose skin is dry has a resistance of about 10,000 Ω. Assume that a person suddenly touches the globe while it is charged. Estimate the maximum current that flows through the person to the ground and the approximate time during which the current flow is significant. A 50 mA current maintained for more than a few seconds can kill a person. Is someone who touches such a globe risking death? (*Hints:* Model the globe as one plate of a capacitor, with the other plate at infinity, and assume that the ground is "infinity." Carefully define what you mean by a "significant" current flow. Will other definitions lead to radically or only modestly different results for the current duration?)

Advanced

E5A.1 Imagine that the charge on an isolated sphere 20 cm in diameter surrounded by air is observed to leak away so that less than 1% of the original charge remains after 10 minutes. Use this to estimate the conductivity of air. (*Hints:* Treat the isolated sphere as a capacitor whose other plate is infinity. One cannot use equation E5.18 to link the air's resistance to its conductivity, because air is not shaped like a wire. I recommend trying to calculate the current that flows at $t = 0$ and relate that to the current density and electric field at the sphere's surface.)

ANSWERS TO SELF-TESTS

E5X.1 Calculating n as in equation E5.11 yields a value of $n = 6.0 \times 10^{28}\ \text{m}^{-3}$. The wire's *diameter* is 0.0015 m, so its cross-sectional area is $\pi(0.00075\ \text{m})^2 = 1.8 \times 10^{-6}\ \text{m}^2$. Calculating $v_d = I/neA$ as in equation E5.12, we get about 3.0×10^{-4} m/s.

E5X.2 The positive charge in the faster moving current to the left will not be fully replaced by positive charge coming from the right. This will leave a deficit of positive charge on the left side of the wire, creating a negative surface charge on the wire there. This surface charge creates an electric field that will speed up positive charges coming in from the right and slow down the charge going away to the left, thus evening out the current flow.

E5X.3 According to equation E5.15,

$$E = \frac{|\Delta\phi|}{L} = \frac{1.5\ \text{V}}{0.5\ \text{m}}\left(\frac{1\ \text{J/C}}{1\ \text{V}}\right)\left(\frac{1\ \text{N}\cdot\text{m}}{1\ \text{J}}\right) = 3.0\ \frac{\text{N}}{\text{C}} \tag{E5.32}$$

The diameter of the wire is irrelevant.

E5X.4 Since $J = \sigma_c E$, $E = J/\sigma_c$. Also $I = JA$ implies that $J = I/A$. Plugging these into equation E5.15 yields:

$$|\Delta\phi_{\text{wire}}| = EL = \frac{J}{\sigma_c}L = \frac{I/A}{\sigma_c}L = I\left(\frac{L}{\sigma_c A}\right). \tag{E5.33}$$

E5X.5 According to equation E5.18,

$$R = L/\sigma_c A$$
$$= \frac{1.0\ \text{m}}{(5.9 \times 10^7\ \Omega^{-1}\text{m}^{-1})\pi(1.0 \times 10^{-4}\ \text{m})^2}$$
$$= 0.54\ \Omega \tag{E5.34}$$

E5X.6 Equation E5.17 implies that $I = |\Delta\phi|/R$ and that $|\Delta\phi| = IR$, so equation E5.20a implies that

$$P = I|\Delta\phi| = I(IR) = I^2R \tag{E5.35a}$$

and
$$P = I|\Delta\phi| = \frac{|\Delta\phi|}{R}|\Delta\phi| = \frac{|\Delta\phi|^2}{R}. \tag{E5.35b}$$

E5X.7 Taking the derivative of equation E5.27, we get:

$$\frac{dV_C}{dt} = \frac{d}{dt}(Ae^{-t/RC}) = Ae^{-t/RC}\left(\frac{-1}{RC}\right) \tag{E5.36}$$

by the chain rule. But $Ae^{-t/RC} = V_C$, so this is the same as equation E5.26.

E5X.8 The units of RC are:

$$\Omega \cdot \text{F} = \frac{\text{V}}{\text{A}} \cdot \frac{\text{C}}{\text{V}}\left(\frac{1\ \text{A}}{1\ \text{C/s}}\right) = \text{s}.$$

E6 Circuits

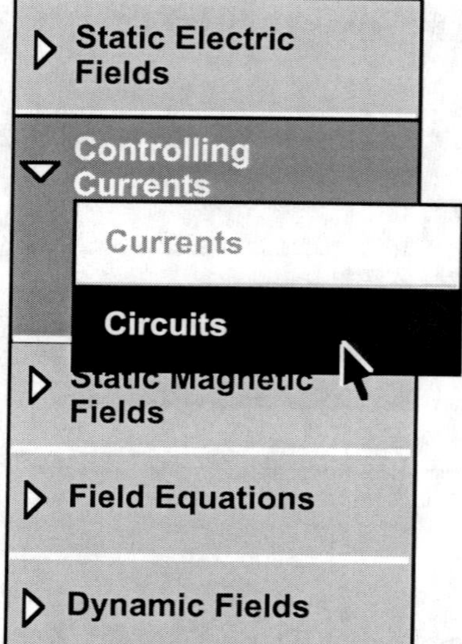

Chapter Overview

Introduction

In chapter E5, we studied a basic electric circuit involving a single wire connected to a capacitor. In such a circuit, current can flow for at most a few seconds. In this chapter (the last in the subdivision on currents), we will explore circuits where current can flow indefinitely, and which involve complicated arrangements of circuit elements.

Section E6.1: An Idealized Model of a Battery

A **battery** is like a capacitor with an internal "conveyor belt" that transports positive charge from the negative plate to the positive plate (*against* the plates' field) as rapidly as needed to maintain the charge on each plate. A battery delivers a certain energy per unit charge or **emf** $\mathscr{E}$ (pronounced "eeyemehf") to the charge carriers it transports against the field (technically, its **electrodes** or **terminals**). This emf is a *fixed characteristic* of most batteries and power supplies. Conservation of energy requires that

$$|\Delta\phi| = \mathscr{E} - \mathscr{E}^{th} \tag{E6.4}$$

Purpose: This equation links the potential difference $|\Delta\phi|$ between a battery's terminals to the battery's characteristic emf $\mathscr{E}$.

Symbols: $\mathscr{E}^{th}$ is the energy per unit charge lost to thermal energy.

Limitations: This assumes no energy loss other than to thermal energy.

Notes: In the **ideal battery approximation**, we assume that $\mathscr{E}^{th} = 0$. An ideal battery will conduct whatever current is necessary to maintain the potential difference $|\Delta\phi| = \mathscr{E}$ between its terminals

Note that while emf and potential have the same SI units (volts), they are conceptually distinct. Potential ϕ refers specifically to *electrostatic potential energy* per unit charge, while emf $\mathscr{E}$ refers to energy per unit charge contributed by something else.

Section E6.2: Batteries in Series

Batteries connected in a sequence with the positive terminal of one connected to the negative terminal of the next are "in series." Batteries connected in series behave as if they were a single battery with an emf equal to the *sum* of the individual batteries' emfs

Section E6.3: Resistances in Series

If we connect a sequence of *two* wires to a battery, the steady-state surface charge distribution on the wires ensures that *the same current flows through each.* Since $|\Delta\phi| = IR$, the potential differences across the wires will be unequal if there resistances are unequal, but their sum must be equal to that across the battery ($|\Delta\phi_{bat}| = |\Delta\phi_1| + |\Delta\phi_2|$).

Potential (like potential energy) is only defined up to a constant, so we can define the potential ϕ at a point in a circuit only if we choose an arbitrary reference point where $\phi \equiv 0$. In *circuits,* we conventionally set $\phi \equiv 0$ at the battery's negative terminal. The potential at a point in a circuit is analogous to the height of a roller coaster track, a charge carrier is analogous to a roller-coaster car, and a battery to the motorized part of the track that lifts the car to the top of the track.

A general set of **circuit elements** is connected **in series** if every charge carrier that flows through any *one* element eventually flows through *all* elements. For such a set,

$$I = I_1 = I_2 = \dots \tag{E6.8a}$$

$$V_{set} = V_1 + V_2 + \dots \tag{E6.8b}$$

$$R_{set} = R_1 + R_2 + \dots \tag{E6.8c}$$

Purpose: These equations characterize a set of circuit elements in series.

Symbols: $I_1, I_2, \dots$ and $V_1, V_2, \dots$ and $R_1, R_2, \dots$ are the currents flowing through, the potential differences across, and the resistances of circuit elements 1, 2, ... respectively. I is the common current flowing through the elements, V_{set} is the potential difference between the two ends of the entire set, and R_{set} is the total resistance of the set.

Limitations: The circuit must have settled into a steady state.

Section E6.4: Notation Conventions and Circuit Diagrams

It is convenient and conventional to define $V_{obj} \equiv |\Delta\phi_{obj}|$ = the potential difference across an object's ends and $V_{ba} = |\phi_b - \phi_a|$ = the potential difference between two points. Be careful that you do not interpret these symbols as being electrostatic potential *energy*

A **circuit diagram** is a visual tool for describing a circuit. Circuit elements are represented in such a diagram by conventional symbols (see figure E6.8). We often use the generic **resistor** symbol to represent any reasonably ohmic device. We use straight black lines (assumed to have zero resistance) to indicate connections between elements. Do *not* assume that such lines connect where they cross unless marked by a black dot.

Section E6.5: Circuit Elements in Parallel

A set of circuit elements are connected **in parallel** if (1) a given charge carrier flowing through the set flows through only *one* of its elements and (2) the potential difference across each element is the same as that across the entire set. For such a set,

$$I_{set} = I_1 + I_2 + \dots \tag{E6.15a}$$

$$V_{set} = V_1 = V_2 = \dots \tag{E6.15b}$$

$$\Rightarrow \quad \frac{1}{R_{set}} = \frac{1}{R_1} + \frac{1}{R_2} + \dots \tag{E6.15c}$$

Purpose: These equations characterize a set of circuit elements in parallel.

Symbols: $I_1, I_2, \dots$ and $V_1, V_2, \dots$ and $R_1, R_2, \dots$ are the currents flowing through, the potential differences across, and the resistances of circuit elements 1, 2, ... respectively. I_{set} is the current flowing through the entire set, V_{set} is the potential difference between the set's ends, and R_{set} is the set's total resistance.

Limitations: The circuit must have settled into a steady state.

Section E6.6: Analyzing Complex Circuits

We can analyze almost any complex circuit by grouping its resistor elements into series and parallel sets, each of which we can replace by a *single* equivalent resistor. By repeating this process, we can eventually reduce *all* elements to a single resistor. If the elements are at least approximately ohmic, we can then calculate the current in that equivalent resistor using Ohm's law, and then work backwards to calculate currents and potential differences for all the elements.

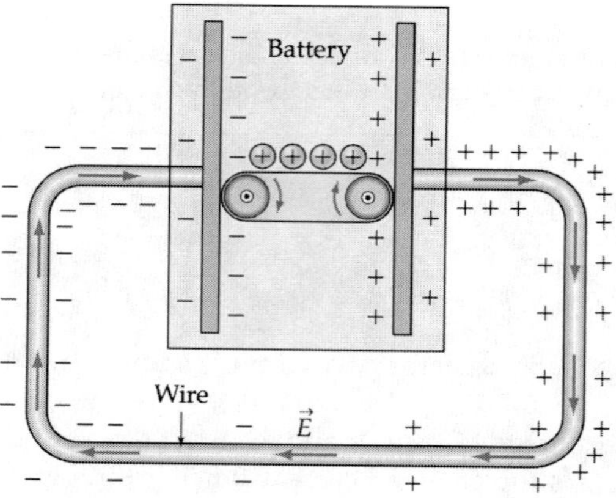

Figure E6.1
In this idealized visualization of a battery, a conveyor belt transports charge from the negative plate of a capacitor to the positive plate against the electric forces exerted by those plates. In the model, the conveyor belt runs at whatever speed is required to maintain a fixed potential difference between the plates.

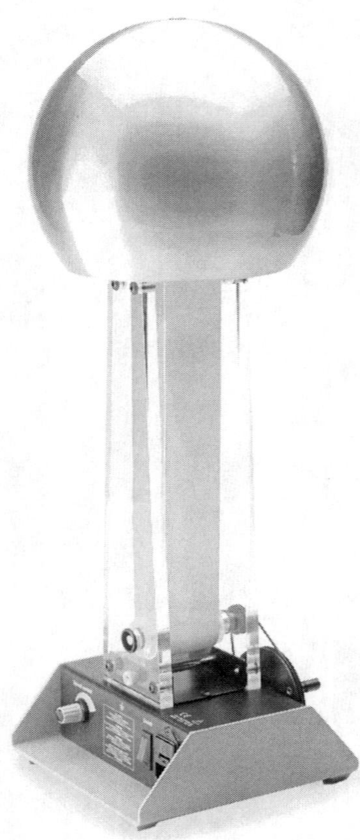

Figure E6.2
A Van de Graaff generator has a literal conveyor belt that carries charge to the upper sphere, but lacks a mechanism for adjusting the rate.

E6.1 An Idealized Model of a Battery

In chapter E5, we saw that when we connect the plates of a charged capacitor with a wire, the capacitor will drive a current through the wire. However, the current decreases exponentially as the plates discharge, and generally does not last very long. How might we maintain a steady flow of current in a wire?

One way to keep charge flowing steadily is to maintain the charges on the capacitor plates by finding some way to physically transport positive charge from the negative plate to the positive plate *against* the electrostatic force that the field exerts on those charges. We can visualize this by imagining that we connect the plates with a motor-driven conveyor belt that picks up positive charges at the negative plate and physically carries them to the positive plate, as shown in figure E6.1. Let us further imagine that the conveyor belt is designed to run at precisely the rate required to maintain a *fixed* potential difference between the plates. Such a mechanism is an idealized model of a **battery.**

A Van de Graaff generator (see figure E6.2) is a mechanical device similar to this idealized model, in that it uses an actual rubber conveyor belt to transport charge between its base and the metal sphere at its top. However, the belt in a typical Van de Graaff generator does not adjust its speed to maintain a fixed potential difference between the sphere and the base, so the generator is not quite an ideal battery according to our description.

Chemical batteries behave like ideal batteries

The batteries we normally encounter in daily life are *chemical* batteries, which use chemical reactions as the "motor" that transports ions between the battery's plates (usually called **electrodes**). As we will see in a moment, feedback effects ensure that these reactions proceed at whatever pace is required to maintain a fairly precisely-defined potential difference between the plates, so such batteries are better realizations of our idealized model.

How a lead-acid battery works

How does a chemical battery work? A practical example of a chemical battery is a lead-acid car battery, which consists of 6 lead-acid *cells* wired in series. (A **cell** is the simplest possible battery configuration, consisting of a single positive electrode and a single negative electrode immersed in the appropriate chemicals. A *battery* is what the end user sees, and may consist of either a single cell or multiple cells internally wired together.) A lead-acid cell consists of a positive electrode of lead dioxide (PbO_2) and a negative electrode of pure lead immersed in an **electrolyte** of sulfuric acid (H_2SO_4) dissolved in water. Sulfuric acid in water disassociates into hydronium ions (H_3O^+) and bisulfate

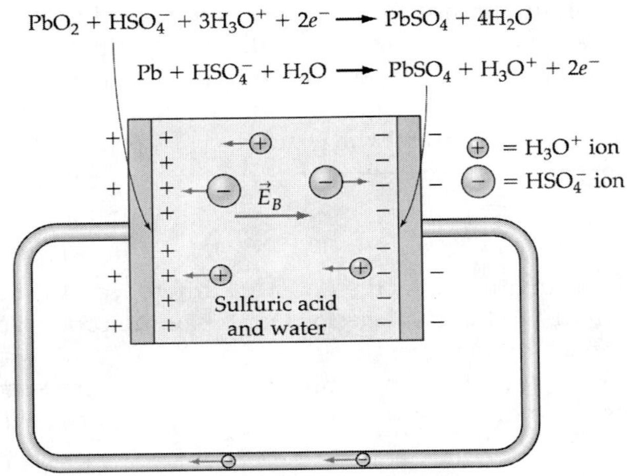

Figure E6.3
This figure illustrates what happens inside a lead-acid cell when it conducts a current. Note that for the reaction to take place, hydronium ions have to diffuse to the left and bisulfate ions to the right against the electric field. (I have drawn the electric field as if it filled the whole space between the electrodes, but technically, the field is only strong in a thin film of fluid surrounding each electrode: see problem E6S.11.)

ions (HSO_4^-). Both electrodes chemically react with the electrolyte as follows:

$$PbO_2 + HSO_4^- + 3H_3O^+ + 2e^- \rightarrow PbSO_4 + 5H_2O \tag{E6.1}$$

$$Pb + HSO_4^- + H_2O \rightarrow PbSO_4 + H_3O^+ + 2e^- \tag{E6.2}$$

The first reaction grabs two electrons from the positive electrode, causing it to become more positive. The second produces two electrons, which pile up on the negative electrode. The net effect of the combined reactions is thus to transport two electrons from the positive electrode to the negative electrode. Note, however, that charge is *actually* transported by hydronium and bisulfate ions diffusing through the electrolyte: this is what serves as the "conveyor belt" that carries charge against the field created by the electrodes (see figure E6.3).

These combined chemical reactions happen to release an energy of about 6.7×10^{-19} J while effectively transporting two electron's-worth of charge between the electrodes, so the energy released per unit charge transported is

$$\mathscr{E} = \frac{6.7\times10^{-19}\,\cancel{\text{J}}}{2(1.6\times10^{-19}\,\cancel{\text{C}})}\left(\frac{1\text{ V}}{1\,\cancel{\text{J}}/\cancel{\text{C}}}\right) = 2.1\text{ V} \tag{E6.3}$$

This reaction goes very quickly (piling up charges on the electrodes) until enough charge has piled up so that the energy cost per unit charge of transporting any more ions (which is the potential difference $|\Delta\phi|$ between the electrodes by definition) would exceed $\mathscr{E}$, the energy per unit charge supplied by the reaction. If a current flow depletes the charges on the electrodes, the reaction restarts, going so quickly that it nearly instantly resupplies enough charge to the electrodes to make the potential difference again $|\Delta\phi| = \mathscr{E}$. So whether current is flowing or not, the reactions in a lead-acid cell strive to maintain a fixed potential difference of 2.1 V between the cell's electrodes.

The definition of *emf*

Like the lead-acid cell, all chemical batteries deliver a characteristic energy per unit charge to the ions that the reaction transports from one electrode to the other against the electrodes' electric field. We call the energy per unit charge delivered to a charged particle from any source other than an electric field an **emf**, short for "electromotive force." This historical term is a misnomer, since an emf is not a force, but rather an *energy per unit charge* delivered from a non-electrostatic source. So I would like you to imagine that emf is simply a new word (which for historical reasons we pronounce "eeyemehf") that expresses a battery's *strength* (one might say "oomph") in delivering energy to the charged particles that travel through it. A lead-acid cell's emf is thus 2.1 V.

Energy losses in real cells prevent them from being ideal

Under realistic conditions, not *all* of the energy released by the chemical reaction in a battery gets converted into electrostatic potential energy this way: some is converted to thermal energy as ions moving through the cell collide with stationary molecules. Conservation of energy implies that the simplistic equality $|\Delta\phi| = \mathcal{E}$ can more accurately be written

$$|\Delta\phi| = \mathcal{E} - \mathcal{E}^{\text{th}} \tag{E6.4}$$

Purpose: This equation links the potential difference $|\Delta\phi|$ between a battery's electrodes to the characteristic emf $\mathcal{E}$ of the process driving charge through the battery.

Symbols: $\mathcal{E}^{\text{th}}$ is the energy per unit charge lost to thermal energy.

Limitations: This equation assumes no energy loss other than to thermal energy.

Thus, while a battery's characteristic chemical emf $\mathcal{E}$ is *independent* of the current flowing through it, $\mathcal{E}^{\text{th}}$ is approximately *proportional* to that current (the more rapidly ions move through the electrolyte, the more energy is lost in collisions). This means that the potential difference $|\Delta\phi|$ between a battery's electrodes is equal to the battery's chemical emf only when *no* current flows through the battery, and $|\Delta\phi|$ generally "droops" a bit as the current increases.

One can minimize this problem by supplying the battery with plenty of electrolyte (having more ions reduces the drift speed required to carry a given current, which reduces thermal losses) and increasing the surface area of the electrodes (so that the ions can more easily get to the electrodes). Battery designers generally work hard to keep $\mathcal{E}^{\text{th}}$ as small as economically possible, and in many situations, $\mathcal{E}^{\text{th}}$ is small enough that we can use the **ideal battery approximation**, where we assume that $\mathcal{E}^{\text{th}} = 0$ independent of the current. A good car battery can supply tens of amperes without a significant decrease in the potential between its electrodes.

A cell's *capacity*

A battery can provide only so much charge to a circuit. For example, when all of the lead and/or lead dioxide and/or sulfuric acid in a lead-acid cell has been used up, the reaction cannot continue, and the cell is "dead". The total number of electrons that a given type of battery can send through a circuit before dying is thus proportional to how many molecules of reactant are available, and thus on how large the battery is.

One of the nice things about a lead-acid cell is that it can be *recharged* simply by forcing a current through the cell in the reverse direction (with a higher-voltage battery or power source). This causes the chemical reactions described in equations E6.1 and E6.2 to go in reverse, until all the lead sulfate is converted back into lead dioxide and lead. Not all cells can be recharged this way: in many cases, the reaction does not work well in reverse. For example, normal alkaline cells (with a characteristic emf of 1.55 V) do not recharge well. Nickel-cadmium cells (with a characteristic emf of 1.2 V) can be recharged many times, but fail eventually because the reverse reaction does not place its reaction products exactly where they started. Nickle-metal-hydride cells (with a characteristic emf of 1.2 V) recharge much more reliably than nickle-cadmium cells and are less polluting when discarded (though they are more expensive).

Other sources of electrical energy generally behave like ideal batteries

Other sources of electrical energy often behave like chemical batteries. The power company that supplies electricity to your home uses non-chemical physical processes to transfer energy to electrons, but these processes also transfer a characteristic amount of energy to each electron. The two vertical terminals in a household electrical outlet behave (for our present purposes) much like the electrodes of a battery with a characteristic emf of 120 V. Electronic power supplies also generally behave like batteries with a certain fixed emf.

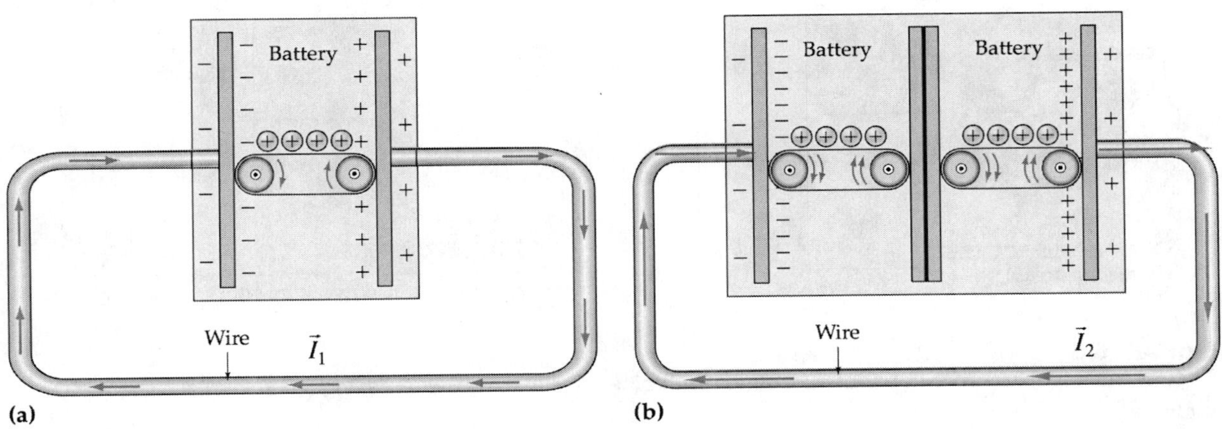

Figure E6.4
Two simple circuits involving (a) one battery and a wire and (b) two batteries and the same wire.

E6.2 Batteries in Series

A simple circuit involving a single battery and a wire

Consider the simple electrical circuit shown in figure E6.4a, which consists of a single wire of resistance R connected to the two electrodes of a battery. In such a case, the potential difference $|\Delta\phi|$ between the wire's ends is the same as that between the battery's electrodes, which (for an ideal battery) is the same as the cell's emf $\mathcal{E}$. As discussed in the last chapter, surface charges on the wire ensure that the electric field everywhere in the wire points directly along the wire and has the uniform magnitude $E_1 = |\Delta\phi|/L \approx \mathcal{E}/L$. This will drive a current through the wire. According to the definition of resistance (equation E5.17), that current's magnitude will be $I_1 = |\Delta\phi|/R \approx \mathcal{E}/R$. For example, if the battery has an emf of 1.5 V, and the wire has a length of 0.2 m and a resistance of 3 Ω, the electric field strength and current flowing in the wire are

$$E_1 = \frac{1.5\,\cancel{\text{V}}}{0.2\,\cancel{\text{m}}}\left(\frac{1\,\cancel{\text{J}}/\text{C}}{1\,\cancel{\text{V}}}\right)\left(\frac{1\,\text{N}\cdot\cancel{\text{m}}}{1\,\cancel{\text{J}}}\right) = 7.5\,\frac{\text{N}}{\text{C}}, \quad I_1 = \frac{1.5\,\cancel{\text{V}}}{3\,\cancel{\Omega}}\left(\frac{1\,\cancel{\Omega}}{1\,\cancel{\text{V}}/\text{A}}\right) = 0.5\text{ A} \qquad \text{(E6.5)}$$

respectively. To maintain the potential difference between the terminals, the battery's "conveyor belt" will carry charge at the same rate through the battery to replace the charge that has flowed away from the positive electrode. Charge will thus circulate around this circuit at a steady rate until the battery dies.

The total emf of two batteries in series is the sum of the two batteries' emfs

Now imagine connecting two batteries in **series** (so that one cell's positive electrode touches the other's negative electrode) and connecting the other two electrodes with the same wire we used before, as shown in figure E6.4b. According to our ideal battery model, a charge carrier with (hypothetically positive) charge q receives an energy of $q\mathcal{E}_L$ as it goes through the left battery and an additional energy $q\mathcal{E}_R$ as it goes through the right battery, so it receives a total energy per unit charge of $\mathcal{E}_{\text{tot}} = \mathcal{E}_L + \mathcal{E}_R$ as it moves from the left battery's negative electrode to the right cell's positive electrode. (The gravitational analogy would be someone lifting a box from the ground to a height of 2.0 m and then handing it to someone else on a ladder who lifts it an additional 1.5 m: the total height through which the people lift the box is the sum of the heights lifted by each person.) So the emfs of batteries *add* if we connect them in series. This, by the way, is how we can connect six lead-acid *cells* with a characteristic emf of 2.1 V to yield an automobile battery with a characteristic emf of 12.6 V.

If the cells in our example are identical, the potential difference between the wire's ends is twice as large as it was in figure E6.4a, so the electric field in the wire is doubled ($E_2 = 15$ N/C), which means that the current flowing through the wire is doubled ($I_2 = 1$ A). The conveyor belts in both batteries

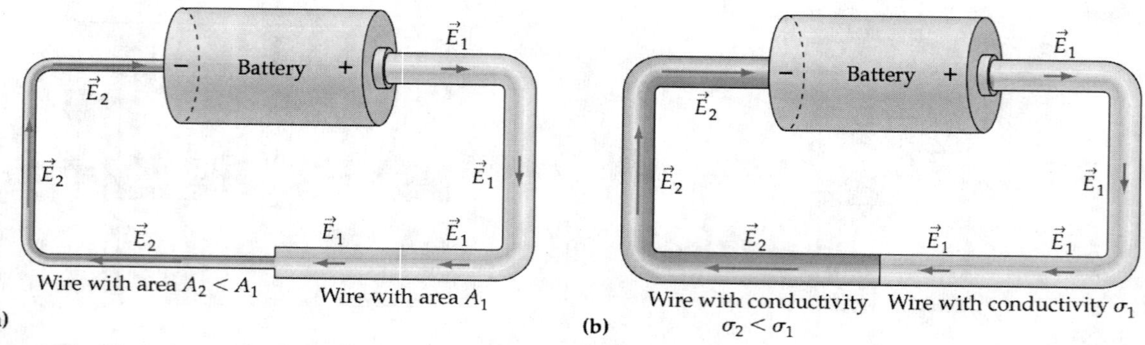

Figure E6.5
Circuits that involve a wire connected in series with otherwise identical wire having (a) a smaller diameter, o (b) a smaller conductivity.

have to run twice as fast as the belt in figure E6.4a to maintain the charge concentrations on the electrodes consistent with the characteristic potential difference that each battery strives to maintain between its electrodes. Remember always that *an ideal battery will drive whatever current is necessary to maintain its characteristic potential difference between its electrodes.*

Self-Test E6X.1

Imagine that we connect two 1.5-V alkaline cells in series with a wire whose length is 0.15 m and which has a resistance of 5 Ω. What is the magnitude of the electric field in the wire? What is the magnitude of the current that flows?

E6.3 Resistances in Series

Consider now the circuit shown in figure E6.5a, which consists of a battery whose terminals are linked by a sequence of two uniform wires with the same length L and conductivity σ_c but different cross-sectional areas A_1 and A_2. Figure E6.5b shows a similar circuit except that the wires have the same length L and cross-sectional area A but different conductivities σ_1 and σ_2.

The currents carried by wires in series must be *equal*

The feedback effects discussed in the previous chapter will ensure that in each case *the current carried by the right wire must be equal to that carried by the left wire.* Why? Imagine that the left wire initially conducts less current than the right wire. Positive charge would then pile up at the wires' junction, because the right wire supplies it with positive charge faster than the left wire carries it away. The excess of positive charge at the junction will slow down incoming positive charges from the right wire and speed up those departing in the other, reducing the difference between the currents. The accumulation of surface charge at the junction will only stop when the two wires' currents are equal.

But this means that the steady-state electric field strength E in the left wire must be greater than that in the right wire in both cases (as illustrated). Why? Since the current I carried by any reasonably thin wire of cross-sectional area A is $I = JA$, (where J is the magnitude of the current density) and $J = \sigma_c E$ (where σ_c is the wire's conductivity), we have $I = A\sigma_c E$ for both wires. Therefore, for I to be the same in both wires in figure E6.5a we must have $E \propto 1/A$, since both wires have the same conductivity. (Qualitatively, E is bigger in the thin wire because it has a smaller volume and so fewer charge carriers than the thick wire. The charge carriers it has thus must move faster in order to carry the same total current.) Similarly, for I to be the same in both wires in figure E6.5b, we must have $E \propto 1/\sigma_c$, since both wires have the cross-sectional area A. (Qualitatively, E must be bigger to push carriers through the left wire at the same speed as carriers flow through the more conductive right wire.)

The potential differences between the two wires' ends must be *unequal*

If the two wires have roughly the same length L, the fact that E is different in the two wires implies that the potential difference $V_L = E_L L$ between the left wire's ends is *not* the same as that for the right wire $V_R = E_R L$ (we can see, in fact, that $V_L > V_R$ in both cases above).

How the potential differences add

Now, once the surface charges on the wires have settled down to their stable steady-state distribution (their **dynamic equilibrium** distribution), the electrostatic potential at any point in space near or inside the wires will have a certain well-defined value ϕ relative to some reference point P. Imagine that point P is the battery's negative terminal. As the battery transports a given charge carrier to the positive plate, the carrier's electrostatic potential *increases* by $\Delta\phi_B$ (the potential difference across the battery). As it moves through the right wire, its potential changes by $\Delta\phi_R = -|\Delta\phi_R|$ (the potential is decreasing because the charge is moving "downhill" in the electric field), and as it moves through the left wire back to point P, its potential changes by the further amount $\Delta\phi_L = -|\Delta\phi_L|$. Since the carrier cannot have a different electrostatic potential at P after going around the circuit than it had before, it follows that

$$\Delta\phi_B + \Delta\phi_R + \Delta\phi_L = \Delta\phi_B - |\Delta\phi_R| - |\Delta\phi_L| = 0 \quad \Rightarrow \quad \Delta\phi_B = |\Delta\phi_R| + |\Delta\phi_L| \qquad \text{(E6.6)}$$

That is, the potential that a carrier gains in the battery must be equal to the potential that it loses as it goes through the wires.

The roller coaster analogy

I find it helpful to visualize this using a gravitational analogy. In chapter E4, we saw that the electrostatic potential ϕ at any point P is analogous to the gravitational potential ϕ_g, which near the earth is $\phi_g = gh$, where h is height above an arbitrary position where ϕ_g is defined to be zero. We can therefore use the following roller-coaster analogy. A charge carrier is analogous to a roller-coaster car. A battery is analogous to the motorized part of the track that lifts the car to the track's highest point, and the rest of the circuit is analogous to the unpowered part the track. Just as a charge carrier gains electrostatic potential energy from the battery and loses $q|\Delta\phi|$ to thermal energy in the wires, the car gains gravitational potential energy from the motor and loses an amount equal to $m(gh)$ to thermal energy as it coasts down the rest of the track. Just as the roller-coaster car returns to the same height after completing one complete trip around the track, so a charge carrier returns to the same potential after going once around the circuit. Since $|\Delta\phi|/L = E$ for a wire, the electric field magnitude E in a wire corresponds to the *slope* of the corresponding section of roller-coaster track. (Note that the section of track corresponding to each wire has a *constant* slope, which is atypical for a real roller-coaster.)

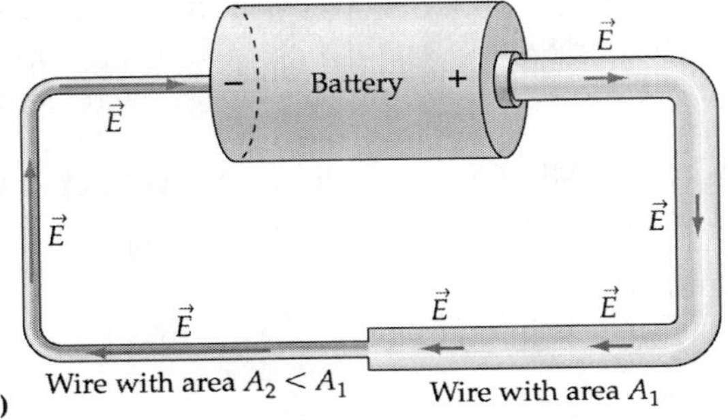

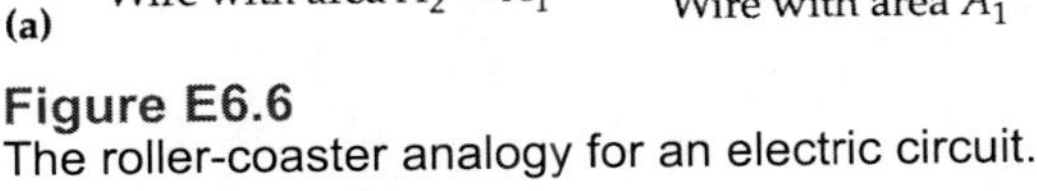

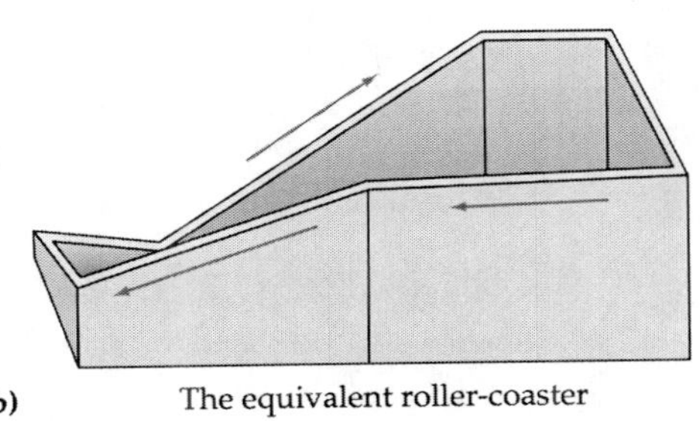

Figure E6.6
The roller-coaster analogy for an electric circuit.

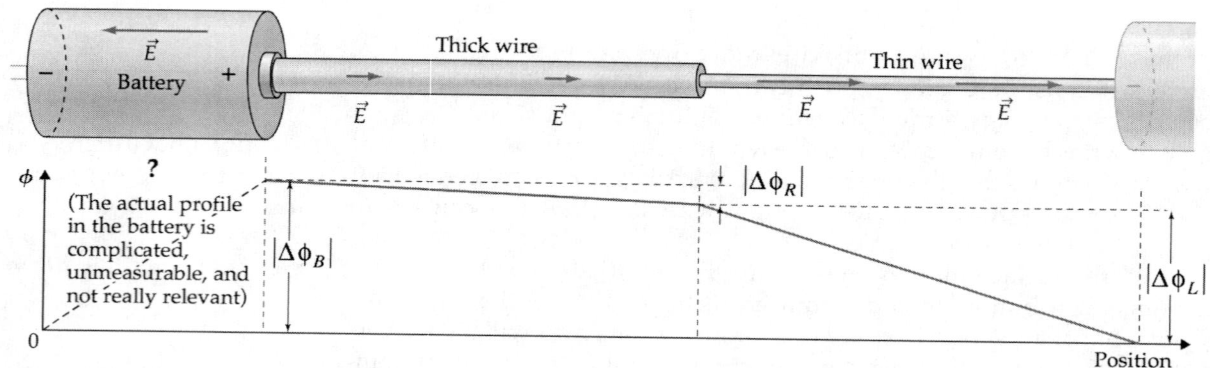

Figure E6.7
A graph of potential versus position for the circuit shown in figure E6.4a.

The potential (or "voltage") at a point in a circuit

It is often useful to talk about the potential (or **voltage**) at a given point in a circuit. Like the electrical potential energy on which it is based, the potential ϕ at any point in space near a charge distribution is only defined up to an overall constant, which we can choose by defining an arbitrary point to have zero potential. Once we have defined this reference position, the potentials of all other points are uniquely defined. In an electrical circuit, it is conventional to define the negative electrode of the battery or power supply to have $\phi = 0$.

Figure E6.7 shows a graph of potential ϕ versus position for the circuit shown in Figure E6.4a. We can make the the graph easier to draw by mentally unwrapping the circuit into a straight line as shown. Note that the slope of ϕ is $|\Delta\phi|/L = E$ = constant for each wire.

The symbol V is commonly used for the potential at a point in a *circuit*, though ϕ is conventional for the same concept in other contexts. Since V can also stand for volume and potential energy (an idea that is uncomfortably close to the concept of potential), I am going to stick with the symbol ϕ for the potential at a point in space, even if we are talking about a point in a circuit.

General definition of a set of circuit elements in series

The two-wire circuits shown in figure E6.4 are examples of **series circuits.** We say that the members of a set of wires and/or other devices (**circuit elements**) excluding batteries are connected "in series" if every charge carrier that flows through any *one* element flows through *all* elements in the set in sequence before returning to the battery. In such a case (as we saw in the two-wire case), surface charges on the conducting elements in the set will adjust themselves so that each element in the set carries the *same* current: $I = I_1 = I_2 = \ldots$.

This in turn implies that the potential difference between the ends of a given element (which we more often call "the potential difference *across*" or "the voltage drop *across*" that element) is generally *different* than that across another element. Indeed, the definition of resistance $R \equiv |\Delta\phi|/I \;\Rightarrow\; |\Delta\phi| = IR$ implies that if the resistance of the ith circuit element is R_i, the potential difference across that element is $|\Delta\phi_i| = IR_i$. Since each charge carrier must go through each element in sequence, the potential difference across the entire series set (analogous to the total altitude decrease one experiences going down a set of ladders) must be the *sum* of the potential differences across each element: $|\Delta\phi_{\text{set}}| = |\Delta\phi_1| + |\Delta\phi_2| + \ldots$.

These equations directly imply the following important and useful relation: total resistance of a set of elements in series is

$$R_{\text{set}} \equiv \frac{|\Delta\phi_{\text{set}}|}{I_{\text{set}}} = \frac{|\Delta\phi_1| + |\Delta\phi_2| + \ldots}{I} = \frac{|\Delta\phi_1|}{I} + \frac{|\Delta\phi_2|}{I} + \ldots$$

$$= \frac{|\Delta\phi_1|}{I_1} + \frac{|\Delta\phi_2|}{I_2} + \ldots = R_1 + R_2 + \ldots \qquad \text{(E6.7)}$$

Therefore, these equations characterize a set of circuit elements in series:

Equations characterizing a set of circuit elements in series

$$I = I_1 = I_2 = \ldots \quad \text{(E6.8a)}$$

$$|\Delta\phi_{set}| = |\Delta\phi_1| + |\Delta\phi_2| + \ldots \quad \text{(E6.8b)}$$

$$R_{set} = R_1 + R_2 + \ldots \quad \text{(E6.8c)}$$

Purpose: These equations describe a set of circuit elements in series.

Symbols: $I_1, I_2, \ldots$ and $|\Delta\phi_1|, |\Delta\phi_2|, \ldots$ and $R_1, R_2, \ldots$ are the currents flowing through, the potential differences across, and the resistances of circuit elements 1, 2, ... respectively. I is the common current flowing through all the elements, $|\Delta\phi_{set}|$ is the potential difference between the entire set's two ends, and R_{set} is the set's total resistance.

Limitations: This equation assumes that the circuit has settled into a steady state (dynamic equilibrium).

These equations are based on *very* basic principles. The current *must* be the same in each element, or charges would pile up somewhere in the circuit. The potential differences across the elements must add by the definition of "potential difference." The last equation follows directly from the definition of resistance. We have *not* even assumed that the circuit elements are ohmic.

We can use these equations to determine completely the current flowing in a series circuit and the potential difference across each element.

Example E6.1 Analysis of a Simple Series Circuit

Problem Suppose that we connect a 50-Ω wire in series with a 10-Ω wire and a 12-V battery. What is the current flowing in this circuit? What is the potential difference across each element?

Translation The series set of non-battery elements here is the two wires. Let $R_1 = 50\ \Omega$, $R_2 = 10\ \Omega$, and $|\Delta\phi_{set}| = |\Delta\phi_B| \equiv$ the battery's potential difference.

Model Assume that the battery is ideal, so $|\Delta\phi_B| = \mathscr{E}_B = 12$ V independent of I.

Solution Equation E6.8c implies that the set's total resistance is $R_{set} = R_1 + R_2 =$ 60 Ω. The current flowing through the set is therefore

$$I = \frac{|\Delta\phi_{set}|}{R_{set}} = \frac{12\ \cancel{V}}{60\ \cancel{\Omega}}\left(\frac{1\ \cancel{\Omega}}{1\ \cancel{V}/\text{A}}\right) = 0.20\ \text{A} \quad \text{(E6.9)}$$

This means that the potential differences across each wire are

$$|\Delta\phi_1| = I_1 R_1 = I R_1 = (0.20\ \cancel{A})(50\ \cancel{\Omega})\left(\frac{1\ \text{V}/\cancel{A}}{1\ \cancel{\Omega}}\right) = 10\ \text{V} \quad \text{(E6.10a)}$$

$$|\Delta\phi_2| = I R_2 = (0.20\ \cancel{A})(10\ \cancel{\Omega})\left(\frac{1\ \text{V}/\cancel{A}}{1\ \cancel{\Omega}}\right) = 2.0\ \text{V} \quad \text{(E6.10b)}$$

Evaluation The units work. Note that $|\Delta\phi_1| + |\Delta\phi_2| = 12\ \text{V} = |\Delta\phi_B|$, as expected.

Self-Test E6X.2

Say that the battery has an emf of 3.0 V, and the wires have resistances of 10 Ω and 2 Ω respectively. What are the potential differences across these wires?

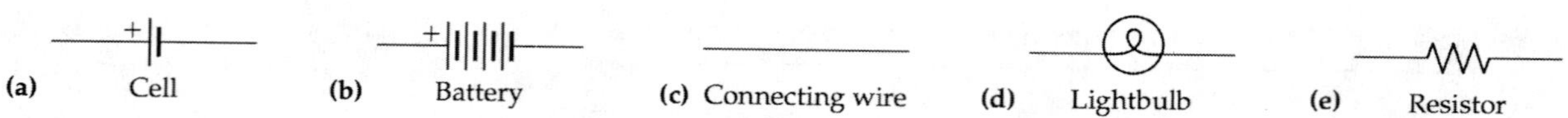

Figure E6.8
Conventional circuit diagram symbols for various circuit elements. Note that a cell's negative terminal is indicated by a shorter fat line and the positive terminal by a longer thin line.

E6.4 Notation Conventions and Circuit Diagrams

A convenient notation for the absolute value of a potential difference

One can see from the previous section that the absolute value of the potential difference between the ends of a circuit element is such a commonly used quantity that the notation $|\Delta\phi|$ becomes cumbersome. For this reason, people often use the symbol V (with a subscript specifying the object) for this quantity.

This notation is risky because V is also conventionally used for potential energy, a concept that people often have trouble distinguishing from potential, and because a simple symbol with no Δ or absolute value indicators invites one to forget that we are talking about the *absolute value* of a potential *difference*.

This notation is convenient and conventional, though, so (having duly warned you of the dangers) I will use it from now on. The following additional conventions help limit the problems. (1) I will use $q\phi$ instead of V_e for electrostatic potential energy from now on. (2) In this text, $V_{\text{obj}} \equiv |\Delta\phi_{\text{obj}}|$ is the *absolute value* of the potential difference between an object's ends: don't forget that V_{obj} is *always* positive. (3) If a and b are two points in a circuit, then $V_{ab} \equiv |\phi_a - \phi_b|$. (4) I will still use ϕ for the potential at a single point in a circuit.

Definition of a circuit diagram

A **circuit diagram** is a tool that helps us describe and visualize an electrical circuit. A real circuit may be a complicated three-dimensional nest of circuit elements, and it can be difficult to see which elements are connected and how. A circuit diagram represents the essential characteristics of the circuit in a two-dimensional diagram that clearly shows how its elements are connected.

Circuit elements are represented in a circuit diagram by conventional symbols that are both suggestive of the element in question and easy to draw. Figure E6.8 illustrates conventional symbols for a *cell*, a *battery*, a low-resistance connecting wire, a *light bulb*, and a *resistor*. (Conventional symbols also exist for many other kinds of elements that we will not consider in this course.)

Figure E6.9
A manufactured resistor.

Technically, a **resistor** is a circuit element manufactured to have a certain specified constant resistance. Such a resistor usually looks like a small cylinder with two connecting wires that emerge along the cylinder's axis; its resistance in ohms is often encoded as a sequence of four or five colored bands (see figure E6.9). Resistors are used in electrical circuits primarily to limit currents and/or control the value of the potential at a certain point in the circuit.

However, we often use the resistor symbol in a circuit diagram to represent any reasonably ohmic device (such as a wire, light bulb, electric motor, heating element or the like) whose resistance is much larger than that of the connecting wires. As long as the device is reasonably ohmic, all the potential differences and currents in a circuit would be the same if we replaced it by an equivalent resistor.

The flexibility one has in drawing connecting lines

Connecting wires in a circuit typically have negligible resistances compared to other circuit elements. On a circuit diagram, we use black lines to show the connections between elements. These connecting lines are assumed to have *zero* resistance and thus zero potential difference between their ends ($|\Delta\phi| = IR = I{\cdot}0 = 0$). The entire purpose of these lines is to display clearly how circuit elements are connected: the shape or length of the lines on a circuit diagram does *not* generally correspond to the shape or length of actual connecting wires in the real circuit. Indeed, if it improves the layout in a circuit diagram, we can either add lines that don't exist in the real circuit or choose not to show wires that do exist as long as the electrical connections between circuit elements are accurately represented.

If a wire's resistance is non-negligible, we indicate its resistance using a resistor symbol. For example, we can represent the circuit in figure E6.5a (the one involving a thick wire, thin wire, and battery in series) using a circuit diagram like figure E6.10. Note that lines have been added in the diagram where no connecting wires exist in the real circuit: it would be much harder to draw resistor symbols connected directly to the battery symbol. Note also that we almost always draw connection lines as vertical or horizontal straight lines that change direction in right angles (this also makes the diagram easier to draw).

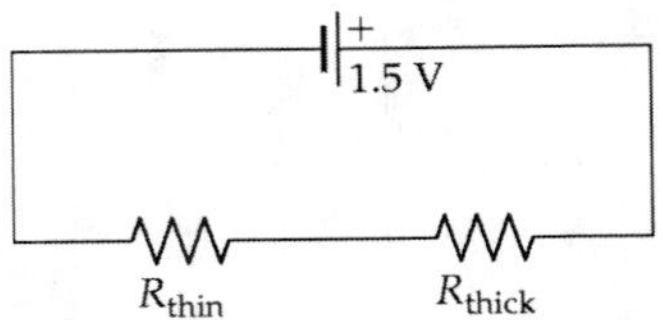

Figure E6.10
A circuit diagram for the circuit in figure E6.4a.

Example E6.2 Drawing a Circuit Diagram

Problem Draw a circuit diagram of the circuit depicted in part (a) of the following figure.

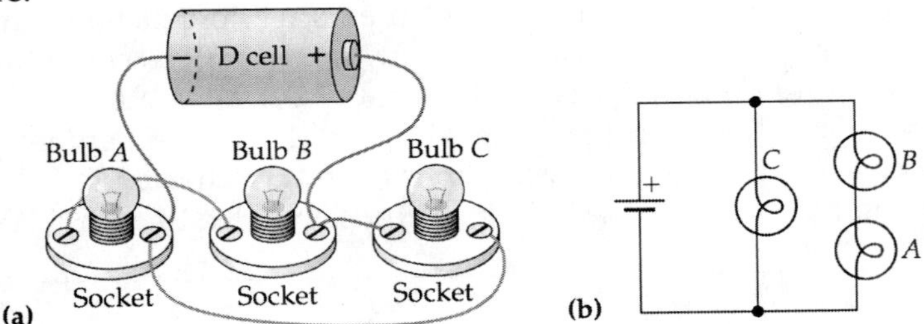

Solution The circuit diagram is shown as part (b). I have straightened and uncrossed the connecting wires, and reoriented the devices to make the circuit's structure clearer. I have ignored the light-bulb sockets: they merely facilitate the connections indicated on the diagram. The black dots on the diagram indicate connections: for example, one socket terminal for bulb C is connected both to one socket terminal for bulb B and the battery's positive electrode. It is irrelevant that the wire from the battery *actually* goes to the B socket first and a connection is made from there to bulb C: if the connecting wires really have zero resistance, it doesn't matter exactly *how* the two bulbs are connected to the battery, it just matters that they are.

There is no one correct way to draw a circuit diagram. I could have reoriented the diagram so that cell and light bulbs were horizontal. I could have drawn the part of the circuit containing bulb C to be outside of the part containing bulbs A and B. Any diagram that correctly represents how the elements are *connected* is equally valid: the *connections* are the important thing.

Self-Test E6X.3

Draw a circuit diagram for the circuit depicted below.

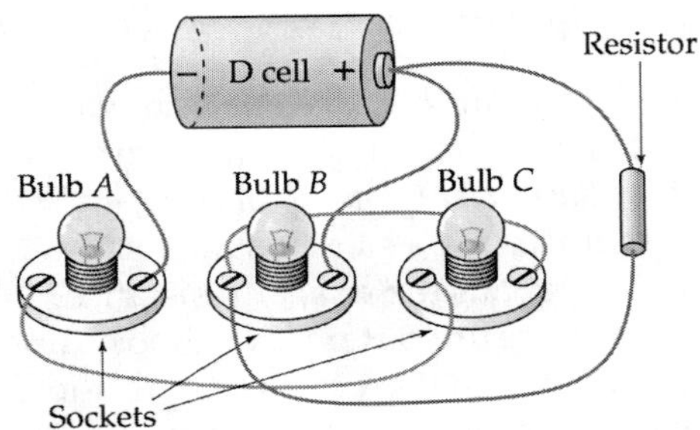

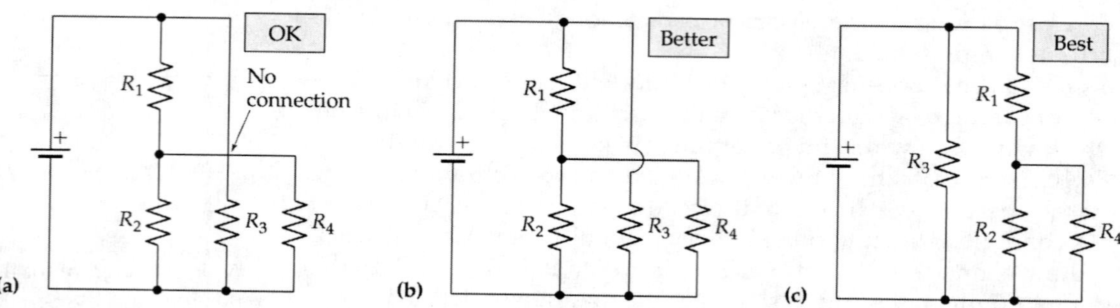

Figure E6.11
Three equivalent circuit diagrams illustrating conventions about crossing lines

About indicating connections

In diagrams for particularly complicated circuits, it may be impossible to indicate the connections between circuit elements without having lines cross each other. If lines do cross on a diagram, they are usually assumed *not* to be connected (see figure E6.11a) unless a black dot at the intersection specifically indicates a connection. A "bridge" (see figure E6.11b) is sometimes used to more clearly communicate that crossing lines are not connected. It is better yet to *avoid* drawing crossed unconnected lines if possible (see figure E6.10c).

Self-Test E6X.4

In figure E6.11, we exchanged the vertical columns involving R_3 and R_1 without affecting the diagram's validity. Can we exchange R_2 and R_4 without changing its validity? How about R_1 and R_2? Explain.

E6.5 Circuit Elements in Parallel

Consider the circuit shown in figure E6.12. In this circuit a given electron flowing out of the battery does *not* move through each of the resistors in sequence, but rather goes through one resistor *or* the other on the way back to the battery but not both. This is clearly not a *series* circuit of the type described earlier: we say that the resistors in this kind of circuit are connected **in parallel**.

The potential differences across parallel elements are the same but not the currents!

The potential difference $V_{ba} \equiv |\phi_b - \phi_a|$ between points a and b on the diagram will be essentially the same as that across each resistor (assuming the potential differences across the connecting wires are negligible):

$$V_{ba} = V_1 = V_2 \quad (= V_{\text{bat}} \text{ in this case}) \tag{E6.11}$$

Though the potential differences V_1 and V_2 across the resistors are the same, if $R_1 \neq R_2$, the *current* that potential difference drives through each resistor are *not*: since the definition of resistance implies that $V = IR$ for any object,

$$I_1R_1 = V_1 = V_2 = I_2R_2 \quad \Rightarrow \quad \text{if } R_1 \neq R_2,\ I_1 \neq I_2 \tag{E6.12}$$

So when the current comes to point b, it divides into two currents, one that goes through R_1 and one that goes through R_2 (these currents rejoin at point a). Equation E6.12 implies that *the current flowing in each parallel path is inversely proportional to that path's resistance* (once a steady state has been reached): *more* current flows through the path that has the *smaller* resistance.

Surface charges direct the correct amount of current along each path

How do the flowing electrons figure out how to choose among these paths in the correct proportions? The explanation is similar to the explanations offered in the last chapter: any deviation from the "correct" current flow sets up surface charges on the circuit's wires that oppose the incorrect flow, pushing

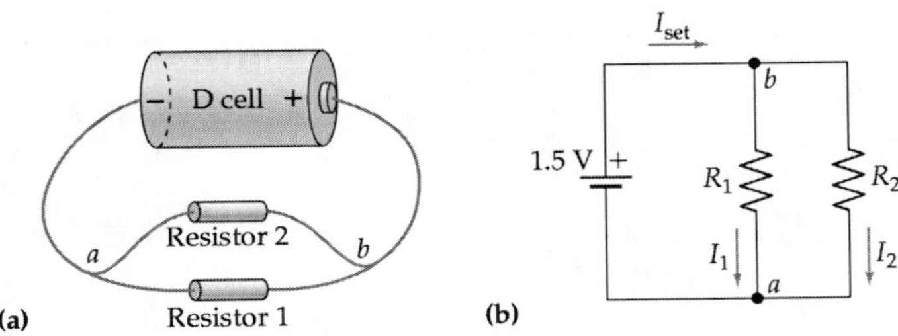

Figure E6.12
(a) A simple circuit involving two resistors in parallel. (b) A circuit diagram of the same circuit.

the flowing currents back toward the balance indicated by equation E6.12. For example, assume that $R_2 > R_1$, and imagine that electrons moving from the battery's negative electrode initially split randomly but equally at point b. But electrons move more slowly through R_2, so they will pile up at the entrance of R_2 like cars piling up at the entrance ramp of a jammed freeway. The piled-up electrons at the entrance of R_2 repel electrons that are still coming toward b, directing more and more of them toward R_1. Eventually (within a few nanoseconds) the balance described by $I_1R_1 = V_1 = V_2 = I_2R_2$ is attained: that is, most of the electrons approaching b are pushed by these surface charges through R_1 but a few continue to flow through R_2.

The equivalent resistance of a parallel pair of resistors

What is the *total* current flowing in this circuit? Once a steady-state current flow has been established, we won't have charge piling up anywhere, so the rate at which charge flows *into* any junction must be equal to the rate at which it flows out. Since "the rate at which charge flows" is simply the current, this means that the total current flowing through the battery (and thus the resistor pair) must be equal to the sum of the currents flowing through each resistor

$$I_{tot} = I_{set} = I_1 + I_2 \tag{E6.13}$$

If V_{set} is the potential difference between the ends of the resistor set, that set's resistance is defined to be

$$R_{set} \equiv \frac{V_{set}}{I_{set}} \quad \Rightarrow \quad \frac{1}{R_{set}} = \frac{I_{set}}{V_{set}} = \frac{I_{tot}}{V_{ba}} \tag{E6.14a}$$

Using equations E6.11 and E6.13, you can easily show that

$$\frac{1}{R_{set}} = \frac{I_1}{V_1} + \frac{I_2}{V_2} = \frac{1}{R_1} + \frac{1}{R_2} \tag{E6.14b}$$

Self-Test E6X.5

Verify equation E6.14*b*.

In general, we say that the members of a set of circuit elements are connected *in parallel* if (1) a given electron flowing through the set flows through only *one* element in the set and (2) the elements' ends are connected together so that the voltage difference across each element is *necessarily* the same as the voltage difference across the entire set (see figure E6.13). Therefore, the fundamental equations that characterize a set of parallel circuit elements are:

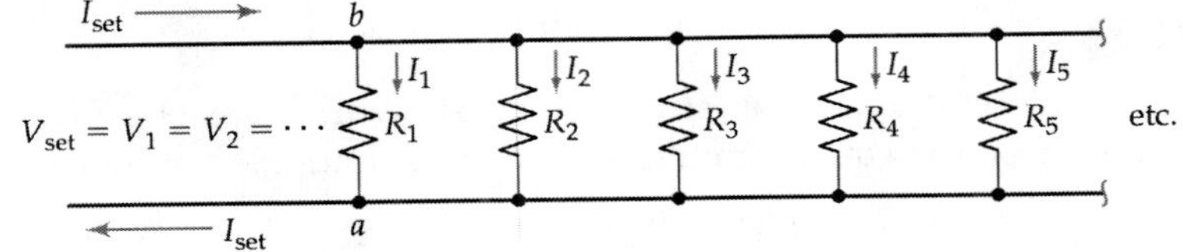

Figure E6.13
Circuit elements connected in parallel. The way that the ends of the elements are connected ensures that the potential difference across each element is the same, and that any current flowing through one element will *not* flow through any other.

Equations that characterize a set of elements in parallel

$$I_{set} = I_1 + I_2 + \ldots \tag{E6.15a}$$

$$V_{set} = V_1 = V_2 = \ldots \tag{E6.15b}$$

$$\Rightarrow \frac{1}{R_{set}} = \frac{1}{R_1} + \frac{1}{R_2} + \ldots \tag{E6.15c}$$

Purpose: These equations characterize a set of circuit elements in parallel.

Symbols: $I_1, I_2, \ldots$ and $V_1, V_2, \ldots$ and $R_1, R_2, \ldots$ are the currents flowing through, the potential differences across, and the resistances of circuit elements 1, 2, ... respectively. I_{set} is the current flowing through the set as a whole, V_{set} is the potential difference between the set's ends, and R_{set} is the total resistance of the entire set.

Limitations: This equation only applies after the circuit has settled into a steady state (dynamic equilibrium).

Self-Test E6X.6

Two nichrome wires with resistance of 3 Ω and 1 Ω are connected in parallel to a 1.5-V alkaline D-cell. What is the combined resistance of the wires? What total current flows through the battery?

E6.6 Analyzing Complex Circuits

How to analyze a complex circuit

Equations E6.8 and E6.15 provide powerful tools for analyzing more complex circuits. The elements in any circuit you are likely to encounter can be grouped into sets of parallel or series elements. Each set can then be replaced by an equivalent *single* resistor whose value we can calculate using equation E6.8c or E6.15c. By repeatedly reducing sets to single resistors, we can eventually reduce *all* elements to a single resistor. If the elements are at least approximately ohmic, we can then predict the current in the equivalent simple circuit using Ohm's law, and then work backwards to calculate currents and potential differences in any part of a circuit. Example E6.3 illustrates the process.

Example E6.3 Analyzing a Complex Circuit

Problem Assume that the light-bulbs in figure E6.14a are reasonably ohmic and all have resistances of 10 Ω. Determine the current flowing through every light bulb and the potential difference across every light bulb in the circuit.

Translation Figure E6.14b defines some useful symbols.

Model: We are assuming that the bulbs are ohmic and the battery is ideal.

Solution The first step is to find the equivalent resistance R_{all} of all the bulbs. According to equation E6.15c, the equivalent resistance R_{BD} of the parallel set consisting of bulbs B and D is

$$\frac{1}{R_{BD}} = \frac{1}{R_B} + \frac{1}{R_D} = \frac{1}{10\ \Omega} + \frac{1}{10\ \Omega} = \frac{2}{10\ \Omega} = \frac{1}{5\ \Omega} \tag{E6.16}$$

So $R_{BD} = 5\ \Omega$. Now this equivalent resistor is in series with bulbs A and C. Equation E6.8c implies that the equivalent resistance of the entire set of bulbs is

$$R_{all} = R_{BD} + R_A + R_C = 5\ \Omega + 10\ \Omega + 10\ \Omega = 25\ \Omega \tag{E6.17}$$

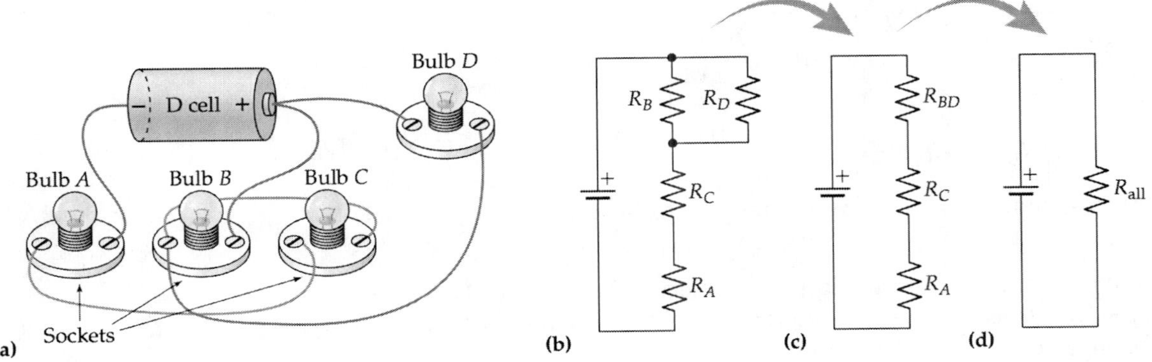

Figure E6.14
(a) A complex circuit. (b) A schematic diagram for this entire circuit (treating the bulbs as resistors). (c) Bulbs B and D are in parallel, so they can be reduced to the single equivalent resistance R_{BD}, whose value can be found using equation E6.15. (d) R_{BD} is in series with bulbs A and C, so the entire set can be replaced by a single equivalent resistor R_{all}, whose value can be found by using equation E6.8c.

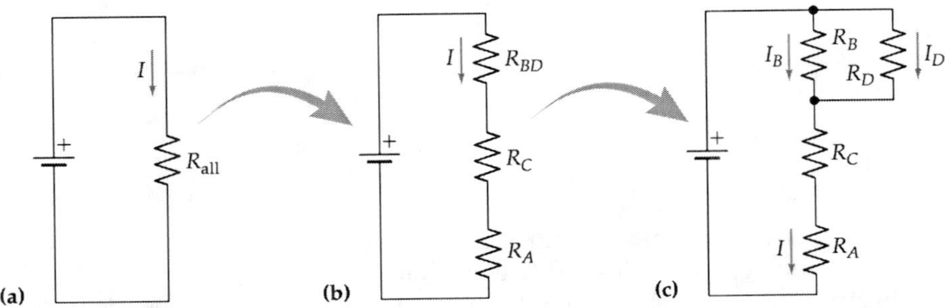

Figure E6.15
Reverse analysis of the circuit in figure E6.14. **(a)** $I = V_{bat}/R_{all}$ gives us the total current I flowing in the circuit. **(b)** We can then use $V = IR$ to find the potential differences across resistors *A*, *C*, and the set *BD*. Note that $V_{BD} = V_B = V_D$ by equation E6.15b. **(c)** We can use $V_B = I_B R_B$ and $V_D = I_D R_D$ to find I_B and I_D. This determines the currents flowing through and potential differences across every element in the circuit!

Now we can begin the reverse analysis illustrated in figure E6.15. The potential difference across the single resistor representing all the bulbs is the same as that across the battery. So the total current I flowing through this equivalent resistor is

$$I = \frac{V_{bat}}{R_{all}} = \frac{1.5\ \cancel{V}}{25\ \cancel{\Omega}}\left(\frac{1\ \cancel{\Omega}}{1\ \cancel{V}/A}\right) = 0.06\ A = 60\ mA \tag{E6.18}$$

This same current flows through all elements in a series set (see equation E6.8a), so $I_A = I_C = I_{BD} = 60\ mA$. We can now apply $V = IR$ individually to each of these three series elements to find the potential difference across each:

$$V_A = I_A R_A = (0.06\ \cancel{A})(10\ \cancel{\Omega})\left(\frac{1\ V/\cancel{A}}{1\ \cancel{\Omega}}\right) = 0.6\ V \tag{E6.19a}$$

$$V_C = I_C R_C = (0.06\ \cancel{A})(10\ \cancel{\Omega})\left(\frac{1\ V/\cancel{A}}{1\ \cancel{\Omega}}\right) = 0.6\ V \tag{E6.19b}$$

$$V_{BD} = I_{BD} R_{BD} = (0.06\ \cancel{A})(5\ \cancel{\Omega})\left(\frac{1\ V/\cancel{A}}{1\ \cancel{\Omega}}\right) = 0.3\ V \tag{E6.19c}$$

Equation E6.15b implies that the potential difference across the parallel pair of bulbs *B* and *D* is the same as that across each individual bulb: $V_B = V_D = V_{BD} =$ 0.3 V. This allows us to compute the current through each:

$$I_B = \frac{V_B}{R_B} = \frac{0.3\,\cancel{\text{V}}}{10\,\cancel{\Omega}}\left(\frac{1\,\cancel{\Omega}}{1\,\cancel{\text{V}}/\text{A}}\right) = 0.03\text{ A} = 30\text{ mA} \tag{E6.20a}$$

$$I_D = \frac{V_D}{R_D} = \frac{0.3\,\cancel{\text{V}}}{10\,\cancel{\Omega}}\left(\frac{1\,\cancel{\Omega}}{1\,\cancel{\text{V}}/\text{A}}\right) = 0.03\text{ A} = 30\text{ mA} \tag{E6.20b}$$

(Because the resistances of these bulbs happen to be the same, the currents through these bulbs also happen to be the same.)

Evaluation All the units came out right. Note also that $V_A + V_{BD} + V_C = 1.5\text{ V} = V_{\text{bat}}$ and $I_B + I_D = I$ as required by equations E6.8b and E6.15a respectively (this is a useful check on the calculations).

Self-Test E6X.7

Imagine that in the circuit shown in figure E6.14a, we remove bulb D from the circuit. What is the total current through the circuit now? What happens to the potential difference across bulb B?

E6.7 The Mystery du Jour

We have now learned a great deal about charges moving through conductors and about how to drive and control such currents. It might seem that we understand the physics of currents pretty thoroughly. However, there is a fundamental aspect of the physics of moving charges that awaits our exploration.

A beam of electrons traveling in a vacuum represents a current. We find that if we pass a beam of electrons near a permanent magnet, the beam is bent, and is bent only when the magnet is near. Electrons in the beam must therefore be responding to some force exerted on each by the magnet. Could this force be due to an electric field that the magnet creates? The answer is *no*.

Consider the experiment shown in figure E6.16, which shows an electron beam traveling in front of one face of a rectangular ceramic refrigerator magnet. The force exerted by the magnet on the electrons causes the beam to be deflected downward in the plane parallel to the magnet's face as shown. This deflection could be explained by an upward electric field, as shown in figure E6.16a. If such a field exists, then if we reverse the electrons' direction of motion, we would predict that they will *still* be deflected downward, as shown in figure E6.16b. However, if we do the experiment, we find that the electrons are deflected *upward*, as shown in figure E6.16c.

Therefore, the electric field model *fails* to explain what is happening to these moving electrons: there must be some new kind of physical effect acting on the electrons. What is this effect and how does it work? This is the mystery we will tackle in the next chapter.

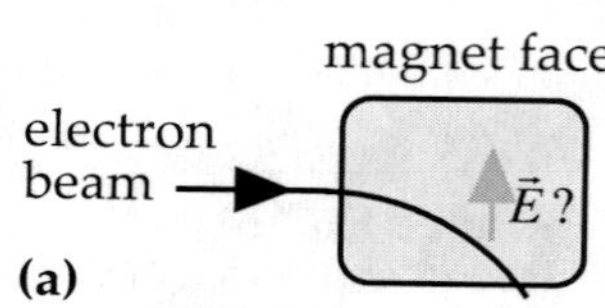

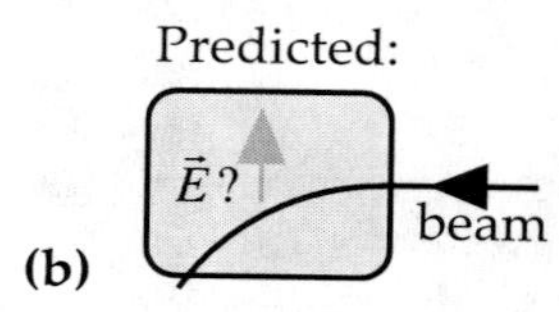

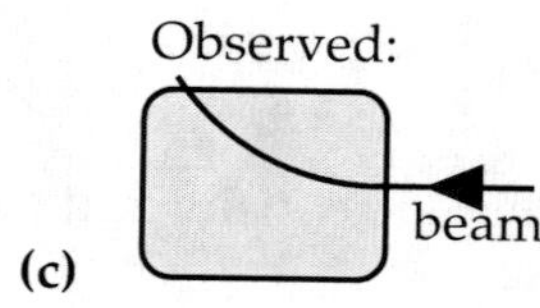

Figure E6.16
(a) The observed deflection of an electron beam passing in front of the face of a refrigerator magnet could be explained by an upward electric field. (b) If this is so, the beam will still be deflected downward if its direction is reversed. (c) However, the beam is observed to be deflected *upward*.

TWO-MINUTE PROBLEMS

E6T.1 The magnitude of the steady-state electric field in a given wire connected to a battery is proportional to the battery's emf, true or false (T or F)?

E6T.2 A battery always drives the same amount of current through a wire connecting its terminals (no matter what the wire's characteristics might be), T or F?

E6T.3 We have seen that we can construct a battery with a high potential difference between its terminals by connecting lower-potential batteries in series (see figure E6.4). We can also construct a battery by connecting the cells in *parallel*, that is connecting all the cells' positive terminals together and all the negative terminals together. What might be the advantage of doing this?

A. Again, the resulting battery will have a higher potential difference between its terminals than each individual cell
B. The resulting battery will last longer than an individual cell in the same circuit would
C. The resulting battery will be more ideal ($\mathscr{E}^{th}$ would be closer to zero for a given current) than a single cell
D. Both A and B
E. Both B and C
F. A, B, and C are all true
T. Their is no advantage to connecting batteries this way

E6T.4 Two identical light bulbs are connected to a battery as shown in the circuit diagram below. The dark black lines represent connecting wires with negligible resistance and the arrows indicate the direction of conventional current flow. Which bulb will conduct the greater current?

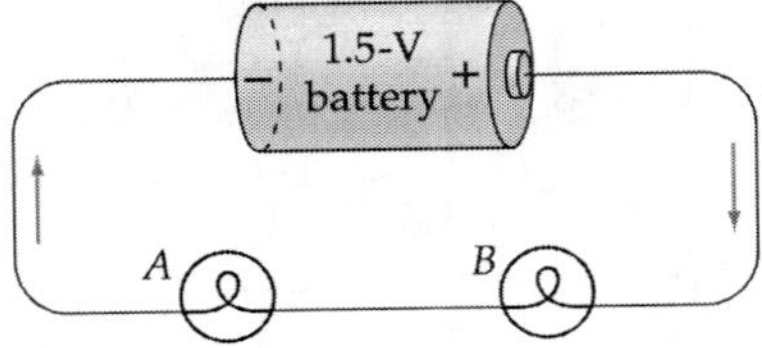

A. Bulb *A*
B. Bulb *B*
C. Each conducts the same *I*
D. Impossible to tell (could be either)

E6T.5 Bulbs *A* and *B* have resistances of 40 Ω and 10 Ω respectively in the diagram above. What is the potential difference across bulb *A*?

A. 1.5 V
B. 1.2 V
C. 0.75 V
D. 0.5 V
E. 0.3 V
F. 0.15 V

E6T.6 Imagine in the circuit described in problem E6T.4, we define ϕ to be zero in between the two bulbs. What is the potential at the battery's negative electrode? (Specify the magnitude of this potential using the answers to problem E6T.5, then specify the sign by $T = +$, $F = -$.)

E6T.7 Consider the circuit shown below. Which of the circuit diagrams below that figure correctly represents the circuit shown?

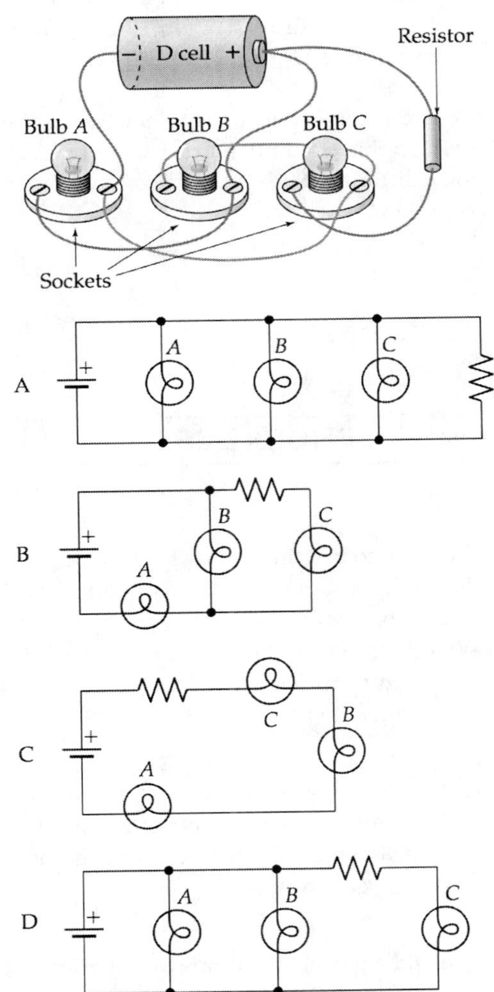

E6T.8 Consider the circuit shown below. If you were to unscrew bulb A from its socket (effectively removing it from the circuit and leaving a gap in its place), bulb B will

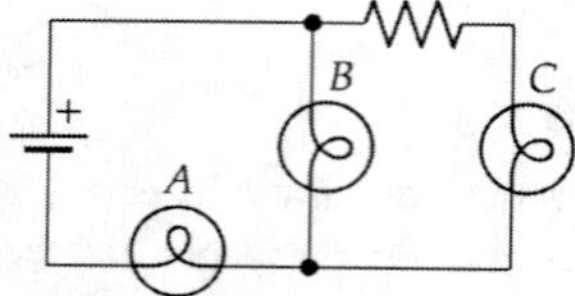

A. get brighter
B. get dimmer
C. remain the same
D. go out

E6T.9 Consider the circuit in problem E6T.8. If you were to unscrew bulb B from its socket (effectively removing it from the circuit and leaving a gap in its place), what will bulb A do? (Select from the answers provided for problem E6T.8.)

E6T.10 Consider the circuit in problem E6T.8. If each element in this circuit has a resistance of 12 Ω, what is the resistance of the entire circuit?
A. 48 Ω
B. 32 Ω
C. 24 Ω
D. 20 Ω
E. 12 Ω
F. 4 Ω

E6T.11 Consider the circuit shown below. If you were to unscrew bulb B from its socket (effectively removing it from the circuit and leaving a gap in its place), bulb A will

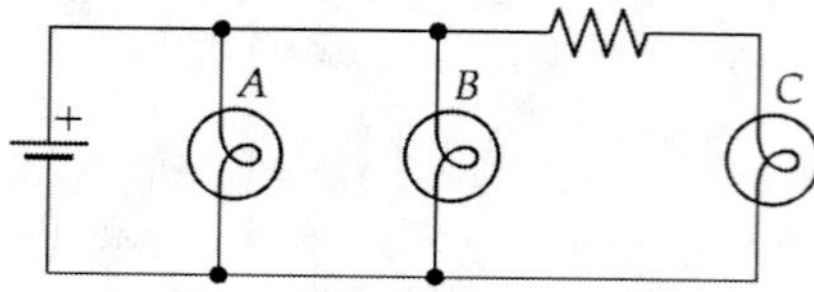

A. get brighter
B. get dimmer
C. remain the same
D. go out

E6T.12 In the circuit shown in problem E6T.11, the three bulbs are in parallel, T or F?

E6T.13 In the circuit shown in problem E6T.11, bulbs A and B are in series, T or F?

E6T.14 Imagine that two wires with the same length and conductivity are connected in *parallel* across a battery. Wire A has half the diameter of wire B. How do the strengths of the electric fields in each wire compare?
A. $E_A > E_B$
B. $E_A = E_B$
C. $E_A < E_B$

HOMEWORK PROBLEMS

Basic Skills

E6B.1 Imagine connecting a 10-Ω lightbulb and a 20-Ω lightbulb in series with a 1.5-V battery (using low-resistance wires that we can essentially ignore). What is the current flowing in this circuit? What is the potential difference across the 20-Ω light bulb?

E6B.2 Imagine that we connect a 1.5-V battery in series with two copper wires. Wire A has a resistance of 0.85 Ω and wire B has a resistance of 2.15 Ω. What current flows in this circuit? What is the potential difference across wire A?

E6B.3 You and a partner are doing an experiment on a circuit involving three objects in series with a 1.5-V battery. Your partner has measured the potential differences across each object and claims they are 0.45 V, 0.92 V and 0.23 V respectively. Explain why these cannot possibly be right.

E6B.4 Draw a circuit diagram for the circuit shown below.

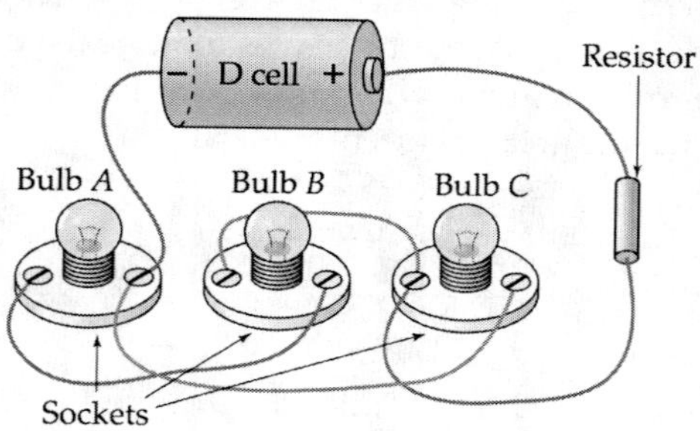

E6B.5 Draw a circuit diagram for the circuit shown below.

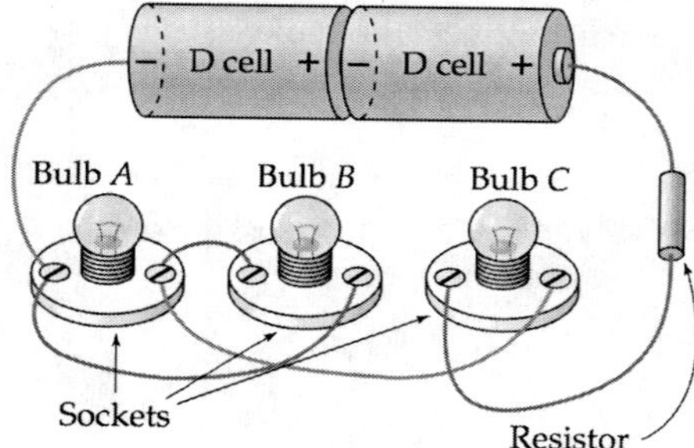

E6B.6 Imagine we connect a 12-Ω light bulb and an 8-Ω light bulb in parallel and connect the set to a 12-V battery. What is the total current flowing through the battery?

E6B.7 Imagine we connect a 10-Ω light bulb to a 6-V battery. What is the current flowing through the battery? Now imagine that we put a 50-Ω resistor in parallel with the light bulb. By what factor does the current through the battery increase?

E6B.8 If all of the light bulbs the circuit diagram below have a resistance of 10 Ω, what is the circuit's total resistance?

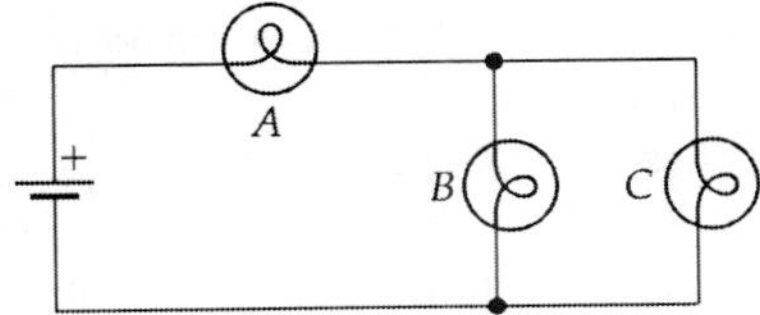

E6B.9 In the circuit diagram shown in problem E6B.8, are bulbs *A* and *B* in series? Explain your response.

E6B.10 If all of the light bulbs in the circuit diagram below have a resistance of 12 Ω, what is the circuit's total resistance?

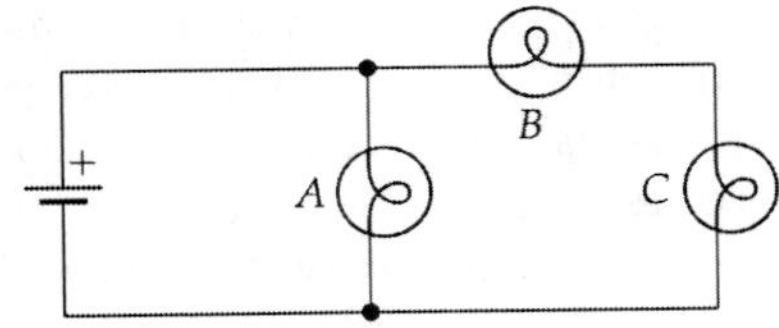

E6B.11 In the circuit shown in problem E6B.10, are bulbs *A* and *B* in parallel? Explain your response.

E6B.12 Imagine that we connect the terminals of a 1.5-V alkaline D cell with a wire 25 cm long, which then conducts a current of 30 A. At what rate will thermal energy be produced in the wire?

Synthetic

E6S.1 A 100-W household light bulb is plugged into a wall outlet using a 100-ft extension cord made with #18 copper wire (which has a diameter of 1.01 mm). If the potential difference across the two terminals of the outlet is 120 V, what is the potential difference across the light bulb?

E6S.2 Imagine a circuit consisting of three light bulbs with resistances 10 Ω, 20 Ω and 30 Ω connected in series with a 1.5-V battery, with the 10–Ω bulb closest to the battery's positive terminal. These circuit elements are all connected with low-resistance wires. Say that we define the terminal of the 20-Ω bulb closest to the positive end of the battery to be where $\phi = 0$. Draw a *quantitatively* accurate graph of potential versus position for this circuit.

E6S.3 Imagine that you connect two circuit elements with resistances R_1 and R_2 in series with a battery having a potential difference V_{bat} across its terminals. Imagine that we define the battery's negative terminal to have potential $\phi = 0$, which means that the battery's positive electrode has a potential $\phi = V_{bat}$. Assume that R_2 is attached to the battery's negative end. Find a formula for the potential at a point in the circuit between the two resistive circuit elements in terms of V_{bat}, R_1, and R_2. You may assume that all circuit elements are connected with wires with essentially zero resistance. Be sure to show your work. (This kind of circuit is called a *voltage divider,* and can be used to establish at the point between the two resistors a potential of any desired value between 0 and V_{bat})

E6S.4 Imagine an electric lawn mower has a motor that can produce 2.0 hp of mechanical power when connected directly to a normal electrical outlet. When using this motor outside, however, one is forced to connect the mower to an outlet using a 100-ft power cord consisting of two strands of #14 copper wire (each strand has a diameter of 1.63 mm). How much mechanical power can one expect out of the mower under these conditions?

E6S.5 Imagine that we measure the potential difference between the terminals of a certain alkaline cell to be 1.55 V when its electrodes are unconnected and 1.49 V when they are connected by a wire carrying a current of 1.0 A.**(a)** *Why* does the potential difference decrease when the cell conducts the current? **(b)** How much thermal energy is being produced in the battery every second in the second case?

E6S.6 Assume that all of the bulbs in the circuit shown in problem E6B.8 have a resistance of 10 Ω, and the cell has an emf of 1.5 V.

(a) Find the potential difference across and current conducted by each bulb.

(b) If bulb *C* were to be removed (leaving a nonconductive gap in its place, what would happen to the brightness of the other bulbs? Explain your reasoning carefully.

E6S.7 Assume that all of the bulbs in the circuit shown in problem E6B.10 have a resistance of 10 Ω, and the cell has a voltage of 1.5 V.

(a) Find the potential difference across and the current conducted by each bulb.

(b) If bulb *A* were to be removed (leaving a nonconductive gap in its place, what would happen to the brightness of the other bulbs? Explain your reasoning carefully.

E6S.8 Assume that all the elements in the circuit shown problem E6B.4 have a resistance of 12 Ω. Find the potential difference across each element and current conducted by each.

E6S.9 Assume that all the elements in the circuit shown in problem E6B.5 have a resistance of 12 Ω. Find the potential difference across each element and the current conducted by each.

E6S.10 A chemical battery's *capacity* expresses the total amount of charge that it send through a circuit, which is proportional to the total number of molecules of chemical reactants it contains. Thus a larger battery generally has more capacity than a small battery of the same type. A battery's capacity is generally expressed in ampere-hours (A·h), which is numerically equal to the number of hours that the battery could supply one ampere of current.

(a) Express 1 A·h in coulombs, as a number of electrons and in terms of moles of electrons.

(b) Imagine that you are designing a battery-powered toaster that uses 6 alkaline D-cells in series. While the toaster is on, it must produce at least 900 W of thermal energy. D-cells have a capacity of about 5 A·h. Roughly how long will your set of batteries run your toaster?

E6S.11 Consider a lead-acid cell of the type discussed in section E6.1.

(a) Explain why there must be essentially *no* electric field inside the conducting sulfuric acid solution except in microscopically thin regions around the electrodes (this is pretty much true even if the battery is conducting a significant current). You might draw a picture of showing how concentrations of various molecules vary near each electrode.

(b) What are the charge carriers in the sulfuric acid solution, and which way do they move? (These carriers travel by diffusion).

(c) Battery capacity is measured in ampere-hours, which specifies how long the battery can supply a current of 1 A (see problem E6S.10). Show that 1 A·h represents 0.0373 moles of electrons.

(d) The cell can only supply a current if there is lead and lead dioxide and bisulfate ions left in the cell to react. Lead, sulfur, oxygen, and hydrogen have atomic weights of 207, 32, 16, and 1 g/mole respectively. Estimate the minimum mass of a cell whose capacity is 100 A·h, the approximate capacity of a car battery.

(e) A typical car battery consists of six lead-acid cells wired in series. What must its mass be to have 100 A·h of capacity? Explain.

E6S.12 When a non-ideal battery conducts current, moving ions in the electrolyte collide with other molecules and convert potential energy to thermal energy in much the same way that electrons moving in a wire do. We can therefore model a non-ideal battery as if it were an ideal battery connected to an "internal resistor" R_{int}. Devise a way to measure the internal resistance of a battery using an external resistor and a voltmeter. (*Hint:* See problem E6S.3).

Rich-Context

E6R.1 Imagine that your uncle has an electric winch that he uses to haul his sailboat out of the water up into a trailer. The winch is connected to the car's 12-V battery and draws 240 W of power. One day, you and your uncle are using the sailboat at a place where you can't get the car close to the landing. So you go to the convenience store and buy four standard thickness (1.01-mm diameter) 25-foot, 2-wire extension cords and connect them together, giving you essentially a 100-ft extension cord. You wheel the trailer down to the landing and park the car on the road about 80 ft away. You then use jumper cables to connect the two prongs on one end of the cord to the car battery, and connect the two wires at the other end of the extension cord to the winch. But when you turn on the winch, nothing happens. You carefully verify that one end of the battery is indeed connected to one end of the winch through the extension cord, and the other end of the battery is connected to the other terminal of the winch through the other wire in the 2-wire extension cord. As you are doing this, you notice that the extension cord is getting *hot*. What is going on? Why doesn't the winch work? Why is the cord getting hot? Explain with the help of a calculation.

E6R.2 An inventor claims to have created a chemical cell that involves nickel and iron plates immersed in a secret solution. The cell has a characteristic voltage of 1.3 V. The cell has a mass of 100 g and the inventor claims a capacity of 250 A·h. A cell with this mass and capacity would sell like hotcakes. But is the inventor's claim physically impossible? Defend your response carefully (there is some serious money at stake here!). (*Hint:* See problem E6S.10.)

E6R.3 Imagine that you have N identical non-ideal batteries, each with emf $\mathscr{E}$ and internal resistance R_{int} (see problem E6S.12). Imagine that we connect these batteries to an external resistor with resistance R. Show that if $R >> R_{\text{int}}$, much more current flows through the external resistor if you connect the batteries in series, but if $R = R_{\text{int}}$, the current is the same whether you connect the batteries in series or parallel!

ANSWERS TO SELF-TESTS

E6X.1 The two 1.5-V cells in series will comprise a battery with an effective emf of $\mathscr{E} = 3.0$ V. If the battery is reasonably ideal, then the potential difference across the wire will be $|\Delta\phi| \approx \mathscr{E}$. If the wire has length L = 0.15 m, the electric field in the wire is

$$E = \frac{|\Delta\phi|}{L} = \frac{3.0\,\cancel{\text{V}}}{0.15\,\cancel{\text{m}}}\left(\frac{1\,\cancel{\text{J}}/\text{C}}{1\,\cancel{\text{V}}}\right)\left(\frac{1\,\text{N}\cdot\cancel{\text{m}}}{1\,\cancel{\text{J}}}\right) = 20\,\frac{\text{N}}{\text{C}} \qquad \text{(E6.21)}$$

The definition of resistance implies that

$$I = \frac{|\Delta\phi|}{R} = \frac{3.0\,\cancel{\text{V}}}{5.0\,\cancel{\Omega}}\left(\frac{1\,\cancel{\Omega}}{1\,\cancel{\text{V}}/\text{A}}\right) = 0.60\text{ A} \qquad \text{(E6.22)}$$

E6X.2 Because resistances in series add, $R_{\text{tot}} = 12\ \Omega$. The total current in the circuit is thus

$$I = \frac{|\Delta\phi_{\text{batt}}|}{R} = \frac{3.0\,\cancel{\text{V}}}{12\,\cancel{\Omega}}\left(\frac{1\,\cancel{\Omega}}{1\,\cancel{\text{V}}/\text{A}}\right) = 0.25\text{ A} \qquad \text{(E6.23)}$$

Since this current flows through each wire individually, the potential difference across the thick wire is $|\Delta\phi_{\text{thick}}| = IR_{\text{thick}} = (0.25\text{ A})(2\text{ V/A}) = 0.5$ V. Similarly, $|\Delta\phi_{\text{thin}}| = 2.5$ V.

E6X.3 One possible circuit diagram looks as shown below. It is possible to reorient the elements in different ways, but the basic connections in your diagram should be the same as in this diagram.

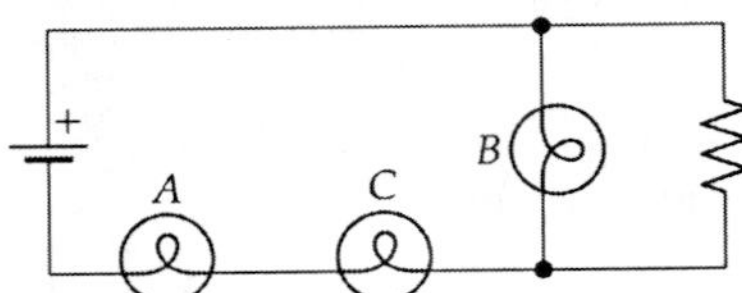

E6X.4 It does not matter whether R_2 or R_4 is on the right. It does matter whether it is R_2 or R_1 that is connected to the battery's positive electrode, though, so exchanging these resistors would make the diagram invalid.

E6X.5 Since $I_{\text{set}} = I_1 + I_2$ and $V_{\text{set}} = V_1 = V_2$, we have

$$\frac{1}{R_{\text{set}}} = \frac{I_{\text{set}}}{V_{\text{set}}} = \frac{I_1 + I_2}{V_{\text{set}}} = \frac{I_1}{V_{\text{set}}} + \frac{I_2}{V_{\text{set}}} = \frac{I_1}{V_1} + \frac{I_2}{V_2} = \frac{1}{R_1} + \frac{1}{R_2} \qquad \text{(E6.24)}$$

E6X.6 The combined resistance is:

$$R_{\text{set}} = \left[\frac{1}{R_1} + \frac{1}{R_2}\right]^{-1} = \left[\frac{1}{3\ \Omega} + \frac{1}{1\ \Omega}\right]^{-1} = \left[\frac{4}{3\ \Omega}\right]^{-1} = \frac{3\ \Omega}{4} \qquad \text{(E6.25)}$$

The current through the battery is thus

$$I_{\text{bat}} = I_{\text{set}} = \frac{V_{\text{set}}}{R_{\text{set}}} = \frac{1.5\,\cancel{\text{V}}}{3\,\cancel{\Omega}/4}\left(\frac{1\,\cancel{\Omega}}{1\,\cancel{\text{V}}/\text{A}}\right) = 2.0\text{ A} \qquad \text{(E6.26)}$$

E6X.7 *Model* Assume that all the bulbs are ohmic and have a resistance of 10 Ω (as in Example E6.3).

Solution Then if we remove bulb D, the remaining bulbs are in series, and so have a total resistance of

$$R_{\text{set}} = R_A + R_B + R_C = 30\ \Omega \qquad \text{(E6.27)}$$

The total current is thus $I = V_{\text{set}} / R_{\text{set}} = 0.05$ A. The potential difference across B was originally 0.3 V (see equation E6.19c), but now has increased to

$$V_B = I_B R_B = (0.05\,\cancel{\text{A}})(10\,\cancel{\Omega})\left(\frac{1\text{ V}/\cancel{\text{A}}}{1\,\cancel{\Omega}}\right) = 0.5\text{ V} \qquad \text{(E6.28)}$$

E7 Magnetic Fields

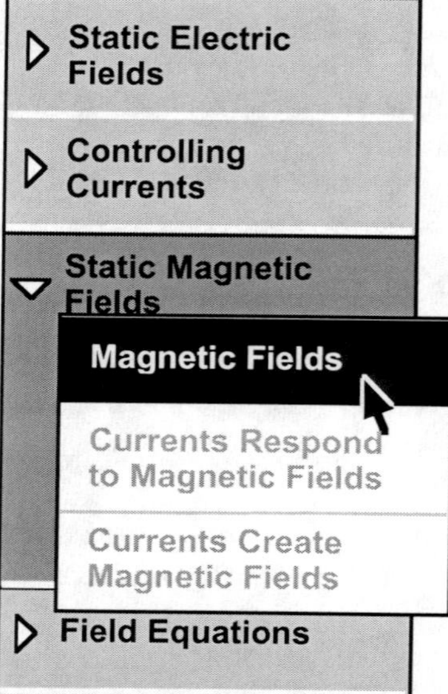

Chapter Overview

Introduction

This chapter opens a new subdivision on static magnetic fields by discussing the behavior of magnets, the definition of the magnetic field vectors $\vec{B}$ and $\vec{\mathbf{B}}$, and how magnetic fields affect moving charged particles.

Section E7.1: The Phenomenon of Magnetism

The following properties of magnets have been known since at least the late 1500s:

1. Every **magnet** has exactly two **magnetic poles**, a **north** pole and a **south** pole.
2. Like poles repel , but unlike poles attract.
3. A magnet's poles cannot be isolated.
4. Magnets strongly attract certain (**ferromagnetic**) substances.
5. A freely suspended magnet (a **magnetic compass**) will align itself so that its north pole points toward the earth's geographic north pole.

Section E7.2: The Definition of the Magnetic Field Direction

We can describe a magnet's **magnetic field** by assigning to every point in space around the magnet a magnetic field vector $\vec{B}$ whose *direction* is the "northward" direction indicated by a compass needle placed at that point and whose *magnitude* reflects how vigorously the compass responds to the field. (We could have defined $\vec{E}$ in a similar way using a suspended electric dipole instead of a compass.)

Indeed, (1) magnets repel and attract each other just like dipoles attract and repel each other. (2) A magnet's magnetic field is very similar to a dipole's electric field at points far from each. (3) A magnet responds to an external magnetic field like a dipole responds to an external electric field. This *analogy* between magnets and electric dipoles is useful, but *magnets are not the same as electric dipoles.* Unlike dipoles, for example, magnetic poles cannot be separated, and magnets have no effect on stationary charges.

Section E7.3: Magnetic Forces on Moving Charges

We find empirically that magnetic fields *do* exert forces on *moving* charges. We can experimentally examine these forces using the electron beam in a **cathode ray tube (CRT)**. Experiments show that a magnetic field $\vec{B}$ exerts a force on a moving charged particle that is perpendicular to both $\vec{B}$ and the particle's velocity $\vec{v}$ in the direction indicated by one's right thumb if one's right index finger points in the direction of $q\vec{v}$ and one's second finger in the direction of $\vec{B}$.

Section E7.4: A Review of the Cross Product

The cross product $\vec{u}\times\vec{w}$ of two arbitrary vectors $\vec{u}$ and $\vec{w}$ is a vector that is also perpendicular to $\vec{u}$ and $\vec{w}$ in the sense indicated by one's right thumb. Such a cross product has the following additional mathematical properties:

$$\text{mag}(\vec{u}\times\vec{w}) = uw\sin\theta \qquad (\theta \text{ is the angle between } \vec{u} \text{ and } \vec{w}) \qquad \text{(E7.2)}$$

$$\vec{u}\times\vec{w} = -\vec{w}\times\vec{u} \qquad (\text{the cross product is } \textit{anticommutative}) \qquad \text{(E7.3a)}$$

$$\vec{u}\times(\vec{w}+\vec{a}) = \vec{u}\times\vec{w} + \vec{u}\times\vec{a} \quad \text{(the cross product is } \textit{distributive}\text{)} \qquad \text{(E7.3b)}$$

$$\vec{u}\times(b\vec{w}) = b(\vec{u}\times\vec{w}) \quad \text{(the cross product is } \textit{linear}\text{)} \qquad \text{(E7.3c)}$$

$$\vec{u}\times\vec{u} = 0 \qquad \text{(E7.3d)}$$

$$\vec{u}\times\vec{w} = 0 \quad \Leftrightarrow \quad \vec{u} \parallel \pm\vec{w} \quad \text{(assuming } \vec{u}\neq 0 \text{ and } \vec{w}\neq 0\text{)} \qquad \text{(E7.3e)}$$

The magnitude of $\vec{u}\times\vec{w}$ is equal to the area of the parallelogram formed by $\vec{u}$ and $\vec{w}$, and is u times the magnitude of the component of $\vec{w}$ perpendicular to $\vec{u}$ or vice versa.

Section E7.5: The Definition of the Magnetic Field Magnitude

Using the cross product, we can define the magnetic field magnitude so that

$$\vec{F}_m = q\vec{v}\times\vec{B} = q\left(\frac{\vec{v}}{c}\times\vec{\mathbf{B}}\right) \qquad \text{(E7.9)}$$

Purpose: This equation specifies the magnetic force $\vec{F}_m$ acting on a charged particle with charge q moving with velocity $\vec{v}$ at a point where the magnetic field vector is $\vec{B}$ or $\vec{\mathbf{B}}$.

Symbols: c is the speed of light.

Limitations: This equation only works for charged *particles*.

Notes: The SI unit for $\vec{B}$ is the *tesla*, where $1\ \text{T}=1\,(\text{N/C})(\text{m/s})^{-1}$; the SI units for $\vec{\mathbf{B}}$ are merely N/C, and $\vec{\mathbf{B}}=c\vec{B}$. This equation works when $v\approx c$ if we define $\vec{F}_m$ to be the rate at which the interaction delivers relativistic momentum.

This equation defines the magnitudes of the magnetic field vectors $\vec{B}$ and $\vec{\mathbf{B}}$ by linking them quantitatively to the previously defined quantities of force, charge, and velocity. Magnetic fields are usually described using $\vec{B}$, but we will find the alternative magnetic field vector $\vec{\mathbf{B}}$ ("B-bar") very useful because it has the same units as $\vec{E}$.

Section E7.6: A Free Particle in a Magnetic Field

Equation E7.9 also implies that an otherwise free particle moving in a uniform magnetic field follows a helical trajectory around and along the magnetic field direction. The following equations describe this trajectory.

$$R = \left|\frac{p_\perp c}{q\mathbf{B}}\right| = \left|\frac{p_\perp}{qB}\right| \qquad \text{(E7.15a)}$$

$$T = \frac{2\pi mc}{|q|\,\mathbf{B}\sqrt{1-v^2/c^2}} \approx \frac{2\pi mc}{|q|\mathbf{B}} \quad (\text{if } v \ll c) \qquad \text{(E7.15b,c)}$$

$$p_\parallel = \text{constant} \qquad \text{(E7.15d)}$$

Purpose: These equation describe features of the helical motion of a particle with charge q and (possibly relativistic) momentum $\vec{p}$ moving in a reasonably uniform magnetic field described by $\vec{\mathbf{B}}$.

Symbols: R is the radius of the helix's circular envelope, T is the time required to go once around the helix, $p_\parallel$ and $p_\perp$ are the components of the particle's relativistic momentum parallel to and perpendicular to $\vec{\mathbf{B}}$ respectively, v is the particle's speed, c is the speed of light, and $B\equiv \mathbf{B}/c$ is the magnetic field strength in teslas.

Limitations: The magnetic field must be nearly uniform over the region spanned by one cycle of the helix.

E7.1 The Phenomenon of Magnetism

A brief history of magnetism

Ancient texts show that magnetism was known and described in Greece as early as 800 BC. *Magnetite,* a certain oxide of iron found in many parts of the world (but especially in the Greek province of Magnesia), can exhibit substantial magnetic effects even in its natural state. In western Europe before the Renaissance, people considered magnets to be occult objects because of the uncanny nature of the forces they exerted. However, magnetic compasses were one of several new navigational tools that helped European sailors freely roam the globe in the 1500s and 1600s, and daily use by sailors eventually undercut superstition about magnetism. The British physicist William Gilbert was one of the first people to investigate magnetism scientifically: because of the comprehensive and careful work described in his book *De Magnete* (1600), magnetism was better understood than electricity for more than a century.

Empirically observed properties of magnets

Gilbert described the following important empirical properties of magnets:

1. Every **magnet** has exactly two **magnetic poles**, a **north** pole and a **south** pole (we will discuss the reason for these names shortly).
2. North poles repel north poles and south poles repel south poles, but unlike poles attract.
3. A magnet's poles cannot be isolated: breaking a magnet in half merely creates two magnets, (each with its own north and south pole).
4. Either pole of a magnet can strongly attract certain (**ferromagnetic**) objects that are not themselves magnets, but most substances are only *very* weakly affected by magnets.
5. A freely suspended magnet (a **magnetic compass**) will align itself so that its north pole points toward the earth's geographic north pole (hence the names for a magnet's poles).

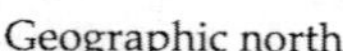

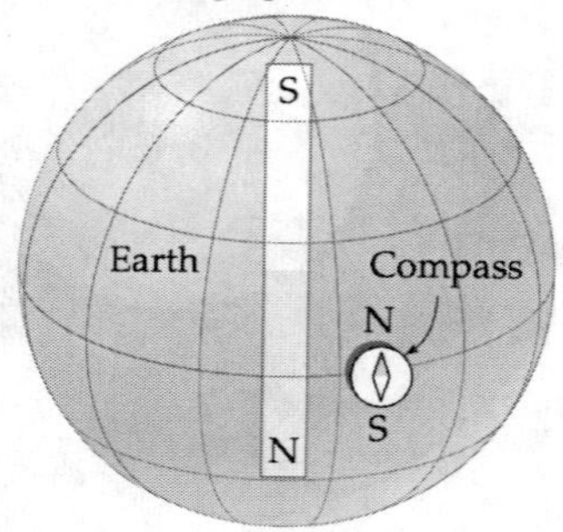

Figure E7.1
The conventional rule for naming magnetic poles says that when a magnet is used as a compass, the pole that ends up pointing toward the earth's geographic north pole is the magnet's north pole. This means that the earth's geographic north pole is a magnetic *south* pole, since it attracts the compass magnet's north pole.

Gilbert also seems to have been the first to recognize that the last item implies that the earth *itself* is a magnet. Since the north pole of a compass magnet is attracted to a magnetic *south* pole, the earth's geographic north pole must be a magnetic south pole, as illustrated in figure E7.1† .

E7.2 The Definition of the Magnetic Field Direction

Just as we can describe the electrostatic interaction between two charged objects using a field theory that assigns an electric field vector $\vec{E}$ to every point in space, so we can describe the magnetic interaction between magnetic poles using a field theory that assigns a magnetic field vector $\vec{B}$ to every point in space. Indeed, we *need* a field theory for magnetic interactions for the same reason we need a field theory for electrostatic interactions: only a field theory can be consistent with special relativity.

Definition of the magnetic field vector at a point

In the case of magnetism, we can define the *direction* of $\vec{B}$ at a given point to be the direction a compass needle at that point would indicate is "northward," and we qualitatively define the *magnitude* of $\vec{B}$ to reflect how vigorously the compass responds to the field at that point (see figure E7.2).

A common way to display a magnet's magnetic field is to sprinkle iron filings on a sheet of paper on top of the magnet. The filings at a given point align

†Actually, the earth's magnetic south pole is located just north of Hudson's Bay in Canada, about 1300 km from the earth's geographic north pole. The location, strength, and even polarity of the earth's magnetic poles are known to vary over geological time, and the details about exactly how the earth maintains its magnetism remain unclear.

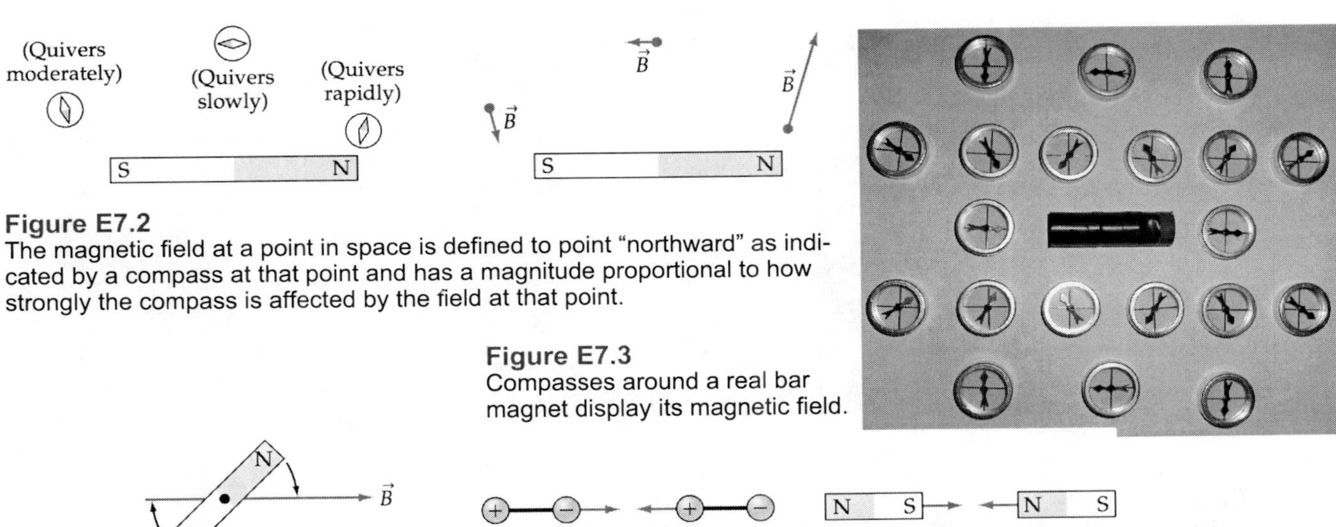

Figure E7.2
The magnetic field at a point in space is defined to point "northward" as indicated by a compass at that point and has a magnitude proportional to how strongly the compass is affected by the field at that point.

Figure E7.3
Compasses around a real bar magnet display its magnetic field.

(a) $\vec{F} = q\vec{E}$ (b)

Figure E7.4
(a) Just as a magnet seeks to align itself with the magnetic field direction in its vicinity (by definition), an electric dipole seeks to align itself with the electric field direction in its vicinity. (b) Electric dipoles attract and repel each other just as magnets do.

themselves with the direction of the magnetic field at that point because the magnet's field actually magnetizes each iron filing, making it a weak magnet that aligns itself with the magnetic field as a compass would (see figure E7.3).

In chapter E2, we defined the electric field vector $\vec{E}$ at a point in terms of the electrostatic force the field exerts on a charged particle at rest, but we *could* have defined $\vec{E}$ in a way very similar to the way we have just defined $\vec{B}$. Figure E7.4a illustrates that the electrostatic forces acting on the charges at a suspended electric dipole's ends will cause that dipole to align itself with the direction of $\vec{E}$ just as a compass aligns itself with the direction of $\vec{B}$. The definitions of $\vec{E}$ and $\vec{B}$ are thus really quite similar.

Magnets are *analogous* to electric dipoles

Magnets and electric dipoles are similar in other ways. The like poles of two magnets repel each other and the unlike poles attract, just as the like ends of two dipoles repel and the unlike ends attract (see figure E7.4b). Indeed, the forces that two magnets exert on each other depend on their relative separation and orientation exactly as the forces between two similarly-shaped electric dipoles would. Moreover, if we use a compass to plot out the magnetic field of a bar or horseshoe magnet we find that (as long as the magnet's pole faces are small compared to the distance separating them) its magnetic field is almost identical to the electric field of an electric dipole (see figure E7.5). I recommend memorizing the fact that magnetic field vectors near a magnet point *away* from its north pole and *toward* its south pole as shown in figure E7.5 (just as $\vec{E}$ points away from a positive charge and toward a negative charge).

But magnets are not the *same* as electric dipoles

We will find the dipole analogy for magnets very useful in what follows. However, it is crucial to understand that this is just an *analogy*: magnets are not the *same* as electric dipoles, nor are magnetic poles the same as electric charges. For example, magnetic poles do not exert forces on charged particles at rest, while the ends of an electric dipole do. The kinds of neutral substances that respond strongly to magnets do not generally respond strongly to electric dipoles. Moreover, while we can easily find or make isolated objects that have

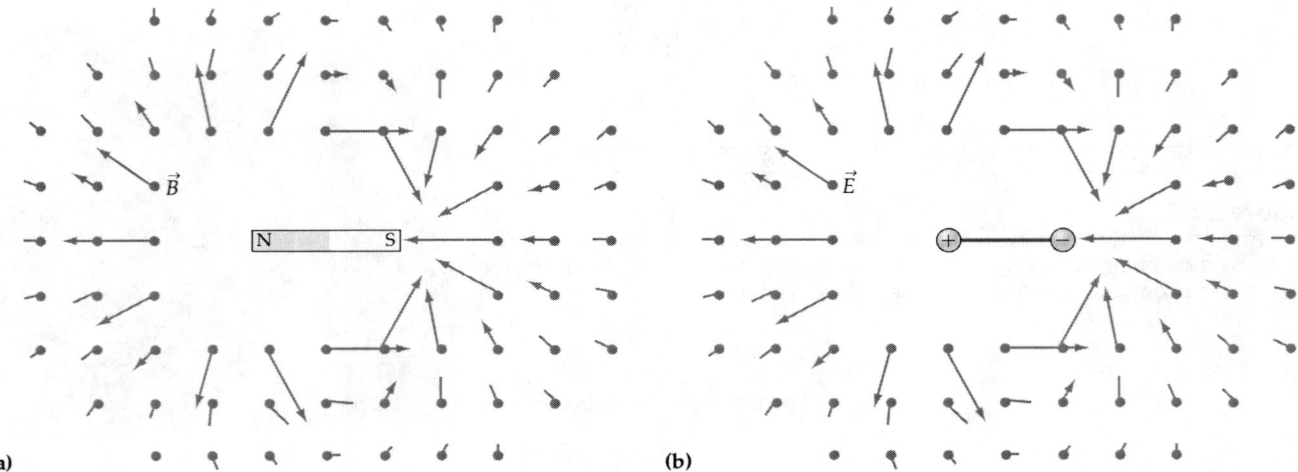

Figure E7.5
(a) The external magnetic field of a bar magnet. (b) The external electric field of an electric dipole.

purely positive or negative charge, it does *not* seem to be possible to find or make an object having an isolated magnetic pole (a **magnetic monopole**). Magnets and electric dipoles may be *analogous*, but they are not identical.

Self-Test E7X.1

We define $\vec{E}$ at a point to be the force per unit charge exerted on a charged particle at rest at that point. Why would it be awkward to define $\vec{B}$ in terms of the magnetic force exerted on an isolated magnetic pole?

E7.3 Magnetic Forces on Moving Charges

While a magnetic field does not exert any force on a electric charge at rest, it turns out that it *will* exert a force on a *moving* charge. We will see that this provides a tool for more precisely defining the magnitude of $\vec{B}$.

Description of a *cathode-ray* tube

One can create a beam of moving electrons using an **electron gun** (see figure E7.6), which consists of two metal plates (a **cathode** and an **anode**) enclosed in a vacuum tube. A power supply connected to these plates gives them a negative and positive charge, respectively. An electric heater makes the cathode so hot that its atoms vibrate so violently as to knock electrons free of the metal. These free electrons accelerate away from the negative cathode toward the positive anode. Most are absorbed by the anode, but a few fly through a hole in the anode, creating a beam of electrons. A phosphor-coated screen placed at the other end of the tube displays a glowing spot where the beam hits it. The resulting device (called a **cathode-ray tube** or **CRT**) is used in TVs, old-

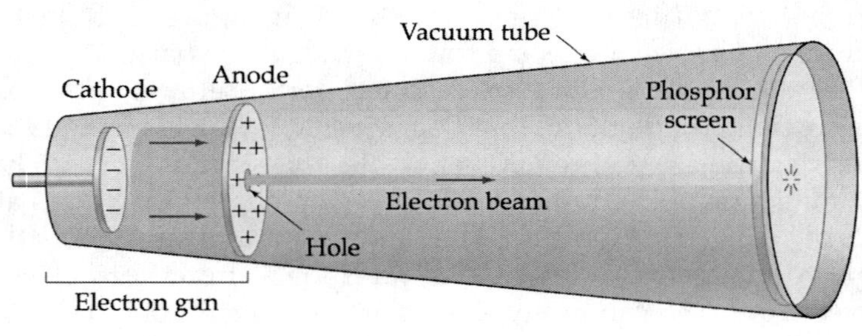

Figure E7.6
A schematic diagram of a cathode-ray tube. Electrons boil off a hot, negatively charged cathode and accelerate toward a positively charged anode. Some go through a hole in the anode, creating an electron beam. A phosphor-coated screen glows when the electron beam hits it.

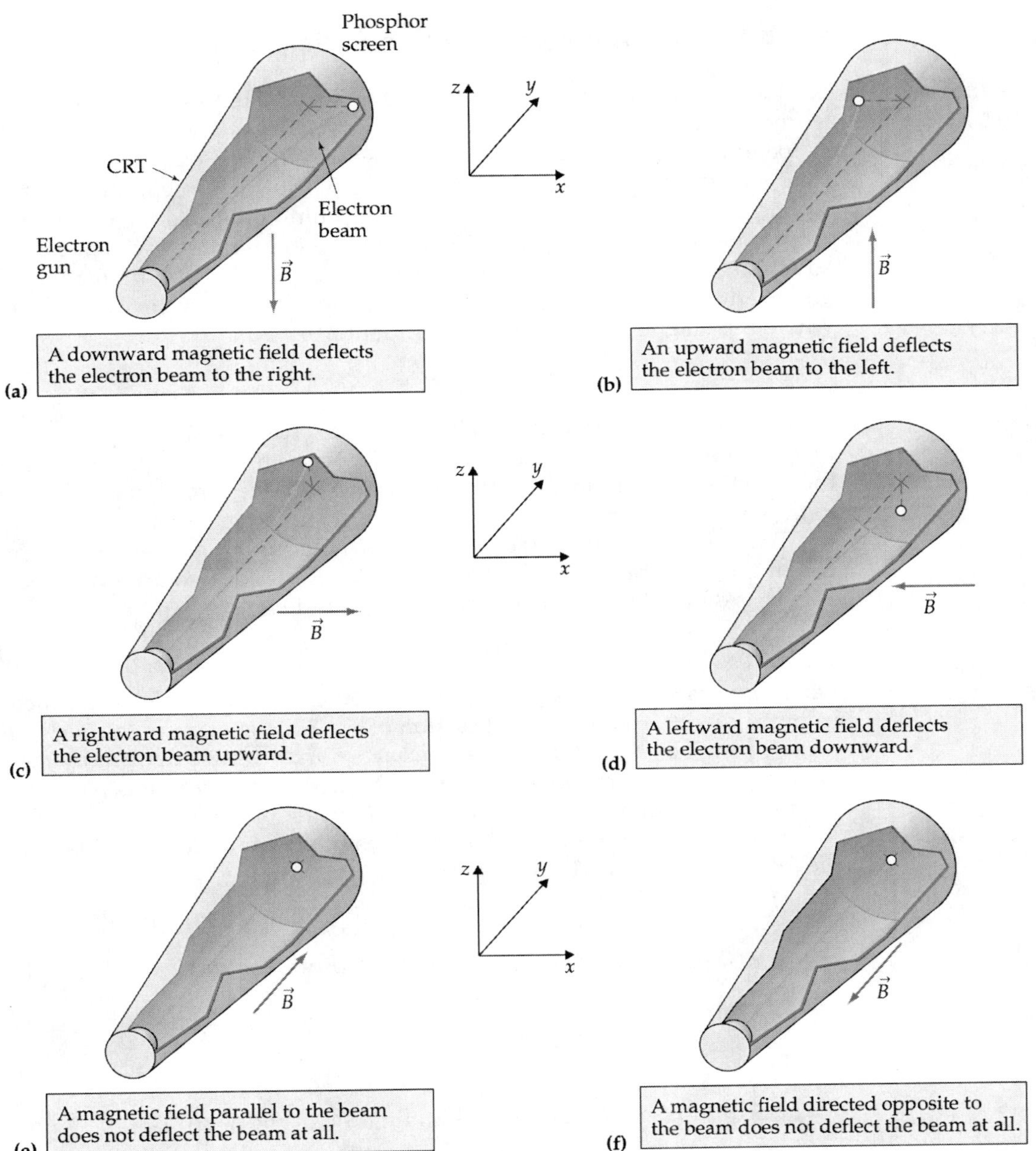

Figure E7.7
How magnetic fields affect an electron beam. In each drawing, the electron gun is closer to you than the phosphor screen is, and the electron beam moves in the $+y$ direction.

style computer monitors, oscilloscopes, radar screens, and many other devices to convert electronic signals into visible images.

Observations about the magnetic forces on moving charges

We can use a simple CRT to investigate what a magnetic field does to moving charges. Figure E7.7 illustrates what happens when such a CRT is placed in magnetic fields with various orientations. The first four cases display the empirical result that when $\vec{v}$ and $\vec{B}$ are not collinear, *the magnetic force on the electron beam is perpendicular to both* $\vec{v}$ *and* $\vec{B}$. We can in fact use the following right hand rule to predict the direction of deflection: If you point your right index finger in the direction of $\vec{v}$ and your second finger in the direction of $\vec{B}$, your right thumb will point in the direction *opposite* to the magnetic force that deflects the negatively charged electrons. If we do analogous experiments with a beam of *positive* ions, we find experimentally that the magnetic force on the beam points in the *same* direction as your right thumb.

E7.4 A Review of the Cross Product

A possible mathematical formula for the magnetic force

Now, where have we seen a right-hand rule like this before? In unit C we learned that the *cross product* $\vec{u} \times \vec{w}$ of two vectors $\vec{u}$ and $\vec{w}$ is a vector that is perpendicular to both $\vec{u}$ and $\vec{w}$ in the sense indicated by *exactly the same right hand rule*: if you point your right index finger in the direction of $\vec{u}$ and your second finger in the direction of $\vec{w}$, your thumb indicates the direction of the cross product (see figure E7.8). Therefore, the observations we have discussed so far suggest that a possible mathematical expression for the magnetic force $\vec{F}_m$ exerted on a particle with charge q moving with velocity $\vec{v}$ at a point where the magnetic field vector is $\vec{B}$ might be

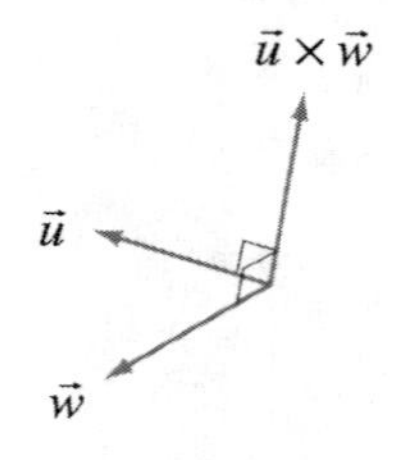

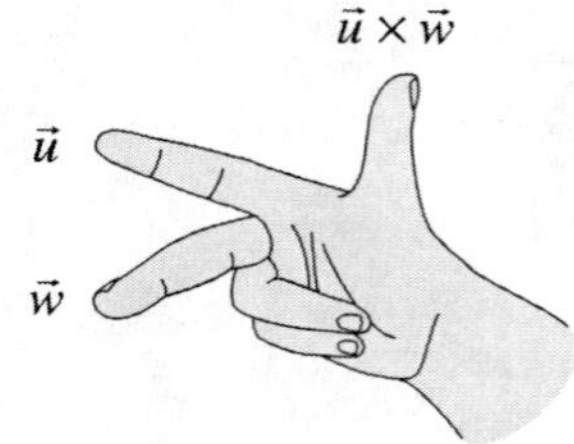

Figure E7.8
The right-hand rule for determining the direction of the cross-product.

$$\vec{F}_m \propto q(\vec{v} \times \vec{B}) \tag{E7.1}$$

Note that since q is negative for electrons, the force would be opposite to the direction indicated by your right thumb if you point your right index finger in the direction of $\vec{v}$ and your right second finger in the direction of $\vec{B}$, consistent with what we observe.

To further unpack the meaning of this hypothesis, let us review the properties of the cross product. The cross product $\vec{u} \times \vec{w}$ of two arbitrary vectors $\vec{u}$ and $\vec{w}$ is defined to be a *vector* whose magnitude is

$$\text{mag}(\vec{u} \times \vec{w}) = uw \sin\theta \tag{E7.2}$$

where $u \equiv \text{mag}(\vec{u})$, $w \equiv \text{mag}(\vec{w})$, and θ is the (smallest possible) angle measured from the direction of $\vec{u}$ to the direction of $\vec{w}$. The direction of the vector $\vec{u} \times \vec{w}$ is defined to be *perpendicular to both* $\vec{u}$ *and* $\vec{w}$ in the sense defined by the right-hand rule mentioned above. Note that the cross product points along the axis around which you would have to rotate $\vec{u}$ to align it with $\vec{w}$.

A review of the properties of the cross product

From this definition, one can fairly easily prove that the cross product has the following mathematical properties:

$$\vec{u} \times \vec{w} = -\vec{w} \times \vec{u} \quad \text{(the cross product is } \textit{anticommutative}\text{)} \tag{E7.3a}$$

$$\vec{u} \times (\vec{w} + \vec{a}) = \vec{u} \times \vec{w} + \vec{u} \times \vec{a} \quad \text{(the cross product is } \textit{distributive}\text{)} \tag{E7.3b}$$

$$\vec{u} \times (b\vec{w}) = b(\vec{u} \times \vec{w}) \quad \text{(the cross product is } \textit{linear}\text{)} \tag{E7.3c}$$

$$\vec{u} \times \vec{u} = 0 \tag{E7.3d}$$

$$\vec{u} \times \vec{w} = 0 \quad \Leftrightarrow \quad \vec{u} \parallel \pm\vec{w} \quad \text{(assuming } \vec{u} \neq 0 \text{ and } \vec{w} \neq 0\text{)} \tag{E7.3e}$$

Note that the second and third properties are like the corresponding properties of the simple product of ordinary numbers, but the others are different. The first follows directly from the right-hand rule: if you point your right index finger in the direction of $\vec{w}$ and your second finger in the direction of $\vec{u}$, your thumb points the opposite direction than it does if you do it the other way around. Because the cross product of two vectors changes sign when we reverse the vectors' order, we say that the cross product is **anticommutative**.

A component expression for the cross product

By breaking up $\vec{u}$ and $\vec{w}$ into component vectors, one can derive from equation E7.2 the following expression for the components of $\vec{u} \times \vec{w}$:

$$\text{If } \vec{a} = \vec{u} \times \vec{w}, \text{ then} \quad \begin{bmatrix} a_x \\ a_y \\ a_z \end{bmatrix} = \begin{bmatrix} u_y w_z - u_z w_y \\ u_z w_x - u_x w_z \\ u_x w_y - u_y w_x \end{bmatrix} \tag{E7.4}$$

There is an easy way to remember this formula. Look at the first line, which tells us that $a_x = u_y w_z - u_z w_y$. Note that the first three subscripts are *xyz*. The

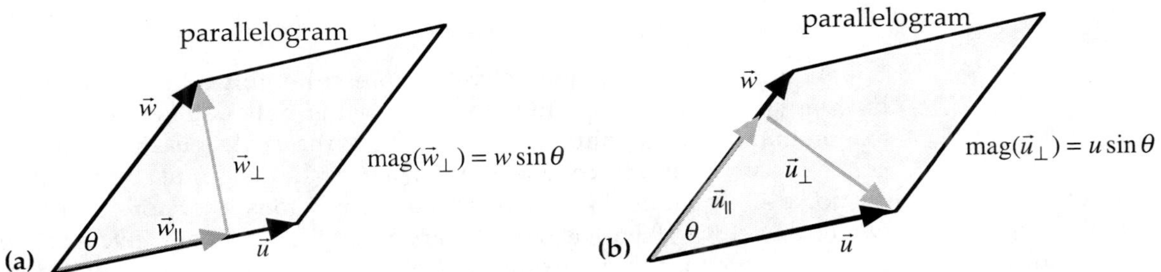

Figure E7.9
We can think of the magnitude of $\vec{u}\times\vec{w}$ as being either $uw_\perp$ or $u_\perp w$, where $w_\perp \equiv \text{mag}(\vec{w}_\perp)$ and $u_\perp \equiv \text{mag}(\vec{u}_\perp)$. In either case, the magnitude of the cross product is equal to the area of the gray parallelogram.

first three subscripts in the next line are *yzx*, which is the same as *xyz* rotated one position to the left (with the first character rotating to the end). The first three subscripts of the third line are *zxy*, again rotated one position to the left. In each line, the negative term is the positive term with the subscripts reversed.

The parallelogram rule as a qualitative interpretation of the cross product magnitude

What is the qualitative meaning of the cross product $\vec{u}\times\vec{w}$? As figure E7.9 shows, we can consider any vector $\vec{u}$ to be the sum of two component vectors $\vec{u}_\parallel$ and $\vec{u}_\perp$ parallel and perpendicular to any other vector $\vec{w}$ respectively. Similarly, we can consider $\vec{w}$ to be the sum of component vectors $\vec{w}_\parallel$ and $\vec{w}_\perp$ parallel and perpendicular to $\vec{u}$. The figure shows that we can interpret the magnitude of the cross product as either being the magnitude of $\vec{u}$ times the magnitude of $\vec{w}_\perp$ or vice versa:

$$\text{mag}(\vec{u}\times\vec{w}) = u_\perp w = w_\perp u \tag{E7.5}$$

where $u_\perp \equiv \text{mag}(\vec{u}_\perp)$ and $w_\perp \equiv \text{mag}(\vec{w}_\perp)$. We also see that *the magnitude of the cross product $\vec{u}\times\vec{w}$ is equal to the "area" of the parallelogram spanned by $\vec{u}$ and $\vec{w}$*, as illustrated in figure E7.9. The area of any parallelogram is the length of an arbitrarily-chosen leg (the parallelogram's **base**) times the parallelogram's width (or **height**) measured in the direction perpendicular to the base. If we construct a parallelogram so that its adjacent legs are vectors $\vec{u}$ and $\vec{w}$, then you can see in figure E7.9 that whichever vector we choose to be the base, equation E7.5 yields the parallelogram's area. This is a very powerful and useful way to think about the cross-product's magnitude.

Returning to our hypothetical equation E7.1, note that if $\vec{v}$ and $\vec{B}$ are either parallel or opposite, then this parallelogram rule (or equation E7.2) implies that $\vec{F}_m \propto q(\vec{v}\times\vec{B})$ will be zero. This is consistent with observed behavior in the situations illustrated in figure E7.7e and E7.7f. Equation E7.1 also predicts (and experiments verify) that the magnetic force is directly proportional to q, v, and the magnetic field strength qualitatively indicated by compass response).

E7.5 The Definition of the Magnetic Field Magnitude

Defining the magnitude of $\vec{B}$

So the equation $\vec{F}_m \propto q(\vec{v}\times\vec{B})$ appears to have solid experimental support: all that remains is to determine the constant of proportionality. We know how to measure the *force* acting on a particle and the particle's *charge* and *velocity*, but our compass-based definition of $\vec{B}$ is too fuzzy to define its numerical value precisely. The historical solution was to *define* the numerical magnitude of $\vec{B}$ so that the constant of proportionality in equation E7.1 is exactly one:

$$\vec{F}_m = q\vec{v} \times \vec{B} \tag{E7.6}$$

Equation E7.6 therefore qualitatively expresses empirical observations about how moving charges respond to magnetic fields, but quantitatively amounts to a definition of the magnitude of $\vec{B}$ in terms of the easily measured quantities of charge, velocity, and force. The SI units of $\vec{B}$ so defined must be N·s/(C·m) for the force in equation E7.6 to come out in newtons: therefore, the **tesla** (T), where 1 T ≡ 1 N·s/(C·m), is the standard SI unit for magnetic field strength.

Defining the magnitude of $\vec{\mathbb{B}}$

However, this is not the only possible choice for the constant of proportionality. If we choose that constant to be $1/c$ (where c is the speed of light), the equation becomes

$$\vec{F}_m = q\left(\frac{\vec{v}}{c} \times \vec{\mathbb{B}}\right) \tag{E7.7}$$

where $\vec{\mathbb{B}}$ is an alternative version of the magnetic field vector. This definition has a crucial advantage: because $\vec{v}/c$ is unitless, $\vec{\mathbb{B}}$ has SI units of N/C, which are the *same* as those for the electric field vector $\vec{E}$! We will find later in this unit that because of this symmetry, the equations of electromagnetism that link electric and magnetic fields are simpler and more beautiful when expressed in terms of $\vec{\mathbb{B}}$ rather than $\vec{B}$. Therefore, we will use $\vec{\mathbb{B}}$ (which we will call "B-bar") instead of $\vec{B}$ to describe the magnetic field throughout this unit. (The symbol is meant to be an ordinary capital "B" with a doubled vertical bar.) The clarity gained comes at only a small cost, because we can easily change any formula involving $\vec{\mathbb{B}}$ (in N/C) to one involving $\vec{B}$ (in teslas) by substituting

$$\vec{\mathbb{B}} = c\vec{B} \tag{E7.8}$$

anywhere that $\vec{\mathbb{B}}$ occurs.

Table E7.1 lists some magnetic field-strength benchmarks in units of N/C, teslas, and another common unit called the **gauss** (where 1 gauss $\equiv 10^{-4}$ T = 30,000 N/C). The magnetic field near a typical refrigerator magnet has a magnitude of roughly 200 gauss = 0.02 T = 6×10^6 N/C = 6 MN/C. The gauss is used partly because it is a nice "laboratory-sized" unit. (The "meganewton per coulomb" would also be a convenient unit if it were not so hard to say.†)

The magnetic force law

In summary, the following **magnetic force law** both describes the observed character of the magnetic forces on a moving charged particle and operationally defines the magnitudes of the magnetic field vectors $\vec{B}$ and $\vec{\mathbb{B}}$:

$$\vec{F}_m = q\vec{v} \times \vec{B} = q\left(\frac{\vec{v}}{c} \times \vec{\mathbb{B}}\right) \tag{E7.9}$$

Purpose: This equation specifies the magnetic force $\vec{F}_m$ acting on a charged particle with charge q moving with velocity $\vec{v}$ at a point where the magnetic field vector is $\vec{B}$ or $\vec{\mathbb{B}}$.

Symbols: c is the speed of light.

Limitations: This equation only works for charged *particles*.

Notes: The SI unit for $\vec{B}$ is the *tesla*, where $1\,\text{T} = 1\,(\text{N/C})(\text{m/s})^{-1}$; the SI units for $\vec{\mathbb{B}}$ are merely N/C, and $\vec{\mathbb{B}} = c\vec{B}$. This equation works in relativistic contexts as long as we define $\vec{F}_m$ to be the rate at which the interaction delivers relativistic momentum.

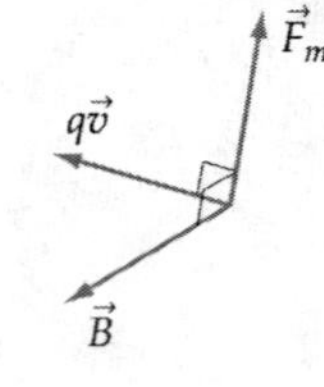

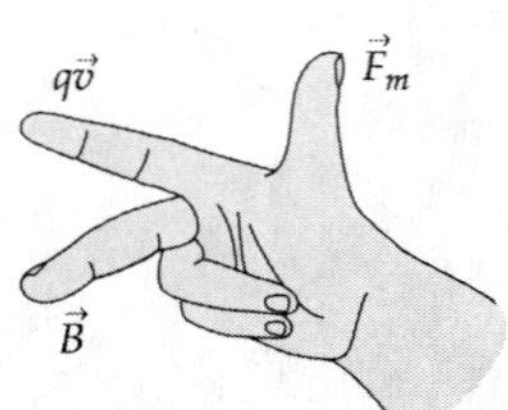

Figure E7.10
The right-hand rule for determining the direction of the magnetic force on a moving charged particle.

Figure E7.10 summarizes the right hand rule for determining the direction of the magnetic force $\vec{F}_m$. As illustrated, I generally find it easiest to think of $q\vec{v}$ as being a single vector that is parallel to $\vec{v}$ if q is positive and opposite to $\vec{v}$

†Perhaps we can call 1 MN/C a "meganick," which is not so hard.

Table E7.1 Some magnetic field strength benchmarks

Situation:	$\mathbf{B}$	B (in gauss)	B (in teslas)
In a magnetically shielded room	~ 10 μN/C	~ 0.3 ngauss	3×10^{-14} T
In interstellar space in our galaxy	~ 0.03 N/C	~ 1 μgauss	~ 0.1 nT
In a magnetic field with a strength of 1 N/C	≡ 1 N/C	33.3 μgauss	3.33 nT
At the surface of the earth	15 kN/C	0.5 gauss	50 μT
Near an interstate power line (above earth's field)	~ 15 kN/C	~ 0.5 gauss	~ 50 μT
In a magnetic field with a strength of 1 gauss	30 kN/C	≡ 1 gauss	≡ 10^{-4} T
At the surface of the sun	~ 3 MN/C	~ 100 gauss	~ 0.01 T
Near a refrigerator magnet	~ 6 MN/C	~ 200 gauss	~ 0.02 T
Within a sunspot	~ 90 MN/C	~ 3000 gauss	~ 0.3 T
In a magnetic field field with a strength of 1 T	300 MN/C	≡ 10 kgauss	≡ 1 T
Inside a moving-coil loudspeaker	~ 450 MN/C	~ 15 kgauss	1.5 T
Strongest superconducting electromagnets	~ 6 GN/C	~ 200 kgauss	~ 20 T
Inside a large laboratory electromagnet	~ 10 GN/C	~ 350 kgauss	~ 35 T
Near the surface of a neutron star	~ 3×10^{16} N/C	~ 10^{12} gauss	~ 10^{8} T

when q is negative. If I point my right index finger in the direction of $q\vec{v}$ and my second finger in the direction of $\vec{B}$, then my right thumb always correctly indicates the direction of $\vec{F}_m$.

Self-Test E7X.2

Given equation E7.9, prove that $\vec{\mathbf{B}} = c\vec{B}$.

Self-Test E7X.3

Given equation E7.1, determine the initial direction of the force acting on the charged particles shown below as they enter regions of space where the magnetic field vectors have the directions shown. The vector attached to the particle indicates the direction of its velocity. *Note*: The symbol × is conventionally used to indicate a magnetic field that is directed *into* the page perpendicular to the plane of the drawing (you are looking at the "feathers" of the magnetic field arrows). A dot is conventionally used to indicate a magnetic field that is directed out of the page (you are looking at the arrows' sharp ends in this case).

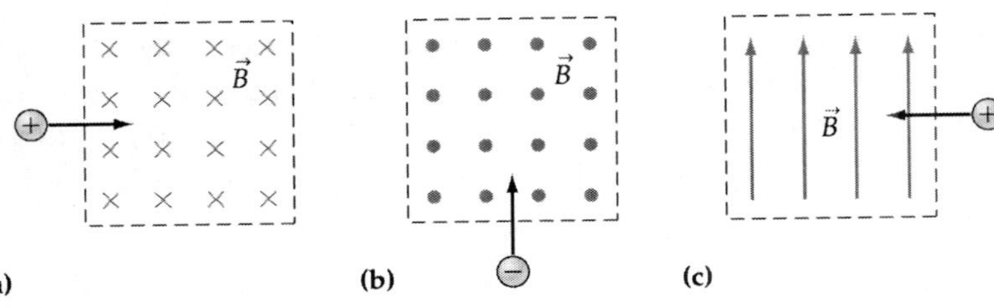

Self-Test E7X.4

What are the directions of the magnetic fields causing the particles shown to experience the forces shown in each drawing? Which of the drawings (if any) are impossible?

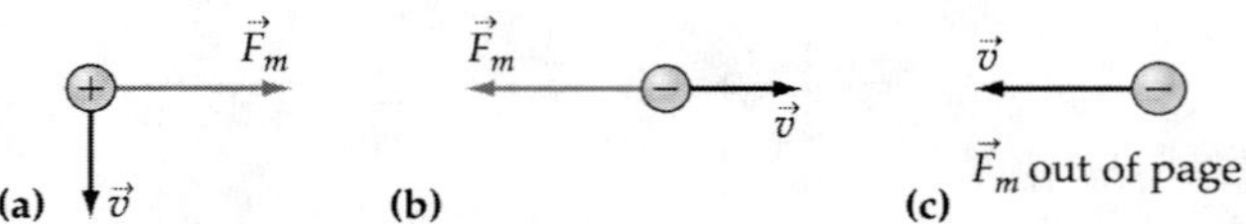

E7.6 A Free Particle in a Magnetic Field

A magnetic field contributes no k-work to a moving particle

Equation E7.9 implies that no matter how the particle moves, the magnetic field exerts a force perpendicular to the particle's velocity, so the rate at which a magnetic force directly contributes k-work to a particle is

$$\frac{[dK]}{dt} = \frac{\vec{F}_m \cdot d\vec{r}}{dt} = \vec{F}_m \cdot \vec{v} = 0 \qquad (\text{since } \vec{F}_m \perp \vec{v}) \tag{E7.10}$$

(see the discussion of k-work in chapter C8). Thus a charged particle's kinetic energy (and so its speed) is not changed by a static magnetic field.

A free particle initially moving perpendicular to $\vec{\mathbb{B}}$ moves in a circle

What the magnetic field *does* do is change such a particle's direction of motion. Consider the case where we have uniform magnetic field (a field whose field vectors $\vec{\mathbb{B}}$ are essentially constant in magnitude and direction at all points in a region of interest) through which a particle with charge q moves with a velocity initially perpendicular to $\vec{\mathbb{B}}$ (see figure E7.11a). Since the magnetic force $\vec{F}_m$ is perpendicular to $\vec{\mathbb{B}}$, it will act in the same plane as $\vec{v}$, but will also always be perpendicular to $\vec{v}$, as shown. Under these circumstances, the magnitude of this force is

$$F_m = q\left(\frac{v}{c}\right)\mathbb{B}\sin\theta = q\left(\frac{v}{c}\right)\mathbb{B} = \text{constant} \tag{E7.11}$$

since the angle θ between $\vec{v}$ and $\vec{\mathbb{B}}$ is always 90°, the value of q is fixed, the particle's speed v is constant (as we've just argued) and $\mathbb{B} \equiv \text{mag}(\vec{\mathbb{B}})$ is constant (since the field is uniform). If no other forces act on the particle, its *acceleration* must also be constant. One can use the Newton computer program (see chapter N4) to show that whenever a particle experiences a constant acceleration perpendicular to its motion, it will necessarily move in a *circle*, as shown in figure E7.11 (see problem E7S.7).

The radius of the particle's circular path is proportional to its momentum and its period is independent of its speed

The acceleration of a particle moving at a constant speed v in a circle of radius R is v^2/R. Newton's second law therefore implies that in this case

$$|q|\left(\frac{v}{c}\right)\mathbb{B} = F_m = ma = m\frac{v^2}{R} \Rightarrow R = \frac{mvc}{|q|\mathbb{B}} = \frac{pc}{|q|\mathbb{B}} \tag{E7.12}$$

This important equation says that the radius R of the circular motion of a particle with a given charge in a given field is proportional to the magnitude of the particle's *momentum* $\vec{p}$. The time T required for the particle to go once around the circle is the circle's circumference divided by the particle's speed, so

$$T = \frac{2\pi R}{v} = \frac{2\pi}{v}\frac{mvc}{|q|\mathbb{B}} = \frac{2\pi mc}{|q|\mathbb{B}} \tag{E7.13}$$

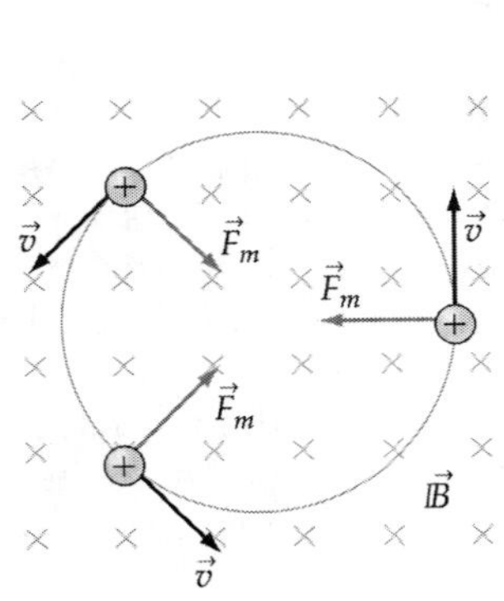

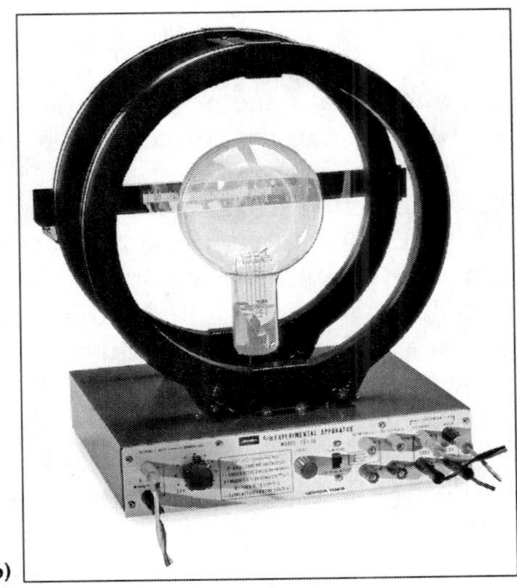

(a) (b)

Figure E7.11
(a) The path of a charged particle whose initial velocity is perpendicular to $\vec{B}$. The crosses indicate that the magnetic field is directed into the plane of the page (b) This photograph shows an electron beam moving in the uniform magnetic field created by the large circular coils (electrons striking gas molecules in the tube causes those molecules to glow). Note that the trajectory of the electrons in this field is nearly a perfect circle.

Note that, surprisingly, T does *not* depend on the particle's initial speed! Therefore, a batch of identical and otherwise free particles moving in a given magnetic field will cycle around in the plane perpendicular to $\vec{B}$ at the same frequency $f = 1/T$, independent of their (assumedly nonrelativistic) speeds. We call this unique frequency the particles' **cyclotron frequency** in that field (after a type of particle accelerator that takes advantage of this fact).

What if the particle is relativistic?

Equation E7.12 turns out to be correct even if the particle is moving close to the speed of light as long as we take p to be the particle's *relativistic* momentum $p \equiv mv/[1 - v^2/c^2]^{1/2}$. On the other hand, equation E7.13 in this case becomes

$$T = \frac{2\pi R}{v} = \frac{2\pi}{v}\frac{pc}{|q|\boldsymbol{B}} = \frac{2\pi}{v|q|\boldsymbol{B}}\frac{mvc}{[1 - v^2/c^2]^{1/2}}$$

$$= \frac{2\pi mc}{|q|\boldsymbol{B}}\frac{1}{[1 - v^2/c^2]^{1/2}} \tag{E7.14}$$

So we see that T is not really *exactly* independent of v, but the v-dependence is negligible unless v becomes an appreciable fraction of c. If $v < 0.14c$, equation E7.13 will be in error by less than 1%.

Self-Test E7X.5

An electron beam whose electrons are traveling at a speed of 3.0×10^7 m/s perpendicular to a uniform magnetic field is observed to travel in a circle with a radius of 12.0 cm. What is the magnitude of the magnetic field? What is the cyclotron frequency of these electrons according to equation E7.13? By what percentage is this expression in error?

What if the particle is *not* moving perpendicular to $\vec{B}$?

Now consider the more general case where the particle is *not* initially moving entirely perpendicular to $\vec{B}$. Since the magnetic force $\vec{F}_m$ is always per-

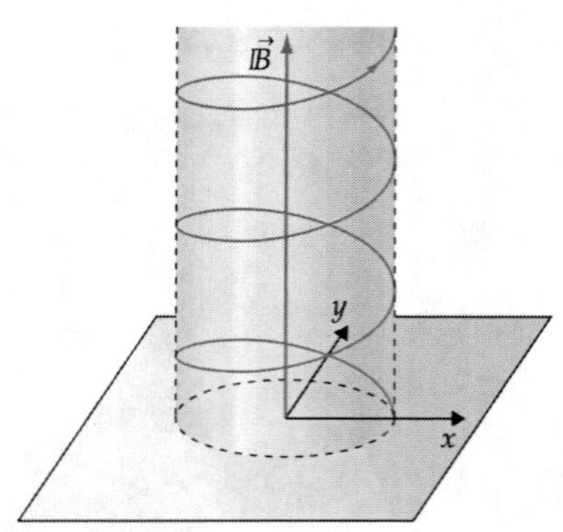

Figure E7.12
The helical path of a negatively charged particle whose velocity is not initially perpendicular to $\vec{\mathbb{B}}$

pendicular to $\vec{\mathbb{B}}$, it has no component in that direction, so the component of the particle's momentum parallel to $\vec{\mathbb{B}}$ is conserved. The projection of the particle's motion in a plane perpendicular to $\vec{\mathbb{B}}$ is still a circular path, and equation E7.12 still yields the correct radius for this circular projection as long as we replace p by $|p_\perp| = |p\sin\theta|$, where $|p_\perp|$ is the absolute value of the component of $\vec{p}$ perpendicular to $\vec{\mathbb{B}}$ and θ is the angle between $\vec{p}$ and $\vec{\mathbb{B}}$ (see problems E7S.10 and E7S.11 for a discussion). In this situation, then, the particle moves in a helical path around and along the direction of $\vec{\mathbb{B}}$ (see figure E7.12). The particle's helical path spirals around the local direction of $\vec{\mathbb{B}}$, so if $\vec{\mathbb{B}}$ changes direction on a scale much larger than R, the central axis of the particle's helical path will trace out a curved trajectory that is everywhere tangent to the field.

To summarize, the most general equations describing the motion of a free particle in a uniform magnetic field are

Equations describing the motion of a free particle in a uniform magnetic field

$$R = \left|\frac{p_\perp c}{q\mathbb{B}}\right| = \left|\frac{p_\perp}{qB}\right| \tag{E7.15a}$$

$$T = \frac{2\pi mc}{|q|\,\mathbb{B}\sqrt{1-v^2/c^2}} = \frac{2\pi m}{|q|\,B\sqrt{1-v^2/c^2}} \tag{E7.15b}$$

$$\approx \frac{2\pi mc}{|q|\,\mathbb{B}} \text{ independent of } v \quad (\text{if } v << c) \tag{E7.15c}$$

$$p_\parallel = \text{constant} \tag{E7.15d}$$

Purpose: These equation describe features of the helical motion of a particle with charge q and (possibly relativistic) momentum $\vec{p}$ moving in a reasonably uniform magnetic field described by $\vec{\mathbb{B}}$.

Symbols: R is the radius of the circular part of the helical motion, T is the time required to go once around the helix, $p_\parallel$ and $p_\perp$ are the components of the particle's relativistic momentum parallel to and perpendicular to $\vec{\mathbb{B}}$ respectively, v is the particle's speed, c is the speed of light, and $B \equiv \mathbb{B}/c$ is the magnetic field strength expressed in teslas.

Limitations: The magnetic field must be nearly uniform over the region spanned by one cycle of the helix.

Applications of these equations in particle physics

These equations have a number of applications in technology and research. The most powerful particle accelerators use magnets to constrain particles to follow a circular trajectory around a closed ring. Because particles travel many times around the ring as they are being accelerated, a circular accelerator can do the same job as a much longer (and thus more expensive) linear accelerator.

After the accelerated particles reach their final speeds, they are deflected by magnetic fields into a target surrounded by a particle detector. Physicists usually place such detectors in a magnetic field because one can determine the particle's momentum from the radius of its trajectory and the sign of its charge from the direction of the trajectory's curvature (see figure E7.13).

Applications of these equations to the earth's aurora

The fact that a charged particle will follow a helical path that tracks the local direction of the magnetic field is important to understanding the phenomenon of the **aurora** (commonly known as the *northern lights* though they are visible in the extreme south as well). On clear night, people near the earth's magnetic poles often see ghostly curtains of light hanging in the sky. This is caused by charged particles from the sun that get captured by the earth's magnetic field. Because these particles follow helical paths along the local direction of the earth's magnetic field, they get channeled into the upper atmosphere where

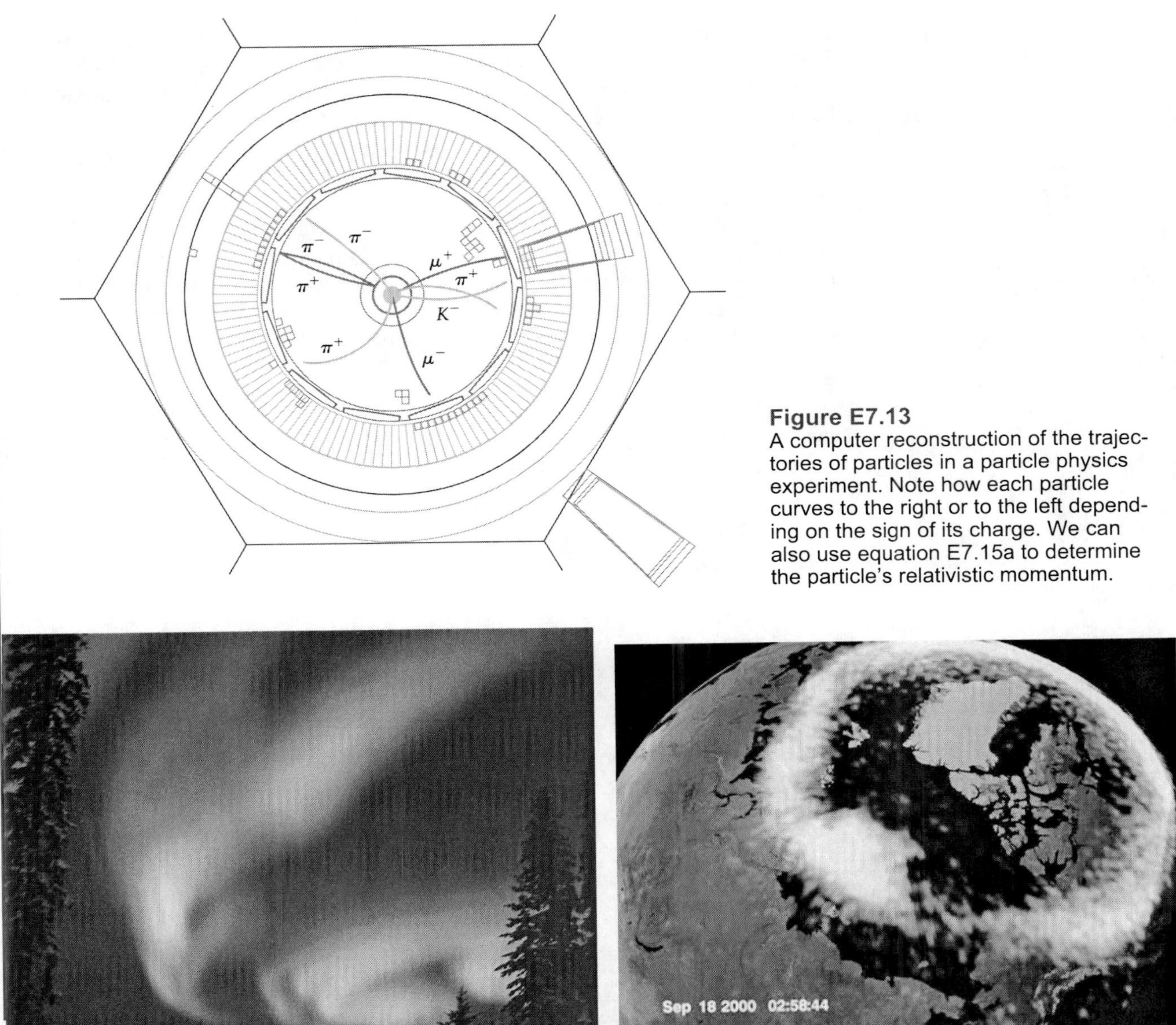

Figure E7.13
A computer reconstruction of the trajectories of particles in a particle physics experiment. Note how each particle curves to the right or to the left depending on the sign of its charge. We can also use equation E7.15a to determine the particle's relativistic momentum.

Figure E7.14
(a) The aurora as viewed from the ground. (b) The aurora as viewed from space. This ultraviolet photograph taken by a NASA satellite shows a circular glowing region around the earth's magnetic pole where protons from the sun are entering the earth's upper atmosphere.

the magnetic field lines are most vertical, i.e. near the earth's magnetic poles. Collisions between these energetic particles and atoms in the upper atmosphere cause the atoms to glow, creating the auroral display (see figure E7.14).

E7.7 The Mystery du Jour

In chapters E5 and E6, we discussed electric currents, which also involve moving charged particles. The logic of equation E7.9 suggests that if charged particles are really moving in a conductor that carries a current, a magnetic field will exert forces on them. But the particles are trapped in a conductor instead of being free particles in space, so how will they respond? Also, we found in chapter E5 that charge carriers in typical conductors also move at terribly small speeds, on the order of millimeters per hour. Will a magnetic field have a discernible effect on the these carriers at all? How might we calculate the effect of a magnetic field on a current-carrying wire? Might it be possible to use this effect to determine whether the charge carriers in a given conductor are positive or negative?

We will begin to address these interesting questions in the next chapter. Along the way, we will also take some first steps toward explaining why magnets behave like electric dipoles and see how we can use magnetic fields to make electric motors and generators, which play crucial roles in modern technology. The story of magnetism just gets more and more interesting!

TWO-MINUTE PROBLEMS

E7T.1 Which of the following statements describes an observation that represents strong physical evidence that magnetic poles are *not* the same as electrical charges?

A. Poles are described as being *north* and *south* while charges are described as being *positive* and *negative*
B. A magnet does not exert a force on a motionless charge
C. Magnetic poles always come in pairs
D. A and B
E B and C
F. A, B, and C
T. Magnetic poles *are* the same as electric charges

In each of problems E7T.2 through E7T.4, a particle whose charge has the specified sign enters a region of space where the magnetic field has the direction shown. What is the initial direction of the magnetic force on the particle?

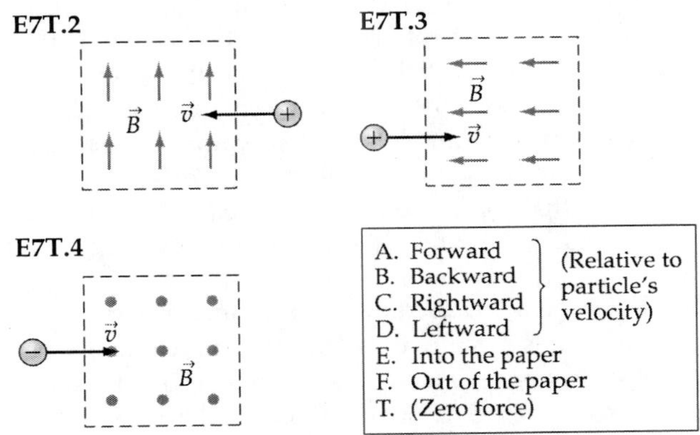

In each problems E7T.5 through E7T.7, determine the direction of the magnetic field that is causing the charged particle to experience the magnetic force shown.

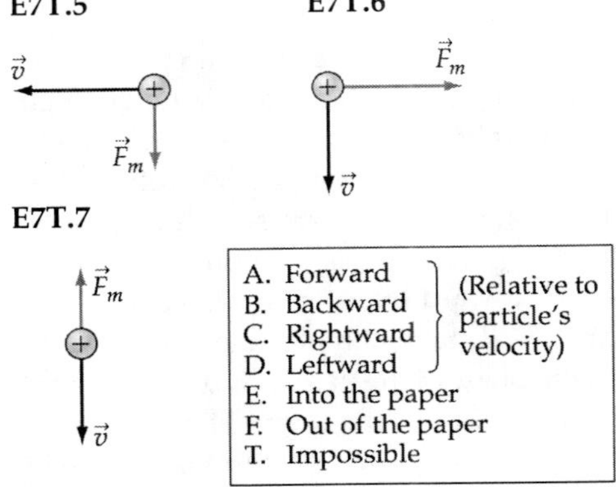

E7T.8 Imagine placing a magnet in a *uniform* magnetic field (a field whose vectors have the same magnitude and direction at all points). Will the field exert a net force on the magnet? If so, what is the direction of this force? [*Hint*: Use the dipole analogy.]

A. Yes, in the direction of the magnetic field
B. Yes, opposite to the direction magnetic field
C. Yes, but direction depends on magnet's orientation
D. No, the net force on the magnet is zero.

E7T.9 Imagine looking at the face of a CRT. The bright spot where the electron beam hits the face is exactly in the center of the screen. You bring a permanent magnet toward the CRT vertically from above. The magnet is oriented vertically with its north pole downward. In which direction will the spot deflect?

A. Up
B. Down
C. The spot does not deflect
D. Right
E. Left
F. Other (specify)

E7T.10 In a magnetic field oriented vertically downward, a particle is observed to move counterclockwise in a horizontal circle when viewed from above. This particle has a

A. Positive charge
B. Negative charge
C. Zero charge
D. One cannot determine the sign of the charge from the information given

HOMEWORK PROBLEMS

Basic Skills

E7B.1 Imagine that you are looking at the face of a CRT. The bright spot indicating where the electron beam hits the face is exactly in the center of the screen. You bring a permanent magnet toward the middle of the CRT horizontally from the right with its south pole closest to the CRT. Which direction will the spot deflect? Explain.

E7B.2 A sample of an unknown radioactive substance is observed to emit particles. In a magnetic field oriented vertically upward, these particles are observed to bend left (according to an observer looking along their direction of motion). Are the emitted particles positively or negatively charged, or is it impossible to tell? Explain.

E7B.3 Electrons produced by a certain device are observed to travel in a circular path with a radius of 2.0 cm when placed in a uniform magnetic field whose strength is 10 MN/C. What is the speed of the electrons emitted by this device? [You may express this speed as a fraction of c.]

E7B.4 Protons produced by a certain device are observed to travel in a circular path with a radius of 1.0 m when placed in a magnetic field whose strength is 0.67 T ($\vec{B}$ = 200 MN/C). What is the speed of the protons emitted by this device? [You may express this speed as a fraction of c.]

E7B.5 Electrons moving perpendicular to the direction of a magnetic field are observed to circulate around the field direction at a frequency of 150 MHz. What is the strength of the magnetic field in N/C, in Tesla, and in gauss?

E7B.6 How long would an electron moving perpendicular to the earth's magnetic field take to complete one orbit around the magnetic field direction (assuming that the electron is traveling at a nonrelativistic speed)?

E7B.7 Imagine that the magnetic field in a particle detector chamber points vertically downward and has a magnitude of 500 MN/C. Imagine that a collision in the target produces (among other things) a subatomic particle whose track bends to its right as we look along the direction of its motion. What is the sign of the particle's charge? If the radius of curvature of this particle's trajectory is $R = 85$ cm and we assume that the *magnitude* $|q|$ of the particle's charge is $e = 1.6\times10^{-19}$ C, what is the particle's relativistic momentum p?

Synthetic

E7S.1 Imagine you are looking at the face of a CRT in an airplane. The plane is initially flying south at the equator, and thus approximately opposite to the earth's magnetic field direction. The electron beam moves in the same direction as the plane, and the electron beam hits the CRT face exactly in the center of the screen. The plane then turns 90° to the east. In what direction will will you see the spot shift due to the effects of the earth's magnetic field? Explain.

E7S.2 Your company is designing a desktop-sized proton accelerator, using a 500-MN/C superconducting magnet to hold the protons in a circular path. Estimate the maximum kinetic energy that your accelerator can give protons. Express your answer in the conventional particle-physics unit of *electron volts*, where 1 eV = 1.6×10^{-19} J. For comparison, the accelerator at Fermi National Laboratory can accelerate protons to energies of over 1 TeV. [*Hint*: Assume that the protons are non-relativistic, do the calculation, and then check that assumption.]

E7S.3 The aurora is caused by electrons and protons from the sun spiraling in along the direction of the earth's magnetic field. The typical speed of the electrons involved is about $0.003c$, and the speed of protons is about $(1.5\times10^{-4})c$. What are the *maximum* radii of the circular part of these particles' motions around the field direction as they spiral into the atmosphere? What are their orbital frequencies? The magnitude of the magnetic field near the earth is approximately 0.5 gauss.

E7S.4 It is possible to use crossed electric and magnetic fields to construct a *velocity selector*, a device that only passes charged particles having a certain velocity. One way of constructing such a velocity selector is shown in below: ions are sent through a region of space where there is a uniform magnetic field (directed upward out of the page) and a uniform electric field acting in the direction shown (upward in the plane of the page). Only ions having a specific speed will be able to travel in a straight line through this apparatus. If the magnetic field strength is $\boldsymbol{B}$ = 3.0 MN/C, what electric field strength would you want to select ions having a speed of exactly $0.01c$? Does your answer depend on the mass of the ion? Does it depend on the sign of the ion's charge? Does it depend on the magnitude of the ion's charge? (Ignore gravity.)

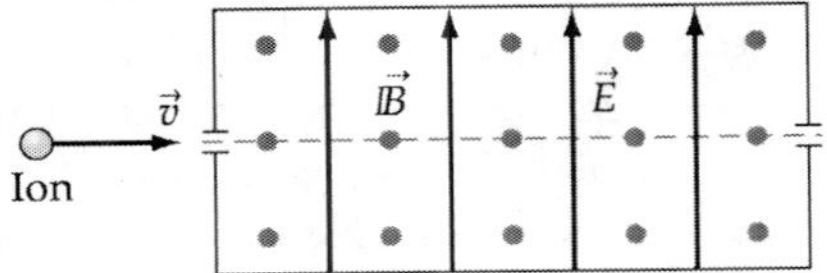

E7S.5 A *mass spectrometer* is a device that uses a magnetic field to sort atoms by mass. In this device, atoms whose mass are to be determined are *ionized* by stripping off one electron. They are then sent through a velocity selector (see the previous problem) that selects ions only with a very specific speed v, and these ions are sent into a region of space filled with a known uniform magnetic field $\vec{B}$ perpendicular to $\vec{v}$. The field causes the atom to follow a circular path whose radius is proportional to the atom's mass. Atoms with different masses will therefore follow somewhat different circular paths and thus end up at different places on a photographic plate, as shown below. Imagine that we give N_2^+ ions, O_2^+ ions and NO^+ ions the same velocity of 30.0 km/s and then send them into a mass spectrometer where the magnetic field strength is B = 8.5 MN/C. How far would the spot on the photographic plate be from the entry point for each ion, assuming that each ion completes half an orbit, as shown in the figure? The atomic mass of a nitrogen atom is 14.0031 amu and oxygen is 15.9949 amu, where 1 amu = 1.6605×10^{-27} kg.

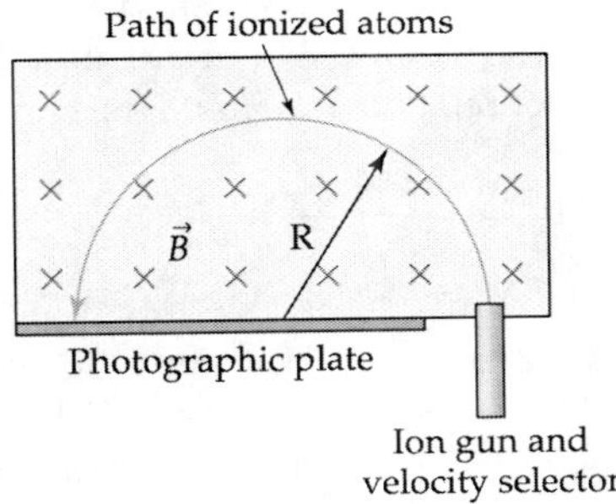

E7S.6 Your college physics department has a garage sale, and you pick up a particle accelerator at a *great* price. The sellers said that they *thought* that the beam produced by the accelerator was an electron beam, but it might be a proton beam. They give you an unmarked bar magnet, a piece of wire, and a battery, and tell you to check it yourself. Carefully and completely describe how you could use these items to determine whether the particles emerging from your new accelerator are electrons or protons charged. (Assume that you can see the beam emerging from the accelerator.)

E7S.7 Set up the Newton computer program to model the situation where a particle's acceleration has magnitude proportional to its speed and perpendicular to its velocity, as in the case of a free particle moving in a uniform magnetic field. (For the sake of simplicity, let us arbitrarily choose the constant of proportionality to be $1.0\ \text{s}^{-1}$.) Submit printouts that demonstrate that in this situation (a) the particle moves in a circular trajectory irrespective of its speed, (b) the radius of its trajectory is proportional to its speed, and (c) the period of the particle's trajectory is independent of its speed.

E7S.8 Prove that equation E7.12 still follows from equation E7.9 if we define $\vec{p} \equiv m\vec{v}/[1-v^2/c^2]^{1/2}$ = relativistic momentum and $\vec{F}_m \equiv d\vec{p}/dt$. (*Hints:* Note that the equation $a = \text{mag}(d\vec{v}/dt) = v^2/R$ only depends on calculus and the characteristics of vectors and so still applies in the relativistic limit. Begin by arguing that the particle's speed is still unaffected by the magnetic field in the relativistic limit.: this will turn out to be important in your proof.)

E7S.10 Consider an otherwise free and nonrelativistic particle with charge q moving in a uniform magnetic field whose field vectors are $\vec{B}$. Imagine that we write its velocity vector $\vec{v}$ in terms of component vectors parallel to and perpendicular to the magnetic field direction: $\vec{v} = \vec{v}_{\parallel} + \vec{v}_{\perp}$.

(a) Prove that

$$\vec{F}_m = q\left(\frac{\vec{v}}{c}\right) \times \vec{B} = q\left(\frac{\vec{v}_{\perp}}{c}\right) \times \vec{B} \tag{E7.16}$$

(b) Argue that $\vec{v}_{\parallel}$ is constant in time, implying that

$$\vec{a} \equiv \frac{d\vec{v}}{dt} = \frac{d\vec{v}_{\perp}}{dt} \tag{E7.17}$$

(c) Equation E7.16 implies that the magnetic force on the charged particle is the same whether it has a velocity component parallel to $\vec{B}$ or not. Equation E7.17 tells us that the particle's acceleration is the same whether it has a component parallel to $\vec{B}$ or not. Argue, therefore, that equation E7.15a is true.

E7S.11 Consider an otherwise free particle with charge q moving in a uniform magnetic field whose field vectors are $\vec{B}$. For the sake of simplicity, let's orient our reference frame so that the magnetic field vectors point entirely in the z direction.

(a) The component definition of the cross product specifies that

$$\vec{u} \times \vec{w} = \begin{bmatrix} u_y w_z - u_z w_x \\ u_z w_x - u_x w_z \\ u_x w_y - u_y w_x \end{bmatrix} \tag{E7.18}$$

Use this and Newton's second law to show that in this situation, the particle's acceleration is

$$\vec{a} = \begin{bmatrix} a_x \\ a_y \\ a_z \end{bmatrix} = \frac{q}{m}\begin{bmatrix} v_y B \\ -v_x B \\ 0 \end{bmatrix} \tag{E7.19}$$

(b) Show that if we integrate these equations from time $t = 0$ to some arbitrary time t, we get

$$b(v_x - v_{0x}) = y - y_0$$

$$\Rightarrow \quad bv_x = y - (y_0 - bv_{0x}) \tag{E7.20}$$

$$b(v_y - v_{0y}) = -x + x_0$$

$$\Rightarrow \; bv_y = -x + (x_0 + bv_{0y}) \tag{E7.21}$$

$$v_z = v_{0z} \tag{E7.22}$$

where x_0, y_0, and z_0 are the components of the particle's position at $t = 0$, v_{0x}, v_{0y}, and v_{0z} are components of its velocity at $t = 0$ and b is a constant whose value you should determine. Note that equation E7.22 shows that the particle's velocity component along the field direction is constant.

(c) Our freedom to choose the origin of our reference frame in the xy plane implies that we can find a coordinate system where $y_0 - bv_{0x}$ and $x_0 + bv_{0y}$ are zero. Draw a sketch showing how we might do this in an example case (perhaps one where either v_{0x} or v_{0y} is zero).

(d) The distance the particle is from the z axis in this *new* coordinate system is $R = [x^2 + y^2]^{1/2}$. Show that equations E7.18 then imply that if v is constant, R is constant, implying that the projection of the particle's motion on the xy plane is a circle of radius R around the z axis.

(e) Argue that this radius is has the value predicted by equation E7.15a. (*Hint:* First argue that $[v_x^2 + v_y^2]^{1/2} = v\sin\theta$.)

Rich-Context

E7R.1 A cathode ray tube (CRT) sits on a table, oriented horizontally. The controls have been adjusted so that the electron beam should make a single spot of light exactly in the center of the screen. You observe, however, that the spot is deflected to the right. As a clever scientist, you suspect that your laboratory is in either an electric or magnetic field, but you do not know which. Carefully describe a set of experiments that only involve reorienting your CRT that will determine (a) that you really are in a field, as opposed to having a broken CRT, and (b) whether the field is an electric field or a magnetic field.

E7R.2 In a *cyclotron* particle accelerator, a charged particle travels in a nearly circular horizontal path in a uniform vertical constant magnetic field $\vec{B}$. Twice each orbit, the particle passes a place where electric fields give it a small boost in energy ε. As the particle's energy increases, its momentum increases, so its orbital radius increases (its spirals outward). Assuming that the particle is non-relativistic and ε is small enough so that each orbit remains nearly circular, find an expression for the orbital radius R as a function of time.

Advanced

E7A.1 A *synchrotron* particle accelerator is much like a cyclotron (see problem E7R.2) except that the magnitude of $\vec{B}$ is increased in synchrony with the particle's energy so that the particle's orbital radius remains constant. Find an expression describing how B must vary with time. Do *not* assume that the particles are nonrelativistic. (*Hint:* First show that

$$B^2 = \frac{E^2 - m^2c^4}{q^2R^2} \tag{E7.23}$$

where E is particle's total relativistic energy $= [p^2c^2 + m^2c^4]^{1/2} = mc^2[1 - v^2/c^2]^{-1/2}$. Take the time derivative of each side and make some appropriate approximations.)

ANSWERS TO SELF-TESTS

E7X.1 It is awkward to define $\vec{B}$ in terms of the magnetic force exerted on an isolated magnetic pole because we cannot in practice isolate magnetic poles the way that we can isolate electric charges. Every magnetic pole comes with a nearby opposite pole, which will complicate making measurements of the force exerted on the first pole.

E7X.2 If we multiply equation E7.6 by c/c, we get

$$F_m = q\vec{v}\left(\frac{c}{c}\right)\times\vec{B} = q\left(\frac{\vec{v}}{c}\right)\times(c\vec{B}) \qquad \text{(E7.24)}$$

If we compare this to equation E7.9, we see that $\vec{\mathbb{B}} = c\vec{B}$.

E7X.3 The directions are upward, to the left, and into the paper.

E7X.4 In the first and third cases, the directions are into the paper and upward, respectively. The second case is impossible.

E7X.5 Equation E7.13 implies that

$$\mathbb{B} = \frac{mvc}{|q|R} = \frac{(9.11\times10^{-31}\ \text{kg})(3\times10^{7}\ \cancel{\text{m}}/\text{s})(3\times10^{8}\ \text{m/s})}{(1.60\times10^{-19}\ \text{C})(0.12\ \cancel{\text{m}})}$$

$$= 4.3\times10^{5}\ \frac{\cancel{\text{kg}}\cdot\cancel{\text{m}}}{\text{C}\cdot\cancel{\text{s}^2}}\left(\frac{1\ \text{N}}{1\ \cancel{\text{kg}}\cdot\cancel{\text{m}}/\cancel{\text{s}^2}}\right) = 430{,}000\ \frac{\text{N}}{\text{C}} \qquad \text{(E7.25)}$$

Equation E7.14 tells us that

$$f = \frac{1}{T} = \frac{|q|\mathbb{B}}{2\pi mc} = \frac{(1.60\times10^{-19}\ \cancel{\text{C}})(430{,}000\ \text{N}/\cancel{\text{C}})}{2\pi(9.11\times10^{-31}\ \text{kg})(3\times10^{8}\ \text{m/s})}$$

$$= 4.0\times10^{7}\ \frac{\cancel{\text{N}}\cdot\cancel{\text{s}}}{\cancel{\text{kg}}\cdot\cancel{\text{m}}}\left(\frac{1\ \cancel{\text{kg}}\cdot\cancel{\text{m}}/\cancel{\text{s}^2}}{1\ \cancel{\text{N}}}\right)\left(\frac{1\ \cancel{\text{Hz}}}{1\ \cancel{\text{s}^{-1}}}\right)\left(\frac{1\ \text{MHz}}{10^{6}\ \cancel{\text{Hz}}}\right)$$

$$= 40\ \text{MHz} \qquad \text{(E7.26)}$$

E8 Currents Respond to Magnetic Fields

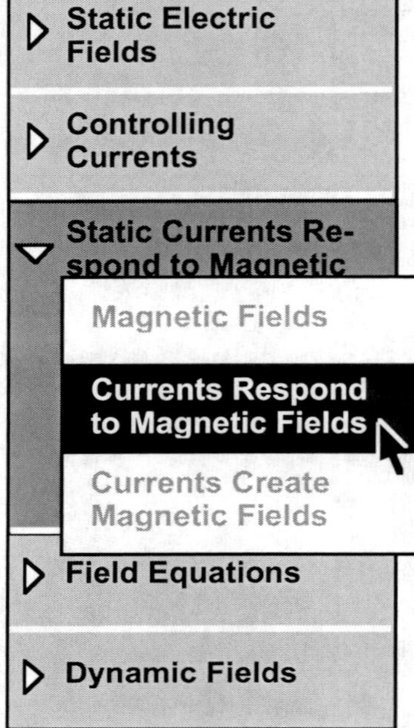

Chapter Overview

Introduction

In chapter E7, we defined the magnetic field and learned how to calculate how a magnetic field affects a free charged particle. In this chapter, we will use the basic principles of the last chapter to discover how magnetic fields exert forces on currents and how magnetic fields can even drive currents in moving conductors.

Section E8.1: The Magnetic Force on a Wire

A magnetic field will exert a magnetic force on charge carriers flowing in a wire that is conducting a current. This force will be transmitted to the wire itself as a result of collisions between the charge carriers and the wire lattice. The result is that a magnetic field will exert a force on a current-carrying segment of wire:

$$\vec{F}_{m,\text{seg}} = \frac{L}{c}\vec{I} \times \vec{\mathbb{B}} = L\vec{I} \times \vec{B} \qquad \text{(E8.3)}$$

Purpose: This equation describes the magnetic force $\vec{F}_{m,\text{seg}}$ on a straight wire segment of length L in a magnetic field described by $\vec{\mathbb{B}}$ or $\vec{B}$.

Symbols: $\vec{I}$ is the steady conventional current in the wire.

Limitations: The wire must be straight and thin, and L must be small enough that $\vec{\mathbb{B}}$ is nearly uniform over the segment.

Section E8.2: The Magnetic Torque on a Loop

Equation E8.3 implies that a current-carrying loop will experience forces that will seek to orient the loop so that its plane is perpendicular to the magnetic field. The loop will in fact twist in a magnetic field exactly as if it had a bar magnet embedded in the loop's plane with its north and south poles sticking out above and below the plane. (The **loop-to-magnet rule** says that if you curl your right fingers in the direction of the loop's current flows, your right thumb indicates the direction of the equivalent magnet.)

If the magnetic field is approximately uniform over the loop's face, the loop will in fact experience a torque

$$\vec{\tau} = \vec{\mu} \times \frac{\vec{\mathbb{B}}}{c} = \vec{\mu} \times \vec{B}, \quad \text{where } \operatorname{mag}(\vec{\mu}) = NAI \qquad \text{(E8.9)}$$

Purpose: This equation describes the torque $\vec{\tau}$ experienced by a loop with area A and N turns of wire that each carry current I in a magnetic field $\vec{B} = \vec{\mathbb{B}}/c$.

Symbols: $\vec{\mu}$, the loop's **magnetic moment**, expresses the strength and south-to-north orientation of the loop's equivalent bar magnet.

Limitations: The loop must be small enough so that $\vec{B}$ is approximately constant over its face.

Notes: This equation applies to arbitrarily shaped flat loops.

The magnetic moment vector is a convenient way to express both the strength and orientation of the loop's equivalent bar magnet.

Section E8.3: Electric Motors

Electric motors take advantage of the fact that a loop will twist in a magnetic field: a current-carrying loop can in fact be made to continually rotate if we switch the direction of current flow every half rotation. This section discusses one practical method for doing this. The section also argues that the k-work given to the loop by the magnetic field during one complete loop rotation is

$$[\Delta K]_{\text{tot}} = 4NAIB = 4\mu B \tag{E8.13}$$

where N is the number of turns of wire carrying current I in the loop, A is its area and B is the magnetic field strength. (This assumes that the loop is small enough so that $\vec{B}$ is constant over its face and that the current in the loop switches direction instantaneously at just the right time.)

Section E8.4: Creating Currents in Moving Loops

The magnetic forces on charge carriers in a conductor moving through a magnetic field can cause the ends of the conductor to become charged, creating a potential difference between its ends as if it were a battery. Such forces will actually drive a current through a closed conducting loop *if* the loop moves through a *nonuniform* magnetic field. The magnitude of the net emf that a charge circling a square loop with sides L would gain under these circumstances is given by

$$\left|\mathscr{E}_{\text{loop}}\right| = \frac{v}{c}|\Delta \mathbb{B}| \tag{E8.16}$$

where v is the loop's speed, c is the speed of light, and $\Delta\mathbb{B}$ is the change in the component of the magnetic field perpendicular to the loop's face between its leading and trailing edges. We will find this expression very useful in chapter E13.

Section E8.5: Eddy Currents in Moving Conductors

Similarly, a nonuniform magnetic field can induce so-called **eddy currents** in a conducting plate moving through that field, and these currents will interact with the magnetic field in such a way as to exert a drag force on the moving plate. This section explores a simple case where a large conducting plate moves between the poles of a horseshoe magnet whose magnetic field we imagine to be uniform in the region between the poles and zero elsewhere (a simplified approximation of the real field in such a case). In such a case, the section discusses how one can estimate the magnetic drag force in such a case: it turns out (within a factor of 2 or so) to be

$$F_{\text{eddy}} \approx \sigma_c V v \frac{\mathbb{B}^2}{c^2} = \sigma_c V v B^2 \tag{E8.20}$$

where $B = \mathbb{B}/c$ is the assumedly uniform magnetic field strength in the region where the field is nonzero, V is the volume of the conducting plate enclosed by this region, v is the plate's speed, and σ_c is its conductivity. Note that this magnetic drag force is proportional to the speed.

E8.1 The Magnetic Force on a Wire

In chapter E7, we learned that a magnetic field will exert forces on charges moving otherwise freely in a vacuum. In this chapter, we will explore how magnetic fields can not only exert forces on established currents in other contexts but can also *create* currents in the right circumstances.

If charge is *really* moving in a current-carrying wire (as claimed in chapter E5), then these moving charges ought to respond to a magnetic field. According to equation E7.9, the magnetic force on a single electron of charge q moving through this wire with drift velocity $\vec{v}_d$ is

$$\vec{F}_m = q\left(\frac{\vec{v}_d}{c}\right) \times \vec{\mathbb{B}} \tag{E8.1}$$

How the magnetic force on the electrons moving in a wire gets transmitted to the wire

Any impulse that this interaction delivers to electrons in a wire is almost instantly transmitted to the wire itself when the electrons next collide with lattice atoms. Remember that the electrons are not really moving freely through the wire like baseballs through air but are rather oozing through the wire lattice like toothpaste being squeezed through a narrow tube. Just as exerting a force on the toothpaste basically amounts to exerting the same force on the tube, exerting a force on the electrons amounts to exerting a force on the wire lattice.

This means that the total magnetic force exerted on a straight wire segment is equal to the force given in equation E8.1 multiplied by the number of flowing electrons in the wire segment (assuming that the electrons all have essentially the same drift velocity). A segment of wire of length L and cross-sectional area A has a volume LA, so if n is the number of free electrons per unit volume in the wire, the total number of flowing electrons in the wire segment is nLA. Thus the total magnetic force on the segment is

$$\vec{F}_{m,\text{seg}} = nLAq\left(\frac{\vec{v}_d}{c}\right) \times \vec{\mathbb{B}} \tag{E8.2}$$

Since $\vec{I} = nqA\vec{v}_d$ for a sufficiently thin and straight segment of wire (see equation E5.9), this becomes

The magnetic force on a wire segment

$$\vec{F}_{m,\text{seg}} = \frac{L}{c}\vec{I} \times \vec{\mathbb{B}} = L\vec{I} \times \vec{B} \tag{E8.3}$$

Purpose: Describes the magnetic force $\vec{F}_{m,\text{seg}}$ exerted on a straight segment of wire of length L in a magnetic field described by $\vec{\mathbb{B}}$ or $\vec{B}$.

Symbols: $\vec{I}$ specifies the direction and magnitude of the steady-state conventional current in the wire.

Limitations: The wire must be straight and thin and L must be small enough so that $\vec{\mathbb{B}}$ is nearly uniform over the segment.

If we need to compute the total magnetic force on a length of curved wire (or even an entire closed loop of wire), we can divide the wire up into sufficiently short straight segments, calculate the force on each using equation E8.3, and then add up the contributions from each segment.

Equation E8.3 makes a specific and quantitative prediction about the force that a magnetic field exerts on a current-carrying wire. One of the things it implies is that the magnetic force on a segment of wire acts *perpendicular* to the direction of the conventional current $\vec{I}$ (which always points along the wire) in a direction indicated by the usual right hand rule for the cross product. The fact that wires are observed to experience a force of exactly this description is solid evidence that charges really *are* moving in a current-carrying wire.

Why magnetic forces are not negligible

However, as we saw in chapter E5, electrons ooze very slowly through a wire, with drift speeds on the order of millimeters per hour. Are we sure that the forces the magnetic field exerts on the wire will be even measurable? The answer is yes! The electrons may move very slowly, but there are a *lot* of moving electrons in even a small piece of wire. Equation E8.3 implies that a magnetic field of 1 T (a large but not unreasonable field) will exert a force of 1 N (not negligible!) on a 1-m piece of wire that carries a modest current of 1 A.

Example E8.1 The Magnetic Force on a Short Wire Segment

Problem Imagine that you hold a horizontal length of wire carrying 30 A of current to your right in a uniform magnetic field that is directed vertically upward and has a magnitude of 3 MN/C (0.01 T). What is the magnitude and direction of the magnetic force acting on each centimeter of the wire in the field?

Translation Let $\vec{I}$ be the current vector = 30 A to the right, let $\vec{\mathbb{B}}$ be the magnetic field vector = 3MN/C upward, and let L = 1 cm be the segment's length.

Model If you point your right index finger to the right (the direction of $\vec{I}$) and your second finger upward (in the direction of $\vec{\mathbb{B}}$) you should find that your thumb points toward you, so the magnetic force acts directly toward you. We can calculate the magnitude of the force using equation E8.3.

Solution Since the current is perpendicular to the magnetic field, the sine of the angle between $\vec{I}$ and $\vec{\mathbb{B}}$ is one, so the magnitude of the force on a 1-cm segment of wire is

$$F_m = \frac{L}{c}\,\text{mag}(\vec{I}\times\vec{\mathbb{B}}) = \frac{L}{c}I\mathbb{B} = \frac{(0.01\text{ m})(30\text{ A})(3\times10^6\text{ N/C})}{3.0\times10^8\text{ m/s}}$$

$$= \frac{0.0030\ \cancel{\text{m}}\cdot\cancel{\text{A}}\cdot\text{N}}{(\cancel{\text{m}}/\cancel{\text{s}})\cancel{\text{C}}}\left(\frac{1\ \cancel{\text{C}}/\cancel{\text{s}}}{1\ \cancel{\text{A}}}\right) = 0.0030\text{ N} \tag{E8.4}$$

Evaluation Note that the units all work out. This force is not very large (about the weight of an object with a mass of 0.3 g), but it is plausible for such a short segment of wire. (A 3 MN/C is not a huge magnetic field either.)

E8.2 The Magnetic Torque on a Loop

A magnetic field will twist a current-carrying loop so its face is perpendicular to $\vec{\mathbb{B}}$

The fact that a magnetic field can exert a force on a current-carrying wire also means that a magnetic field will try to twist a current-carrying loop around an axis perpendicular to the magnetic field. Consider, for the sake of simplicity, a rectangular loop in a uniform horizontal magnetic field (see figure E8.1a on the next page). The right hand rule for the cross product implies that when the loop is oriented as shown, the magnetic force on the upper leg is oriented vertically upward and the magnetic force on the lower leg is vertically downward, as shown (check this!). These forces seek to twist the loop so that its face is perpendicular to the direction of $\vec{\mathbb{B}}$.

Self-Test E8X.1

Use your right hand to show that the forces on the near and far legs point along the axis shown and therefore do not twist the loop around this axis.

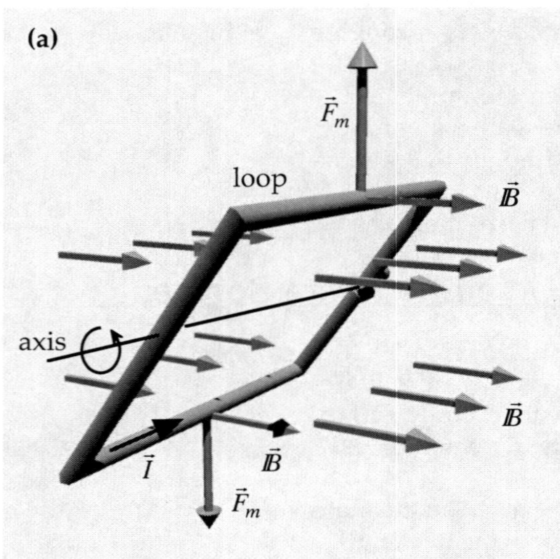

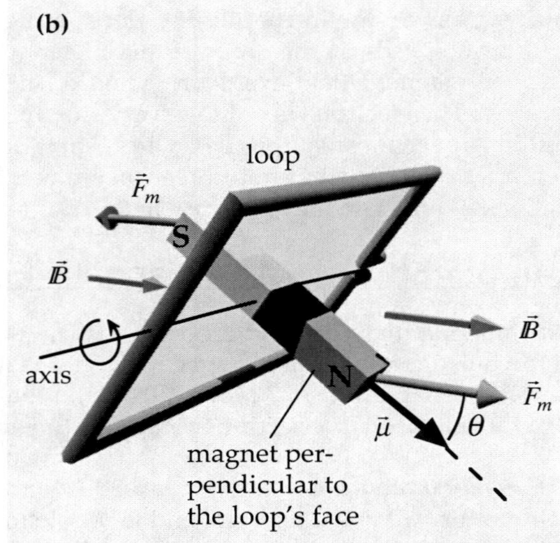

Figure E8.1
(a) A rectangular current-carrying loop in a uniform magnetic field will experience forces on the two legs perpendicular to the field that seek to twist the loop so that its face is perpendicular to the magnetic field. (b) In this regard, the loop behaves as if had a bar magnet imbedded in the plane of its face that points perpendicular to that face with the north end in the direction that one's right thumb points when one's fingers curl in the direction of the current flow. The vector $\vec{\mu}$ indicates the south-to-north axis of the magnet.

The loop behaves like a bar magnet in this regard

Indeed, the loop behaves as a bar magnet would in the same magnetic field. Pretend that the loop's face is a clear plastic slab and we imbed a magnet in that face so that it is perpendicular to the slab with its north pole on the side indicated by your right thumb when your right fingers curl with the current flow (see figure E8.1b). The horizontal magnetic field would exert a rightward horizontal force on the magnet's north pole and a leftward horizontal force on the south pole, as shown. You can see from the diagram that these hypothetical forces would again twist the loop to align its face perpendicular to the magnetic field, just as the actual forces do in figure E8.1a.

We can characterize the "strength" of the loop's magnetic response by measuring the torque $\vec{\tau}$ that the field exerts on the loop around an axis through the loop's central point O. As we saw in unit C, a force $\vec{F}$ acting at a point whose position is $\vec{r}$ relative to the origin O exerts a torque around O that is given by $\vec{\tau} = \vec{r} \times \vec{F}$. As you may recall, the direction of $\vec{\tau}$ indicates the axis around which the force seeks to twist the object, and $\text{mag}(\vec{\tau})$ expresses the strength of the twisting effect.

How to calculate the torque the field exerts on the loop

Let's calculate the magnitude of the torque exerted on our loop. Imagine that the loop's upper and lower legs have length L and the side legs have length W, as shown in figure E8.2. We can think of total force on the top leg as being exerted at its midpoint, which is a distance $r = W/2$ from the loop's central point O. Since the magnetic field is perpendicular to the current in this leg, equation E8.3 implies that the magnetic force on the top leg has magnitude

$$F_m = \text{mag}(\vec{F}_m) = \frac{L}{c}\text{mag}(\vec{I} \times \vec{B}) = \frac{L}{c} I B \sin 90° = LI\frac{B}{c} \tag{E8.5}$$

The magnitude of the magnetic torque exerted on the top leg is thus

$$\tau_{\text{top}} = rF_m \sin\theta = \frac{W}{2} LI\frac{B}{c}\sin\theta = \frac{1}{2} AI\frac{B}{c}\sin\theta \tag{E8.6}$$

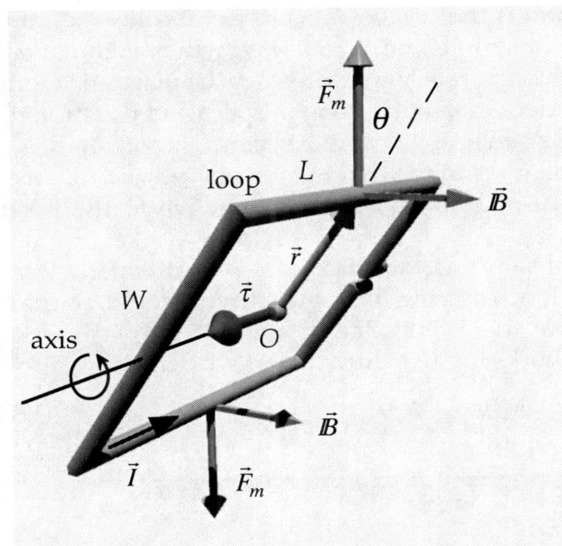

Figure E8.2
This diagram illustrates how one can calculate the torque that the magnetic field exerts on the loop. The torque vector $\vec{\tau}$ indicates the direction of the axis of rotation.

where $A = LW$ is the loop's area. The force on the bottom leg exerts a torque of the same magnitude and direction (as you can check with your right hand), so the total torque on the loop is twice as large:

$$\tau = AI\frac{\mathbb{B}}{c}\sin\theta \tag{E8.7}$$

Note that the angle θ here is the same as the angle that the equivalent magnet shown in figure E8.1b makes with the horizontal. This makes it possible to express equation E8.7 in an especially compact way. Imagine that we define a vector $\vec{\mu}$ whose direction points from the south pole to the north pole of the equivalent magnet in figure E8.1b, and whose magnitude is equal to AI. Then we can write equation E8.7 as follows:

Definition of a loop's *magnetic moment* vector $\vec{\mu}$

$$\tau = \mu\frac{\mathbb{B}}{c}\sin\theta \tag{E8.8}$$

Moreover, as we have just noted, the angle between the magnetic field and the direction of $\vec{\mu}$ is θ (as shown in figure E8.1b). Finally, you can check with your right hand that the direction of the cross product of $\vec{\mu}$ and $\vec{B}$ is the same as the torque vector shown in figure E8.2. Therefore, we can express the torque on the loop this way

The torque on a current-carrying loop in a magnetic field

$$\vec{\tau} = \vec{\mu}\times\frac{\vec{\mathbb{B}}}{c} = \vec{\mu}\times\vec{B}, \quad \text{where } \text{mag}(\vec{\mu})=AI \tag{E8.9}$$

Purpose: This equation describes the torque $\vec{\tau}$ experienced by a loop of area A that carries current I in a magnetic field $\vec{B} = \vec{\mathbb{B}}/c$.

Symbols: $\vec{\mu}$ is called the loop's **magnetic moment**, and expresses the strength and south-to-north orientation of the loop's equivalent bar magnet.

Limitations: The loop must be small enough so that $\vec{B}$ is approximately constant over its face.

Notes: Though we derived this equation for a rectangular loop, it applies to flat loops with arbitrary shapes. Note also the analogy to the similar equation $\vec{\tau} = \vec{p}_e \times \vec{E}$ for an electric dipole (see equation E2.18).

The beauty of this equation is that it allows us to express how a loop responds to a magnetic field in a simple and direct way, which is much easier than analyzing the forces on the separate legs. Moreover, the magnetic moment $\vec{\mu}$ neatly expresses both the orientation of the loop in space and the strength of its response to the magnetic field in a single simple vector. The vector $\vec{\mu}$ is also directly and conveniently analogous to the dipole moment $\vec{p}_e \equiv q\vec{d}$ of an electric dipole, where $\vec{d}$ is the displacement from the negative to the positive charge.

Generalizing to loops that have N turns

If the loop has N turns of wire instead of one, *each* turn experiences the same forces that a single-turn loop carrying the same current would, so the *total* force at each point on the loop is N times larger and the torque is N times larger. So, equation E8.9 still works for an N-turn loop if we define

$$\text{mag}(\vec{\mu}) = NAI \tag{E8.10}$$

Self-Test E8X.2

Argue that the *net* magnetic force on the loop is zero, so that in a uniform magnetic field, the loop's center of mass does not accelerate.

E8.3 Electric Motors

The basic operation of an electric motor

Electric motors represent an important application of this effect. Figure E8.3 shows an electric motor stripped down to its two most basic elements, which are displayed here in simplified form as a pair of permanent magnet poles that create an approximately uniform horizontal magnetic field between them, and a rectangular current-carrying loop of wire that is free to rotate around a horizontal axis (we'll worry about how to get current to the loop shortly). If the loop is oriented as shown in figure E8.3a and conducts current

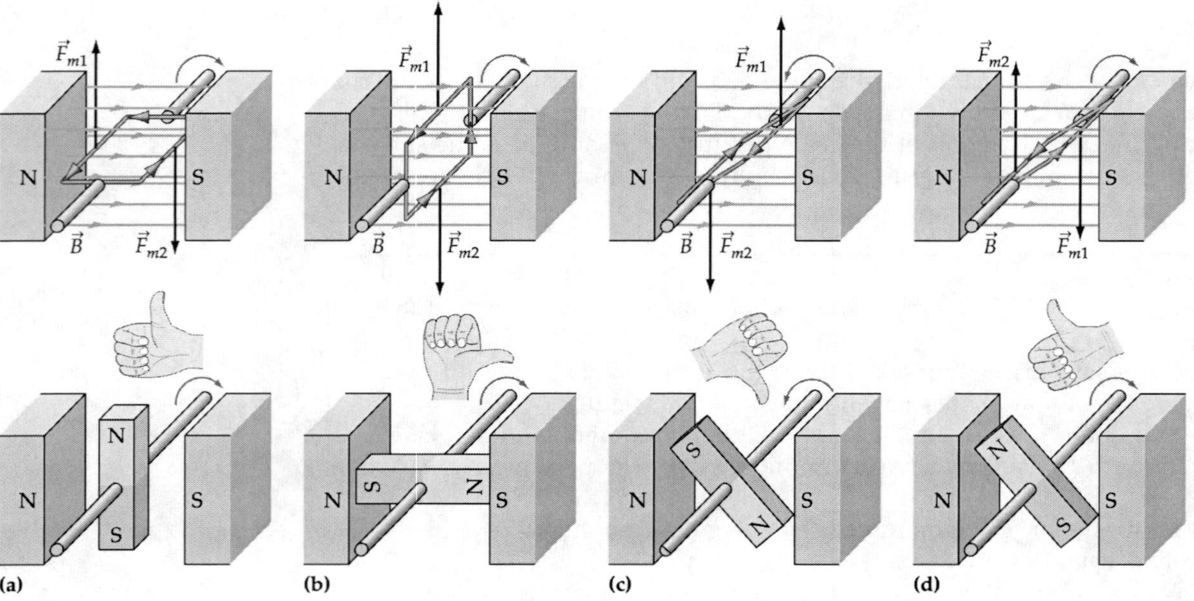

Figure E8.3
The basic elements of an electric motor are a set of permanent magnets that create a magnetic field and a current-carrying loop of wire that is free to rotate in that field. The loop behaves in the magnetic field as if it were a magnet oriented as shown below each drawing. In the last drawing, the current in the loop has been reversed.

in the direction shown, the two loop legs parallel to the axis of rotation each experience a vertical magnetic force (as you can easily check with your right hand) that seeks to twist the loop *clockwise*. When the loop reaches the vertical orientation shown in figure E8.3b, these forces no longer twist the loop but rather try to pull it apart. If the loop were to continue to rotate clockwise, the forces on these legs would seek to twist the loop counterclockwise (see figure E8.3c). The loop therefore seeks to orient itself as shown in figure E8.3b.

The loop rule

In each of these three orientations, the loop in fact responds to the magnetic field just as the permanent magnet shown below each loop would. Note that if you curl your right fingers around the loop in the direction that its current flows, your thumb points toward the north pole of the analogous permanent magnet (see figure E8.3a): we will call this the **loop rule**.

Self-Test E8X.3

Explain why the magnetic forces on the legs perpendicular to the axis of rotation do nothing to aid or hinder rotation.

Such a loop would not make a good motor, because it gets stuck in the orientation shown in figure E8.3b. The trick to making a motor is finding a way to reverse the direction of the current just as the loop passes through the position shown in figure E8.3b, so that magnetic forces on the loop *continue* to twist it clockwise (see figure E8.3d) instead of counterclockwise as in figure E8.3c. If we reverse the loop's current every half-rotation, the loop will rotate endlessly.

How a commutator keeps the loop rotating

There are a number of ways to perform this reversal. The most straightforward is illustrated in figure E8.4. In this scheme, we attach the loop's ends to two half-rings that each wrap halfway around the motor's axle (these half rings, which together are called the motor's **commutator**, are shown in figure E8.4a). A stationary **brush** touches each ring: as the axle turns, the half-rings rotate under the brushes, but maintain good electrical contact with them. Note that if we connect the two brushes to the two terminals of a battery as shown, current will always flow into the rightward leg and out the leftward leg, ensuring that the magnetic forces on the loop always seek to turn it clockwise.

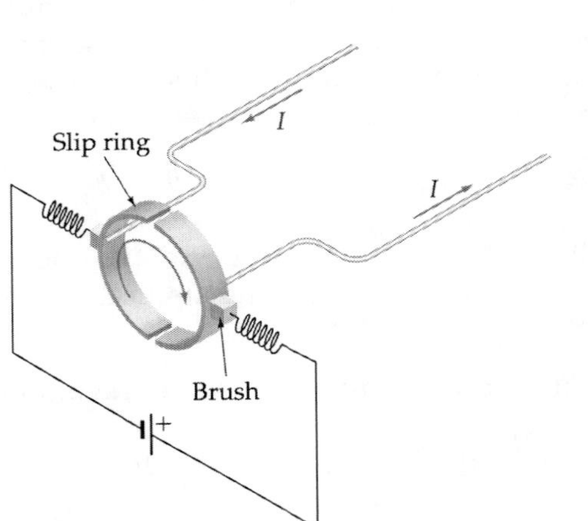

Figure E8.4
(a) A *commutator* can both feed current to a rotating loop and reverse the current's direction each half turn so that the loop continues to rotate. The brushes slide on the commutator's metal half rings as the axle turns, feeding current into the loop's left leg and taking it out of the right leg. (b) An actual photograph of an electric motor. The commutator is at the lower left of the motor's axle, and the brushes in this case touch the commutator on its top and bottom instead of its sides. The loop here consists of many turns of wire wrapped around an iron bar.

We can make our motor more powerful by wrapping N sequential turns of wire around the loop instead of a single turn. In such a case, the total magnetic force on the N strands of wire in each leg will be N times greater than on a single-strand leg carrying the same current. Figure E8.4b shows an actual electric motor with a commutator and a rotating loop that has multiple turns of wire.

Example E8.2 The Energy Released as a Motor Turns

Problem Consider a motor whose rotating loop consists of N turns of wire wound in a rectangular loop of length L and width W. If the loop carries current I as it rotates in a magnetic field of strength $\boldsymbol{B}$, how much energy does it produce per revolution?

Translation Figure E8.5 shows the situation.

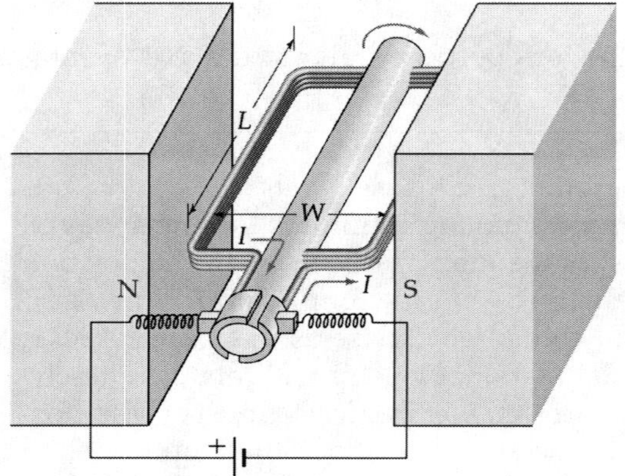

Figure E8.5
A picture of the loop described in example E8.2, with some useful symbols defined.

Model Note that no matter how the loop is oriented, the current flowing in the two legs parallel to the axis of rotation is perpendicular to the magnetic field. According to equation E8.3, the magnitude of the magnetic force on each of N strands in each these legs is therefore

$$F_m = \frac{L}{c}\,\text{mag}(\vec{I} \times \vec{B}) = \frac{L}{c} I \boldsymbol{B} \sin 90° = \frac{LI}{c}\boldsymbol{B} \quad \text{(per strand)} \tag{E8.11}$$

The total force is N times this. Now, as the loop rotates a half revolution, each leg moves a total displacement $\Delta\vec{r}$ parallel to the force whose magnitude is equal to the loop's width W. If the magnetic field is uniform over the size of the loop, the magnetic force on the legs will be constant over this displacement, so the total k-work flowing into each leg during the displacement will be

$$[\Delta K] = \sum_{\text{all steps}} \vec{F}_m \cdot d\vec{r} = \vec{F}_m \cdot \Big(\sum_{\text{all steps}} d\vec{r}\Big) = \vec{F}_m \cdot \Delta\vec{r} = F_m W \cos\theta = F_m W \tag{E8.12}$$

since the magnetic force is parallel to the total displacement $\Delta\vec{r}$. The k-work contributed during a full revolution is simply double the amount contributed per half revolution.

Solution Therefore, the total energy contributed to the loop per revolution is

$$[\Delta K]_{\text{tot}} = 2F_{m,\text{tot}} W = 2\frac{2NLI}{c}\boldsymbol{B}W = 4NAI\frac{\boldsymbol{B}}{c} = 4NAIB \tag{E8.13}$$

where $A = LW$ is the loop's area.

Evaluation The result is proportional to the number of turns, the current, and the magnetic field strength, which all makes sense. The result also has SI units of $(\text{m}^{\cancel{2}})(\cancel{\text{C}}/\cancel{\text{s}})(\text{N}/\cancel{\text{C}})(\cancel{\text{s}}/\cancel{\text{m}}) = \text{N·m} = \text{J}$, which is appropriate.

Self-Test E8X.4

Imagine that the loop in a certain motor consists of a coil with 150 turns spanning an area of 2.0 cm^2. Imagine that in operation, the loop carries an average current of about 1.0 A and rotates at 1500 rpm in a magnetic field of magnitude 200 MN/C. How much mechanical power does the motor provide?

E8.4 Creating Currents in Moving Loops

We have seen that a magnetic field can exert magnetic forces on a conductor carrying a current. However, under the right circumstances, magnetic fields can also *create* currents in moving conductors. In this section, we will consider how this is possible.

A metal bar moving in a magnetic field

First consider a metal bar of length L moving with a velocity $\vec{v}$ in a uniform magnetic field whose field vectors at all points have the common value $\vec{B}$. Assume that the length of the bar, $\vec{v}$, and $\vec{B}$ are mutually perpendicular, as shown in figure E8.6. As the bar moves, it carries its conduction electrons with it. Therefore, these electrons are moving in the magnetic field, and thus will experience a magnetic force $\vec{F}_m$ toward the bar's left end whose magnitude is

$$F_m = \frac{ev\mathbf{B}}{c} = evB \qquad \text{(E8.14)}$$

where e is the magnitude of an electron's charge.

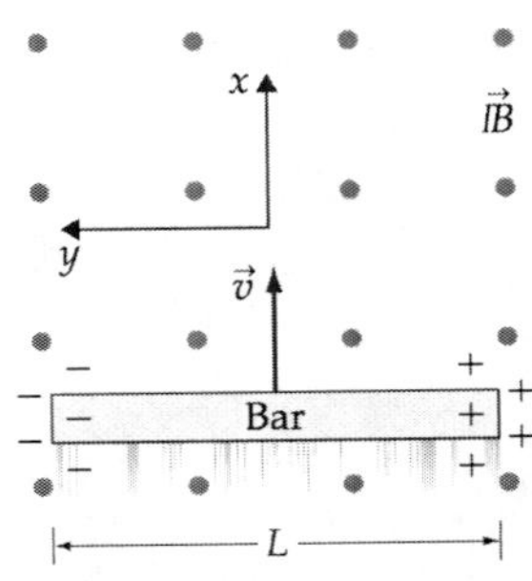

Figure E8.6
The ends of a conducting bar moving perpendicular to a magnetic field become charged.

Self-Test E8X.5

Check with your right hand that the electrons are indeed pushed toward the bar's left end.

This magnetic force will cause electrons to pile up on the bar's left end, leaving a deficit of electrons on its right end, as shown in the diagram. This will continue until the charges reach a static equilibrium configuration where they create an electric field that exerts an electrostatic force on every charge in the bar that is equal in magnitude but opposite in direction to the magnetic force. The magnitude of this field (by the definition of $\vec{E}$) will then be $E = F_e/|q| = F_m/e = v\mathbf{B}/c$ everywhere in the bar. According to chapter E4, this implies that there will be a potential difference between the bar's negative and positive ends of

$$\Delta\phi = \sum_{\text{all steps}} -\vec{E}\cdot d\vec{r} = -\vec{E}\cdot\Big(\sum_{\text{all steps}} d\vec{r}\Big) = -\vec{E}\cdot\Delta\vec{r} = \frac{v\mathbf{B}}{c}L = vBL \qquad \text{(E8.15)}$$

Self-Test E8X.6

An airplane with a wingspan of 80 m flies at 280 m/s due east in a region where the earth's magnetic field has a magnitude of 0.5 gauss and points nearly directly downward. What is the potential difference between the ends of the plane's wings? Which wing becomes positively charged?

The ends of such a bar therefore become charged with a characteristic potential difference between them, just like the electrodes of a battery. Can we ex-

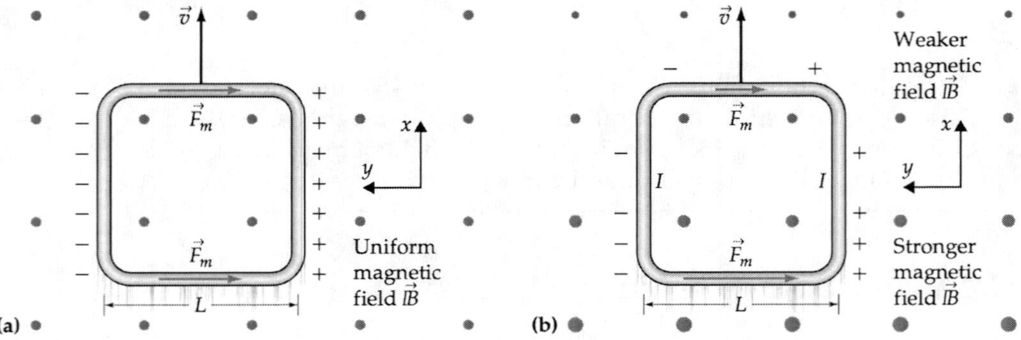

Figure E8.7
(a) A loop moving through a uniform magnetic field with its face perpendicular to the field. No current flows in the loop in this case, because electrons experience equal magnetic forces in the front and rear legs. (The gray arrows show the direction in which the magnetic force would act on a positive charge. (b) If the loop moves in a nonuniform field, the stronger magnetic force in one leg pushes conventional current counterclockwise around the loop.

ploit this magnetic battery to drive a current around a circuit? Figure E8.7a illustrates what happens when we try to complete the circuit by closing the loop. The problem is that *both* horizontal legs in this circuit act as opposing magnetic batteries, *both* driving electrons toward the loop's left side. (Note that charges on the two legs parallel to the motion are driven to those legs' left sides but not along their length, so these legs neither oppose nor aid the flow of current.) The result, as illustrated in the diagram, is that the loop's left side becomes negatively charged and its right side positively charged, but no current flows.

Induction in a loop moving in a nonuniform magnetic field

What if the magnetic field is *not* uniform, but decreases in strength in the $+x$ direction as shown in figure E8.7b? In this case, the magnetic field's magnitude $\boldsymbol{B}_r$ at the the rear leg's position is stronger than its magnitude $\boldsymbol{B}_f$ at the front leg's position. The unbalanced magnetic forces exerted on the electrons in these legs *will* cause electrons to flow clockwise around the loop, even though electrons are pushed *against* the magnetic force in the front leg. How is this possible? The leftward magnetic force on electrons in the rear leg packs excess electrons onto the surface of the loop's *left* leg. This surface charge pushes electrons forward into the front leg. At first, they are driven back by the opposing magnetic force, but as electrons pile up behind them in the left leg (driven there by the stronger magnetic force exerted in the rear leg), there is eventually a sufficiently strong electrostatic repulsion from the surface charges on left leg to push electrons through the front leg against the magnetic force. A steady-state situation is soon established where electrons flow clockwise at a steady rate through the loop. You can show that the net emf (energy per unit charge) contributed by the magnetic force to a charge q flowing around the loop is

$$|\mathscr{E}_{\text{loop}}| \equiv \left|\frac{1}{q}\sum_{\text{loop}} \vec{F}_m \cdot d\vec{r}\right| = \left(\frac{v}{c}\right)\left|\boldsymbol{B}_r - \boldsymbol{B}_f\right|L = vL\left|B_r - B_f\right| \tag{E8.16}$$

We say in such a situation that the magnetic field **induces** a current in the loop. Note that current will *only* flow if the field through which the loop moves is *not* uniform, so that $\boldsymbol{B}_r \neq \boldsymbol{B}_f$.

Self-Test E8X.7

Verify that equation E8.16 is correct.

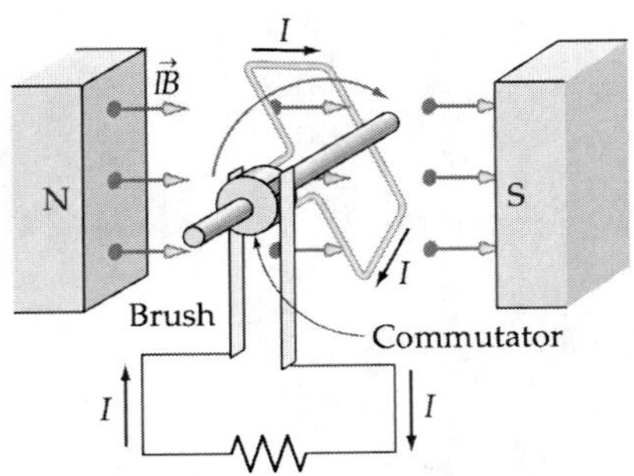

Figure E8.8
A schematic diagram of an electric generator.

Generators

Magnetic forces on electrons in a loop *rotating* in a uniform magnetic field can also induce a current to flow through the loop. Imagine that we take the electric motor shown in figure E8.4, connect its brushes to a resistive load of some type, and then compel the loop to rotate clockwise in the magnetic field, as shown in figure E8.8b. Note that as the left leg of the loop moves upward in the magnetic field, the magnetic forces on charge carriers in that leg will drive conventional current away from us. Similarly, as the right leg moves downward, magnetic forces drive current toward us. Thus the left brush will become negative and the right brush positive, and current will flow leftward through the resistor, as if it were connected to a battery. Since the right brush is always connected by the commutator to whichever leg of the loop is rightward (and the left brush likewise to the leftward leg) as the loop turns, current will *always* flow leftward through the resistor. Such a device constitutes a simplified electrical **generator**. Generators used by power companies throughout the world employ this general principle to create currents.

E8.5 Eddy Currents in Moving Conductors

A magnetic field can also create a current in a conducting surface that moves through that magnetic field. Such currents, called **eddy currents**, generally act to resist the conductor's motion through the field (though these currents also provide the lift forces in magnetic levitation trains).

A simple example where we can estimate the magnetic drag due to an eddy current

As a simple example, consider a horseshoe magnet having square poles that are separated by a very small gap. Imagine that we can model the magnetic field in the gap as having an essentially uniform magnitude $\mathbb{B}$ in a square region whose sides have a length of approximately L, and essentially zero magnitude outside this region (this will be only an approximation, but it makes the calculations much simpler). Now imagine that we pull an aluminum plate through the gap with speed v, as shown in figure E8.9a on the next page. Assume that the aluminum plate is much larger than the rectangular region, has thickness w, and a conductivity of σ_c.

Assume that we define coordinates so that the plate moves in the $+x$ direction and the magnetic field points in the y direction. As the plate drags charge carriers through the magnetic field, the carriers experience magnetic forces that push them in the $+z$ direction through the region where $\mathbb{B} \neq 0$, as shown in figure E8.9b. Since the drift velocity of carriers is very small even in a large cur-

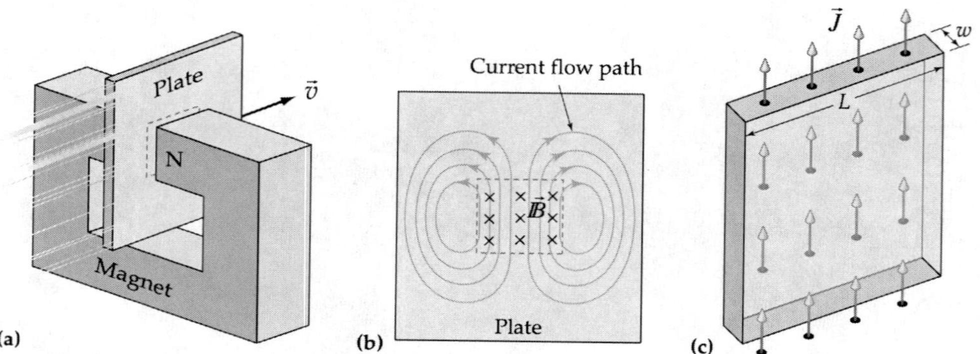

Figure E8.9
(a) An aluminum plate being pulled through the gap between the square poles of a horseshoe magnet. **(b)** As the plate moves to the right, the magnetic field in the square region enclosed by the dotted line exerts a magnetic force on charge carriers within that region that pushes conventional current upward in this region. This *eddy current* curves back around outside this region to complete the circuit. **(c)** This diagram shows just the part of the plate where the magnetic field is nonzero. The current density $\vec{J}$ will be essentially uniform and upward throughout the volume of this region. If the magnet's poles have sides of length L, this region will be a flat box with sides L and a thickness equal to the plate's thickness w. The current goes into the box's bottom face and emerges from its top face.

rent (see example E5.1), the velocity of the carriers even when the current is flowing will be essentially $\vec{v}$, which is perpendicular to the magnetic field. Therefore, by the magnetic force law, the magnitude of the magnetic force on a given carrier of charge q will be

$$F_m = \text{mag}(\vec{F}_m) = \text{mag}\left(q\frac{\vec{v}}{c}\times\vec{\boldsymbol{B}}\right) = q\left(\frac{v}{c}\right)\boldsymbol{B}\sin 90° = \frac{qv\,\boldsymbol{B}}{c} \tag{E8.17}$$

Now, we saw in chapter E5 that when an electric field $\vec{E} = \vec{F}_e/q$ exerts forces on charge carriers in a conductor, the current density is $\vec{J} = \sigma_c\vec{E} = \sigma_c\vec{F}_e/q$. By analogy (since it really shouldn't matter what force is doing the pushing) the magnitude of the current density that should be created when the *magnetic* field exerts a magnetic force $\vec{F}_m$ on the charge carriers in the aluminum conductor should have the magnitude

$$J \approx \sigma_c\frac{F_m}{q} = \frac{\sigma_c v\,\boldsymbol{B}}{c} \tag{E8.18}$$

The current completes the circuit by circling around and flowing in the opposite direction outside of this region, as illustrated in figure E8.9b.

(Equation E8.18 is only an approximation, because the surface charges on the plate that redirect the current outside the region affected by the magnetic field create electric forces that partially oppose the magnetic forces on the charge carriers. A detailed calculation shows that the actual average current is smaller than this estimate by very roughly a factor of 2. However, this estimate yields a useful first approximation.)

This current flows in the bottom and out the top of the rectangular volume in the aluminum plate where $\boldsymbol{B} \neq 0$, as shown in figure E8.9c. If we assume that the current density is approximately uniform through this region, the total current flowing in the region will be the magnitude of the current density J times the cross-sectional area through which the current moves, which according to figure E8.9c has area Lw. The current flowing through the rectangular volume where $\boldsymbol{B} \neq 0$ is therefore

$$I \approx \frac{\sigma_c v w L}{c} \mathbb{B} \tag{E8.19}$$

(This is also only approximate, because it is impossible to create a field that is truly uniform within a certain region and then suddenly falls to zero outside the region. But this is again a reasonable first estimate.)

Finally, we can treat this rectangular volume of aluminum as a sort of chunky wire carrying a current in a magnetic field. Note that the current (because it lies in the plane of the plate) is perpendicular to the magnetic field. If we plug this current into equation E8.3, we find with only a bit of work that

$$F_{\text{eddy}} \approx \sigma_c V v \frac{\mathbb{B}^2}{c^2} = \sigma_c V v B^2 \tag{E8.20}$$

where V is the volume of metal immersed in the magnetic field. As noted previously, this is only an estimate, but should be good to within a factor of two or so. You can check with your right hand that the magnetic force on this current will point opposite to the plate's velocity $\vec{v}$, so this will act like a drag force that is proportional to the plate's speed v.

A final estimate of the drag force in this situation

Self-Test E8X.8

Fill in the missing steps between equations E8.19 and E8.20.

Self-Test E8X.9

Imagine that the region where $B \neq 0$ is 4 cm on a side, that $B = 0.1$ T in this region, that the speed of the aluminum plate is 10 cm/s, and the plate is 0.5 cm thick. Show that the drag force in this case is about 0.3 N.

E8.6 The Mystery du Jour

We have seen in this chapter that magnetic fields exert forces on current-carrying wires and loops, and that magnetic fields can even create currents in certain situations. This is analogous to the way that electric fields exert forces on charged particles, so it seems that currents are to magnetic fields what charged particles at rest are to electric fields.

But how far can we push this analogy? Since charged particles also *create* electric fields, the analogy suggests that currents should create magnetic fields. Is this true?

Hans Christian Oersted showed in 1820 that a current in a wire affected a nearby compass, presenting the world with the first evidence that currents do indeed create magnetic fields. But how does this work? What laws govern the creation of magnetic fields by currents? The answers to such questions will be our focus in the next chapter.

TWO-MINUTE PROBLEMS

E8T.1 Imagine that you hold a short segment of wire vertically in a magnetic field that is directed horizontally toward you. If the wire segment carries conventional current in an upward direction, what is the direction of the magnetic force exerted on the wire?

A. Right
B. Left
C. Up
D. Down
E. Toward you
F. Away from you

E8T.2 An east-facing loop carries a counterclockwise current as viewed from the east. It is placed in a magnetic field whose vectors point vertically upward. The loop is free to rotate around any axis. How will the loop respond to the magnetic field? (*Hint:* Find the orientation of this loop's equivalent magnet).

A. When viewed from above, it will twist 90° clockwise to face south.
B. When viewed from above, it will twist 90° counterclockwise to face north.
C. When viewed from the south, it will twist 90° clockwise to face downward.
D. When viewed from the south, it will twist 90° counterclockwise to face upward.
E. The loop will be unaffected by the field.
F. It will respond in some other way (specify).

E8T.3 A jet flies in a region of the earth where the magnetic field points nearly straight upward. Which part of the airplane becomes negatively charged?

A. Its nose
B. Its tail
C. Its top
D. Its bottom
E. Its left wing
F. Its right wing
T. No part becomes charged.

E8T.4 A large bar magnet is embedded in a table so that its north pole sticks somewhat above the table and its south pole sticks out an equal distance below the table. A ring of wire lying flat on the table is pushed so that it slides directly toward the magnet. What is the direction of the current induced in the ring when viewed from above? (Assume the magnet's field is not affected by the table.)

A. clockwise
B. counterclockwise
C. there is no induced current
D. insufficient information

E8T.5 Imagine that we move the plate in figure E8.9a in the $+y$ direction (that is, toward the magnet's north pole) instead of sideways between the poles. We obviously can't do this for long, but while the plate is moving toward that pole, does an eddy current flow in the plate? If so, in what direction?

A. No current flows.
B. A current flows in the $+x$ direction.
C. A current flows in the $-x$ direction.
D. A current flows in the $+z$ direction
E. A current flows in the $-z$ direction
F. A current flows in some other direction (specify).

E8T.6 Consider the situation just described in problem E8T.5. Is there a magnetic force on the plate? If so, in what direction?

A. There is no magnetic force.
B. $\vec{F}_{\text{eddy}}$ points in the $-x$ direction.
C. $\vec{F}_{\text{eddy}}$ points in the $+y$ direction.
D. $\vec{F}_{\text{eddy}}$ points in the $-y$ direction.
E. $\vec{F}_{\text{eddy}}$ points in the $+z$ direction
F. $\vec{F}_{\text{eddy}}$ points in the $-z$ direction
T. $\vec{F}_{\text{eddy}}$ points in some other direction (specify).

HOMEWORK PROBLEMS

Basic Skills

E8B.1 A wire carries a current of 300 A. What is the maximum possible force per unit length that could be exerted on the wire by the earth's magnetic field? Why is what you found a *maximum* possible value (what might make the actual force smaller)?

E8B.2 A wire has a mass of 10 g per meter. What is the *minimum* amount of current it would have to carry if the magnetic force exerted by a horizontal 30 MN/C magnetic field on a horizontal length of this wire is able to lift the wire off the ground?

E8B.3 A square loop 1.0 cm on a side conducts a current of 3.0 A clockwise when viewed from the east. The loop is placed in a vertically downward magnetic field having a strength of 20 MN/C. How will the loop seek to orient itself in this magnetic field? How much energy does it take to flip the loop 180° from this preferred orientation?

E8B.4 A circular coil consisting of 60 turns of wire that carry a current of 1.5 A is placed in a horizontal magnetic field with strength 50 MN/C. After experimenting with various orientations of the loop, we find that it takes 2.0 J of energy to turn it 180° from the loop's preferred orientation. What is this loop's radius?

E8B.5 An airplane develops a 0.25-V potential difference between the tips of its wings when flying in a region where the earth's magnetic field points essentially vertically upward. If the plane's wingspan is 35 m, how fast is it flying?

E8B.6 Consider a copper sheet that is 1 mm thick moving at 1 m/s between the poles of a horseshoe magnet. Assume that the magnetic field between the poles has a magnitude of 100 MN/C and that the poles are circular with a diameter of 5 cm. What is the approximate magnetic drag force on the plate?

Synthetic

E8S.1 A long straight wire having a mass of 0.025 kg per meter is suspended by threads (see the picture at the top of the next column). When the wire carries a 20-A current, it experiences a horizontal magnetic force that deflects it to an equilibrium angle of 10° (see the drawing below). What is the magnitude and direction of the magnetic field? (Assume that the field vectors are perpendicular to the wire.)

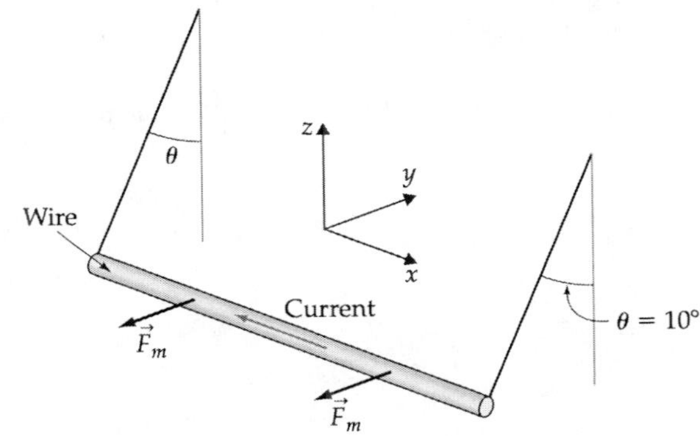

E8S.2 A bar magnet oriented with its long axis aligned with the direction of a nonuniform magnetic field produced by another bar magnet will experience a net force toward that magnet, as shown in part (a) of the drawing below. Explain why using an electric dipole analogy. Also explain why a current-carrying loop oriented analogously will *also* experience a net force toward the magnet [see part (b) of the drawing below]. This is an example of how current loops and bar magnets behave alike.

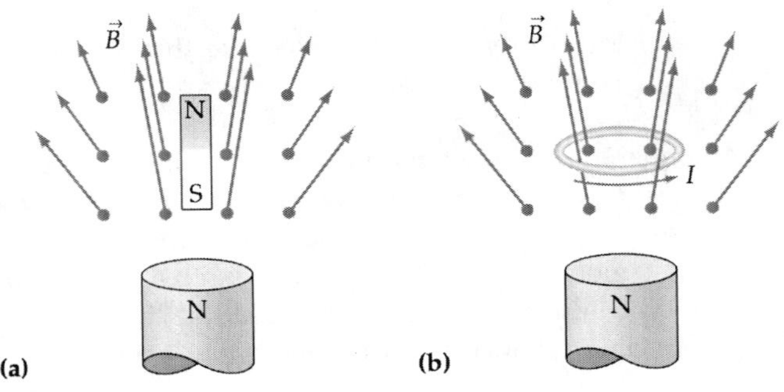

E8S.3 One can use the fact that sea water conducts electricity to construct *magnetohydrodynamic* boat engine that uses magnetic forces (instead of a propeller) to thrust water backward. (This would be advantageous in creating very quiet submarine drives.) An example of such an engine is illustrated in the drawing on the next page. The engine consists of a channel through which sea water flows. The side walls of the channel are powerful permanent magnets that create a strong magnetic field perpendicular to the flow of water. Electrodes on the top and bottom faces of the channel drive a very large current through the sea water as it flows through the channel. For the sake of argument, assume that the channel has a width and height of $w = h = 50$ cm and a length of $L = 2.0$ m, the average magnetic field strength in the channel is 1 tesla (a *large* magnetic field), and that we want to exert a total thrust force of F_{Th} = 100 N (22 lbs) on the water flowing through the channel. Assume that the magnetic field and the current density in the water are uniform.

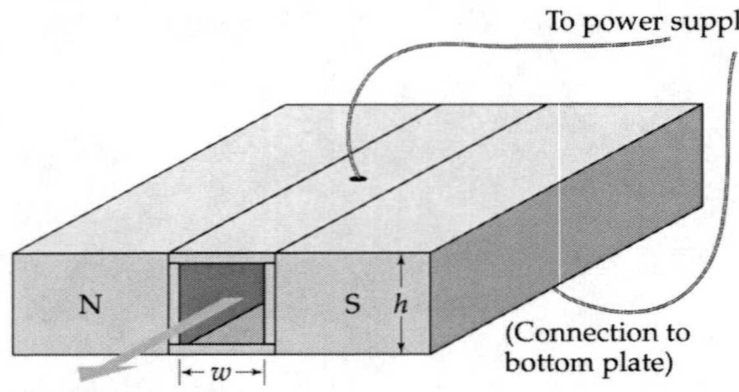

(a) Estimate the total current that must flow through the water to obtain this thrust.

(b) What direction must the current flow to push the water in the direction shown?

(c) Use data in Table E5.1 to estimate the total resistance of the sea water in the channel.

(d) How much power is wasted in the form of thermal energy to get this thrust?

(e) Why do you think drives like this are not in common use?

E8S.4 Imagine that we construct a motor using a coil consisting of 300 turns of wire wound in the form of a square 2.5 cm on a side. The permanent magnets in the motor create a field with strength 40 MN/C in which the coil rotates. We would like the motor to be able produce 5.0 W of mechanical energy when it is turning at 1200 rpm. How much current do we need to supply to the motor?

E8S.5 Imagine constructing a motor that would operate in the earth's magnetic field instead of using permanent magnets. Let's say that we would be satisfied if such a motor generated a paltry 1 W of power while turning at a (very rapid) rate of 100 rev/s. Assume also that the rotor has 1000 turns of wire, and that the wire carries a healthy 1 A of current.

(a) If the loop were a square loop, about how big would it have to be?

(b) Does such a motor seem practical to you? Discuss why or why not.

E8S.6 The drawing below shows a way to take advantage of the way that a conducting bar moving in a magnetic field becomes a magnetic battery. Imagine that we have two metal rails 20 cm apart connected by a light bulb. The rails are placed in a 1.0-T magnetic field oriented vertically downward. We then constrain a bar to slide on the rails toward the light bulb in this magnetic field. How fast must the bar move to put a potential difference of 3.0 V across the bulb? What direction does the current flow?

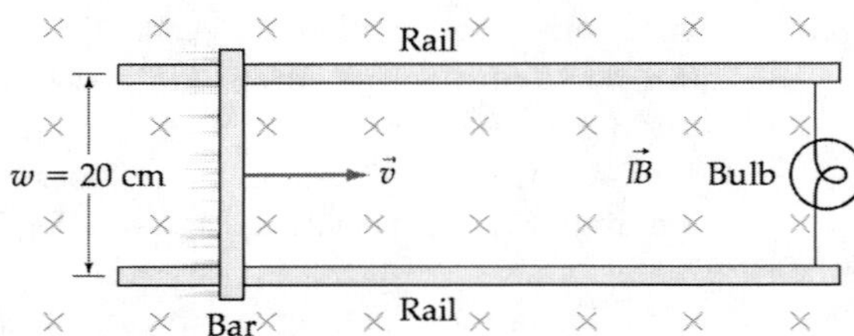

E8S.7 Imagine that we have a conductor with a rectangular cross-section whose height in the z direction is h and its width in the y direction is w. This conductor carries a conventional current $\vec{I}$ in the $+x$ direction along its length in a magnetic field $\vec{B}$ directed in the $-y$ direction, as illustrated below.

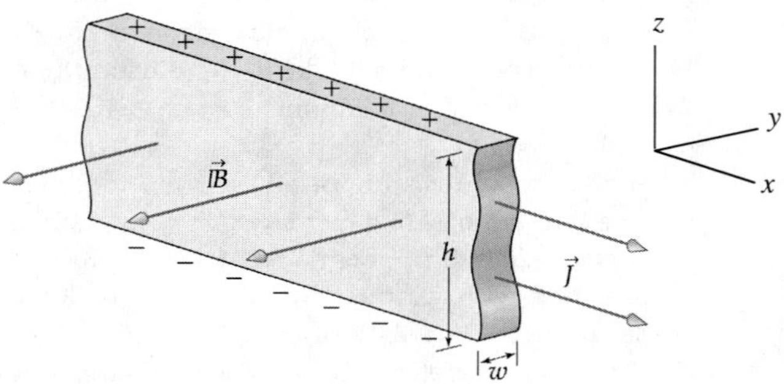

(a) The moving charge carriers will experience magnetic forces that will push them either upward or downward, depending on their charge and their direction of motion. Yet when a steady-state current flow is established, the charges must move directly along the conductor. Argue that whatever the charge q of the charge carriers, this only becomes possible once surface charges have been established on the top and bottom edges that create an electrostatic field such that

$$\vec{E} = -\frac{\vec{v}}{c} \times \vec{B} \quad \text{(E8.21)}$$

(b) Argue that this means that the potential difference between the conductor's bottom surface to its top surface is given by

$$\Delta\phi = \frac{B\,I}{nqwc} \quad \text{(E8.22)}$$

where n is the number density (number per unit volume) of charge carriers.

(c) The fact that a current-carrying conductor in a magnetic field develops a potential difference between its top and bottom edges is called the *Hall effect*. The Hall effect is useful (1) because we can use it to measure the strength of a magnetic field using only simple measurements of current and potential difference, and (2) because the *sign* of this potential difference depends on the actual sign of of the charge carriers. This means we can *determine* whether it is electrons or positive ions that are actually flowing in any substance by measuring the Hall potential difference. If it is really electrons that flow in copper, and we have a copper conductor of width 1 mm carrying a a current of 10 A in a magnetic field of 100 MN/C, what would we predict the Hall-effect potential difference between the conductor's top and bottom to be?

E8S.8 A generator constructed as described in section E8.4 uses a 200-turn coil in the form of a square that is 5.0 cm on a side. When the coil is rotated at 3600 rpm, its emf oscillates between 0 V and +30 V.

(a) Explain qualitatively why the emf is not constant for such a generator and sketch a qualitative graph of the emf versus time. (*Hint:* The emf is zero at the instant that the loop's legs are moving parallel to the magnetic field. Why? When is the emf maximum?)

(b) What is the magnitude of the magnetic field in this generator?

E8S.9 Consider a generator constructed as shown below.

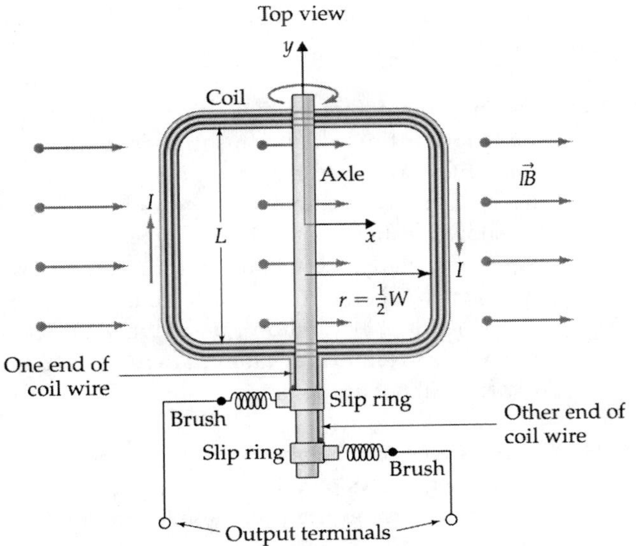

The loop in this generator rotates at an angular rate of ω. The slip rings in this design ensure that the same leg of the rotating loop is always connected to the same output terminal. Show that the potential difference between the output terminals is given by $\mathscr{E} = \mathscr{E}_0 \cos\theta$ (where $\theta = \omega t$ is the angle that the plane of the loop makes with the magnetic field direction at time t), and determine $\mathscr{E}_0$ in terms of the loop's length L, width W, the magnetic field strength $\boldsymbol{B}$, and the loop's angular rotation rate ω.

E8S.10 A device called a *homopolar generator* is shown below. A metal disk rotates in the presence of a magnetic field perpendicular to the disk. Sliding contacts connect the axle and the outer surface of the disk to an external circuit.

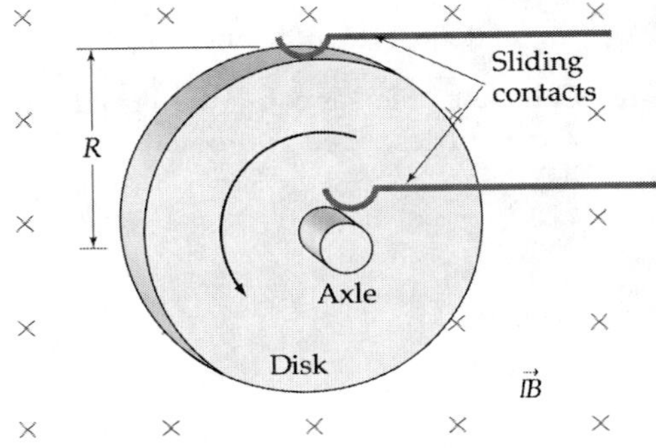

(a) Explain why this device produces an emf between the two contacts. Is this emf oscillating or constant?

(b) Determine the magnitude of this emf in terms of the disk's radius R, the magnetic field strength B, and the angular rate of rotation ω. (Hint: Divide the disk up into rings of infinitesimal thickness dr, compute the emf created across each ring, then sum.)

E8S.11 The magnetic drag force due to eddy currents on a conducting plate moving through a magnetic field means that a plate dropped vertically between the poles of a magnet will reach a terminal speed, just like an object falling in air. Imagine that we drop a long strip of aluminum whose mass is 0.60 kg and whose thickness is 0.5 cm so that it falls vertically between the poles of a horseshoe magnet (just imagine rotating figure E8.9a so that the plate moves vertically downward). If the poles are round and have a diameter of 5 cm, and the magnetic field strength between the poles is 0.2 T, what is the plate's terminal speed? (*Hint*: Remember that the terminal speed is the speed where the drag force balances the gravitational force on the object: the net force on the object will then be zero and it will no longer increase its downward speed.)

Rich-Context

E8R.1 Consider the magnetohydrodynamic boat drive described in problem E8S.3. Imagine that the channel has height h, width w, and length L, and that the average magnetic field strength in the channel is B. Say that we would like to exert given thrust force F on sea water that has conductivity σ_c while the boat is moving at some reasonable speed v through the water (assume this v is the speed of the water relative to the channel). Ignore friction.

(a) Find an expression for the rate at which the boat gains k-work from the drive's interaction with the water divided by the rate at which the drive expends thermal energy (this is a measure of the drive's efficiency).

(b) Calculate this ratio for the specific drive parameters described in problem E8S.3.

E8R.2 In section E7.6, we saw that a magnetic field cannot do any k-work on a free charged particle. In example E8.2 in section E8.3, however, we calculate the (nonzero) k-work that a magnetic field contributes to loop turning in the magnetic field. Can a magnetic field contribute k-work or not? Solve this puzzle by considering in detail what happens to charge carriers in a wire (according to the Drude model) as they are deflected by the magnetic field. Exactly how (at the microscopic level) does the magnetic field actually exert a force on a current-carrying wire? Is it really the magnetic field that does the k-work on the wire's atom, or is it some other kind of interaction? If so, what kind of interaction? Explain your responses to all of these questions carefully and completely.

ANSWERS TO SELF-TESTS

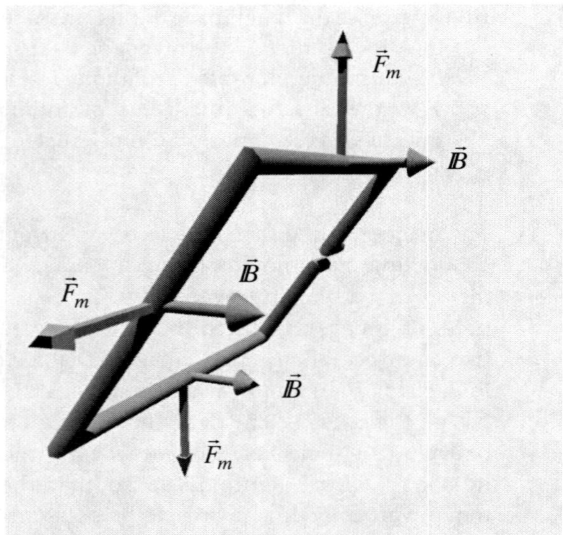

Figure E8.10
This diagram illustrates the magnetic force on the closest leg of the loop.

E8X.1 The magnetic force on either one of the side legs will point perpendicular to both the magnetic field direction and the current direction. One can check with one's right hand that the magnetic force on either leg must point directly away from the the other side leg when the current flows in the direction specified in figure E8.1 (see figure E8.10). Since such forces lie in the plane of the loop, they exert no torque on the loop.

E8X.2 The magnetic forces on the top and bottom legs of the loop must be equal in magnitude (because the magnitudes of the current and the magnetic field are the same at each leg) and opposite in direction (as shown in figure E8.10). The forces on the side legs are similarly equal in magnitude and opposite in direction. Therefore the net force on the loop is zero when it is in a uniform magnetic field. Therefore, while the loop may attempt to twist, its center of mass will not accelerate.

E8X.3 In the orientation shown in figure E8.3a, the current in these legs flows parallel to the magnetic field, so there is no force exerted on these legs at all. In the other orientations, the right hand rule for the cross product implies that the forces on these legs are parallel to the axis of rotation. These forces therefore cannot influence the rotation at all.

E8X.4 According to equation E8.13, for each revolution, the k-work done on the coil is

$$4NAI\frac{\mathbb{B}}{c} = 4(150)(2.0\text{ cm}^2)(1.0\text{ A})\frac{200\times10^6\text{ N/C}}{3.0\times10^8\text{ m/s}}$$

$$= 80\ \cancel{\text{cm}}^2\cancel{\text{A}}\cdot\frac{\cancel{\text{N}}}{\cancel{\text{C}}(\cancel{\text{m}}/\cancel{\text{s}})}\left(\frac{1\ \cancel{\text{m}}}{100\ \cancel{\text{cm}}}\right)^2\left(\frac{1\ \cancel{\text{C}}/\cancel{\text{s}}}{1\ \cancel{\text{A}}}\right)\left(\frac{1\text{ J}}{1\ \cancel{\text{N}}\cdot\cancel{\text{m}}}\right)$$

$$= 0.08\text{ J} \qquad \text{(E8.23)}$$

If the motor coil turns at 1500 rpm (revolutions per minute), the total energy released is

$$\frac{1500\ \cancel{\text{rev}}}{\cancel{\text{min}}}\left(\frac{1\ \cancel{\text{min}}}{60\ \cancel{\text{s}}}\right)\left(\frac{0.08\ \cancel{\text{J}}}{\cancel{\text{rev}}}\right)\left(\frac{1\text{ W}}{1\ \cancel{\text{J}}/\cancel{\text{s}}}\right) = 2.0\text{ W} \qquad \text{(E8.24)}$$

E8X.5 The drawing below shows how to use your right hand. Note that electrons have a negative charge, so the direction of $q\vec{v}$ points opposite to the direction of $\vec{v}$.

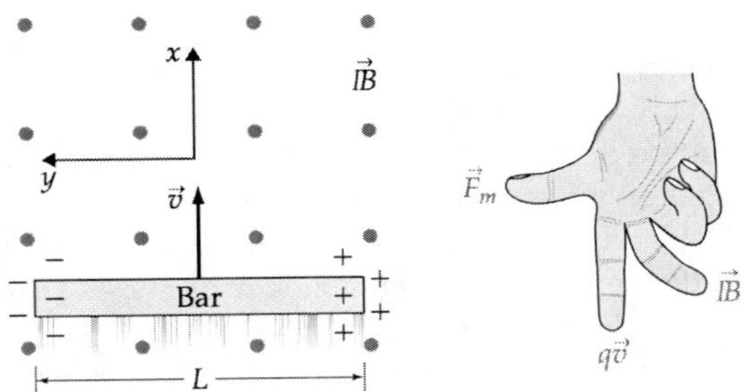

E8X.6 The right hand rule implies that positive charges will move to the north, so the plane's left wing becomes positively charged. Plugging the given values into equation E8.15 yields

$$\Delta\phi = \frac{v\mathbb{B}L}{c} = \frac{(280\ \cancel{\text{m/s}})(0.5\text{ gauss})(80\text{ m})}{3.0\times10^8\ \cancel{\text{m/s}}}$$

$$= 3.7\times10^{-5}\ \cancel{\text{gauss}}\cdot\cancel{\text{m}}\left(\frac{30{,}000\ \cancel{\text{N}}/\cancel{\text{C}}}{1\ \cancel{\text{gauss}}}\right)\left(\frac{1\ \cancel{\text{J}}}{1\ \cancel{\text{N}}\cdot\cancel{\text{m}}}\right)\left(\frac{1\text{ V}}{1\ \cancel{\text{J}}/\cancel{\text{C}}}\right)$$

$$= 1.1\text{ V} \qquad \text{(E8.25)}$$

E8X.7 The magnetic force vectors on (hypothetical) positive charge carriers all point to the right in figure E8.7b. Let us divide the loop up into a sequence of infinitesimal steps $d\vec{r}$ that go counterclockwise around the loop. These displacement vectors will be parallel to the magnetic force in the rear leg, opposite to the magnetic force in the front leg, and perpendicular to the magnetic force in the other legs. Equation E8.14 implies that the magnitude of the magnetic force at any point is $F_m = qv\mathbb{B}/c$. This has the same value at all points on the rear leg, so by the definition of the dot product

$$\frac{1}{q}\sum_{\text{rear leg}}\vec{F}_m\cdot d\vec{r} = \frac{1}{q}\sum_{\text{rear leg}}\frac{qv\mathbb{B}_r}{c}dr\cos(0°)$$

$$= \frac{v\mathbb{B}_r}{c}\sum_{\text{rear leg}}dr = \frac{v\mathbb{B}_r}{c}L \qquad \text{(E8.26)}$$

For the front leg, $\vec{F}_m$ and $d\vec{r}$ are opposite, so

$$\frac{1}{q}\sum_{\text{front leg}}\vec{F}_m\cdot d\vec{r} = \frac{1}{q}\sum_{\text{front leg}}\frac{qv\mathbb{B}_f}{c}dr\cos(180°)$$

$$= -\frac{v\mathbb{B}_f}{c}\sum_{\text{rear leg}}dr = -\frac{v\mathbb{B}_f}{c}L \qquad \text{(E8.27)}$$

For either of the other legs

$$\frac{1}{q}\sum_{\text{front leg}}\vec{F}_m\cdot d\vec{r} = \frac{1}{q}\sum_{\text{front leg}}F_m dr\cos(90°) = 0 \qquad \text{(E8.28)}$$

Putting all these sums together, we get

$$\frac{1}{q}\sum_{\text{loop}}\vec{F}_m\cdot d\vec{r} = \frac{qv\mathbb{B}_rL}{c} - \frac{qv\mathbb{B}_fL}{c}$$

$$= \frac{qvL}{c}(\mathbb{B}_r - \mathbb{B}_f) \qquad \text{(E8.29)}$$

Taking the absolute value yields equation E8.16.

E8X.8 Equation E8.3 tells us that

$$F_m \equiv \text{mag}(\vec{F}_m) = \text{mag}\left(\left[\frac{L}{c}\right]\vec{I}\times\vec{\mathbb{B}}\right)$$

$$= \frac{LI\mathbb{B}}{c}\sin 90° = \frac{LI\mathbb{B}}{c} \qquad \text{(E8.30)}$$

since the angle between the current and the magnetic field is 90°. Plugging the expression for I from equation E8.19 into this expression yields

$$F_m \approx \frac{L\mathbb{B}}{c}\left(\frac{\sigma_c vwL}{c}\mathbb{B}\right) = \sigma_c vwL^2\left(\frac{\mathbb{B}}{c}\right)^2 \qquad \text{(E8.31)}$$

But wL^2 is simply V, the volume of the region in the plate where the magnetic field is nonzero, so this expression is equivalent to equation E8.20.

E8X.9 Plugging in the numbers yields

$$F_m = \left(3.6\times10^7\frac{\text{C}^2\cancel{\text{s}}}{\cancel{\text{m}}^3\text{kg}}\right)\left(0.1\frac{\cancel{\text{m}}}{\cancel{\text{s}}}\right)(0.04\ \cancel{\text{m}})^2(0.005\text{ m})(0.1\text{ T})^2$$

$$= 0.29\frac{\cancel{\text{C}}^2\cancel{\text{T}}^2\cancel{\text{m}}}{\cancel{\text{kg}}}\left(\frac{1\text{ N}\cdot\cancel{\text{s}}}{1\ \cancel{\text{T}}\cdot\cancel{\text{C}}\cdot\cancel{\text{m}}}\right)^2\left(\frac{1\ \cancel{\text{kg}}\cdot\cancel{\text{m}}/\cancel{\text{s}}^2}{1\text{ N}}\right)$$

$$= 0.29\text{ N} \qquad \text{(E8.32)}$$

(This is about an ounce of force: not much, but it should be discernible.)

E9 Currents Create Magnetic Fields

Chapter Overview

Introduction

In chapter E8, we saw that magnetic fields can create currents in moving conducting loops or plates. In this chapter, we will see that *currents can create magnetic fields*, and indeed are ultimately the *only* known sources of magnetic fields.

Section E9.1: The Magnetic Field of a Moving Charge

In 1820, Hans Oersted discovered that moving charges create magnetic fields. A moving point charge creates a magnetic field described by

$$\vec{B} = \frac{\mu_0 c^2}{4\pi}\frac{q}{r_{PC}^2}\left(\frac{\vec{v}}{c}\times\hat{r}_{PC}\right) = \frac{kq}{r_{PC}^2}\left(\frac{\vec{v}}{c}\times\hat{r}_{PC}\right) \tag{E9.1}$$

Purpose: This equation describes the magnetic field vector $\vec{B}$ created at a point P by a charge q moving through a point C at velocity $\vec{v}$.

Symbols: $\vec{r}_{PC}$ is the position of P relative to C, $r_{PC} = \text{mag}(\vec{r}_{PC})$, $\hat{r}_{PC}$ is the direction of $\vec{r}_{PC}$, c is the speed of light, and $\mu_0 = 4\pi k / c^2$ is the magnetic permeability constant (k is the Coulomb constant).

Limitations: This equation is an approximation that is most accurate when $\vec{v}$ is constant and nonrelativistic.

Section E9.2: The Magnetic Field of a Wire Segment

Like the electric field, the magnetic field obeys the superposition principle: *the total magnetic field vector at a given point is the sum of the magnetic field vectors contributed by all individual moving charges at that point.*

This means that we can find the magnetic field of an arbitrary wire by dividing the wire into segments of length dL, where dL is small enough so that we can treat each segment as a point particle. Since one can show that the total of $q\vec{v}$ for all the charge carriers in such a segment carrying current $\vec{I}$ is equal to $\vec{I}\,dL$, the field of a wire is

$$\vec{B} = \frac{\mu_0 c}{4\pi}\sum_{\text{all } i}\frac{dL}{r_{Pi}^2}\left(\vec{I}\times\hat{r}_{Pi}\right) = \frac{k}{c}\sum_{\text{all } i}\frac{dL}{r_{Pi}^2}\left(\vec{I}\times\hat{r}_{Pi}\right) \tag{E9.7}$$

Purpose: This equation describes the magnetic field vector $\vec{B}$ created at a point P by an arbitrarily shaped wire carrying current $\vec{I}$.

Symbols: $\vec{r}_{Pi}$ is the position of P relative to the ith segment, $r_{Pi} = \text{mag}(\vec{r}_{Pi})$, $\hat{r}_{Pi} = \vec{r}_{Pi}/r_{Pi}$ is the direction of $\vec{r}_{Pi}$, dL and $\vec{I}_i$ are the ith segments length and current [note that $\text{mag}(\vec{I}_i) = \text{mag}(\vec{I})$], c is the speed of light, and $\mu_0 = 4\pi k / c^2$ is the magnetic permeability constant.

Limitations: This equation strictly applies only to static magnetic fields, and assumes that the charge carriers are not moving at relativistic speeds (a good assumption for realistic wires). Also, dL must be small compared to r_{Pi} and small enough so that all segments are essentially straight.

Note: This is the **Biot-Savart law** (pronounced "Bee-oh Sahvahr").

Section E9.3: The Magnetic Field of a Long, Straight Wire

Using the Biot-Savart law, we can show that the magnitude of $\vec{\mathbb{B}}$ at a point a distance r from the nearest point on a long, straight wire carrying a steady current I is

$$\mathbb{B} \approx \frac{2kI}{cr} = \frac{\mu_0 c}{2\pi}\frac{I}{r} \tag{E9.12}$$

This approximation is valid if r is much smaller than the distance to any parts of the circuit that are not part of the long, straight segment. The **wire rule** says that if you point your right thumb in the direction of the wire's current, your fingers will curl in the direction of the magnetic field around the wire.

Section E9.4: The Magnetic Field of a Circular Loop

The Biot-Savart law also implies that the magnitude of $\vec{\mathbb{B}}$ at the center of a circular loop of radius R carrying a current I is

$$\mathbb{B} = \frac{2\pi kI}{cR} = \frac{\mu_0 cI}{2R} \tag{E9.13}$$

The magnetic field vectors at other points are harder to compute, but it turns out that far from the loop, the magnetic field looks like that of a small bar magnet aligned with the loop axis, which in turn is much like the electric field of a dipole. The **loop rule** says that if you curl your right fingers in the direction in which current flows in the loop, your thumb indicates the direction of $\mathbb{B}$ at the loop's center and the direction from the south to north poles of the equivalent magnet. (For a table of the right hand rules associated with magnetism, see table E9.1.)

Section E9.5: *All* Magnets Involve Circulating Charges

Most atoms behave as little dipole-like magnets because they contain orbiting or spinning electrons that create current loops. While these atomic magnets are randomly oriented in most materials and thus create no net magnetic field, in **ferromagnetic** materials, one can easily align these atomic magnets to create a permanent magnet. Because such a magnet is simply a sum of atomic current loops, a magnet, like a loop, creates a dipole-like magnetic field and responds to external magnetic fields as a dipole would to the corresponding electric field.

Section E9.6: Magnetic Symmetry Arguments

Just as in the case of electric fields, one can use symmetry arguments to determine a great deal about the magnetic field of a symmetric current distribution in advance of doing any calculations. Symmetry arguments for magnetic fields, like those for electric fields, are based on the principle that any transformation that leaves the current distribution unchanged should also leave the magnetic field unchanged. Unlike charge, however, current is a vector. Therefore a transformation leaves a current distribution unchanged only if the *direction* of current flow is unchanged.

The magnetic field also obeys a second principle, called the **mirror rule,** that does not apply to electric fields:

> If we can slice a current distribution with a mirror so that the distribution (taking account of current-flow directions) is *unchanged* by inserting the mirror, the magnetic field vector at any point on the mirror's surface must be either *perpendicular* to that surface or zero.

This rule is usually the easiest way to determine the *directions* of magnetic field vectors around a symmetric current distribution.

E9.1 The Magnetic Field of a Moving Charge

Oersted's discovery

In the winter of 1819-20, Hans Christian Oersted, a professor at the university in Copenhagen, gave a course in electrostatics and magnetism. At the time, the latter simply entailed the study of lodestones and other natural magnets, as no one yet knew anything about how magnets affected moving charges. Even so, Oersted had a metaphysical belief in the "unity of all forces", and particularly felt that magnetism might possibly be a variant form of electricity. One day, searching for some way to demonstrate this, Oersted tried before his class an experiment where he placed a wire above a compass and ran a current through it in a direction perpendicular to the compass needle. He intuitively expected to see the compass needle turn to be more parallel to the flowing current, but (as is the case with so many purportedly great physics demonstrations) nothing happened. After class, it occurred to him to try again with the compass needle initially oriented parallel to the wire. This time (after everyone had gone home, of course) the needle swung decisively away from the current. Oersted's article (July 1820) describing this experiment was the first published indication of the link between electricity and magnetism.

This discovery opened the floodgates for research

The study of magnetism had not advanced at all for more than 200 years (since the publication of Gilbert's *De Magnete* in 1600) at the time of Oersted's discovery. But within weeks of learning of Oersted's discovery in September of 1820 at the Paris Academy of Sciences, Jean Biot (rhymes with "Cleo") and Felix Savart (rhymes with "bazaar") had quantitatively measured the magnitude of the magnetic field in the vicinity of a current-carrying wire (using the "quivering compass" method of chapter E7) and discovered that the field at a point near the wire depended on $1/R$, where R is the perpendicular distance between the point and the wire. Within a few short years, Andre Marie Ampère, Michael Faraday, and others had provided to the physics community a fairly complete description of the magnetic fields generated by currents. Within 12 years of Oersted's discovery, Faraday had discovered magnetic induction, within 60 years, James Clerk Maxwell was able to provide a complete description of the behavior of electromagnetic fields, a theory that rapidly led to the discovery of radio waves and prompted Einstein to develop the theory of special relativity. Oersted's discovery thus turned out to be the impetus needed to open the floodgates of research, research which ultimately vindicated his intuition about the unity of electricity and magnetism.

The wire rule

Biot and Savart's empirical measurements of the magnetic field near a long, straight, current-carrying wire showed that the magnetic field is directed circularly around the wire as shown in figure E9.1. Note that in this figure the wire runs perpendicular to the plane of the page: the "×" indicates that the current it carries flows into the plane of the diagram. The direction of the magnetic field can be determined by a simple right-hand rule: if you point your right thumb in the direction of the conventional current carried by the wire, your fingers will curl in the direction of the magnetic field. Thus if the current is flowing *into* of the plane of the paper, as shown in figure E9.1, the magnetic field will curl clockwise; if the current were to flow out of the plane of the paper, the field would curl counterclockwise.

The right-hand rule just described is not the same as the right-hand rule that defines the cross product or the right hand rule used in chapter E8 to indicate the direction of the north pole of a magnet equivalent to a loop. To help us distinguish these rules, let us call the rule described in figure E9.1 the **wire rule**, and the others the **cross product rule** and the **loop rule**. We will see later that the wire and loop rules are really just convenient variants of the cross-product rule.

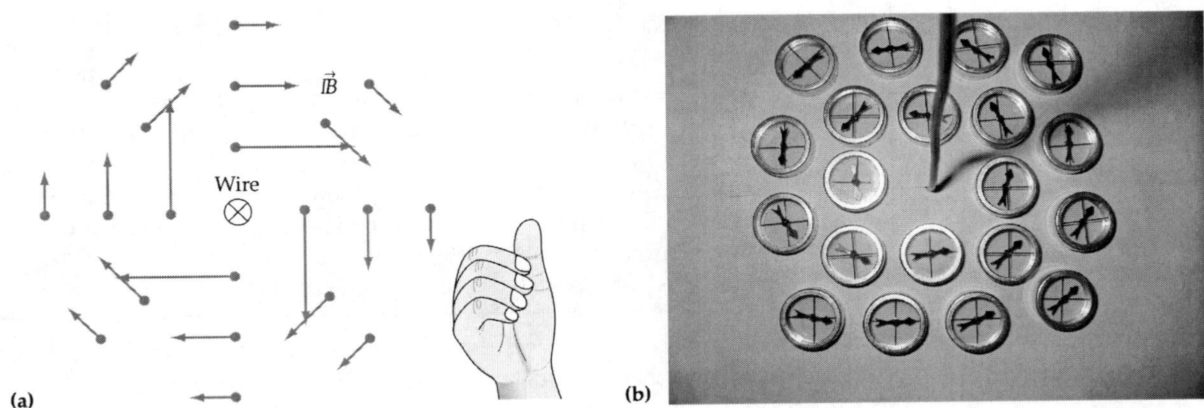

Figure E9.1
The magnetic field around a long straight wire. The hand illustrates the wire rule linking the directions of the magnetic field vector and the current that creates the field. (b) The wire in this photograph is carrying a large current toward the viewer. The surrounding compasses display the magnetic field created by the wire. (Check that the right hand rule works for this wire also!)

Self-Test E9X.1

Explain why Oersted's class demonstration failed but his after-lecture experiment succeeded in displaying the magnetic effect of a current.

We also know that currents consist of moving charges. Does it then follow that *any* moving charge will create a magnetic field? For example, will a beam of electrons moving through a vacuum create a magnetic field? How about a static charge on a rotating disk?

Rowland shows that moving *static* charges can create a magnetic field

In 1875, Henry Rowland at Johns Hopkins University performed a clever experiment to measure the magnetic field produced by a static charge on the perimeter of rubber disk rotating at 60 turns per second. This was very difficult, because the sensitive compasses used to register the disk's tiny magnetic field (~ 10^{-5} of the earth's magnetic field) had to be completely shielded from electrostatic effects due to the charge of the disk. Even so, Rowland was able to show that the magnetic field produced by the rotating static charge on the edge of the disk was *exactly* the same as that produced by the equivalent current in a ring of the same dimensions. This makes it clear that *magnetic fields are indeed generated by charges in motion*. Subsequent experiments with electron beams and the like have underlined the truth of this statement.

Figure E9.1 suggests that a moving charge produces a magnetic field that goes around the direction of motion in a plane perpendicular to the velocity. Careful measurements indicate that the strength of the magnetic field generated by a moving point charge is proportional to the charge's speed and (like the electric field of a point charge) inversely proportional to the square of the distance that one is from the charge:

The magnetic field created by a moving charged particle

$$\vec{B} = \frac{\mu_0}{4\pi}\frac{q}{r_{PC}^2}(\vec{v} \times \hat{r}_{PC}) \quad \text{or} \quad \vec{\mathbb{B}} = \frac{\mu_0 c^2}{4\pi}\frac{q}{r_{PC}^2}\left(\frac{\vec{v}}{c} \times \hat{r}_{PC}\right) \qquad \text{(E9.1a)}$$

Purpose: This equation describes the magnetic field vector $\vec{\mathbb{B}}$ or $\vec{B}$ created at a point P by a charge q at point C moving with velocity $\vec{v}$.

Symbols: $\vec{r}_{PC}$ is the position of point P relative to C, $r_{PC} = \text{mag}(\vec{r}_{PC})$, $\hat{r}_{PC}$ is a directional representing the direction of $\vec{r}_{PC}$, c is the speed of light, and μ_0 is an empirical constant called the **magnetic permeability**: $\mu_0 = 4\pi \times 10^{-7}\ \text{T·s·m/C} = 4\pi \times 10^{-7}\ \text{N·s}^2/\text{C}^2$.

Limitations: Technically, $\vec{v}$ should be constant and nonrelativistic.

The cross product in parentheses may look daunting, but all that it does is compactly express three important ideas: (1) that the magnetic field strength is indeed proportional to the particle's speed, (2) that the direction of $\vec{\mathbb{B}}$ is perpendicular to both $\vec{v}$ and $\vec{r}_{PC}$, and (3) that the magnitude of $\vec{\mathbb{B}}$ is also proportional to the sine of the angle between $\vec{v}$ and $\vec{r}_{PC}$. The fact that $\vec{\mathbb{B}}$ is perpendicular to $\vec{v}$ means that the field at a point P (for example) must lie somewhere in a plane that is perpendicular to $\vec{v}$ and contains P: this is illustrated in Figure E9.2. The fact that $\vec{\mathbb{B}}$ is *also* perpendicular to $\vec{r}_{PC}$ means that $\vec{\mathbb{B}}$ must be perpendicular to the projection of $\vec{r}_{PC}$ on that plane, which in turn means that $\vec{\mathbb{B}}$ points tangent to a circle going around the charge's direction of motion (consistent with the wire rule) as illustrated in figure E9.2.

Self-Test E9X.2

Convince yourself that the directions of $\vec{\mathbb{B}}$ shown in figure E9.2 are consistent not only with the cross product rule but also the wire rule. (This shows that the wire rule is really just the cross product rule in disguise.)

Expressed in the right units, this equation looks eerily like Coulomb's law!

Note that except for the term in parentheses, equation E9.1a is very similar to Coulomb's law for the electric field of a point particle:

$$\vec{E} = \frac{1}{4\pi\varepsilon_0}\frac{q}{r_{PC}^2}\hat{r}_{PC} = \frac{kq}{r_{PC}^2}\hat{r}_{PC} \qquad \text{(E9.2)}$$

The empirical constant of proportionality $\mu_0/4\pi$ in equation E9.1 is to the magnetic field what the empirical Coulomb constant $k = 1/4\pi\varepsilon_0$ is to the electric field in equation E9.2: each expresses how strong a field a given amount of charge creates.

The relationship between μ_0 and $k = 1/4\pi\varepsilon_0$

Now here is something that will really make the little hairs on the back of your neck stand up: if you compute the value of the constant $\mu_0 c^2/4\pi$, you will find that it has exactly the same *value and units as the Coulomb constant* $k = 1/4\pi\varepsilon_0$! Therefore, we can write the second version of equation E9.1 as

$$\vec{\mathbb{B}} = \frac{kq}{r_{PC}^2}\left(\frac{\vec{v}}{c} \times \hat{r}_{PC}\right) = \frac{1}{4\pi\varepsilon_0}\frac{q}{r_{PC}^2}\left(\frac{\vec{v}}{c} \times \hat{r}_{PC}\right) \qquad \text{(E9.1b)}$$

There is something very deep and eerie going on here: when we express the equation for the magnetic field of a point particle in the right units, we see that it is just a strangely warped, velocity-dependent version of Coulomb's law! This is a tantalizing moonlit glimpse of a deep substructure connecting $\vec{E}$ and $\vec{\mathbb{B}}$, a substructure whose bold lines we will see in the broad light of day in chapter E13. (Note that this vital clue is almost completely obscured when we use the historical SI units for the magnetic field.)

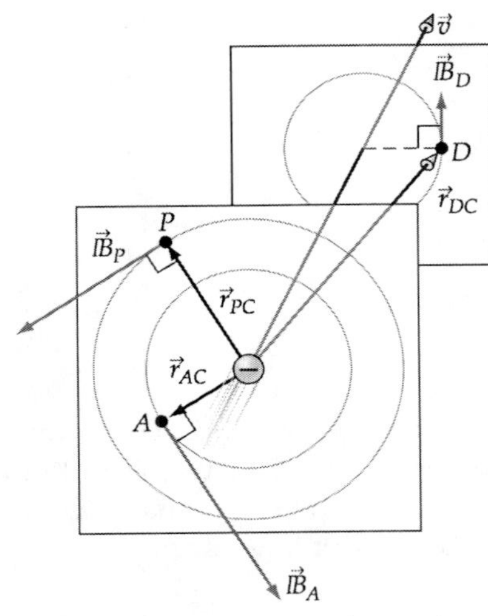

Figure E9.2
The magnetic field vectors created at selected points by a moving charged particle. The particle is moving more or less away from the viewer.

Self-Test E9X.3

Show that $k = \mu_0 c^2 / 4\pi$. (Note that this and $\vec{\mathbf{B}} = c\vec{B}$ makes it easy to convert any equation in this chapter involving k and $\vec{\mathbf{B}}$ to one involving μ_0 and $\vec{B}$.)

Self-Test E9X.4

Imagine that a tiny Styrofoam ball has been given a charge of 10 nC and is moving in a straight line at 30 m/s. What are the maximum magnitudes of the magnetic field quantities $\vec{B}$ and $\vec{\mathbb{B}}$ produced by that ball at a point 10 cm from its path as it passes by? What is the maximum magnitude of the electric field $\vec{E}$ produced by the ball at that point? What is $E/\mathbb{B}$?

E9.2 The Magnetic Field of a Wire Segment

Experiments indicate that, like the electric field, the magnetic field obeys the superposition principle: the total magnetic field vector at a point near a set of *moving* particles with charges $q_1, q_2, q_3, \ldots$ is the simple vector sum of the magnetic field vectors that would be produced at that point by each individual moving charge acting alone:

The superposition principle

$$\vec{\mathbf{B}} = \vec{\mathbf{B}}_1 + \vec{\mathbf{B}}_2 + \vec{\mathbf{B}}_3 + \ldots \qquad \text{(E9.3)}$$

Purpose: This equation states that the magnetic field obeys the superposition principle.

Symbols: $\vec{\mathbf{B}}$ is the total magnetic field vector at a specified point at a given time and $\vec{\mathbf{B}}_1, \vec{\mathbf{B}}_2, \vec{\mathbf{B}}_3, \ldots$ are the magnetic field vectors that would be created at that same point and time by moving the charges 1, 2, 3, … individually.

Limitations: None known.

This provides a means (at least in principle) of calculating the magnetic field produced by a current flowing in an arbitrarily shaped wire. Imagine that we want to know the magnetic field at a point P near a wire of cross-sectional area A carrying a current I, as shown in figure E9.3. The basic trick is to divide

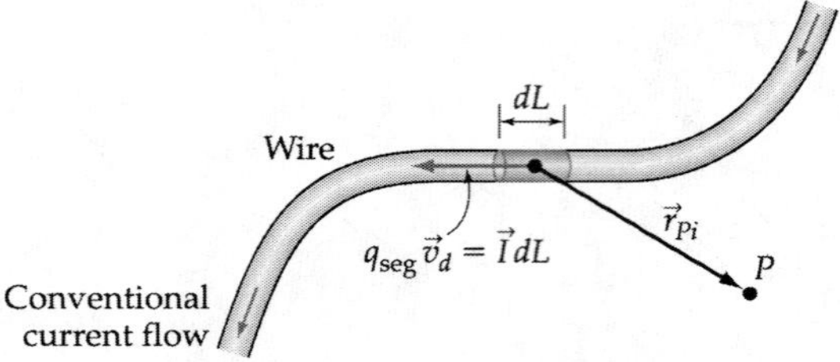

Figure E9.3
To find the magnetic field at a point *P* due to a current flowing in a wire, divide the wire up into segments so small that they can be considered point charges, calculate each segment's contribution to the field at *P*, and then sum the contributions.

the curved wire into tiny segments, each so small that segment's current can be considered a moving point charge. We then use equation E9.1 to compute the field at *P* produced by each segment, and sum over all the segments. In principle, we should be able to calculate the magnetic field of *any* curved wire this way.

Let's see more carefully how we might do this in practice. Consider dividing the wire into infinitesimal segments of length *dL*. The volume of each segment is *AdL*, so the total amount of moving charge in a segment is

$$q_{seg} = \rho A\, dL \tag{E9.4}$$

where ρ is the density of mobile charge in the wire. The current flowing in this segment of wire (as we saw in chapter E5) is

$$\vec{I} = \vec{J}A = \rho\vec{v}_d A \tag{E9.5}$$

where $\vec{v}_d$ is the drift velocity of the charge carriers. This means that

$$q_{seg}\vec{v}_d = \rho A dL\, \vec{v}_d \;=\; (\rho A\vec{v}_d)dL \;=\; \vec{I}dL \tag{E9.6}$$

This will be true for all segments, so plugging this into the fundamental equation E9.1, and summing over all segments, we find that the total magnetic field vector produced by the wire at point *P* is

The Biot-Savart law

$$\vec{\mathbb{B}} = \frac{k}{c}\sum_{all\ i}\frac{dL}{r_{Pi}^2}\left(\vec{I}_i \times \hat{r}_{Pi}\right) \quad \text{or} \quad \vec{B} = \frac{\mu_0}{4\pi}\sum_{all\ i}\frac{dL}{r_{Pi}^2}\left(\vec{I}_i \times \hat{r}_{Pi}\right) \tag{E9.7}$$

Purpose: Describes the magnetic field $\vec{\mathbb{B}}$ produced at a point *P* by an arbitrarily shaped wire carrying a current *I*.

Symbols: $\vec{r}_{Pi}$ is *P*'s position relative to the *i*th segment, $r_{Pi} = \text{mag}(\vec{r}_{Pi})$, $\hat{r}_{Pi} \equiv \vec{r}_{Pi}/r_{Pi}$ is directional representing the direction of $\vec{r}_{Pi}$, dL and $\vec{I}_i$ are the segment's length and conventional current vector respectively, $k = 1/4\pi\varepsilon_0$ is the Coulomb constant, $\mu_0 = 1/\varepsilon_0 c^2 = 4\pi k/c^2$ is the permeability constant, and *c* is the speed of light.

Limitations: This equation strictly applies only to static magnetic fields. Also, *dL* must be small enough so that all segments are essentially straight.

Notes: This is called the **Biot-Savart law**.

In principle, we can apply this formula to any wire or loop carrying a constant current. In practice, this is difficult except in the simplest cases. Even so, we can extract some useful qualitative principles from this formula. The effect of the *i*-th segment at point *P* is proportional to $1/r_{Pi}^2$: this means that the magnetic field at point *P* will primarily be determined by the parts of the wire that are closest to *P*. Moreover, while information about the *direction* of the field implied in equation E9.7 looks tough to decipher, remember that this cross product turns out to be consistent with the wire rule (which is generally easier to remember and use).

Self-Test E9X.5

What are the approximate magnitudes of the magnetic field vectors at points B and C compared to the magnetic field strength at point A?

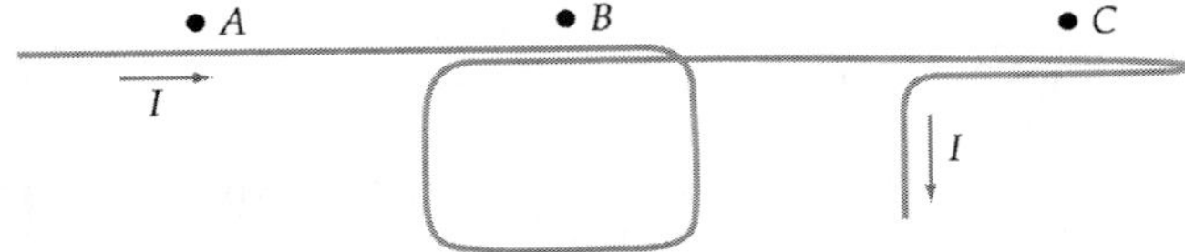

E9.3 The Magnetic Field of a Long, Straight Wire

Application to a long and straight wire

One of the easiest applications of equation E9.7 is to the problem of a *long straight wire*. Consider a point P a distance r from such a wire. Let us choose our x axis to coincide with the wire (with the $+x$ direction pointing in the same direction as the current) and let $x = 0$ be the point on the wire closest to P. We will divide the wire into infinitesimal segments of length dx. Figure E9.4 illustrates the situation.

Note that for such a wire, both the magnitude and direction of the current are the same in every segment: $\vec{I}_i = \vec{I}$ for all i. Now, equation E9.7 implies that the magnetic field vector contributed by a given segment will point in same direction as $\vec{I} \times \hat{r}_{Pi}$. Since both $\vec{I}$ and $\hat{r}_{Pi}$ lie in the plane of the figure, the vector $\vec{\boldsymbol{B}}_i$ contributed by each segment at P must point perpendicular to the plane of the figure (in fact, toward the viewer for the point P shown). Since the $\vec{\boldsymbol{B}}_i$ vectors contributed by all segments are parallel, the magnitude of the total magnetic field vector $\vec{\boldsymbol{B}}$ at P is simply the sum of the magnitudes of the $\vec{\boldsymbol{B}}_i$ vectors contributed by the segments. So in this particular case, equation E9.7 becomes

$$\boldsymbol{B} = \frac{k}{c}\sum_{\text{all } i}\frac{dx}{r_{Pi}^2}\,\text{mag}(\vec{I}_i \times \hat{r}_{Pi}) = \frac{k}{c}\sum_{\text{all } i}\frac{dx}{r_{Pi}^2}\,I\sin\theta_i \tag{E9.8}$$

where θ_i is the angle between $\vec{r}_{Pi}$ and $\vec{I}$ (remember that the directional $\hat{r}_{Pi} \equiv \vec{r}_{Pi}/r_{Pi}$ has a magnitude of 1). Since we can see from figure E9.4 that $\sin\theta_i = r/r_{Pi}$ and that $r_{Pi}^2 = r^2 + x_i^2$, this becomes

$$\boldsymbol{B} = \frac{kI}{c}\sum_{\text{all } i}\frac{dx}{r_{Pi}^2}\frac{r}{r_{Pi}} = \frac{kIr}{c}\sum_{\text{all } i}\frac{dx}{r_{Pi}^3} = \frac{kIr}{c}\sum_{\text{all } i}\frac{dx}{(r^2 + x_i^2)^{3/2}} \tag{E9.9}$$

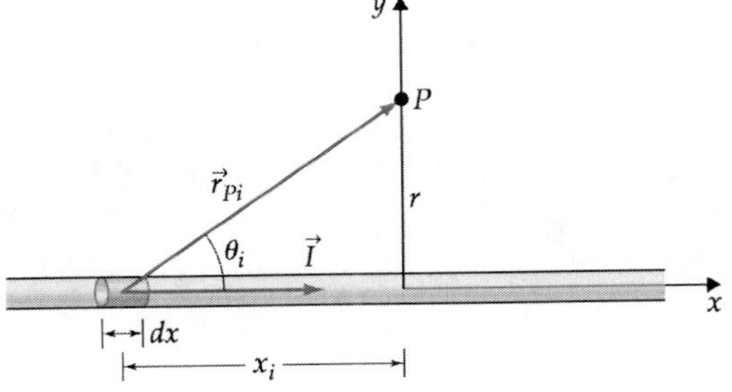

Figure E9.4
A diagram defining symbols that are useful for calculating the magnetic field at a point P near a long, straight wire.

In the limit that dx becomes infinitesimal, the sum becomes an integral

$$\boldsymbol{B} = \frac{kIr}{c}\int_{x_1}^{x_2}\frac{dx}{(r^2+x^2)^{3/2}} \tag{E9.10}$$

We have seen this integral before (see the inside front cover and example E2.3): the result is

$$\boldsymbol{B} = \frac{kIr}{c}\left[\frac{x}{r^2\sqrt{r^2+x^2}}\right]_{x_1}^{x_2} = \frac{kI}{cr}\left[\frac{x_2}{\sqrt{r^2+x_2^2}} - \frac{x_1}{\sqrt{r^2+x_1^2}}\right] \tag{E9.11}$$

If the ends of the straight segment and all other parts of the circuit are very far away from P compared to r ($x_1^2 >> r^2$ and $x_2^2 >> r^2$, with x_1 negative and x_2 positive), then this becomes

The magnetic field of a long, straight wire.

$$\boldsymbol{B} \approx \frac{kI}{cr}\left[\frac{x_2}{\sqrt{x_2^2}} - \frac{x_1}{\sqrt{x_1^2}}\right] = \frac{kI}{cr}[1-(-1)] = \frac{2kI}{cr} = \frac{\mu_0 c}{2\pi}\frac{I}{r} \tag{E9.12}$$

This result can serve as a useful approximation in a number of situations. Note that this result is consistent with the empirical results described by Biot and Savart, as discussed in section E9.1. We will refer to this result again in chapters E11 and E12.

Self-Test E9X.6

How much current would a long straight wire have to carry to produce a magnetic field that at a distance of 10 cm from the wire has a magnitude comparable to the that of the earth's magnetic field (15 kN/C)?

Self-Test E9X.7

What is the magnitude (in terms of k, I, c, and r) and the direction of the magnetic field at the point P shown? Assume that the wire continues to essentially infinity in both the horizontal and vertical directions. (*Hint:* Argue that the horizontal half of the wire contributes *nothing* to the field at point P. Why?)

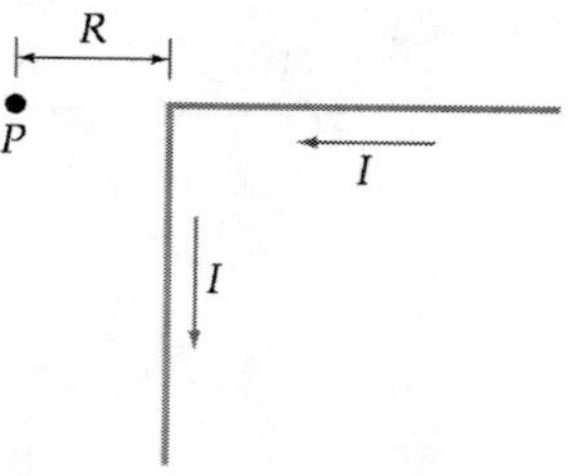

E9.4 The Magnetic Field of a Circular Loop

In chapter E8, we saw that a current-carrying loop of wire behaves in a magnetic field as if it were a bar magnet. Our discussion so far this chapter makes it clear that a current-carrying loop will also produce a magnetic field. What does this magnetic field look like?

Example E9.1 The Field at the Center of a Current-Carrying Loop

Problem Calculate the magnitude of the magnetic field at the center of a circular loop of radius R carrying a current I.

Translation Figure E9.5 shows the situation and defines some useful symbols.

Model Note that all segments on the loop are the same distance R from the loop. Moreover, note that since both $\vec{I}$ and $\vec{r}_{Pi}$ lie in the plane of the drawing for each segment, each segment will contribute a magnetic field vector $\vec{B}_i$ that is perpendicular to the plane of the loop (as illustrated in figure E9.5). Therefore, as in the case of the long wire, we can find the magnitude of $\vec{B}$ at the center by summing the *magnitudes* of the vectors $\vec{B}_i$ contributed by the segments. Finally, note that $\vec{I}_i$ is perpendicular to $\vec{r}_{Pi}$ for all segments, so $\text{mag}(\vec{I}_i \times \hat{r}_{Pi}) = I \sin 90° = I$ for all segments.

Solution Therefore, the total magnetic field at the loop's center is

$$B = \frac{k}{c}\sum_{\text{all } i}\frac{dL}{r_{Pi}^2}\text{mag}(\vec{I}_i \times \hat{r}_{Pi}) = \frac{k}{c}\sum_{\text{all } i}\frac{dL}{R^2}I = \frac{kI}{cR^2}\sum_{\text{all } i} dL = \frac{2\pi kI}{cR} = \frac{\mu_0 cI}{2R} \quad \text{(E9.13)}$$

Evaluation This expression has units of $(\text{N}\cdot\cancel{\text{m}}^2/\text{C}^{\cancel{2}})(\cancel{\text{C}}/\cancel{\text{s}})(\cancel{\text{s}}/\cancel{\text{m}})/\cancel{\text{m}} = \text{N/C}$, which are the correct units for $\vec{B}$.

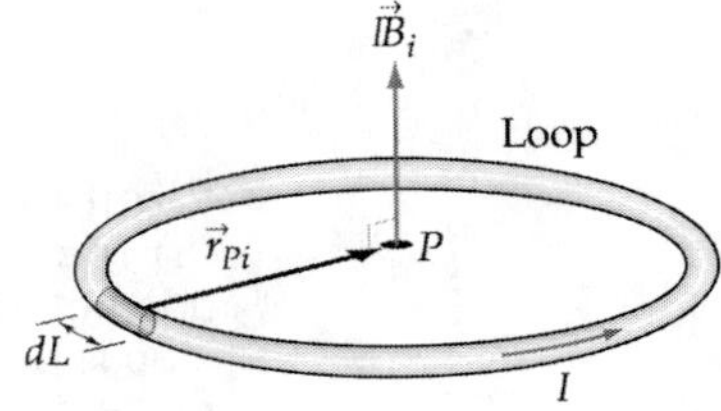

Figure E9.5
This diagram shows the part of the magnetic field contributed at the center of a circular loop by the loop's *i*th segment.

The magnetic field vector at any point *other* than the loop's center is more difficult to calculate. Computing the magnetic field at a point along the loop's axis is not so bad (see problem E9S.3) but doing so at any point off the axis presents a real mathematical challenge. However, one can pretty easily write a computer program that performs the sum given by equation E9.7 directly for any point P. When one does this, one finds that the magnetic field vectors created by a loop at points close to the loop are as shown in figure E9.6a on the next page. Figure E9.6b indicates that at points far from the loop compared to its radius, the magnetic field vectors are essentially the same as those for a small bar magnet, which in turn are analogous to the electric field vectors produced by a dipole (see problems E9S.3, E9S.4, and E9A.1 for more discussion of this issue).

The loop rule introduced in section E8.3 tells us that if you wrap your right fingers in the direction that current flows in a loop, your right thumb indicates the direction of the north pole of the bar magnet that *responds* to a magnetic field in the same way that a loop does. Figure E9.6 makes it clear that this rule also describes the orientation of the bar magnet that *creates* a magnetic field that is the same as the loop's magnetic field at large distances. It is also useful to note that in this context, if you curl your right fingers in the direction of the current flowing in the loop, your right thumb indicates the direction of the magnetic field vectors $\vec{B}$ at points inside the loop.

Since the field vectors shown in figure E9.6 ultimately come from a calculation involving equation E9.7, which employs the cross product rule to determine the direction of $\vec{B}$, we see that the loop rule is actually just another application of the cross product rule. But it is actually easier, in my opinion, to memorize the loop and wire rules separately rather than always to work everything out using the cross product rule. Table E9.1 summarizes the right-hand rules we have introduced so far.

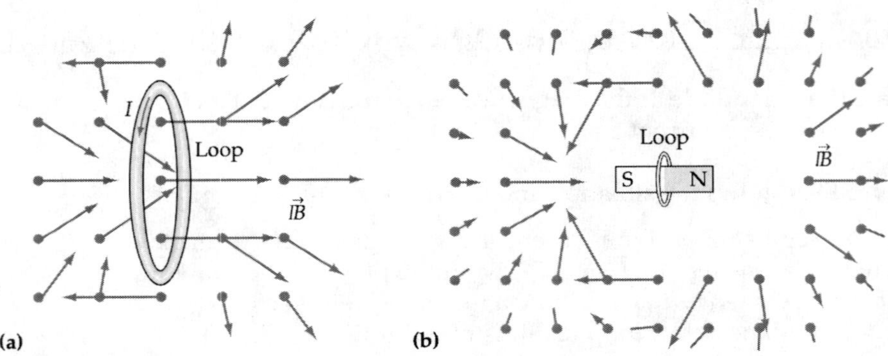

Figure E9.6
(a) The magnetic field close to a circular current-carrying loop is complicated and not particularly dipole-like. (b) However, the magnetic field far from the loop is equivalent to the electric field produced by a dipole, and thus (according to the dipole model) to the magnetic field produced by a permanent bar magnet in the orientation shown

E9.5 *All* Magnets Involve Circulating Currents

What creates a permanent magnet's magnetic field?

So, a current-carrying loop not only *responds* to a magnetic field like a small permanent bar magnet would (which is analogous to how an electric dipole would respond to an analogous electric field), but it also *creates* a magnetic field like the distant field of a permanent magnet (which is analogous to the electric field of an electric dipole). But what creates the field of a permanent magnet?

Ampère was perhaps the first physicist to intuit (in the early 1800s) that a permanent magnet's field might be produced by microscopic current loops. However, how these currents could circulate indefinitely remained a mystery for a long time.

Orbiting electrons in atoms act as current loops

We now know that atoms are constructed of electrons circulating around an atomic nucleus. A classical model of the atom imagines the electrons orbiting the nucleus like planets orbiting the sun. Quantum mechanics teaches us to

Table E9.1 Right-hand Rules

Rule	Fingers	Thumb	Figure
Cross-product rule	Point index finger in the direction of the first vector in the product and second finger in the direction of the second vector.	Indicates the direction of the cross product	$\vec{u} \times \vec{v}$, $\vec{u}$, $\vec{v}$
Loop rule (= loop-to-magnet rule)	Curl fingers in the direction of the current flowing around the loop.	Indicates (1) the-S-to-N direction of the analogous bar magnet, and (2) the direction of the magnetic field at the loop's center	$\vec{B}$, I, =, N, S
Wire rule	Fingers curl in the direction of the magnetic field that the wire creates.	Thumb indicates the direction of the conventional current flowing in the wire	$\vec{B}$, $\vec{I}$

be careful about such a description, but even in quantum mechanics, an electron can have nonzero orbital angular momentum, which is just a quantum-mechanical way of saying that the electron is circulating around the nucleus.

Now, circulating electrons are essentially tiny current loops. Most atomic electrons are members of pairs that circulate in opposite directions (thus yielding zero net circulating current), but many atoms have at least one unpaired electron with nonzero orbital angular momentum that represents a tiny permanent current loop. Unlike a macroscopic current flowing in a wire, the circulating electrons in an atom flow in a vacuum without losing energy and thus do not require a power supply.

The magnetic fields created by these atomic current loops can combine to create a stronger magnetic field if the loops are aligned in the same direction. If we could align all of the atomic current loops in a cylindrical bar, we would create a powerful permanent bar magnet whose total field would be the sum of atomic-level dipole-like fields. Figure E9.7 illustrates how microscopic atomic magnets can combine to create what looks like a single north pole at one end of the magnet and a single south pole at the other end.

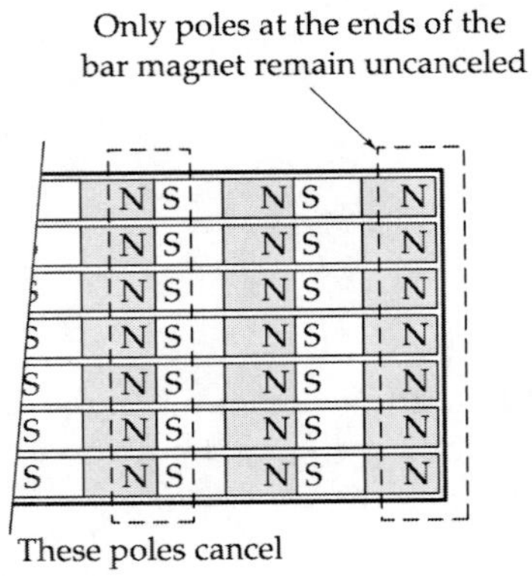

Only poles at the ends of the bar magnet remain uncanceled

These poles cancel

Figure E9.7
This close-up side view of one end of a bar magnet shows (schematically) how the tiny dipoles inside a permanent magnet essentially add up to poles at the magnet's ends.

In most substances, however, these atomic magnets are oriented randomly, so the net magnetic field produced by the substance is essentially zero. However, in a very few substances (**ferromagnetic** substances such as iron, nickel and cobalt), it turns out to be energetically favorable for adjacent atoms to align their effective current loops in the *same* direction. (This is a bit strange, since if you put two bar magnets next to each other pointing in the same direction, their adjacent like poles repel each other, exerting forces that tend to reorient the magnets in *opposite* directions. Clearly, some non-magnetic effect must overcome this tendency.) In a typical piece of iron, the iron atoms tend to form small regional "clubs" called **domains**, within which all atoms agree on a given orientation (see figure E9.8). In an unmagnetized piece of iron, the alignments of the various domains are random, and thus the net magnetic field is still zero. But if one puts a piece of iron in a strong external magnetic field, domains whose orientations are basically aligned with the field tend to grow (by "recruiting" along their boundaries) and domains that are not aligned with the field shrink. The result is that the iron develops its own net magnetic field whose average direction is the same as the direction of the applied field.

In ferromagnetic materials, these atomic current loops tend to be aligned

This is why a coil of wire wrapped around piece of iron creates a stronger magnetic field than the same coil wrapped around a piece of wood. In the first case, the coil's field is augmented by the net magnetic field of the iron atoms as they line up with coil's field.

(a)

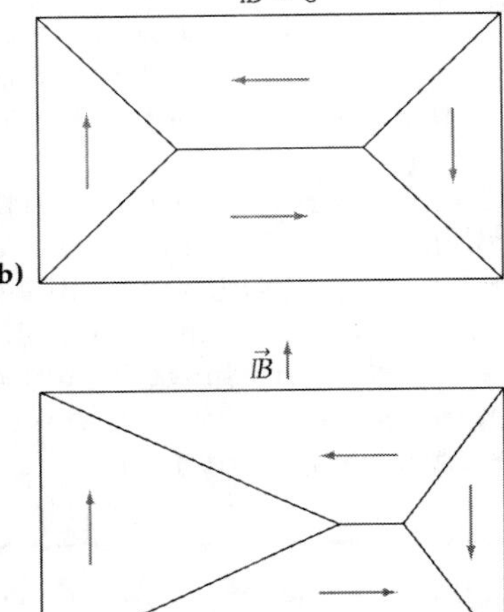

Figure E9.8
(a) A photograph showing the magnetic domains in a tiny rectangle of permalloy (80% nickel, 20% iron). (b) A schematic diagram of the domains in such a substance. The arrows show the orientation of the atomic magnets inside the domains. (c) When the object is placed in an external magnetic field, the domains most most nearly aligned with the field grow, while others shrink.

When you remove the external magnetic field, most ferromagnetic materials retain a residual magnetic field (some materials better than others), because once the atoms have chosen to align themselves in a given direction, they tend to stay oriented that way. So an unmagnetized piece of iron exposed to a strong external magnetic field will subsequently remain permanently magnetized: we have created a *permanent magnet*. The atoms will remain aligned unless the temperature becomes too large (and the jostling due to thermal effects destroys the alignment) or a strong magnetic field in a different direction is imposed.

All magnetic fields are caused by moving charged particles

The fundamental point of this discussion is that the magnetic field of a permanent magnet, like that of a current loop, is ultimately produced by charges in motion. *Moving or spinning* charges are the only known source of magnetic fields.* Since each atomic current loop in a permanent magnet both *responds* to an external magnetic field like an electric dipole responds to an external electric field (see section E8.2) and *creates* a magnetic field that (far from the atom) is like an electric dipole's electric field (see section E9.4), a permanent magnet comprised of such atomic current loops will *also* respond to a field and create a field in a similar way (the sum of little dipole-like magnets is just a big dipole-like magnet). This is fundamentally why the dipole model for permanent magnets introduced in chapter E7 works so well in practical situations.

E9.6 Magnetic Symmetry Arguments

Differences between symmetry arguments for the electric and magnetic fields:

In chapter E3, we saw that symmetry arguments were a powerful tool for determining the characteristics of the electric field produced by a symmetric charge distribution in advance of doing any calculations. We can use similar symmetry arguments to determine the characteristics of the magnetic fields produced by symmetric current distributions. There are, however, two crucial differences between symmetry arguments involving the electric and those involving magnetic fields.

... current is a vector while charge is a scalar

The first difference is that current is a *vector* having a direction, whereas charge is a *scalar* with no direction. We can only say that a transformation leaves a current distribution unchanged if that transformation changes neither the shape *nor* the direction of the current (in the case of charge distributions, we only needed to worry about the shape).

... the mirror rule (which has no analogy in electrostatics)

The second difference is that the cross product that appears in the basic equation for the magnetic field of a point particle implies that mirror reflections of magnetic fields obey the following **mirror rule**:

> If we can slice a current distribution with a mirror so that the distribution (taking account of current-flow directions) is *unchanged* by inserting the mirror, any magnetic field vector at any point on the mirror's surface must be either *perpendicular* to that surface or zero.

(Thanks to my colleague David Tanenbaum for this elegant expression of the rule). Figure E9.9 illustrates the application of this rule to the case of a moving point charge (which we will visualize as a small ball). If we arrange a mirror so that it slices the charge in half in the plane that contains the charge's velocity vector $\vec{v}$, then the reflection of the visible half of the charge (including the charge's velocity vector) looks identical to the part of the charge hidden by the mirror. We already know what the magnetic field vectors surrounding a point

---

*Spinning charges will be discussed in more depth in Unit Q.

charge look like; we can see that each vector on the mirror's surface is indeed perpendicular to the mirror's surface.

One can prove mathematically that this mirror rule follows from equation E9.1 for the magnetic field of a point particle, the superposition principle, and the definition of the cross product (see problem E9A.2). Since the formula for the *electric* field of a charged particle does not involve a cross product, the mirror rule does *not* apply to electric fields.

Once you get used to it, you will find that the mirror rule is generally the most effective way to determine the directions of magnetic field vectors created by a current distribution. We will generally use symmetry arguments involving rotation, flipping, and/or sliding to determine constraints on the *magnitudes* of magnetic fields.

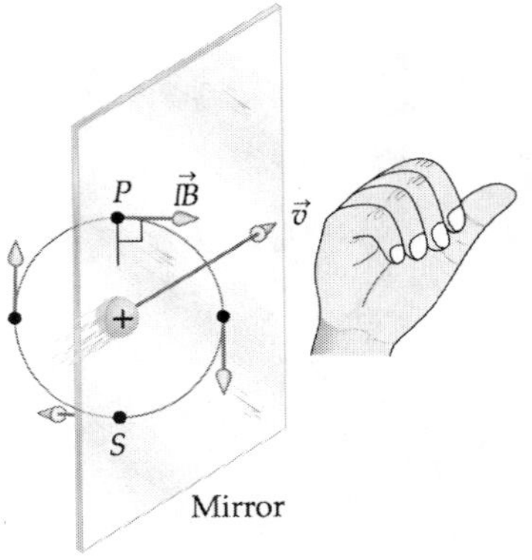

Figure E9.9
The current distribution represented by a moving charge is unaffected if we bisect it with a mirror containing its velocity vector. Note that the magnetic field vectors at points on the mirror's surface do indeed point perpendicular to that surface.

Self-Test E9X.8

In the moving point-charge example, imagine placing the mirror so that it slices the charge in half in the plane *perpendicular* to the charge's velocity. Explain why this does not satisfy the condition on mirror placement specified in the mirror rule.

The following examples illustrate the application of the mirror rule to some important types of current distributions.

Example E9.2 An Axial Current Distribution

Problem Consider a cylindrically symmetric current distribution (one that is unchanged by rotating the distribution around its central axis or sliding along that axis) that involves currents that flow only parallel to its central axis. We call such a distribution an **axial current distribution**. An infinite cylindrical wire or pipe carrying current parallel to its length is an example of such a distribution. Argue that the magnetic field vector created at a given point P by such a distribution must point tangent to a circle perpendicular to the axis but centered on it, and that its magnitude can at most depend on the distance r that P is from the axis.

Solution Figure E9.10a on the next page shows that if we place a mirror in any plane perpendicular to the current distribution's central axis, the distribution's mirror image *looks* exactly like the part of the distribution behind the mirror except that the current direction is reversed. The mirror rule, therefore, does *not* apply to such a mirror. However, figure E9.10b shows that if we place the mirror so that its plane contains the central axis and the arbitrary point P where we would like to evaluate the field, the current distribution's mirror image (including the current) looks *exactly* like the part behind the mirror. The mirror rule therefore implies that the magnetic field vector P must point perpendicular to the mirror. But as figure E9.10b shows, such a vector is indeed tangent to a circle going around the axis in a plane perpendicular to the axis. Since P was arbitrary, this applies to all points inside and outside the distribution.

Now consider rotating the current distribution an arbitrary amount around the central axis. As figure E9.10c shows, this rotation carries the vector originally at point P to a point S that is the same distance r from the central axis. The current distribution is unchanged by such a rotation (by hypothesis), so the magnetic field should be unchanged. This will only be true if the field vector originally at P has the same magnitude as the vector that was originally at S. Sliding the distribution along the axis also leaves it unchanged, and a combi-

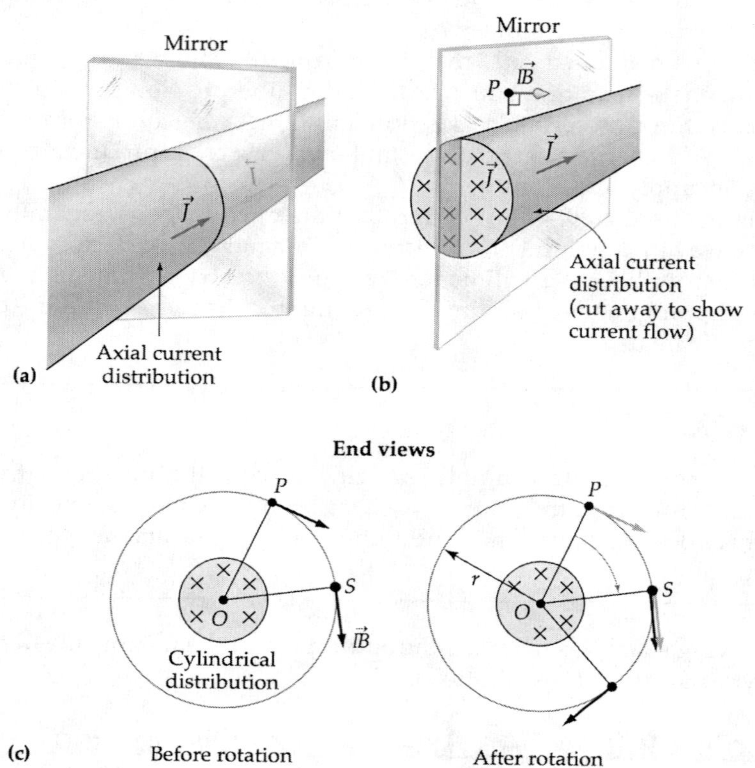

Figure E9.10
(a) If we place a mirror perpendicular to the central axis of an axial current distribution, the distribution looks the same *except* that the current is reversed in the mirror image. (b) If we place a mirror so that it bisects the distribution in a plane that contains its central axis, the distribution looks exactly the same. Therefore its magnetic field is perpendicular to the mirror at points on the plane of the mirror. (The distribution goes on indefinitely in the direction toward the viewer, but I have sliced it to display the mirror image more clearly.) (c) Rotation around the distribution's central axis moves the field vector at P to a new position S the same distance r from O. If the field is to remain unchanged by this rotation, the vectors originally at P and S must have the same magnitude.

nation of a rotation and a slide will carry the vector at P to any arbitrary point that is the same distance r from the axis. Therefore the field vectors at *all* points a given distance r from the axis must have the same magnitude, implying that the magnitude of the magnetic field at a point can *at most* depend on r.

Example E9.3 A Solenoidal Current Distribution

Problem A **solenoid** is a coil of wire closely wound around a cylindrical form. Consider an infinite solenoid wrapped around a cylindrical pipe of uniform radius and infinite length. Such a coil (like the distribution in example E9.2) is essentially unchanged by rotating it around its central axis or sliding it along that axis, but the currents in this case flow *perpendicular* to the axis (contrary to the situation in example E9.2). We call such a distribution an **solenoidal** current distribution. Argue that the magnetic field created by such a solenoidal distribution is parallel to the distribution's central axis at all points, and has a magnitude at a given point P that can, at most, depend on the distance that P is from the axis.

Solution Figure E9.11a shows that if we place a mirror perpendicular to the solenoid's central axis, the reflected image looks exactly the same as the part of the solenoid behind the mirror. Since we can slide the solenoid along the axis an arbitrary amount without changing it, we can slide it until any arbitrary point P lies in the plane of such a mirror. The mirror rule then implies that the magnetic field at this arbitrary point P is perpendicular to the mirror and thus is parallel to the axis.

As in example E9.2, the solenoid's current distribution is unaffected by rotating it around the axis or sliding it along the axis. Since the combination of a rotation and a slide can carry the magnetic field vector at point P to any arbitrary point S that is the same distance r from the solenoid's central axis, the field vector originally at P must have the same magnitude as that originally at point S if the field is to be unchanged by such a transformation. Therefore, the magnitude of the magnetic field vector at a given point P can at most depend on the distance r that P is from the solenoid's central axis.

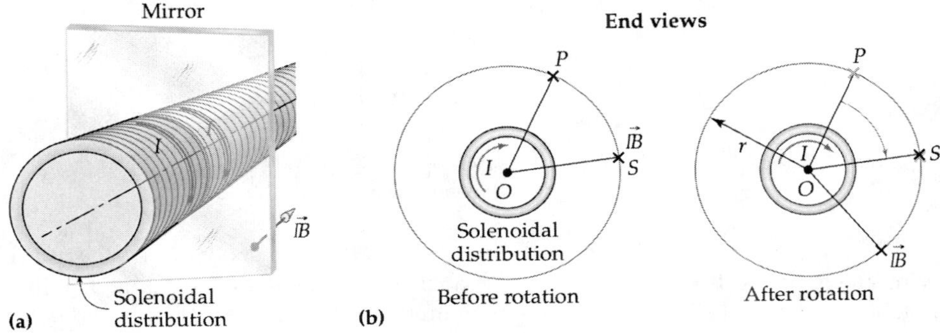

Figure E9.11
(a) In the case of a solenoidal distribution, we have to place the mirror perpendicular to the distribution's central axis to preserve the current direction in the mirror image. Therefore the magnetic field in this case is parallel to the axis. (b) Rotation about the distribution's central axis moves the field vector from P to a new position S the same distance r from O. If the field is to remain unchanged by this rotation, the vectors originally at P and Q must have the same magnitude.

Self-Test E9X.9

Argue why placing a mirror so that its plane contains the solenoid's central axis (as we did in example E9.3) does *not* help us determine anything about field in this case.

E9.7 Mystery du Jour

The material in this chapter brings up the core issue of the unit: why are the electric and magnetic fields so similar, even down to the constant in the equations for the electric and magnetic field of a charged particle? We also *still* have not seen how to write laws of electricity and magnetism that are possibly consistent with the principle of relativity. We will begin to face these problems squarely in the next chapter.

TWO-MINUTE PROBLEMS

E9T.1 Imagine placing two long wires parallel to each other. If currents flow through the wires in the directions shown, will the wires attract, repel, or exert no forces on each other?

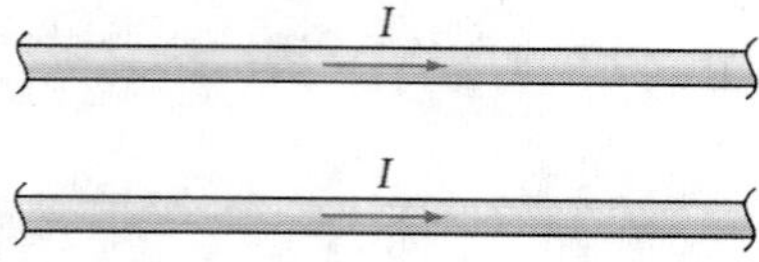

A. Attract
B. Repel
C. Exert no forces

E9T.2 Imagine placing two long wires parallel to each other. If currents flow through the wires in the directions shown, will the wires attract, repel, or exert no forces on each other?

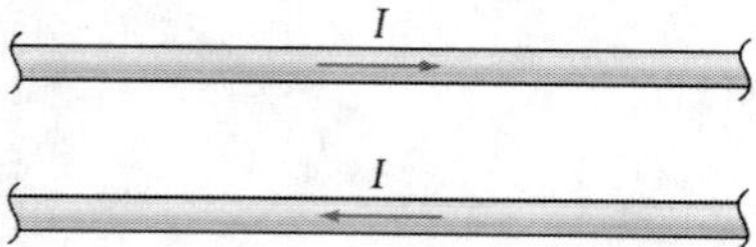

A. Attract
B. Repel
C. Exert no forces

E9T.3 Consider the loop of flexible wire shown below. If a current is passed through the loop, will it tend to expand (becoming more circular), scrunch up even more tightly, or do nothing?

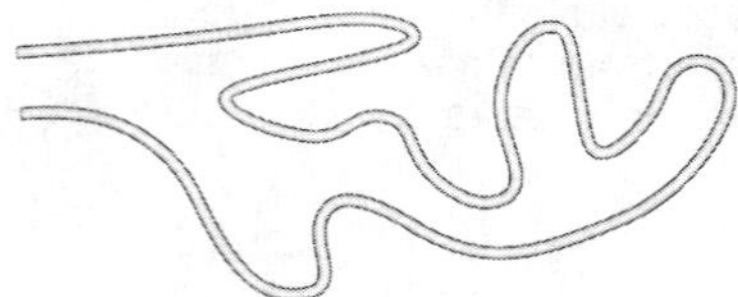

A. Expand
B. Scrunch up
C. Do nothing
D. The answer depends on the current's direction.

E9T.4 The picture below shows an end view of a loop conducting a current whose direction is shown. The magnetic field at the loop's center points

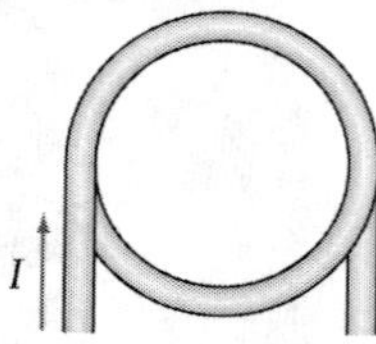

A. Toward us
B. Away from us
C. To the left
D. To the right
E. Nowhere, because there is no field
F. In a direction we don't have enough information to determine

E9T.5 A wire bent in the shape shown below carries a current in the direction marked. What is the magnitude $\boldsymbol{B}$ of the magnetic field at point a due to the *horizontal segments* of the wire?

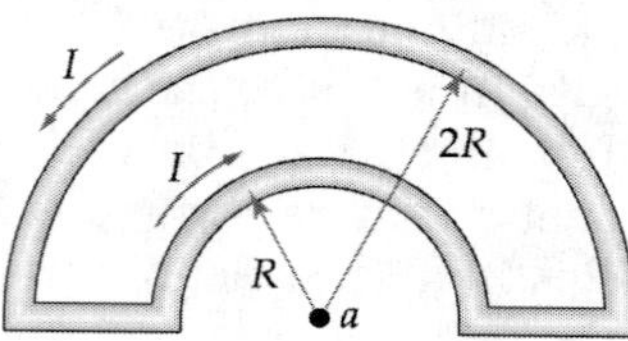

A. kI/cR
B. $\pi kI/cR$
C. $\pi kI/2cR$
D. $2\pi kI/cR$
E. kI/c
F. zero
T. other (specify)

E9T.6 A wire bent in the shape shown in problem E9T.5 carries a current in the direction marked. What is the magnitude of the magnetic field at the point a due to the entire loop? (Select from the answers provided for problem E9T.5.)

E9T.7 Consider a wire bent in the hairpin shape shown below. The wire carries a current I. What is the approximate magnetic field magnitude $\boldsymbol{B}$ at point a?

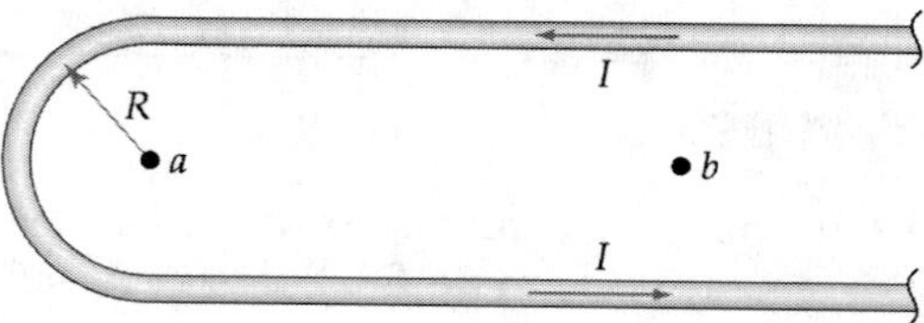

A. kI/cR
B. $2kI/cR$
C. $2\pi Ik/cR$
D. $(2+\pi)kI/cR$
E. zero
F. other (specify)

E9T.8 Consider a wire bent in the hairpin shape shown in problem E9T.7. The wire carries a current I. What is the approximate magnitude of the magnetic field at point b? (Select from the answers provided for problem E9T.7.)

E9T.9 Consider a circular loop that carries a uniform current. Define the loop's central plane to be the plane that slices the loop exactly in half as one would slice a bagel. Which of the following ways to place a mirror satisfy the conditions of the mirror rule?

A. Placing a mirror in any plane containing the loop's central axis
B. Placing a mirror in the loop's central plane (dividing the loop in half like a bagel)
C. Placing a mirror in any plane parallel to the loop's central plane
D. All of the above
E. A and B
F. None of the above.

HOMEWORK PROBLEMS

Basic Skills

E9B.1 A bullet with a charge of +10 nC is fired along the x axis with a speed of 520 m/s. Imagine that you sit at the position $y = 1.0$ m, $x = 0$. What is the magnitude and direction of the *maximum* magnetic field that you feel as a result of the bullet's motion? Where is the bullet when its field at your position is maximum?

E9B.2 An electron travels at $0.1c$ along the x axis. An atom sits along the y axis 2.5 nm away from the x axis. What is the magnitude and direction of the *maximum* magnetic field that the atom feels as a result of the electron? Where is the electron when it exerts this maximum effect?

E9B.3 How much current would a long straight wire have to carry to create magnetic field whose strength is $B = 100$ MN/C at a point 1 cm from the wire?

E9B.4 A long straight wire carries a current of 200 A. What is the magnetic field strength at a point 3 cm from the wire?

E9B.5 A circular loop of wire has a radius of 12 cm and carries a current of 0.5 A. What is the magnitude of the magnetic field at its center? How does this compare to the magnitude of the earth's magnetic field?

E9B.6 Imagine that you have a loop of wire 10 cm in diameter. How much current would have to flow through the wire to create a field at the loop's center that is twice as strong as the earth's magnetic field ($\approx$ 0.5 gauss)?

E9B.7 Imagine winding N turns of wire in a circular loop of radius R, and assume the wire is so thin that the width of a bundle of N wires is $<< R$. Each turn in this coil acts like a loop of radius R, and so the magnetic field at the coil's center is N times larger than that for a single loop of the same size. If the wire can safely carry 1.0 A of current, how many turns are needed to produce a magnetic field with strength 0.0033 T in the center of a coil 10 cm in diameter?

E9B.8 How does the model of a permanent magnet described in section E9.5 explain why we cannot isolate a magnet's poles by breaking a magnet in half?

E9B.9 Consider an infinite planar current distribution. Use a rotation argument to prove that if the magnetic field points in the $+z$ direction at points on one slide of the slab's central plane, it must point in the $-z$ direction at points on the other side.

E9B.10 Consider a circular loop of wire that carries a uniform current. Use a rotation argument to prove that the magnetic field vector at any point along the loop's central axis must point parallel to that axis.

E9B.11 In example E9.3, we used a mirror placed perpendicular to the solenoid's axis to determine the direction of the magnetic field. Explain why this is the only possible choice for mirror placement that satisfies the conditions of the mirror rule in the case of an infinite solenoid.

E9B.12 Consider a planar slab that is infinite in the yz direction but has a uniform thickness in the x direction. Imagine that the slab carries a uniformly distributed current density $\vec{J}$ in the $+y$ direction. Explain why any mirror whose plane is *not* parallel the current direction cannot satisfy the conditions of the mirror rule in this case.

Synthetic

E9S.1 Use the Biot-Savart law to calculate the field in the center of the loop shown in the diagram for problem E9T.5, except assume that the radius of the larger loop is $3R/2$.

E9S.2 Imagine that we have a circular plastic disk of radius 20 cm. By rubbing its edge with fur, we create a total negative charge of about 30 nC uniformly distributed around the disk's edge. We then spin the disk at a rate of 60 turns per second. What is the approximate magnitude of the magnetic field that rotating charge creates at the disk's center? How does this compare to the earth's magnetic field?

E9S.3 Consider a circular loop of wire of radius R that carries a current I. Let us set up our coordinate system so that the loop lies in the yz plane and the x axis goes through the loop's center (the x axis will then correspond to the loop's central axis).

(a) Use the Biot-Savart law to show that the magnetic field strength $\boldsymbol{B}$ at a point along the x axis is given by

$$\boldsymbol{B} = \frac{2\pi k I R^2}{c[x^2 + R^2]^{3/2}} \qquad \text{(E9.14)}$$

(b) Argue that at large distances r from the loop's center, the loop's magnetic field $\vec{\boldsymbol{B}}$ at points along the loop's central axis is exactly analogous to the electric field $\vec{E}$ at distant points along an electric dipole's central axis (see equation E2.16) if we substitute qd for $\pi R^2 I/c$, where q is the absolute value of the electric charge at either end of a dipole of length d.

E9S.4 Consider a square loop of wire with sides of length L and which carries current I. Let us set up our coordinate system so that the loop lies in the yz plane and the x axis goes through the loop's center (the x axis will then correspond to the loop's central axis).

(a) Use the Biot-Savart law and the small angle approximation $\sin\phi \approx \tan\phi \approx \phi$ when $\phi << 1$ to compute the total magnetic field at a point P along the x axis that is a distance $x >> L$. (*Hints:* Since each leg is very small compared to the distance x, we can treat each leg as a single segment in the sum in the Biot-Savart law. Draw a picture of the situation looking at the loop from above the xy plane, and argue that the $\boldsymbol{B}_y$ and $\boldsymbol{B}_z$ components contributed by the four legs cancel out in pairs, but that the $\boldsymbol{B}_x$ components contributed by all four legs are identical and add.)

(b) Show that formula for the magnitude of the magnetic field created by the square loop at point along its central axis such that $x >> L$ is same as that created by a *circular* loop at a point along its central axis such that $x >> R$ (see equation E9.14) if IL^2 for the square loop is the same as $I\pi R^2$ for the circular loop. (This is a special case of a general result that a loop's magnetic field in the large-distance limit does not depend on the loop's shape, but only on the product of its area and the current it carries.)

E9S.5 Imagine that we have two parallel current-carrying coils of radius R that are perpendicular to and centered on the x axis, with one coil's center at $x = \frac{1}{2}D$ and the other at $x = -\frac{1}{2}D$ (so the two coils are a distance D apart). These coils both carry the same magnitude of current I in the same direction (see figure E9.12). We would like to adjust the value of D so that the magnetic field created by the coils is as constant as possible along the x axis in the neighborhood of $x = 0$.

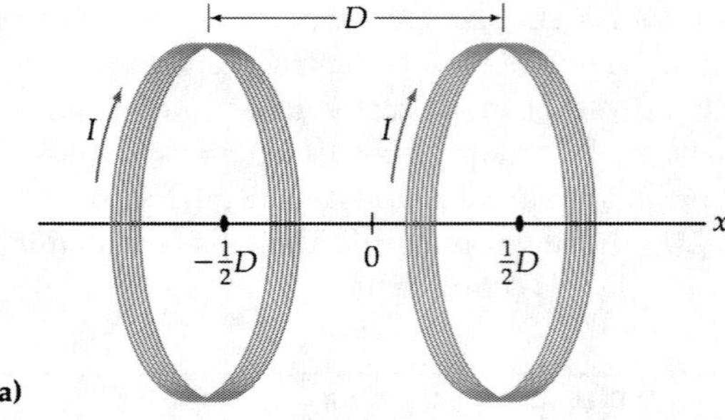

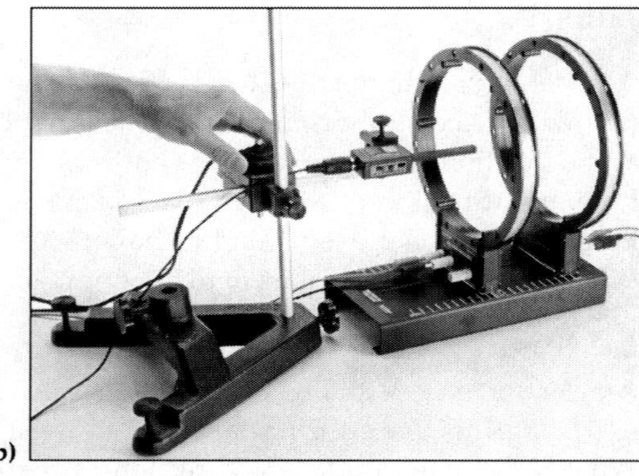

Figure E9.12
(a) A schematic diagram of a pair of Helmholtz coils (see problem E9S.5). (b) A photograph showing Helmholtz coils being used in an experiment.

(a) Use equation E9.14 to show that the first derivative of $\boldsymbol{B}_x$ with respect to x is zero for all values of D just because the arrangement of coils is symmetric about the origin. (*Hint:* Argue that x in equation E9.14 should be replaced by $x \pm \frac{1}{2}D$ in this problem, where the sign in front of the $\frac{1}{2}D$ depends on which of the two coils we are talking about.)

(b) Show that if we place the coils a certain distance D apart, the second derivative of $\boldsymbol{B}_x$ will also be zero at $x = 0$. Find this distance in terms of R. (This optimal spacing gives the most constant field possible with two coils: coils arranged with this optimal spacing are called *Helmholtz coils.*)

E9S.6 Use a symmetry argument to prove that the magnetic field must be zero at points along the central axis of an axially symmetric current distribution.

E9S.7 Consider an infinite conducting planar slab which (for the sake of argument) has a fixed width in the x direction but is infinite in the y and z directions. Let this slab be uniformly filled with current moving in the $+y$ direction.

(a) Use a reflection argument to prove that the magnetic field everywhere must point in the $\pm z$ direction.

(b) Use either another reflection argument or a different kind of symmetry argument to prove that the field vectors at points on the slab's central plane must be zero.

E9S.8 A toroidal coil (see see the figure below) is a coil of wire wound around a donut-shaped form. (Mathematicians call a donut shape a *torus*. One can also think of a toroidal coil as being a solenoid that has been bent into a circle.) Let us define coordinates so that the z axis coincides with the toroid's central axis and let r be the distance that a given point is from that central axis.

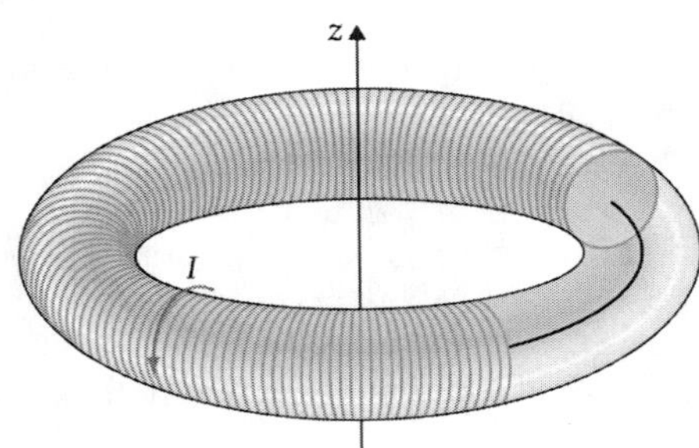

(a) Use the mirror rule to prove that at any point inside or outside the coil, its magnetic field must point tangent to a circle going through the point that is perpendicular to and centered on the z axis.

(b) Use a rotational symmetry argument to prove that the magnitude of this field can depend at most on r and z.

Rich-Context

E9R.1 A particle accelerator injects $N = 10^{15}$ protons traveling at speed $v = 0.2c$ into a region where there is a uniform magnetic field with a strength of $\boldsymbol{B}_{\text{ext}}$ = 300 MN/C (B_{ext} = 1.0 T). As discussed in chapter E7, the protons will travel in a circle in this region. They will therefore act as a current loop that creates its own magnetic field $\vec{\boldsymbol{B}}_{\text{pro}}$.

(a) Will this field reinforce or oppose $\vec{\boldsymbol{B}}_{\text{ext}}$?

(b) *Assuming* that the magnitude of $\vec{\boldsymbol{B}}_{\text{pro}}$ is small compared to $\boldsymbol{B}_{\text{ext}}$, derive a *symbolic* expression for $\boldsymbol{B}_{\text{pro}}$ at the center of the proton loop in terms of k, c, N, $\boldsymbol{B}_{\text{ext}}$, and the proton's charge and mass e and m.

(c) Show that in this case, $B_{\text{pro}}/B_{\text{ext}} \approx 1/400$ at the loop's center, justifying the initial assumption.

(d) If v were smaller, would $B_{\text{pro}}/B_{\text{ext}}$ get smaller or larger? Explain your answer *physically* (not by just appealing to the equation).

E9R.2 Imagine that you are designing circular coil that must have a radius of 10 cm, create a magnetic field of magnitude 0.01 T at its center, must have a cross-sectional area of less than $0.25\ \text{cm}^2$ and must use as little power as possible. The question is, should you use many turns of thin wire in this coil or one turn of wire with a cross-sectional area $0.25\ \text{cm}^2$? Assume that you are using copper wire.

(a) Show that, to a first approximation anyway, the power this coil will use is fixed by the design requirements, and the number of turns of wire is therefore irrelevant for minimizing the power. What assumptions go into this result?

(b) Since the number of turns N does not affect the power much, we can choose N to satisfy other constraints. What would be the appropriate number of turns if you intend to connect this coil directly to a 12-V car battery and why?

E9R.3 Just how strong can a permanent magnet be? Specifically, imagine a small cylindrical permanent magnet that is 2.0 cm long and 1.0 cm in diameter. What is the maximum magnetic field we could reasonably expect such a magnet to create at a point, say, 10 cm from its center along its long axis? This might seem impossible to guess, but as a matter of fact, we can arrive at a pretty good guess by making only some pretty basic assumptions.

(a) Consider an electron of mass m traveling at speed v in a circular orbit of radius r around an atom. The magnitude of the angular momentum of such an electron is $L = mvr$. The current that this orbiting electron represents is its charge divided by the time it takes to go around once. Show that the magnitude of the orbiting electron's magnetic moment is

$$\mu = IA = \frac{eL}{2m} \tag{E9.15}$$

(b) Quantum mechanics tells us that the electron's orbital angular momentum L is quantized in steps of $\hbar = h/2\pi = 1.054\times10^{-34}$ J·s (h is Planck's constant). Show that this means that an atom's magnetic moment must be quantized in steps of $\mu_B = 9.26\times10^{-24}\ \text{A}\cdot\text{m}^2$ (this quantity is called the *Bohr magneton*).

(c) Iron has a mass of about 55 g per mole of atoms. Most of the other ferromagnetic elements are close to iron on the periodic table, so ferromagnetic alloys will have very roughly this molar mass. Iron also has a density of about 7900 kg/m^3. Roughly how many atoms will there be in our magnet?

(d) In a typical atom, most electrons orbit in pairs having opposite angular momenta, so they contribute nothing to the atom's magnetic moment. The electron also has a spin angular momentum whose magnetic moment is quantized in roughly the same-sized steps as the orbital magnetic moment. So we will likely have one or at most two electrons contributing to the magnetic moment per atom. Let's be very generous and imagine that the total magnetic moment per atom is $4\mu_B$ ($1\mu_B$ is probably more realistic). Also let's assume that *all* of the atomic magnetic moments in our magnet are perfectly aligned. Use this information and equation E9.14 to compute the magnetic field of our magnet at a point P that is 10 cm from its center along its axis. (*Hints:* All of the atomic loops will be very small compared to their separation from point P. Note also that the loops are all roughly the same distance from P and that P lies pretty close to the central axis of each.)

(e) Analyze the assumptions that went into this calculation. What would we have to assume to get a magnet of the same volume that is, say, 10 times stronger? Could using metals higher on the periodic table help? Is it realistic to assume higher total magnetic moment per atom? Why or why not?

E9R.4 Consider a uniformly charged infinite slab moving with velocity $\vec{v}$ perpendicular to its surface (see the drawing below).

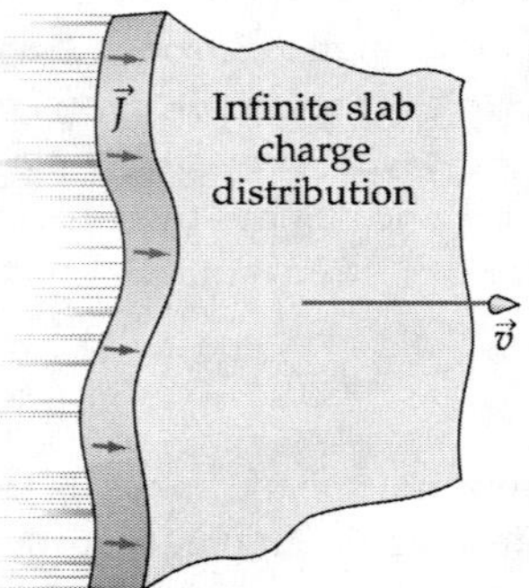

Since any moving charge constitutes a current, this moving slab represents a *current* distribution. In this situation, it turns out that symmetry arguments *completely determine* the magnetic field at all points inside and outside the slab. Describe this slab's field and provide the symmetry arguments that support your description.

Advanced

E9A.1 Calculate the magnetic field $\vec{B}$ at a point P a displacement $\vec{r}_{PQ}$ away from a square loop with side L centered at point Q as a function of the angle θ between $\vec{r}_{PQ}$ and the loop's central axis, assuming that $\text{mag}(\vec{r}_{PQ}) \equiv r >> L$. Show that the formulas for the radial and perpendicular components $\boldsymbol{B}_r$ and $\boldsymbol{B}_\perp$ are the same as those for E_r and $E_\perp$ given in problem E2A.1 if we substitute qd for IL^2/c. (*Hints:* To find the radial and perpendicular components B_r and $B_\perp$ of the magnetic field, I think that it is easiest to orient the coordinate system so that the x axis always goes from Q to P, and so that the two of the loop's legs are parallel to the z axis. Then the loop's central axis will lie in the xy plane and we will have $B_r = B_x$ and $B_\perp = B_y$. In this coordinate system, evaluate $\vec{I}_i \times \hat{r}_{PQ}$ for all four legs using the *component* form of the cross product:

$$\vec{u} \times \vec{w} = \begin{bmatrix} u_y w_z - u_z w_y \\ u_z w_x - u_x w_z \\ u_x w_y - u_y w_x \end{bmatrix} \quad \text{(E9.16)}$$

and use the binomial approximation.)

E9A.2 In this problem, we will prove the mirror rule from equation E9.1 and the properties of the cross product. Imagine that we have a charge distribution that is not affected by a mirror reflection across a certain plane. Without loss of generality, we can choose coordinates so that the yz ($x = 0$) plane is the plane of the mirror.

(a) Argue that if the current distribution is to be unchanged by the mirror reflection across the yz plane, then for every moving charged particle whose position is $[x, y, z]$, there must be another charged particle whose position is $[-x, y, z]$ and whose velocity is the same. Argue also that the x-velocities of both must be zero.

(b) Use equation E9.1 and the component definition of the cross product to show that the total magnetic field that this *pair* of particles contribute at an arbitrary point $[0, Y, Z]$ on the mirror's plane must have zero y and z components.

(c) Using the superposition principle, argue that *any* charge distribution that is symmetrical across the yz plane must therefore have a field that obeys the mirror rule.

ANSWERS TO SELF-TESTS

E9X.1 The compass needle will align itself with the wire's magnetic field. A needle initially perpendicular to the wire is *already* aligned with its field and thus will not move when the current is turned on, but one initially *parallel* will visibly swing to align itself with the field.

E9X.2 In applying the cross-product rule, point your right index finger in the direction of $q\vec{v}$ and your long finger in the direction of $\hat{r}_{PC}$ for the point P in question. When applying the wire rule, point your thumb parallel to $q\vec{v}$.

E9X.3 According to the value of μ_0 given

$$\frac{\mu_0 c^2}{4\pi} = \frac{(4\pi\times10^{-7}\,\text{T}\cdot\text{s}\cdot\text{m/C})(2.998\times10^8\ \text{m/s})^2}{4\pi}$$

$$= 8.99\times10^9\,\frac{\cancel{\text{T}}\cdot\text{m}^{\cancel{3}2}}{\cancel{\text{s}}\cdot\text{C}}\left(\frac{1\,(\text{N/C})(\cancel{\text{s}}/\cancel{\text{m}})}{1\,\cancel{\text{T}}}\right)$$

$$= 8.99\times10^9\,\frac{\text{N}\cdot\text{m}^2}{\text{C}^2} = k \qquad \text{(E9.17)}$$

E9X.4 Note that the maximum value of $\text{mag}(\vec{v}\times\hat{r})$ is v. Plugging in the numbers, we get

$$E_{\max} = \frac{kq}{r_{\min}^2} = \frac{(8.99\times10^9\ \text{N}\cdot\cancel{\text{m}}^2\text{C}^{-\cancel{2}})(10\times10^{-9}\ \cancel{\text{C}})}{(0.1\ \cancel{\text{m}})^2}$$

$$= 9000\ \text{N/C} \qquad \text{(E9.18)}$$

$$B_{\max} = \frac{\mu_0 qv}{4\pi r_{\min}^2} = \frac{(4\pi\times10^{-7}\ \text{T}\cdot\cancel{\text{m}}\cdot\cancel{\text{s}}/\text{C})(10\times10^{-9}\ \text{C})(30\ \cancel{\text{m}}/\cancel{\text{s}})}{4\pi(0.1\ \cancel{\text{m}})^2}$$

$$= 3.0\times10^{-12}\ \text{T} \qquad \text{(E9.19)}$$

$$\mathbb{B}_{\max} = \frac{kq}{r_{\min}^2}\frac{v}{c} = E_{\max}\frac{v}{c} = 9000\,\frac{\text{N}}{\text{C}}\left(\frac{30\ \cancel{\text{m/s}}}{3.0\times10^8\ \cancel{\text{m/s}}}\right)$$

$$= 9.0\times10^{-4}\ \text{N/C} \qquad \text{(E9.20)}$$

Note that $\mathbb{B}/E = v/c = 10^{-7}$ here.

E9X.5 Since only the segments of the wire closest to the point really affect the field at the point, we can guess that $B_B \approx 2B_A >> B_C$.

E9X.6 Solving equation E9.13 for I and plugging in numbers yields

$$I = \frac{\mathbb{B}cr}{2k} = \frac{(15{,}000\ \cancel{\text{N}}/\cancel{\text{C}})(3.0\times10^8\ \cancel{\text{m}}/\text{s})(0.1\ \cancel{\text{m}})}{2(8.99\times10^9\ \cancel{\text{N}}\cdot\cancel{\text{m}}^2/\text{C}^{\cancel{2}})}$$

$$= 25\,\frac{\text{C}}{\text{s}} = 25\ \text{A}. \qquad \text{(E9.21)}$$

E9X.7 The magnetic field at the point in question is $\mathbb{B} = kI/cR$ (half of a full line). The horizontal segment of the wire contributes nothing because I is parallel to $\hat{r}_{Pi}$ for all segments along the wire, so $\vec{I}\times\hat{r}_{Pi} = 0$ for that part of the wire.

E9X.8 If the mirror is placed perpendicular to the charge's velocity, that velocity will appear reversed in the mirror, as shown below. This means that the *current* distribution represented by the moving charge is *not* the same after the mirror is placed as it was before, even if the mirror exactly bisects the charge at an instant. Therefore, this mirror does not satisfy the conditions imposed by the mirror rule.

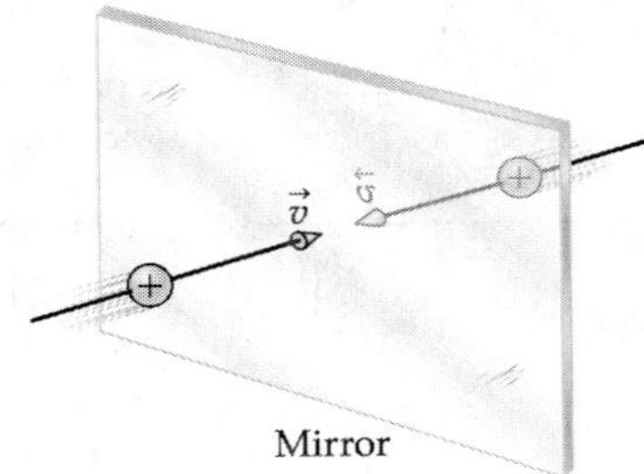

E9X.9 If the plane of the mirror contains the symmetry axis, the figure below shows that the solenoid current distribution does *not* look the same before and after we place the mirror, because the current direction is reversed in the mirror image. Therefore, the conditions of the mirror rule do not apply, and this means that placing the mirror this way does not tell us anything useful about the current distribution.

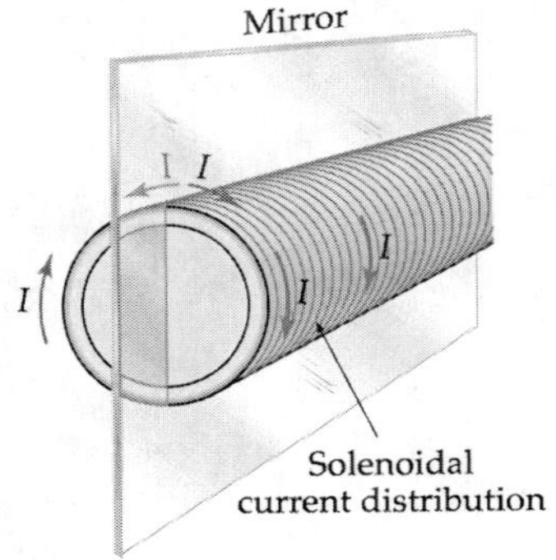

E10 Gauss's Law

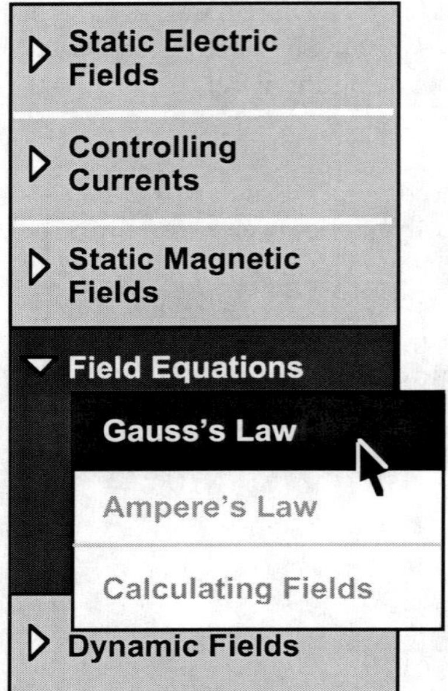

Chapter Overview

Introduction

In previous chapters, we have developed an "action-at-a-distance" model of the electric and magnetic fields, a model that is inconsistent with relativity and does not correctly handle time-dependent fields. In this subsection of the unit, we will discuss an entirely different approach, one that describes electric and magnetic fields using *local field equations* that are consistent with relativity.

Section E10.1: What is a Field Equation?

The fundamental problem with an action-at-a-distance model is that it links the behavior of charged particles at one point instantaneously to changes in their fields at distant points, which is forbidden by relativity. We can get around this problem if we can re-express the laws of electricity and magnetism in terms of **local field equations** that link a characteristic of the field *at a point* with the density of charge or current *at the same point*, ignoring the effect of distant charges or currents on the field. Such laws do not require forbidden instantaneous communication.

Section E10.2: The Divergence of an Electric Field

This section describes how we can visualize measuring an electric field's **divergence** at a point with a **div-meter** consisting of a box whose faces flex outward or inward in response to the perpendicular component of the electric force acting on positive test particles embedded in those faces. The divergence is proportional to the change in the box's volume. A charge inside the box will either puff out its faces or pull them in (yielding nonzero divergence) but the field of a charged particle outside the box plausibly produces zero net change in the box's volume and so zero divergence. This makes the divergence suitable for use in a local field equation.

Section E10.3: The Divergence in Terms of Tile Vectors

We can quantify the spatial orientation of a small patch of surface by using a **normal** or **nose** vector $\hat{n}$, a unit vector perpendicular to the surface. If we are interested only in this patch's area dA and its orientation, then we can quantify all that we need to know about the patch with a tile vector $d\vec{A} = dA\,\hat{n}$.

We can use this idea to write down a quantitative expression for the divergence that is independent of size or other characteristics of the div-meter:

$$\text{div}(\vec{E}) \equiv \lim_{L\to 0} \frac{1}{L}\left[\vec{E}_1\cdot\hat{n}_1 + \vec{E}_2\cdot\hat{n}_2 + \ldots + \vec{E}_6\cdot\hat{n}_6\right] \tag{E10.10}$$

$$\equiv \lim_{V\to 0} \frac{1}{V}\left[\vec{E}_1\cdot d\vec{A}_1 + \vec{E}_2\cdot d\vec{A}_2 + \ldots + \vec{E}_6\cdot d\vec{A}_6\right] \tag{E10.11}$$

Purpose: These equations mathematically define the divergence $\text{div}(\vec{E})$ of an electric field at a given point P.

Symbols: $\vec{E}_i$ is the electric field vector at the center of the ith face of a cube with side L and volume $V = L^3$ centered on point P, $\hat{n}_i$ and $d\vec{A}_i \equiv L^2\hat{n}_i$ are the nose and tile vectors for that face, respectively. This means that $\vec{E}_i\cdot\hat{n}_i$ is the outward component of the electric field evaluated at the center of the ith face.

Limitations: In the limit that $L \to 0$, this equation is an exact definition. However, if L is not infinitesimal, it must be small compared to the scale over which the electric field varies significantly.

We can use this expression to prove mathematically that the divergence does not register the electric fields created by distant charges.

Section E10.4: The Divergence as a Derivative.

This section argues that the divergence is a kind of derivative of the electric field:

$$\text{div}(\vec{E}) = \frac{\partial E_x}{\partial x} + \frac{\partial E_y}{\partial y} + \frac{\partial E_z}{\partial z} \quad \text{(E10.19)}$$

Purpose: This is the definition of the divergence $\text{div}(\vec{E})$ in terms of partial derivatives of the electric field function $\vec{E}(x,y,z)$.

Symbols: E_x, E_y, and E_z are the components of $\vec{E}$.

Limitations: This equation follows from equation E10.10.

Section E10.5: Gauss's Law

Gauss's law is the local field equation that links the electric field to charge:

$$\text{div}(\vec{E}) = \frac{\rho}{\varepsilon_0} \quad (= 4\pi k\rho) \quad \text{(E10.20)}$$

Purpose: This local field equation links the divergence of the electric field $\vec{E}$ at a point with the charge density ρ at that point.

Symbols: $\text{div}(\vec{E})$ is the divergence of the electric field at the point (as defined by equation E10.10 or E10.19), $\varepsilon_0 = (4\pi k)^{-1}$ is the permittivity constant, and k is the Coulomb constant.

Limitations: This law has no limits (until one gets into the realm of quantum field theory): it applies even to rapidly varying fields.

The section illustrates some simple applications of this law. For static electric fields, this equation yields exactly the same results as the methods based on Coulomb's law discussed in chapter E3 (sometimes much more quickly!).

Section E10.6: Gauss's Law for the Magnetic Field

By analogy, one can imagine measuring the divergence of the magnetic field using a box whose faces have embedded isolated north magnetic poles instead of charges. The magnetic divergence is then defined precisely as in equations E10.10 or E10.19, except with $\boldsymbol{B}$s appearing where the Es appear in these equations.

Gauss's law for the magnetic field asserts that

$$\text{div}(\vec{\boldsymbol{B}}) = 0 \quad \text{(E10.26)}$$

Purpose: This local field equation states that one cannot create a magnetic field having a nonzero divergence at any point in space.

Symbols: $\text{div}(\vec{\boldsymbol{B}})$ is the divergence of the magnetic field.

Limitations: This law has no limits (until we get to the realm of quantum field theory): it applies even to rapidly varying fields.

This law tells us that there are no **magnetic monopoles** (isolated magnetic poles) that play for magnetism the role that charged particles play for electrostatics. This law constrains the types of magnetic fields that can exist in nature.

E10.1 What Is a Field Equation?

A review of the methods we have used to calculate fields so far in the course

Our discussion of electric and magnetic phenomena in the past nine chapters has been based on only *four* equations. Two of these equations implicitly *define* the vectors $\vec{E}$ and $\vec{B}$ at a given point in space in terms of the electric and magnetic forces that a test charge experiences at that point:

$$\vec{F}_e = q\vec{E} \qquad \text{and} \qquad \vec{F}_m = q\left(\frac{\vec{v}}{c}\right) \times \vec{B} \tag{E10.1}$$

The other two equations specify how to calculate the electric or magnetic field at a point P due to a charged particle at point C:

$$\vec{E}_P = \frac{kq}{r_{PC}^2}\hat{r}_{PC} \qquad \text{and} \qquad \vec{B}_P = \frac{kq}{r_{PC}^2}\left(\frac{\vec{v}}{c} \times \hat{r}_{PC}\right) \tag{E10.2}$$

where $k \equiv (4\pi\varepsilon_0)^{-1}$. Almost everything we have discussed to this point is a consequence of these four equations and the principle of superposition.

These methods are not consistent with relativity

Equations E10.2 present an "action-at-a-distance" model of the electric and magnetic fields: they connect the field vectors at a given point in space with charges at distant points in space. These equations accurately describe static (time-independent) fields, and approximately describe slowly varying fields. But as we first saw in chapter E2, these equations are *not* consistent with relativity, because (taken literally) these equations claim that the field at a given point *at an instant* depends on the location of a distant charge *at the same instant*. Thus, if I wiggle a charge, its electric and magnetic field vectors everywhere in space *instantly* respond to its change in location. If this were really true, it would allow for instantaneous communication in a manner forbidden by relativity.

These equations therefore must (and are in fact are known to) break down when the charges that create the fields *accelerate* rapidly and thus create rapidly varying electric and magnetic fields. Our task in the next three chapters is thus to replace equations E10.2 with a set of **field equations** that *can* accurately describe rapidly varying fields in a manner consistent with relativity.

One can avoid the problem by using *local field equations* to describe the fields

What will such a field equation look like? The basic feature of equations E10.2 that makes them inconsistent with relativity is that they connect the field *here* with distant charges *there*: this is exactly what creates the instantaneous communication problem. A relativistically consistent field equation *avoids* this problem by connecting characteristics of the electric or magnetic field at a point with the presence of charge or current *at the same point*, not a distant point. A field equation will thus have this general form:

$$\begin{pmatrix}\text{a quantity that describes}\\ \text{some } \textit{characteristic} \text{ of the}\\ \text{field at a point in space}\end{pmatrix} = \begin{pmatrix}\text{a quantity that describes}\\ \text{the presence of charge or}\\ \text{or current } \textit{at the same point}\end{pmatrix} \tag{E10.3}$$

We call an equation like this a **local field equation,** because it links a *local* field characteristic with the *local* presence of charge or current. Such an equation must completely ignore distant charges or currents, focusing instead on how *local* charges or currents modify the character of the field.

The quantity on the left side of such a field equation cannot be the field vector itself, because we know (from equations E10.2, which are valid for static fields at least!) that the field vector at a point depends on the placement of *distant* charges. What we are looking for is some quantitative *characteristic* of the field that is *zero* at a point unless there is local charge or current *at that point*.

E10.2 The Divergence of an Electric Field

One field characteristic that turns out to be important for constructing local field equations for both the electric and magnetic fields is a quantity that physicists call the field's *divergence.* In this section, I will operationally define this quantity by describing how to *measure* it for an electric field.

Imagine a cubical box whose sides have a length L that is small compared to the scale over which $\vec{E}$ varies significantly, and with identical positive test charges glued to the centers of each of the box's six faces. Imagine that the box's edges and vertexes form a rigid framework, and the box faces do not permit their embedded charges to move from side to side parallel to the face. However, imagine that each face is flexible and bows outward or inward a bit as that face's test charge responds to the component of the electrostatic force perpendicular to that face, and that this bowing changes the box's volume by a tiny amount *directly proportional* to that force component. Assume that we know the constant of proportionality between the force component on each face and the resulting volume change and that we know the box's "zero-field" volume when the box and its test charges are isolated from all other charges.

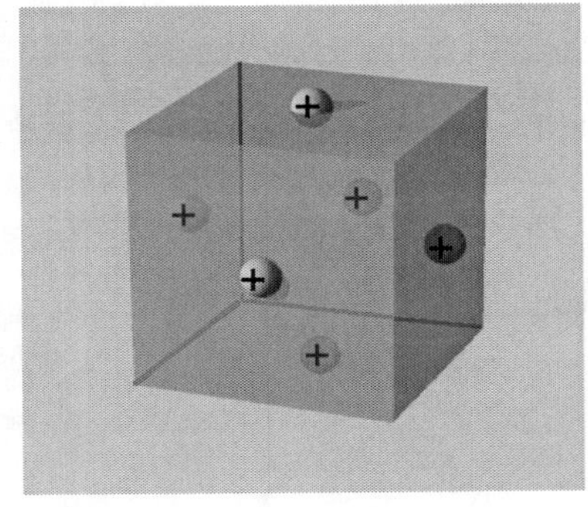

Figure E10.1
An illustration of a div-meter. An electrostatic force on a charge that acts perpendicular to the charge's face will bow the face outward or inward, changing the box's volume.

Figure E10.1 illustrates such a device, which we will call a **div-meter.** The **divergence** at point P of an electric field is proportional to the box's total volume change when we place the box's center at P. The divergence is positive if the box is puffed out by the electrostatic forces on its test charges and negative if it is pulled in by those forces. The divergence of the electric field at a point therefore expresses what we might call the "net outwardness" of the field in the vicinity of that point.

The definition of *divergence*

Why are we interested in the divergence? It turns out that our div-meter responds only to charges that are *inside* the box, completely ignoring all distant charges! Clearly, any positive charge inside the box will puff out all sides of the box, and any negative charge will pull in those sides, producing a positive or negative divergence respectively. However, the electric field of any charged particle *outside* the box produces no net volume change. For example, consider how the single external charge shown in figure E10.2 will affect the div-meter. The face nearest the external charge is pushed inward, and the opposite face is bowed outward a bit less, and the side faces are also bowed outward a small amount due to the small field component perpendicular to those faces. It turns out (as we will prove in section E10.3) that because of the inverse-square nature of the electric field, the effect of the bigger inward bowing of the near face cancels the sum of the effects of the smaller outward bowings of the other faces. Since the electric field obeys the superposition principle, the definition of the divergence implies that the divergence of the field created by any *set* of external charges will be zero (see problem E10S.5).

The divergence registers local charges but ignores distant charges

Therefore, the divergence is precisely the kind of quantity we want on the left side of a local field equation of the type described by equation E10.3: it responds to local charges but ignores distant charges.

Figure E10.2
How a div-meter is affected by an external charge.

Self-Test E10X.1

As an example, consider placing a div-meter at a point somewhere in the uniform electric field between two parallel uniformly charged plates so that two div-meter faces are perpendicular to the field and the other four are parallel to the field. By considering the bowing of the div-meter's faces, argue that the *divergence* of this electric field is zero (even though the electric field itself could be very strong at the point in question).

E10.3 The Divergence in Terms of Tile Vectors

The definitions of a *tile* and its associated *nose vector*

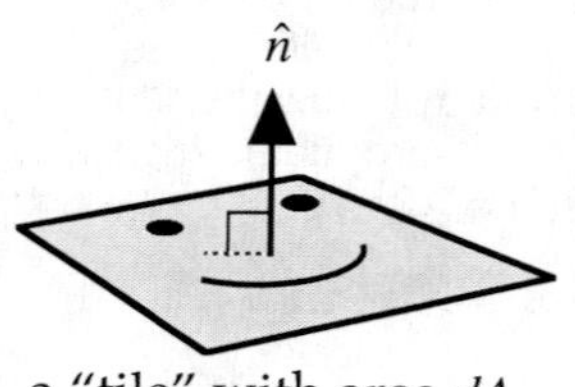

Figure E10.3
A tile and its nose vector.

In order to proceed further, we need a precise mathematical expression for the divergence of the electric field at a point. The mathematical concept of what I will call a *tile vector* will help us move toward this goal.

Let us define a **tile** to be a tiny flat patch of area in a three-dimensional space, small enough that the electric field is nearly uniform at all points on its surface. We can conveniently describe this tile's *orientation* in the three-dimensional space with a unit vector (that is, a directional) $\hat{n}$ perpendicular to the tile's flat surface, as shown in figure E10.3. Such a unit vector is technically called a **normal** vector, from the (now archaic) sense of *normal* as meaning "upright" or "perpendicular," but I like to think of this vector as being the tile's "nose" vector, because this vector points in the direction the tile is facing (as figure E10.3 whimsically illustrates).

In the circumstances where we will use the tile concept, the tile's exact *shape* is not relevant. In such cases, the only other useful piece of information about the tile is its size or (more specifically) its area. Let us denote the tile's area as dA, where the differential notation reminds us that the tile is supposed to be infinitesimally small compared to the scale over which $\vec{E}$ varies significantly. We can, therefore, compactly express everything we need to know about a tile with a **tile vector** $d\vec{A}$ such that

The definition of the tile's *tile vector*

$$d\vec{A} \equiv (dA)\hat{n} \tag{E10.4}$$

The magnitude of this vector is the tile's area dA and its direction is the tile's nose vector perpendicular to the tile's surface. The vector $d\vec{A}$ describes the tile in that, given the vector, we can construct a tile with the appropriate area and direction in space.

Reviewing the characteristics of the dot product

Before we go on, let us review some important characteristics of the dot product $\vec{u}\cdot\vec{w}$ of two vectors. As we saw in unit C, the dot product is a scalar quantity defined to be

$$\vec{u}\cdot\vec{w} \equiv uw\cos\theta = u_x w_x + u_y w_y + u_z w_z \tag{E10.5}$$

where θ is the angle between the vectors. From this definition, one can prove that the dot product has the following mathematical properties:

$$\vec{u}\cdot\vec{w} = \vec{w}\cdot\vec{u} \quad \text{(the dot product is } \textit{commutative}\text{)} \tag{E10.6a}$$

$$\vec{u}\cdot(\vec{w}+\vec{a}) = \vec{u}\cdot\vec{w} + \vec{u}\cdot\vec{a} \quad \text{(the dot product is } \textit{distributive}\text{)} \tag{E10.6b}$$

$$\vec{u}\cdot(b\vec{w}) = b(\vec{u}\cdot\vec{w}) \quad \text{(the dot product is } \textit{linear}\text{)} \tag{E10.6c}$$

$$\vec{u}\cdot\vec{u} = u^2 \tag{E10.6d}$$

$$\vec{u}\cdot\vec{w} = 0 \iff \vec{u}\perp\vec{w} \quad \text{(assuming } \vec{u}\neq 0 \text{ and } \vec{w}\neq 0\text{)} \tag{E10.6e}$$

One of the most important features of the dot product for our present purposes is that if $\hat{n}$ is a unit vector (directional) then, because a unit vector has a magnitude of 1,

$$\vec{u} \cdot \hat{n} = u \cos\theta = \text{the scalar component of } \vec{u} \text{ in the } \hat{n} \text{ direction} \quad \text{(E10.7)}$$

This is illustrated in figure E10.4. Note that if $\vec{u}$ is more aligned with $\hat{n}$ than not ($\theta < 90°$), then this component is positive; if it is more antialigned with $\hat{n}$ ($\theta > 90°$) then the component is negative, as we would expect a "component in the $\hat{n}$ direction" to be.

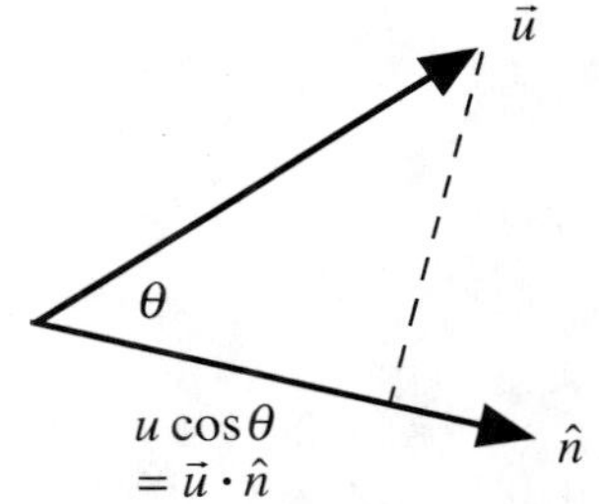

Figure E10.4
This diagram illustrates why $\vec{u} \cdot \hat{n}$ (where $\hat{n}$ is a unit vector) gives you the component of $\vec{u}$ in the direction of $\hat{n}$.

As a simple example, consider a unit vector $\hat{n} = [1, 0, 0]$ in the $+x$ direction. Then $\vec{u} \cdot \hat{n} = u_x(1) + u_y(0) + u_z(0) = u_x$, the vector's normal x component. This component is positive if $\vec{u}$ points at least partly in the $+x$ direction and negative if it points partly in the $-x$ direction.

Now we are in a position to define the divergence more precisely. We qualitatively defined the divergence at a point P as being proportional to the sum of the outward components of the electrostatic forces on charged test particles at the centers of the faces of a tiny box centered on P. Think of these six faces as outward-facing tiles with nose vectors $\hat{n}_1, \hat{n}_2, \ldots, \hat{n}_6$ as shown in figure E10.5. Assume that the electric field in the neighborhood of P exerts forces $\vec{F}_1, \vec{F}_2, \ldots, \vec{F}_6$ on the charged test particles respectively. Since the nose vectors are unit vectors and since the dot product of a force vector with a unit vector yields the component of that force in the unit vector's direction, the sum of the outward force components acting on our div-meter's test particles is

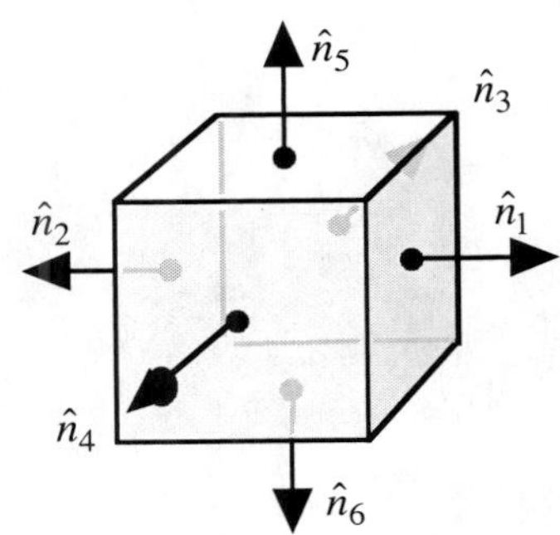

Figure E10.5
The nose vectors for the tiles representing the faces of a div-meter box.

$$\begin{aligned} \text{div}(\vec{E}) &\propto F_{\text{out},1} + F_{\text{out},2} + \ldots + F_{\text{out},6} \\ &= \vec{F}_1 \cdot \hat{n}_1 + \vec{F}_2 \cdot \hat{n}_2 + \ldots + \vec{F}_6 \cdot \hat{n}_6 \end{aligned} \quad \text{(E10.8)}$$

We need only define the constant of proportionality. Note that for a given electric field, the magnitudes of the forces the test particles experience will be proportional to the particles' common charge magnitude q, so if we want the divergence to depend only on the electric field and not on how charged our div-meter's test particles are, we should divide by q.

The div-meter's size also makes a difference. Note (as discussed in self-test E10X.1) that an electric field that is precisely uniform over the region spanned by the div-meter will exert an inward force on one face that has the same magnitude as the outward force on the opposite face, so the terms in equation E10.8 cancel in pairs (that is, $\vec{F}_1 \cdot \hat{n}_1 + \vec{F}_2 \cdot \hat{n}_2 = 0$, and so on.) Most electric fields are not uniform, so the electrostatic forces experienced by the div-meter's test particles will *not* exactly cancel in pairs this way. However, as the div-meter box becomes smaller, the field will be more and more uniform over the region the div-meter spans, so the pairs in equation E10.8 will more nearly cancel. For sufficiently small boxes, it turns out that the degree to which a div-meter can register a field's nonuniformity is proportional to the linear size of its box. Therefore, if we want the divergence to be a quantity independent of the size of our particular div-meter, we should divide by the length L of the side of our div-meter box. The resulting ratio should then approach a well-defined value as $L \to 0$.

Therefore, we define an electric field's divergence at a point P to be

A definition of the divergence that ignores the characteristics of the div-meter

$$\text{div}(\vec{E}) \equiv \lim_{L \to 0} \frac{1}{qL}\left[\vec{F}_1 \cdot \hat{n}_1 + \vec{F}_2 \cdot \hat{n}_2 + \ldots + \vec{F}_6 \cdot \hat{n}_6\right] \quad \text{(E10.9)}$$

The electric field $\vec{E}_1$ at the center of face 1 is defined to be $\vec{E}_1 \equiv \vec{F}_1 / q$ (and similarly for the other faces) so we can write this expression more compactly as follows:

$$\text{div}(\vec{E}) \equiv \lim_{L\to 0}\frac{1}{L}\left[\vec{E}_1\cdot\hat{n}_1 + \vec{E}_2\cdot\hat{n}_2 + \ldots + \vec{E}_6\cdot\hat{n}_6\right] \tag{E10.10}$$

Note that the area of each face is L^2 and the div-meter's volume is $V = L^3$, so if we multiply the top and bottom of this expression by L^2, and use $d\vec{A}_1 \equiv L^2\hat{n}_1$ and so on, we can also express this definition in terms of the tile vectors for the div-meter faces:

The quantitative definition of the divergence

$$\text{div}(\vec{E}) \equiv \lim_{L\to 0}\frac{1}{L}\left[\vec{E}_1\cdot\hat{n}_1 + \vec{E}_2\cdot\hat{n}_2 + \ldots + \vec{E}_6\cdot\hat{n}_6\right] \tag{E10.10}$$

$$\equiv \lim_{V\to 0}\frac{1}{V}\left[\vec{E}_1\cdot d\vec{A}_1 + \vec{E}_2\cdot d\vec{A}_2 + \ldots + \vec{E}_6\cdot d\vec{A}_6\right] \tag{E10.11}$$

Purpose: These equations define the divergence $\text{div}(\vec{E})$ of an electric field at a given point P.

Symbols: $\vec{E}_i$ is the electric field vector at the center of the ith face of a cube with side L and volume $V = L^3$ centered on point P, $\hat{n}_i$ and $d\vec{A}_i \equiv L^2\hat{n}_i$ are the nose and tile vectors for that face, respectively. This means that $\vec{E}_i\cdot\hat{n}_i$ is the outward component of the electric field evaluated at the center of the ith face.

Limitations: In the limit that $L \to 0$, this equation is an exact definition. However, if L is not infinitesimal, it must be small compared to the scale over which the electric field varies significantly.

We will find equation E10.10 to be the more useful form of this definition in the next section, but equation E10.11 will be more useful in chapter E11.

Remember that the whole point of the divergence is that it serves as a detector of local charge: when the div-meter box physically contains charge, the divergence is nonzero and when it does not contain charge, it is zero. I will now use our formal definition of the divergence to prove that the divergence does indeed ignore the electric field created by a charged particle outside the box.

The proof that the divergence ignores the field created by an external charged particle

Figure E10.6 illustrates a point P a distance r from a particle with charge Q. Without loss of generality, we can choose coordinates so that the particle lies at the origin and point P lies along the $+x$ axis. We can also choose to orient our div-meter so that it is aligned with the coordinate axis directions. The nose vectors for the div-meter sides are then

$$\hat{n}_1 = \begin{bmatrix}1\\0\\0\end{bmatrix},\ \hat{n}_2 = \begin{bmatrix}-1\\0\\0\end{bmatrix},\ \hat{n}_3 = \begin{bmatrix}0\\1\\0\end{bmatrix},\ \hat{n}_4 = \begin{bmatrix}0\\-1\\0\end{bmatrix},\ \hat{n}_5 = \begin{bmatrix}0\\0\\1\end{bmatrix},\ \hat{n}_6 = \begin{bmatrix}0\\0\\-1\end{bmatrix} \tag{E10.12}$$

We can write the electric field at the center of ith face as

$$\vec{E}_i = \frac{kQ}{r_i^3}\vec{r}_i \tag{E10.13}$$

where $\vec{r}_i$ is the position of that point relative to the charge. This means that

$$\vec{E}_1\cdot\hat{n}_1 = \frac{kQ}{(r+\frac{1}{2}L)^3}\begin{bmatrix}r+\frac{1}{2}L\\0\\0\end{bmatrix}\cdot\begin{bmatrix}1\\0\\0\end{bmatrix} = \frac{kQ}{(r+\frac{1}{2}L)^3}\left[(r+\tfrac{1}{2}L)1+0+0\right]$$

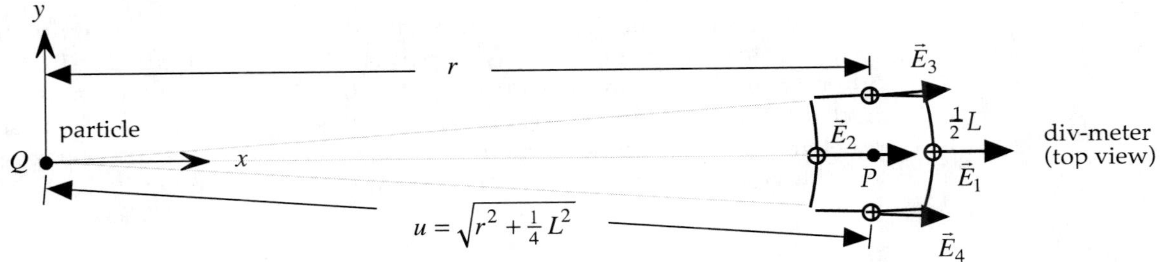

Figure E10.6
How to calculate the divergence of the field created at point *P* by a distant charged particle. The *z* axis points directly toward us in this drawing.

$$\vec{E}_2 \cdot \hat{n}_2 = \frac{kQ}{(r-\frac{1}{2}L)^3}\begin{bmatrix} r-\frac{1}{2}L \\ 0 \\ 0 \end{bmatrix} \bullet \begin{bmatrix} -1 \\ 0 \\ 0 \end{bmatrix} = -\frac{kQ}{(r-\frac{1}{2}L)^2} \tag{E10.14b}$$

$$\vec{E}_3 \cdot \hat{n}_3 = \frac{kQ}{u^3}\begin{bmatrix} r \\ \frac{1}{2}L \\ 0 \end{bmatrix} \bullet \begin{bmatrix} 0 \\ 1 \\ 0 \end{bmatrix} = +\frac{kQL}{2u^3} \tag{E10.14c}$$

$$\vec{E}_4 \cdot \hat{n}_4 = \frac{kQ}{u^3}\begin{bmatrix} r \\ -\frac{1}{2}L \\ 0 \end{bmatrix} \bullet \begin{bmatrix} 0 \\ -1 \\ 0 \end{bmatrix} = \frac{kQ}{u^3}(-\tfrac{1}{2}L)(-1) = +\frac{kQL}{2u^3} \tag{E10.14d}$$

where $u \equiv [r^2 + \frac{1}{4}L^2]^{1/2}$. You can quite easily show that $\vec{E}_5 \cdot \hat{n}_5 = \vec{E}_6 \cdot \hat{n}_6 = +kQL/2u^3$ as well, as the symmetry of the situation suggests.

Self-Test E10X.2

Verify this last statement.

Therefore, the divergence of this field becomes

$$\begin{aligned}
\text{div}(\vec{E}) &= \lim_{L\to 0}\frac{1}{L}\left[\frac{kQ}{(r+\frac{1}{2}L)^2} - \frac{kQ}{(r-\frac{1}{2}L)^2} + \frac{4kQL}{2(r^2+\frac{1}{4}L^2)^{3/2}}\right] \\
&= \lim_{L\to 0}\frac{kQ}{L}\left[\frac{(r-\frac{1}{2}L)^2 - (r+\frac{1}{2}L)^2}{(r+\frac{1}{2}L)^2(r-\frac{1}{2}L)^2} + \frac{2L}{(r^2+\frac{1}{4}L^2)^{3/2}}\right] \\
&= \lim_{L\to 0}\frac{kQ}{L}\left[\frac{\cancel{r^2} - Lr + \cancel{\tfrac{1}{4}L^2} - \cancel{r^2} - Lr - \cancel{\tfrac{1}{4}L^2}}{(r^2-\frac{1}{4}L^2)^2} + \frac{2L}{(r^2+\frac{1}{4}L^2)^{3/2}}\right] \\
&= \lim_{L\to 0} kQ\left[\frac{-2r}{(r^2-\frac{1}{4}L^2)^2} + \frac{2}{(r^2+\frac{1}{4}L^2)^{3/2}}\right] \\
&= kQ\left[\frac{-2r}{r^4} + \frac{2}{r^3}\right] = 0 \qquad \text{Q. E. D.}
\end{aligned} \tag{E10.15}$$

So we see that the divergence we have defined does indeed ignore the electric field of an external charged particle. One can use the distributive property of the dot product to prove that the divergence will ignore the electric field created by any *set* of external charged particles as well (but see problem E10S.5 for an easier method). The divergence therefore *only* registers charge in the immediate neighborhood of its central point P.

E10.4 The Divergence as a Derivative

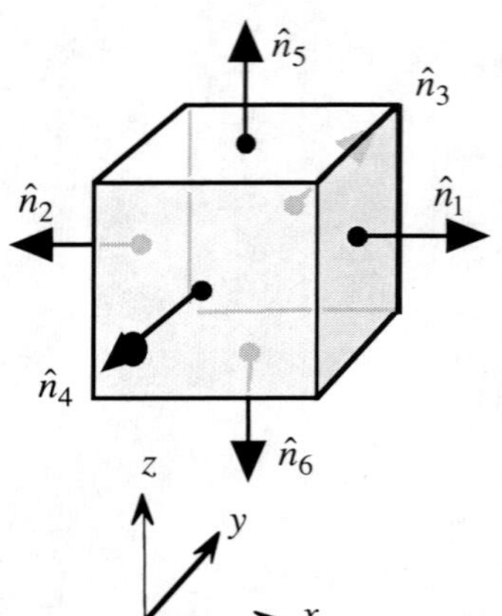

Figure E10.7
Standard orientation for a div-meter.

We can express the divergence in an even more compact form. Imagine that we orient a div-meter so that its sides are parallel to the coordinate axis directions (see figure E10.7), so that its faces' nose vectors are given by equation E10.12. Let the coordinates of point P be $[x, y, z]$ and assume that we know the electric field as a vector function $\vec{E}(x, y, z)$. The first two dot products appearing in the definition of the divergence are therefore

$$\vec{E}(\vec{r}_1)\cdot\hat{n}_1 = \begin{bmatrix} E_x(\vec{r}_1) \\ E_y(\vec{r}_1) \\ E_z(\vec{r}_1) \end{bmatrix} \cdot \begin{bmatrix} 1 \\ 0 \\ 0 \end{bmatrix} = E_x(\vec{r}_1) + 0 + 0 = E_x(x + \tfrac{1}{2}L, y, z) \tag{E10.16a}$$

where $\vec{E}(\vec{r}_1)$ stands for the electric field vector evaluated at the position $\vec{r}_1 = [x + \frac{1}{2}L, y, z]$ of the center of face 1. Similarly

$$\vec{E}(\vec{r}_2)\cdot\hat{n}_2 = \begin{bmatrix} E_x(\vec{r}_2) \\ E_y(\vec{r}_2) \\ E_z(\vec{r}_2) \end{bmatrix} \cdot \begin{bmatrix} -1 \\ 0 \\ 0 \end{bmatrix} = -E_x(\vec{r}_2) + 0 + 0 = -E_x(x - \tfrac{1}{2}L, y, z) \tag{E10.16b}$$

The calculations are similar for the other four faces. The divergence is thus

$$\text{div}(\vec{E}) \equiv \lim_{L\to 0} \frac{1}{L}\left[\vec{E}_1\cdot\hat{n}_1 + \vec{E}_2\cdot\hat{n}_2 + \ldots\right]$$

$$= \lim_{L\to 0}\left[\frac{E_x(x + \frac{1}{2}L, y, z) - E_x(x - \frac{1}{2}L, y, z)}{L} + \ldots\right] \tag{E10.17}$$

with a similar ratio for each of the other coordinate directions. The numerator is the change in E_x evaluated at two points a distance L apart in the x direction, with the y and z coordinates held constant. The ratio, in the limit that $L \to 0$, is the *definition* of the partial derivative of E_x with respect to x:

$$\lim_{L\to 0}\left[\frac{E_x(x + \frac{1}{2}L, y, z) - E_x(x - \frac{1}{2}L, y, z)}{L}\right] \equiv \frac{\partial E_x}{\partial x} \tag{E10.18}$$

The argument for the other two coordinate directions is entirely analogous. Therefore we can write the divergence very simply as

The divergence in terms of partial derivatives of $\vec{E}$

$$\text{div}(\vec{E}) = \frac{\partial E_x}{\partial x} + \frac{\partial E_y}{\partial y} + \frac{\partial E_z}{\partial z} \tag{E10.19}$$

Purpose: This is the definition of the divergence $\text{div}(\vec{E})$ in terms of partial derivatives of the electric field function $\vec{E}(x, y, z)$.
Symbols: E_x, E_y, and E_z are the components of $\vec{E}$.
Limitations: This equation is a definition.

Self-Test E10X.3

Argue that $\lim_{L\to 0} L^{-1}\left[\vec{E}_3 \cdot \hat{n}_3 + \vec{E}_4 \cdot \hat{n}_4\right] = \partial E_y / \partial y$.

Why didn't I simply start with this definition? Two reasons: (1) I think that the approach starting with the div-meter gives you a much more solid understanding of what the divergence *means* physically than the much more abstract equation E10.19. (2) The image of the div-meter as comprised of faces with nose vectors is essential for understanding the techniques we will develop in chapter E12.

Interpreting the divergence as a specialized derivative

However, equation E10.19 is valuable in making it clear that the divergence is simply a type of derivative of the electric field with respect to the three spatial coordinates. We will see that our intuition and experience with solving equations involving time derivatives in newtonian physics will have useful and clarifying analogies here.

Self-Test E10X.4

In self-test E10X.1, you argued from the basic definition of the div-meter that an electric field that is uniform in direction and magnitude will have zero divergence. Use equation E10.19 to prove the same thing.

E10.5 Gauss's Law

The local field equation that describes how the electric field is connected to electric charge is **Gauss's law**, which claims that

$$\operatorname{div}(\vec{E}) = \frac{\rho}{\varepsilon_0} \quad (= 4\pi k\rho) \qquad \text{(E10.20)}$$

Purpose: This local field equation links the divergence of the electric field $\vec{E}$ at a point with the charge density ρ at that point.

Symbols: $\operatorname{div}(\vec{E})$ is the divergence of the electric field at the point (as defined by equation E10.10 or E10.19), $\varepsilon_0 = (4\pi k)^{-1}$ is the permittivity constant, and k is the Coulomb constant.

Limitations: There are no limits (until one gets into the realm of quantum field theory): this equation applies even to rapidly varying fields.

This equation, which is one of the four fundamental electromagnetic equations known as **Maxwell's equations**, is completely equivalent to Coulomb's law for static electric fields, but has the advantage (by virtue of being a *local* field equation) of working for dynamic fields as well.

Self-Test E10X.5

Check that the right and left sides of Gauss's Law have the same units.

The following examples illustrate that with this simple law, we can easily prove some claims (including one that I made in chapter E4) that are very difficult to prove using the methods of chapter E3.

Example E10.1 The Excess Charge on a Conductor

Problem Prove (as claimed in chapter E4) that any excess charge on a conductor must reside on its *surface* when the conductor is in *static* equilibrium. (*Hint:* We have seen that $\vec{E} = 0$ inside the conductor in equilibrium).

Model and ***Solution*** If the electric field is zero throughout a conductor's interior, then equation E10.19 implies that the divergence of that field is also zero, since the partial derivatives of a constant field are zero. But Gauss's law implies that the density of charge at all such points is zero, so a conductor in static equilibrium *must be electrically neutral throughout its interior*. Therefore, any excess charge must be on the conductor's surface. (Since the charge cannot leave the conductor, it can be trapped at rest against the surface even if there is a nonzero electric field acting on it.) We will see in chapter E12 that we can extend this argument to include the surface charges on a conductor carrying a steady current.

Example E10.2 A Unidirectional Electric Field in Empty Space

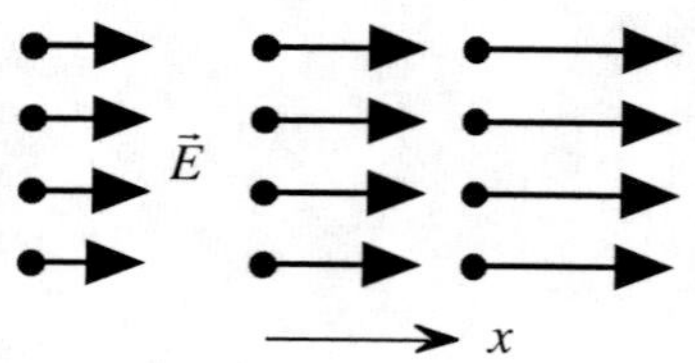

Figure E10.8
The electric field shown is impossible in a region of empty space, no matter what charges might surround that region.

Problem Prove that it is *impossible* to find a charge distribution that can create an electric field in a region of empty space that points in a given fixed direction *and* varies in strength along that direction (see figure E10.8).

Model and ***Solution*** Let us take advantage of our freedom to choose coordinates to take the x direction to be the direction in which our electric field points. Then $E_y = E_z = 0$, and Gauss' law in this case reads

$$\frac{\partial E_x}{\partial x} = 0 \qquad \text{(E10.21)}$$

since the density of charge in empty space is zero. This equation implies that E_x, and thus the magnitude of $\vec{E}$, is constant with respect to x: it can neither increase nor decrease along the direction of the field.

Example E10.3 The Electric Field of an Infinite Slab

Problem Consider a planar slab that stretches infinitely in the y and z directions but has a finite thickness W in the x direction. Assume that the slab has charge uniformly distributed throughout its interior. Prove that the electric field created by this slab must (a) point in the $\pm x$ direction everywhere, (b) vary linearly with x inside the slab, and (c) have a *constant* magnitude $E = \frac{1}{2}\sigma/\varepsilon_0$ outside (where σ is the slab's charge per unit area).

Translation Let the charge density inside the slab be ρ. Let us define $x = 0$ to coincide with the slab's central plane (midway between its surfaces).

Model We can use symmetry arguments to prove that the slab's field must point in the $\pm x$ direction, be independent of y and z, and be zero at $x = 0$. Consider first an arbitrary point P with a nonzero x coordinate, and let O be point on the slab's central plane closest to P. Since the slab is infinite, it is unchanged by a rotation about the OP axis, so this rotation should not change the field vector at point P. As figure E10.9a shows, the field vector is unchanged by this rotation only if it points along the OP axis, i.e. in the $\pm x$ direction. This argument works for points P inside *and* outside the slab.

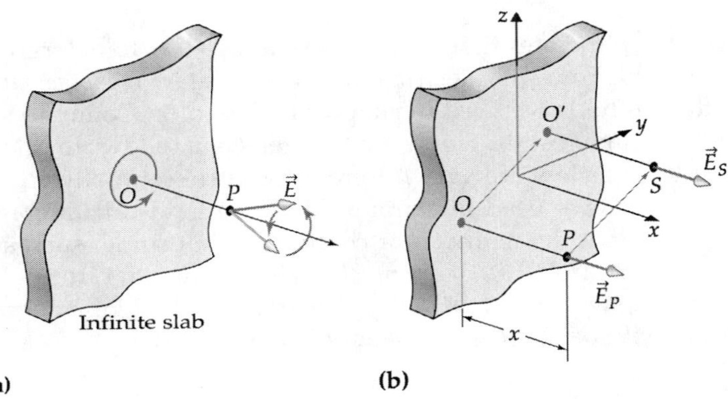

Figure E10.9
This figure illustrates the symmetry transformations considered in example E10.3: (a) rotating the slab around an axis perpendicular to that slab and (b) sliding the slab parallel to its central plane.

Now consider sliding the slab in the y and/or z direction (see figure E10.9b). Such a transformation can carry the field vector originally at P to any arbitrary point S with different y and z coordinates but the same x coordinate. Since this transformation does not change the slab, it cannot change the field, so the field vector originally at S must have the same magnitude as that originally at P. Therefore, the magnitude of the field at a point cannot depend on that point's y and z coordinates.

Finally, consider a point O on the slab's central plane (at $x = 0$). The first argument implies that if the field vector at O is nonzero, it must point in the $\pm x$ direction. But a 180° flip of the slab around an axis going through O parallel to the y axis would change neither the slab nor the location of O, but would reverse a vector with $E_x \neq 0$ at that point. Only the zero vector would be unchanged by both transformations.

If charge is uniformly distributed throughout the slab's interior, the charge density ρ must be *constant* in the interior. Since $\vec{E} = [E_x, 0, 0]$ everywhere, Gauss's law at points in the slab's interior reduces to

$$\frac{\partial E_x}{\partial x} = \frac{\rho}{\varepsilon_0} = \text{constant} \quad \Rightarrow \quad E_x = \frac{\rho}{\varepsilon_0}x + C \quad \text{(inside the slab)} \qquad \text{(E10.22)}$$

where C is a constant of integration. But since $\vec{E} = 0$ at $x = 0$, the value of C must be zero. Therefore, we see that $E_x = (\rho/\varepsilon_0)x$ inside the slab. This means that the values of E_x at the slab's surfaces (at $x = \pm\frac{1}{2}W$) must be

$$E_x = \frac{\rho}{\varepsilon_0}(\pm\tfrac{1}{2}W) = \pm\frac{\rho W}{2\varepsilon_0} \qquad \text{(E10.23)}$$

Note that the total charge on a chunk of slab with area A will be ρAW, the charge density times the chunk's volume AW. Therefore ρW = charge per unit area on the slab = σ, and $E_x = \pm\frac{1}{2}\sigma/\varepsilon_0$ on the slab's surfaces.

At points *outside* the slab, the charge density ρ is zero. This means that Gauss's law outside the slab implies that

$$\frac{\partial E_x}{\partial x} = 0 \quad \Rightarrow \quad E_x = \text{constant} \quad \text{(outside the slab)} \qquad \text{(E10.24)}$$

This constant value must match the value of E_x at the slab's surface, so the magnitude of $\vec{E}$ outside the slab must be $E = \frac{1}{2}\rho W/\varepsilon_0 = \frac{1}{2}\sigma/\varepsilon_0$.

Evaluation This is what we set out to show. The result is for the external field magnitude is consistent with equation E3.20 for the field at the center of a very large disk, which makes sense.

Example E10.3 illustrates that we can use Gauss's law to determine an object's electric field. For *static* electric fields, Gauss's law is *mathematically equivalent* to the methods we used in chapter E3 based on Coulomb's law, and will yield the same results. However, the steps one follows to calculate the fields with Gauss's law are very different (both conceptually and procedurally) than those we used in chapter E3. Some field calculations are much easier to do with the methods of chapter E3, but some (such as the case considered in example E10.3) are *much* easier to do with Gauss's law.

In chapter E12, we will develop a powerful method of integrating Gauss's law that will make it easier to apply in a variety of cases.

E10.6 Gauss's Law for the Magnetic Field

Constructing a magnetic div-meter

The div-meter discussed in section E10.2 measures the divergence of an *electric* field. To measure the divergence of a magnetic field, we want to construct some kind of device that measures the quantity

$$\text{div}(\vec{\boldsymbol{B}}) \equiv \lim_{L \to 0} \frac{1}{L}\left[\vec{\boldsymbol{B}}_1 \cdot \hat{n}_1 + \vec{\boldsymbol{B}}_2 \cdot \hat{n}_2 + \ldots + \vec{\boldsymbol{B}}_6 \cdot \hat{n}_6 \right]$$

$$= \frac{\partial \boldsymbol{B}_x}{\partial x} + \frac{\partial \boldsymbol{B}_y}{\partial y} + \frac{\partial \boldsymbol{B}_z}{\partial z} \qquad \text{(E10.25)}$$

where L is the length of the side of a cubical box and $\hat{n}_1, \hat{n}_2, \ldots, \hat{n}_6$ are the outward nose vectors for the box's six faces.

Now, the north pole of a bar magnet is magnetically repelled by other north poles and attracted to south poles in a manner analogous to the way that a positive charge is electrostatically repelled by other positive charges and attracted to negative charges. To measure the divergence of a *magnetic* field, therefore, we should replace the positive test charges of the electrical div-meter with isolated magnetic north poles (see figure E10.10a). This is not possible in reality, because (as we saw in chapter E7) we cannot isolate the two poles of a magnet. However, even though there are realistic ways to construct a magnetic div-meter (see problem E10S.6 for an example of such a device) this imaginary div-meter represents the best way to *visualize* what a real magnetic div-meter would measure.

A magnetic div-meter does not register a moving charged particle even at its center!

Imagine a positively charged particle moving at a constant velocity along a line that goes horizontally through the poles on the left and right faces of the div-meter, as shown in figure E10.10b. According to what we learned in chapter E8, the magnetic field of such a moving charge points circularly around the axis along which it is moving and goes to zero on that axis. Therefore, when the particle moves through the div-meter, the magnetic field vectors at the div-meter poles on the right and left faces are zero (since these poles lie along the axis of motion) and the magnetic field vectors at the other four poles are parallel to their respective faces. Therefore, *none* of the div-meter's magnetic poles are deflected outward or inward: the magnetic divergence is zero. The magnetic field of a moving charged particle has this property whether the particle is inside or outside the div-meter. Therefore a magnetic div-meter ignores the magnetic field of *any* moving charged particle, whether it is inside the box or not.

Since any magnetic field is the sum of the fields created by individual particles, and the div-meter ignores the magnetic fields of individual particles, the divergence of any magnetic field should be zero (problem E10S.5 discusses this in more detail.) **Gauss's law for the magnetic field** elevates

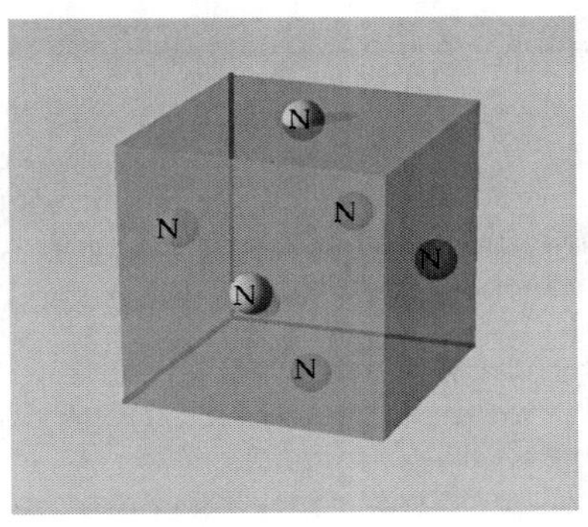

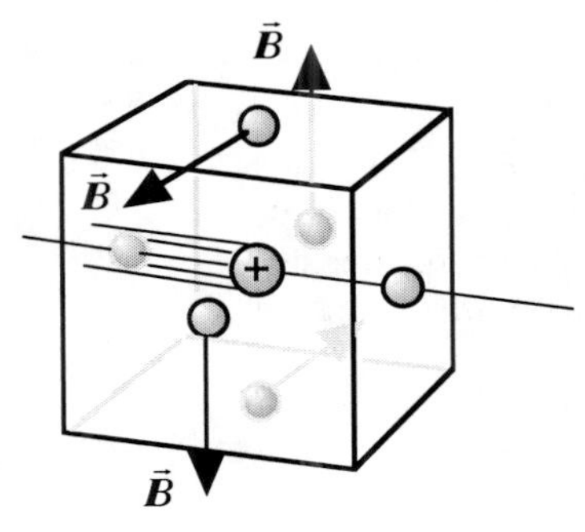

Figure E10.10
(a) An illustration of a div-meter for the magnetic field. A magnetic force on one of the imaginary isolated north poles acting perpendicular to the face in which the pole is embedded, will bow the face outward or inward.
(b) A moving charged particle passing through such a div-meter creates a magnetic field that has no outward component at any face and thus has no divergence.

this concept to the level of a fundamental assertion that applies to arbitrary current distributions, even if they vary rapidly with time.

The statement of Gauss's law for the magnetic field

$$\text{div}(\vec{B}) = 0 \qquad \text{(E10.26)}$$

Purpose: This local field equation states that one cannot create a magnetic field having a nonzero divergence at any point in space.
Symbols: div($\vec{B}$) is the divergence of the magnetic field.
Limitations: This law has no limits (until we get to the realm of quantum field theory): it applies even to rapidly varying fields.

If we compare this to Gauss's law for the electric field $\text{div}(\vec{E}) = \rho/\varepsilon_0$, we find that Gauss's law for the *magnetic* field essentially asserts that nothing plays exactly the role for the magnetic field that charge plays for the the electric field. A **magnetic monopole** (an isolated magnetic north or south pole) placed inside the div-meter *would* cause the div-meter to puff out or be drawn in, so Gauss's law for the magnetic field says that:

What this law means: no magnetic "charges"

Magnetic monopoles do not exist.

(It is ironic that imagining a div-meter with isolated magnetic poles is the easiest way to see that Gauss's magnetic law says such poles cannot exist!)

This law puts constraints on the kinds of fields that are physically possible

Note that it is perfectly possible to *imagine* magnetic fields that have a nonzero divergence. Gauss's law for the magnetic field simply asserts that such magnetic fields *do not exist in nature*. It puts an important physical constraint on the types of magnetic fields that are physically possible: *no* combination of moving charged particles can *ever* create a magnetic field that has nonzero divergence *anywhere*.

Self-Test E10X.6

Imagine a unidirectional magnetic field whose vectors in a certain region of space all point in the $+x$ direction whose magnitude increases with x. Argue that such a field is physically *impossible*.

E10.7 The Mystery du Jour

We need to search further for a local field equation that connects $\vec{B}$ to currents

But magnetic fields *are* somehow connected to moving charged particles. Gauss's law for the magnetic field does *not* make such a connection in the way that Gauss's law for the electric field connects the field to electric charge. We need to search further for a local field equation that links the magnetic field to moving charge. This will be our task in the next chapter.

TWO-MINUTE PROBLEMS

E10T.1 The electric field in a certain region of space has a constant magnitude and direction at all points within the region. Let the charge density in the region be ρ. From this information we can conclude
A. that ρ is positive
B. that ρ is zero
C. that ρ is negative
D. that the field is physically impossible
E. nothing useful.

E10T.2 Consider a uniformly charged disk and a uniformly charged wire. These two charge distributions create very different electric fields. The divergence of the disk's electric field at every point in the empty space outside the disk is nonetheless equal to the divergence of the electric field at every point outside the infinite wire (T or F).

E10T.3 Imagine that in a certain region of space (which might be inside a charge or current distribution), a field has constant x and z components and a y component proportional to y^2. Is this a possible electric or magnetic field in this case?
A. Possible electric field; impossible magnetic.
B. Possible magnetic field; impossible electric.
C. Possible electric or magnetic field.
D. Impossible electric or magnetic field.
E. We cannot answer the question with the information given.

E10T.4 A magnetic field points in the $+x$ direction and has a magnitude that depends on y. This is a possible magnetic field (T or F).

E10T.5 The magnetic field at a point just outside the north pole of a permanent magnet must have zero divergence (T or F).

HOMEWORK PROBLEMS

Basic Skills

E10B.1 Can the divergence of an electric field be nonzero at any point in a vacuum? Explain your response.

E10B.2 Imagine that the electric field in a certain region of space is given by $\vec{E} = [ax, ay, az]$, where a is a constant. Find the divergence of this field in terms of a.

E10B.3 Imagine that the electric field in a certain region of space is $\vec{E} = [ar^2x,\ ar^2y, ar^2z]$, where a is a constant and $r^2 = x^2 + y^2 + z^2$. Show that the divergence of this field is $4ar^2$.

E10B.4 Imagine that the electric field vectors inside a certain object point in the same direction and that E_x increases linearly with x: $E_x = ax$. What is the density of charge in this object in terms of the constant of proportionality a?

E10B.5 Imagine that the electric field inside a plastic sphere is the radial field $\vec{E} = [ar^2x,\ ar^2y, ar^2z]$, where where a is a constant and $r^2 = x^2 + y^2 + z^2$. How does the charge density in this sphere depend on a and r? (*Hint:* See problem E10B.3.)

Synthetic

E10S.1 The electric field that a particle with charge Q at the origin creates at a point with coordinates x, y, z is

$$\vec{E} = \frac{kQ}{r^3}\vec{r} = \frac{kQ}{r^3}\begin{bmatrix} x \\ y \\ z \end{bmatrix} \tag{E10.27}$$

Prove that the derivative form of the divergence implies that the divergence of this field is zero at all points except the origin.

E10S.2 (a) Argue that any electric field that points radially away from the origin and has a magnitude that depends only on the distance r one is from the origin has the form

$$\vec{E} = f(r)\begin{bmatrix} x \\ y \\ z \end{bmatrix} \tag{E10.28}$$

where $f(r)$ is some arbitrary function of r.

(b) Use equation E10.19 to prove that for this

$$\text{div}(\vec{E}) = r\frac{df}{dr} + 3f \tag{E10.29}$$

(c) In empty space, the divergence of such a field must be zero. Show that this means

$$\frac{df}{f} = -\frac{3\,dr}{r} \tag{E10.30}$$

(d) Integrate both sides of this to show that $f(r)$ must be a/r^3, where a is a constant of integration. Therefore argue that a purely radial field in empty space must be the same as the field of a charged particle at the origin (see equation E10.27).

E10S.3 Use the result of problem E10S.2d to prove the shell theorem. (*Hints:* Argue that far from the shell with charge Q, the shell's external electric field must be indistinguishable from that of a particle with charge Q, and go from there. Also use symmetry to argue that the field in the empty space enclosed by the shell must be zero at the center, and use that to show that the field must be zero *everywhere* inside the shell.)

E10S.4 It would be cool if we could create an electric field that in the neighborhood of a point P in empty space points directly toward that point, because we could use such a field to stably suspend a charged particle in midair. Use the div-meter concept to argue that such a field is (alas) physically impossible.

E10S.5 (a) Argue from the derivative definition of the divergence that if $\vec{E} = \vec{E}_1 + \vec{E}_2 + \ldots$ then

$$\text{div}(\vec{E}) = \text{div}(\vec{E}_1) + \text{div}(\vec{E}_2) + \ldots \qquad \text{(E10.31)}$$

(b) We know from section E10.3 that at any point outside a charged particle, the divergence of its electric field is zero. Argue that equation E10.31 and the superposition principle together imply that the divergence of the electric field created by any *set* of charged particles is zero (as long as all particles are outside the div-meter).

(c) Argue similarly that the divergence of the magnetic field created by any set of moving charged particles must be zero.

E10S.6 One can realistically measure the magnetic divergence at a point as follows. Consider placing a thin bar magnet at the point in question, aligned so that its north pole points in the $+x$ direction relative to its south pole. Define the "outward" direction at each pole to be the direction away from the magnet's center.

(a) Argue that the x-component of the *net* force that an external magnetic field exerts on the magnet in this case is

$$F_x \propto \boldsymbol{B}_{\text{out,N}} + \boldsymbol{B}_{\text{out,S}} \qquad \text{(E10.32)}$$

where $\boldsymbol{B}_{\text{out,N}}$ is the outward component of the magnetic field at the magnet's north pole, and so on. (One could find the constant of proportionality in this expression by measuring the force when the magnet is placed in a known magnetic field.)

(b) From this, describe how one could measure the divergence of an unknown magnetic field at the point of interest.

ANSWERS TO SELF-TESTS

E10X.1 As we have discussed in chapter E3, the electric field between two uniformly charged parallel plates is uniform in magnitude and direction, and points perpendicularly away from the positive plate and toward the negative plate. This field will therefore push in the div-meter's face that is closest to the positive plate, but bow out the face closest to the negative plate. Since the field is uniform, though, these two effects will exactly cancel, yielding no net div-meter volume change.

E10X.2 The equations for these products are the same as equations E10.14c and E10.14d except that the dot product of the two column vectors is

$$\begin{bmatrix} r \\ 0 \\ \pm\frac{1}{2}L \end{bmatrix} \cdot \begin{bmatrix} 0 \\ 0 \\ \pm 1 \end{bmatrix} = (\pm\tfrac{1}{2}L)(\pm 1) = \tfrac{1}{2}L \qquad \text{(E10.33)}$$

E10X.3 We have

$$\vec{E}(\vec{r}_3)\cdot\hat{n}_3 = \begin{bmatrix} E_x(\vec{r}_3) \\ E_y(\vec{r}_3) \\ E_z(\vec{r}_3) \end{bmatrix} \cdot \begin{bmatrix} 0 \\ 1 \\ 0 \end{bmatrix} = E_y(\vec{r}_3) \qquad \text{(E10.34)}$$

where $\vec{r}_3 = [x, y+\frac{1}{2}L, z]$. Similarly $\vec{E}_4(\vec{r}_4)\cdot\hat{n}_4 = E_y(\vec{r}_4) = E_y(x, y-\frac{1}{2}L, z)$. From there,

$$\lim_{L\to 0}\left[\frac{E_y(x, y+\frac{1}{2}L, z) - E_y(x, y-\frac{1}{2}L, z)}{L}\right] \equiv \frac{\partial E_y}{\partial y} \qquad \text{(E10.35)}$$

E10X.4 If the field is uniform in magnitude and direction, its components will be constant, so all of the partial derivatives in equation E10.19 will be zero. Therefore the total divergence is zero.

E10X.5 According to the definition of the divergence, the units of the divergence are the units of electric field (N/C) divided by the unit of distance (m). The units of the right side are the units of k (units of $1/\varepsilon_0$) times those of charge density:

$$\frac{\text{N}\cdot\text{m}^2}{\text{C}^2}\frac{\text{C}}{\text{m}^3} = \frac{\text{N}}{\text{C}\cdot\text{m}} \qquad \text{(E10.36)}$$

The units of both sides are therefore consistent.

E10X.6 According to equation E10.25, the divergence of such a magnetic field would be

$$\text{div}(\vec{\boldsymbol{B}}) = \frac{d\boldsymbol{B}_x}{dx} \qquad \text{(E10.37)}$$

But if the magnetic field increases in the x direction, $d\boldsymbol{B}_x/dx \neq 0$, meaning that the divergence is not zero. According to Gauss's law for the magnetic field, this is not possible.

E11 Ampere's Law

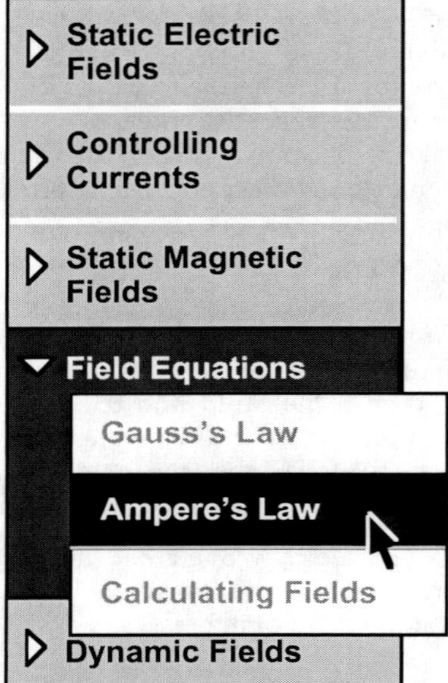

Chapter Overview

Introduction

In this chapter, we continue to work through the process of finding local field equations for the electric and magnetic fields. This chapter focuses on Ampere's Law, which describes the connection between magnetic fields and currents.

Section E11.1: The Curl of a Magnetic Field

Visualize a **curl-meter** consisting of a square plate that has (imagined) isolated north magnetic poles embedded in the middle of its four edges and that can rotate around an axis perpendicular to its surface. This device measures the component of a vector we call the **curl** of the magnetic field along its axis direction. Such a curl-meter will clearly twist in response to the magnetic field of a current-carrying wire going through curl-meter's plate, but it plausibly ignores the field created by distant current-carrying wires. This makes the curl a suitable "field characteristic" for a local field equation connecting a magnetic field to currents.

Section E11.2: The Curl in Terms of Edge Vectors

Imagine defining a unit-length **edge vector** $\hat{e}$ for each edge of the curl-meter plate that points parallel to that edge in the counterclockwise direction when the plate's nose vector faces us. We can also define a side vector $d\vec{S}$ whose direction is the same but whose magnitude is equal to the length of the edge. Using such vectors, we can express the curl in a mathematically well-defined way

$$\vec{\text{curl}}(\vec{B})\cdot\hat{n} \equiv \lim_{L\to 0}\frac{1}{L}(\vec{B}_1\cdot\hat{e}_1 + \vec{B}_2\cdot\hat{e}_2 + \vec{B}_3\cdot\hat{e}_3 + \vec{B}_4\cdot\hat{e}_4) \qquad \text{(E11.2a)}$$

$$= \lim_{A\to 0}\frac{1}{A}(\vec{B}_1\cdot d\vec{S}_1 + \vec{B}_2\cdot d\vec{S}_2 + \vec{B}_3\cdot d\vec{S}_3 + \vec{B}_4\cdot d\vec{S}_4) \qquad \text{(E11.2b)}$$

Purpose: These equations define $\vec{\text{curl}}(\vec{B})\cdot\hat{n}$, the component along the $\hat{n}$ direction of a magnetic field's curl vector $\vec{\text{curl}}(\vec{B})$ measured at point P.

Symbols: L is the side length and A is the area of a tiny square with nose vector $\hat{n}$ centered on P, and $\vec{B}_i$ is the magnetic field evaluated at the center of the square's ith side, and $\hat{e}_i$ and $d\vec{S}_i \equiv L\hat{e}_i$ are that side's edge and side vectors respectively. Note that $\vec{B}_i\cdot\hat{e}_i$ is the counterclockwise component of $\vec{B}$ at the center of the ith side.

Limitations: In the limit that $L \to 0$, this equation is an exact definition. However, if L is not infinitesimal, it must be small compared to the scale over which the magnetic field varies significantly.

Using this expression, we can prove mathematically that the curl does not register the magnetic field created by any distant infinite current-carrying wires.

Section E11.3: The Curl as a Derivative

This section argues that the curl is equivalent to a specific combination of partial derivatives of the magnetic field:

$$\text{cũrl}(\vec{B}) \equiv \left[\frac{\partial B_z}{\partial y} - \frac{\partial B_y}{\partial z}, \quad \frac{\partial B_x}{\partial z} - \frac{\partial B_z}{\partial x}, \quad \frac{\partial B_y}{\partial x} - \frac{\partial B_x}{\partial y}\right] \qquad \text{(E11.9)}$$

Purpose: This is the definition of the $\text{cũrl}(\vec{B})$ vector in terms of partial derivatives of the magnetic field function $\vec{B}(x, y, z)$.

Symbols: B_x, B_y, and B_z are the components of $\vec{B}$.

Limitations: This equation is a definition.

Section E11.4: Ampere's Law

The local field equation that links the magnetic field to the currents that create the field is **Ampere's Law:**

$$\text{cũrl}(\vec{B}) = \frac{1}{\varepsilon_0}\left(\frac{\vec{J}}{c}\right) \quad \left[= 4\pi k\left(\frac{\vec{J}}{c}\right)\right] \qquad \text{(E11.11)}$$

Purpose: This local field equation links the curl of a static magnetic field $\vec{B}$ at a point with the current density $\vec{J}$ at the same point.

Symbols: $\text{cũrl}(\vec{B})$ is the curl of $\vec{B}$ at the point (see equation E11.10), k is Coulomb's constant, $\varepsilon_0 = (4\pi k)^{-1}$ is the permittivity constant and c is the speed of light.

Limitations: This only applies to static fields.

Notes: Each one of the terms in this equation is a vector, so this equation actually represents three separate component equations. The value of $1/\varepsilon_0 c = 4\pi k/c$ is 377 Ω.

As an example the section shows how we use Ampere's law (and the assumption that $B = 0$ at infinity) to calculate the magnetic field created by an infinite solenoid

$$B = \frac{1}{\varepsilon_0}\frac{NI}{cL} \text{ inside,} \quad B = 0 \text{ everywhere outside} \qquad \text{(E11.17)}$$

Purpose: This equation specifies the magnitude B of the magnetic field inside and outside an infinite solenoid.

Symbols: N is the number of turns of wire per length L along the solenoid, I is the current carried by each turn, $\varepsilon_0 = (4\pi k)^{-1}$ is the permittivity constant and c is the speed of light.

Limitations: This strictly only applies to infinite solenoids. It is reasonably accurate at points not close to the ends of a finite solenoid if its length is much larger than its radius.

Note: We will find this equation useful in chapter E14.

Section E11.5: The Curl of the Electric Field

By analogy, we can imagine measuring the curl of an electric field using a curl-meter with positive charged particles replacing the isolated north poles. Such a device measures the same quantity defined by equations E11.2 or E11.9 except with E replacing B. We can also measure the curl using a closed conducting loop of wire. For static electric fields, energy conservation requires that

$$\text{cũrl}(\vec{E}) = 0 \qquad \text{(E11.19)}$$

Section E11.6: The Mystery du Jour

In general, how can we calculate fields using these local field equations?

E11.1 The Curl of a Magnetic Field

Gauss's law $\text{div}(\vec{E}) = 4\pi k\rho$ is a local field equation that describes the connection between the electric field and charge in a relativistically self-consistent way. However, Gauss's law for the magnetic field, $\text{div}(\vec{B}) = 0$ only puts a constraint on the type of magnetic fields that are possible: it does not tell us how the magnetic field is connected to the currents that create it. We need a new kind of "field characteristic" to describe this link.

The curl-meter

Consider the device shown in figure E11.1. This **curl-meter** consists of a set of four (imagined) isolated north magnetic poles affixed to the sides of a square. The square can rotate around an axle whose direction is perpendicular to the square in the direction indicated by the arrowhead. The **curl** $\vec{\text{curl}}(\vec{B})$ of a magnetic field at a point P is a *vector* quantity whose component in the direction of the axle arrow is proportional to the *net torque* the field exerts on the square about the axle when the square's center is placed at P. If the square's rotation is opposed by a spring, as shown in the drawing, we can measure the torque by measuring how much opposing torque the spring must apply to the square to keep it from rotating.

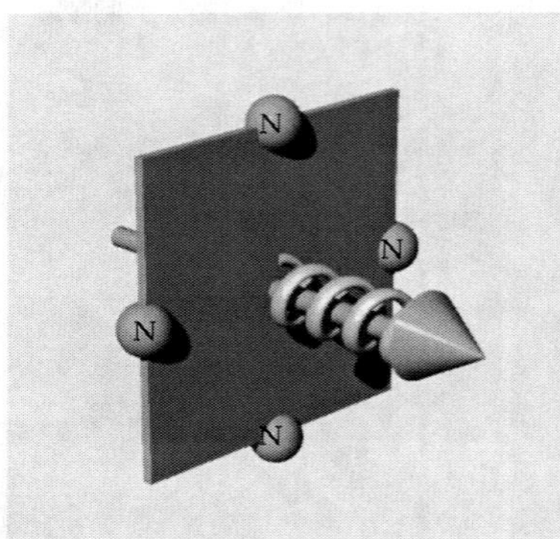

Figure E11.1
A picture of a curl-meter. The balls represent isolated magnetic north poles. A magnetic field at a point has a positive component of curl in the axis direction indicated by the arrow if the curl-meter twists counterclockwise when it is placed with its center at that point.

We define the component of the curl along the axle direction to be positive if the field seeks to turn the square *counterclockwise* when we view it with the axis pointing at us, and negative if the field seeks to turn the square *clockwise*. (The positive sense of rotation is the direction your right fingers curl when you point your right thumb along the axis.) To measure the curl vector's x, y, and z components, we simply take a measurement with the axle pointed in the $+x$ direction, another with it pointed in the $+y$ direction, and a third with it pointed in the $+z$ direction. You might think of the three components of the vector $\vec{\text{curl}}(\vec{B})$ as expressing the magnetic field's "twistedness" around each of the three coordinate axes.

The curl-meter shown in figure E11.1 is, of course, impossible to build as described, because isolated magnetic north poles do not exist. However, as in the case of the magnetic div-meter, there are realistic ways to construct a magnetic curl-meter, but realistic curl-meters have complexities that obscure the basic concept. The curl-meter in figure E11.1 is the best way to *visualize* what a curl-meter does.

Why we are interested in the curl

Why are we interested in the curl? Imagine that a current-carrying wire passes through the plane of a curl-meter's square in a direction parallel to its axle. As figures E11.2a and E11.2b show, the magnetic field that the wire creates will will clearly twist the curl-meter counterclockwise if the current flows in the direction of the axle arrow and clockwise if it flows opposite to the arrow. On the other hand, the magnetic field created by a distant wire (see figure E11.2c) exerts no net torque on the curl-meter: even though the clockwise component of the magnetic field is stronger on the near side of the curl-meter than the counterclockwise component on the far side, it turns out that because of the inverse-r dependence of the field of a wire, the small counterclockwise contributions from the magnetic field vectors the on curl-meter's other two sides cancel the difference. Therefore the curl-meter registers the presence of *local* current while ignoring *distant* currents, making it a good candidate for use in a local field equation.

Self-Test E11X.1

Consider placing a curl-meter at a point somewhere in a uniform magnetic field. Use the curl-meter visualization to argue that all three components of the curl of such a magnetic field are zero.

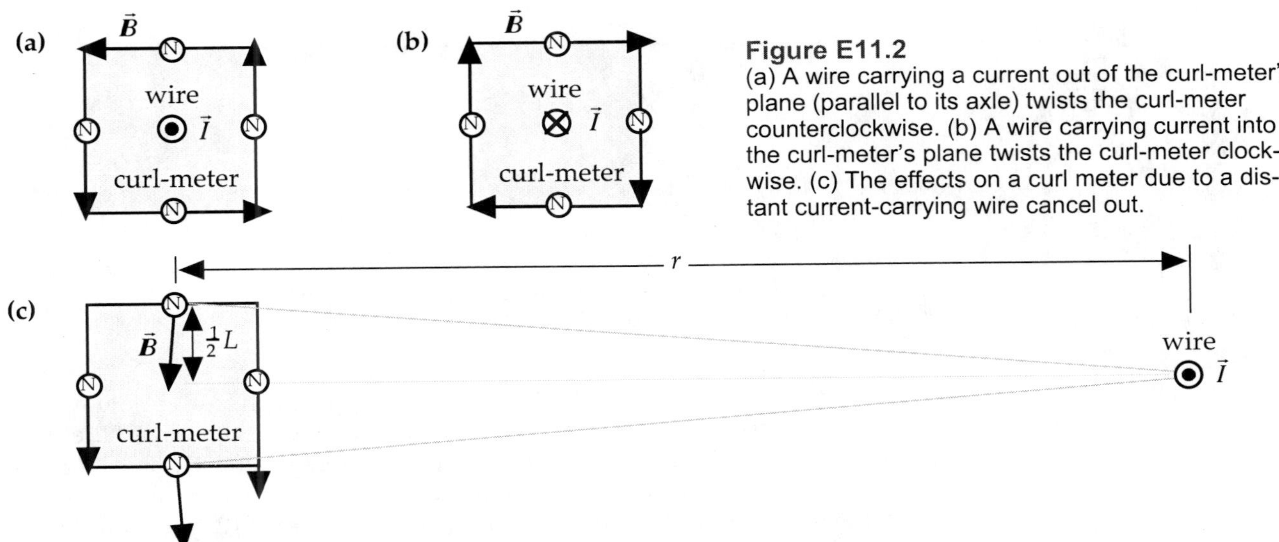

Figure E11.2
(a) A wire carrying a current out of the curl-meter's plane (parallel to its axle) twists the curl-meter counterclockwise. (b) A wire carrying current into the curl-meter's plane twists the curl-meter clockwise. (c) The effects on a curl meter due to a distant current-carrying wire cancel out.

E11.2 The Curl in Terms of Edge Vectors

To go further, we need a precise mathematical expression for the curl of a magnetic field at a point. We can do this with the help of a new mathematical idea I will call an *edge vector*. Let us think of our curl-meter as being a tiny tile with side length L and its nose vector $\hat{n}$ along the curl-meter's rotation axis. Visualize assigning to each of this tile's four edges a unit-length **edge vector** $\hat{e}$ directed along that edge counterclockwise around the tile (when the tile's nose is toward us), as illustrated in figure E11.3.

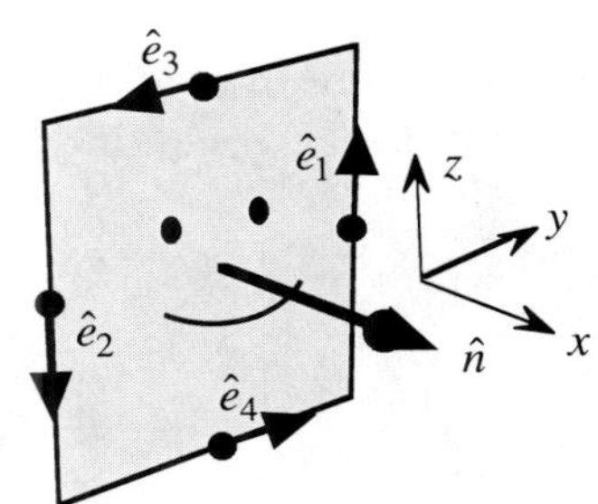

Figure E11.3
Thinking about a curl meter as a tile with nose and edge vectors. This drawing shows a curl-meter oriented to measure the curl's x component.

The contribution to the torque about the curl meter's axis that a particular magnetic pole makes expresses how effectively the magnetic force exerted on that pole twists the curl-meter counterclockwise about that axis. The force's effectiveness clearly increases in proportion to its counterclockwise component at the pole, which in turn is proportional to the magnetic *field's* counterclockwise component at that pole. The latter is $\vec{B}_i \cdot \hat{e}_i$, where $\vec{B}_i$ is the magnetic field evaluated at the ith pole and $\hat{e}_i$ is the edge vector at that pole. (Note that if the magnetic field has a *clockwise* component, this dot product is negative and the contribution to the torque is negative, signaling that the field is trying to twist that pole clockwise instead of counterclockwise.) The torque on this pole also increases directly with the pole's distance $\frac{1}{2}L$ from the axis. The *net* torque twisting the curl-meter about the axis (and so the curl's component *along* that axis) will therefore be proportional to $\frac{1}{2}L(\vec{B}_1 \cdot \hat{e}_1 + \vec{B}_2 \cdot \hat{e}_2 + \vec{B}_3 \cdot \hat{e}_3 + \vec{B}_4 \cdot \hat{e}_4)$.

However, as in the case of the divergence, we want to define the curl in such a way as to be independent of the curl-meter's size. Now, in a *uniform* magnetic field, $\vec{B}_1 = \vec{B}_2 = \vec{B}_3 = \vec{B}_4$, so $\vec{B}_1 \cdot \hat{e}_1 + \vec{B}_2 \cdot \hat{e}_2 + \vec{B}_3 \cdot \hat{e}_3 + \vec{B}_4 \cdot \hat{e}_4 = \vec{B}_1(\hat{e}_1 + \hat{e}_2 + \hat{e}_3 + \hat{e}_4) = 0$, since $\hat{e}_1 = -\hat{e}_2$ and $\hat{e}_3 = -\hat{e}_4$. The curl will therefore only be nonzero for *nonuniform* fields. A large curl-meter spans a larger region of the nonuniform field, so the difference between $\vec{B}_1$ and $\vec{B}_2$ is likely to be larger than it would be for a small curl-meter. Indeed, when a curl-meter is sufficiently small, $\vec{B}_1 \cdot \hat{e}_1 + \vec{B}_2 \cdot \hat{e}_2$ and $\vec{B}_3 \cdot \hat{e}_3 + \vec{B}_4 \cdot \hat{e}_4$ will both grow roughly linearly with L in a nonuniform field. Therefore, if we were to define the curl vector's component in the $\hat{n}$ direction to be

$$\begin{pmatrix} \text{the component of } \vec{\text{curl}}(\vec{B}) \\ \text{along the } \hat{n} \text{ direction} \end{pmatrix} = \frac{1}{L}(\vec{B}_1 \cdot \hat{e}_1 + \vec{B}_2 \cdot \hat{e}_2 + \vec{B}_3 \cdot \hat{e}_3 + \vec{B}_4 \cdot \hat{e}_4) \quad \text{(E11.1)}$$

its value should be roughly independent of L for small curl-meters.

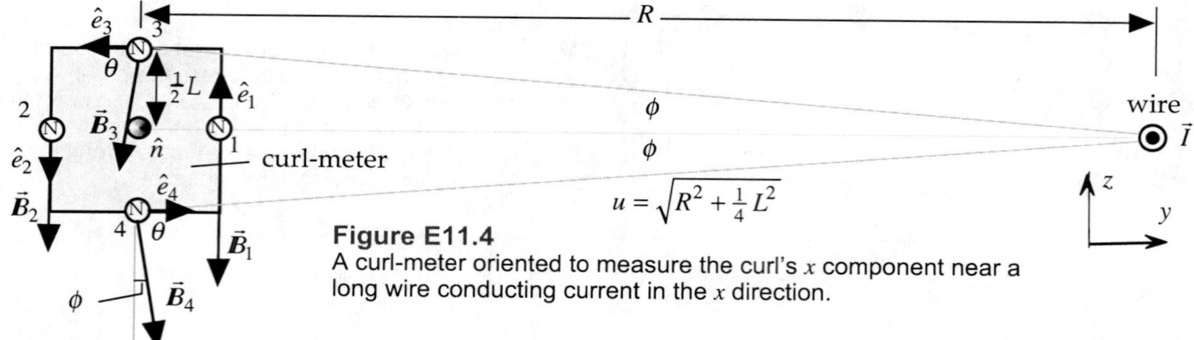

Figure E11.4
A curl-meter oriented to measure the curl's x component near a long wire conducting current in the x direction.

However, to evaluate the curl "at a point" precisely, we should technically take this ratio's limit as $L \to 0$. Note also that we can write "the component of $\vec{\text{curl}}(\vec{B})$ along the direction of $\hat{n}$" more compactly as $\vec{\text{curl}}(\vec{B}) \cdot \hat{n}$ (since the dot product of *any* vector with a unit vector like $\hat{n}$ yields that vector's component along $\hat{n}$). Finally, in chapter E12, we will find a slightly modified definition of the curl useful. Define the **side vector** of a tile's ith side to be $d\vec{S}_i = L\hat{e}_i$ (the $d\vec{S}$ notation is traditional and reminds us that the tile's side length L is supposed to be very small). Then our formal definition of the curl vector's component in the $\hat{n}$ direction becomes

The formal definition of the curl in terms of edge and side vectors

$$\vec{\text{curl}}(\vec{B}) \cdot \hat{n} \equiv \lim_{L \to 0} \frac{1}{L}(\vec{B}_1 \cdot \hat{e}_1 + \vec{B}_2 \cdot \hat{e}_2 + \vec{B}_3 \cdot \hat{e}_3 + \vec{B}_4 \cdot \hat{e}_4) \quad \text{(E11.2a)}$$

$$= \lim_{A \to 0} \frac{1}{A}(\vec{B}_1 \cdot d\vec{S}_1 + \vec{B}_2 \cdot d\vec{S}_2 + \vec{B}_3 \cdot d\vec{S}_3 + \vec{B}_4 \cdot d\vec{S}_4) \quad \text{(E11.2b)}$$

Purpose: These equations define $\text{curl}(\vec{B}) \cdot \hat{n}$, the component along the $\hat{n}$ direction of a magnetic field's curl vector $\vec{\text{curl}}(\vec{B})$ measured at point P.

Symbols: L is the side length and A is the area of a tiny square with nose vector $\hat{n}$ centered on P, and $\vec{B}_i$ is the magnetic field evaluated at the center of the square's ith side, and $\hat{e}_i$ and $d\vec{S}_i \equiv L\hat{e}_i$ are that side's edge and side vectors respectively. Note that $\vec{B}_i \cdot \hat{e}_i$ is the counterclockwise component of $\vec{B}$ at the center of the ith side.

Limitations: In the limit that $L \to 0$, this equation is an exact definition. However, if L is not infinitesimal, it must be small compared to the scale over which the magnetic field varies significantly.

The proof that the curl x component ignores the magnetic field of distant linear current

Remember that the whole point of the curl is that it serves as a detector of *local* current: the curl-meter registers nonzero curl when current flows *through* its square, but nothing when the current flows outside the square. I will now use the formal definition of the curl above to show that the curl of the static magnetic field created by an external straight wire is indeed zero.

Consider a point P a distance R from a very long straight wire carrying a current I out of the plane of the drawing. We know from chapter E9 that the magnetic field created by such a wire points circularly around the wire and has a magnitude of $B = (\mu_0 c / 2\pi)(I / r)$ at a point a distance r from the wire. Let us choose the $+x$ direction to be the direction that current flows in the wire, and consider a curl-meter whose axis (nose vector) is parallel to the current, as shown in figure E11.4.

Note that the magnetic field at the center of side 2 points *parallel* to that side's edge vector $\hat{e}_2$, so $\vec{B}_2 \cdot \hat{e}_2 = B_2[1]\cos 0° = B_2$. The magnetic field at the center of side 1 points *opposite* to that side's edge vector $\hat{e}_1$, so $\vec{B}_1 \cdot \hat{e}_1 = B_1[1]\cos 180° = -B_1$. The magnetic field vectors at the centers of sides 3 and 4 make the same angle θ with the corresponding edge vectors which is the same as 90°-ϕ. Figure E11.5 illustrates the useful trigonometric identity $\cos\theta = \cos(90° - \phi) = \sin\phi$. Note also that $\sin\phi = \frac{1}{2}L/u = L/2u$, where u is the distance from the wire to the centers of sides 3 and 4. So $\vec{B}_3 \cdot \hat{e}_3 = B_3[1]\cos\theta = B_3\sin\phi = B_3 L/2u$, and similarly $\vec{B}_4 \cdot \hat{e}_4 = B_4 L/2u$. If we use $B = (\mu_0 cI/2\pi)(1/r)$ to determine the magnitudes of the magnetic field at the various points, we find that the x component of the curl is

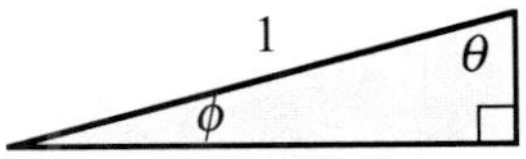

$$\vec{\text{curl}}(\vec{B})_x \equiv \lim_{L\to 0}\frac{1}{L}(\vec{B}_1\cdot\hat{e}_1 + \vec{B}_2\cdot\hat{e}_2 + \vec{B}_3\cdot\hat{e}_3 + \vec{B}_4\cdot\hat{e}_4)$$

$$= \lim_{L\to 0}\frac{1}{L}\left(-B_1 + B_2 + B_3\frac{L}{2u} + B_4\frac{L}{2u}\right)$$

$$= \frac{\mu_0 cI}{2\pi}\lim_{L\to 0}\frac{1}{L}\left(-\frac{1}{R-\frac{1}{2}L} + \frac{1}{R+\frac{1}{2}L} + \frac{1}{u}\frac{L}{2u} + \frac{1}{u}\frac{L}{2u}\right) \tag{E11.3}$$

Combining the last two terms and putting the first two terms over the common denominator $(R-\frac{1}{2}L)(R+\frac{1}{2}L) = R^2 - \frac{1}{4}L^2$, we find that

$$\vec{\text{curl}}(\vec{B})_x = \frac{\mu_0 cI}{2\pi}\lim_{L\to 0}\frac{1}{L}\left(\frac{-R-\frac{1}{2}L+R-\frac{1}{2}L}{R^2-\frac{1}{4}L^2} + \frac{L}{u^2}\right)$$

$$= \frac{\mu_0 cI}{2\pi}\lim_{L\to 0}\frac{1}{\cancel{L}}\left(\frac{-\cancel{L}}{R^2-\frac{1}{4}L^2} + \frac{\cancel{L}}{R^2+\frac{1}{4}L^2}\right)$$

$$= \frac{\mu_0 cI}{2\pi}\left(\frac{-1}{R^2} + \frac{1}{R^2}\right) = 0 \tag{E11.4}$$

So the x component of the curl of this field is indeed zero.

What about the other components of the curl? Figure E11.6 illustrates the curl-meter oriented to measure the curl's y component. Note that the magnetic field at the center of side 2 points *parallel* to that side's edge vector $\hat{e}_2$, so $\vec{B}_2 \cdot \hat{e}_2 = B_2[1]\cos 0° = B_2$. The magnetic field at the center of side 1 points *opposite* to the edge vector $\hat{e}_1$, so $\vec{B}_1 \cdot \hat{e}_1 = B_1[1]\cos 180° = -B_1$. However, poles 1 and 2 are the same distance R from the nearest points on the straight wire, so $B_1 = B_2$, which means $\vec{B}_1\cdot\hat{e}_1 + \vec{B}_2\cdot\hat{e}_2 = -B_1 + B_2 = 0$. The edge vectors for sides 3 and 4 point in the $\pm\hat{x}$ direction, but the magnetic field vectors at these points point perpendicular to the wire and therefore have zero x components. Therefore, the magnetic field vectors at these points are perpendicular to the edge vectors, which in turn implies that $\vec{B}_3\cdot\hat{e}_3 + \vec{B}_4\cdot\hat{e}_4 = 0$. Therefore the y-curl of the magnetic field of this wire is identically zero.

Figure E11.5
This diagram illustrates the identity $\cos\theta = \cos(90° - \phi) = \sin\phi$. Note that $\phi + \theta + 90° = 180°$, so $\theta - 90° - \phi$.

The proof that the curl y component ignores the magnetic field of distant linear current

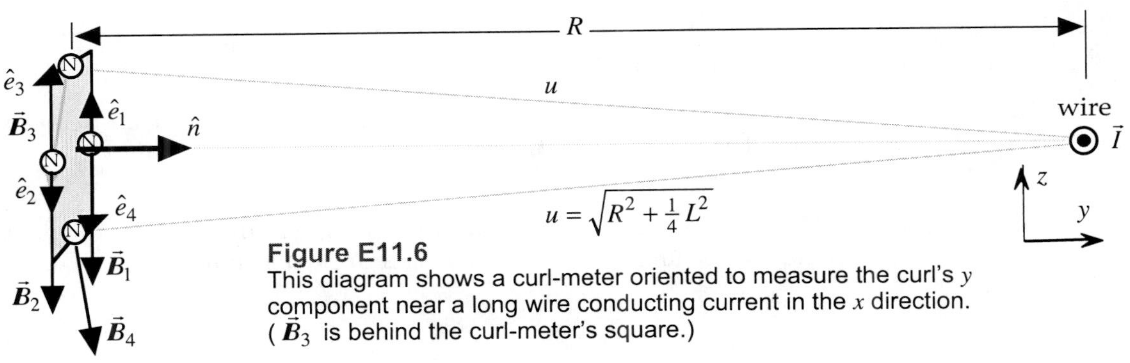

Figure E11.6
This diagram shows a curl-meter oriented to measure the curl's y component near a long wire conducting current in the x direction. ($\vec{B}_3$ is behind the curl-meter's square.)

Self-Test E11X.2

Argue that in this case $\widetilde{\text{curl}}(\vec{B})_z = 0$ as well. (*Hint:* This is the easy one.)

E11.3 The Curl as a Derivative

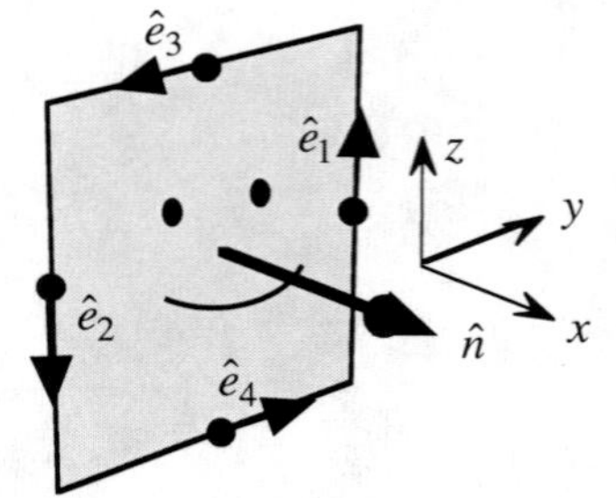

Figure E11.7
This drawing shows a curl-meter oriented to measure the curl's x component.

As in the case of the divergence, we can express the curl in an even more compact form. Imagine that we orient a curl-meter so that its nose points in the x direction and its sides are parallel to the other two coordinate axis directions (see figure E11.7). We see that in this case, $\hat{e}_1 = +\hat{z}$, $\hat{e}_2 = -\hat{z}$, $\hat{e}_3 = -\hat{y}$, and $\hat{e}_4 = +\hat{y}$. Let the coordinates of point P at the curl-meter's center be $[x, y, z]$ and assume that we know the magnetic field as a vector function $\vec{B}(x,y,z)$. The formal definition of the curl then implies

$$\widetilde{\text{curl}}(\vec{B})_x \equiv \lim_{L\to 0}\frac{1}{L}[\vec{B}_1\cdot\hat{e}_1 + \vec{B}_2\cdot\hat{e}_2 + \vec{B}_3\cdot\hat{e}_3 + \vec{B}_4\cdot\hat{e}_4]$$

$$= \lim_{L\to 0}\frac{1}{L}[\vec{B}_1\cdot\hat{z} - \vec{B}_2\cdot\hat{z} - \vec{B}_3\cdot\hat{y} + \vec{B}_4\cdot\hat{y}]$$

$$= \lim_{L\to 0}\frac{1}{L}[B_{1z} - B_{2z} - B_{3y} + B_{4y}] \tag{E11.5}$$

Now, the coordinates of pole 1 are $[x, y+\frac{1}{2}L, z]$, so $\vec{B}_1 = \vec{B}(x, y+\frac{1}{2}L, z)$. Similarly, we have $\vec{B}_2 = \vec{B}(x, y-\frac{1}{2}L, z)$, $\vec{B}_3 = \vec{B}(x, y, z+\frac{1}{2}L)$, and $\vec{B}_4 = \vec{B}(x, y, z-\frac{1}{2}L)$. The first two terms in equation E11.5 are therefore

$$\lim_{L\to 0}\frac{1}{L}[B_{1z} - B_{2z}] = \lim_{L\to 0}\left[\frac{B_z(x, y+\frac{1}{2}L, z) - B_z(x, y-\frac{1}{2}L, z)}{L}\right] \tag{E11.6}$$

This is the limit as $L\to 0$ of the difference in B_z evaluated at two points L apart in the y direction (holding x and z constant) divided by L. This is therefore the *definition* of the partial derivative $\partial B_z/\partial y$. Similarly,

$$\lim_{L\to 0}\frac{1}{L}[-B_{3y} + B_{4y}] = \lim_{L\to 0}\left[-\frac{B_y(x,y,z+\frac{1}{2}L) - B_z(x,y,z-\frac{1}{2}L)}{L}\right] \tag{E11.7}$$

is the definition of the partial derivative $-\partial B_y/\partial z$. Therefore

$$\text{curl}(\vec{B})_x = \frac{\partial B_z}{\partial y} - \frac{\partial B_y}{\partial z} \tag{E11.8}$$

You can show similarly that $\text{curl}(\vec{B})_y = \partial B_x/\partial z - \partial B_z/\partial x$ and $\text{curl}(\vec{B})_z = \partial B_y/\partial x - \partial B_x/\partial y$.

Self-Test E11X.3

Using the same general approach that I have used above, prove that $\text{curl}(\vec{B})_y = \partial B_x/\partial z - \partial B_z/\partial x$.

To summarize, we can compactly express the three components of the curl vector at any point P in a magnetic field as follows:

$$\text{c\breve{u}rl}(\vec{B}) \equiv \begin{bmatrix} \dfrac{\partial B_z}{\partial y} - \dfrac{\partial B_y}{\partial z} \\ \dfrac{\partial B_x}{\partial z} - \dfrac{\partial B_z}{\partial x} \\ \dfrac{\partial B_y}{\partial x} - \dfrac{\partial B_x}{\partial y} \end{bmatrix} \qquad \text{(E11.9)}$$

The curl in terms of partial derivatives of $\vec{B}$

Purpose: This is the definition of the curl $\text{c\breve{u}rl}(\vec{B})$ in terms of partial derivatives of the magnetic field function $\vec{B}(x, y, z)$.
Symbols: B_x, B_y, and B_z are the components of $\vec{B}$.
Limitations: This equation is a definition.

We see that like the divergence, a field's curl is mathematically a kind of derivative of that field. The most important *difference* between the divergence and the curl (besides the detailed form of the derivative) is that the divergence is a scalar quantity (i.e. a single number) while the curl is a *vector* quantity (with three components). In the applications we will consider, generally only one component of the curl is nonzero, but it is important to recognize the curl's vector character.

How to remember the components of the curl

It may seem that equation E11.9 is impossibly hard to remember, but compare this equation to the component definition of the cross product:

$$\begin{bmatrix} \text{curl}(\vec{B})_x \\ \text{curl}(\vec{B})_y \\ \text{curl}(\vec{B})_z \end{bmatrix} \equiv \begin{bmatrix} \dfrac{\partial}{\partial y}B_z - \dfrac{\partial}{\partial z}B_y \\ \dfrac{\partial}{\partial z}B_x - \dfrac{\partial}{\partial x}B_z \\ \dfrac{\partial}{\partial x}B_y - \dfrac{\partial}{\partial y}B_x \end{bmatrix}, \qquad \begin{bmatrix} (\vec{u} \times \vec{w})_x \\ (\vec{u} \times \vec{w})_y \\ (\vec{u} \times \vec{w})_z \end{bmatrix} = \begin{bmatrix} u_y w_z - u_z w_y \\ u_z w_x - u_x w_z \\ u_x w_y - u_y w_x \end{bmatrix} \qquad \text{(E11.10)}$$

Note that in both cases, the subscripts of the left side and the first term on the right (treating the derivative denominator as a subscript) go in the order *xyz*, *yzx*, or *zxy*, and the second term on the right is negative and has its subscripts reversed when compared to the first. So if you memorize this rule, you will have memorized the components of both the cross product and the curl. (For this reason, the curl is sometimes written $\vec{\nabla} \times \vec{B}$, where $\vec{\nabla}$ is the "vector" $[\partial/\partial x, \partial/\partial y, \partial/\partial z]$.)

Self-Test E11X.4

In self-test E11X.1, you argued from the basic definition of the curl-meter that a magnetic field that is uniform in direction and magnitude will have a zero curl. Prove this much more directly using equation E11.9.

E11.4 Ampere's Law

The local field equation that describes how *static* magnetic fields are related to current is Ampere's Law, which claims that

Ampere's law

$$\text{c\~{u}rl}(\vec{B}) = \frac{1}{\varepsilon_0}\left(\frac{\vec{J}}{c}\right) \quad \left[= 4\pi k\left(\frac{\vec{J}}{c}\right)\right] \tag{E11.11}$$

Purpose: This local field equation links the curl of a static magnetic field $\vec{B}$ at a point with the current density $\vec{J}$ at the same point.
Symbols: $\text{c\~{u}rl}(\vec{B})$ is the curl of $\vec{B}$ at the point (see equation E11.10), k is Coulomb's constant, $\varepsilon_0 = (4\pi k)^{-1}$ is the permittivity constant and c is the speed of light.
Limitations: This only applies to static fields.
Notes: Each one of the terms in this equation is a vector, so this equation actually represents three separate component equations. The value of $1/\varepsilon_0 c = 4\pi k/c$ is 377 Ω.

Just as Gauss's law connects the electric field to charge density, so Ampere's law connects the magnetic field to current density. Note that $\vec{J}/c$ plays exactly the same role for $\text{c\~{u}rl}(\vec{B})$ that charge density ρ plays for $\text{div}(\vec{E})$ (the equation even involves the same constant of proportionality!)

Self-Test E11X.5

Show that $1/\varepsilon_0 c = 4\pi k/c$ really is equal to 377 Ω.

We can use Ampere's law instead of the Biot-Savart law to calculate magnetic fields

For static fields, Ampere's law is mathematically equivalent to the Biot-Savart law used in chapter E9 and we can use it in place of the Biot-Savart law to calculate the magnetic fields of steady-state current distributions (though the steps we follow to do the calculations are quite different). In chapter E12, we will develop a powerful method of integrating Ampere's law that will make it easier to apply in many situations, but the following examples illustrate a couple of cases where Ampere's law quickly yields results that would be very difficult to prove using the methods of chapter E9.

Example E11.1 A Unidirectional Magnetic Field in Empty Space

Problem Prove that a unidirectional static magnetic field in empty space must also be uniform (i.e. independent of position).

Model and *Solution* Choose coordinates so that the magnetic field points entirely in the x direction, so $B_y = B_z = 0$. Gauss's law for the magnetic field then reduces to

$$\text{div}(\vec{B}) = \frac{\partial B_x}{\partial x} = 0 \tag{E11.12}$$

This implies that since $B = |B_x|$, the magnetic field magnitude cannot depend on x. Since there is no current in empty space, Ampere's law implies

$$\text{c\~{u}rl}(\vec{B}) \equiv \begin{bmatrix} \dfrac{\partial B_z}{\partial y} - \dfrac{\partial B_y}{\partial z} \\ \dfrac{\partial B_x}{\partial z} - \dfrac{\partial B_z}{\partial x} \\ \dfrac{\partial B_y}{\partial x} - \dfrac{\partial B_x}{\partial y} \end{bmatrix} = \begin{bmatrix} 0 \\ \dfrac{\partial B_x}{\partial z} \\ -\dfrac{\partial B_x}{\partial y} \end{bmatrix} = 0 \tag{E11.13}$$

This implies that the magnetic field also cannot depend on y or z. Therefore the magnetic field must be independent of position.

Example E11.2 The Magnetic Field of an Infinite Solenoid

Problem Consider an infinite solenoid consisting of N turns of wire along a given length L of solenoid, each turn carrying a current I. Use Ampere's law to determine the magnetic field magnitude inside the solenoid.

Translation Let the solenoid's inner radius be R. For the sake of argument, choose the x axis to coincide with the solenoid's central axis. Let us also assume that the windings have a thickness W.

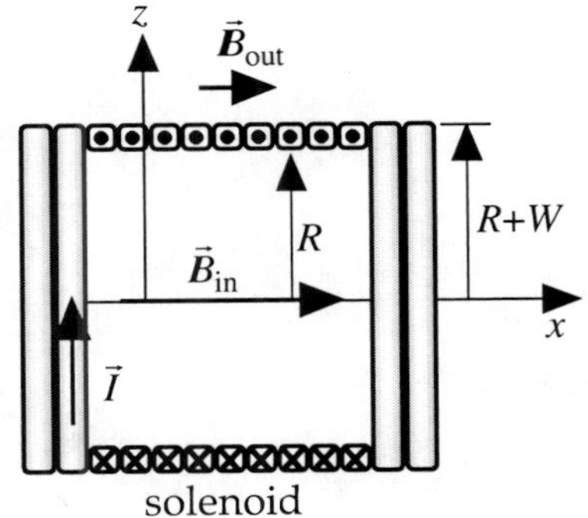

Figure E11.8
This diagram shows a cutaway side view of a portion of an infinite solenoid. The circles with dots represent wires crossing the xz plane that carry current toward the viewer (that is, in the $-y$ direction). The circles with crosses correspond to wires carrying current away from the viewer.

Model We saw in example E9.3 that symmetry in this situation implies that the magnetic field at all points inside and outside the solenoid must point parallel to the solenoid's central axis, which in this case is the x direction, so $\vec{B} = [B_x, 0, 0]$ everywhere. According to example E11.1 such a field must have a constant magnitude in the empty spaces both inside and outside the solenoid: let the constant field x components in these regions be $B_{in,x}$ and $B_{out,x}$ respectively. The only place that the field magnitude can change is in the region $R \ge r \ge R+W$ where current is actually flowing.

In order to apply Ampere's law to this region, we need to compute the magnitude of the current density $\vec{J}$. According to equation E5.9, the magnitude of the current density in this region is $J = I_{tot}/A$, where I_{tot} is the total current carried by a given cross-sectional area A of wire. If we have N turns per length L along the solenoid, and the windings have thickness W, then the magnitude of the current density must be

$$J = \frac{NI}{LW} \tag{E11.14}$$

Consider points in the $+z$ side of the xz plane within the coil windings (that is, where $R \ge z \ge R+W$). Note that in this region, current is flowing in the $-y$ direction.

Solution Ampere's law in this region therefore implies that

$$\vec{\text{curl}}(\vec{B}) \equiv \begin{bmatrix} \dfrac{\partial B_z}{\partial y} - \dfrac{\partial B_y}{\partial z} \\[2ex] \dfrac{\partial B_x}{\partial z} - \dfrac{\partial B_z}{\partial x} \\[2ex] \dfrac{\partial B_y}{\partial x} - \dfrac{\partial B_x}{\partial y} \end{bmatrix} = \begin{bmatrix} 0 \\[2ex] \dfrac{\partial B_x}{\partial z} \\[2ex] -\dfrac{\partial B_x}{\partial y} \end{bmatrix} = \frac{1}{\varepsilon_0}\begin{bmatrix} 0 \\[2ex] -\dfrac{J}{c} \\[2ex] 0 \end{bmatrix} = \frac{1}{\varepsilon_0}\begin{bmatrix} 0 \\[2ex] -\dfrac{NI}{cLW} \\[2ex] 0 \end{bmatrix} \tag{E11.15}$$

The bottom component tells us that B_x in the yz plane does not depend on y. Gauss's magnetic law in this case (equation E11.12) tells us that B_x cannot depend on x. So in the yz plane, B_x can only depend on z. Integrating the middle row of equation E11.15 from the coil's inner surface, where $B_x(0,0,R) = B_{in,x}$, to its outer surface, where $B_x(0,0,R+W) = B_{out,x}$, yields

$$\int_R^{R+W} \frac{\partial B_x}{\partial z} dz = -\frac{1}{\varepsilon_0}\frac{NI}{cLW}\int_R^{R+W} dz \;\Rightarrow\; B_{out,x} - B_{in,x} = -\frac{1}{\varepsilon_0}\frac{NI}{cL\cancel{W}}\cancel{W}$$

$$\Rightarrow B_{out,x} - B_{in,x} = -\frac{1}{\varepsilon_0}\frac{NI}{cL} \;\Rightarrow\; B_{in,x} = B_{out,x} + \frac{1}{\varepsilon_0}\frac{NI}{cL} \tag{E11.16}$$

We see, therefore, that Ampere's law implies that the x component of the magnetic field inside the solenoid must be $NI/\varepsilon_0 cL$ larger than that outside the solenoid. If we assume that $B_{out} = 0$, the magnetic field inside the solenoid must be $B_{in} = NI/\varepsilon_0 cL$.

Why doesn't Ampere's law completely determine the solenoid's field?

It may seem surprising at first that Ampere's law cannot completely determine the solenoid's magnetic field without the additional assumption that $\boldsymbol{B}_{\text{out}} = 0$. But remember that the curl completely ignores the magnetic field created by all distant currents. If the solenoid happened to be immersed in a uniform external magnetic field created by distant currents we haven't accounted for, Ampere's law will completely ignore this field. This means that Ampere's law by its very nature cannot tell us about the absolute magnitude of the magnetic field *anywhere*: it only tells us about how the magnetic field is modified by the currents we take into account.

However, if we can in some way determine the value of the magnetic field that the known current distribution *must* create at a certain point, then we can use Ampere's law to calculate the field that the same distribution must create at all other points. In many cases, we would use symmetry to find a place where the field created by the known distribution must be zero, but this case, symmetry does not help. It is not plausible, though, that the magnetic field the *solenoid* creates in its exterior could be nonzero all the way out to infinity, so if the solenoid's external field must be a constant, the most plausible constant is zero. This result is supported by experimental determinations of the external magnetic fields created by long but finite solenoids. If we make this assumption, then Ampere's law tells us that a solenoid's magnetic field must be

The magnetic field strength inside an infinite solenoid

$$\boldsymbol{B} = \frac{1}{\varepsilon_0}\frac{NI}{cL} \text{ inside, } \quad \boldsymbol{B} = 0 \text{ everywhere outside} \qquad \text{(E11.17)}$$

Purpose: This equation specifies the magnitude $\boldsymbol{B}$ of the magnetic field inside and outside an infinite solenoid.

Symbols: N is the number of turns of wire per length L along the solenoid, I is the current carried by each turn, $\varepsilon_0 = (4\pi k)^{-1}$ is the permittivity constant and c is the speed of light.

Limitations: This strictly only applies to infinite solenoids. It is reasonably accurate for points far from the ends of a finite solenoid if its length is much larger than its radius.

Note: We will find this equation useful in chapter E14.

Note also that equation E11.16 implies that this field must point in the $+x$ direction, which is the direction we would get from the loop rule. Therefore, except for the one extra assumption we have to make, Ampere's law tells us *everything* about the solenoid's magnetic field.

The field described by equation E11.17 pretty closely approximates the field deep inside a finite solenoid if the solenoid's radius is much smaller than its length. Indeed, a long solenoid represents the most practical way to create a strong and nearly uniform magnetic field in a large volume. The solenoids used in medical magnetic resonance imaging (MRI) machines are long and narrow (and thus claustrophobia-provoking) partly because good MRI images depend on having a strong and nearly uniform field over the imaging region (see figure E11.9).

E11.5 The Curl of the Electric Field

How the curl of an electric field is defined

The curl-meter discussed in section E11.1 measures the curl of a *magnetic* field. To measure the curl of an electric field, all that we need to do is replace the north poles of the magnetic curl-meter with positive charged

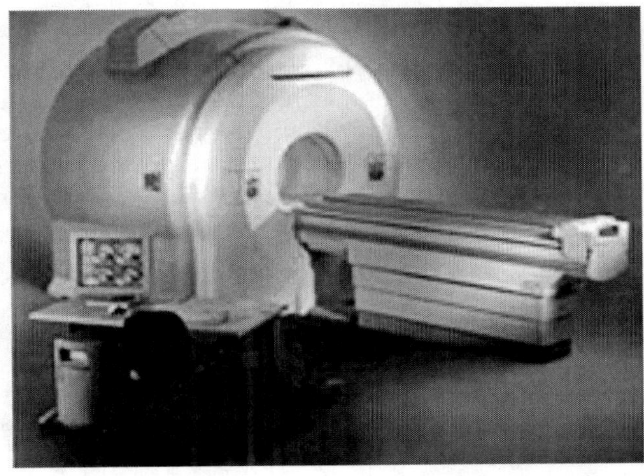

Figure E11.9
An MRI machine. The patient lies on the platform to the right, which is then slid in the large solenoid to the left.

particles. The quantity measured by a curl-meter modified this way will be $\widetilde{\text{curl}}(\vec{E})$, which is the same as the quantity defined by equations E11.2 or E11.9 as long as we replace $\boldsymbol{B}$ with E everywhere.

How an electric curl-meter responds to the electric field of a charged particle

Figure E11.10 shows electric curl-meters placed both on top of and far from a charged particle. If the charged particle is at the curl-meter's center, its electric field vectors at the positions of the curl-meter's edge charges are perpendicular to the edges and therefore have no counterclockwise components. Thus the electric curl in this case must be zero. If the charged particle is *outside* the curl-meter square, then the electric field vectors at the top and bottom curl-meter charges have positive and negative counterclockwise components that are equal in magnitude and therefore cancel. The field vectors at the other two curl-meter charges have no counterclockwise components. The net electric curl in this case is also zero.

Self-Test E11X.6

The result of figure E11.10a is the same no matter how the curl-meter is oriented. The situation in figure E11.10b is essentially the same whether the curl-meter is oriented in the x direction (as shown) or the z direction. Argue that the curl is still zero if the curl-meter is oriented in the y direction.

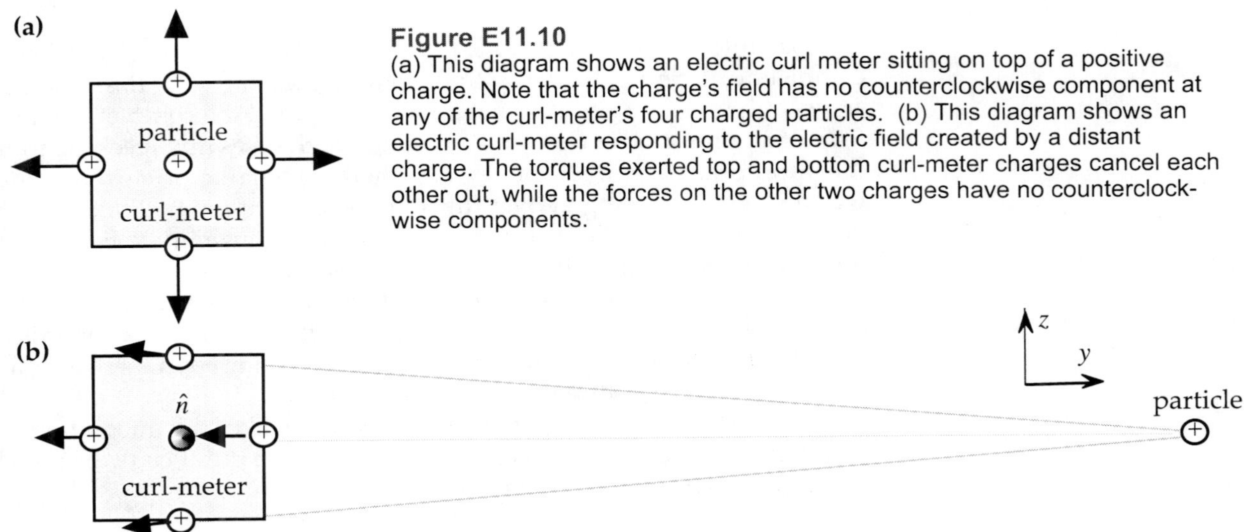

Figure E11.10
(a) This diagram shows an electric curl meter sitting on top of a positive charge. Note that the charge's field has no counterclockwise component at any of the curl-meter's four charged particles. (b) This diagram shows an electric curl-meter responding to the electric field created by a distant charge. The torques exerted top and bottom curl-meter charges cancel each other out, while the forces on the other two charges have no counterclockwise components.

We see that whether the charged particle is inside or outside the curl-meter square, the net torque exerted by its field on the curl-meter is zero no matter how the curl-meter is oriented. This means that not only does the curl-meter ignore the electric field created by distant charges, but it ignores the electric field created by local charges as well! The superposition principle then implies that *all components of the curl of an electric field created by any combination of local or nonlocal charges is zero.*

Ampere's law for the electric field

$$\vec{\text{curl}}(\vec{E}) = 0 \quad \text{(for static electric fields)} \tag{E11.18}$$

Like Gauss's law for the magnetic field $\text{div}(\vec{B}) = 0$, this field equation imposes a basic constraint on the character of a static electric field, but does not say anything about how the field is linked to charged particles.

A loop as a curl-meter

Note that an electric field that can twist the positive curl-meter charges counterclockwise (or clockwise) around an axis would similarly push charge carriers around a closed loop of wire in a plane perpendicular to that axis (see figure E11.11). Conversely, if we observe an electric field driving charge carriers flowing around a closed conducting loop, then that field would also twist the curl meter and thus have nonzero curl. Indeed, since only an *electric* field can exert a force on charge carriers at rest, the mere existence of a current flowing in a closed conducting loop *at rest* would *require* the existence of an electric field with nonzero curl. Therefore we can use a closed loop of wire as a practical electric curl -meter.

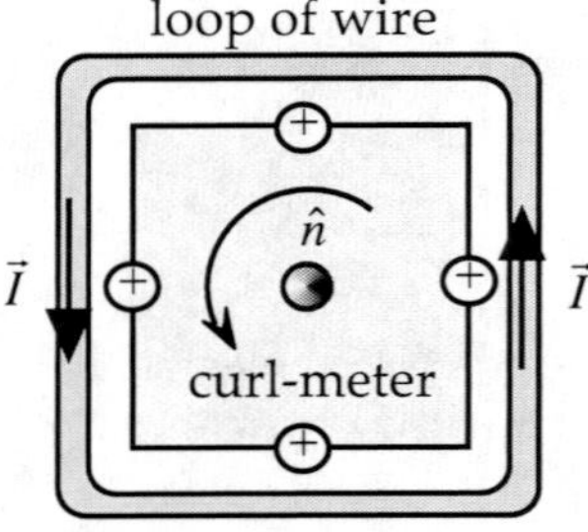

Figure E11.11
An electric field that exerts a nonzero torque on a curl-meter will also drive a continuous current in a closed loop.

Ampere's law for the electric field expresses *conservation of energy* for a static electric field

Equation E11.18 (Ampere's law for the electric field) thus asserts that *it is impossible to create a static electric field that drives charge carriers around a closed conducting loop*. There is a good reason for this: if a static electric field *could* drive a current in a conducting loop, it would violate conservation of energy. A current flowing in the loop would generate thermal energy in the conductor. If the electric field alone is driving this current, then the energy must come from the field (nothing else is involved). But if the field is *static*, its total energy cannot change. So a static electric field with nonzero curl would continuously generate thermal energy from nowhere. Therefore, $\vec{\text{curl}}(\vec{E}) = 0$ is *required* if a static electric field is to conserve energy.

Note that this conclusion does not follow if either the electric or magnetic field is *not* static, as changing fields channel energy from one form to another. We will consider such cases in chapter E13.

E11.6 The Mystery du Jour

Example E10.3 illustrates that we can use Gauss's law to calculate the complete electric field of an infinite charged planar slab. Example E11.2 showed that we can use Ampere's law to calculate the complete magnetic field of an infinite solenoid. The method in both cases involved integrating the appropriate law over the region where the charge or current density was not zero. The integral over the derivative representing the divergence or curl respectively allowed us to calculate the change in the field created by the charge or current density respectively.

However, both of these examples involved fields that symmetry required to be unidirectional, which made the analysis much easier. It is difficult to see how we could generalize the methods I used in these examples to more complicated three-dimensional problems.

Fortunately, there is a very clever trick that makes the integration easy in a number of cases. What is this trick, and where did it come from? This will be our topic in the next chapter.

TWO-MINUTE PROBLEMS

E11T.1 Imagine that within a certain region of space, a magnetic field points entirely in the $+y$ direction but has a magnitude that increases as x increases. The curl of this field

A. must be zero
B. must have a positive x component
C. must have a positive y component
D. most have a positive z component
E. must have a negative component in some direction
F. cannot be determined from this information

E11T.2 A long current-carrying wire and a permanent magnet have very different magnetic fields. The curl of these fields nevertheless has the same value at every point in the empty space surrounding these objects (T or F).

E11T.3 Which of the following quantities must be zero in all circumstances at a point in empty space near a static current distribution?

A. the magnetic field's curl
B. the magnetic field's divergence
C. both
D. neither

E11T.4 A magnetic field at points in a certain region which may or may not be inside a current-carrying object points in the $+x$ direction and has a magnitude that increases as a point's y coordinate increases. In this region

A. a current must be flowing in the $+x$ direction
B. a current must be flowing in the $-x$ direction
C. a current must be flowing in the $+y$ direction
D. a current must be flowing in the $-y$ direction
E. a current must be flowing in the $+z$ direction
F. a current must be flowing in the $-z$ direction
T. there must be no current flowing

E11T.5 The electric field just outside a large charged flat plate must have zero curl (T or F).

E11T.6 A static electric field at points in a certain region (which may or may not be inside a charged object) points in the $+x$ direction and has a magnitude that grows as a point's y coordinate increases. This is a possible electric field (T or F).

HOMEWORK PROBLEMS

Basic Skills

E11B.1 Can the curl of a magnetic field ever be nonzero at a point in truly empty space? Why or why not?

E11B.2 Calculate the curl of a magnetic field having the form $\vec{B} = [ayz, 0, 0]$, where a is a constant. (Remember to calculate all components!)

E11B.3 Calculate the curl of a magnetic field having the form $\vec{B} = [ar^2x,\ ar^2y,\ ar^2z]$, where a is a constant and $r^2 = x^2 + y^2 + z^2$. (Remember to calculate all components!)

E11B.4 Calculate the curl of a unidirectional field pointing in the $+x$ direction and having an x component $B_x = ayz$, where a is a constant. (Remember to calculate all components!)

E11B.5 Imagine that the magnetic field inside a certain object has the form $\vec{B} = [0,\ 0,\ ay]$, where a is a constant. What is the magnitude and direction of the current density inside this object?

E11B.6 Imagine that an electric field in a certain region of space has the form $\vec{E} = [-az,\ 0,\ ax]$, where a is a constant. Is this a physically possible static electric field?

E11B.7 Imagine a solenoid consisting of 30,000 turns of wire wrapped around a cylinder 0.6 m in diameter and 3.0 m long.

(a) Is the infinite solenoid approximation a reasonably good approximation here for points close to the solenoid's center? Explain.

(b) Using that approximation, calculate how much current the wire will have to carry to create a magnetic field with a strength of $B =$ 1.0 T ($\boldsymbol{B}$ = 300 MN/C) inside the solenoid far from either end.

Synthetic

E11S.1 Prove that any unidirectional and static electric field in empty space must be uniform.

E11S.2 Argue from the derivative form of the curl that if $\vec{B} = \vec{B}_1 + \vec{B}_2 + \ldots$ then

$$\tilde{\text{curl}}(\vec{B}) = \tilde{\text{curl}}(\vec{B}_1) + \tilde{\text{curl}}(\vec{B}_2) + \ldots \quad \text{(E11.19)}$$

E11S.3 In problem E10S.2, we argued that a purely radial electric field that depends only on the distance r one is from the origin will have the form

$$\vec{E} = f(r)\begin{bmatrix} x \\ y \\ z \end{bmatrix} \quad \text{(E11.20)}$$

Show that such a field has identically zero curl.

E11S.4 As we discussed in example E9.2, the magnetic field created by an axial current distribution must point circularly around the distribution's central axis and have a magnitude that depends only on the distance r one is from the central axis. Let us define our coordinate axes so that the x axis coincides with the distribution's central axis.

(a) Argue that such a field must have the form

$$\vec{B} = f(r)\begin{bmatrix} 0 \\ z \\ -y \end{bmatrix}, \text{ where } r = \sqrt{y^2 + z^2} \quad \text{(E11.21)}$$

(b) Show that the curl of such a field is

$$\tilde{\text{curl}}(\vec{B}) = -\begin{bmatrix} r(df/dr) + 2f \\ 0 \\ 0 \end{bmatrix} \quad \text{(E11.22)}$$

(c) In empty space, the curl of such a field must be zero. Show that this means that

$$\frac{df}{f} = -\frac{2dr}{r} \quad \text{(E11.23)}$$

(d) Integrate both sides of this to show that the only field of this type that has zero curl is

$$f = \frac{a}{r^2} \quad \text{(E11.24)}$$

where a is a constant of integration. Show also that this field has a magnitude of a/r.

(e) Symmetry requires that a circular field like this must be zero along the central axis. Argue therefore that the magnetic field of an infinite current-carrying cylindrical pipe must be zero everywhere inside the pipe's hollow interior.

E11S.5 Consider a hypothetical static electric field that within a certain region points entirely in the $+x$ direction but has a magnitude that depends on z. Is such a static field possible? If not, explain why not. If so, are there any restrictions on how $\vec{E}$ can depend on y?

E11S.6 Consider a hypothetical static electric field that within a certain region points entirely in the $+z$ direction but has a magnitude that depends on z.

(a) Does Ampere's law for the electric field forbid such a field or otherwise put any restrictions on it? Explain.

(b) Does Gauss's law for the electric field forbid this field or otherwise put restrictions on the places which it can appear? Explain.

Rich-Context

E11R.1 Use symmetry and Ampere's law to determine the magnetic field inside and outside a planar conducting slab that is infinite in the y and z directions but has finite width W in the x direction. Assume that a current with uniform current density $\vec{J}$ in the $+y$ direction flows in the slab's interior. (*Hints:* See problem E9S.7, and also argue that the magnetic field must be independent of y and z. Then follow the approach in example E11.2 for applying Ampere's law.)

E11R.2 You want to construct a solenoid 20 cm long that has an interior magnetic field strength $\mathbb{B}$ of about 1.5 MN/C. The coil has to be wound as a single layer of wire around a form whose diameter is 3.0 cm. You have two spools of wire handy. #18 wire has a diameter of about 1.02 mm and can carry a current of 6.0 A before overheating. #26 wire has a diameter of 0.41 mm and can carry up to 1.0 A. Which kind of wire should you use and why? What potential difference do you want to put across the coil's ends?

E11R.3 The solenoid used in a typical MRI machine might have an inside diameter of 60 cm, a length of 3.0 m, and generates a field with a magnitude of 1.5 T in its interior. Imagine that this solenoid uses copper wires 3 mm in diameter that are able to carry 50 A of current. Roughly estimate the power that such a magnet will dissipate and compare it to the average electrical power used by a household of four (about 1000 W). Comment about why most modern MRI machines use superconducting magnets, which dissipate no power but require expensive cooling to near absolute zero. (Note that in order to get the required number of turns per meter, you are going to have to wind multiple layers of turns: be sure to take this into account.)

ANSWERS TO SELF-TESTS

E11X.1 Define the $+x$ direction to coincide with the uniform field's direction. If we orient the curl-meter so that its nose vector points in the the $+x$ direction (see figure E11.12a), the field vectors are all perpendicular to the curl-meter's plane, and so exert no torque on the curl-meter. If we orient the curl-meter's nose in the $+y$ direction (see figure E11.12b, which shows a rear view), we see that the field exerts no torque on the two side poles and equal and opposing torques on the upper and lower poles, so the net torque is zero. The same argument applies when we orient the curl-meter so that its axis faces the $+z$ direction. Therefore, all three curl components are zero for a uniform magnetic field.

E11X.2 If we reorient the curl meter in figure E11.6 so that its nose vector points in the $+z$ direction, then the magnetic field vectors will be perpendicular to the plane of the plate at each of the four poles, so their dot products with the edge vectors will be zero, so the curl is zero.

E11X.3 If the curl-meter's nose vector points in the $+y$ direction then its four counterclockwise-facing edge vectors are $\hat{e}_1 = -\hat{z}$, $\hat{e}_2 = +\hat{z}$, $\hat{e}_3 = +\hat{x}$, and $\hat{e}_4 = -\hat{x}$ (see figure E11.12b). The curl's y-component is thus

$$\lim_{L \to 0} \frac{1}{L}[\,\vec{B}_1 \cdot \hat{e}_1 + \vec{B}_2 \cdot \hat{e}_2 + \vec{B}_3 \cdot \hat{e}_3 + \vec{B}_4 \cdot \hat{e}_4\,]$$

$$= \lim_{L \to 0} \frac{1}{L}[-\vec{B}_1 \cdot \hat{z} + \vec{B}_2 \cdot \hat{z} + \vec{B}_3 \cdot \hat{x} - \vec{B}_4 \cdot \hat{x}]$$

$$= \lim_{L \to 0} \frac{1}{L}[-B_{1z} + B_{2z} + B_{3x} - B_{4x}] \quad \text{(E11.25)}$$

Now, pole 1 has coordinates $[x+\frac{1}{2}L, y, z]$, so $\vec{B}_1 = \vec{B}(x+\frac{1}{2}L, y, z)$. Similarly

$$\vec{B}_2 = \vec{B}(x-\tfrac{1}{2}L, y, z), \quad \text{(E11.26a)}$$

$$\vec{B}_3 = \vec{B}(x, y, z+\tfrac{1}{2}L), \quad \text{(E11.26b)}$$

$$\vec{B}_4 = \vec{B}(x, y, z-\tfrac{1}{2}L). \quad \text{(E11.26c)}$$

The first two terms in equation E11.26 are thus

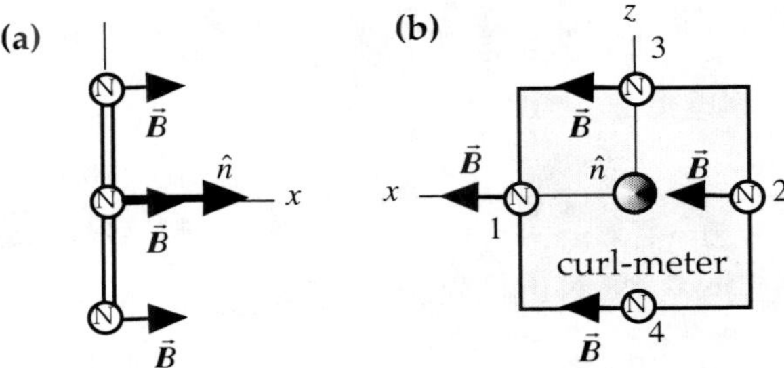

Figure E11.12
(a) A side view of a curl-meter whose axis faces the $+x$ direction in a uniform magnetic field pointing in that direction. **(b)** A rear view of a curl-meter whose axis faces in the $+y$ direction in the same field.

$$\lim_{L \to 0}\left[-\frac{B_z(x+\frac{1}{2}L,y,z) - B_z(x-\frac{1}{2}L,y,z)}{L}\right]$$

$$\equiv -\frac{\partial B_z}{\partial x} \quad \text{(E11.27)}$$

Similarly, the other two terms are

$$\lim_{L \to 0}\left[\frac{B_x(x,y,z+\frac{1}{2}L) - B_x(x,y,z-\frac{1}{2}L)}{L}\right]$$

$$\equiv \frac{\partial B_x}{\partial z} \quad \text{(E11.28)}$$

E11X.4 If a field is uniform (that is, independent of position), its partial derivatives are all zero. Therefore, equation E11.9 implies that curl is zero.

E11X.5 Calculating the magnitude simply involves typing the numbers into a calculator. The tricky parts are the units. The units of $4\pi k/c$ are

$$\frac{\cancel{N}\cdot\cancel{m}^2}{\cancel{C}^2}\frac{\cancel{s}}{\cancel{m}}\left(\frac{1\,\cancel{J}}{1\,\cancel{N}\cdot\cancel{m}}\right)\left(\frac{1\,\text{V}}{1\,\cancel{J}/\cancel{C}}\right)\left(\frac{1\,\cancel{C}/\cancel{s}}{1\,\text{A}}\right)$$

$$= \frac{\cancel{V}}{\cancel{A}}\left(\frac{1\,\Omega}{1\,\cancel{V}/\cancel{A}}\right) = \Omega \quad \text{(E11.29)}$$

E11X.6 In this case, all the field vectors at all four curl-meter charges have no counterclockwise components, so they exert zero torque on the curl-meter (see figure E11.13 below).

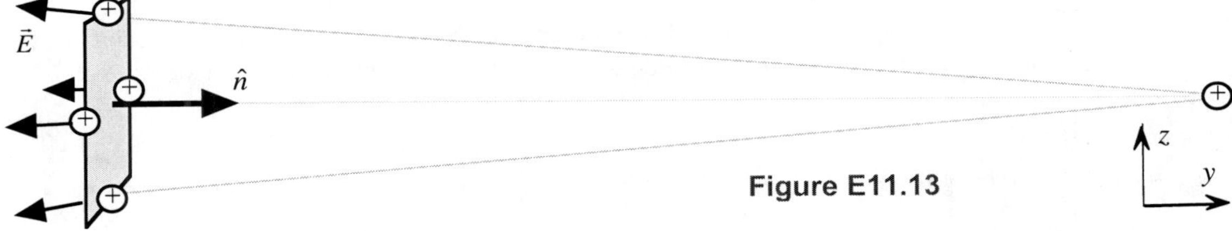

Figure E11.13

E12 Calculating Fields

▷ Static Electric Fields
▷ Controlling Currents
▷ Static Magnetic Fields
▼ Field Equations
Gauss's Law
Ampere's Law
Calculating Fields
▷ Dynamic Fields

Chapter Overview

Introduction

This chapter completes the subsection on field equations by discussing clever methods for integrating Gauss's law and Ampere's law. These methods make easy the calculation of the electric and magnetic fields of certain kinds of objects.

Section E12.1: Integrating Gauss's Law

In this section we consider summing the tile-vector form of Gauss's law over a set of cubical **cells** filling a certain specified volume. It turns out that the contributions from adjoining cell faces cancel each other out, so that only contributions from exterior faces count in the final sum. This means that we can write Gauss's law in this **integral form**:

$$\oint \vec{E} \cdot d\vec{A} = \frac{1}{\varepsilon_0} Q_{\text{enc}} \tag{E12.7}$$

Purpose: This equation links the behavior of the electric field on the surface of an arbitrary volume to the charge enclosed by that surface.

Symbols: $\vec{E}$ is the electric field at a point on the volume's surface, $d\vec{A}$ is the tile vector associated with an infinitesimal tile (patch of surface area) centered on that point, $\oint$ instructs us to perform a sum over all such infinitesimal patches on the volume's surface, $\varepsilon_0 = (4\pi k)^{-1}$ is the permittivity constant, and Q_{enc} is the charge within the volume.

Limitations: Each tile must be small enough so that it is approximately flat and $\vec{E}$ is approximately constant over its surface. The surface must completely enclose the volume (but can otherwise have an arbitrary shape and size, and may be either real or imaginary).

Section E12.2: Using the Integral Form of Gauss's Law

Following a four-step process helps one use this tool to calculate fields rapidly:

1. ***Use Symmetry.*** You should first use symmetry and/or other arguments to determine the field's precise direction at all points and also what the field's magnitude does *not* depend on.

2. ***Choose a Gaussian Surface.*** You should then pick a useful imaginary closed surface (which we will call a **gaussian surface**) shaped so that it is easy to calculate $\vec{E} \cdot d\vec{A}$ at all points on the surface.

3. ***Calculate*** $\oint \vec{E} \cdot d\vec{A}$. Sum $\vec{E} \cdot d\vec{A}$ for all tiles on the surface.

4. ***Apply the Integral Form of Gauss's Law*** to determine any remaining unknown features of the field.

The section provides some advice about how to construct gaussian surfaces from surface elements on which $\vec{E} \cdot d\vec{A} = 0$ or some other easily-calculated value.

Section E12.3: The Shell Theorem

This section illustrates the use of the four-step process by using Gauss's law to prove the shell theorem.

Section E12.4: Integrating Ampere's Law

In this section we consider summing the edge-vector form of Ampere's law over a set of tiles that span a certain surface. It turns out that the contributions from adjoining tile edges cancel each other out, so that only contributions from exterior edges count in the final sum. **Ampere's law in integral form** then becomes

$$\oint \vec{\mathbb{B}} \cdot d\vec{S} = \frac{1}{\varepsilon_0}\left(\frac{i_{\text{enc}}}{c}\right) \quad \left[\text{or } \oint \vec{B} \cdot d\vec{S} = \mu_0 i_{\text{enc}}\right] \qquad \text{(E12.18)}$$

Purpose: This equation links the behavior of a static magnetic field on the closed boundary of a surface to the total signed current i_{enc} flowing through that surface.

Symbols: $\oint$ is a shorthand notation for "sum over all infinitesimal steps around a closed curve" (the surface's boundary in this case), $d\vec{S}$ is one such step, $\vec{B}$ or $\vec{\mathbb{B}} = c\vec{B}$ is the magnetic field vector evaluated at a given step, $\varepsilon_0 = (4\pi k)^{-1}$ is the permittivity constant, $\mu_0 = 1/\varepsilon_0 c^2$ is the permeability constant, and c is the speed of light.

Limitations: This equation only applies to *static* magnetic fields. Each step must be small enough so that $\vec{\mathbb{B}}$ is nearly uniform along its length and so that each step can be straight but still match the surface's boundary well. The surface can have arbitrary shape, but the sum on the left must be performed for all steps around the shape's boundary.

Note: The absolute value of $i_{\text{enc}} \equiv \int \vec{J} \cdot d\vec{A}$ is always the total current I (charge per unit time) that passes through the surface, but i_{enc} is negative if the current density $\vec{J}$ is flowing (in general) against the direction of the tile vectors $d\vec{A}$ for tiles on the surface in question.

Make sure that you assign tile vectors for the surface so that the step vectors go counterclockwise around the surface when those tile vectors face you.

Section E12.5: Using the Integral Form of Ampere's Law

The four steps for using Ampere's law to calculate magnetic fields are:

1. ***Use Symmetry.***
2. ***Choose an Amperian Loop.*** Choose a loop surrounding a surface so that it will be easy to calculate $\vec{\mathbb{B}} \cdot d\vec{S}$ at all steps along the loop.
3. ***Calculate*** $\oint \vec{\mathbb{B}} \cdot d\vec{S}$.
4. ***Apply the Integral Form of Ampere's Law*** to determine the field.

Section E12.6: The Field of an Axial Current Distribution

This section illustrates the use of Ampere's law by showing how one can use the law to calculate the magnetic field of an axial current distribution.

Section E12.7: The Mystery du Jour

The laws of electromagnetism that we have developed so far are incomplete, because we have as yet no explanation for how a moving magnet can drive a current in a loop at rest. Explaining this will be our goal in the next chapter.

E12.1 Integrating Gauss's Law

In chapter E10, we introduced Gauss's law and showed that we can use this law to calculate the electric field of a suitably simple object. Calculating the electric field involved integrating Gauss's law over any region that contains charge. If the field is unidirectional, this is not too hard, but cases where the field is more complex, this approach becomes too difficult. In this section we will discuss a brilliant trick that allows us to integrate Gauss's law rapidly (and without much actual calculation) in more complex situations.

Dividing up a region of space into infinitesimal cells

Figure E12.1 shows a small region of space that I have divided into four even tinier cubical sections I will call **cells**. Equations E10.11 and Gauss's law together imply that for each of these cells

$$\frac{1}{dV}\left[\vec{E}_1 \cdot d\vec{A}_1 + \vec{E}_2 \cdot d\vec{A}_2 + \ldots + \vec{E}_6 \cdot d\vec{A}_6\right] = \text{div}(\vec{E}) = \frac{\rho}{\varepsilon_0} \tag{E12.1}$$

where dV is the cell's infinitesimally small volume, $\vec{E}_i$ is the electric field vector evaluated at the cell's ith face, and $d\vec{A}_i$ is that face's *tile vector*, which has a magnitude equal to the face's area and whose direction points perpendicularly outward from the face. (I have not included taking the limit as $dV \to 0$ in this expression because I am assuming that the cell is already infinitesimally small.) If we multiply both sides of this equation by dV, we get

$$\vec{E}_1 \cdot d\vec{A}_1 + \vec{E}_2 \cdot d\vec{A}_2 + \ldots + \vec{E}_6 \cdot d\vec{A}_6 = \frac{\rho\, dV}{\varepsilon_0} = \frac{dQ}{\varepsilon_0} \tag{E12.2}$$

where dQ is the infinitesimal amount of charge enclosed by the cell.

Summing up Gauss's law for that set of cells

Now, imagine that we were to sum this expression over all four cells, which I have labeled *A, B, C, D*. The total expression is

$$\begin{aligned}
&\vec{E}_{A1} \cdot d\vec{A}_{A1} + \vec{E}_{A2} \cdot d\vec{A}_{A2} + \ldots + \vec{E}_{A6} \cdot d\vec{A}_{A6}\\
&+ \vec{E}_{B1} \cdot d\vec{A}_{B1} + \vec{E}_{B2} \cdot d\vec{A}_{B2} + \ldots + \vec{E}_{B6} \cdot d\vec{A}_{B6}\\
&+ \vec{E}_{C1} \cdot d\vec{A}_{C1} + \vec{E}_{C2} \cdot d\vec{A}_{C2} + \ldots + \vec{E}_{C6} \cdot d\vec{A}_{C6}\\
&+ \vec{E}_{D1} \cdot d\vec{A}_{D1} + \vec{E}_{D2} \cdot d\vec{A}_{D2} + \ldots + \vec{E}_{D6} \cdot d\vec{A}_{D6}\\
&= \frac{1}{\varepsilon_0}(dQ_A + dQ_B + dQ_C + dQ_D)
\end{aligned} \tag{E12.3}$$

The contributions for interior cell walls cancel out

However, note that the tile vectors for adjoining cell walls are equal in magnitude but opposite in direction (for example, $d\vec{A}_{A3} = -d\vec{A}_{B4}$ and $d\vec{A}_{C5} = -d\vec{A}_{A6}$). However, the electric field vectors evaluated at the centers of these walls are the same (for example $\vec{E}_{A3} = \vec{E}_{B4}$ and $\vec{E}_{A6} = \vec{E}_{C5}$. Therefore the terms in the sum above that are contributed by adjacent cell walls cancel:

$$\vec{E}_{A3} \cdot d\vec{A}_{A3} + \vec{E}_{B4} \cdot d\vec{A}_{B4} = \vec{E}_{A3} \cdot (d\vec{A}_{A3} - d\vec{A}_{A3}) = 0 \tag{E12.4a}$$

$$\vec{E}_{C5} \cdot d\vec{A}_{C5} + \vec{E}_{A6} \cdot d\vec{A}_{A6} = \vec{E}_{C5} \cdot (d\vec{A}_{C5} - d\vec{A}_{C5}) = 0 \tag{E12.4b}$$

and so on. This means that the only important terms in the sum on the left side of equation E12.3 are those for the *exterior* faces of the four-cell set: all contributions from interior faces cancel each other out. So equation E12.3 becomes

$$\begin{aligned}
&\left[\textstyle\sum \vec{E}_i \cdot d\vec{A}_i\right] \text{ for all } \textit{external} \text{ faces of a set of cells}\\
&= \frac{1}{\varepsilon_0}\sum dQ_i = \frac{1}{\varepsilon_0}(\text{total charge enclosed})
\end{aligned} \tag{E12.5}$$

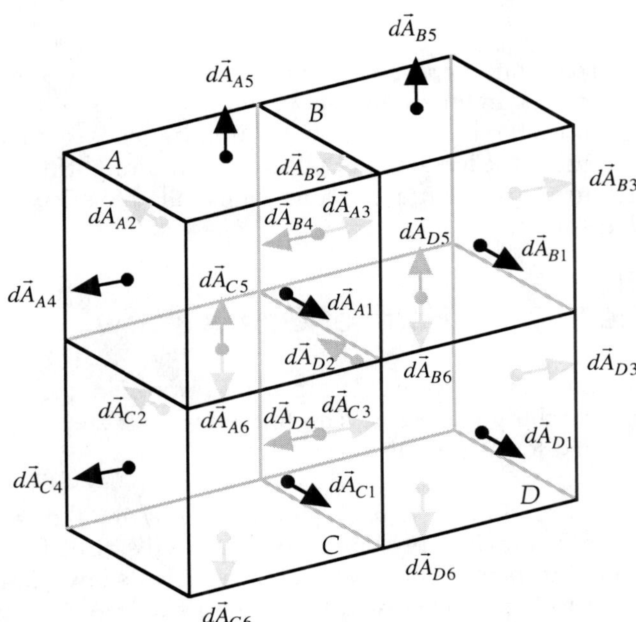

Figure E12.1
Four adjoining cells with their tile vectors. Note that the tile vectors associated with adjoining cell walls are equal in magnitude but point in opposite directions.

This equation applies to any number of cells. Since we can divide up any volume of arbitrary size and shape in space into a huge number of imaginary infinitesimal cells,

$$\left[\sum \vec{E}_i \cdot d\vec{A}_i\right] \text{ for all infinitesimal tile vectors on a volume's } \textit{surface}$$
$$= \frac{1}{\varepsilon_0}(\text{charge enclosed by that surface}) \tag{E12.6}$$

It turns out (see problem E12S.6) the surface tiles do not literally have to be the square faces at right angles that would correspond to the external faces of a set of tiny cubes, but can be chosen tangent to the volume's actual surface.

This very important equation is usually written in the following more compact form, which is called **Gauss's law in integral form**:

Gauss's law in integral form

$$\oint \vec{E} \cdot d\vec{A} = \frac{1}{\varepsilon_0} Q_{\text{enc}} \tag{E12.7}$$

Purpose: This equation links the behavior of the electric field on the surface of an arbitrary volume with the charge enclosed by that surface.

Symbols: $\vec{E}$ is the electric field at a point on the volume's surface, $d\vec{A}$ is the tile vector associated with an infinitesimal tile (patch of surface area) centered on that point, $\oint$ instructs us to perform a sum over all such infinitesimal patches on the volume's surface, $\varepsilon_0 = (4\pi k)^{-1}$ is the permittivity constant, and Q_{enc} is the charge within the volume.

Limitations: Each tile must be small enough so that it is approximately flat and $\vec{E}$ is approximately constant over its surface. The surface must completely enclose the volume (but can otherwise have an arbitrary shape and size, and may be either real or imaginary).

This expression provides a convenient and powerful way to integrate Gauss's law over a region containing charge.

How to interpret the integral symbol

Don't let the strange-looking integral sign distress you. Interpret it as simply an instruction to perform a sum over many infinitesimal quantities. The circle in the integral sign is a traditional way of reminding us that we are to perform this sum over a surface that *completely encloses* a certain volume (we call such a surface a **closed surface**). In the examples we will consider in this class, we will never have to perform a nasty integral: we will rather choose our volumes cleverly so that summing the left side of the equation is straightforward.

The quantity $\oint \vec{E} \cdot d\vec{A}$ for a given surface is sometimes called the **flux** of the electric field through that surface.

E12.2 Using the Integral Form of Gauss's Law

A four-step process for using Gauss's law in integral form

The integral form of Gauss's law provides a powerful tool for calculating the electric field created by charged objects. The following four-step process represents a practical manual for using this tool.

1. ***Use Symmetry.*** You should first use symmetry and/or other arguments to determine as much as possible about the field's direction and magnitude at all points before you attempt to use Gauss's law. Gauss's law will be easiest to apply when you know the field's precise direction at all points and you know at least what the field's magnitude does *not* depend on.

2. ***Choose a Gaussian Surface.*** You should then pick a useful imaginary closed surface (which we will call a **gaussian surface**) shaped so that it is easy to calculate $\vec{E} \cdot d\vec{A}$ at all points on the surface.

3. ***Calculate*** $\oint \vec{E} \cdot d\vec{A}$. Then calculate the sum of $\vec{E} \cdot d\vec{A}$ at all points on the surface. If you have chosen your surface well, this should be easy.

4. ***Apply the Integral Form of Gauss's Law*** to determine any remaining unknown features of the field.

Choosing a gaussian surface

A key part of this process is choosing the appropriate Gaussian surface; if you do this well, the rest of the solution is pretty easy, but an inappropriately chosen surface can make your life miserable. The appropriate surface is not always obvious, but there are some basic guidelines that you can follow.

The trick is usually to construct your closed surface from pieces of surface (let us call them **surface elements**) that are shaped so that calculating $\vec{E} \cdot d\vec{A}$ is as easy as possible. Calculating the $\vec{E} \cdot d\vec{A}$ is *easiest* when $\vec{E} = 0$ everywhere on the surface element, because then $\vec{E} \cdot d\vec{A}$ is trivially zero.

It is also very easy to calculate $\vec{E} \cdot d\vec{A}$ for a surface element that it is *parallel* to the field. Since the tile vector $d\vec{A}$ for any arbitrary tile on the surface element is perpendicular to that tile, this means that $d\vec{A}$ will also be perpendicular to the field vector $\vec{E}$. Since the dot product of two perpendicular vectors is zero, $\vec{E} \cdot d\vec{A} = 0$ for all tiles on that surface element.

Finally, it is fairly easy to calculate $\vec{E} \cdot d\vec{A}$ for tiles on a surface element that is always perpendicular to the field and arranged so that the field has the same magnitude at every point on the surface. Then the field vectors and tile vectors will be parallel (or antiparallel) at all points on this surface element, so for every tile $\vec{E} \cdot d\vec{A} = E\,dA\cos\theta = \pm E\,dA$, since the angle θ between $\vec{E}$ and $d\vec{A}$ either 0° or 180°. The sign is positive if the field vectors point toward the closed surface's exterior (because then $\theta = 0°$) and negative if the field vectors point toward its interior (because then $\theta = 180°$). Since we have designed the surface portion so that $E = \text{mag}(\vec{E})$ has the same value at each tile, the total flux through this portion of surface is simply

$$\sum_{\text{all tiles}} \vec{E} \cdot d\vec{A} = \pm E \sum_{\text{all tiles}} dA = \pm EA \tag{E12.8}$$

where A is the total area of the surface element.

So the scheme is that you should to try to construct your closed surface entirely out of surface elements that fall into one of these three categories. Assume that some kind of symmetry argument determines the direction of the field and specifies that its magnitude depends on some single variable. If at all possible, you should construct your closed surface entirely out of surface elements such that

1. the field is zero everywhere on the surface element,
2. the surface element everywhere parallel to the field, and/or
3. the surface element is both perpendicular to the field and has constant value of the variable on which the field magnitude might depend.

Having at least one surface element of the last type is usually essential, because only when the sum of $\vec{E} \cdot d\vec{A}$ is *not* zero for a surface element does Gauss's law nontrivially link the field's magnitude on that surface to the presence of charge inside it. Therefore it is often best to start by constructing a surface element of this type, and then use elements of the other type to complete the surface (if necessary) so that it entirely encloses a volume.

In some situations, you may not be able find a surface that satisfies *both* of the criteria for a surface of type 3. Under such circumstances, you should choose to satisfy whichever criterion makes evaluating $\vec{E} \cdot d\vec{A}$ easiest, but doing the sum will not be nearly as straightforward as in the case shown in equation E12.8 (it will usually involve doing an actual integral).

E12.3 The Shell Theorem

In chapter E3, I claimed that the electric field *outside* a uniformly charged spherical shell is as if the shell's total charge were located at its center, and the electric field in the empty space *inside* the shell is zero. We can easily use Gauss's law to prove these assertions, and indeed show that these descriptions apply to spherically symmetric charge distributions in general.

Example E12.1 The Field Outside a Spherical Charge Distribution

Problem Use Gauss's law to prove that the electric field at a point P *outside* of *any* spherically symmetric charge distribution is as if the distribution's total electric charge were concentrated at its center.

Use Symmetry We saw in example E3.3 that the symmetry implies that the electric field vector $\vec{E}$ at any point P inside or outside *any* spherically symmetric charge distribution must point either directly away from or toward the distribution's center O. Moreover, $E = \text{mag}(\vec{E})$ can depend at most on the distance r that P is from the center.

Choose a Gaussian Surface In this case, we can choose our Gaussian surface to be a sphere whose center coincides with the distribution's center and whose radius r is the same as that of the point P where we want to evaluate the field. Note that if P is outside the distribution, then $r > R$, where R is distribution's outer radius (see figure E12.2). The distribution's electric field $\vec{E}$, since it points radially outward or inward, is perpendicular to this surface, and since this is a surface of constant r, $E = \text{mag}(\vec{E})$ will be constant on the surface and have the

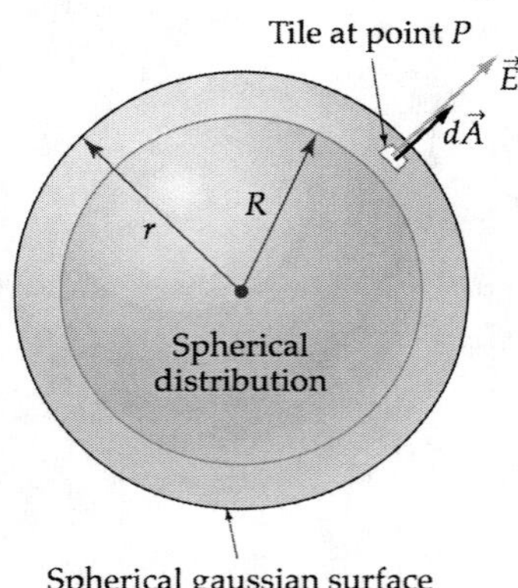

Figure E12.2
This figure shows an appropriate gaussian surface for determining the field at a point *P* outside a spherical charge distribution.

same magnitude as the electric field at *P*. Such a surface is itself closed, so we do not need any additional surface elements to construct a closed surface.

Calculate $\oint \vec{E} \cdot d\vec{A}$. The value of $\vec{E} \cdot d\vec{A}$ an arbitrary tile on such a surface is $\vec{E} \cdot d\vec{A} = E\,dA\cos 0° = E\,dA$ if $\vec{E}$ points outward and $E\,dA\cos 180° = -E\,dA$ if it points inward. Let us define E_r to be the component of $\vec{E}$ in the radial (outward) direction at *P* (and thus at all points on our gaussian surface):

$$E_r = \begin{cases} +E \text{ if } \vec{E} \text{ is outward} \\ -E \text{ if } \vec{E} \text{ is inward} \end{cases} \quad \text{and} \quad \vec{E} = E_r\hat{r} \tag{E12.9}$$

We see then that $\vec{E} \cdot d\vec{A} = E_r\,dA$ in both cases. Since $E_r = \pm E$ is the same at all points on a surface of constant *r*, the net flux through all tiles on our Gaussian surface is simply

$$\oint \vec{E} \cdot d\vec{A} = E_r \oint dA = 4\pi r^2 E_r \tag{E12.10}$$

since the total area of a spherical surface of radius *r* is $4\pi r^2$.

Apply Gauss's Law Gauss's law then implies that

$$\oint \vec{E} \cdot d\vec{A} = \frac{Q_{\text{enc}}}{\varepsilon_0} \Rightarrow 4\pi r^2 E_r = \frac{Q_{\text{enc}}}{\varepsilon_0} \Rightarrow E_r = \frac{Q_{\text{enc}}}{4\pi\varepsilon_0 r^2} \tag{E12.11}$$

Now, a gaussian surface having the same radius as our external point *P* encloses the distribution's net charge *Q* by definition, and since $\vec{E} = E_r\hat{r}$, we have

$$\vec{E} = \frac{Q}{4\pi\varepsilon_0 r^2}\hat{r} = \frac{kQ}{r^2}\hat{r} \tag{E12.12}$$

Evaluation This is exactly the field we would expect at the point *P* if the distribution's total charge were a point charge located at the distribution's center.

Example E12.2 The Field Inside a Charged Spherical Shell

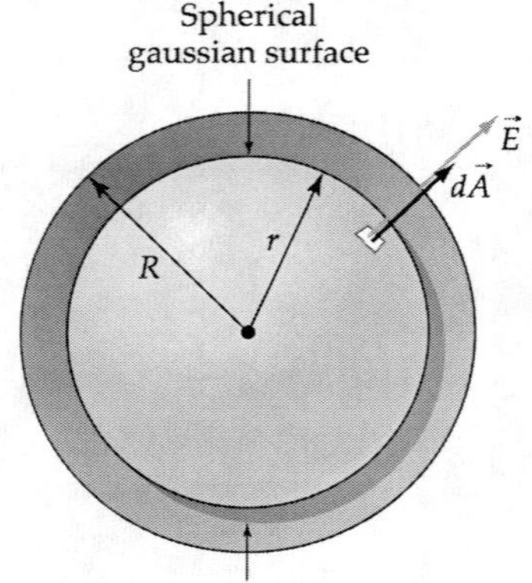

Figure E12.3
This figure shows an appropriate gaussian surface for determining the field at a point *P* inside a spherical charge distribution. (The field vector here is hypothetical.)

Problem Consider now a spherical shell that has a uniformly distributed charge on its surface. Use Gauss's law to prove that the electric field at *any* point *P inside* the surface charge is zero.

Model The situation here is exactly the same as in example E12.1 except that the point *P* where we want to evaluate the field is *inside* the surface charge. Since we want to use a spherical gaussian surface that has the same radius as *P*, our Gaussian surface will thus have a radius $r < R$, where *R* is the radius of the surface charge (see figure E12.3). Even so, the net flux through this gaussian surface is still $4\pi r^2 E_r$ (see equation E12.10, and Gauss's law still implies that $E_r = Q_{\text{enc}}/4\pi\varepsilon_0 r^2$ (see equation E12.11). The difference is that since there is no net charge inside the sphere by hypothesis, our gaussian sphere in this case encloses no net charge: $Q_{\text{enc}} = 0$.

Solution Equation E12.11 therefore implies that $E_r = 0$. This argument applies to any arbitrary point *P* inside the surface, so the electric field due to the surface charge must be zero *everywhere* inside the spherical object.

Evaluation This is what we set out to show.

If you compare the relative simplicity of this argument with the complexity of the mathematical arguments in problem E3S.7, you can perhaps appreciate the value of Gauss' law! In situations with lots of symmetry, an argument based on Gauss' law is usually *much* simpler than a calculation using the methods of chapter E3.

Note also that if we model a point particle as being essentially a very tiny sphere, then symmetry implies that the field of such a particle at rest must be radial and equation E12.12 clearly indicates that the combination of symmetry and Gauss' law implies that its field is $\vec{E} = (kq/r^2)\hat{r}$ at a point a distance r from the particle's center. We see, therefore, that Gauss' law does indeed imply Coulomb's law for the electric field of a point particle at rest.

Gauss's law is equivalent to Coulomb's law for a charged particle at rest

Now *you* try the method! The following exercises walk you through the equivalent steps for calculating the external field of a planar slab that extends infinitely in the y and z directions but has finite width W in the x direction, and which carries a uniformly distributed charge with charge density ρ (see example E10.3). Try to figure out each step on your own, and then look at the answer in at the end of the chapter before proceeding to the next self-test.

The electric field of an infinite, uniformly charged slab

Self-Test E12X.1

Use Symmetry Argue that the electric field at any point inside or outside the slab must have the form $\vec{E} = [E_x, 0, 0]$, where E_x is independent of y and z and is zero on the slab's central plane (which is midway between its surfaces).

Self-Test E12X.2

Choose a Gaussian Surface Select an appropriate gaussian surface that includes a point P outside the distribution in the $+x$ direction. (*Hint:* Take advantage knowing the direction of $\vec{E}$ and where it is zero.)

Self-Test E12X.3

Calculate $\oint \vec{E} \cdot d\vec{A}$. Show that summing $\vec{E} \cdot d\vec{A}$ over your surface leads to

$$\oint \vec{E} \cdot d\vec{A} = E_x A \qquad \text{(E12.13)}$$

where A is the area of the gaussian surface element that contains point P.

Self-Test E12X.4

Apply Gauss's Law Use Gauss's law in integral form to show that the electric field outside the slab (on the $+x$ side) is given by $E_x = \frac{1}{2}\sigma / \varepsilon_0$, independent of x, where $\sigma =$ charge per unit area $= \rho W$.

E12.4 Integrating Ampere's Law

In section E12.1 I introduced a trick for integrating Gauss's law. We can use an analogous trick for evaluating Ampere's law. Consider a surface (real or imaginary) in space. In this case, we need not consider a closed surface (that is, a surface that completely encloses a volume) but rather any surface with a well-defined boundary. Imagine dividing this surface up into tiny square tiles, each with its own nose vector and side vectors. Figure E12.4 illustrates a simple flat rectangular surface divided up into four tiles.

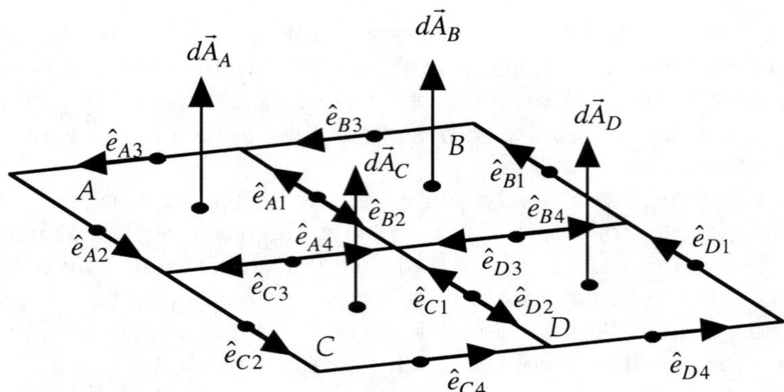

Figure E12.4
Four adjoining tiles and their edge vectors. The four vertical vectors are the tile's vectors. The vectors in the horizontal plane are the tiles' edge vectors. Note that the edge vectors at the center of each interior edge are opposite in direction.

Summing the curls over the tiles on a surface

If we sum the definition of the curl given by equation E11.2a over the four tiles shown in figure E12.4, we get

$$\text{c}\vec{\text{url}}(\vec{\boldsymbol{B}}_A)\cdot\hat{n}_A + \text{c}\vec{\text{url}}(\vec{\boldsymbol{B}}_B)\cdot\hat{n}_B + \text{c}\vec{\text{url}}(\vec{\boldsymbol{B}}_C)\cdot\hat{n}_C + \text{c}\vec{\text{url}}(\vec{\boldsymbol{B}}_D)\cdot\hat{n}_D$$

$$= \frac{1}{L}\Big[\, \vec{\boldsymbol{B}}_{A1}\cdot\hat{e}_{A1} + \vec{\boldsymbol{B}}_{A2}\cdot\hat{e}_{A2} + \ldots + \vec{\boldsymbol{B}}_{D6}\cdot\hat{e}_{D6}\Big] \tag{E12.14}$$

where again I have dropped the limit because we will assume that the tile side-length L is infinitesimal (so the limit has effectively been taken already). Notice that again the terms in the sum that come from all *internal* edges cancel in pairs: for example, since $\vec{\boldsymbol{B}}_{A1} = \vec{\boldsymbol{B}}_{B2}$ and $\hat{e}_{A1} = -\hat{e}_{B2}$, we have

$$\vec{\boldsymbol{B}}_{A1}\cdot\hat{e}_{A1} + \vec{\boldsymbol{B}}_{B2}\cdot\hat{e}_{B2} = \vec{\boldsymbol{B}}_{A1}\cdot(\hat{e}_{A1}+\hat{e}_{B2}) = \vec{\boldsymbol{B}}_{A1}\cdot 0 = 0 \tag{E12.15}$$

If we multiply both sides of equation E12.14 by the area $dA = L^2$ of a tile, then the equation becomes

$$\sum_{\text{all tiles } j} \text{c}\vec{\text{url}}(\vec{\boldsymbol{B}})_j\cdot d\vec{A}_j = \sum_{\substack{\text{all } exterior\\ \text{tile sides } i}} \vec{\boldsymbol{B}}_i\cdot d\vec{S}_i \tag{E12.16}$$

where $d\vec{A}_j = dA\,\hat{n}_j$ is the tile vector for the jth tile, and $d\vec{S}_i \equiv L\,\hat{e}_i$ is the counter-clockwise-oriented side vector for the *i*th exposed tile edge along the surface's periphery.

Generalizing to an infinite number of tiles

This last expression works for any number of tiles. Now, we can *always* divide an arbitrary surface in space into a sum of infinitesimal tiles, and (as discussed in problem E12S.11), we don't have to exactly follow the jagged contour of the square boxes but can evaluate $\vec{\boldsymbol{B}}_i\cdot d\vec{S}_i$ for infinitesimal steps tangent to a surface's smooth boundary. If we substitute Ampere's law $\text{c}\vec{\text{url}}(\vec{\boldsymbol{B}}) = \varepsilon_0^{-1}(\vec{J}/c)$ into the above, reverse the order of the equation, and express the sums in the more conventional integral notation, we get the much prettier equation

$$\oint \vec{\boldsymbol{B}}\cdot d\vec{S} = \frac{1}{\varepsilon_0 c}\int \vec{J}\cdot d\vec{A} \tag{E12.17}$$

Again, don't be spooked by the integral symbols: these are simply meant to represent sums over infinitesimal quantities. Also, the circle in the left-hand integral sign is only a reminder that we are doing the sum over the closed curve that represents the outer boundary of our surface (we do *not* use a circle in the integral sign on the right because we are *not* doing this sum of tile vectors over a necessarily closed surface, as we did in the integral form of Gauss's law).

Interpreting the $\int \vec{J}\cdot d\vec{A}$ term

The term on the right has a fairly simple conceptual interpretation. Remember that if a total current I flows through a cross-sectional area A in a wire, we have $I = JA$, where J is the magnitude of the current density $\vec{J}$. So if $\vec{J}$ near a given tile happens to be perpendicular to that tile's face (that is, parallel to its tile vector) then $\vec{J} \cdot d\vec{A} = J\,dA$ = the infinitesimal total current dI flowing through that tile. In fact, we can *always* interpret $|\vec{J} \cdot d\vec{A}|$ as being the current flowing through the tile's surface, no matter how $\vec{J}$ and $d\vec{A}$ are oriented. For example, if $\vec{J}$ and $d\vec{A}$ are perpendicular, then charge carriers are flowing parallel to the tile's surface, so none of the flowing charge is actually going *through* the tile. The fact that $\vec{J} \cdot d\vec{A} = 0$ in this context therefore makes perfect sense. If $\vec{J}$ and $d\vec{A}$ are opposite, then again $|\vec{J} \cdot d\vec{A}| = |-JA| = dI$ = the current flowing through the tile. (This also works for more general orientations.)

However, note that $\vec{J} \cdot d\vec{A}$ is a *signed* quantity: it can be negative if the angle between $\vec{J}$ and $d\vec{A}$ is greater than 90°. In such a case, $\vec{J} \cdot d\vec{A}$ is a quantity whose absolute value is equal to the total current through the tile's surface but whose sign indicates that it is flowing *backwards* through that surface, i.e. *against* the direction indicated by the tile vector.

Therefore, we can interpret $i_{enc} \equiv \int \vec{J} \cdot d\vec{A}$ as the "signed current enclosed" by the surface in question. This quantity is a scalar whose absolute value is equal to the total current flowing through all the tiles on the surface we are considering, and whose sign indicates whether charge is (on the average) moving through tiles in the direction that their tile vectors point (positive) or opposite to that direction (negative).

Having discussed this important quantity, we can now present our final version of the integral form of Ampere's law:

The integral form of Ampere's law

$$\oint \vec{\mathbb{B}} \cdot d\vec{S} = \frac{1}{\varepsilon_0}\left(\frac{i_{enc}}{c}\right) \quad \left[\text{or } \oint \vec{B} \cdot d\vec{S} = \mu_0 i_{enc}\right] \tag{E12.18}$$

Purpose: This equation links the behavior of a static magnetic field on the closed boundary of a surface with the total signed current i_{enc} flowing through that surface.

Symbols: $\oint$ is a shorthand notation for "sum over all infinitesimal steps around a closed curve" (the surface's boundary in this case), $d\vec{S}$ is one such step, $\vec{B}$ or $\vec{\mathbb{B}} = c\vec{B}$ is the magnetic field vector evaluated at a given step, $\varepsilon_0 = (4\pi k)^{-1}$ is the permittivity constant, $\mu_0 = 1/\varepsilon_0 c^2$ is the permeability constant, and c is the speed of light.

Limitations: This equation only applies to *static* magnetic fields. Each step must be small enough so that $\vec{B}$ is nearly uniform along its length and so that each step can be straight but still match the surface's boundary well. The surface can have arbitrary shape, but the sum on the left must be performed for all steps around the shape's boundary.

Note: The absolute value of $i_{enc} \equiv \int \vec{J} \cdot d\vec{A}$ is always the total current I (charge per unit time) that passes through the surface, but i_{enc} is negative if the current density $\vec{J}$ is flowing (in general) against the direction of the tile vectors $d\vec{A}$ for tiles on the surface in question.

Note that the direction one chooses for the tile vectors in the case of a general surface is somewhat arbitrary, unlike the case in Gauss's law, where the "outward" direction of a closed surface is always well-defined. It does not matter which sense you choose as long as you choose a self-consistent common direction for all tiles on the surface. Once you *have* chosen such a direction, however, the integral form of Ampere's law assumes that the step vectors $d\vec{S}$ go counterclockwise around the surface's boundary, just as they would for an individual tile. Figure E12.5 illustrates how this should go for a finite surface.

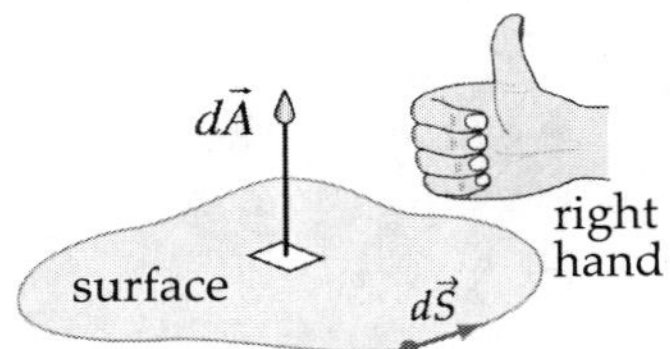

Figure E12.5
Step vectors $d\vec{S}$ should go counterclockwise around the edge of a surface when its tile vectors generally point upward. The diagram also shows a right hand rule for these directions.

E12.5 Using the Integral Form of Ampere's Law

A four-step process for calculating fields using the integral form of Ampere's law

When using Ampere's law to calculate the magnetic field of a static current distribution one uses a four-step process that is basically identical to the steps we used when applying Gauss law. The steps, when adapted for Ampere's law, read as follows:

1. ***Use Symmetry.*** You should first use symmetry and/or other arguments to determine as much as possible about the field's direction and magnitude at all points. Ampere's law will be easiest to apply when you know the field's precise direction at all points and you know at least what the field's magnitude does *not* depend on.
2. ***Choose an Amperian Loop.*** You should then pick an imaginary surface with boundary shaped so that it is easy to calculate $\oint \vec{B} \cdot d\vec{S}$ around that boundary. We call the closed boundary curve an **amperian loop**.
3. ***Calculate*** $\oint \vec{B} \cdot d\vec{S}$ around the amperian loop. If you have chosen your boundary curve well, this should be easy.
4. ***Apply Ampere's Law*** to finish determining the field.

Choosing an amperian loop

As with Gauss's law, the crucial part of this process is the second step; choosing your amperian loop well is the key to making your solution easy. As is the case with Gaussian surfaces, the appropriate amperian loop is not always obvious, but there are some basic guidelines that you can follow.

Calculating $\oint \vec{B} \cdot d\vec{S}$ for a particular section of the loop is *easiest* if either $\vec{B} = 0$ or $\vec{B}$ is perpendicular to the step vectors at all points on that section, because either way, $\vec{B} \cdot d\vec{S} = 0$ for all steps in the section, meaning that that section contributes nothing to the sum. It is also very easy to calculate the contribution made by a loop section chosen so that $\vec{B}$ is either *parallel* or *antiparallel* to the step vectors $d\vec{S}$ in that section *and* $B = \text{mag}(\vec{B})$ is constant at all steps along the section. Then $\vec{B} \cdot d\vec{S} = B\,dS \cos\theta = \pm B\,dS$ (since θ is either 0° or 180°), and the section's contribution to the sum is simply

$$\int \vec{B} \cdot d\vec{S} = \pm B \int dS = \pm BL \qquad \text{(E12.19)}$$

where L is the total length of the segment. If your symmetry argument tells you that B can at most depend on some variable (call it x), then B will be constant along any curve of constant x.

So the trick is to construct a complete closed loop out of sections that each fit into one of the categories above.

E12.6 The Field of an Axial Current Distribution

How we can apply the method to an infinite cylindrical current distribution

Consider now an axial current distribution, which consists of an infinite cylindrical object (i.e. an object that is unchanged either by rotation around its central axis or sliding along its central axis) that carries a steady current parallel to that axis. Infinite cylindrical wires, straight pipes, or straight coaxial cables could qualify as axial distributions. What does Ampere's law tell us about the external magnetic field of such a distribution?

Use Symmetry In example E9.2, we showed that the magnetic field created by an axial current distribution must point circularly around the distribution's central axis (that is, tangent to circles whose planes are perpendicular to that axis) and that its magnitude must depend at most on the distance r one is from that central axis (see Figure E12.6).

Choose an Amperian Loop Since the magnetic field can at most depend on r, a convenient Amperian loop would be a circle of radius r around the central axis (see the gray loop in figure E12.6) that lies in a plane perpendicular to that axis and goes through the point P where we would like to evaluate the field. The magnetic field strength $\mathbb{B} \equiv \text{mag}(\vec{\mathbb{B}})$ is the same at all points along this loop, and if we choose the step vectors to point counterclockwise around the loop, then $\vec{\mathbb{B}}$ is either parallel or antiparallel to the step vector at every point.

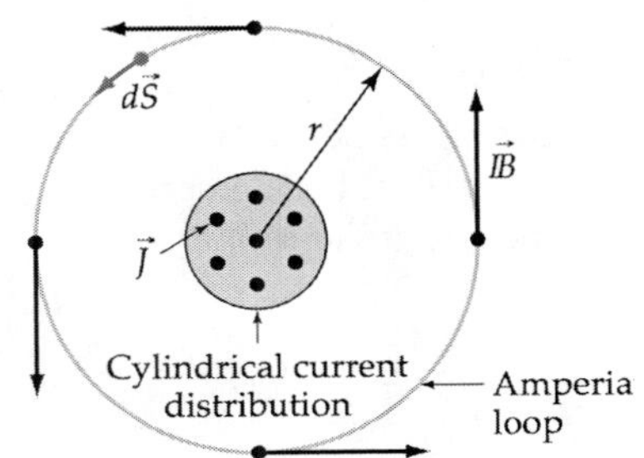

Figure E12.6
Magnetic field vectors and an appropriate amperian loop for an infinite cylindrical current distribution. This is a cross-sectional view, with the dots indicating current flowing toward us.

Calculate $\oint \vec{\mathbb{B}} \cdot d\vec{S}$. The net magnetic circulation around the loop is therefore $\oint \vec{\mathbb{B}} \cdot d\vec{S} = \pm \mathbb{B} \oint dS = \pm \mathbb{B}(2\pi r)$, where the positive result applies if the field goes counterclockwise around the loop and the negative result if the field goes clockwise.

Apply Ampere's Law If the point P is outside the charge distribution, then our amperian loop completely encloses whatever total current I the distribution carries. Ampere's law in this case then tells us that

$$\oint \vec{\mathbb{B}} \cdot d\vec{S} = \frac{1}{\varepsilon_0}\left(\frac{i_{\text{enc}}}{c}\right) \quad \Rightarrow \quad \pm \mathbb{B}(2\pi r) = \frac{1}{\varepsilon_0}\left(\frac{I}{c}\right) \tag{E12.20}$$

We know that i_{enc} is positive here since in figure E12.6, the step vectors go counterclockwise around the loop from our viewpoint, implying that the tile vectors for tiles on the surface enclosed by the loop point at us, and the current also flows toward us, so $\vec{J} \cdot d\vec{A}$ will be positive. To make the signs agree on both sides of this expression, we must choose the positive sign in front of $\mathbb{B}$, so $\vec{\mathbb{B}}$ must go counterclockwise around the circle.

Self-Test E12X.5

Show that this result is consistent with the wire rule.

Solving for $\mathbb{B}$, we find that the magnetic field strength at points along this loop (and thus at the point P) is

The magnetic field outside an infinite cylindrical current distribution

$$\mathbb{B} = \frac{I}{2\pi\varepsilon_0 c r} \quad \text{or} \quad B = \frac{\mu_0 I}{2\pi r} \tag{E12.21}$$

As discussed previously, this equation is a useful approximation whenever the point P is much closer to the distribution's central axis than to the nearest point where the distribution starts to deviate from being axially symmetric.

Self-Test E12X.6

The magnetic field inside an infinite pipe is zero

Use Ampere's law to prove that if the cylindrical current distribution is a circular pipe with a hollow interior, the magnetic field is *zero* in the hollow interior. (*Hint:* Remember that symmetry implies that a nonzero magnetic field *inside* the distribution would have to point circularly around the axis just as it does outside the distribution.)

Self-Test E12X.7

Consider a planar conducting slab that is infinite in the y and z directions but has a finite width W in the x direction and conducts a uniformly distributed current in the $+y$ direction. What would be a good amperian loop for calculating this slab's magnetic field?

E12.7 The Mystery du Jour

The complete set of field equations for static electric and magnetic fields

In chapters E10 and E11, we discussed the following local field equations:

$$\text{div}(\vec{E}) = \frac{\rho}{\varepsilon_0} \tag{E12.22a}$$

$$\text{div}(\vec{B}) = 0 \tag{E12.22b}$$

$$\vec{\text{curl}}(\vec{B}) = \frac{1}{\varepsilon_0}\left(\frac{\vec{J}}{c}\right) \tag{E12.22c}$$

$$\vec{\text{curl}}(\vec{E}) = 0 \tag{E12.22d}$$

Two of these field equations (E12.22a and E12.22c) connect the behavior of the field at a point to the presence of charge or current at that point. Two of these field equations (E12.22b and E12.22d) describe restrictions on the type of fields that are physically possible. These equations seem very pleasing, symmetrical, and complete. By virtue of being local field equations, it is at least possible that they are consistent with special relativity. In this chapter, we have also learned powerful techniques for integrating these equations to calculate the fields created by charged or current-carrying objects. What can we lack?

You may have noticed, however, that particularly when talking about the last two equations, I have been careful to say that these equations only apply to static fields. The fact is that the two curl equations are not yet consistent with the theory of relativity, and so do not yet correctly handle dynamic fields.

How we know that these equations are not complete

One can easily see that something is wrong as follows. Consider the case of a loop moving through a nonuniform magnetic field discussed in section E8.4. There we saw that because charge carriers are dragged along with the loop, they experience magnetic forces that drive a current through the wire. The magnetic force law provides a very clear explanation of this effect in that context, an explanation well-supported by experiment.

However, consider analyzing this situation in the reference frame in which the loop is at rest. In this frame, the loop is not moving, so the charges are not moving in the magnetic field. Charge carriers at rest cannot respond to a magnetic field, so (no matter what the magnetic field is in that frame), the magnetic field cannot drive them around the loop. Yet the principle of relativity asserts that the same thing must be observed to happen in both frames, and experiments support this conclusion (the wire gets hot no matter how we observe it). Therefore, *something* must be driving the charge carriers through the wire even when the loop is at rest. Only an *electric* field can exert a force charge carriers that are initially at rest. But as discussed at the end of chapter E11, if an electric field is driving this current, it must have nonzero curl, which violates equation E12.22d! Something is wrong or incomplete here.

Our task in the next chapter is to add the missing terms to the last two equations above that will allow them to become fully relativistically consistent. Once we have these terms in place, we will have a complete and beautifully powerful theory of electromagnetism.

TWO-MINUTE PROBLEMS

E12T.1 Imagine that we know from some kind of symmetry argument the electric field in a certain region everywhere points in the $+y$ direction and has a magnitude that depends only on y. For which of the following closed Gaussian surfaces would it be easiest to calculate the net flux of a electric field fitting this description?

A. A cubical surface oriented so that two opposite faces are perpendicular to the y axis
B. A spherical surface centered on the origin
C. A cylindrical can-like surface oriented with its central axis perpendicular to the y axis
D. A pyramid-like surface whose bottom plane is perpendicular to the y axis.

E12T.2 Imagine that we place a positively charged particle inside an arbitrarily shaped closed gaussian surface, as shown part a of the drawing below, and calculate the value of $\oint \vec{E} \cdot d\vec{A}$ for this surface and the magnitude of the electric field at point P. We then bring in an identical particle, park it just *outside* the gaussian surface, as shown in part b of the drawing and again calculate $\oint \vec{E} \cdot d\vec{A}$ for the surface and mag($\vec{E}$) at point P.
(a) How does mag($\vec{E}$) at point P change?
(b) How does $\oint \vec{E} \cdot d\vec{A}$ for the surface change?

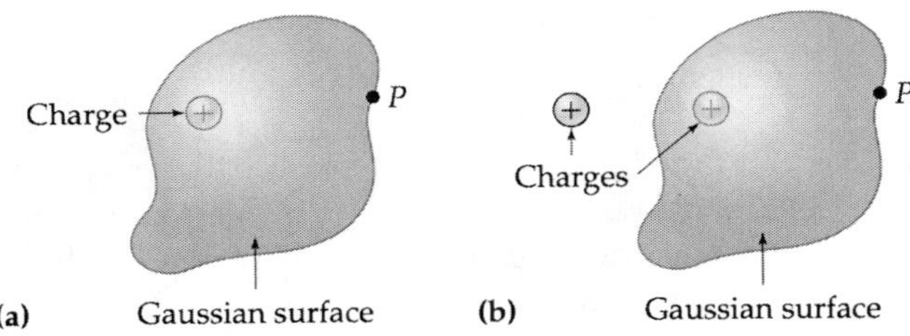

A. The quantity increases.
B. The quantity decreases.
C. The quantity remains the same.
D. The quantity changes, but whether it increases or decreases depends on details not given.
E. The quantity may nor may not change, depending on details not given.

Situation for problems E12T.3 and E12T.4: The drawing below shows field-arrow diagrams for some hypothetical electric or magnetic fields. Assume that the field is independent of position in the direction perpendicular to the drawing. What can we say from these field diagrams about the charge or current present within the region enclosed by the dashed line? (*Hints:* The gray surface in each drawing represents the cross-section of a possible gaussian surface or amperian loop that you might use to help you answer the question. In drawing *c*, the vectors all have the same magnitude and point circularly around the point O.)

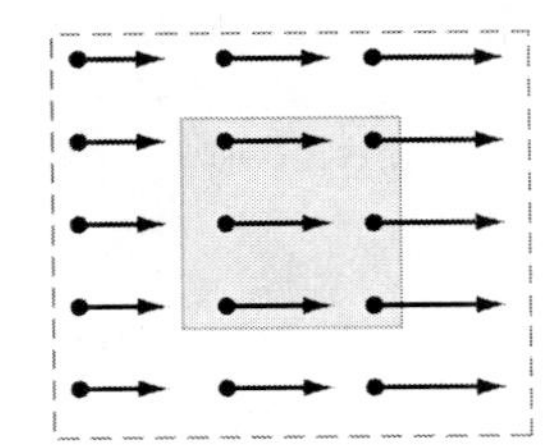

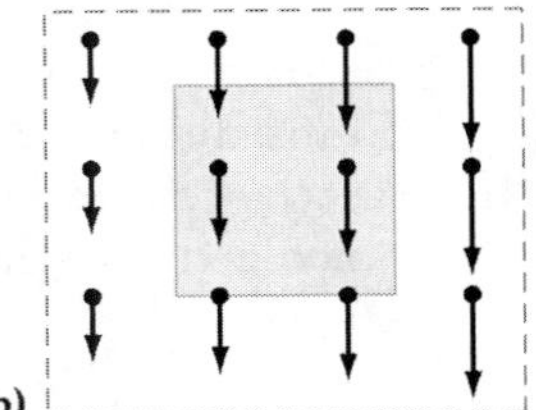

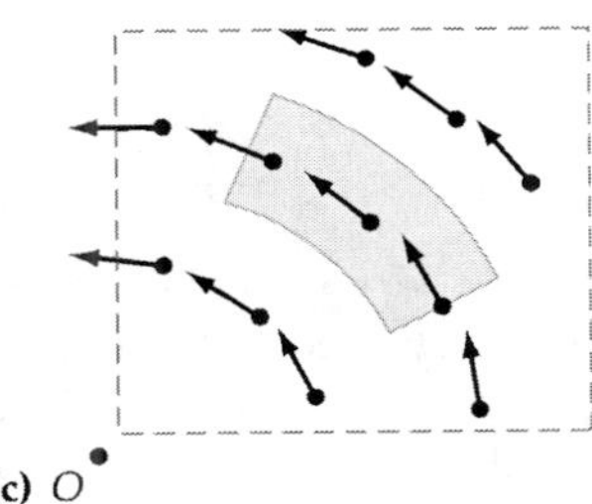

E12T.3 If the field is electric, there is within the region
E12T.4 If the field is magnetic, there is within the region

A. no charge/current *anywhere*
B. positive charge or positive i_{enc} *somewhere*
C. negative charge or negative i_{enc} *somewhere*
D. charge or i_{enc} *somewhere*, whose sign depends on details not given.
E. positive charge or positive i_{enc} *everywhere*
F. negative charge or negative i_{enc} *everywhere*
T. nothing definitive we can say

E12T.5 A friend claims that in a certain region of space, a certain static magnetic field being measured in an experiment points radially outward from some central point with a radial component of $\boldsymbol{B}_r \propto r^{-1}$. Such a field cannot exist because

A. It violates Gauss's law for electric fields
B. It violates Gauss's law for magnetic fields
C. It violates Ampere's law
D. It cannot be a static field
E. (Specify another reason)

E12T.6 Consider an amperian loop in a plane perpendicular to our line of sight, and imagine that the step vectors $d\vec{s}$ along the loop point clockwise as we view them. The quantity i_{enc} is positive if current flowing through the surface enclosed by the loop

A. goes toward our right
B. goes toward our left
C. goes away from us
D. goes toward us
E. goes clockwise around the loop
F. goes in some other direction (specify)

HOMEWORK PROBLEMS

Basic Skills

E12B.1 The drawing below shows two electric dipoles, each consisting of point charges q and $-q$ separated by a distance d. What is the value of $\oint \vec{E} \cdot d\vec{A}$ for each of the five closed surfaces shown in cross-section in the diagram?

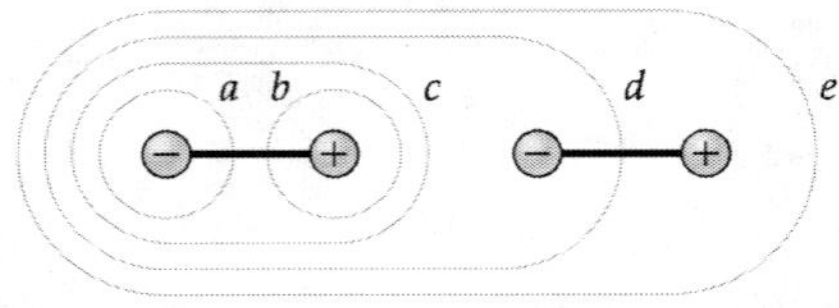

E12B.2 The drawing below shows two small permanent magnets. What is $\oint \vec{B} \cdot d\vec{A}$ for each of the five closed surfaces shown in cross-section in the diagram? (*Hint:* What would be the integral form of Gauss's law for the magnetic field?)

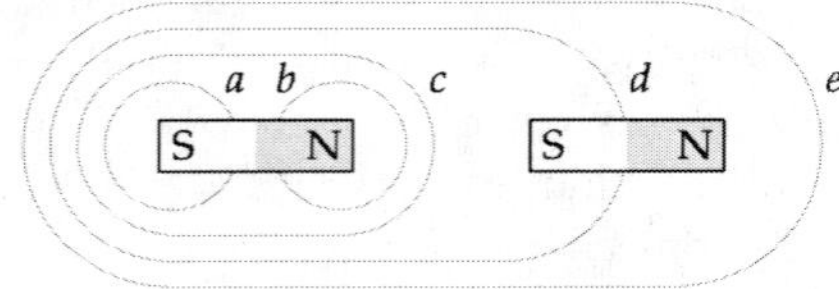

E12B.3 Check that Ampere's law has the same units on both sides.

E12B.4 The drawing below shows a cross-sectional view of a nested pair of thin infinite cylindrical pipes. The inner pipe has a radius of R and carries a uniformly distributed current toward the viewer. The outer pipe has a radius of $2R$ and carries the same total uniformly distributed current directly away from the viewer. Draw a graph of the electric field as a function of r for $r = 0$ to $r = 3R$.

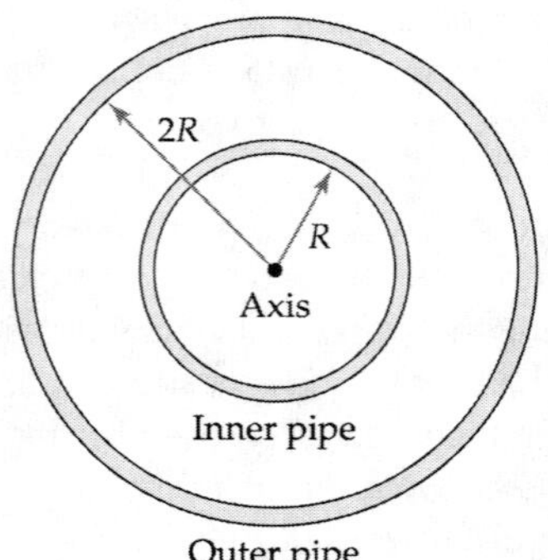

E12B.5 Imagine that the magnetic field in a certain region of space points in the +z direction and has a magnitude $B = ax^2$, where a is some constant. Consider a square Amperian loop with sides of length L in the xz plane with one corner at the origin. Assume that the step vectors $d\vec{S}$ go counterclockwise around this loop when we view it with the y axis facing us. Evaluate $\oint \vec{B} \cdot d\vec{S}$ for this loop in terms of a and L.

E12B.6 Imagine that the magnetic field vectors in a certain region of space are always tangent to a circle drawn around the x axis perpendicular to that axis. The field has a magnitude of $B = ar^2$, where r is the distance from the x axis and a is some constant. Consider a circular Amperian loop of radius R centered on and perpendicular to the x axis. Evaluate the circulation for this loop in terms of a and R, and explain why there are two possible values for the result.

E12B.7 The drawing below shows four wires, each carrying current perpendicular to the plane of the figure. The currents all have the same magnitude I. What is the value of $\oint \vec{B} \cdot d\vec{S}$ for each of the five closed loops shown in the diagram?

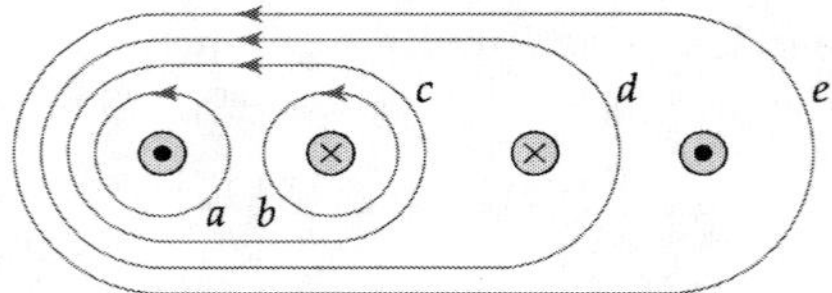

E12B.8 The drawing below shows four charges that have the same magnitude of charge q. What is the value of $\oint \vec{E} \cdot d\vec{S}$ for each of the five closed loops shown in the diagram?

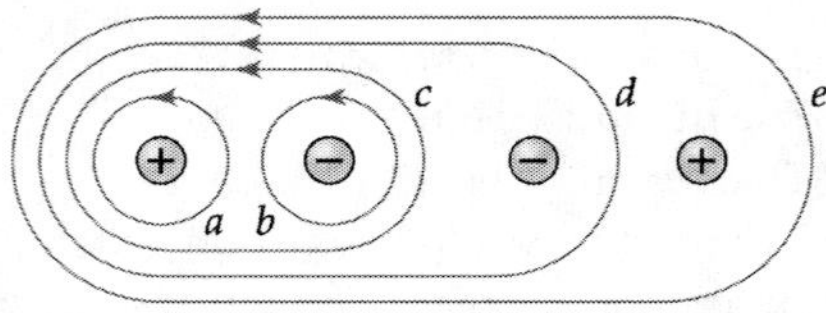

Synthetic

E12S.1 Consider a spherical ball of radius R with a charge Q uniformly distributed throughout its interior.

(a) Use symmetry and Gauss's law to find the electric field (magnitude and direction) *inside* the ball in terms of k, Q, R, and the distance r one is from the center.

(b) Draw a graph showing how the electric field magnitude depends on r from $r = 0$ to $r = 3R$.

E12S.2 Consider an infinite cylindrical rod of radius R that has charge with a uniform density ρ_0 throughout its interior.

(a) Use Gauss's law to determine the electric field (magnitude and direction) at points *outside* the rod in terms of k, ρ_0, R and the distance r one is from the rod's axis.

(b) Use Gauss's law to determine the electric field (magnitude and direction) at points *inside* the rod in terms of k, ρ_0, R and the distance r one is from the rod's axis.

(c) Draw a graph showing how the electric field magnitude depends on r from $r = 0$ to $r = 5R$.

E12S.3 Consider a uniformly charged infinite cylindrical pipe. Use Gauss's law to show that the electrical field in the hollow space enclosed by the pipe must be zero.

E12S.4 Consider the electric field at points just outside the surface of an arbitrary conducting object in static equilibrium.

(a) In chapter E4, we argued that the field vectors at points just outside a charged conductor must point perpendicular to the surface. Explain in your own words why this must be true.

(b) On an arbitrarily shaped conductor, the surface charge density may vary from place to place on the conductor. Consider a patch of area small enough so that the charge per unit area σ is essentially constant over the patch, and consider a small, pillbox-like gaussian surface that encloses such a patch, as shown in the drawing below. Use Gauss' law to show that the magnitude of the electric field at an arbitrary point P just outside the conductor is $E = \sigma / \varepsilon_0$, where σ is the charge per unit area on the patch of conductor nearest to P. Explain your reasoning very carefully

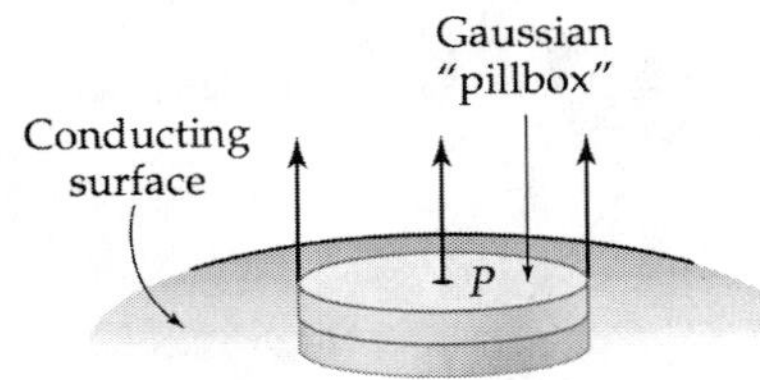

E12S.5 Imagine that in a different universe the radial component of the electric field of a point charge were given by $E_r = kQ / r^3$ instead of $E_r = kQ / r^2$ (assume that the field still points directly toward or a way from the charge, though). Show that Gauss's law would *not* be true in such a universe.

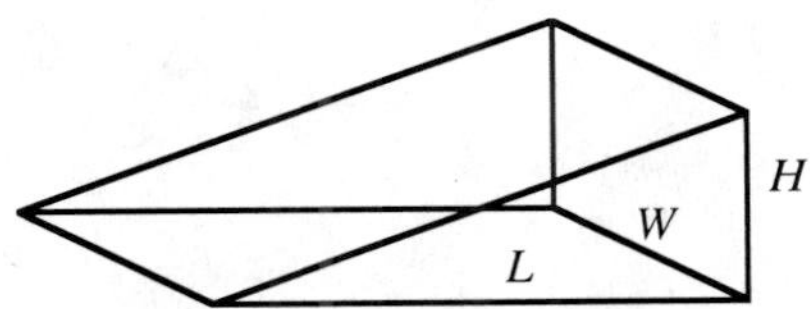

E12S.6 Prove that for arbitrary (small) values of L and H, the value of $\vec{E} \cdot d\vec{A}$ for the slanted tile shown in the drawing above is the same as the sum of $\vec{E} \cdot d\vec{A}$ for the horizontal and vertical tiles, as long as the surfaces are small enough that $\vec{E} \approx$ constant in the region. (*Hint:* You will find the component definition of the dot product useful if you define an appropriate coordinate system.) This illustrates that we can replace the jagged surface of a volume constructed of tiny cubes with a set of tiles matching a smoother surface enclosing the same volume.

E12S.7 Coulomb's law $\vec{F}_e = (kq_1q_2 / r^2)\hat{r}$ is very similar to Newton's law of gravitation $\vec{F}_g = -(Gm_1m_2 / r^2)\hat{r}$. Since (for static particles anyway) Coulomb's law is equivalent to Gauss's law, it follows that there should be a Gauss's law for gravitation as well.

(a) By comparing the definitions of the electric field vector $\vec{E}$ with that of the gravitational field vector $\vec{g}$, argue that the gravitational counterpart to the formula for the electric field of a point particle must be

$$\vec{g} = -\frac{Gm}{r^2}\hat{r} \tag{E12.23}$$

(b) Considering the ingredients of Gauss's law for the electric field and their gravitational counterparts, argue that Gauss' law for the gravitational field must be

$$\oint \vec{g} \cdot d\vec{A} = -4\pi G m_{\text{enc}} \tag{E12.24}$$

(c) Show that this formula works for a spherical Gaussian surface of arbitrary radius r surrounding a particle of mass m at its center.

E12S.8 Consider an infinite cylindrical wire of radius R whose central axis coincides with the x axis. The wire carries a current in the $+x$ direction that has a uniform current density $\vec{J}_0$. Use the four-step process to find the magnitude and direction of the magnetic field *inside* this wire.

E12S.9 Consider a planar conducting slab that extends infinitely in the y and z directions but has a finite width W in the x direction. Assume that a constant current flows in the $+y$ direction whose current density has the uniform magnitude J_0. Determine the magnetic field (magnitude and direction) at all points inside and outside the slab, and draw a quantitatively accurate graph of $\boldsymbol{B}(x)$ for $-W \geq x \geq +W$.

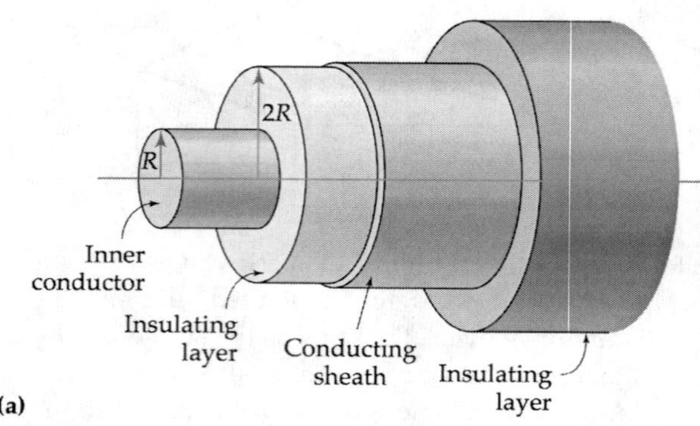

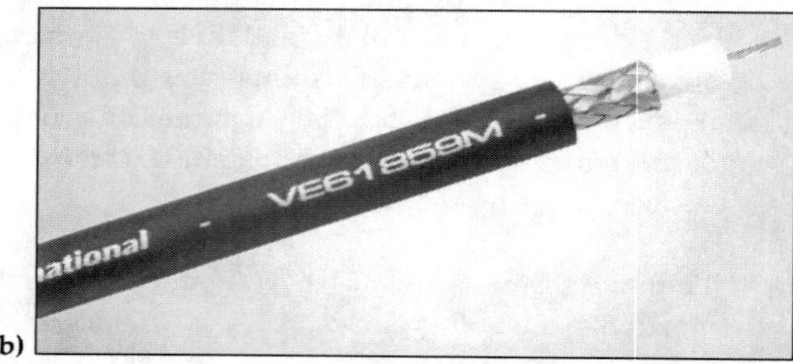

Figure E12.7
(a) A drawing showing the inner layers of a coaxial cable. The cable has been cut and stripped so that you can see inside, but you should consider it to be infinite and straight. (b) A photograph of a real coaxial cable.

E12S.10 Consider an infinite straight coaxial cable consisting of a cylindrical wire, surrounded by a layer of insulation, which is surrounded by a conducting sheath (like a pipe), which is surrounded by another insulating layer, as shown below. Assume that the radius of the inner conductor is R, the inner radius of the outer sheath is $2R$, and that the sheath has a negligible thickness. Assume that the inner wire carries a current of I toward the viewer, and the sheath carries the same magnitude of current in the opposite direction. Use the four-step process presented in this chapter to calculate the magnetic field inside the inner wire, between the wire and the sheath, and outside the cable, and present your results by drawing a quantitatively accurate graph of $\boldsymbol{B}(r)$ for $0 \le r \le 3R$.

E12S.11 Prove that for arbitrary (small) values of $\text{mag}(d\vec{S}_A)$ and $\text{mag}(d\vec{S}_B)$, the value of $\vec{B}\cdot d\vec{S}$ for the diagonal step shown in the drawing below is the same as the sum of $\vec{B}\cdot d\vec{S}$ for the horizontal and vertical steps if these steps are small enough that $\vec{B} \approx$ constant in the region. (*Hint:* You will find the component definition of the dot product useful if you define an appropriate coordinate system.) This shows that we can replace the jagged boundary of a surface constructed of square tiles with a set of steps matching a smoother curve enclosing the same surface.

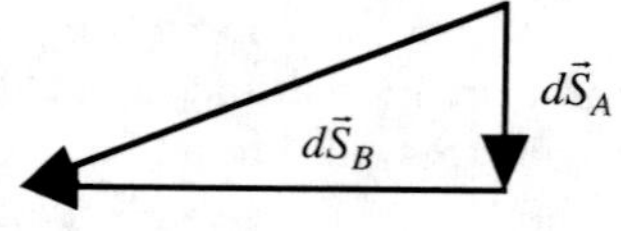

Rich-Context

E12R.1 Imagine that you have some coaxial cable that consists of a central core of wire of radius $R_1 = 0.40$ mm surrounded by an insulating layer, which in turn is surrounded by pipe-like conducting sheath with an inner radius of $R_2 = 1.2$ mm. It is often very important in computer or cable television applications to know the capacitance of the cables used. What is the capacitance per unit length of this particular cable? (*Hints:* Calculating the potential difference between the inner and outer conductors requires doing a simple integral.)

E12R.2 The space colony on the asteroid Tenebria has built a shuttle that travels in a straight tunnel drilled from the main colony dome through the asteroid's center to the main mining site on the exact opposite side of the spherical asteroid (see the drawing below). The asteroid has a diameter of 16 km and consists entirely of rock with an approximately constant density of 3200 kg/m^3. The shuttle requires no fuel: rather, it freely falls in the asteroid's own interior gravitational field throughout its trip from the dome to the mining site and back.

(a) Use Gauss's law for the gravitational field (see problem E12S.7) and the mathematics discussed in the chapter on harmonic oscillation (chapter N11) in unit N to determine how long it takes the shuttle to travel from the dome to the mining site.

(b) Compare this to the time required for a spaceship orbiting the asteroid just above its surface to travel between the two sites.

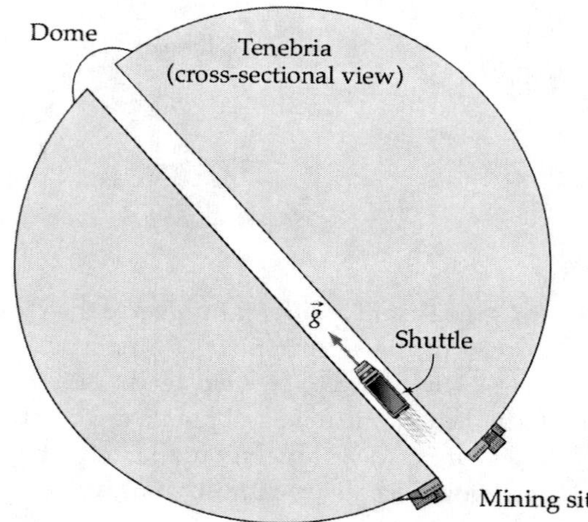

ANSWERS TO SELF-TESTS

E12X.1 See example E10.3 for the arguments required.

E12X.2 A suitable gaussian surface would be a rectangular box with one face lying on the slab's central plane, four sides parallel to the x direction (perpendicular to the slab), and an end cap parallel to the slab's surface having the same x coordinate as the point P. Note that $x = x_P$ = constant on the last surface.

E12X.3 The value of $\vec{E}\cdot d\vec{A}$ is zero for all tiles on the box's face that sits on the slab's central plane, because we have seen that $\vec{E}=0$ on the slab's central plane. The value of $\vec{E}\cdot d\vec{A}$ is zero for all tiles on the box's sides because these sides are parallel to the x axis and therefore parallel to $\vec{E}$, which means that the tile vectors $d\vec{A}$ for all tiles on these surfaces are *perpendicular* to $\vec{E}$. The tile vectors on the end cap all point in the $+x$ direction, Therefore $\vec{E}\cdot d\vec{A}$ = $E_x dA_x + E_y dA_y + E_z dA_z = E_x dA + 0 + 0$. Since the end cap is a surface of constant x, E_x is constant for all tiles on the surface. Therefore

$$\int \vec{E}\cdot d\vec{A} = E_x \int dA = E_x A \quad \text{(E12.25)}$$

where A is the total area of the end cap.

E12X.4 Assuming that the point P is outside the surface, the box extends from the slab's central plane to well outside of the slab. Since the distance between the central plane and the slab's surface is $\frac{1}{2}W$, the total volume the box encloses within the slab is $\frac{1}{2}WA$, so the total charge enclosed is $Q_{\text{enc}} = \frac{1}{2}\rho WA$. Gauss's law therefore implies that

$$E_x A = \tfrac{1}{2}\rho AW / \varepsilon_0$$

$$\Rightarrow \; E_x = \tfrac{1}{2}\rho W / \varepsilon_0 = \tfrac{1}{2}\sigma / \varepsilon_0 \quad \text{(E12.26)}$$

E12X.5 The wire rule says that if you stick your right thumb in the direction of the current carried by a wire, your curled right fingers indicate the direction that the magnetic field will go around the wire. In figure E12.6, the current is coming toward the viewer, so if you point your right thumb toward yourself, you should see your fingers wrapping counterclockwise around your thumb. This is consistent with the direction implied by Ampere's law, so Ampere's law is consistent with the wire rule.

E12X.6 Imagine a circular Amperian loop like that shown in figure E12.6, except with a radius r small enough so that the loop is entirely within the hollow space inside the pipe. The symmetry argument made in example E9.2 applies to *all* points inside or outside an infinite cylindrical current distribution, so it applies to the empty space inside the cylindrical pipe. If there is any magnetic field at all inside the pipe, summing $\vec{B}\cdot d\vec{S}$ around this loop will yield $\pm \mathbf{B}(2\pi r)$, just as it would be for a loop outside the distribution. But our loop in this case encloses only empty space, so i_{enc} = 0. Ampere's law thus implies that $\pm(2\pi r)\mathbb{B}$ = 0 for all r, which implies that $\vec{B}=0$ everywhere inside the pipe. (**Note:** Technically, Ampere's law does *not* require $\vec{B}$ to be zero at r = 0, but symmetry does. Here is a quick argument. The mirror rule implies that $\vec{B}$, if nonzero, must be perpendicular to any plane that contains the pipe's central axis, as discussed in example E9.2. At any point P off the axis, there is only a single plane that contains both the axis and P, so the direction of the magnetic field is well-defined. But there are an infinite number of possible mirror planes that contain both P and the axis if P lies *on* the axis. Since the magnetic field at P cannot be perpendicular to all of these planes, it must be zero.)

E12X.7 Choose a rectangular loop with one leg lying on the slab's central axis (where the magnetic field is zero), two sides perpendicular to the slab (and thus perpendicular to the magnetic field, so $\vec{B}\cdot d\vec{S}$ = 0 for steps along this leg0, and a leg parallel to the slab at whatever x-position one would like to calculate the field ($\vec{B}$ will be constant at points along this leg and be either parallel or antiparallel to the step vectors $d\vec{S}$ along this leg).

E13 Maxwell's Equations

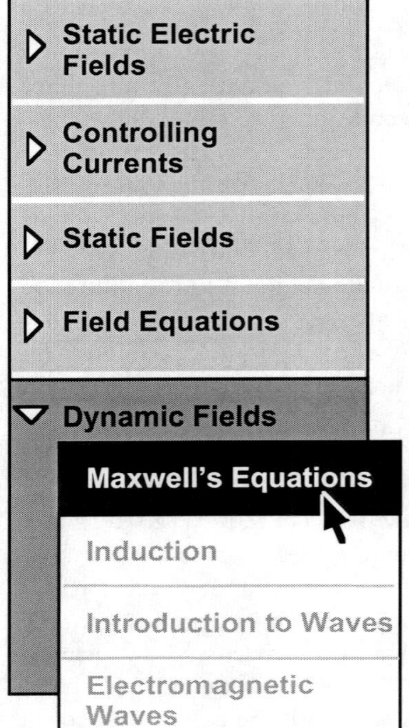

Chapter Overview

Introduction

In this chapter, we will see how relativity teaches us that the electric and magnetic fields are simply different manifestations of a unified electromagnetic field. We will also discover Faraday's law, the last of the four local electromagnetic field equations that comprise Maxwell's equations for the electromagnetic field.

Section E13.1: A Loop at Rest in a Varying Magnetic Field

This section introduces the mystery we hope to solve in this chapter. We can easily explain why charges in a loop that moves in a nonuniform magnetic field experience forces that push them around the loop. The principle of relativity implies that the charges should still flow in the rest frame of the loop. But in this frame, magnetic forces cannot act on the charges: only an electric field can exert forces on charges at rest. But where does this electric field come from, and why does it appear in this frame but not the original frame?

Section E13.2: Relativity and the Electromagnetic Field

We have a similar problem with a moving charged particle. In a frame where it is moving, it creates a magnetic field. But in its own rest frame it does not. It seems that here also we have a field whose existence depends on our choice of frame.

The solution to such puzzles is to recognize that the interaction between charged particles is mediated by an **electromagnetic field** that manifest itself as differing mixtures of electric and magnetic fields in different reference frames, This electromagnetic field exerts a force on a charged particle that we can calculate in *any* frame by using the **Lorentz force law:**

$$\vec{F}_{\text{em}} = q\left[\vec{E} + \frac{\vec{v}}{c} \times \vec{B}\right] \tag{E13.2}$$

Purpose: This equation describes the electromagnetic force $\vec{F}_{\text{em}}$ exerted by an electromagnetic field on a particle with charge q in frame where the particle moves with velocity $\vec{v}$.

Symbols: $\vec{E}$ and $\vec{B}$ are the electric and magnetic manifestations of the electromagnetic field in the frame in question, and c is the speed of light.

Limitations: This equation strictly applies only to *particles*.

Note: This equation is valid even at relativistic particle velocities if we define $\vec{F}_{\text{em}} \equiv d\vec{p}/dt$, where t is the coordinate time and $\vec{p}$ is the particle's relativistic momentum $m\vec{v}/[1-(v/c)^2]^{1/2}$.

If this force is zero (or nonzero) in any inertial frame, it must be zero (or nonzero) in *all* inertial frames, because all observers will agree about whether

Section E13.3: How the Fields Transform

If one knows the electric and magnetic fields in one frame (the "unprimed" frame), one can calculate them in a frame (the "primed" frame that is moving with speed v in the $+x$ direction with respect to the unprimed frame as follows:

$$\begin{bmatrix} E'_x \\ E'_y \\ E'_z \end{bmatrix} = \begin{bmatrix} E_x \\ \gamma(E_y - \beta\, B_z) \\ \gamma(E_z + \beta\, B_y) \end{bmatrix} \quad \text{and} \quad \begin{bmatrix} \boldsymbol{B}'_x \\ \boldsymbol{B}'_y \\ \boldsymbol{B}'_z \end{bmatrix} = \begin{bmatrix} \boldsymbol{B}_x \\ \gamma(\, B_y + \beta E_z) \\ \gamma(\, B_z - \beta E_y) \end{bmatrix} \tag{E13.3}$$

Purpose: These equations describe how, given $\vec{E}$ and $\vec{\boldsymbol{B}}$ in one inertial reference frame, we can calculate $\vec{E}'$ and $\vec{\boldsymbol{B}}'$ in another frame moving at a speed v in the $+x$ direction relative to the first.

Symbols: $[E_x, E_y, E_z]$ are the components of $\vec{E}$ (and similarly for $\vec{\boldsymbol{B}}$, $\vec{E}'$, and $\vec{\boldsymbol{B}}'$); $\beta = v/c$, and $\gamma \equiv (1 - v^2/c^2)^{-1/2}$.

Limitations: Both frames must be inertial and their corresponding coordinate axes must point in the same directions.

Note: The value of $\gamma \approx 1$ when $v << c$.

The remainder of the section illustrate how observers in different frames will offer coherent (but different) explanations of electromagnetic phenomena.

Section E13.4: Faraday's Law

With this background, we can analyze the moving loop case in full. We find that the electric field in the loop's frame is linked to the changing magnetic field in that frame. **Faraday's law** is the local field equation that describes the link:

$$\vec{\text{curl}}(\vec{E}) + \frac{1}{c}\frac{d\vec{\boldsymbol{B}}}{dt} = 0 \tag{E13.11}$$

Purpose: This local field equation links the curl of an electric field $\vec{E}$ at a point to the time derivative of the magnetic field $\vec{\boldsymbol{B}}$ at the same point in a given reference frame.

Symbols: $\vec{\text{curl}}(\vec{E})$ is the curl of $\vec{E}$, c is the speed of light.

Limitations: This equation applies without limits (until we venture into quantum field theory): it applies even to rapidly varying fields.

This equation states that a changing magnetic field can act as the source of an electric field. In the absence of a time-dependent magnetic field, it implies that an electric field can be described by a meaningful electrostatic potential ϕ.

Section E13.5: The Ampere-Maxwell Relation

Similarly, by examining the field of a moving charged particle, we discover that

$$\vec{\text{curl}}(\vec{\boldsymbol{B}}) - \frac{1}{c}\frac{d\vec{E}}{dt} = \frac{1}{\varepsilon_0}\left(\frac{\vec{J}}{c}\right) \tag{E13.19}$$

Purpose: This local field equation links the curl of a magnetic field $\vec{\boldsymbol{B}}$ at a point to the time derivative of the electric field $\vec{E}$ and the the current density $\vec{J}$ at that same same point in a given reference frame.

Symbols: ε_0 is the permittivity constant and c is the speed of light.

Limitations: This equation applies without limits (until we venture into quantum field theory): it applies even to rapidly varying fields.

Section E13.6: Maxwell's Equations

Equations E13.11 and E13.19, combined with Gauss's laws for the electric and magnetic fields, comprise **Maxwell's equations.** The section discusses a bit of the history of these equations, which represent one of the greatest achievements of the human mind.

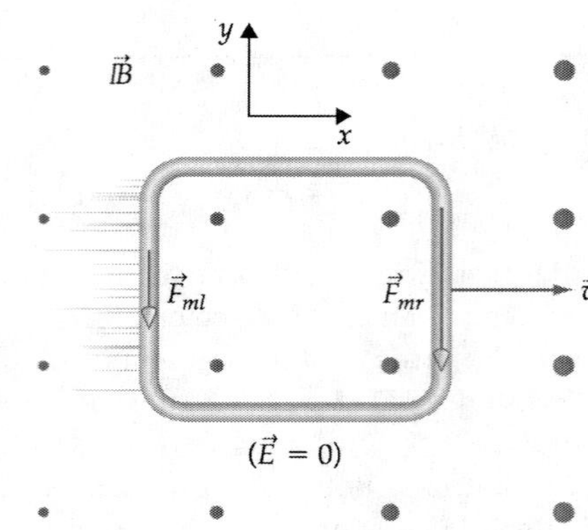

Figure E13.1
Charge carriers inside a loop moving through a nonuniform magnetic field experience different magnetic forces in the front and rear legs. This difference drives a current counterclockwise around the loop.

E13.1 A Loop at Rest in a Varying Magnetic Field

A review of the problem of a square loop moving through a nonuniform magnetic field

In section E8.4, we saw that a nonuniform magnetic field creates a current in a loop that moves through it. This is because (as illustrated in figure E13.1) as the loop carries its charge carriers through the field with essentially the same velocity as the loop's overall velocity $\vec{v}$, the charge carriers experience a magnetic force of magnitude $F_m = qv\boldsymbol{B}/c$ that is larger for charge carrier's in the loop's leg where the magnetic field is stronger than it is in opposite leg where the field is weaker. The net effect of these magnetic forces is that charge carriers are pushed around the loop in the direction favored by the larger force.

We cannot explain why the current flows in the frame of the loop itself

This all makes perfect sense in a reference frame where the loop is moving. However, consider the situation as viewed in the reference frame where the loop is at rest (call this the primed frame). In this frame, the loop and its charge carriers are at rest ($v' = 0$), so the magnetic force on those charge carriers is $F_m' = \text{mag}(q[\vec{v}'/c]\times \vec{\boldsymbol{B}}') = \text{mag}(q\vec{0}\times \vec{\boldsymbol{B}}') = 0$. One might conclude therefore that current will *not* flow around the loop in this frame.

But that conclusion would be absurd! One easy way to display the absurdity is to measure the loop's temperature. If current flows in the loop, collisions between the current carriers and the wire's atomic lattice will cause the wire to get warm. Now, the loop must either get warm in *both* frames or remain cold in both frames: the loop's temperature is not something about which observers in different frames can disagree. Since it is clear that current flows around the loop (and thus heats the loop) in the frame where the loop is moving, current *must* be observed to flow around the loop (and thus heat the loop) in the frame where it is at rest as well.

The problem is really only that we cannot in this frame explain *why* the current flows. Because the charge carriers are *not* moving in this frame, they cannot be affected by *any* magnetic field, no matter what the characteristics of that magnetic field might be. It is not relevant that the source of the nonuniform field may be moving with respect to the loop in this frame: the moving source simply creates a magnetic field that changes with time at fixed points around the loop as the source moves away. But even a *changing* magnetic field cannot exert forces on charges at rest.

We must have an electric field in the loop's frame. But how is this possible?

Now, an electric field *can* exert forces on charges at rest. We in fact *define* the electric field at a point to be the force per unit charge that a test charge placed *at rest* at that point feels. Therefore (by this definition!) there must be an *electric* field pushing charges around the loop in the loop's rest frame. We could in fact explain what we observe if we assume that in the loop's frame, there is an electric field that exerts the same downward forces that the magnetic field does in figure E13.1.

But where does this electric field come from? Moreover, how is it that this field exists in the loop's rest frame but not in the frame where the loop is moving (where the magnetic field suffices to explain the circulating current)? Is an electric field less real than a current in that it can be created or erased by simply going to a different reference frame?

E13.2 Relativity and the Electromagnetic Field

The existence of a moving particle's magnetic field is frame-dependent!

If you think about it, we have a similar problem with the fields created by a moving charged particle. According to equations E2.9 and E9.1, the electric and magnetic fields created at a point P by a particle with charge q moving at a constant velocity $\vec{v}$ past a point C (assuming $v << c$) are

$$\vec{E} = \frac{kq}{r_{PC}^2}\hat{r}_{PC} \quad \text{and} \quad \vec{B} = \frac{kq}{r_{PC}^2}\left(\frac{\vec{v}}{c} \times \hat{r}_{PC}\right) \tag{E13.1}$$

where $\vec{r}_{PC}$ is the position of point P relative to point C. While these action-at-a-distance equations are not fully consistent with special relativity and fail when v becomes a significant fraction of c, they make it abundantly clear (within their range of validity) that observers in different reference frames will disagree about the relative strength of the electric and magnetic fields in a given situation. For example, in a frame where a charged particle has a constant velocity $\vec{v}$, equation E13.1 clearly implies that the particle creates a nonzero magnetic field at point P. But in a frame traveling with that particle, the same equation predicts that the particle creates *no* magnetic field in that frame. Here we see that the existence of the particle's magnetic field depends on one's choice of reference frame (just as the existence of an electric field seems to depend on one's choice of frame in the case of the moving loop). However, there has to be *something* real about the electric and magnetic fields, because both produce real and observable effects under the right circumstances. How can we resolve this puzzle?

The special theory of relativity is founded on the **principle of relativity**, which makes the following claim

The principle of relativity

The laws of physics are the same in all inertial reference frames.

Experimental results must be frame-independent, but explanations need not be

This principle requires that *all* observers in all reference frames agree on the physical *outcome* of an experiment or physical process. For example, observers in all reference frames must agree about whether a given particle is experiencing a force, since the effects of the force on, say, a spring attached to the particle are clear in all reference frames. However, it is important to notice that the principle of relativity does *not* require that all observers agree on a particular *explanation* for that force (or even on its numerical value), as long as the explanation in each frame is based on the same physical laws and yields the predicted experimental outcomes are the same.

Electric and magnetic fields are but manifestations of a unified electromagnetic field

Example: a charge moving near a current-carrying wire

How might the explanations for a given outcome differ in different reference frames? Here is an example. Consider the situation shown in figure E13.2a. Here we have an electron moving parallel to a long wire whose free electrons flow in the same direction. To make the subsequent discussion a bit simpler, let's assume that the electron outside the wire is also moving at the same *speed* as the electrons inside the wire. In the frame shown in the diagram, the wire is at rest (so we will call this the *wire frame*). Let's *assume* that in its rest frame, the wire is electrically neutral (that is, that the free electron density is the same as the positive ion density of the lattice

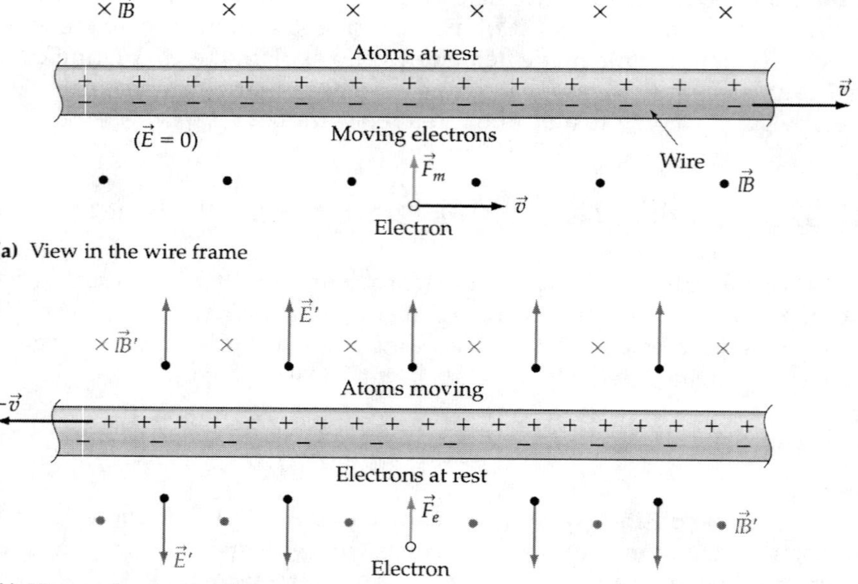

Figure E13.2
(a) An electron moving near a wire through which electrons flow with the same velocity feels a magnetic force (gray arrow) toward the wire. (The positive and negative charges are uniformly distributed in the wire, but have been separated to make the picture clearer.

(b) In an inertial frame moving with the electrons, the wire still creates a magnetic field, but the outside electron is at rest and so feels no magnetic force. In this frame, however, there is an electric field created by Lorentz contraction effects. For observers in this frame, the existence of this field explains why the electron feels a force toward the wire.

atoms).* If this is true, the wire creates no electric field in the wire frame. It does, however, create a magnetic field having the direction shown in the diagram, and this field exerts on the external moving electron a magnetic force directed toward the wire.

Self-Test E13X.1

Verify that the direction of the magnetic field produced by the wire and the magnetic force on the electron is correct in figure E13.2a.

Now consider the same situation as observed in a frame moving with the electrons (figure E13.2b). The wire still creates a magnetic field in this frame, because there is still a conventional current flowing to the left, though in this frame the current is due to the wire's positive atoms flowing leftward instead of the electrons flowing rightward. But since the electron outside the wire is at rest in this frame, there can be *no* magnetic force acting on it: $\vec{F}_m = q(\vec{v}/c)\times \vec{\mathbb{B}} = 0\times \vec{\mathbb{B}} = 0$. Yet an observer in this frame must agree that the outside electron is pulled toward the wire, as *all* observers can see that it accelerates in that direction. How does the observer in the electrons' frame explain this?

Special relativity implies that an object's length will be observed to be shorter in a frame where that object is moving than in a frame where it is at rest. (This phenomenon is called *Lorentz contraction,* and is discussed fully in chapter R7 of unit R. For our purposes now, it is enough to know that this effect exists.) This means that in the *wire's* frame (figure E13.2a), the distances between the flowing electrons (considered collectively as a moving object) are Lorentz-contracted due to their motion. In the *electrons'* frame (figure E13.2b),

*For real current-carrying wires, the situation is actually more complicated than this simple model would suggest, because there are surface charges on the wire and the electrons in the wire also respond in a complicated way to the magnetic field that they themselves create. However, the point of my argument is not to provide a good model of a current-carrying wire but rather to show how electric and magnetic fields must be interrelated to be logically consistent with the principle of relativity. Making the assumption that the wire is neutral in its own frame simplifies the argument.

their separations are *not contracted* and thus their charge density is a bit *lower* than it was in the wire's frame. On the other hand, the distances between the wire's positive *atoms* are Lorentz-contracted in that frame (since they are moving leftward in that frame), so they have a *higher* density in that frame than in the wire frame. Since we are assuming the wire is electrically neutral in the wire frame, this means it must have a net positive charge in the electrons' frame! This creates an *electric* field in that frame that attracts the electron toward the wire, explaining in this frame the acceleration that all observers see.

We see that observers in the different reference frames *disagree* about how much electric field and how much magnetic field is actually present, and they disagree about whether the force the electron experiences is a magnetic force or an electrostatic force. However, they all agree that the charges in the wire create *some* kind of field that pushes the electron toward the wire.

The concept of an *electromagnetic field*

The solution to our puzzle is to understand that the electric and magnetic fields are but two different aspects of an **electromagnetic field** whose reality and effects are frame-independent, but whose division into electric and magnetic parts are not. The degree to which we interpret a given electromagnetic field to be purely electric, purely magnetic, or some combination of both depends on our frame of reference. For example, the electromagnetic field of a point particle is purely electric in the frame in which it is at rest, while it consists of some mixture of electric and magnetic fields in the frame where the particle is moving. The electromagnetic field in the moving loop case is purely magnetic in the frame where the loop is moving and the magnetic field is static, but is partly electric in the frame where the loop is at rest.

No matter how the electric and magnetic parts of the electromagnetic field are manifested in a given frame, we can always compute the electromagnetic force acting on a particle using the **Lorentz force law:**

The **Lorentz force law** describes the electromagnetic force on a charged particle in any reference frame

$$\vec{F}_{\text{em}} = q\left[\vec{E} + \frac{\vec{v}}{c} \times \vec{\boldsymbol{B}}\right] \tag{E13.2}$$

Purpose: This equation describes the electromagnetic force $\vec{F}_{\text{em}}$ exerted by an electromagnetic field on a particle with charge q in frame where the particle moves with velocity $\vec{v}$.

Symbols: $\vec{E}$ and $\vec{\boldsymbol{B}}$ are the electric and magnetic manifestations of the electromagnetic field in the frame in question, and c is the speed of light.

Limitations: This equation strictly applies only to *particles*.

Note: This equation is valid even at relativistic particle velocities if we define $\vec{F}_{\text{em}} \equiv d\vec{p}/dt$, where t is the coordinate time and $\vec{p}$ is the particle's relativistic momentum $m\vec{v}/[1-(v/c)^2]^{1/2}$.

How we define an electromagnetic field's electric and magnetic parts

Note that this law (which is a combination of equations E2.3 and E7.9) essentially *defines* how an electromagnetic field manifests itself as electric and magnetic fields in a given frame. The *electric field* $\vec{E}$ in a given frame is the part of the electromagnetic field that exerts a force on a charge at *rest* (in that frame!). The magnetic field is that part that exerts a force proportional to a charge's *speed* (in that frame!). Since the distinction between the electric and magnetic fields hinges on whether the charge is moving or not, and since whether a charge is moving or not depends on one's choice of frame, the way we divide the electromagnetic field into electric and magnetic parts in a given frame *necessarily* depends on our choice of frame.

Gravitomagnetism

It is an interesting side-note to this discussion that the same kinds of arguments apply to the gravitational interaction as well. Einstein's general theory of relativity requires that a rapidly moving mass produce a "gravitomagnetic field" in addition to its normal gravitational field for pretty much the same reasons that a moving charge must produce a magnetic field in addition to an electric field. We don't notice gravitomagnetic effects in daily life because they are so weak, but astronomers recently announced tentative evidence of a gravitomagnetic effect called *frame dragging* in observations of matter falling into what is believed to be a rapidly spinning neutron star. A satellite called the *Gravity Probe B*, launched in April 2004, is currently measuring the excruciatingly tiny effects of the rotating earth's gravitomagnetic field on perhaps the most perfect gyroscope ever made (which will behave essentially like a gravitomagnetic compass). When the results are analyzed, this experiment will provide humanity's first direct measurement of a gravitomagnetic field.

E13.3 How the Fields Transform

In the last section, I argued that an electromagnetic field at a given point in space and time manifests itself in one frame as a pair of field vectors $\vec{E}$ and $\vec{B}$, but in a different frame by a different pair of vectors $\vec{E}'$ and $\vec{B}'$. In the example shown in figure E13.2, this was due to frame-dependent differences in the charge densities on the wire. However, assuming that $\vec{E}$, $\vec{B}$ and $\vec{E}'$, $\vec{B}'$ are really just different "camera angles" on the same real electromagnetic field at point in space and time in question, then given $\vec{E}$ and $\vec{B}$ in an inertial reference frame S and the velocity $\vec{v}$ of some other inertial frame S' relative to S we should be able to *determine* $\vec{E}'$ and $\vec{B}'$ in S' without having to know anything about the charge and/or current distributions that create these fields.

It turns out that if you know the electric and magnetic fields $\vec{E}$ and $\vec{B}$ at a point in a given ("unprimed") reference frame, you can calculate $\vec{E}'$ and $\vec{B}'$ at the same point in a different ("primed") frame moving with speed v in the $+x$ direction relative to the first as follows:

The transformation equation for the electromagnetic field

$$\begin{bmatrix} E'_x \\ E'_y \\ E'_z \end{bmatrix} = \begin{bmatrix} E_x \\ \gamma(E_y - \beta B_z) \\ \gamma(E_z + \beta B_y) \end{bmatrix} \quad \text{and} \quad \begin{bmatrix} B'_x \\ B'_y \\ B'_z \end{bmatrix} = \begin{bmatrix} B_x \\ \gamma(B_y + \beta E_z) \\ \gamma(B_z - \beta E_y) \end{bmatrix} \qquad \text{(E13.3)}$$

Purpose: These equations describe how, given $\vec{E}$ and $\vec{B}$ in one inertial reference frame, we can calculate $\vec{E}'$ and $\vec{B}'$ in another frame moving at a speed v in the $+x$ direction relative to the first.

Symbols: $[E_x, E_y, E_z]$ are the components of $\vec{E}$ (and similarly for $\vec{B}$, $\vec{E}'$, and $\vec{B}'$); $\beta = v/c$, and $\gamma \equiv (1 - v^2/c^2)^{-1/2}$.

Limitations: Both frames must be inertial and their corresponding coordinate axes must point in the same directions.

Note: The value of $\gamma \approx 1$ when $v << c$.

We see that as we change reference frames, the components of the electric and magnetic fields that are perpendicular to the direction of the frames' relative velocity are mixed together into a new combination.

It is not my purpose here to derive this formula, but I want you (1) to see how it vividly displays how electric and magnetic fields mix when one changes frames, and (2) how it, in conjunction with the Lorentz force law, enables us to explain a given phenomenon in two different frames. Example E13.1 illustrates the latter issue.

Example E13.1 The Velocity Selector in the Particle's Frame

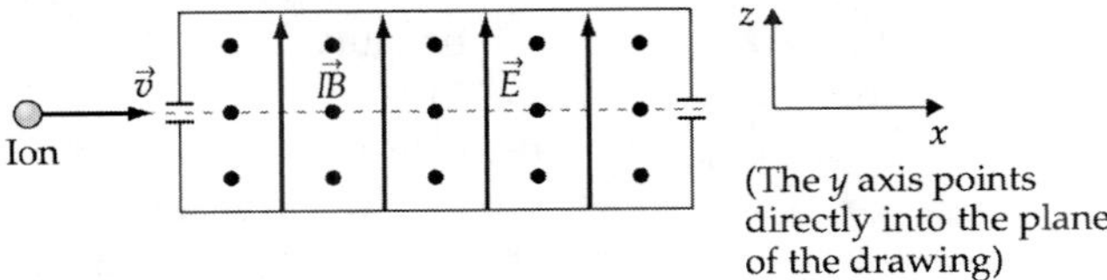

Figure E13.3
A schematic diagram of a *velocity selector.* In the white region, the electric field is uniform and points in the $+z$ direction, while the magnetic field is uniform and points in the $-y$ direction. A charged particle will travel in a straight line through the region if and only if it has a velocity in the x direction such that $v/c = E/\boldsymbol{B}$.

Problem Figure E13.3 shows a schematic diagram of a **velocity selector** (see also problem E7S.4). Charge and current distributions outside the boxed region create electric and magnetic fields $\vec{E}$ and $\vec{\boldsymbol{B}}$ that are uniform and point in the $+z$ and $-y$ directions (respectively) inside the box. If a positive ion moves through the box along the x axis with speed v, the electric field exerts an upward force on it while the magnetic field exerts a downward force on it (as you can check with your right hand). The Lorentz force law thus implies the net z-force on the charge in the frame of the box is

$$F_{\text{em},z} = q\left[E - \frac{v}{c}\boldsymbol{B}\sin 90°\right] = q\left[E - \frac{v}{c}\boldsymbol{B}\right] \tag{E13.4}$$

The electromagnetic force on the particle in this situation will be zero if and only if its speed is such that $v/c = E/\boldsymbol{B}$. So consider a particle moving with this particular speed in the box frame. Show that the electromagnetic force on this particle is zero in its own rest frame as well.

Model Note that we have $\boldsymbol{B}_y = -\boldsymbol{B}$ and $E_z = +E = (v/c)\boldsymbol{B} = \beta\,\boldsymbol{B}$ in the box frame in this case. The particle's frame moves with a speed v in the $+x$ direction with respect to the box frame, so we can use equation E13.3 to calculate the electric and magnetic fields in the particle's frame.

Solution The electric field in the particle's frame is

$$\begin{bmatrix} E'_x \\ E'_y \\ E'_z \end{bmatrix} = \begin{bmatrix} E_x \\ \gamma(E_y - \beta\,\boldsymbol{B}_z) \\ \gamma(E_z + \beta\,\boldsymbol{B}_y) \end{bmatrix} = \begin{bmatrix} 0 \\ \gamma(0 - \beta 0) \\ \gamma(\beta\,\boldsymbol{B} - \beta\,\boldsymbol{B}) \end{bmatrix} = \begin{bmatrix} 0 \\ 0 \\ 0 \end{bmatrix} \tag{E13.5}$$

The Lorentz force law therefore implies that in the particle's frame

$$\vec{F}_{\text{em}} = q\left[\vec{E}' + \frac{\vec{v}'}{c}\times\vec{\boldsymbol{B}}'\right] = q\left[0 + 0\times\vec{\boldsymbol{B}}'\right] = 0 \tag{E13.6}$$

no matter what the magnetic field might be in the particle's frame.

Evaluation We see that in its own frame, the particle cannot respond to the magnetic field in the box, but the electric field is also zero, so the net force is zero, as the principle of relativity requires.

Self-Test E13X.2

Calculate the magnetic field in the particle's frame this situation.

Bottom line: same conclusions, different explanations

An observer in the box frame in example E13.1 would say that the particle experiences zero net force because the electric and magnetic fields exert equal and opposite forces on it, while an observer in the particle's frame would say that it experiences zero net force because there is no electric field and the magnetic field cannot exert a force on a particle at rest. The point is that in spite of the differing explanations, *both* observers agree on the result: the Lorentz force law predicts that the net force on the particle is zero. This illustrates how observers in different frames can use different arguments but arrive at the same physical conclusion.

E13.4 Faraday's Law

Now we are in a position to return to the problem of explaining the current in the moving loop of figure E13.1 in the loop's own rest frame. We see that in this frame, there must be an electric field that drives the current around the loop. But what is the source of this electric field? Our goal in this section is to find a field equation that describes the source of this field in a way that works in all reference frames.

Explaining the loop problem in its own frame

Imagine an electric curl-meter that has positive charges where we put north magnetic poles in section E11.1 (see figure E13.4a). Figure E13.4b illustrates that if the electric field in the loop frame is to successfully drive a current around the loop against the loop's resistance, *it must have a nonzero curl in the vicinity of the loop.* This contradicts Ampere's law for the electric field! Our goal is therefore to revise that field equation so that it correctly predicts that the curl of the electric field is nonzero in the loop's frame.

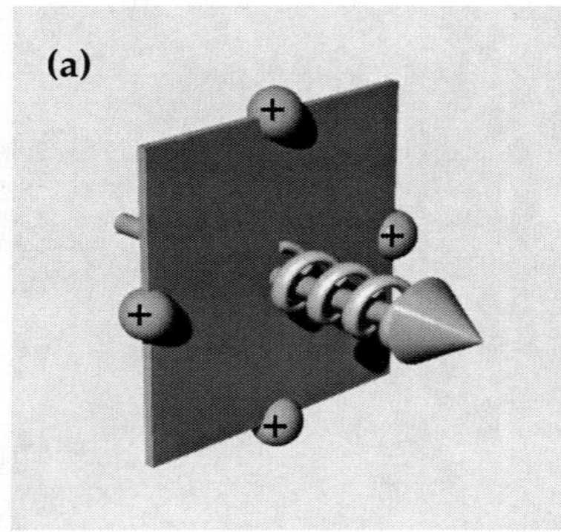

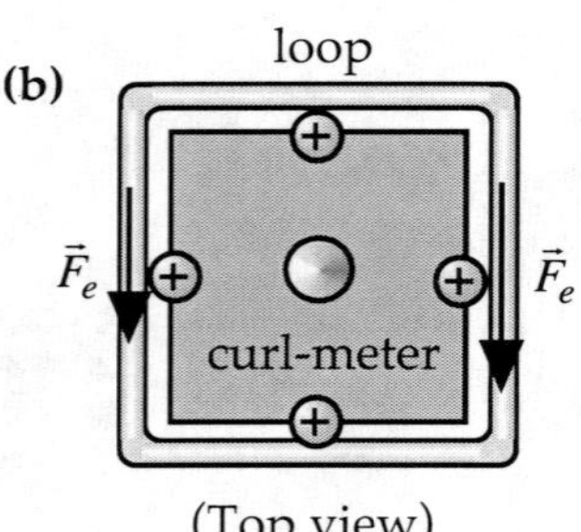

Figure E13.4
(a) An electric curl-meter has positive point charges where a magnetic curl-meter has isolated north poles.
(b) If electrical forces on charge carriers in a loop would tend to push those carriers around the loop (clockwise in the case shown) the charges in a curl-meter centered on the loop would be twisted the same way.

We can calculate this curl pretty easily in that frame. Assume that the electric field is zero in the original frame shown in figure E13.1 and that the magnetic field in the loop's plane in that frame points purely in the $+z$ direction. Equation E13.3 then implies that the electric and magnetic fields in the loop's frame (the "primed" frame in this case) are

$$\begin{bmatrix} E'_x \\ E'_y \\ E'_z \end{bmatrix} = \begin{bmatrix} E_x \\ \gamma(E_y - \beta\, \boldsymbol{B}_z) \\ \gamma(E_z + \beta\, \boldsymbol{B}_y) \end{bmatrix} = \begin{bmatrix} 0 \\ \gamma(0 - \beta\, \boldsymbol{B}_z) \\ \gamma(0 - \beta 0) \end{bmatrix} = \begin{bmatrix} 0 \\ -\gamma\beta\, \boldsymbol{B}_z \\ 0 \end{bmatrix} \tag{E13.7a}$$

$$\begin{bmatrix} \boldsymbol{B}'_x \\ \boldsymbol{B}'_y \\ \boldsymbol{B}'_z \end{bmatrix} = \begin{bmatrix} \boldsymbol{B}_x \\ \gamma(\boldsymbol{B}_y + \beta E_z) \\ \gamma(\boldsymbol{B}_z - \beta E_y) \end{bmatrix} = \begin{bmatrix} 0 \\ \gamma(0 + \beta 0) \\ \gamma(\boldsymbol{B}_z - \beta 0) \end{bmatrix} = \begin{bmatrix} 0 \\ 0 \\ \gamma\, \boldsymbol{B}_z \end{bmatrix} \tag{E13.7b}$$

This means that $E'_y = -\beta\, \boldsymbol{B}'_z$, and since $\boldsymbol{B}_z$ increases as x' increases in the loop frame, so does E_y, as figure E13.5a illustrates. The derivative definition of the curl in this case implies that

$$\text{c\~url}(\vec{E}') = \begin{bmatrix} \dfrac{\partial E'_z}{\partial y'} - \dfrac{\partial E'_y}{\partial z'} \\ \dfrac{\partial E'_x}{\partial z'} - \dfrac{\partial E'_z}{\partial x'} \\ \dfrac{\partial E'_y}{\partial x'} - \dfrac{\partial E'_x}{\partial y'} \end{bmatrix} = \begin{bmatrix} 0 - 0 \\ 0 - 0 \\ \dfrac{\partial E'_y}{\partial x'} - 0 \end{bmatrix} = \begin{bmatrix} 0 \\ 0 \\ -\beta \dfrac{\partial \boldsymbol{B}'_z}{\partial x'} \end{bmatrix} \tag{E13.8}$$

where in the last step, I used $E'_y = -\beta\, \boldsymbol{B}'_z$.

Now the major thing that is different about the original frame and the loop's frame in this situation is that the magnetic field was position-de-

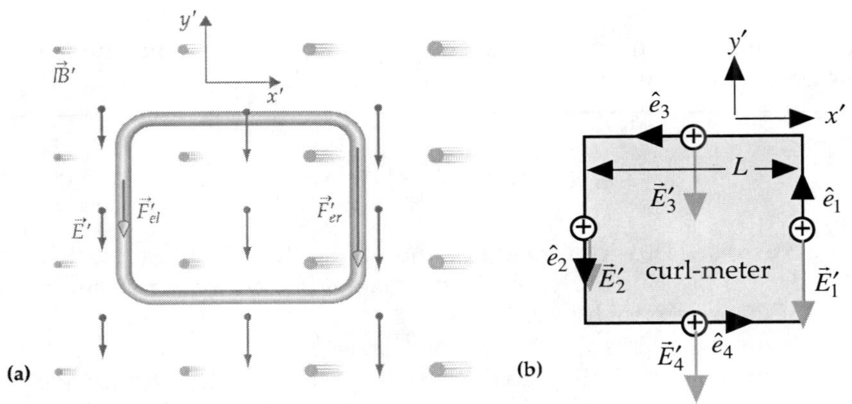

Figure E13.5
(a) This picture shows the square loop of figure E13.1 viewed in its own rest frame. In this frame, there is an electric field in the $-y'$ direction that drives current around the loop.
(b) A curl-meter superimposed on this field shows that it does indeed have a negative curl in the z' direction (that is, it seeks to twist the curl-meter clockwise around an axis in that direction.)

pendent but static (presumably because the source of the field is fixed while the loop moves toward it), but in the loop frame, the magnetic field at a given position is *time-dependent* (because the source of the magnetic field gets closer as time passes). Note that in the time $dt' = L/v$ required for the source to move a distance $dx' = L$ closer to the loop, the magnetic field that was at the curl-meter's right side is now the field at the left side. This means the change $d\boldsymbol{B}'_z$ in the magnetic field as one travels a distance L from one side of the curl-meter to the other is the same as the change one would experience if one would wait at the curl-meter's center (or any other fixed position) for time $dt' = L/v$ to pass. Therefore

$$\frac{\partial \boldsymbol{B}'_z}{\partial t'} = \frac{\partial \boldsymbol{B}'_z}{\partial x'/v} = v\frac{\partial \boldsymbol{B}'_z}{\partial x'} \quad\Rightarrow\quad \frac{1}{c}\frac{\partial \boldsymbol{B}'_z}{\partial t'} = \frac{v}{c}\frac{\partial \boldsymbol{B}'_z}{\partial x'} = \beta\frac{\partial \boldsymbol{B}'_z}{\partial x'} \tag{E13.9}$$

If we substitute this into equation E13.8, we have

$$\tilde{\text{curl}}(\vec{E}')_z = -\frac{1}{c}\frac{\partial \boldsymbol{B}'_z}{\partial t'} \quad\text{or}\quad \tilde{\text{curl}}(\vec{E}')_z + \frac{1}{c}\frac{\partial \boldsymbol{B}'_z}{\partial t'} = 0 \tag{E13.10}$$

Therefore it seems that in this case, the mysterious electric field that appears in the loop's frame is satisfying the z component of a field equation that in full form (and written without the primes) would look like this:

$$\tilde{\text{curl}}(\vec{E}) + \frac{1}{c}\frac{\partial \vec{B}}{\partial t} = 0 \quad\text{or}\quad \tilde{\text{curl}}(\vec{E}) = -\frac{1}{c}\frac{\partial \vec{B}}{\partial t} \tag{E13.11}$$

This field equation is satisfied both in the loop's frame (as we have just seen) *and* in the original frame: because the magnetic field is static in the original frame and we have no electric field, the equation reads $0 + 0 = 0$.

If you compare this to $\tilde{\text{curl}}(\vec{B}) = (1/\varepsilon_0)(\vec{J}/c)$ (Ampere's law for the magnetic field), you will see that the negative time-derivative of the magnetic field acts as a source for the electric field in a manner analogous to the way that current acts as the source of a magnetic field. In the loop's frame, the electric field created by the changing magnetic field is necessary to explain the current flow, so this modified version of Ampere's law for the electric field is absolutely necessary to make the moving loop situation consistent with relativity. Yet postulating this equation in no way affects our analysis in the original frame where the magnetic field is static, because the equation predicts no electric field in that frame.

While we have only shown that equation E13.11 works in this particular case, it in fact is a general local field equation that works in all situations and all reference frames. We call this equation **Faraday's law**, after

Michael Faraday, who discovered the fact that a changing magnetic field could create a current in 1831. Here is the formal box for this equation:

Faraday's Law

$$\text{c\bar{u}rl}(\vec{E}) + \frac{1}{c}\frac{\partial \vec{\boldsymbol{B}}}{\partial t} = 0 \qquad \text{(E13.11)}$$

Purpose: This local field equation links the curl of an electric field $\vec{E}$ to the time derivative of the magnetic field $\vec{\boldsymbol{B}}$ as measured in a given reference frame.

Symbols: $\text{c\bar{u}rl}(\vec{E})$ is the curl of $\vec{E}$, c is the speed of light.

Limitations: This equation applies without limits (until we venture into quantum field theory), even to rapidly varying fields.

This law constrains the electromagnetic field to be consistent with energy conservation

In situations and reference frames where there is no changing magnetic field, Faraday's law tells us that $\text{c\bar{u}rl}(\vec{E}) = 0$. Like Gauss's law for the magnetic field, this puts a basic restriction on the kinds of electric fields that can exist, an intrinsic restriction that does not depend on the characteristics of the charge distribution that creates the electric field. The restriction that $\text{c\bar{u}rl}(\vec{E}) = 0$ is really a consequence of conservation of energy: it tells us that an electric field (in the absence of a changing magnetic field) cannot *spontaneously* drive a current around a conducting loop, an action that would create thermal energy in the wire with no corresponding loss in any other kind of energy. As we will see in the next chapter, a magnetic field (like an electric field) contains energy, so when a magnetic field changes, we can tap some of its energy to drive the current in the loop without violating conservation of energy.

When the electric curl is zero, we can represent the field using the electric potential ϕ

Moreover, the statement that $\text{c\bar{u}rl}(\vec{E}) = 0$ means that we can describe an electric field with a meaningful electric potential ϕ. This can be proven mathematically using multivariable calculus, but we can see the converse physically as follows. Assume that $\text{c\bar{u}rl}(\vec{E}) \neq 0$. As figure E13.4b shows, this means that the electric field will drive a current around a closed loop. But current will flow from high potential to low potential, so as a charge goes once completely around the loop should have a lower potential at the end than at the beginning. But the starting point and ending points are the same: how can this point have both a high and low potential? It would be as absurd as a bike path that is a closed loop but goes downhill all the way! Therefore, we *cannot* describe the electric field with a potential ϕ that has a unique and well-defined value at each point unless $\text{c\bar{u}rl}(\vec{E}) = 0$, i.e. if there is no changing magnetic field present.

This equation is one of the most important pieces of electromagnetic field theory. As we will see in the next chapter, this equation stands at the very foundation of 20th and 21st century technology.

E13.5 The Ampere-Maxwell Relation

Why Ampere's law cannot be correct as it stands

Ampere's law for the magnetic field is also inconsistent with the principle of relativity in its present form. We can see this quite directly. Consider a particle with charge q that in a certain frame is observed to be moving in the $+x$ direction with speed v. Equation E13.1 implies that the magnetic field created by that particle at a point P is directed circularly around the velocity direction (the $+x$ direction here) and has a magnitude of

$$\boldsymbol{B} = \frac{kq}{r_{PC}^2}\text{mag}\left(\frac{\vec{v}}{c} \times \hat{r}_{PC}\right) = \frac{kqv}{cr_{PC}^2}\sin\theta \qquad \text{(E13.12)}$$

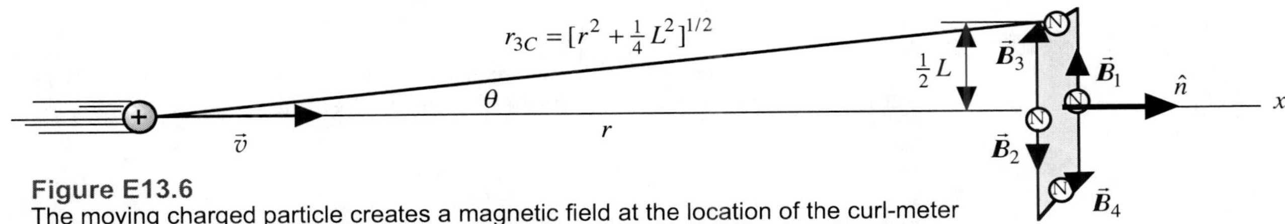

Figure E13.6
The moving charged particle creates a magnetic field at the location of the curl-meter that has a positive x component, yet there is no current passing through that location. This violates Ampere's law. (The side of the curl-meter has length L.)

where $\vec{r}_{PC}$ is the position of point P relative to the charged particle and θ is the angle between $\vec{v}$ and $\hat{r}_{PC}$. Now imagine placing a curl-meter on the x axis at a point in the empty space a distance r in front of the particle, and imagine that we orient the curl-meter with its axis in the $+x$ direction. Figure E13.6 illustrates the field will twist the curl-meter counterclockwise, implying $\text{curl}(\vec{\boldsymbol{B}})_x > 0$. But the current density $\vec{J}$ at this point in empty space is *zero*. This magnetic field, therefore, violates Ampere's law for the magnetic field, which requires that

$$\vec{\text{curl}}(\vec{\boldsymbol{B}}) = \frac{1}{\varepsilon_0}\left(\frac{\vec{J}}{c}\right) = 0 \tag{E13.13}$$

We therefore are going to need to modify this equation as well to make it consistent with relativity.

Finding the time-derivative term that fixes the problem

The main difference between this situation and static situations where Ampere's law works fine is that the electric field at the curl-meter's center is not constant, but rather grows with time as the charge approaches. Let's see if adding a time-derivative term analogous to the term we added to Ampere's law for the electric field also solves the problem here.

Equation E13.12 implies that the magnitude of the magnetic field at the top magnetic pole (pole 3) in figure E13.6 is given by

$$\boldsymbol{B}_3 = \frac{kqv}{cr_{3C}^2}\sin\theta = \frac{kqv}{cr_{3C}^2}\left(\frac{\frac{1}{2}L}{r_{3C}}\right) = \frac{kqvL}{cr_{3C}^3} = \frac{kqvL}{c(r^2 + \frac{1}{4}L^2)^{3/2}} \tag{E13.14}$$

Since this vector is parallel to the counterclockwise edge vector $\hat{e}_3$ at that pole, $\vec{\boldsymbol{B}}_3 \cdot \hat{e}_3 = +\boldsymbol{B}_3$. Because of symmetry, the situation is exactly the same at all of the other poles, so the x component of the curl in this case is

$$\text{curl}(\vec{\boldsymbol{B}})_x \equiv \lim_{L\to 0}\frac{1}{L}\left[\vec{\boldsymbol{B}}_1\cdot\hat{e}_1 + \vec{\boldsymbol{B}}_2\cdot\hat{e}_2 + \vec{\boldsymbol{B}}_3\cdot\hat{e}_3 + \vec{\boldsymbol{B}}_4\cdot\hat{e}_4\right]$$

$$= \lim_{L\to 0}\frac{1}{L}\left[4\frac{kqvL}{2c(r^2 + \frac{1}{4}L^2)^{3/2}}\right] = \frac{2kqv}{cr^3} \tag{E13.15}$$

Now, only the x component of the electric field at the curl-meter's center is nonzero, and it is changing (increasing) because the distance r between the particle and curl-meter is decreasing. Therefore

$$\frac{1}{c}\frac{\partial E_x}{\partial t} = \frac{1}{c}\frac{dE_x}{dr}\frac{dr}{dt} = \frac{1}{c}\left(\frac{d}{dr}\frac{kq}{r^2}\right)(-v) = +\frac{1}{c}\frac{2kqv}{r^3} \tag{E13.16}$$

since $dr/dt = -v$ (dr/dt must be negative because r is decreasing with time). Putting equations E13.15 and E13.16 together, we find that:

$$\text{curl}(\vec{\boldsymbol{B}})_x = \frac{1}{c}\frac{\partial E_x}{\partial t} \quad \Rightarrow \quad \text{curl}(\vec{\boldsymbol{B}})_x - \frac{1}{c}\frac{\partial E_x}{\partial t} = 0 \tag{E13.17}$$

when $\vec{J} = 0$. Therefore, in this case, it looks like the field is satisfying one component of the three-component local field equation

$$\vec{\text{curl}}(\vec{\boldsymbol{B}}) - \frac{1}{c}\frac{\partial \vec{E}}{\partial t} = 0 \tag{E13.18}$$

Self-Test E13X.3

Check that the other two components of this equation are (trivially) satisfied for the situation shown in figure E13.6. (*Hint*: Mentally reorient the curl-meter so that its nose vector points in the other two coordinate axis directions while keeping its center at the same point.)

Now, equation E13.18 works when $\vec{J} = 0$ but $\vec{E}$ varies with time. When $\vec{J} \neq 0$ but $\vec{E}$ is static ($\partial\vec{E}/\partial t = 0$) then we have $\vec{\text{curl}}(\vec{\boldsymbol{B}}) = (1/\varepsilon_0)(\vec{J}/c)$. This means that a local field equation that would apply in *both* circumstances would be the **Ampere-Maxwell relation**:

The **Ampere-Maxwell relation**

$$\vec{\text{curl}}(\vec{\boldsymbol{B}}) - \frac{1}{c}\frac{\partial \vec{E}}{\partial t} = \frac{1}{\varepsilon_0}\left(\frac{\vec{J}}{c}\right) \tag{E13.19}$$

Purpose: This local field equation links the curl of a magnetic field $\vec{\boldsymbol{B}}$ at a point to the time derivative of the electric field $\vec{E}$ and the the current density $\vec{J}$ at that same same point in a given frame.

Symbols: ε_0 is the permittivity constant and c the speed of light.

Limitations: This equation applies without limits (until we venture into quantum field theory), even to rapidly varying fields.

A changing electric field can create a magnetic field

Writing this relation as I have in equation E13.19 puts the derivatives of the electromagnetic field quantities on one side and the current density on the other, as well as emphasizing the similarity to Faraday's law. But we can see one interesting consequence of this equation if we move the time derivative to the other side of the equation:

$$\vec{\text{curl}}(\vec{\boldsymbol{B}}) = \frac{1}{\varepsilon_0}\left(\frac{\vec{J}}{c}\right) + \frac{1}{c}\frac{\partial \vec{E}}{\partial t} \tag{E13.20}$$

We have seen before that we can consider current density to be the physical *source* of a magnetic field. This equation emphasizes that a changing electric field can also act as the source of a magnetic field! In fact, this equation implies that a changing electric field can create a magnetic field even in completely empty space (where $\vec{J} = 0$)!

It is not easy to display the effect of this term

In practice, however, it is *much* easier to create significant magnetic fields using actual currents instead of changing electric fields.

Self-Test E13X.4

A wire with a square cross-section 1 mm on a side conducting 1 A of current carries a current density of magnitude $J = 10^6$ A/m^2. Show that an electric field would have to change at a rate of $\approx 10^{17}$ (N/C)/s to have a comparable effect on the curl of a magnetic field.

Considering that air breaks down when the electric field strength exceeds 3 MN/C, we would have to reduce such an electric field to zero in less than 10^{-10} s (a tenth of a nanosecond) to create the same magnetic field that a quite ordinary current density can create (and even then, our magnetic field would not last very long!).

We will see in chapter E16, though, that this term nonetheless is of enormous practical importance in phenomena with which you have daily experience...

But this term is nonetheless very important

E13.6 Maxwell's Equations

We have now a complete set of four local field equations that describe the electromagnetic field, two that describe the connection between the electric and magnetic fields and their sources, and two that describe the constraints on these fields independent of the nature of their sources.

$$\mathrm{div}(\vec{E}) = \frac{\rho}{\varepsilon_0} \qquad \mathrm{div}(\vec{\boldsymbol{B}}) = 0 \qquad \text{(E13.21)}$$

$$\vec{\mathrm{curl}}(\vec{\boldsymbol{B}}) - \frac{1}{c}\frac{\partial \vec{E}}{\partial t} = \frac{1}{\varepsilon_0}\left(\frac{\vec{J}}{c}\right) \qquad \vec{\mathrm{curl}}(\vec{E}) + \frac{1}{c}\frac{\partial \vec{\boldsymbol{B}}}{\partial t} = 0 \qquad \text{(E13.22)}$$

Purpose: These equations provide a complete and relativistically valid description of dynamic electromagnetic fields $\vec{E}$ and $\vec{\boldsymbol{B}}$.

Symbols: $\vec{J}$ and ρ are the current and charge density at a point, respectively, $\varepsilon_0 = (4\pi k)^{-1}$ is the permittivity constant, and c is the speed of light.

Limitations: There are no known limitations on these equations (until quantum considerations become important).

Maxwell's Equations

Physicists call these equations **Maxwell's Equations**. Note the beautiful symmetry of these equations: two divergence equations on the top, two curl-based equations (each with a time derivative term involving the opposite field) on the bottom; two equations describing connections to sources on the left and two field-constraint equations on the right. Adding any other equation to this set, or even another term to any of the equations, would break this beautiful symmetry. They form a complete and perfect set, whose very elegance bespeaks their credibility. These equations represent one of the greatest achievements of the human mind.

The crowning touches to these equations were the time-derivative terms that we added in this chapter. I want you to know, however, that Maxwell's equations were not actually discovered theoretically using the logic I have displayed in this chapter. They were actually developed by painstaking generalization of experimental data, after many discarded hypotheses, false trails, and mistaken reasoning (like most of the great discoveries of science) and definitely without the help of the grand unifying perspective that relativity provides.

Any history of Maxwell's equations is complicated by the fact that even the "traditional" form of these equations given by equations E13.21 and E13.22 did not appear in print until decades after Maxwell's critical 1864 paper. (Oliver Heaviside is primarily responsible for distilling the twenty equations appearing in Maxwell's original paper to the four equations listed here.) So it is difficult to say who "discovered" each of these equations and when they were first written.

A short history of Maxwell's equations

It is less difficult to pinpoint who performed the crucial experiments and had the crucial insights that ultimately led to these equations. The basic physics behind Gauss's law and the equation $\vec{\text{curl}}(\vec{E}) = 0$ are implicit in Coulomb's law (1785), though it took considerable mathematical work by C. F. Gauss, P. S. de Laplace, and others over a number of decades before such concise expressions were discovered.

Ampère and Faraday

As mentioned in chapter E9, Oersted's discovery in 1820 of the link between electricity and magnetism opened floodgates of research. In the decade immediately following, the two leading figures in this research were Andre-Marie Ampère (at the Paris Academy of Sciences) and Michael Faraday (at the Royal Institute in London). Soon after Oersted's announcement, Ampère had completely mapped out the magnetic field produced by a wire and had laid the experimental foundation for what came to be known as Ampere's Law, which he expressed mathematically in 1825.

Ampère and Faraday were in some sense opposites. Ampère was a trained scientist with significant mathematical skills, but was not as intuitive as Faraday, and Ampère missed being able to make some significant discoveries because of this. Faraday's extraordinary physical intuition about electricity and magnetism and his ability to construct ingenious experiments enabled him to contribute more to knowledge about the relationship between electricity and magnetism than any other single person.

Faraday's great discovery

Faraday made his most important discovery in 1831, when he first observed that a changing magnetic field could produce an electrical current in a nearby wire. This is the crucial insight that led ultimately to the equation we now call Faraday's law. Others had actually observed this effect before (Joseph Henry in 1830 and even Ampère in 1822), but Faraday, guided by his intuition, was the first to really recognize it for what it was and carefully work out its details.

Maxwell's contribution

Yet Faraday's almost complete lack of mathematical training and skill prevented him from expressing his ideas clearly and precisely in the language of mathematics. James Clerk Maxwell, a physicist and mathematician working at King's College in London, admired Faraday's work and set out to set it on a firm mathematical basis. Toward this end, Maxwell constructed an intricate mechanical model of the behavior of electromagnetic field, and found that his model logically required the time-dependent term in Ampère's Law that not only hadn't been observed but had little hope of *being* observed with equipment then available. When this piece was added, though, Maxwell was able in 1864 to express everything then known about electricity and magnetism in a mathematically coherent whole. Maxwell went on in 1865 to predict that light was an electromagnetic wave, a consequence of Maxwell's equations that we will explore in chapter E16.

The inspired genius of Maxwell's synthesis

When viewed in the context of theoretical and mathematical disarray at the time, Maxwell's compression of humanity's total understanding of electricity and magnetism into a handful of powerful equations ranks as one of the greatest intellectual achievements in physics. Relativity not only failed to unseat Maxwell's equations (like it did so many other ideas of physics) it was in a real sense *inspired* by them: since Einstein was convinced that equations so beautiful must be correct, he developed special relativity to explain how they could work in all reference frames (his original paper on relativity was titled *On the Electrodynamics of Moving Bodies*).

The line of reasoning that historically led Maxwell to his equations was thus quite complex (this is part of why it was such an astonishing achievement!). Exploring the history, though interesting in its own right, would have obscured the ultimate beauty and simplicity of these equations. The approach I have presented in the past few chapters has taken full advantage of 21st-century insights to make the argument clearer and cleaner.

TWO-MINUTE PROBLEMS

E13T.1 Two charged particles move with the same velocities in the laboratory frame, as shown.

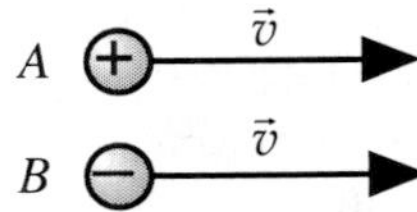

(a) In the laboratory reference frame, does particle A exert a magnetic force on particle B in this frame? If so, what direction?
(b) Answer the same question in the frame where particle A and particle B are at rest.

A. Particle B experiences a magnetic force toward A.
B. Particle B experiences a magnetic force away from A.
C. Particle B experiences a magnetic force toward the right in the drawing.
D. Particle B experiences a magnetic force toward the left in the drawing.
E. Particle B experiences a magnetic force out of plane of drawing.
F. Particle B experiences a magnetic force into plane of drawing.
T. Particle B experiences no magnetic force in this frame.

E13T.2 Imagine that in one inertial reference frame, there is a uniform electric field and no magnetic field. It is possible to find another inertial reference frame where there is a magnetic field but no electric field, T or F?

E13T.3 Imagine that in a certain region of space, when observed in a certain reference frame, an electric field is uniform in magnitude and direction. What can we conclude about the magnetic field in that region and in that frame?

A. $\vec{B} = 0$
B. $\vec{B}$ is uniform in space.
C. $\vec{B}$ is constant in time.
D. $\vec{B}$ is both uniform in space and constant in time.
E. There are no restrictions on $\vec{B}$.
F. There are other restrictions on $\vec{B}$ (specify)

E13T.4 If the electric and magnetic fields are both zero in any given frame, they are zero in all frames T or F?

E13T.5 Any time that we have a varying magnetic field in a given frame, we cannot describe the electric field in that frame using a potential function $\phi(x, y, z)$, T or F?

E13T.6 A conducting loop lies in the xy plane of a certain reference frame. The loop is immersed in a magnetic field that points in the $-z$ direction but is increasing in strength. Which way will current flow in the loop, if we look down on the loop with the $+z$ axis pointing up at us?
A. clockwise
B. counterclockwise
C. no current will flow

E13T.7 Imagine that at a certain point in empty space, the curl of the magnetic field has a positive x component. What can we conclude about the electric and/or magnetic field at this point?
A. E_x must be positive at that point
B. E_x must be negative at that point
C. E_x must be zero at that point
D. E_x must be increasing at that point
E. E_x must be decreasing at that point
F. The field described is not possible
T. None of the above.

HOMEWORK PROBLEMS

Basic Skills

E13B.1 What is the total electromagnetic force on a particle with charge $q = 10$ nC moving with a speed $v = \frac{3}{5}c$ in the $+x$ direction in a region where the electric and magnetic fields are $\vec{E} = [0, 0, 3000 \text{ N/C}]$ and $\vec{B} = [0, 5000 \text{ N/C}, 0]$?

E13B.2 In a certain reference frame, there is a uniform electric field $\vec{E} = [0, 0, E]$, where E = 100 N/C and no magnetic field. What is the magnitude and direction of the electric field $\vec{E}'$ in a frame moving with speed $v = \frac{3}{5}c$ in the $+x$ direction? Is there a magnetic field $\vec{B}'$ in this frame? If so, what is its magnitude (in both N/C and tesla) and direction?

E13B.3 In a certain reference frame, there is no electric field and a uniform magnetic field $\vec{B} = [0, B, 0]$ with B = 100 N/C. What is the magnitude and direction of the magnetic field $\vec{E}'$ in a frame moving with speed $v = \frac{3}{5}c$ in the $+x$ direction? Is there a magnetic field in this frame? If so, what is its magnitude (in N/C and tesla) and direction?

Synthetic

E13S.1 Consider a metal bar parallel to the y axis moving with speed v in the $+x$ direction in a uniform magnetic field that points in the $+z$ direction (see figure E8.6 on page 151). As discussed in section E8.4, a charge q in this bar will experience a magnetic force $F_m = qvB/c$ along the bar. This force will cause charges to accumulate at the bar's ends until they create an electric field that exerts a force equal and opposite to the magnetic force at every point in the bar. This means that in this equilibrium situation, $\vec{F}_{em} = 0$ at all points in the bar's interior. Prove that F'_{em} is also zero in the bar's rest frame, but discuss how an observer in that frame would explain this differently than an observer in the original frame.

E13S.2 Imagine that the electric field within a certain region of space is accurately modeled by the expression $\vec{E} = [0, axe^{-bt}, 0]$, where a and b are positive constants.

(a) What are the units of a and b?

(b) Find an expression for $\partial B_z/\partial t$ at all points within the region in this case.

E13S.3 Use equations E13.3 to show that $\vec{E} \cdot \vec{B} = \vec{E}' \cdot \vec{B}'$ no matter what the fields might be and no matter what β is. This means that $\vec{E} \cdot \vec{B}$ is a quantity that has the same numerical value in all reference frames. (*Hint*: write the dot product out in component form.)

E13S.4 Use equations E13.3 to show that $E^2 - B^2 = (E')^2 - (B')^2$ no matter what the fields might be and no matter what β is. This means that $E^2 - B^2$ is a quantity that has the same numerical value in all reference frames. (*Hint*: $E^2 \equiv [\text{mag}(\vec{E})]^2 \equiv E_x^2 + E_y^2 + E_z^2$.)

E13S.5 Use equations E13.3 to prove that if there is no magnetic field at a given point P in an inertial reference frame S, then in any frame S' moving with velocity $\vec{v}$ relative to S, there the magnetic field at P will be

$$\vec{B}' = -(\vec{v}/c) \times \vec{E}' \qquad \text{(E13.23)}$$

(*Hint*: I do mean there to be a prime on the $\vec{E}'$!)

Rich-Context

E13R.1 The electric field of a charged particle in its own rest frame is $\vec{E} = (kq/r_{PC}^2)\hat{r}_{PC}$.

(a) Use equations E13.3 to calculate the magnetic field in a frame where the charge is moving with a constant speed $\vec{v}$ and show that the result is

$$\vec{B} = \frac{kq}{r_{PC}^2}\left(\frac{\vec{v}}{c} \times \hat{r}_{PC}\right) \qquad \text{(E13.24)}$$

in some limit. What is the limit?

(b) Reflect on the implied limitations of this equation, which we first saw in chapter E9.

E13R.2 (Requires knowing some relativity.) The electric field vectors of a positively charged particle in its rest frame all point directly away from that particle. Prove that this statement is *still* true in a frame where the particle moves with a constant velocity $\vec{v}$, in spite of the way that equation E13.3a messes up the electric field components. (*Hint:* Let's say that the point where we want to evaluate the field is P. You will want to consider the angle that a line between P the charge's position at an instant makes with respect to the x axis in each frame. Why are these angles *not* the same?)

ANSWERS TO SELF-TESTS

E13X.1 This is a matter of applying appropriate right-hand rules. In both parts of figure E13.2, the conventional current is flowing toward the left. Your fingers will curl in the direction of the magnetic field if you point your thumb in the direction of the conventional current. The magnetic field thus points upward in the region below the wire and downward in the region above, as shown. The electron is negatively charged, so the vector $q\vec{v}/c$ points to the left in figure E13.2a. Since $\vec{F}_m = q(\vec{v}/c)\times \vec{B}$, your right thumb will indicate the direction of $\vec{F}_m$ if you point your right index finger in the direction of $q\vec{v}/c$ and your second finger in the direction of $\vec{B}$. When you do this, you should find that $\vec{B}$ points toward the wire, as shown.

E13X.2 According to equation E13.3, the magnetic field in the charge's frame is

$$\begin{bmatrix} \boldsymbol{B}'_x \\ \boldsymbol{B}'_y \\ \boldsymbol{B}'_z \end{bmatrix} = \begin{bmatrix} \boldsymbol{B}_x \\ \gamma(\boldsymbol{B}_y + \beta E_z) \\ \gamma(\boldsymbol{B}_z - \beta E_y) \end{bmatrix}$$

$$= \begin{bmatrix} 0 \\ \gamma(-\boldsymbol{B} + \beta(v/c)\boldsymbol{B}) \\ \gamma(0 - \beta 0) \end{bmatrix}$$

$$= \begin{bmatrix} 0 \\ -\gamma\, \boldsymbol{B}(1-\beta^2) \\ 0 \end{bmatrix}$$

$$= \begin{bmatrix} 0 \\ -\boldsymbol{B}(1-\beta^2)^{1/2} \\ 0 \end{bmatrix} \qquad \text{(E13.25)}$$

since $v/c = \beta$ and $\gamma \equiv (1-\beta^2)^{-1/2}$. So the magnetic field is not zero in this frame, but it cannot exert any force on a charged particle at rest. (If *both* the electric and magnetic fields were zero in this or any frame, then equations E13.3 imply that there would be no electric or magnetic field in *any* frame.)

E13X.3 If we reorient the curl-meter in figure E13.6 so that it faces in the $+y$ direction, the magnetic field is strictly zero at the two poles lying on the x axis and is perpendicular to the curl-meter square (and thus its edge vectors) at the other two poles. Therefore there the component of the curl in the y direction must be zero. Note also that E_y is zero at the curl-meter's center, so $\partial E_y / \partial t = 0$. So the y component of equation E13.18 reads $0 - 0 = 0$ and is thus trivially satisfied. The same analysis applies if we orient the curl-meter to face the z direction.

E13X.4 Note from the inside front cover that $1/\varepsilon_0 c = 4\pi k/c = 377\ \Omega$. If the two terms are to have roughly the same effect on the curl, then we must have

$$\frac{J}{\varepsilon_0 c} \approx \frac{1}{c}\mathrm{mag}\left(\frac{d\vec{E}}{dt}\right)$$

$$\Rightarrow \mathrm{mag}\left(\frac{\partial \vec{E}}{\partial t}\right) = \frac{c}{\varepsilon_0 c} J$$

$$= \left(3\times 10^8\ \frac{\mathrm{m}}{\mathrm{s}}\right)(377\ \Omega)10^6\ \frac{\mathrm{A}}{\mathrm{m}^2}$$

$$\approx 10^{17}\ \frac{\cancel{\Omega}\cdot\cancel{\mathrm{A}}}{\cancel{\mathrm{m}}\cdot\mathrm{s}}\left(\frac{1\ \cancel{\mathrm{V}}/\cancel{\mathrm{A}}}{1\ \cancel{\Omega}}\right)\left(\frac{1\ \cancel{\mathrm{J}}/\mathrm{C}}{1\ \cancel{\mathrm{V}}}\right)\left(\frac{1\ \mathrm{N}\cdot\cancel{\mathrm{m}}}{1\ \cancel{\mathrm{J}}}\right)$$

$$= 10^{17}\ \frac{\mathrm{N/C}}{\mathrm{s}} \qquad \text{(E13.26)}$$

E14 Induction

- Static Electric Fields
- Controlling Currents
- Static Magnetic Fields
- Field Equations
- Dynamic Fields
  - Maxwell's Equations
  - **Induction**
  - Introduction to Waves
  - Electromagnetic Waves

Chapter Overview

Introduction

In this chapter, we will be exploring the fascinating implications and important technological applications of Faraday's law, one of the new equations we discovered in chapter E13. In the process, we will learn how to calculate the energy density of an electromagnetic field, a result we will find useful in chapter E16.

Section E14.1: Magnetic Flux and Induced EMF

Faraday's law implies that *a changing magnetic flux in the interior of a closed conducting loop will induce a current in that loop*, a phenomenon we call **induction**. The effective emf driving that current through the loop is given by **Faraday's law of induction**:

$$\mathcal{E}_{\text{loop}} = -\frac{1}{c}\frac{d\Phi_{\mathbb{B}}}{dt} \quad \text{or} \quad \mathcal{E}_{\text{loop}} = -\frac{d\Phi_B}{dt} \qquad \text{(E14.4)}$$

Purpose: This equation describes the effective emf $\mathcal{E}_{\text{loop}}$ induced in a conducting loop by time-dependent magnetic flux $\Phi_{\mathbb{B}}$ or Φ_B going through the loop.

Symbols: $\Phi_{\mathbb{B}} \equiv \int \vec{\mathbb{B}} \cdot d\vec{A}$ and $\Phi_B \equiv \int \vec{B} \cdot d\vec{A}$ are alternative expressions of the magnetic flux through the loop, and c is the speed of light.

Limitations: There are no known limitations at the macroscopic level (i.e. as long as the quantum nature of the electromagnetic field is unimportant).

Note: The emf is defined so that $\mathcal{E}_{\text{loop}} \equiv \oint \vec{E} \cdot d\vec{S}$ in the frame of the loop, where $\vec{E}$ is the electric field evaluated at a loop step represented by $d\vec{S}$. A positive value of $\mathcal{E}_{\text{loop}}$ means that conventional current flows in the direction of the loop's step vectors.

Section E14.2: Lenz's Law

One *can* calculate the direction of an induced current by carefully following the loop rule conventions in equation E14.2, but it is generally easier to use it to calculate the *magnitude* of the induced emf and determine the direction by using Lenz's law:

An induced current seeks to *oppose* the change that creates it.

For example, the current induced in a loop flows in the direction that creates a magnetic field that reinforces a decreasing external magnetic field or opposes an increasing field.

This law is a consequence of conservation of energy. As discussed in the section, if an induced current were to reinforce a change instead of opposing it, it would be possible to create energy from nothing.

Section E14.3: Self-Induction

A time-varying current flowing through a coil creates a changing magnetic field within the coil, which in turn induces an emf *in the coil itself* that opposes the original variation in current. The strength of this effect is characterized by the coil's **inductance**:

$$|\mathscr{E}| = L\left|\frac{dI}{dt}\right| \quad \text{(E14.7)}$$

Purpose: This equation defines the (self-)inductance L of a coil or loop.

Symbols: dI/dt is the time-rate-of-change of the current I in the coil or loop, and $|\mathscr{E}|$ is the resulting induced emf in the coil or loop.

Limitations: Since this is a definition, there are no limitations.

Notes: The value of a coil's self-inductance L turns out to be a fixed characteristic of the shape, size, and number of turns in the coil.

An example in this section illustrates how we can calculate L for a long solenoid.

Section E14.4: "Discharging" an Inductor

Imagine that we use a battery to drive a current through coil with inductance L connected in series with a resistor R. If we suddenly remove the battery from such an **LR circuit**, the induced emf seeks to oppose the change by continuing to push current through the coil and the resistor. A simple calculation shows that the current driven by the coil in this case decays exponentially with time according to:

$$I(t) = I_0 e^{-tR/L} \quad \text{(E14.16)}$$

Purpose: This equation describes the current I as a function of time t in a coil of inductance L whose self-induced emf is pushing the current through both the coil and a resistor with resistance R connected in series

Symbols: t is the elapsed time, I_0 is the current at time $t = 0$.

Limitations: This assumes L is independent of I (which *is* generally true).

Section E14.5: The Energy in a Magnetic Field

A detailed analysis of the energy in *LR* circuit shows that a magnetic field must store energy. The total energy per unit volume stored in an electromagnetic field is

$$u_{EM} = \tfrac{1}{2}\varepsilon_0(E^2 + \mathbb{B}^2) = \frac{\varepsilon_0 E^2}{2} + \frac{B^2}{2\mu_0} \quad \text{(E14.22)}$$

Purpose: This equation expresses the energy density u_{EM} (energy per unit volume) of an electromagnetic field at a point where the electric and magnetic field magnitudes are E and $\mathbb{B} = cB$ respectively.

Symbols: $\varepsilon_0 = 1/4\pi k$ and $\mu_0 = 4\pi k/c^2$, where k is the Coulomb constant and$c$ is the speed of light.

Limitations: There are no known limitations at the macroscopic level (i.e. as long as the quantum nature of the electromagnetic field is unimportant).

Section E14.6: Transformers

A **transformer** consists of a pair of nested coils, a *primary* and a *secondary*. If the primary is connected to a source of **alternating** (sinusoidally-varying) **current**, an alternating current will be induced in the secondary. If the secondary is attached to something that uses electricity, their interacting magnetic fields transfer energy from the primary to the secondary without any direct electrical connection between the coils! By varying the ratio of turns in the two coils, one can set the secondary's output emf to be any arbitrary multiple or fraction of the primary's emf. Transformers make our technological civilization possible by making it practical to ship electric power over large distances economically at high emfs while still delivering the power at useful and safe low emfs.

E14.1 Magnetic Flux and Induced EMF

Faraday's law $\text{c\u{u}rl}(\vec{E}) = -(1/c)(\partial\vec{B}/\partial t)$ is the most interesting of the two Maxwell equations we discovered in the last chapter because it has some fascinating implications and useful applications. (The correction to Ampere's law, by contrast, is difficult to even observe.) Our purpose in this chapter is to explore some of these implications and applications.

The integral form of Faraday's law

We will find it easiest to use this equation in its integral form. In chapter E12, we saw that we could express the differential form of Ampere's law for static fields in a mathematically equivalent integral form as follows:

$$\text{c\u{u}rl}(\vec{B}) = \frac{1}{\varepsilon_0}\left(\frac{\vec{J}}{c}\right) \quad \Rightarrow \quad \oint \vec{B}\cdot d\vec{S} = \frac{1}{\varepsilon_0 c}\int \vec{J}\cdot d\vec{A} \tag{E14.1}$$

(see equation E12.17), where the sum implied by the integral on the left side is over step vectors $d\vec{S}$ that go completely around the periphery of some surface and the sum implied by the integral on the right is over all tile vectors $d\vec{A}$ on the enclosed surface. By analogy, we can express Faraday's law in a mathematically equivalent integral form as follows:

$$\text{c\u{u}rl}(\vec{E}) = -\frac{1}{c}\frac{\partial\vec{B}}{\partial t} \quad \Rightarrow \quad \oint \vec{E}\cdot d\vec{S} = -\frac{1}{c}\int \frac{\partial\vec{B}}{\partial t}\cdot d\vec{A} \tag{E14.2}$$

The integral version of the equation simply states that the sum of $\vec{E}\cdot d\vec{S}$ around any closed loop is equal to the sum of $(-1/c)(\partial\vec{B}/\partial t)\cdot d\vec{A}$ over all tile vectors on the surface enclosed by that loop.

The magnetic flux Φ_B

Both sides of this equation can be expressed more simply. Since the tile vectors on the given surface do not change with time, since the integral is really just a sum, and since the derivative of a sum is the same as the sum of the derivatives, we can rewrite the right side of equation E14.2 as follows:

$$-\frac{1}{c}\int \frac{\partial\vec{B}}{\partial t}\cdot d\vec{A} = -\frac{1}{c}\int \frac{\partial}{\partial t}(\vec{B}\cdot d\vec{A}) = -\frac{1}{c}\frac{d}{dt}\int \vec{B}\cdot d\vec{A} \tag{E14.3}$$

The quantity $\int \vec{B}\cdot d\vec{A}$ is traditionally called the **flux** of $\vec{B}$ through the surface in question and given the compact notation $\Phi_B \equiv \int \vec{B}\cdot d\vec{A}$ (Φ is the Greek letter phi, for "phlux," I suppose). I can also drop the partial derivative symbol in the last step, because the flux of $\vec{B}$ through a *given* surface depends *only* on time, so the partial derivative symbol is no longer necessary.

The right-hand side of equation E14.2 has a surprisingly simple physical interpretation. Note that $\vec{E}\cdot d\vec{S} = (\vec{F}_e/q)\cdot d\vec{S} = (\vec{F}_e\cdot d\vec{S})/q$ is the k-work delivered per unit charge by the electric field to a charge carrier moving along the displacement represented by the step vector $d\vec{S}$. The sum of $\vec{E}\cdot d\vec{S}$ for all step vectors around the loop is therefore the total energy per unit charge, i.e. the emf $\mathscr{E}_{\text{loop}}$, transferred to a charge carrier by the electric field as the carrier travels once around the loop. In particular, if the loop in question happens to correspond to a conducting loop, this equation implies that a changing magnetic flux *through* the loop will drive a current *around* that loop exactly as if the loop were connected to a battery with emf

Faraday's law of induction

$$\mathscr{E}_{\text{loop}} = -\frac{1}{c}\frac{d\Phi_{\mathbb{B}}}{dt} \quad \text{or} \quad \mathscr{E}_{\text{loop}} = -\frac{d\Phi_B}{dt} \tag{E14.4}$$

Purpose: This equation describes the effective emf $\mathscr{E}_{\text{loop}}$ induced in a conducting loop by time-dependent magnetic flux $\Phi_{\mathbb{B}}$ or Φ_B going through the loop.

Figure E14.1
As we move the magnet into or out of the coil, the magnetic flux through the coil changes, inducing a current in the coil.

> **Symbols:** $\Phi_{\mathbb{B}} \equiv \int \vec{\mathbb{B}} \cdot d\vec{A}$ and $\Phi_B \equiv \int \vec{B} \cdot d\vec{A}$ are alternative expressions of the magnetic flux through the loop, and c is the speed of light.
>
> **Limitations:** There are no known limitations at the macroscopic level (i.e. as long as the quantum nature of the electromagnetic field is unimportant).
>
> **Note:** The emf is defined so that $\mathscr{E}_{\text{loop}} \equiv \oint \vec{E} \cdot d\vec{S}$ in the frame of the loop, where $\vec{E}$ is the electric field evaluated at a loop step represented by $d\vec{S}$. A positive value of $\mathscr{E}_{\text{loop}}$ therefore means that conventional current flows in the direction of the loop's step vectors.

Physicists call this phenomenon **induction** and equation E14.4 **Faraday's law of induction.** Michael Faraday is generally credited as being first to recognize and describe this law in qualitative terms in 1831. Figure E14.1 shows how a changing magnetic field can create a current.

Self-Test E14X.1

Argue that $\Phi_B = c\Phi_{\mathbb{B}}$.

The following example illustrates how we can use this law.

Example E14.1 Induction in a Loop Inside a Solenoid

Problem Imagine that we place a loop with a radius $r = 2.0$ cm inside a long solenoid with radius $R = 3.0$ cm. The magnetic field inside the solenoid points in the $+x$ direction and has a uniform magnitude $B = 1.0$ T. The loop is perpendicular to the solenoid's axis (the x axis here) The field inside suddenly drops to zero within 0.1 s. What is the approximate emf induced in the loop during this time?

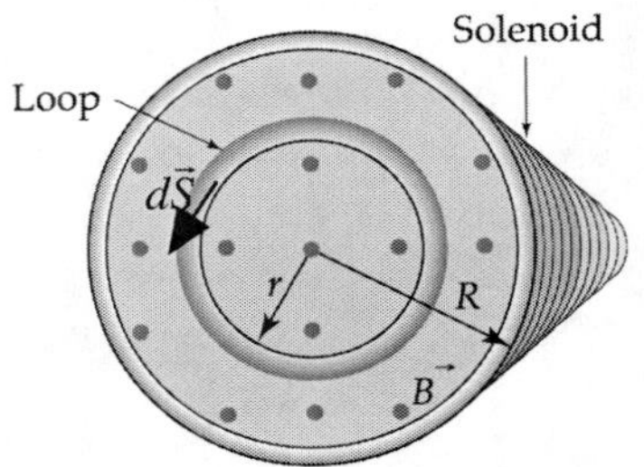

Figure E14.2
A cross-sectional cutaway view of the solenoid and loop, with the x axis facing us. The dots indicate that the magnetic field faces us.

Translation Figure E14.2 shows a cross-sectional drawing of the situation with the x axis pointing toward the viewer.

Model Since the magnetic field inside a long solenoid is approximately uniform, this loop should be small enough so that $\vec{B} \approx$ constant over its face. If we define the loop's $d\vec{S}$ vectors to point counterclockwise around the loop as shown in the diagram, the loop rule tells us that enclosed surface's tile vectors point in the $+x$ direction. Since magnetic field inside the solenoid is uniform and also points in the $+x$ direction, the flux through the loop is $\Phi_B = \int \vec{B} \cdot d\vec{A} = \int +B\,dA\cos 0° = B\int dA = B(\pi r^2)$, because the loop's total area is πr^2. We are not given any details about how the magnetic field falls to zero, so let's assume that it falls to zero at a roughly *constant* rate (as a first approximation anyway):

$$\frac{d\Phi_B}{dt} \approx \frac{\Delta\Phi_B}{\Delta t} = \frac{\Phi_{B,\text{final}} - \Phi_{B,\text{initial}}}{\Delta t} = \frac{0 - \pi r^2 B}{\Delta t} = -\frac{\pi r^2 B}{\Delta t} \tag{E14.5}$$

Solution According to equation E14.4, the induced emf in the loop is thus

$$\mathcal{E}_{\text{loop}} = -\frac{d\Phi_B}{dt} \approx +\frac{\pi r^2 B}{\Delta t} = \frac{\pi(0.03\text{ m})^2(1.0\text{ T})}{0.1\text{ s}}$$

$$= 0.028\,\frac{\cancel{\text{T}}\cdot\cancel{\text{m}}^2}{\cancel{\text{s}}}\left(\frac{1\,\cancel{\text{N}}\cdot\cancel{\text{s}}\cdot\cancel{\text{C}}^{-1}\cancel{\text{m}}^{-1}}{1\,\cancel{\text{T}}}\right)\left(\frac{1\,\cancel{\text{J}}}{1\,\cancel{\text{N}}\cdot\cancel{\text{m}}}\right)\left(\frac{1\text{ V}}{1\,\cancel{\text{J}}\cdot\cancel{\text{C}}^{-1}}\right) = 0.028\text{ V} \tag{E14.6}$$

Since $\mathcal{E}_{\text{loop}} > 0$ and since we have defined the loop's $d\vec{s}$ vectors to point counterclockwise, we see that the induced current flows counterclockwise.

Evaluation Note that 1.0 T is a *huge* magnetic field, so the effect is pretty small!

Self-Test E14X.2

In the situation described in this exercise, what will be the approximate magnitude of the induced current I during the change if the loop has a resistance of 0.10 Ω? (*Hint*: Use the definition of resistance.)

E14.2 Lenz's Law

We can find the direction of the induced current flow by using Faraday's law of induction...

As example E14.1 illustrates, equation E14.4 provides us with a way of finding both the magnitude and flow direction of the induced current in a loop. However, it is usually easier to use the *absolute value* of equation E14.4 to determine the *magnitude* of an induced emf or current and use another method to determine its direction. *Lenz's law* provides both the most straightforward way to determine this direction and additional insight into the physical implications of the signs in Faraday's law of induction.

... but Lenz's law provides a memorable alternative

This law (first proposed by Heinrich Lenz in 1834) asserts that:

Lenz's law: An induced current seeks to *oppose* the change that creates it.

Let's see how this works in a specific situation. Imagine pushing the north end of a magnet toward a conducting ring, as shown in figure E14.3 (remember that magnetic field vectors point away from the north end of a magnet). Pushing the magnet toward the loop makes the average x component of the applied magnetic field inside the loop increase. Lenz's law means that the magnetic field produced by the current induced in the loop should *oppose* this change. In this case, this means that the loop should produce a magnetic field in the $-x$ direction to try to counteract the growing applied magnetic field in the $+x$ direction. Knowing the direction of the induced field, we can then determine the direction of the induced current using the loop rule introduced in chapter E8: if you curl your right fingers in the direction of the current, your thumb points in the direction of the loop's north pole, which is also the direction of the induced magnetic field.

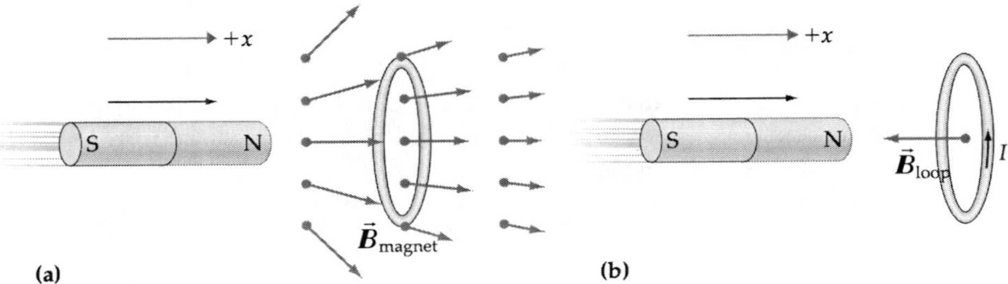

Figure E14.3
(a) If we push a bar magnet toward the ring, the average magnetic field within the ring increases in the $+x$ direction. (b) Lenz's law implies that the induced current will oppose the change by creating a magnetic field in the $-x$ direction.

Not only does Lenz's law imply that the induced field opposes the change in the applied field, the loop actually exerts a magnetic force on the bar magnet that opposes its motion! Note that the induced current in the loop above makes the loop equivalent to a bar magnet whose north magnetic pole faces the oncoming north pole of the bar magnet. The loop and bar magnet's north poles repel each other, meaning that you actually have to *push* on the magnet to keep it moving toward the loop.

Lenz's law expresses the law of conservation of energy

This is in fact a necessary consequence of conservation of energy. The changing magnetic field is creating an electric field that drives current through the loop. Electrons flowing in the loop pick up energy from the electric field and convert it to thermal energy through collisions with the metal atoms in the loop. Where does this energy come from? It has to come from the energy that we transfer to the bar magnet by pushing it against the opposing induced field of the loop. As we push the magnet through a distance, we transfer energy from our arm muscles to the system: this energy ends up as thermal energy in the loop.

The link between Lenz's law and conservation of energy is especially vivid when you consider what would happen if the induced current would act to *support* the change in the applied magnetic field. In our case, just nudging the bar magnet a bit toward the loop would set up an induced field that would tend to attract the magnet. This would cause the magnet to speed up toward the loop, which would create a stronger induced current in the loop, which would tug harder on the magnet and so on. In such a case, the kinetic energy of both the magnet and ring would increase spontaneously even while thermal energy is being dissipated by the growing current in the loop. Energy would therefore be created from (apparently) nowhere if this "inverted" version of Lenz's law were true.

It is important to recognize that Lenz's law does not *add* anything to Faraday's law of induction: it is simply a vivid way of expressing what is already implicit there. As pointed out at the beginning of this section, we can determine the induced current's direction by remembering the various sign conventions in Faraday's law of induction. But you will probably find it easier to use the absolute value of Faraday's law to find the *magnitude* of the induced emf and/or current, and use Lenz's law to find the direction.

Self-Test E14X.3

Determine the sign of $d\Phi_B/dt$ in the situation shown in figure E14.3 and use the sign conventions in Faraday's law to show that Faraday's law makes same prediction the direction of the induced current as Lenz' law.

Self-Test E14X.4

Imagine that the bar magnet in figure E14.3 is pulled *away* from the ring. Does the current go in the same direction or the opposite direction? Does the loop attract or repel the magnet?

E14.3 Self-Induction

A current-carrying coil can induce an emf in itself!

One of the most fascinating implications of Faraday's law is that a loop or coil that conducts a changing current can induce an emf *in itself* that opposes changes in the applied current. To consider an extreme example, imagine a loop that carries a current I supplied by a battery. This creates a magnetic field that goes through the face of the loop, creating a nonzero magnetic flux through the loop. Imagine that we now disconnect the loop from the battery, so the current suddenly drops to zero. This causes the magnetic field and thus the flux through the loop to decrease very rapidly. But by Faraday's law, this changing flux will induce an emf in the loop, and by Lenz's law, this emf will seek to drive a current through the loop in the *same* direction that the battery did, so as to prop up the failing magnetic field. In situations where the current falls to zero almost instantly (as when a switch is opened), the induced emf can be so large that it causes current to arc briefly between the opening contacts of the switch; the loop will do *anything* to keep the current flowing at least for a short time.

The self-**inductance** L of any coil or loop is defined by the equation

Definition of a coil's (self-) inductance L

$$|\mathscr{E}| = L\left|\frac{dI}{dt}\right| \tag{E14.7}$$

Purpose: This equation defines the (self-)inductance L of a coil or loop.

Symbols: dI/dt is the time-rate-of-change of the current I in the coil or loop, $|\mathscr{E}|$ is the resulting induced emf in the coil or loop.

Limitations: This is a definition, so there are no limitations.

Notes: The value of a coil's self-inductance L turns out to be a fixed characteristic of the shape, size, and number of turns in the coil.

Equation E14.7 specifies only the magnitude of the induced emf. The direction of the emf is most easily determined by Lenz's law.

Self-Test E14X.5

L is measured in the SI unit of henrys (H). What is the henry in terms of more basic units?

Self-Test E14X.6

If the current in a 100-mH coil decreases from 1 A to zero in a time interval of about 1 ms, what is the approximate emf induced in the coil during the time the current decreases?

Example E14.2 The Inductance of a Long Solenoid

Problem Consider a long solenoid consisting of N turns of wire around a cylindrical form having a radius of r and length $\ell >> r$. Use an infinite solenoid model to *estimate* the inductance of the real solenoid.

Model The magnetic field everywhere inside an *infinite* solenoid with N turns per length ℓ points parallel to its axis and has a uniform strength given by

$$B = \frac{1}{\varepsilon_0}\frac{NI}{c\ell} \tag{E14.8}$$

(see equation E11.17). Each turn of wire in this coil is essentially a loop whose enclosed surface is perpendicular to this field direction, so tile vectors $d\vec{A}$ on this surface can be chosen to be parallel to the field, implying that $\vec{B}\cdot d\vec{A} = +\,B\,dA$. The magnitude of the magnetic field is also approximately uniform over the enclosed surface, so the magnetic flux going through a given turn in the coil is

$$\Phi_B = \int_S \vec{B}\cdot d\vec{A} = B\int_S dA = B(\pi r^2) = \frac{\pi r^2 N}{\varepsilon_0 c\ell} I \tag{E14.9}$$

since the turn spans an area of πr^2.

Solution Combining this with Faraday's law of induction, we find that the induced emf in one turn of the coil is given by

$$|\mathscr{E}_{\text{per turn}}| = \left|\frac{1}{c}\frac{d\Phi_B}{dt}\right| = \frac{\pi r^2 N}{\varepsilon_0 c^2 \ell}\left|\frac{dI}{dt}\right| \tag{E14.10}$$

because all of the factors in equation E14.9 are independent of time except for the current I. Since the turns of the coil are essentially a series of loops in series, the total emf induced in the coil is the sum of the emfs induced in each turn, so

$$|\mathscr{E}_{\text{tot}}| = N|\mathscr{E}_{\text{per turn}}| = \frac{\pi r^2 N^2}{\varepsilon_0 c^2 \ell}\left|\frac{dI}{dt}\right| \tag{E14.11}$$

Comparing this to equation E14.7, we see the coil's inductance is roughly

$$L = \frac{\pi r^2 N^2}{\varepsilon_0 c^2 \ell} = \frac{\mu_0 \pi r^2 N^2}{\ell} \quad (\text{since } \mu_0 = \frac{1}{\varepsilon_0 c^2}) \tag{E14.12}$$

Note that this only depends on fixed features of the coil, as I claimed before.

Evaluation Now, this is only an approximation, since the magnetic field inside a finite coil will get weaker as we get close to its ends, meaning that equation E14.9 overestimates the flux through a turn near the coil's ends, meaning that the inductance given by equation E14.12 is an overestimate of the coil's actual inductance. But the inductance of a long, skinny coil (whose length ℓ is much greater than its radius R) will be pretty close to this value.

Self-Test E14X.7

Use the result found above to estimate the inductance of a coil consisting of 500 turns of wire wound around a cylindrical form 1.0 cm in diameter and 10 cm long.

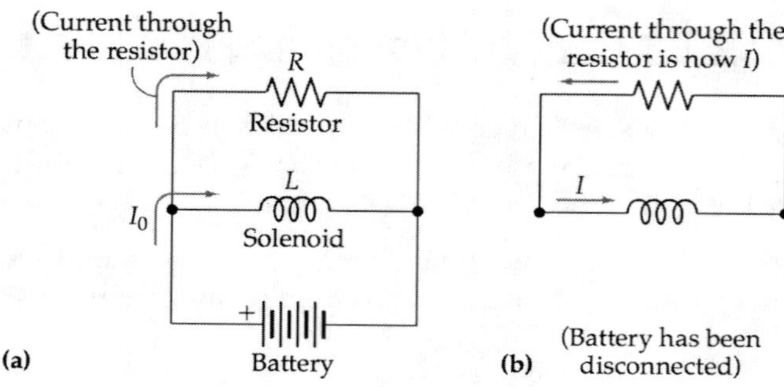

Figure E14.4
(a) A solenoid coil connected in parallel to a resistor and a battery. After the circuit settles down to a steady state, the solenoid conducts a steady current.
(b) If the battery is disconnected at $t = 0$, an emf will be induced in the solenoid that will continue to drive current through the resistor for a while.

E14.4 "Discharging" an Inductor

How to "discharge" an inductor

Imagine that we connect a coil to a battery in parallel with a resistor, as shown in figure E14.4a. After a steady state is achieved, the coil will conduct a certain current I (that depends on its resistance) and will have some magnetic field in its interior. Now, imagine that we cut the connection with the battery but leave the resistor connected (see figure E14.4b). As the current through the coil begins to decrease, the magnetic field in the coil will begin to decrease, and the change in the magnetic field induces an emf in the coil that (by Lenz' law) opposes the change by continuing to push current through the coil. According to equation E14.7, the magnitude of this emf is

$$|\mathscr{E}| = L\left|\frac{dI}{dt}\right| \tag{E14.13}$$

So in this situation, the coil's self-generated emf continues to drive current through both the coil and the resistor after the battery has been removed. How long can this last? Assume that our coil's resistance is very small compared to that of the resistor; then the total resistance in the circuit shown in figure E14.4b is essentially R. The current that flows in this circuit at any given time is thus $I = |\mathscr{E}|/R$. If we solve this for $|\mathscr{E}|$ and plug this into the above, we get

$$IR = L\left|\frac{dI}{dt}\right| = L\left(-\frac{dI}{dt}\right) \tag{E14.14}$$

Note that $|dI/dt| = -dI/dt$ in this case because I is decreasing, so dI/dt is negative, so $-dI/dt$ is positive. We can rewrite equation E14.12 in the form

$$\frac{dI}{dt} = -\frac{R}{L}I \tag{E14.15}$$

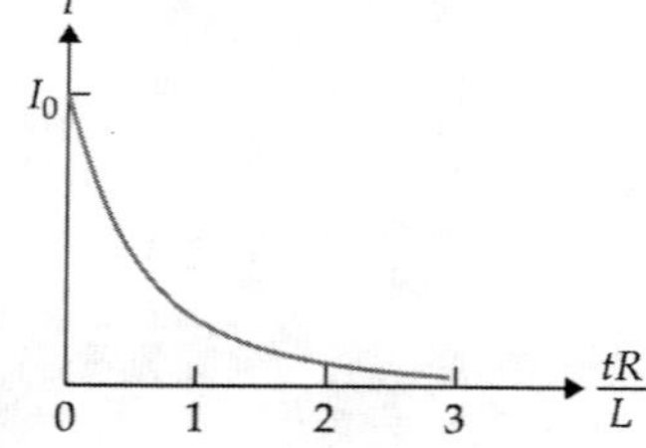

Figure E14.5
A graph of the current as a function of time when an inductor (such as our solenoid) pushes current through a resistor in an effort to maintain the current flowing in the inductor.

This says that the current I is that function of time whose time derivative is a negative constant times itself. We encountered a similar equation in the context of a discharging capacitor (see equation E5.28). There we found that a decaying exponential was the solution. Similarly, you can verify that in this case, the solution to equation E14.13 is

The formula for the time-dependence of the current

$$I(t) = I_0 e^{-tR/L} \tag{E14.16}$$

Purpose: This equation describes the current I as a function of time in a coil of inductance L whose self-induced emf pushes the current through the coil and a resistor with resistance R connected in series

Symbols: t is the elapsed time, e = 2.7183... is the basis of the natural logarithms, and I_0 is the current at time $t = 0$.

Limitations: This equation assumes L is independent of I.

Note: A graph of this function is shown in figure E14.5.

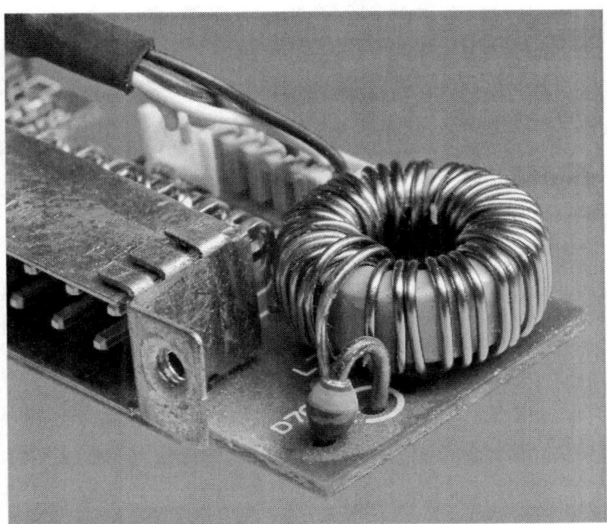

Figure E14.6
This photograph shows a toroidal inductor in an electronic circuit.

Self-Test E14X.8

Verify that $I(t) = I_0 e^{-tR/L}$ is indeed a solution to equation E14.16.

Self-Test E14X.9

Check that L/R has units of seconds. (Note that this is the time required for the current in the inductor to decay to $1/e$ times its previous value.)

Just as Lenz's law implies that an inductor opposes any decrease in the current flowing through it, it also opposes any increase in that current. This means that when we connect an inductor to a battery, it can take some time for the current through the inductor to reach its maximum value (see problem E14S.2). Inductors are used in electrical circuits to smooth out current variations or as parts of timing circuits. Figure E14.6 shows a photograph of an inductor in an electronic circuit.

E14.5 The Energy in a Magnetic Field

So we see that a coil, like a capacitor, can act for a short period of time as if it were a battery, driving a current through a resistor. But driving a current through a resistor takes energy (which is ultimately converted to thermal energy in the resistor). Where does this energy come from?

The energy dissipated in the resistor must come from the magnetic field!

It makes sense that this energy is coming from the internal energy of the magnetic field, which is decreasing in magnitude as the current decreases. Let's accept this as a hypothesis and see if we can figure out how much energy is stored per unit volume in a magnetic field.

First we need to determine the total energy that is dissipated by the resistor. At every instant during the decay, the *power* involved in the conversion of electrical energy to thermal energy in the resistor is given by

$$\frac{dU^{\text{th}}}{dt} \equiv P = |\mathscr{E}|I = I^2R = I_0^2(e^{-tR/L})^2R = I_0^2e^{-2tR/L}R \tag{E14.17}$$

The total energy stored in the magnetic field of an inductor

You can find the total energy dissipated in the resistor by integrating this expression from $t = 0$ to $t = \infty$: if you do this, you should find that

$$U_{\text{tot}}^{\text{th}} = \tfrac{1}{2}LI_0^2 \tag{E14.18}$$

This is, therefore, the energy stored in the magnetic field at time $t = 0$.

Self-Test E14X.10

Verify equation E14.18.

Our hypothesis is that this energy came from the internal energy of the magnetic field that was in the solenoid at time $t = 0$. We can most easily relate this to the magnetic field strength if we assume the coil is a solenoid whose length $\ell >>$ its radius r. In this case, the coil is well-approximated by an infinite solenoid, so its magnetic field at time $t = 0$ has a uniform magnitude $\mathbb{B}_0$ throughout its solenoid's interior and is essentially zero outside. According to equation E11.17, the relationship between $\mathbb{B}_0$ and the initial current I_0 is

$$\mathbb{B}_0 = \frac{NI_0}{\varepsilon_0 c\ell} \quad \Rightarrow \quad I_0 = \frac{\varepsilon_0 c\ell}{N} \tag{E14.19}$$

If you now plug this into equation E14.18, and substitute for the inductance L the formula given by equation E14.12, you can show that the energy in the solenoid's magnetic field at time $t = 0$ must have been

$$U_0^{\text{field}} = \frac{\varepsilon_0 \pi r^2 \ell \mathbb{B}_0^2}{2} \tag{E14.20}$$

Self-Test E14X.11

Verify equation E14.20.

The density of energy in the solenoid's magnetic field

But in an *infinite* solenoid, the field is uniform throughout its interior and zero outside. So in the limit that our solenoid becomes infinite, the energy density stored in the magnetic field is simply the total energy that we have just calculated divided by the volume $\pi r^2 \ell$ of the solenoid's cylindrical interior

$$u_B = \frac{U_0^{\text{field}}}{\pi r^2 \ell} = \frac{1}{\pi r^2 \ell}\frac{\varepsilon_0 \pi r^2 \ell \mathbb{B}_0^2}{2} = \frac{\varepsilon_0 \mathbb{B}_0^2}{2} \tag{E14.21}$$

This equation is essentially identical to the equation $u_E = \frac{1}{2}\varepsilon_0 E^2$ for the energy density of an electric field (equation E3.26)! This may not come as a great surprise if you have really been convinced that the electric and magnetic fields are just two aspects of a greater whole, but it is a gratifying sign that this equation is probably correct. Though our "derivation" of this equation does not assure it, this formula does apply even to a magnetic field that is *not*

$$u_{EM} = \frac{\varepsilon_0}{2}(E^2 + \mathbb{B}^2) = \frac{\varepsilon_0 E^2}{2} + \frac{B^2}{2\mu_0} \quad \text{(E14.22)}$$

Purpose: This equation expresses the energy density u_{EM} (energy per unit volume) of an electromagnetic field at a point where the electric and magnetic field magnitudes are E and $\mathbb{B} = cB$ respectively.

Symbols: $\varepsilon_0 = 1/4\pi k$ and $\mu_0 = 4\pi k/c^2$, where k is the Coulomb constant and c is the speed of light.

Limitations: There are no known limitations at the macroscopic level (i.e. as long as the quantum nature of the electromagnetic field is unimportant).

A general expressionfor the energy in an electromagnetic field

This formula will be useful to us in chapter E16.

E14.6 Transformers

An idealized transformer

Consider now two independent long skinny solenoid coils of wire, one (which we will call the **primary** coil) consisting of N_1 turns of wire wrapped around a cylindrical form of radius R and length ℓ, and the other (the **secondary** coil consisting of N_2 turns wrapped directly on top of the first. For the sake of simplicity, imagine that both coils have negligible resistance.

Imagine now that we connect the ends of the primary coil to a source of a sinusoidally varying emf

$$\mathscr{E}_s(t) = \mathscr{E}_0 \sin \omega t \quad \text{(E14.23)}$$

where $\mathscr{E}_s(t)$ is the emf imposed on the primary coil as a function of time and $\mathscr{E}_0$ is a constant specifying the *amplitude* of that oscillating emf. Let us assume for the present that we leave the two ends of the secondary coil unconnected to anything, so that no current can flow through that coil.

If the primary coil's resistance is small, the induced emf is the same as the applied emf

The oscillating emf connected to the primary coil drives an oscillating current through that coil that creates an oscillating magnetic field inside *both* coils. This oscillating magnetic field, in turn, induces an oscillating *opposing* emf in both coils. In the case of the primary coil, this opposing emf acts to limit the current flowing in that coil. Indeed, if the primary coil's resistance is negligible, the opposing induced emf must almost exactly balance the emf imposed by the outside source so that energy is conserved in the coil (negligible resistance means that only a negligible amount of energy is being converted to thermal energy in the wire). Therefore, we must have

$$\mathscr{E}_0 \sin \omega t = \mathscr{E}_s(t) \approx \mathscr{E}_1(t) \quad \text{(E14.24)}$$

where $\mathscr{E}_1(t)$ is the emf induced in the primary coil.

Now, since the same magnetic field goes through each turn of each coil and the turns in each coil have essentially the same area, the magnetic flux Φ_B going through each turn in the primary *and* the secondary has the same value at all times. By Faraday's law of induction, this means that the emf induced in each turn of each coil must be the same:

$$\mathscr{E}_{\text{turn}} = -\frac{d\Phi_B}{dt} \quad \text{(E14.25)}$$

Since the total induced emfs in the primary and secondary coils are $\mathscr{E}_1 = N_1\mathscr{E}_{\text{turn}}$ and $\mathscr{E}_2 = N_2\mathscr{E}_{\text{turn}}$, it follows that the emf induced in the secondary coil is related to the emf induced (and imposed) on the primary as follows:

The ratio of induced emfs is equal to the ratio of the number of the coils' turns

$$\frac{\mathcal{E}_2}{N_2} = \mathcal{E}_{\text{turn}} = \frac{\mathcal{E}_1}{N_1} \Rightarrow \mathcal{E}_2(t) = \left(\frac{N_2}{N_1}\right)\mathcal{E}_1(t) \tag{E14.26}$$

We see, therefore, that if we connect a low-resistance primary coil to a source of sinusoidally varying emf, we induce a sinusoidally varying emf in the secondary coil whose magnitude is related to that of the primary-coil emf by the ratio of the number of turns in the two coils. What we have here is a simple example of a **transformer**. A transformer is any device that uses induction to transfer electrical energy from one coil to another while changing the emf at which that electrical energy is delivered.

Why transformers are important

Why is being able to change the emf advantageous? For safety reasons, we would like to deliver electrical power to people at low enough emfs so that accidentally touching a bare wire will not certainly be instantly fatal. It also turns out to be economically advantageous to generate electrical power at relatively low emfs. On the other hand, shipping power at low emfs over large distances is very wasteful. This is because the amount of electrical power delivered to a device when we apply an emf $\mathcal{E}$ to it is given by

$$P = |\mathcal{E}|\, I \tag{E14.27}$$

where I is the current flowing through the device. Therefore, the lower the emf, the greater the current that has to flow to supply a given power. Driving a large current through a wire causes more thermal energy to be wasted in the wire than would be the case if we could supply the same power using lower currents (see problem E14S.4). If we ship the power at very high emfs, only a very small current is needed to carry substantial amounts of energy, and thus less energy is lost to thermal energy in the wires. Interstate power lines therefore carry energy at emfs of up to 500 kV.

Transformers that can shift emf levels thus make it economically feasible to transport electrical power over long distances and yet generate it and deliver it at usefully low emfs. The transformer is therefore one of the core inventions that makes our technological civilization possible.

Transformers depend on alternating current

Note that the transformer design described above assumes that the current in the primary coil is oscillating sinusoidally. The current flowing in a transformer indeed *must* be oscillating to create an oscillating magnetic field that in turn creates the oscillating induced emf; remember that only a *changing* magnetic field can induce an emf. We call a sinusoidally oscillating current an **alternating current** (**AC**). Electrical power is delivered to our homes as alternating current precisely because it is so much easier to use induction-based transformers to shift the emf of an alternating current than it is to shift the emf of a steady current (called a **direct current** or **DC**).

There are some aspects of transformer design that are interesting to consider more carefully. According to the definition of inductance, the induced emf in the primary (which is equal to the applied emf) is

$$L_1 \frac{dI_1}{dt} = \mathcal{E}_1(t) = \mathcal{E}_0 \sin \omega t \tag{E14.28}$$

If we divide both sides by L and integrate with respect to time, we get

$$I_1(t) = -\frac{\mathcal{E}_0}{L_1\omega}\cos \omega t = \frac{\mathcal{E}_0}{L_1\omega}\sin(\omega t - \tfrac{1}{2}\pi) \tag{E14.29}$$

High primary inductance keeps primary current (and thus thermal losses) small

since $-\cos\theta = \sin(\theta - \frac{1}{2}\pi)$. This tells us two very interesting things about the current flowing in the primary coil: (1) it lags the applied emf by a quarter-cycle of the sine wave as shown in figure E14.7 (a full cycle of the wave would correspond to ωt changing by 2π) and (2) the current becomes smaller as the inductance of the coil increases. Because losses to thermal energy in the primary coil are going to be primarily determined by the current it carries, there is a significant advantage to making the inductance of the primary coil as large as possible. For this reason, transformer coils are usually wrapped not around long empty cylindrical forms but rather around specially shaped iron cores that both greatly increase the inductance of the transformer coils and confine the magnetic fields created mostly to the interior of the iron (see figure E14.8).

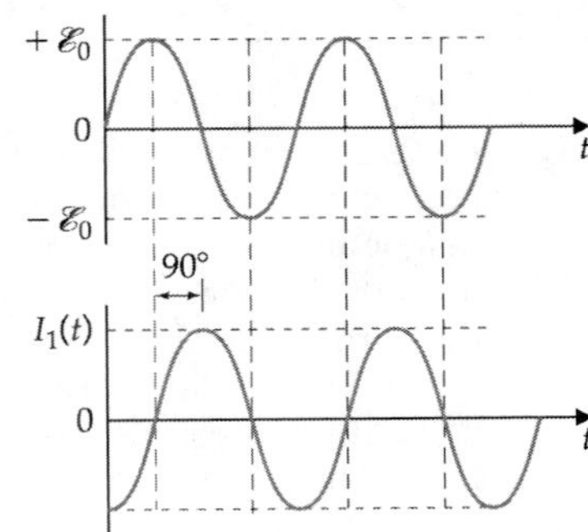

Figure E14.7
The current in the primary of a transformer lags behind the emf by a quarter cycle (when no current flows in the secondary).

The average power that the primary coil absorbs from its source will be given by the average value of

$$P_1(t) = \mathcal{E}_1(t)I_1(t) = -\frac{\mathcal{E}_0^2}{L\omega}\sin\omega t\cos\omega t = -\frac{\mathcal{E}_0^2}{2L\omega}\sin(2\omega t) \qquad \text{(E14.30)}$$

The average value of $\sin(2\omega t)$ over a cycle is *zero*, since it will spend as much time in positive territory as in negative territory. We see then that because the current lags the emf by a quarter cycle, the primary coil *on the average* does not draw any power (other than small thermal energy losses that we are neglecting) from the source of its emf.

Inductive feedback from the secondary regulates the power drawn by the primary

However, this analysis assumes that the transformer *secondary* coil does not conduct any current. When we connect this coil to some kind of load, *it* will begin to conduct an alternating current. This alternating current creates an additional oscillating magnetic field inside both coils that in turn induces an additional emf in both coils. The details are tricky to analyze, but the new oscillating magnetic field ultimately has the effect of causing the primary coil to draw additional current from the source of its emf and shifts the time relationship between the current and emf in the primary coil so that the primary actually draws *power* from the source. This power is then converted to power in the secondary circuit that is in turn dissipated by whatever that coil is connected to.

The point is that inductive feedback effects ensure that the primary coil draws essentially exactly the power from the source of the primary coil's emf that is required to power the device connected to the secondary coil. A well-designed transformer experiences losses to thermal energy that are typically on the order of 1% of the power transformed.

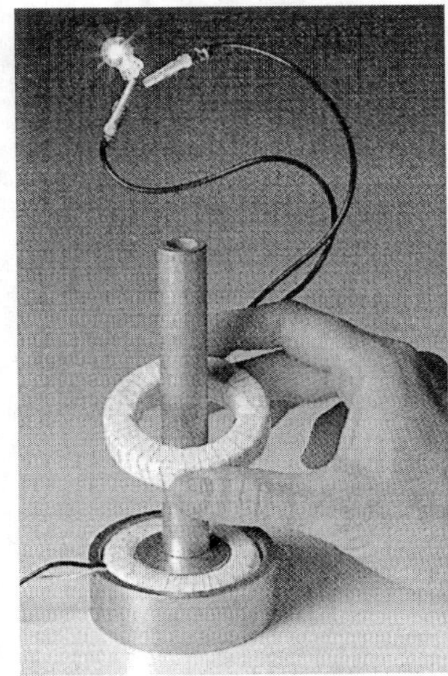

Alternating current flowing through the lower coil creates a sinusoidal magnetic field (mediated by the metal rod) that induces a current in the upper coil. The flowing induced current causes the bulb to glow. This illustrates how energy can be transported from one coil to another across empty space.

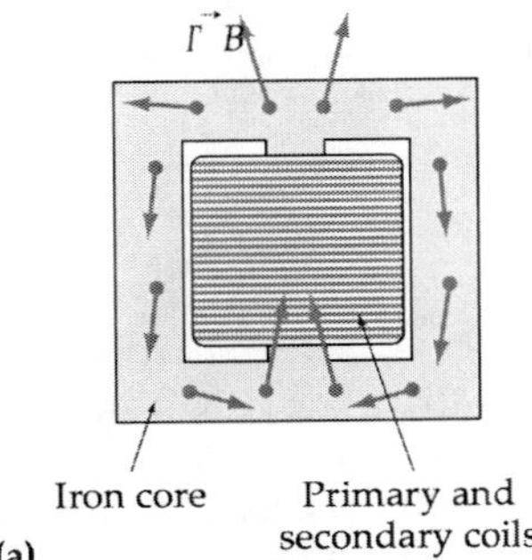

Figure E14.8
(a) A schematic diagram of a common transformer design. The magnetic field created by the coils is mostly confined to the interior of the specially shaped iron core. (b) An actual transformer that uses this design.

TWO-MINUTE PROBLEMS

E14T.1 Imagine that you place a loop with its face perpendicular to a uniform, static magnetic field. If the magnetic field points directly at you as you look at the loop, in what direction does the induced current flow around the loop?
A. It flows clockwise.
B. It flows counterclockwise.
C. There is no induced current.
D. Something else happens (specify).
E. There is not enough information to determine the flow direction.

E14T.2 In the situation described in problem E14T.1, imagine that the magnetic field magnitude is *increasing*. What is the direction of the induced current now?
A. It flows clockwise.
B. It flows counterclockwise.
C. There is no induced current.
D. Something else happens (specify).
E. There is not enough information to determine the flow direction.

E14T.3 Loop *A* and a long, straight, current-carrying wire lie near each other on a tabletop in the top view shown below. Loop *B* is perpendicular to the wire and concentric with it. Assume that the current in the wire suddenly decreases.
(a) In what direction does the induced current flow in loop *A*?
(b) In what direction does the induced current flow in loop *B*?

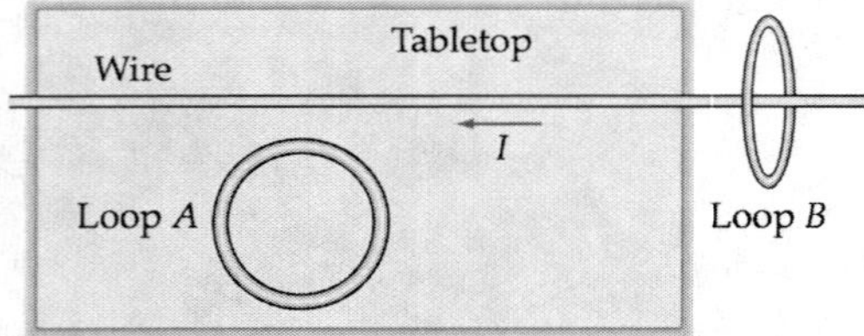

A. It flows clockwise.
B. It flows counterclockwise.
C. There is no induced current.
D. Something else happens (specify).
E. There is not enough information to determine the flow direction.

E14T.4 Two identical concentric loops are arranged as shown in the drawing at the top of the next column. One loop has a steady current flowing through it (provided by the power supply shown). When the power is turned off, in what direction does the induced current flow in loop 2?

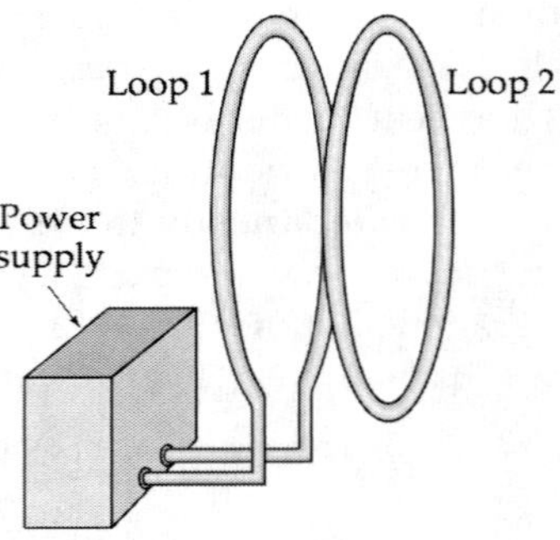

A. It flows clockwise.
B. It flows counterclockwise.
C. There is no induced current.
D. Something else happens (specify).
E. The answer depends on what direction the current was flowing in loop 1.

E14T.5 In the situation described in problem E14T.4 and shown above, will the two loops briefly attract or repel each other when the current is cut off?
A. They will attract each other.
B. They will repel each other.
C. They will neither attract nor repel each other.
D. The answer depends on the direction current was flowing in loop 1.

E14T.6 Imagine that we wrap a solenoid coil around a hollow cardboard cylinder. Now imagine that we insert an iron core into the solenoid. What will happen to the coil's inductance when we insert the iron core? (Explain.)
A. The inductance increases.
B. The inductance decreases.
C. The inductance is unchanged.
D. We do no have enough information to determine how the inductance changes

E14T.7 A coil with a self-inductance of 1 H is connected in parallel to a 10-Ω light bulb and a 5-V battery. Very roughly how long would it keep the light bulb lit if the battery was disconnected from the circuit? (Choose the nearest answer.)
A. 100 s
B. 20 s
C. 2 s
D. 0.2 s
E. 0.02 s

E14T.8 If we increase the resistance in the circuit shown in Figure E14.4b, how would this change the rate of decay of the current through the coil?
A. The current will decay more quickly.
B. The current will decay more slowly.
C. There will be no change in the rate of decay.
D. There is not enough information to answer definitively.

HOMEWORK PROBLEMS

Basic Skills

E14B.1 The face of a loop with a radius of 10 cm is perpendicular to a magnetic field that decreases in magnitude from about 200 MN/C to zero in 0.5 s. What is the magnitude of the induced emf in the loop? If you look at the loop with the magnetic field coming towards you, in what direction (counterclockwise or clockwise) does the current flow around the loop?

E14B.2 The face of a loop with a radius of 3 cm is perpendicular to a magnetic field that increases in magnitude from zero to about $B = 0.10$ T ($\mathbb{B} = 300$ MN/C) in 1.0 ms. What is the magnitude of the induced emf in the loop? If you look at the loop with the magnetic field coming towards you, in what direction (counterclockwise or clockwise) does the current flow around the loop?

E14B.3 The magnetic field *inside* a long solenoid is approximately uniform, while the magnetic field outside the solenoid is approximately zero. Imagine that we have a solenoid that is 3.0 cm in diameter and has an internal field strength of $B = 0.17$ T ($\mathbb{B} = 50$ MN/C). This solenoid goes through the center of a square loop 10 cm on a side, with the axis of the solenoid perpendicular to the loop. What is the magnetic flux going through the square loop?

E14B.4 Imagine that a horizontal conducting ring falls toward the south pole of a vertical bar magnet. As we look at the ring from above, which way does the induced current flow? Does the bar magnet exert a force on the falling ring? Explain your reasoning carefully.

E14B.5 Imagine that I have two coils of wire arranged as shown below. When I connect the battery to deliver power to coil *A*, which end (left or right) of the light-bulb connected to coil *B* becomes positive? What about when I disconnect the battery? What about when coil *A* conducts a steady current?

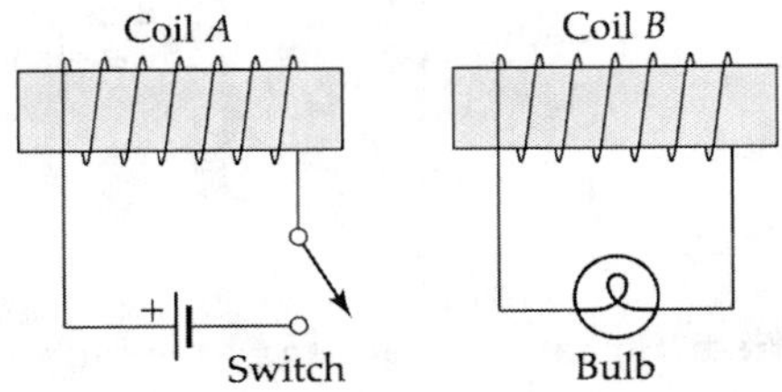

E14B.6 A coil has 1000 turns of wire wrapped around a cylindrical form 1.0 cm in diameter and 10 cm long. What is the approximate inductance L of this coil?

E14B.7 A coil has an inductance of 0.5 H. It is conducting a current of 10 mA. If this current drops to zero within a time span of 0.02 s, what is the emf induced in the coil?

E14B.8 Imagine that we connect a 10-mH coil to a battery through a resistor, and it settles down to conducting 1.0 A. How much energy is now stored in its magnetic field?

E14B.9 The magnetic field between the poles of a very strong horseshoe magnet has a magnitude of $B =$ 1.0 T ($\mathbb{B} = 300$ MN/C), which is fairly well confined to a region about 5 cm in diameter and 2 cm long. Estimate the total energy stored in this magnetic field.

Synthetic

E14S.1 Imagine that we have a coil consisting of N turns of wire shaped like a circular loop with radius R. We place this coil in a uniform magnetic field that points perpendicular to the face of the coil. Imagine that the field strength decreases exponentially in time according to the formula

$$\mathbb{B}(t) = \mathbb{B}_0 e^{-at} \qquad \text{(E14.31)}$$

where a is a constant. Find an expression for the induced emf in the loop as a function of time t, N, R, $\mathbb{B}_0$, and a (and whatever other constants you might need).

E14S.2 Self-inductance in a coil means that it also takes time to get a current started in a coil, because (by Lenz' law) as the current in the coil increases, an emf will be created to oppose the change. If we connect a resistor with resistance R in series with a coil with negligible resistance and inductance L and a battery with voltage V_B, show that the current flowing through the coil as a function of time is

$$I(t) = \frac{V_B}{R}(1 - e^{-tR/L}) \qquad \text{(E14.32)}$$

Hints: The potential difference across the resistor plus the emf across the coil must be equal to the emf across the battery. You might also find it helpful to define a new variable $H(t) = V_B/R - I$: if you do this, note that $dH/dt = -dI/dt$.)

E14S.3 Imagine that you want to wind a solenoid that would be able to keep a 10-Ω light bulb lighted for longer than 1 s after the circuit shown in figure E14.4b is disconnected from the battery. If the form around which you wrap the coil has a radius of 5 cm, and you can wrap 2000 turns of superconducting (zero resistance) wire around each linear meter of the form, how long will you have to make the form? Will this solenoid be approximately infinite (in the sense that its length is much greater than its radius)?

E14S.4 Imagine that we connect a given device (such as a motor or a light bulb) to a power supply (ps) with an emf $\mathcal{E}_{ps}$ by two long wires, each with a given resistance R. Note that because of potential differences across the wires, the emf $\mathcal{E}_{dev}$ delivered to the device will be smaller than $\mathcal{E}_{ps}$. Argue that the power that is wasted in the wires in delivering a certain fixed power to the device is proportional to $1/\mathcal{E}_{dev}^2$. (This is why power companies like to ship power over long distances at high emfs.)

E14S.5 Imagine that we have set up a static magnetic field that in the xy plane points the $+z$ direction and decreases linearly with increasing x according to

$$\boldsymbol{B}_z = \boldsymbol{B}_0\left(1-\frac{x}{L}\right) \qquad \text{(E14.33)}$$

between $x = 0$ and $x = L$. Imagine that we also have a square loop with sides of length $w << L$ lying flat in the xy plane whose electrical resistance is R. The situation is shown below.

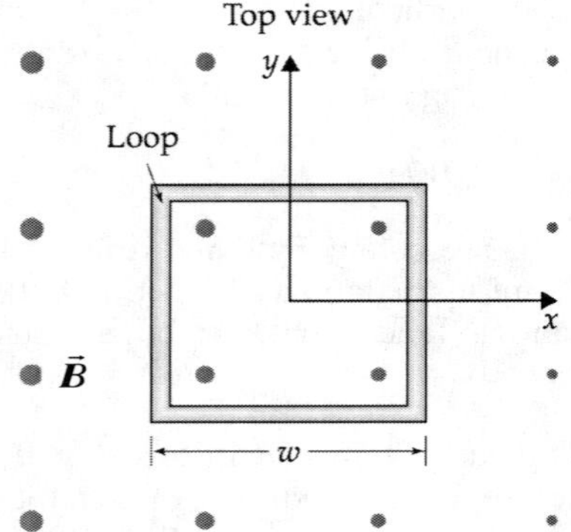

(a) Use Lenz's law and energy concepts to argue qualitatively that if we pull on this loop, we will have to exert some force F to cause the loop to move through this field in the $+x$ direction, even at a constant speed v. (*Hint:* Newton's laws will not particularly help you here. Think about energy flows. If you are pulling on the loop and moving it through a displacement, you are transferring energy to the loop, right? Where is this energy going and why?)

(b) Now let's make this discussion quantitative. Explain carefully why the rate at which energy is transferred to the loop from your hand is Fv (assuming the force directly opposes the displacement), and argue carefully that this must be equal to $\mathcal{E}_{loop}^2/R$..

(c) Show that as the loop moves at speed v in the $+x$ direction, the rate-of-change of flux through this loop has an absolute value of

$$\left|\frac{d\Phi_B}{dt}\right| = \frac{\boldsymbol{B}_0 w^2}{L}v \qquad \text{(E14.34)}$$

(d) By combining the results from parts (b) and (c), show that the magnitude of the force must be

$$F = \frac{\boldsymbol{B}_0^2 w^4}{RL^2c^2}v \qquad \text{(E14.35)}$$

(e) Explain qualitatively (and separately) why it makes good physical sense that the force *should* increase as $\boldsymbol{B}_0$, w, and v increase.

(f) Explain qualitatively (and separately) why it makes good physical sense that the force should decrease as R or L increase.

(g) Now imagine moving the loop at a constant speed v in the $-x$ direction from $x = L$ toward $x = 0$. Will you have to push on the loop to do this, or will you have to pull back to prevent it from speeding up? Will the force you need to apply at a given speed be the same as that you apply when you pull it out at the same speed?

E14S.6 Imagine that a coil consisting of 75 turns of wire shaped as a circular loop with a of radius of 12 cm is placed with its face perpendicular to the direction of an alternating (sinusoidal) magnetic field whose frequency is 60 Hz and whose maximum magnitude is B_{max} = 0.13 T ($\boldsymbol{B}_{max}$ = 40 MN/C). Will this coil be able (in principle) to illuminate a normal 120 V light bulb? (*Note*: The emf of "120 V" household alternating current actually oscillates sinusoidally between ±170 V. Technically, 120 V is the square root of the average of the squared emf, the square ensuring that what you are averaging is always positive.)

Rich-Context

E14R.1 Consider the circuit shown below. Assume that the coil has a huge inductance (so that $L/R \approx 1$ s) and that both the coil and the resistor have a resistance about 20 times smaller than that of the bulb. Use Lenz's law and the idea of self-inductance to answer the following questions. *Be sure to explain your reasoning in detail in each case.*

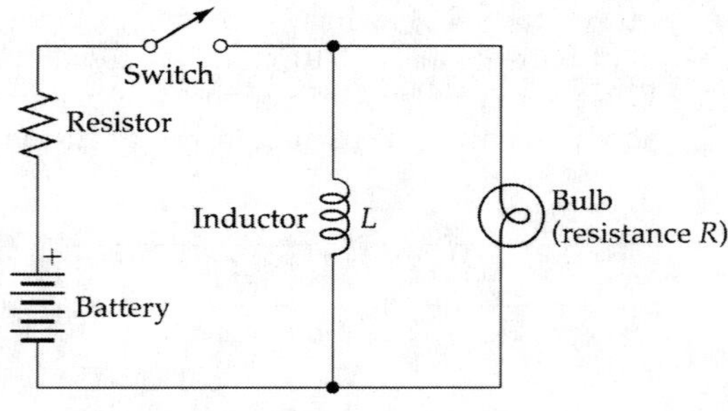

(a) Predict what will happen to the bulb's brightness when the switch is closed. (*Hint:* Before the switch is closed, the coil has zero current flowing through it, and the coil is initially going to want to keep it that way when the switch is closed. How can the coil arrange to have essentially zero current flowing through it? If we define the coil's effective resistance to be the potential difference across it divided by the current flowing through it, what is the coil's effective resistance at the instant that the switch is closed? How does this effective resistance change with time? You might study problem E14S.2 for some ideas.)

(b) Predict what will happen to the bulb's brightness when the switch is opened.

(c) When the switch contacts are opened one often sees bright sparks arcing across the gap between the opening contacts. Why?

E14R.2 A kilogram of gasoline stores contains about 46 MJ of useful energy. Anyone who can develop an energy-storage device that can store electrical energy with anything approaching the same density as gasoline will be the world's richest person (and save the planet, too!). An inductor stores electrical energy. Estimate the magnitude of the magnetic field inside a long solenoid that would store energy at about the same density as gasoline. Is this a reasonable approach toward solving the world's energy problems? (*Hint:* Make a suitable estimate for the density of gasoline: the exact answer is not important. Remember that gasoline floats on water.)

Advanced

E14A.1 Design a transformer whose coils are wrapped around a cylindrical form 20 cm long and 3.0 cm in diameter that changes 120-V household alternating current in the primary coil to 6.0 V in the secondary coil. Assume that you use an iron core that increases the inductance of each coil by a factor of 20 above the value it would normally have. Assume also that you must use #26 copper wire (which has a diameter of 0.41 mm) for both coils. Your secondary coil must be able to provide 300 mA of current without the emf at its ends dropping below 5.7 V.

(a) How many turns must the primary coil have?

(b) How much power is wasted in the primary even when the secondary is disconnected?

(c) How could the design be improved if we could use wire having a different diameter?

[*Hints*: Use the infinite solenoid approximation. You can also *usually* treat alternating currents and emfs in Ohm's law and power calculations as if they were direct currents: *assume* this. Be sure to state any other approximations that you use.]

ANSWERS TO SELF-TESTS

E14X.1 By definition, $\vec{\mathbb{B}} = c\vec{B}$. Therefore

$$\Phi_{\mathbb{B}} \equiv \int \vec{\mathbb{B}}\cdot d\vec{A} = \int c\vec{B}\cdot d\vec{A} = c\int \vec{B}\cdot d\vec{A} \equiv c\Phi_B \qquad \text{E14.36)}$$

E14X.2 $I = \mathscr{E}/R = 28\text{ mV}/0.10\ \Omega = 280\text{ mA}$.

E14X.3 *Model:* We have some freedom to decide which way the loop's segment vectors go around the loop. Let us choose to orient these vectors so that they point counterclockwise around the loop as it is shown in figure E14.2. *Solution:* If I curve my right fingers in the direction that these vectors go around the loop, my right thumb points in the $-x$ direction. This means that since the magnetic field points mostly in the $+x$ direction, $\vec{\mathbb{B}}\cdot d\vec{A}$ for all tiles and thus $\Phi_{\mathbb{B}}$ will be *negative*. Since the field strength is increasing, $\Phi_{\mathbb{B}}$ becomes increasingly negative with time, so $d\Phi_{\mathbb{B}}/dt$ is also negative. Equation E14.4 then says that $\mathscr{E}_{\text{loop}}$ is *positive*, so it will drive current counterclockwise around the loop in the same direction as the $d\vec{S}$ vectors. *Evaluation:* This is the same direction that we deduced using Lenz's law (see figure E14.2b).

E14X.4 Lenz's law implies that the induced current will again resist the change, this time by flowing in a clockwise direction to create a magnetic field in the $+z$ direction to support the failing magnetic field from the departing bar magnet. This means that the loop will attract the magnet.

E14X.5 Looking at equation E14.7, we see that the inductance must have units of emf over current per time, or V·s/A. Since 1 Ω = 1 V/A, 1 H = 1 V·s/A = 1 Ω·s.

E14X.6 Plugging numbers into equation E14.7 yields 100 V.

E14X.7 Plugging numbers into equation E14.12 yields about 0.25 mH.

E14X.8 Taking the time-derivative of the proposed solution $I(t)$, we get:

$$\frac{dI}{dt} = \frac{d}{dt}(I_0e^{-tR/L}) = I_0e^{-tR/L}\left(-\frac{R}{L}\right)$$
$$= -\frac{R}{L}(I_0e^{-tR/L}) = -\frac{R}{L}I \qquad \text{(E14.37)}$$

This is what equation E14.15 says we should get, so this is a solution o that equation.

E14X.9 According to the answer to equation E14X.5, 1 H = 1 Ω·s, so L/R has units of (Ω·s)/Ω = s. This is necessary, because the argument $-tR/L = -t/(L/R)$ in the exponential has to be a unitless number.

E14X.10 Integrating, we get:

$$U_{\text{tot}}^{\text{th}} = \int_0^{\infty}\frac{dU^{\text{th}}}{dt}dt = \int_0^{\infty} I_0^2e^{-2tR/L}R\,dt = I_0^2R\left[\frac{-L}{2R}e^{-2tR/L}\right]_0^{\infty}$$
$$= -\tfrac{1}{2}LI_0^2[0-1] = \tfrac{1}{2}LI_0^2 \qquad \text{E14.38)}$$

E14X.11 Following the suggested steps, we get

$$U_0^{\text{field}} = U_{\text{tot}}^{\text{th}} = \tfrac{1}{2}LI_0^2 = \frac{\pi r^2N^2}{2\varepsilon_0c^2\ell}\left(\frac{\varepsilon_0\mathbb{B}_0c\ell}{N}\right)^2$$
$$= \frac{\pi r^2N^2}{2\varepsilon_0c^2\ell}\frac{\mathbb{B}_0^2\varepsilon_0^2c^2\ell^2}{N^2} = \frac{\varepsilon_0\pi r^2\ell}{2}\mathbb{B}_0^2 \qquad \text{(E14.39)}$$

E15 Introduction to Waves

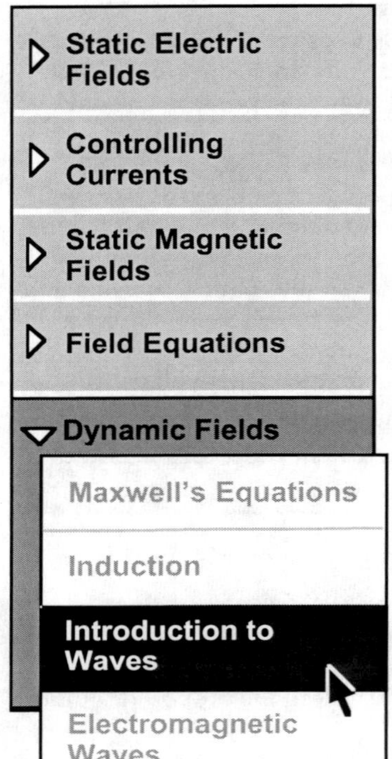

Chapter Overview

Introduction

Maxwell's crowning achievement was his discovery that his equations allowed for the possibility of waves moving through an electromagnetic field. In chapter E16 we will explore the nature of these wave-like solutions of Maxwell's equations. When we talk about "electromagnetic waves," though, we are really constructing an analogy to mechanical waves (such as water waves) with which we have more experience. The purpose of *this* chapter is, therefore, to discuss how we can describe such waves physically and mathematically, so that we can better appreciate the analogy.

Section E15.1: What is a Wave?

In general, a **wave** is *a disturbance that moves through a medium while the medium remains essentially at rest*. Examples include **water waves, sound waves, tension waves** on a vibrating string or spring, **seismic waves**, and "the wave" at a stadium.

In this chapter, we will focus primarily on **mechanical waves**, where the disturbance involves some kind of physical displacement of the medium. Almost all such waves can be classified as being either **transverse** or **longitudinal**, which involve displacements of the medium that are *perpendicular* to or *parallel to* the wave motion respectively. Such mechanical waves can carry energy from place to place.

Section E15.2: A Sinusoidal Wave

Fourier's theorem states that a wave of any shape can be treated as a superposition of **sinusoidal waves**. Therefore, if we fully understand how sinusoidal waves behave in a given situation, we essentially understand how *any* wave would behave.

In this unit, we will consider only **one-dimensional waves**, waves whose disturbance function $f(t,x)$ depends on time and only one spatial coordinate. The equations describing a one-dimensional sinusoidal wave and is associated quantities are

$$f(t,x) = A\sin(kx - \omega t) \tag{E15.7}$$

$$\text{where} \quad k \equiv \frac{2\pi}{\lambda}, \quad \omega \equiv \frac{2\pi}{T}, \quad f = \frac{\omega}{2\pi} = \frac{1}{T} \tag{E15.8}$$

Purpose: These equations describe an idealized one-dimensional sinusoidal wave that varies with time t and position x along the x axis.

Symbols: $f(t,x)$ quantifies the "disturbance" the wave represents at point x at time t, A is the wave's **amplitude**, k (not the Coulomb k!) its **wavenumber,** λ its **wavelength**, ω its **angular frequency**, T its **period**, and f its **frequency** (don't confuse this with the disturbance function).

Limitations: This is an idealization of a real wave.

The value of the disturbance oscillates from $+A$ to $-A$, where A is the wave's *amplitude*. The ***wavenumber*** k expresses (in radians per meter) how rapidly the wave oscillates with increasing position at a given instant. It is related to the ***wavelength*** λ, which specifies the distance between wave crests at a given instant. The ***angular frequency*** ω specifies (in radians per second) how rapidly the wave oscillates with increasing time at a given position. It is related to the ***frequency*** f of the wave (the number of complete oscillations per unit time at a given position), and the wave's ***period*** T (which is the time required for a complete oscillation at a given position).

Section E15.3: The Phase Velocity of a Wave

Another important feature of the sinusoidal wave $f(t,x) = A\sin(kx-\omega t)$ is that its shape moves to the right as time passes. Many of the waves we encounter in nature are **traveling waves** of this type. In this section, we see that a given crest of a sinusoidal wave moves in the $+x$ direction with a **phase speed** v of

$$v = \frac{\omega}{k} = \frac{\lambda}{T} = \lambda f \qquad \text{(E15.12)}$$

Purpose: This equation describes how we can calculate a sinusoidal wave's phase speed v from information about its angular velocity ω, its wavenumber k, its wavelength λ, its period T and/or its frequency f.

Limitations: This expression applies only to sinusoidal traveling waves.

(A wave's **phase velocity** $\vec{v}$ specifies the direction as well as the rate of the motion.)

Section E15.4: The Wave Equation

One of the most important equations in physics is the **wave equation**:

$$0 = b\frac{\partial^2 f}{\partial t^2} - \frac{\partial^2 f}{\partial x^2} \qquad \text{(E15.14)}$$

$$\text{where } v = \frac{1}{\sqrt{b}} \qquad \text{(E15.19)}$$

Purpose: If this equation (where b is a constant independent of t and x) accurately describes the behavior of a disturbance $f(t,x)$ in a medium, that disturbance will travel through the medium as a traveling wave moving in the $\pm x$ direction with phase speed v.

Limitations: This equation applies only to cases where the disturbance depends only on one spatial coordinate x.

Note: Remember that when we evaluate the partial derivative of $f(t,x)$ with respect to one of the variables t or x, we treat the other variable as if it were a constant.

A medium where disturbances obey this wave equation has a number of nice properties: (1) the medium supports sinusoidal traveling waves, (2) it obeys the principle of superposition, and (3) waves of arbitrary shape preserve their shape as they move.

This section explores examples of several kinds of wave-carrying media and show that they do obey the wave equation. We will also see why the wave equation implies the existence of *traveling* waves.

We will find this equation every useful in chapter E16.

E15.1 What Is a Wave?

Drop a pebble in a still pond; the splash of the pebble creates a series of concentric ripples that move out from the disturbance at a sedate and constant pace. When these ripples arrive at the location of a small object floating in the pond (such as a leaf or small stick) some distance away, they cause the object to bob up and down. The fact that the object bobs up and down instead of being swept in the direction of the wave's motion indicates that the pond water that carries the wave does not substantially move along with the wave. The waves move *through* the medium of the water: while the water itself is disturbed by the passing wave and moves slightly in response to it, there is no net displacement of the water in the direction of the wave.

There are many kinds of waves in the natural world

A **wave** in general can be described as being *a disturbance that moves through a medium while the medium remains basically at rest*, at least compared to the velocity of the wave. Examples of such waves in nature are abundant: **water waves** (from tiny ripples to tsunamis), **sound waves** (ranging from tiny whispers to explosion shock waves), **tension waves** on a vibrating string or spring, **seismic waves** that radiate through the Earth's crust from an earthquake, and so on. Figure E15.1 shows some physical waves.

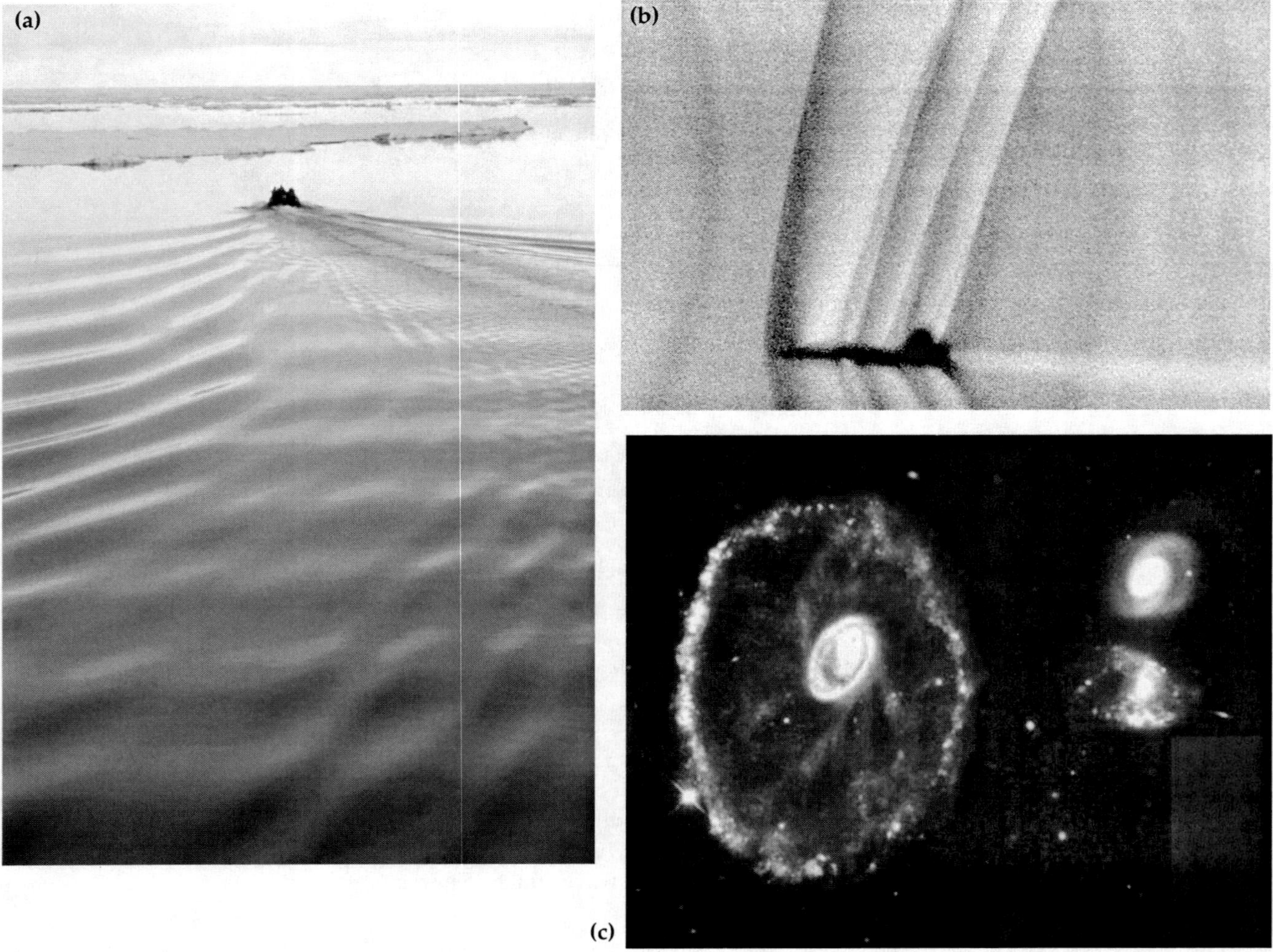

Figure E15.1
Various examples of waves. (a) Water waves from a boat moving through still water. (b) A Schlieren photograph of the shock waves in the air surrounding a supersonic jet. (c) A Hubble photograph of the Cartweel Galaxy. A head-on collision with another galaxy has caused a circular shock wave to move radially outward through the galaxy's gas. The wave compresses the gas, causing a burst of star formation just behind the wave's leading edge

The list given above by no means exhausts the kinds of waves that occur in nature. A crowd doing "The wave" in a stadium provides a good example of a disturbance that moves through a medium (in this case, the human beings involved the wave) without a net motion of the medium in the direction of the wave's motion. If you observe a traffic jam from a helicopter, you can sometimes see waves of disturbance radiate through obstructed traffic at speeds much higher than any of the individual cars are moving. Recently, astrophysicists have discovered that star formation in galaxies often moves in waves away from some disturbance in the galaxy's structure (say as the result of a collision with another galaxy). The growth of cells in a Petri dish can sometimes proceed in waves. The list goes on and on.

Indeed, waves occur so commonly in the physical world and in such a wide variety of contexts that a general study of wave behavior is an indispensable part of a physicist's education. Studying wave behavior in this course would be worthwhile in and of itself even if we weren't using it here as a stepping stone for the study of electromagnetic waves.

While waves of star formation or biological growth are definitely "disturbances in a medium", we will focus in the next few sections on **mechanical waves**, where the disturbance involves some kind of *physical displacement* of the medium. Almost all such waves can be classified as being either **transverse** or **longitudinal** waves. A transverse wave causes the medium to displace in a direction *perpendicular* to the direction of the wave motion. A ripple generated on a rope by a sideways flick of the wrist or "The Wave" in a stadium are examples of transverse waves. A longitudinal wave causes the medium to move back and forth *parallel* to the direction that the wave is moving. Sound waves (which are waves of compression and rarification in air) and/or "car waves" in a traffic jam are examples of longitudinal waves. Transverse and longitudinal waves are illustrated in figure E15.2.

Water waves are somewhat peculiar in that as a wave passes, a given "piece" of water actually moves in a small vertical circle around its rest position (see Figure E15.3). Those of you who have played in the surf at a beach know that in front of a wave crest, water moves backwards toward the wave and upward as the crest approaches, but after it has passed the water moves forward with the wave and downward. Thus water waves exhibit *both* longitudinal and transverse motions (though the net displacement of the water after the wave has passed is still zero). Most mechanical waves, though, are either clearly longitudinal or clearly transverse.

Waves carry energy

One of the most important features of mechanical waves is that they carry not only information that a disturbance has occurred but also *energy* away from the disturbance. For example, the water waves moving away

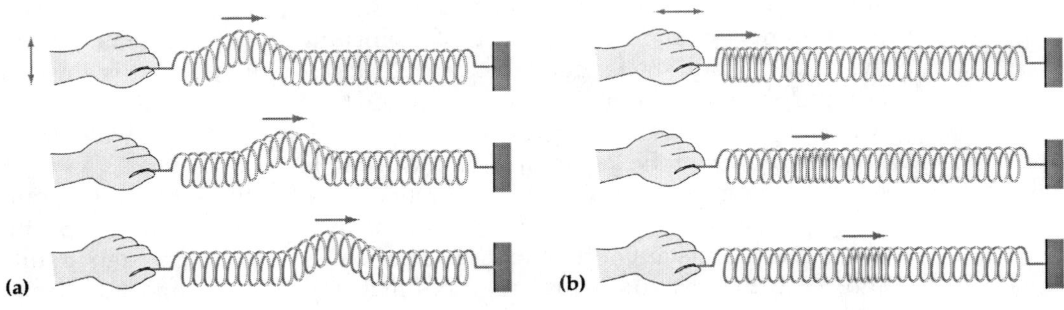

Figure E15.2
(a) A transverse wave moving along a stretched spring. As the wave passes, each element of the spring is displaced perpendicular to the wave's motion. (b) A longitudinal wave on a stretched spring. As the wave passes, each element of the spring is displaced parallel to the wave's motion.

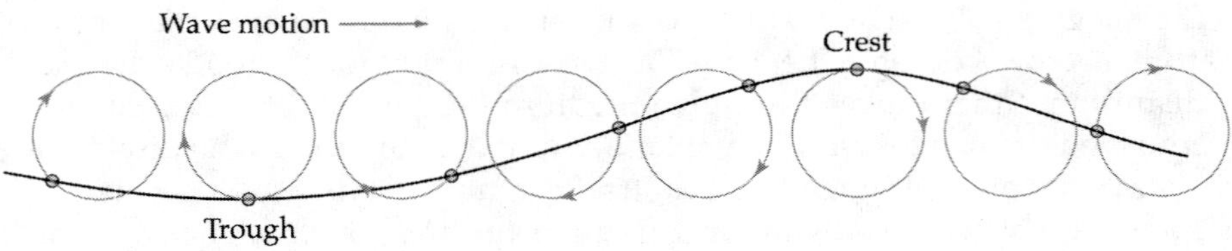

Figure E15.3
This diagram illustrates how particles on the surface of a body of water go around in nearly circular paths as a water wave passes.

from a splash can cause a distant floating bottle to bob up and down as the waves pass; the waves thus transfer energy from the splash and convert it to kinetic energy in the bobbing bottle.

Self-Test E15X.1

An earthquake occurs when part of the earth's crust suddenly slips relative to its surroundings. Such an event radiates energy in the form of two different types of *seismic waves* in the crust of the earth. *P waves* cause the crust to oscillate back and forth toward and away from the earthquake epicenter. *S waves* cause the crust to oscillate up and down. Which of these types is a transverse wave? Which is a longitudinal wave?

Self-Test E15X.2

Describe some evidence that seismic waves carry energy.

E15.2 A Sinusoidal Wave

Why sinusoidal waves are worth studying

A **sinusoidal wave** is a special kind of wave that is especially easy to describe mathematically. Realistic waves are often *approximately* sinusoidal, so a sinusoidal wave represents a convenient simplified model of such waves. But sinusoidal waves are important for another reason. A mathematical theorem called **Fourier's theorem** that states that any wave, no matter how complicated in shape or behavior, can be treated as a superposition of sinusoidal waves. This means that if we fully understand how *sinusoidal* waves behave in a given situation, we essentially understand how *any* wave would behave.

Fourier's theorem: any wave = a sum of sinusoidal waves

Fourier's theorem is an extremely important and useful theorem which you will certainly encounter more than once if you proceed in the study of physics and/or engineering. Its proof, unfortunately, is somewhat beyond our means and would be tangential to our purposes in any case. It is sufficient for our purposes at present for you to understand that not only do sinusoidal waves represent a good approximation to many kinds of real waves, but they actually represent the key to understanding all kinds of waves.

The general mathematical representation of a wave

We can represent *any* wave mathematically by describing a function $f(t,x,y,z)$ that quantifies the disturbance of the medium at every position in space at every instant of time. In this text, I am essentially going to ignore the y and z coordinates and focus on waves that depend on x and t alone: we can pretty much learn everything we need to know about wave behavior from such **one-dimensional** waves without the added complexity of dealing with the y and z coordinates.

A one-dimensional sinusoidal wave has the simple mathematical form

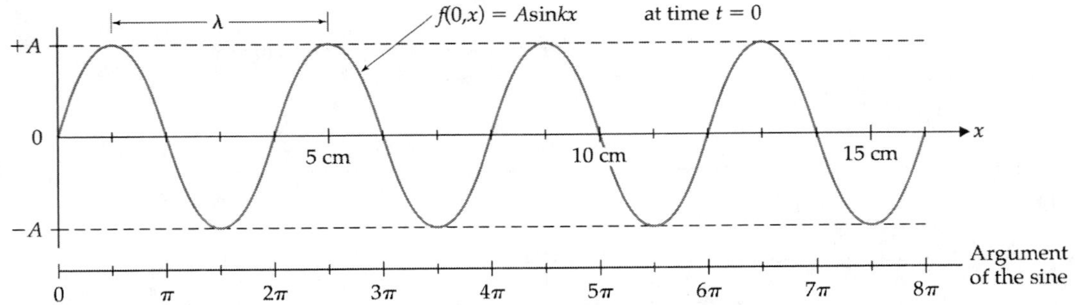

Figure E15.4
A graph of a sinusoidal wave as a function of x at time $t = 0$. In this case, $k = 2\pi/(4\text{ cm}) \approx 1.57\text{ cm}^{-1}$.

$$f(t,x) = A\sin(kx - \omega t) \qquad \text{(E15.1)}$$

A sinusoidal wave

where $f(t,x)$ quantifies the disturbance of the medium at time t and position x, and A, k, and ω are constants. (Please do not confuse k in this context with the k that we have previously encountered as the Coulomb constant.) What does this sinusoidal wave look like?

A "snapshot" of the wave helps us define its amplitude, wavelength, and wavenumber

We can take a "snapshot" of this wave at time $t = 0$ by setting $t = 0$ in equation E15.1 and drawing a graph of how the disturbance $f(x)$ depends on x at this time. Such a graph is shown in Figure E15.4. Notice how the wave looks like an undulating sequence of hills and valleys (called **crests** and **troughs**). We can see also that the wave disturbance value oscillates between $+A$ and $-A$. The quantity A, which is called the **amplitude** of the wave, thus characterizes the maximum strength of the disturbance.

The distance between two adjacent crests in such a graph is called the **wavelength** λ of the sinusoidal wave This wavelength is related to the constant k as follows. The first crest of the wave to the right of $x = 0$ occurs where $kx_1 = \pi/2$, as you can see from Figure E15.4. The next crest happens when $kx_2 = 5\pi/2 = 2\pi + \pi/2$. The distance between these crests is thus:

$$\lambda \equiv x_2 - x_1 = \frac{1}{k}\left(\frac{5\pi}{2} - \frac{\pi}{2}\right) = \frac{2\pi}{k} \qquad \text{(E15.2)}$$

You can think of the quantity k as expressing the number of radians-worth of oscillation the wave goes through in a unit distance:

$$k = \frac{2\pi}{\lambda} = \frac{\text{radians/cycle}}{\text{distance/cycle}} = \frac{\text{radians}}{\text{distance}} \qquad \text{(E15.3)}$$

This quantity is called the **wavenumber** of the wave.

A wave's behavior at a fixed position defines its period, frequency, and angular frequency

Now let us consider what happens to the wave in time as we watch it from a particular *place*, say, $x = 0$. A graph of the sinusoidal wave as a function of time at $x = 0$ is shown in Figure E15.5. Note that we see the wave move up and down between $+A$ and $-A$ as time passes.

The **period** of the wave T is defined to be the time between adjacent crests. By analogy to how we determined the wavelength, you can show that the period is related to ω as follows

$$T = \frac{2\pi}{\omega} \qquad \text{(E15.4)}$$

Self-Test E15X.3

Verify equation E15.4

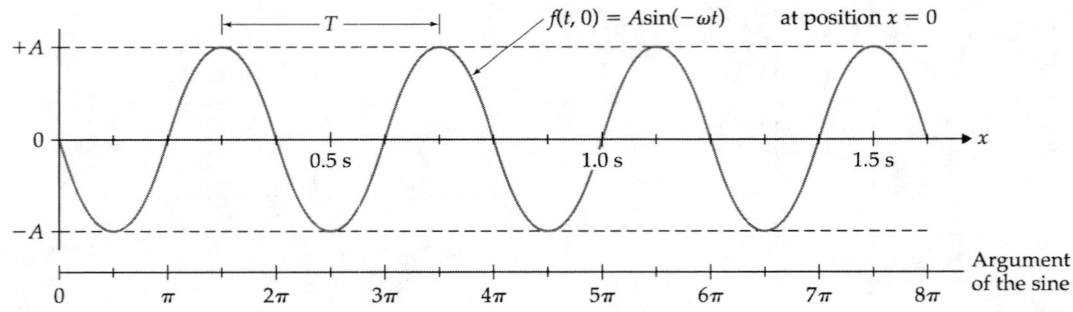

Figure E15.5
A graph of a sinusoidal wave as a function of t at position $x = 0$. In this case, $\omega = 2\pi/(0.4\text{ s}) \approx$ 15.7 (radians) per second.

The quantity ω can be thought of as expressing the number of radians-worth of oscillation that the wave moves through per unit time:

$$\omega = \frac{2\pi}{T} = \frac{\text{radians/cycle}}{\text{time/cycle}} = \frac{\text{radians}}{\text{time}} \tag{E15.5}$$

The constant ω is called the **phase rate** (see chapter N11) or more commonly the **angular frequency** of the oscillation.

The ordinary **frequency** of the oscillation f (in cycles per second, or Hz) is defined to be equal to $1/T$:

$$f = \frac{\text{cycles}}{\text{second}} = \frac{1}{\text{seconds/cycle}} = \frac{1}{T} = \frac{\omega}{2\pi} \tag{E15.6}$$

[Note that the f here is not related to the function $f(t,x)$ considered earlier.]

Self-Test E15X.4

If a sinusoidal water wave has a wavelength of 2.0 cm and a frequency of 2.0 Hz, what are the values (with appropriate units) of the waves' wavenumber k and angular frequency ω?

So in summary, here is the constellation of equations that describe a one-dimensional sinusoidal wave:

A summary of the one-dimensional sinusoidal wave formula and associated quantities

$$f(t,x) = A\sin(kx - \omega t) \tag{E15.7}$$

$$\text{where} \quad k \equiv \frac{2\pi}{\lambda}, \quad \omega \equiv \frac{2\pi}{T}, \quad f = \frac{\omega}{2\pi} = \frac{1}{T} \tag{E15.8}$$

Purpose: These equations describe an idealized one-dimensional sinusoidal wave that varies with time t and position x along the x axis.

Symbols: $f(t,x)$ quantifies the "disturbance" the wave represents at point x at time t, A is the wave's **amplitude**, k (not the Coulomb k!) its **wavenumber**, λ its **wavelength**, ω its **angular frequency**, T its **period**, and f its **frequency** (don't confuse this with the disturbance function).

Limitations: This is an idealization of a real wave.

E15.3 The Phase Velocity of a Wave

Features (such as crests) of a traveling wave move at a rate we call the *phase velocity*

The wave $f(t,x) = A\sin(kx-\omega t)$ has one other important feature: *it moves* as time progresses. Figure E15.6 shows successive snapshots of such a wave at various different times. You can see in this diagram that a given crest of the wave progresses to the right as time passes. We call a wave whose basic spatial shape is translated in space like this as time passes a **traveling wave**: most of the waves we encounter in nature are traveling waves.

Why does the sinusoidal wave given by $f(t,x) = A\sin(kx-\omega t)$ move like this? Consider a given crest of the wave, say, the first crest to the right of $x = 0$

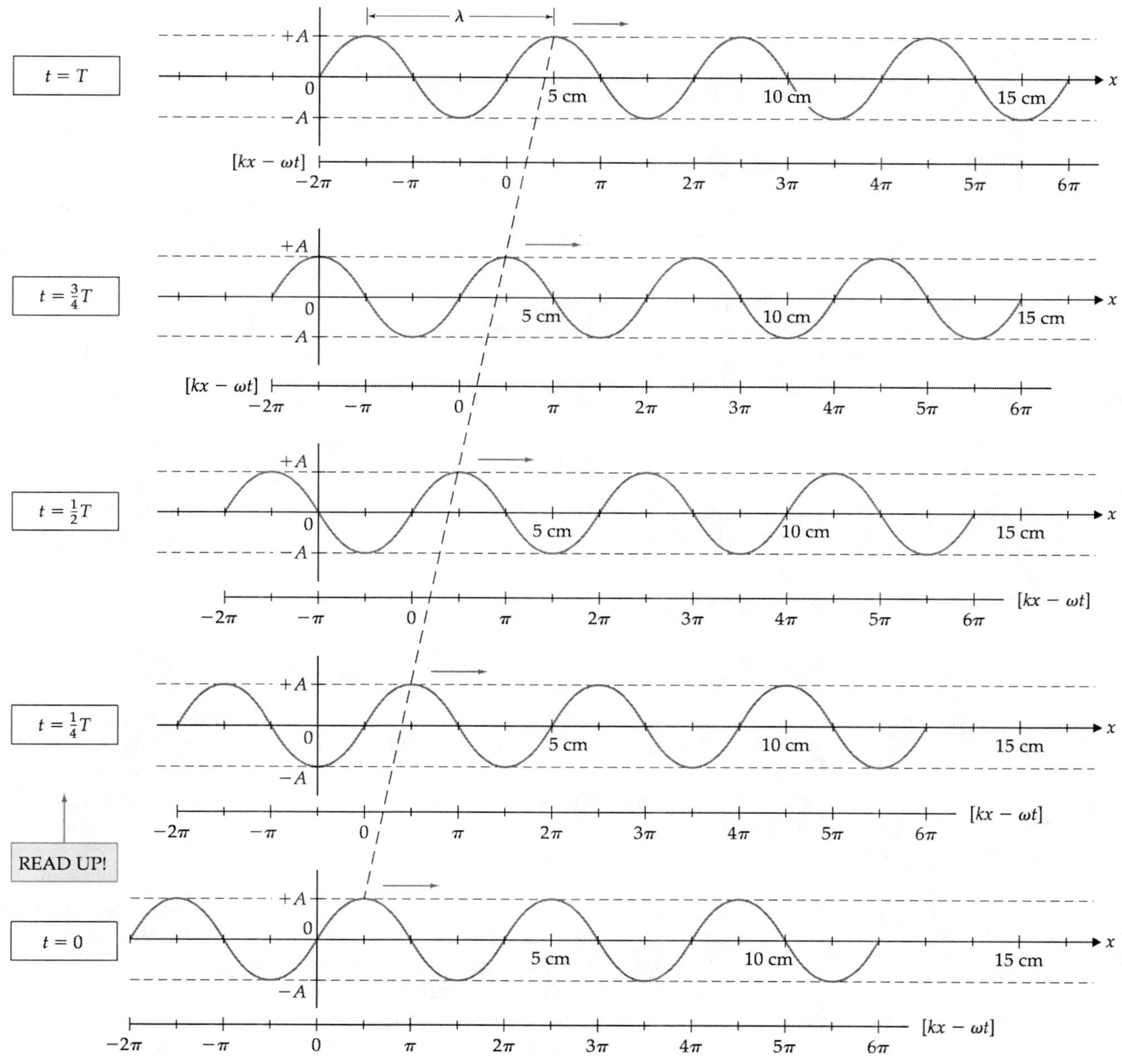

Figure E15.6
A successive series of snapshots of a sinusoidal wave (read from the bottom up!). Note how the crest that was originally at x = 1 cm moves to the right as time passes.

at time $t = 0$. This particular crest is the place where the argument of the sine (the quantity in the parentheses that the sine function operates on) has the value $\pi/2$ (the first positive angle where sine becomes +1). So for all time, the location x_{crest} of *this* particular crest is specified by the condition that

$$\frac{\pi}{2} = kx_{crest} - \omega t \qquad \text{(E15.9)}$$

Now, at time $t = 0$, this crest is located where $kx_{crest} = \pi/2$, that is at $x_{crest} = \pi/2k$. But as t increases, x_{crest} must also increase in proportion to keep the *difference* in equation E15.9 fixed. In fact, if we take the time derivative of both sides of equation E15.9, we find that

$$0 = k\frac{dx_{crest}}{dt} - \omega \quad \Rightarrow \quad \frac{dx_{crest}}{dt} = +\frac{\omega}{k} \qquad \text{(E15.10)}$$

This crest thus moves in the $+x$ direction with speed ω/k.

Self-Test E15X.5

Show that the crest corresponding to the place where the argument of the sine is $5\pi/2$ moves with the same velocity.

Definition of the phase velocity of a sinusoidal wave

The velocity of a given feature (like a given crest) of a traveling wave is called the wave's **phase velocity** (don't confuse this with the wave's *phase rate* w). We see that our sinusoidal traveling wave has a phase velocity in the $+x$ direction whose magnitude (the wave's **phase speed**) is

$$v = |v_x| = +\frac{\omega}{k} \quad \text{(phase speed of our sinusoidal wave)} \qquad \text{(E15.11)}$$

This equation, in combination with equations E15.8, implies the following relationships between the phase speed and the wave's wavelength, period, and frequency:

$$v = \frac{\omega}{k} = \frac{\lambda}{T} = \lambda f \qquad \text{(E15.12)}$$

Purpose: This equation describes how we can calculate a sinusoidal wave's phase speed v from information about its angular velocity ω, its wavenumber k, its wavelength λ, its period T and/or its frequency f.

Limitations: This expression applies only to sinusoidal traveling waves.

We can understand $v = \lambda f$ more intuitively as follows. Consider figure E15.5, and imagine that we sit at the position $x = \pi/2$ and watch the sine wave pass by. At time $t = 0$, there was a crest at this position. After time T has passed, the wave goes through one complete oscillation at our position, so there is again a crest passing our position. Meanwhile, the original crest has moved exactly one wavelength λ ahead in space. The speed of this crest is thus indeed l/T, as claimed by equation E15.12.

Example E15.1 Wavelength from Speed and Frequency

Problem The sound wave from a flute playing the A above middle C has a frequency of 440 Hz. If sound waves move at a speed of 340 m/s in air at 20°C, what is the approximate wavelength of this wave (assuming it is sinusoidal)?

Solution According to equation E15.12, we have:

$$\lambda = \frac{v}{f} = \frac{340 \text{ m}/\cancel{\text{s}}}{440 \cancel{\text{Hz}}}\left(\frac{1 \cancel{\text{Hz}}}{1 \text{ cycle}/\cancel{\text{s}}}\right) = 0.77 \text{ m} = 77 \text{ cm}. \quad \text{(E15.13)}$$

Self-Test E15X.6

Seismic *P*-waves radiating from an earthquake travel at a speed of very roughly 6 km/s near the Earth's surface. If such waves for a given earthquake have a period of 0.2 s, what is their wavelength?

E15.4 The Wave Equation

One of the most important equations in physics is the **wave equation**:

The wave equation

$$0 = b\frac{\partial^2 f}{\partial t^2} - \frac{\partial^2 f}{\partial x^2} \quad \text{(E15.14)}$$

Purpose: If this equation (where b is a constant independent of t and x) accurately describes the behavior of a disturbance $f(t,x)$ in a medium, that medium will support traveling waves.

Limitations: This equation applies only to cases where the disturbance depends only on one spatial coordinate x.

Note: The partial derivative symbols remind us that when we evaluate the derivative of $f(t,x)$ with respect to one of the variables t or x, we treat the other variable as if it were a constant.

This equation appears again and again in all areas of physics: it accurately describes mechanical disturbances of a stretched string or spring, pressure or density disturbances in solids, liquids, and gases, plasma oscillations in the ionosphere, electrical disturbances in a coaxial cable, , some kinds of quantum-mechanical wave functions, and so on and so on. Physicists rapidly learn to recognize this equation as the basic indicator that traveling sinusoidal disturbance waves are possible in the medium in question.

A proof that our sinusoidal traveling wave is a solution of the wave equation

Let us show that our sinusoidal traveling wave $f(t,x) = A\sin(kx - \omega t)$ is indeed a solution of this equation. If we take the derivative of $f(t,x)$ with respect to x (while treating t as constant), we find that the chain rule tells us that

$$\frac{\partial f}{\partial x} = A\frac{\partial}{\partial x}\sin(kx - \omega t) = A\cos(kx - \omega t)\frac{\partial}{\partial x}(kx - \omega t)$$
$$= A\cos(kx - \omega t)(k) = kA\cos(kx - \omega t) \quad \text{(E15.15)}$$

If we take the derivative again, we get

$$\frac{\partial^2 f}{\partial x^2} = kA\frac{\partial}{\partial x}\cos(kx - \omega t) = -k^2 A\sin(kx - \omega t) \tag{E15.16}$$

In a similar way, you can show that

$$\frac{\partial^2 f}{\partial t^2} = -\omega^2 A\sin(kx - \omega t) \tag{E15.17}$$

Self-Test E15X.7

Verify that equation E15.17 is correct.

Plugging these results into the left side of equation E15.14, we get

$$b\frac{\partial^2 f}{\partial t^2} - \frac{\partial^2 f}{\partial x^2} = -b\omega^2 A\sin(kx - \omega t) + k^2 A\sin(kx - \omega t)$$

$$= \left(k^2 - b\omega^2\right)A\sin(kx - \omega t) \tag{E15.18}$$

This will satisfy the wave equation as long as $k^2 - b\omega^2 = 0$. We see that a medium obeying the wave equation can indeed support traveling waves as long as the relationship between the values of k and ω for those waves is such that $k^2 = b\omega^2$, where b is whatever constant appearing in the wave equation.

What will be the phase speed of these waves? Equation E5.11 tells us that the phase speed of the wave is $v = \omega/k$. This means that valid sinusoidal traveling-wave solutions to the wave equation will *all* move at the speed

The relationship between the wave speed and the constant b in the wave equation

$$v = \frac{\omega}{k} = \frac{\omega}{\omega\sqrt{b}} = \frac{1}{\sqrt{b}} \tag{E15.19}$$

independent of their wavelength or frequency. Therefore, *the value of the constant b appearing in a given medium's wave equation uniquely determines the phase speed of waves moving through that medium.* This is a *very* important conclusion.

One can in fact show (see problem E15S.4) that an arbitrary *sum* of sinusoidal traveling waves also satisfies this equation (as long as $k^2 = b\omega^2$ for each wave in the sum, i.e. each wave moves at speed $v = [b]^{-1/2}$). Since the Fourier theorem tells us that any arbitarily shaped traveling wave can be written as a sum of sinusoidal traveling waves, this means that *any* traveling wave will satisfy the wave equation as long as it moves with phase speed $v = [b]^{-1/2}$.

How the wave equation emerges from basic physics in the context of a taut string

How would we know whether this equation "accurately describes the behavior of a disturbance" in a given medium? Let's see how this works by considering the special case of a transverse wave on a stretched string.

Example E15.2 Waves on a Stretched String

Problem Imagine that we place a string under tension by exerting a tension force of magnitude F_T on its ends. Assume that the string has a mass per unit length of μ. Show that small transverse disturbances on this string obey the wave equation and determine the phase speed v of traveling waves on this string.

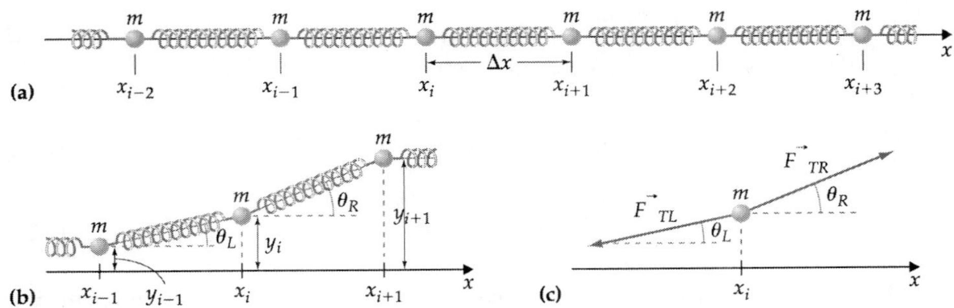

Figure E15.7
(a) We can model a stretched string as being a sequence of particles with mass *m* connected by springs. The diagram shows the string in its equilibrium state. (b) This diagram shows a possible set of vertically disturbed positions for the *i*th particle and its nearest neighbors. (c) This diagram displays the forces that are exerted on the *i*th particle by the springs connecting it to its nearest neighbors.

Translation and Model We will model the string as being a series of particles of mass m connected by identical springs, as shown in figure E15.7a. (We can eventually take the limit that the distance Δx between the masses goes to zero to better model a continuous string.) In our model, saying that the tension on the string has a magnitude of F_T means that each spring is stretched sufficiently so that each of its ends exerts a force of magnitude F_T on the mass to which that end is connected.

Figure E15.7a shows the string in its "undisturbed" configuration, where the string is straight and each mass is at rest on the x axis. We consider the string's ith mass (the one at position x_i) to be "disturbed" if it is displaced vertically away from the x axis to a nonzero y coordinate y_i. A listing of the y coordinates $y_i(t, x_i)$ for all the masses on the string at a given time t completely describes the wave on that string at that time. In this case, therefore, $y_i(t, x_i)$ corresponds to the disturbance function we more generally described earlier as being $f(t, x)$.

How will the masses respond to being disturbed? Figure E15.7b shows some of the masses in a disturbed configuration. The forces acting on the ith mass in this case are the leftward and rightward tension forces $\vec{F}_{TL}$ and $\vec{F}_{TR}$ shown in figure E15.7c. Newton's second law for that mass therefore reads

$$m\vec{a}_i = \vec{F}_{\text{net},i} = \begin{bmatrix} F_{TL,x} + F_{TR,x} \\ F_{TL,y} + F_{TR,y} \\ F_{TL,z} + F_{TR,z} \end{bmatrix} = \begin{bmatrix} -F_{TL}\cos\theta_L + F_{TR}\cos\theta_R \\ -F_{TL}\sin\theta_L + F_{TR}\sin\theta_R \\ 0 \end{bmatrix} \tag{E15.20}$$

At this point, I am going to make an approximation. During a realistic oscillation, the angle that any part of the string makes with the horizontal direction is going to be very small (imagine, for example, a vibrating guitar string: it remains almost straight even as it vibrates, right?). Indeed, I have greatly exaggerated the string's curvature in figure E15.7 just to make the angles visible at all. In this "small oscillation" limit, no individual spring will be stretched much more or less than the general stretching that gives the string its tension F_T. Therefore, the magnitude of the force that each individual spring exerts will be essentially equal to F_T. Moreover, in this small oscillation limit, the angles θ_L and θ_R are small. This means that $\cos\theta_L \approx \cos\theta_R \approx 1$, so the x component of the net force on the ith mass is $(F_{\text{net},i})_x = F_{TL}\cos\theta_L - F_{TR}\cos\theta_R \approx F_T - F_T \approx 0$. It is therefore an good approximation in this limit to assume that the x-position of any mass on this string is essentially fixed.

In the small angle limit, we also have $\sin\theta_L \approx \tan\theta_L$ and $\sin\theta_R \approx \tan\theta_R$. If we take the angles to be positive when measured counterclockwise from the x direction, then

$$\sin\theta_L \approx \tan\theta_L = \frac{y_i - y_{i-1}}{\Delta x} = \frac{\Delta y_L}{\Delta x} \qquad \text{(E15.21a)}$$

$$\sin\theta_R \approx \tan\theta_R = \frac{y_{i+1} - y_i}{\Delta x} = \frac{\Delta y_R}{\Delta x} \qquad \text{(E15.21b)}$$

where Δx is the horizontal distance between masses, y_i is the vertical position of the ith mass, y_{i-1} is the same for the adjacent mass to the left, y_{i+1} is the same for the adjacent mass to the right, $\Delta y_L \equiv y_i - y_{i-1}$, and $\Delta y_R \equiv y_{i+1} - y_i$. If we plug this back into equation E15.20, we see that the only significant component of the ith mass' acceleration is the y component, whose value is

$$a_{i,y} = \frac{(F_{\text{net},i})_y}{m} \approx \frac{F_T}{m}\left[\sin\theta_R - \sin\theta_L\right] \approx \frac{F_T}{m}\left(\frac{y_{i+1} - y_i}{\Delta x} - \frac{y_i - y_{i-1}}{\Delta x}\right)$$

$$= \frac{F_T \Delta x}{m}\left[\frac{1}{\Delta x}\left(\frac{\Delta y_R}{\Delta x} - \frac{\Delta y_L}{\Delta x}\right)\right] \qquad \text{(E15.22)}$$

Now, let us look at the quantity in square brackets in this expression in the limit that the spacing Δx between masses becomes very small. In that limit, $y_i(t, x_i)$ will become a continuous function $y(t,x)$. Now, $\Delta y_R / \Delta x$ describes the string's slope for the step just to the right of the ith mass: this ratio best approximates the derivative dy/dx of the continuous function at a point halfway between the ith and (i+1)th mass, i.e., at $x = x_i + \frac{1}{2}\Delta x$. Similarly, $\Delta y_L / \Delta x$ describes the string's slope for the step just left of the ith mass and best approximates dy/dx at $x = x_i - \frac{1}{2}\Delta x$. Therefore, in the limit that $\Delta x \to 0$,

$$\lim_{\Delta x \to 0}\left[\frac{1}{\Delta x}\left(\frac{\Delta y_R}{\Delta x} - \frac{\Delta y_L}{\Delta x}\right)\right] = \lim_{\Delta x \to 0}\left[\frac{(dy/dx)_{x_i + \Delta x/2} - (dy/dx)_{x_i - \Delta x/2}}{\Delta x}\right]$$

$$\equiv \frac{\partial^2 y}{\partial x^2} \quad \text{(evaluated at position } x_i \text{ and time } t) \qquad \text{(E15.23a)}$$

since this amounts to the definition of the derivative of the derivative of y with respect to x. By the definition of acceleration, we also have

$$a_{i,y} \equiv \frac{d^2 y_i}{dt^2} = \frac{\partial^2 y}{\partial t^2} \quad \text{(evaluated at position } x_i \text{ and time } t) \qquad \text{(E15.23b)}$$

Finally, in this same limit

$$\lim_{\Delta x \to 0}\frac{m}{\Delta x} \equiv \mu \equiv \text{mass per unit length on the string} \qquad \text{(E15.24)}$$

Solution Plugging these results back into equation E15.22, we therefore have, in the limit that $\Delta x \to 0$,

$$\frac{\mu}{F_T}\frac{\partial^2 y}{\partial t^2} = \frac{\partial^2 y}{\partial x^2} \quad \Rightarrow \quad 0 = \frac{\mu}{F_T}\frac{\partial^2 y}{\partial t^2} - \frac{\partial^2 y}{\partial x^2} \qquad \text{(E15.25a)}$$

This has the same mathematical form as the wave equation [considering that our disturbance function is $y(x,t)$ instead of $f(x,t)$] with $b = F_T/\mu$. We can thus conclude that traveling-wave solutions are possible for transverse disturbances on a stretched string and such waves will move with the phase speed

$$v = \sqrt{\frac{F_T}{\mu}} \tag{E15.25b}$$

Evaluation This result makes good intuitive sense: experience with stretched strings suggest that that the speed of waves on the string would increase if we increase the string tension and/or decrease the string's density.

Self-Test E15X.8

Show that F_T/μ has the units of a squared speed, and calculate the speed of transverse waves on a string whose mass per unit length is 2.0 g/m and whose tension force is 100 N (roughly 22 lbs).

Example E15.2 illustrates how basic physical principles applied to a segment of a stretched string leads directly to the wave equation (in the small-oscillation limit, at least). One finds that the same kind of thing happens in a variety of media (particularly in the small-oscillation limit): this equation is a very common outcome of such analyses! (See the problems for other examples.)

The wave equation is a powerful and useful mathematical tool, but it is somewhat abstract. How can we recognize more intuitively when a medium can support travelning waves? Also, we have seen that sinusoidal traveling waves are a solution to the wave equation, but *must* waves travel in media that obey the wave equation? If so, why? The answers to these questions are linked.

At its most fundamental level, the wave equation links the acceleration $\partial^2 f/\partial t^2$ of a medium's displacement at a point to the curvature $\partial^2 f/\partial x^2$ of the displacement in that point's neighborhood. Useful mnemonics might be that "the tow is equal to the bow" or "the kick is equal to the kink." The point is that a medium whose elements interact in a way that seeks to flatten out any disturbance (attempting to restore the graph of the disturbance to a straight line) qualitatively satisfies the wave equation, and it strictly satisfies the wave equation if the restoring force applied on an element of the medium is exactly proportional to how far it is out of line.

A simple example of such a medium is the torsion-rod wave machine shown in figure E15.8. The medium in this case consists of transverse rods connected to a longitudinal wire spine. The spine in this case strongly twists each rod in direct proportion to the degree to which that rod is out of line with its

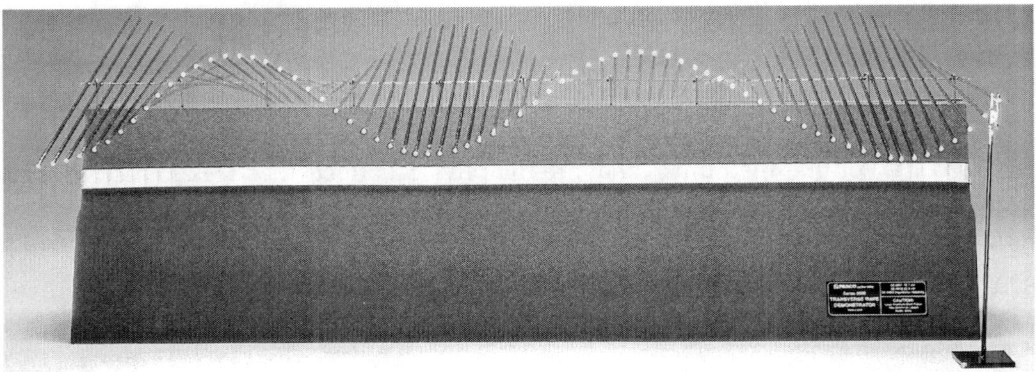

Figure E15.8 A torsion rod wave machine.

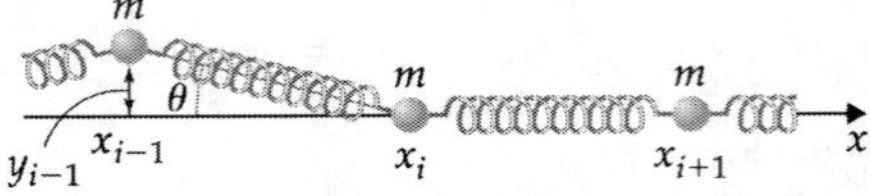

Figure E15.9
Disturbing the mass element at position x_{i-1} creates a kink in the disturbance at position x_i that accelerates the mass element there. But this creates a kink at position x_{i+1} that accelerates the mass element there, and so on.

neighbors, and the spine also twists the rod in a direction that will bring it more in line. Similarly, figure E15.7 on page 281 shows that a mass element on a stretched string only experiences a net force if it is out of the line defined by its nearest neighbors. So a medium obeying the wave equation is easily recognized by its tendency to flatten out any disturbance.

Why do disturbances in such a medium move? Imagine that we are given a stretched string in equilibrium (with all mass elements horizontal and at rest) and we suddenly displace the (i–1)th mass element, as shown in figure E15.9. In that figure, note that this creates a kink in the slope of the displacements in the neighborhood of the ith mass element. By the wave equation, this element will therefore be accelerated upward to try to move this element into the line defined by its neighbors. But its motion upward then creates a kink in the slope at the (i+1)th element, which then accelerates upward, and so on. You can see how this progression causes a disturbance wave to move outward from the initial disturbance.

Moreover, the *speed* at which this disturbance wave moves depends entirely on how rapidly the out-of-line mass element is accelerated: the bigger the acceleration, the more rapidly each mass element will respond to a kink in the disturbance, and the more rapidly the next element will see a kink developing, and so on. Indeed, if we rewrite the wave equation as follows

$$0 = b\frac{\partial^2 f}{\partial t^2} - \frac{\partial^2 f}{\partial x^2} \quad \Rightarrow \quad \frac{\partial^2 f}{\partial t^2} = \frac{1}{b}\frac{\partial^2 f}{\partial x^2} \tag{E15.26}$$

you can easily see that the constant of proportionality that expresses how large an acceleration $\partial^2 f/\partial t^2$ is caused by a given disturbance curvature $\partial^2 f/\partial x^2$ is simply $1/b = v^2$. This supports the line of reasoning just given: the stronger the acceleration caused by a given disturbance curvature, the more rapidly disturbance waves will move through the medium.

E15.5 The Mystery du Jour

We are finally in a position to appreciate fully one of the most profound and important consequences of our dynamic electromagnetic field equations: the existence of electromagnetic waves that are able to move through space, carrying energy from point to point. We now understand what mechanical traveling waves are like, how to describe them mathematically, and how to recognize media that support traveling waves. But what *are* electromagnetic waves? In what medium would such travel? What corresponds to "displacements" of that medium? What are the physical effects that seek to restore that medium to flatness? These are the questions that we will resolve in the crowning chapter of this unit.

TWO-MINUTE PROBLEMS

E15T.1 The speed of a transverse wave traveling on a spring is necessarily equal to the actual speed of a given part of the spring as it moves in response to the passing wave. (T or F)

E15T.2 Sound waves move through air at about 340 m/s. The sound waves produced by bats doing echolocation can have frequencies in excess of 60 kHz. What would be the wavelength of such a sound wave?

A. 2×10^7 m
B. 180 m
C. 28 m
D. 1.3 m
E. 6 mm
F. Some other wavelength (specify)

E15T.3 A sinusoidal sound wave with a frequency of 510 Hz moves through water. The wave is observed to have wavelength 2.94 m. What is the phase speed of sound waves in water according to this information?

A. 1.5 km/s
B. 173 m/s
C. 0.6 mm/s
D. Some other phase speed (specify)

E15T.4 A sinusoidal water surface wave has a wavelength of 10 cm and a frequency of 0.318 Hz. What is *k*?

A. 62.8 cm
B. 31.4 cm
C. 3.18 cm
D. 0.628 cm^{-1}
E. Some other value (specify)

E15T.5 A sinusoidal water surface wave has a wavelength of 10 cm and a frequency of 0.318 Hz. What is *w*?

A. 0.32 s^{-1}
B. 1.0 s^{-1}
C. 2.0 s^{-1}
D. 3.2 cm/s
E. Some other value (specify)

E15T.6 Imagine that sinusoidal waves of with wavelength λ_0 on a certain stretched string are observed to have a frequency f_0. Imagine now that we stretch the string more tightly, so that the phase speed of disturbance waves on the string increases. How will the frequency f_{new} of waves with the same frequency λ_0 on the tighter string compare to the original frequency f_0?

A. $f_{new} > f_0$
B. $f_{new} = f_0$
C. $f_{new} < f_0$
D. We need more information to determine the relationship.

E15T.7 One can show theoretically that the wave equation for sound waves in air is

$$0 = \frac{\rho_0}{p_0\gamma}\frac{\partial^2 f}{\partial t^2} - \frac{\partial^2 f}{\partial x^2} \quad \text{(E15.27)}$$

where p_0 is the ambient mean air pressure, ρ_0 is the ambient mean density of air, and γ is a unitless constant called the *adiabatic index* (its value is ≈ 1.40 for air). What is the phase speed v of sound waves?

A. $v = \rho_0 / p_0\gamma$
B. $v = [\rho_0 / p_0\gamma]^2$
C. $v = [\rho_0 / p_0\gamma]^{1/2}$
D. $v = p_0\gamma / \rho_0$
E. $v = [p_0\gamma / \rho_0]^2$
F. $v = [p_0\gamma / \rho_0]^{1/2}$
T. something else (specify)

E15T.8 The wave equation for one-dimensional S-waves from an earthquake is

$$0 = \frac{\rho}{\mu}\frac{\partial^2 f}{\partial t^2} - \frac{\partial^2 f}{\partial x^2} \quad \text{(E15.28)}$$

where ρ is the density of rock, and μ is a quantity known as the shear modulus of rock, which has units of N/m^2. What is the phase speed v of these S-waves?

A. $v = \mu / \rho$
B. $v = [\mu / \rho]^{1/2}$
C. $v = [\mu / \rho]^2$
D. $v = \rho / \mu$
E. $v = [\rho / \mu]^{1/2}$
F. $v = [\rho / \mu]^2$
T. something else (specify)

HOMEWORK PROBLEMS

Basic Skills

E15B.1 Sound waves move through air at a speed of about 340 m/s. Compute the wavelength of the following sound waves:
(a) an organ pipe playing middle C (260 Hz)
(b) the highest audible pitch (≈ 20,000 Hz)
(c) the lowest audible pitch (≈15 Hz)

E15B.2 In the next chapter, we will find out that electromagnetic waves move at the speed of light. What are the wavelengths of the following kinds of electromagnetic waves?
(a) radio waves on the AM band (≈ 1000 kHz)
(b) radio waves on the FM band (≈ 100 MHz)
(c) EM waves in a microwave oven (≈ 30 GHz)

E15B.3 Sound waves move through air at a speed of about 340 m/s. What would be the frequency of a sound wave that has a wavelength of 1 m? 1 inch? 1 mm?

E15B.4 Visible light has wavelengths between 700 nm and about 400 nm. If light really is an electromagnetic wave, then what are the corresponding frequencies of these waves?

E15B.5 A sinusoidal traveling water wave has a wavelength of 25 cm and a frequency of 0.60 Hz. What are k and ω for this wave? What is the phase speed of this wave?

E15B.6 A sinusoidal wave moving down a taut rope has a wavelength of 2.0 m and a period of about 0.5 s. What are k and w for this wave? What is the phase speed of the wave?

E15B.7 Consider the sinusoidal traveling wave shown below (this is a snapshot at a certain instant of time). Assume the wave travels at 1.0 m/s.
(a) What is the wave's amplitude?
(b) What is its wavenumber k?
(c) What is its angular velocity ω?
(d) What is its period?
(e) What is its frequency?

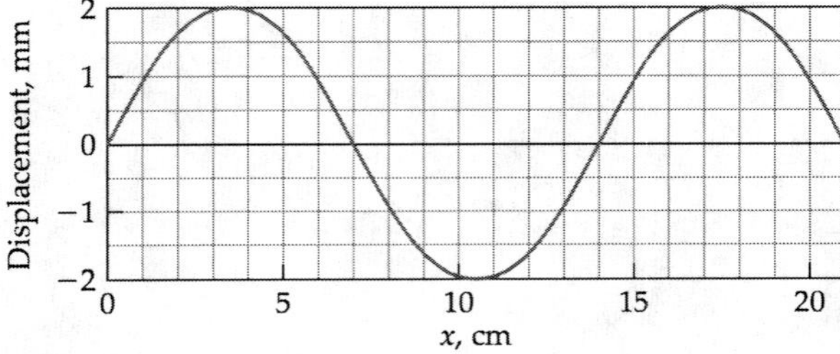

Synthetic

E15S.1 Sinusoidal water waves are created 120 km offshore by an earthquake near a small island. Observers in helicopters above the island report that the waves have an amplitude of about 2.0 m, a wavelength of 15 m, and a frequency of about 0.5 Hz. How long do lifeguards on the mainland have to evacuate beaches before the waves arrive?

E15S.2 magine that a geologist is measuring the waves produced by small earthquakes using two seismographs, one 12 km from the volcano, and another 17 km from the volcano. During one earthquake, the waves feel like the gentle rocking of a boat at a frequency of about 1.5 Hz and an amplitude of about 1 cm. The geologist later notices that the closer seismograph registered the waves about 0.85 s sooner than the other. What was the approximate wavelength of the waves during this episode?

E15S.3 Consider the function $f(x,t) = A\sin(kx+\omega t)$. Does this function describe a *traveling* sinusoidal wave? If not, why not? If so, what is the speed (in terms of w and k) and the direction of motion of this wave? Does this wave satisfy the wave equation? Explain your responses carefully.

E15S.4 Argue that if $f(t,x)$ and $g(t,x)$ separately satisfy the wave equation for a given medium, then $h(t,x) = f(t,x) + g(t,x)$ also satisfies the wave equation. (By extension, any sum of sinusoidal waves will satisfy the wave equation.)

E15S.5 By rocking a boat, a person produces water waves on a previously undisturbed lake. This person observes that the boat oscillates 12 times in 20 s, each oscillation producing a wave crest 5 cm above the undisturbed level of the lake, and that the waves reach the shore (12 m away) in about 6 s. At any given instant of time, about how many wave crests are there between the boat and the shore?

E15S.6 Consider a series of identical masses m arranged along the x axis that are connected by identical springs with spring-constant k_s. The masses are all free to slide in the $\pm x$ direction on a frictionless surface. Assume that when all the masses are in their equilibrium positions, their centers are equal distances Δx apart and the springs between them are all relaxed. Let's define the position x_i of the ith mass (when all masses are in equilibrium) to be its "home" position. We can then define the "disturbance" s_i of the ith mass at a given time to be its horizontal displacement from its home position, where s_i is positive if the mass is displaced in the $+x$ direction from home, and negative if it is displaced in the $-x$ direction from home.

(a) Make a careful drawing of the mass at a given arbitrary position x and its two adjacent neighbors and argue that the x component of the net force on the mass at a given instant of time is

$$F_x = k_s \Delta s_R - k_s \Delta s_L \tag{E15.29}$$

where $\Delta s_R \equiv s_{i+1} - s_i$ describes how much larger the distance between the mass at x_i and the mass to the right is than the usual separation Δx, and $\Delta s_L \equiv s_i - s_{i-1}$ is the same for distance to the left of that mass. (A positive value of Δs_R or Δs_L means that the spring between the masses is stretched; a negative value means that it is compressed.)

(b) Argue (using the definition of the double derivative) that if Δx is reasonably small,

$$\frac{1}{\Delta x^2}[\Delta s_R - \Delta s_L] \approx \frac{\partial^2 s}{\partial x^2} \tag{E15.30}$$

where in the last step, we are imagining $s(x,t)$ to be a smooth function that matches the value of s_i at each home position x_i.

(c) Use this to argue that

$$F_x \approx k_s \Delta x^2 \frac{\partial^2 s}{\partial x^2} \tag{E15.31}$$

(d) Show that Newton's second law and the previous results together imply that longtitudinal disturbances in this set of interconnected masses obey the wave equation

$$0 = b\frac{\partial^2 s}{\partial t^2} - \frac{\partial^2 s}{\partial x^2} \tag{E15.32}$$

and find the wave speed v in terms of k_s, m, and Δx. (This means that disturbances in this system will move like traveling waves up and down the x axis. If we consider the masses to be atoms and the springs to be interatomic bonds, this could represent a simplified model of a one-dimensional elemental solid.)

E15S.7 Figure E15.8 on page 303 shows a torsional wave machine of a type commonly used for classroom demonstrations of traveling waves. The wave machine consists of rods of length L and mass m separated by distance Δx along a wire spine. The disturbance function in this case is the angle $\theta(t,x)$ that the rod at position x makes with the horizontal plane at time t. When a segment of the spine of length Δx is twisted through a small angle $\Delta\theta$, the segment exerts a torque on the rod at each end whose magnitude is

$$\tau = k_t \frac{\Delta\theta}{\Delta x} \tag{E15.33}$$

where k_t is a constant expressing the spine's stiffness (a kind of a spring constant for twisting). Assume that the x axis is along the spine and the positive direction of that axis is toward the right.

(a) Argue that the x component of the net torque on the rod at x_i is

$$\tau_{\text{net},x} = k_t(\Delta\theta_R - \Delta\theta_L) \tag{E15.34}$$

where $\Delta\theta_R = \theta(x_{i+1}) - \theta(x_i)$ is the angle that the rod to the right of x_i is twisted relative to the angle of the rod at x_i, and $\Delta\theta_L = \theta(x_i) - \theta(x_{i-1})$ is the angle that the rod at x_i is twisted relative to the next rod to the left. (Conventionally, counterclockwise angles are positive and clockwise angles are negative.)

(b) Argue (using the definition of the double derivative) that if the distance Δx between adjacent rods is reasonably small,

$$\frac{1}{\Delta x^2}[\Delta\theta_R - \Delta\theta_L] \approx \frac{\partial^2\theta}{\partial x^2} \tag{E15.35}$$

(c) As we saw in unit C, the definition of torque is $\vec{\tau}_{\text{net}} \equiv d\vec{L}/dt$, $\vec{L} = \frac{1}{12}ML^2\vec{\omega}$ for a long, thin rod of mass m and length L, and $\omega \equiv d\theta/dt$. Use this information to argue that the rightward component of the torque on the rod is related to its angle according to the expression

$$\tau_{\text{net},x} \propto \frac{\partial^2\theta}{\partial t^2} \tag{E15.36}$$

and find the constant of proportionality.

(d) Link equation E15.34 and E15.36 to show that an angular disturbance on this medium obeys the wave equation and to determine the speed of disturbance waves in terms of m, L, and k_t

E15S.8 Consider a series of identical disk-shaped magnets strung along like beads along a thin rod. The magnets are able to slide frictionlessly along the rod, and are oriented so that each magnet repels both its nearest neighbors. Assume that when all the magnets are at rest at their equilibrium positions, their centers are equal distances Δx apart. Let's define the position x_i of the ith magnet (when all the magnets are in this equilibrium state) to be its "home" position,. We can then define the "disturbance" s_i for the ith magnet at a given time to be its horizontal displacement from its home position, where s_i is positive if the magnet is displaced in the $+x$ direction from home, and negative if it is displaced in the $-x$ direction. The magnets all have mass m, and let the repulsive force that a magnet exerts on either neighbor be F_0 when they are separated by Δx. Assume also that we define the x axis to be along the rod, with the $+x$ direction to the right.

(a) Make a careful drawing of the magnet at a given arbitrary position x_i and its two adjacent neighbors. It turns out that if the distance between the magnets is large compared to their thckness and diameter, the repulsive force between two magnets separated by a distance r is roughly $\propto 1/r^4$ (see problem E2S.8). *Assuming* that this is true, use the binomial approximation to explain carefully why the x component of the repulsive force that the ith magnet receives from the magnet to its right is

$$F_{R,x} = -F_0\left(\frac{\Delta x}{r}\right)^4 = -F_0\left(\frac{\Delta x}{\Delta x + \Delta s_R}\right)^4$$

$$\approx -F_0\left(1 - 4\frac{\Delta s_R}{\Delta x}\right) = 4F_0\frac{\Delta s_R}{\Delta x} - F_0 \quad \text{(E15.37a)}$$

if $\Delta s_R \equiv s_{i+1} - s_i \ll \Delta x$. Similarly explain why the x component of the force that it receives from the magnet to the left is

$$F_{L,x} \approx +F_0\left(1 - 4\frac{\Delta s_L}{\Delta x}\right) = F_0 - 4F_0\frac{\Delta s_L}{\Delta x} \quad \text{(E15.37b)}$$

where $\Delta s_L \equiv s_i - s_{i-1} \ll \Delta x$.

(b) Argue that the x component of the *net* force on the ith magnet at a given instant of time is

$$F_x = k_s \Delta s_R - k_s \Delta s_L \quad \text{(E15.38)}$$

(c) Argue (using the definition of the double derivative) that if Δx is reasonably small,

$$\frac{1}{\Delta x^2}[\Delta s_R - \Delta s_L] \approx \frac{\partial^2 s}{\partial x^2} \quad \text{(E15.39)}$$

where in the last step, we are imagining $s(x,t)$ to be a smooth function that matches the value of s_i at each home position x_i.

(d) Use this to argue that

$$F_x \approx k_s \Delta x^2 \frac{\partial^2 s}{\partial x^2} \quad \text{(E15.40)}$$

(e) Show that Newton's second law for the ith magnet and the previous results together imply that longtitudinal disturbances in this set of interacting magnets obey the wave equation

$$0 = b\frac{\partial^2 s}{\partial t^2} - \frac{\partial^2 s}{\partial x^2} \quad \text{(E15.41)}$$

and find the speed v at which magnet disturbance waves move up and down the x axis in terms of F_0, m, and Δx.

Rich-Context

E15R.1 Waves do not have to be sinusoidal! Consider the following disturbance function, which might be a good model for a disturbance consisting of a single pulse:

$$f(t,x) = Ae^{-(kx+\omega t)^2} \quad \text{(E15.42)}$$

(a) Sketch a graph of what this wave looks like at $t = 0$ assuming that $k = 1.0/\text{cm}$. (Label the vertical axis in units of A.)

(b) Argue that this is a traveling wave, and find the speed of the peak. Does this wave move in the $+x$ direction or the $-x$ direction?

(c) Does this wave satisfy the wave equation? Defend your answer. (*Hint:* You can save yourself a lot of writing if you define $u \equiv kx + \omega t$ and then show that $du/dx = k$ and $du/dt = \omega$. Then you won't have to ever write out "$kx + \omega t$" when you compute the derivatives.)

E15R.2 Consider a sinusoidal wave moving down a taut elastic string. Find a formula for the ratio of the maximum speed of motion of a point on the string to the phase speed of the wave. Express the ratio in terms of A, k, and ω for the wave and anything else that you need.

E15R.3 Figure E15.10 on the next page shows a drawing of a torsional wave machine that consists of a series of square aluminum rods spaced along a set of two parallel strands of fishing line flanking a stiff central wire. The rods have length L and a mass per unit rod length of μ. The distance between adjacent rods is Δx. The rods pivot around the central wire. The two side strands of fishing line, which are separated by a distance a, are put under the same tension F_T. The disurbance in this case is described by the function $\theta(x,t)$, where $\theta_i \equiv \theta(x_i,t)$ is the angle that the rod at position x_i makes with the horizontal plane at time t. Show that for small angles, such a disturbance obeys the wave equation, and determine the wave speed. (*Hints:* Instead of Newton's second law, you will have to use $\vec{\tau}_{\text{net}} = d\vec{L}/dt$. Problem E15.8 presents an outline for a similar wave machine that you could adapt to this device.)

Advanced

E15A.1 Consider a completely arbitrary function $f(u)$ where $u \equiv kx - \omega t$. **(a)** Argue that no matter what the shape of the function is, its features will move in the $+x$ direction with speed $v = \omega/k$. **(b)** Show that no matter what $f(u)$ might be (as long as it has at least two derivatives), this disturbance function satisfies the wave equation.

ANSWERS TO SELF-TESTS

E15X.1 *P*-waves are longitudinal, *S*-waves transverse.

E15X.2 Earthquake waves shake objects, which means that the waves must have given the objects kinetic energy. This energy ultimately comes from the sudden relaxation of strains in rock due to the slippage along a fault at the epicenter. This energy may be carried many miles from the epicenter by the wave.

E15X.3 The first crest to pass $x = 0$ after $t = 0$ is when $-\omega t_1 = -3\pi/2$ [since $\sin(-3\pi/2) = +1$]. The next crest passes when $-\omega t_2 = -7\pi/2$. Thus $T \equiv t_2 - t_1 = -2\pi/(-\omega) = 2\pi/\omega$, as claimed.

E15X.4 $k = 3.14/\text{cm}$ and $\omega = 12.57/\text{s}$

E15X.5 (The calculation is essentially identical with what we did before except that we now substitute $5\pi/2$ everywhere that we had $\pi/2$ before.)

E15X.6 Solving equation E15.12 for λ and plugging in the numbers, we get $\lambda = 1.2$ km

E15X.7 The first derivative of $f = A\sin(kx - \omega t)$ is

$$\frac{\partial f}{\partial t} = A\frac{\partial}{\partial t}\sin(kx-\omega t) = A\cos(kx-\omega t)\frac{\partial}{\partial t}(kx-\omega t)$$
$$= -\omega A\cos(kx-\omega t) \tag{E15.43}$$

Taking the derivative again, we get

$$\frac{\partial^2 f}{\partial t^2} = -\omega A\frac{\partial}{\partial t}\cos(kx-\omega t)$$
$$= +\omega A\sin(kx-\omega t)\frac{\partial}{\partial t}(kx-\omega t)$$
$$= -\omega^2 A\sin(kx-\omega t) \tag{E15.44}$$

E15X.8 We can do both parts at once here:

$$v = \sqrt{\frac{F_T}{\mu}} = \sqrt{\frac{100\ \cancel{\text{N}}}{2.0\ \cancel{\text{g}}/\text{m}}\left(\frac{1\ \cancel{\text{kg}}\cdot\text{m/s}^2}{1\ \cancel{\text{N}}}\right)\left(\frac{1000\ \cancel{\text{g}}}{1\ \cancel{\text{kg}}}\right)}$$
$$= \sqrt{50{,}000\ \frac{\text{m}^2}{\text{s}^2}} = 220\ \text{m/s} \tag{E15.45}$$

Note that the units do work out correctly!

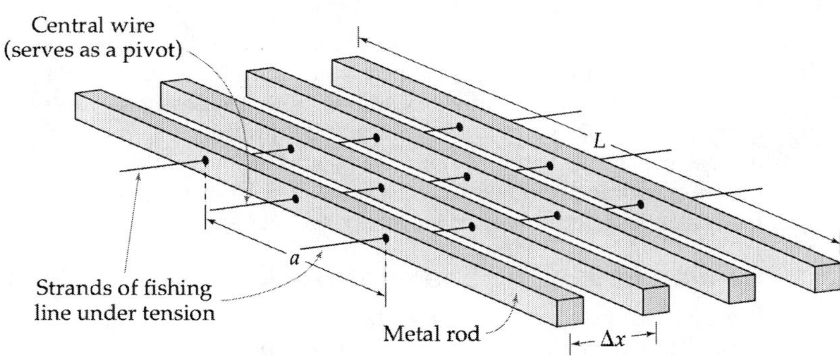

Figure E15.10
A schematic diagram indicating the construction of a certain wave machine. The square metal rods can rotate about the central wire, but the two stretched fishing lines on either side of the central wire try to keep the rods level. How fast do waves move on this wave machine? (See problem E15R.3.)

E16 Electromagnetic Waves

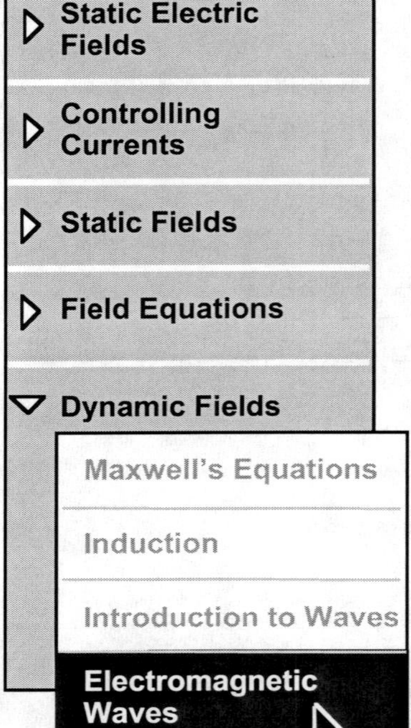

Chapter Overview

Introduction

Maxwell's greatest triumphs were his prediction of the existence of electromagnetic waves that could move through empty space at the speed of light and his identification of light as an electromagnetic wave. We close this unit by exploring what Maxwell's equations can tell us about the existence and characteristics of electromagnetic waves.

Section E16.1: Electromagnetic Waves

For the sake of simplicity, we consider in this section a **plane wave** disturbance of the form $\vec{E} = [0, 0, E_z(x,t)]$, where E_z has the same value at all points on a given plane parallel to the yz plane. By working through Maxwell's equations for empty space, we find that this disturbance will obey the wave equation for waves moving at the speed c. We also find that the electric disturbance must be accompanied by a magnetic disturbance as well. Examination of the equations uncovers the following basic properties of electromagnetic waves:

1. Maxwell's equations allow for the existence of superposable electromagnetic waves that travel at the speed of light through empty space.
2. A wave's $\vec{E}$ and $\vec{\mathbb{B}}$ vectors have equal magnitudes at any given point in space and instant of time.
3. These vectors are perpendicular to each other and to the direction of motion, which is the direction indicated by $\vec{E} \times \vec{\mathbb{B}}$.

Section E16.2: What is Waving?

Mechanical waves are disturbances in a medium. What is the medium for electromagnetic waves? In the late 1800s, physicists simply assumed that such a medium (which they called the "ether") must exist. But independent evidence for the ether failed to materialize. Einstein helped the scientific community face up to the idea that electromagnetic waves move through *empty space*, and that the only thing that remotely resembles a medium for electromagnetic waves is the field itself. The undisturbed state of the electromagnetic field, however, is simply no field at all!

Section E16.3: The Energy in an Electromagnetic Wave

We can use the formula $u_{EM} = \frac{1}{2}\varepsilon_0(E^2 + \mathbb{B}^2)$ for the energy density in an electromagnetic field to calculate the intensity (energy delivered per unit area per unit time) by a sinusoidal electromagnetic wave:

$$\text{Average EM wave intensity} = c\varepsilon_0(E^2)_{\text{avg}} = \tfrac{1}{2}c\varepsilon_0 E_0^2 \qquad \text{(E16.14)}$$

Purpose: This equation describes the energy per unit time per unit area deposited on a surface that absorbs a sinusoidal electromagnetic wave.

Symbols: E_0 is the amplitude of the wave's oscillating electric field, c is the speed of light and k is the Coulomb constant.

Limitations: This equation applies only to sinusoidal waves.

Section E16.4: The Power Radiated by a Charge

A charged particle moving at a constant velocity cannot create an electromagnetic wave, because whether or not such a wave exists is a frame-independent idea, and in the rest frame of the particle, there clearly is no electromagnetic wave. Accelerating charged particles, however, can and do radiate electromagnetic waves. The formula for the power radiated by an accelerating charged particle is:

$$P = \frac{2}{3}\frac{kq^2a^2}{c^3} \tag{E16.20}$$

Purpose: This is the **Larmor formula** for the power P that a particle with charge q whose acceleration is a radiates in the form of electromagnetic waves.

Symbols: k is the Coulomb constant, c is the speed of light.

Limitations: This applies only to nonrelativistic point particles.

This formula applies quite generally to nonrelativistic accelerated particles, and has many interesting applications.

Section E16.5: Why the Sky is Blue

One such application is the explanation of why the sky is blue. Sunlight is scattered by air molecules in a process known as **Raleigh scattering:** the oscillating electric field in the light from the sun causes the electrons in a molecule to oscillate sympathetically, which causes it to reradiate electromagnetic waves of the same angular frequency ω. The power of the light reradiated by this oscillating electron, by the Larmor formula, ends up being proportional to ω^4. This means that the colors of light corresponding to high frequencies (blue and violet) are much more effectively reradiated than those corresponding to low frequencies (red and orange). This is what gives light scattered by the sky its characteristic blue color.

Section E16.6: Maxwell's Rainbow

This section provides an overview of the spectrum of electromagnetic waves as we now understand it, naming the various frequency ranges involved. (Almost none of this spectrum was known when Maxwell published his theory in 1865!)

E16.1 Electromagnetic Waves

In this section, we will show that Maxwell's equations imply that disturbances in an electromagnetic field in empty space obey the wave equation and start exploring the physical properties of such electromagnetic waves.

Unlike mechanical waves, electromagnetic waves do not correspond to physical displacements of anything; rather, they are dynamic disturbances of the values of the electric and magnetic field vectors. We will talk more about this in the next section.

Maxwell's equations in empty space

Now, the behavior of electromagnetic fields of any kind is described by Maxwell's equations. In empty space (where $\rho = 0$ and $\vec{J} = 0$) these equations read as follows:

$$\text{div}(\vec{E}) = 0 \qquad \text{div}(\vec{\boldsymbol{B}}) = 0 \tag{E16.1a}$$

$$\vec{\text{curl}}(\vec{\boldsymbol{B}}) - \frac{1}{c}\frac{\partial \vec{E}}{\partial t} = 0 \qquad \vec{\text{curl}}(\vec{E}) + \frac{1}{c}\frac{\partial \vec{\boldsymbol{B}}}{\partial t} = 0 \tag{E16.1b}$$

A hypothetical plane wave disturbance

Consider, for the sake of simplicity, a disturbance of the electric field where only the z component of the electric field is a function of x and t: $\vec{E}(x,t) = [0, 0, E_z(x,t)]$. We call the wave represented by this disturbance a **plane wave**, because the electric field has the same value at all points on any plane parallel to the yz plane. Note that the derivative definitions of the divergence and the curl imply that in this case, since only E_y is nonzero and since it depends on x alone

$$\text{div}(\vec{E}) = \frac{\partial E_x}{\partial x} + \frac{\partial E_y}{\partial y} + \frac{\partial E_z}{\partial z} = 0 \text{ automatically} \tag{E16.2a}$$

$$\vec{\text{curl}}(\vec{E}) = \begin{bmatrix} \dfrac{\partial E_z}{\partial y} - \dfrac{\partial E_y}{\partial z} \\ \dfrac{\partial E_x}{\partial z} - \dfrac{\partial E_z}{\partial x} \\ \dfrac{\partial E_y}{\partial x} - \dfrac{\partial E_x}{\partial y} \end{bmatrix} = \begin{bmatrix} 0 \\ -\dfrac{\partial E_z}{\partial x} \\ 0 \end{bmatrix} \tag{E16.2b}$$

A disturbance in the electric field must be accompanied by one in the magnetic field

If we plug equation E16.2b into Faraday's law (the second of equations E16.1b), we find that the y component of that law requires that

$$-\frac{\partial E_z}{\partial x} = -\frac{1}{c}\frac{\partial \boldsymbol{B}_y}{\partial t} \tag{E16.3}$$

This implies that at least the y component of the magnetic field cannot be zero in this disturbance: our chosen disturbance in the electric field is necessarily accompanied by a disturbance in the magnetic field. The x and z components of Faraday's law, on the other hand, state that $\partial \boldsymbol{B}_x/\partial t = 0$ and $\partial \boldsymbol{B}_x/\partial t = 0$, which means that $\boldsymbol{B}_x$ and $\boldsymbol{B}_z$ must be constant in time. This condition will be satisfied if both are zero, so let us assume that our electric field disturbance is accompanied by a magnetic field disturbance of the form $\vec{\boldsymbol{B}}(x,t) = [0, \boldsymbol{B}_y(x,t), 0]$ and which satisfies equation E16.3.

For a magnetic field of this form, the general definitions of the divergence and curl of a magnetic field imply that

$$\text{div}(\vec{\boldsymbol{B}}) = \frac{\partial \boldsymbol{B}_x}{\partial x} + \frac{\partial \boldsymbol{B}_y}{\partial y} + \frac{\partial \boldsymbol{B}_z}{\partial z} = 0 \text{ automatically} \tag{E16.4a}$$

$$\text{c\bar{u}rl}(\vec{B}) = \begin{bmatrix} \dfrac{\partial \boldsymbol{B}_z}{\partial y} - \dfrac{\partial \boldsymbol{B}_y}{\partial z} \\ \dfrac{\partial \boldsymbol{B}_x}{\partial z} - \dfrac{\partial \boldsymbol{B}_z}{\partial x} \\ \dfrac{\partial \boldsymbol{B}_y}{\partial x} - \dfrac{\partial \boldsymbol{B}_x}{\partial y} \end{bmatrix} = \begin{bmatrix} 0 \\ 0 \\ \dfrac{\partial \boldsymbol{B}_y}{\partial x} \end{bmatrix} \tag{E16.4b}$$

If we plug this into the Ampere-Maxwell law (the first of equations E16.1b), we find that the z component of that law requires that

$$\frac{\partial \boldsymbol{B}_y}{\partial x} = \frac{1}{c}\frac{\partial E_z}{\partial t} \tag{E16.5}$$

Self-Test E16X.1

Show that the other two components of the Ampere-Maxwell law simply state that $0 = 0$ for the disturbance form we have chosen.

If we now take the x-derivative of both sides of equation E16.3 and the time-derivative of both sides of equation E16.5 and divide the latter by c, we find that

$$\frac{\partial^2 E_z}{\partial x^2} = \frac{1}{c}\frac{\partial}{\partial x}\left(\frac{\partial \boldsymbol{B}_y}{\partial t}\right) \quad \text{and} \quad \frac{1}{c}\frac{\partial}{\partial t}\left(\frac{\partial \boldsymbol{B}_y}{\partial x}\right) = \frac{1}{c^2}\frac{\partial^2 E_z}{\partial t^2} \tag{E16.6}$$

Now, one can show mathematically that the order in which one evaluates partial derivatives of different variables is irrelevant: for any physically reasonable function $f(x,t)$ we have

$$\frac{\partial}{\partial t}\left(\frac{\partial f}{\partial x}\right) = \frac{\partial}{\partial x}\left(\frac{\partial f}{\partial t}\right) \tag{E16.7}$$

Self-Test E16X.2

Check this for $f(x,t) = bx^2t$ and $f(x,t) = x/(x+bt)$, where b is a constant.

Thus the two equations in equation E16.6 are equal, implying that

$$\frac{\partial^2 E_z}{\partial x^2} = \frac{1}{c^2}\frac{\partial^2 E_z}{\partial t^2} \quad \Rightarrow \quad 0 = \frac{1}{c^2}\frac{\partial^2 E_z}{\partial t^2} - \frac{\partial^2 E_z}{\partial x^2} \tag{E16.8}$$

The electric field disturbance must satisfy a wave equation

We see that our hypothetical disturbance must obey the wave equation. Therefore, *electromagnetic wave solutions to Maxwell's equations exist in empty space.* We can read the speed of such waves directly from the wave equation: *electromagnetic disturbances in empty space move at the speed of light c.*

Therefore, electromagnetic waves moving at speed c must exist

As we noted before, our disturbance in the electric field *must* be accompanied by a disturbance in the magnetic field. We can determine how these fields must be related as follows. Imagine that our electric-field disturbance is in fact sinusoidal: $E_z(x,t) = E_0 \sin(\omega t - kx)$, with $\omega/k = c$. Equation E16.3 then implies that

$$\frac{1}{c}\frac{\partial \boldsymbol{B}_y}{\partial t} = \frac{\partial E_z}{\partial x} = -kE_0 \cos(\omega t - kx) \tag{E16.9a}$$

$$\Rightarrow \boldsymbol{B}_y(x,t) = -\frac{kc}{\omega} E_0 \sin(\omega t - kx) + g(x) \tag{E16.9b}$$

where $g(x)$ is some function of x alone. (To see that equation E16.9b is correct, take the partial derivative of both sides of that equation and see that we recover equation E16.9a.). Now, note that $kc/\omega = 1$ (we were given that $\omega/k = c$). Also note that the $g(x)$ term represents an arbitrary *static* magnetic field. This term is there because it is possible for an electromagnetic wave to move through a region of empty space where there is a pre-existing static field, so Maxwell's equations should and do allow for that. But this static field is therefore *not* part of the moving wave we are interested in. So dropping this term and using $\omega / k = v = c$,, we find that

$$\mathbb{B}_y(x,t) = -E_0 \sin(\omega t - kx) = -E_z(x,t) \tag{E16.10}$$

The magnetic and electric disturbances have the same magnitude at every point

implying that $E = \mathbb{B}$ at all x and t. Since we can construct any wave out of an appropriately weighted sum of sinusoidal waves (see section E15.2), this is a general result that applies to all electromagnetic waves: $E = \mathbb{B}$ *at at any given place in an electromagnetic wave at all times.*

Now, when I began this calculation, I chose to consider a *transverse* wave whose electric field at every point was perpendicular to the wave's direction of motion (the x direction in this case). The magnetic part of the wave turned out to be perpendicular to that direction as well. Is it possible to have longitudinal electromagnetic waves?

Electromagnetic waves are transverse waves

Equation E16.2a excludes this possibility. If E_x is nonzero and depends on x and t, then it violates Gauss's law for empty space. Therefore, an electromagnetic wave can *never* have a component in the direction of its motion. The magnetic version of Gauss's law similarly excludes magnetic disturbances having a component in the direction of the disturbance's motion. *Electromagnetic waves are always transverse.*

Self-Test E16X.3

Why exactly would having a nonzero $E_x(x,t)$ violate Gauss's law?

While we can't have an electric field component in the direction of the wave's motion, there is nothing special about the z direction: we could have just as easily chosen the electric field to be in the $+y$ direction. If we had, we would have found that the accompanying magnetic field would point in the $+z$ direction (see problem E16S.1). (We could have also found the same result simply by rotating the coordinate system 90° around the x axis.)

Figure E16.1 illustrates the electric and magnetic field vectors for a sinusoidal wave solution with $E_z \neq 0$ evaluated at points along the x axis at a specific instant of time. Note that we found that in general the magnetic field must be perpendicular to the electric field. The diagram illustrates that we can always determine the relative directions of the two fields by noting that the wave moves in the direction of $\vec{E} \times \vec{\mathbb{B}}$.

Summary of electromagnetic wave properties

In summary, we have seen in this section that

1. Maxwell's equations allow for the existence of superposable electromagnetic waves that travel at the speed of light through empty space.
2. A wave's $\vec{E}$ and $\vec{\mathbb{B}}$ vectors have equal magnitudes at any given point in space and instant of time.
3. These vectors are perpendicular to each other and to the direction of motion, which is the direction indicated by $\vec{E} \times \vec{\mathbb{B}}$.

Maxwell's greatest triumph was his prediction that electromagnetic waves having these properties should exist, and his identification of light as a type of electromagnetic wave. In 1887 and 1888, Heinrich Hertz was finally (after much effort) able to vindicate Maxwell's predictions by producing the first arti-

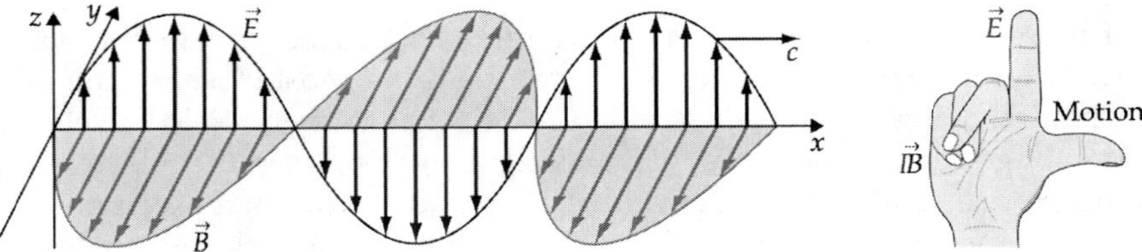

Figure E16.1
A snapshot at a given time of an electromagnetic wave whose electric field points in the z direction. The electric and magnetic field vectors have been evaluated at various points along the x axis (they will look the same at all values of y and z for a given value of x). The hand illustrates that $\vec{E} \times \vec{B}$ points in the direction that the wave is moving.

ficial electromagnetic waves (what we would now call radio waves) and showing that they had exactly the characteristics described in this section. By 1901, Guglielmo Marconi had used such waves to send a message across the Atlantic Ocean, and the wireless age had begun. Thus the musings of a middle-class Scottish college professor began to change the world...

E16.2 What is Waving?

The ether hypothesis

We saw in chapter E15 that *mechanical* waves always involve disturbances of some kind of medium. What is the "medium" in the case of electromagnetic waves? In the late 19th century, physicists were convinced that electromagnetic waves simply must be disturbances of a previously undetected physical medium (which they called the "ether") in the same way that sound waves move through air.

This hypothesis was logical, sensible, and firmly and conservatively based on what was known about other kinds of waves. However, the hypothesis proved to be completely wrong. Experiment after experiment performed in the late 1800s failed to uncover any demonstrable sign of the ether. In particular, the hypothesis implies that such waves would move through the ether with speed c only in the rest frame of the ether: an observer moving at some speed relative to the ether would measure light to travel slower or faster than c. However, careful experiments performed in the 1880s designed to measure the earth's motion through the ether (the most famous of which were the various Michelson-Morely experiments) failed to detect any change in the speed of light at different points in the earth's orbit. Hypotheses designed to explain these failures in the context of an ether model became more and more bizarre.

There is no ether

Einstein was one of the first physicists to really appreciate that electromagnetic waves were fundamentally different than mechanical waves. Electromagnetic waves do *not* require any medium, but rather move freely through a vacuum. Moreover, because one cannot detect, even in principle, whether one is at rest or moving relative to empty space (he argued), Maxwell's equations must apply equally well in *all* reference frames, meaning that the speed of light must be the same in all reference frames. This was the crucial line of reasoning that led to his formulation of the theory of special relativity.†

†As discussed in chapter E13, I have, for the sake of clarity and faithfulness to the modern perspective, inverted this argument in this book, using relativity to help us see why Maxwell's equations have to have the form they do.

Is perhaps the medium the field itself?

So if there is no medium, what is "waving" in an electromagnetic wave? One way to describe what is going on is that the thing most closely analogous to a mechanical wave's medium here is the "electromagnetic field" itself and that electromagnetic waves represent traveling disturbances in that electromagnetic field. (We certainly do see the values of $\vec{E}$ and $\vec{B}$ vary at a given point as the wave goes by, so those varying vectors are what are most closely analogous to the varying displacements of points on a string.) The strange part is that the undisturbed state of that field is *no* field (pure vacuum)! If we are willing to accept that, then this way of looking at things is not so bad.

EM waves as metaphor

But perhaps a more honest way to describe what is going on is to admit that the concept of an electromagnetic wave is simply a descriptive *metaphor*. An electromagnetic wave is *like* a mechanical wave and obeys the same mathematics as a mechanical wave, so mechanical waves we see in nature serve as useful analogies to help us understand and visualize electromagnetic waves. But while an electromagnetic wave is like a mechanical wave in many important and helpful ways, we get into trouble when we push the metaphor too far and start asking questions about the medium and what is waving. That way lies madness (as our 19th century predecessors found.)

E16.3 The Energy in an Electromagnetic Wave

Electromagnetic waves must carry energy

A microwave oven operates by generating electromagnetic waves having a wavelength of roughly 1 cm. The fact that food placed in a microwave oven gets warm is clear evidence that such waves can carry energy. In this section we will use the results of the last section to quantify the energy carried by an electromagnetic sinusoidal wave.

In section E14.5 we found that the density of energy in an electromagnetic field is given by

$$u_{EM} = \tfrac{1}{2}\varepsilon_0(E^2 + \mathbb{B}^2) \tag{E16.10}$$

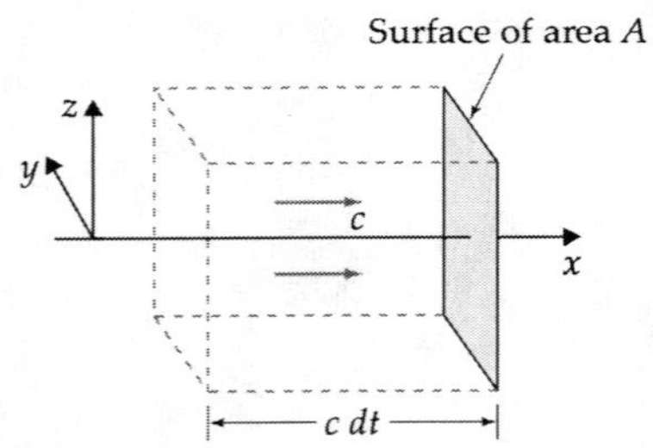

Figure E16.2
All of the electromagnetic energy within the box shown will hit the plate within time *t*.

Since $E = \mathbb{B}$ everywhere in an electromagnetic wave, a sinusoidal wave's total energy density at any specific point in space is

$$u_{EM} = \tfrac{1}{2}\varepsilon_0(E^2 + \mathbb{B}^2) = \varepsilon_0 E^2 = \varepsilon_0 {E_0}^2 \sin^2(k_w x - \omega t) \tag{E16.11}$$

where E_0 is the amplitude of the electric field wave, k_w is its wavenumber (to distinguish it from the Coulomb constant k) and ω is its angular frequency Now imagine that we have a flat surface of area A oriented perpendicular to the direction that the wave is moving, as shown in figure E16.2. All of the energy contained within the box of volume $Ac\,dt$ will hit the plate within time dt, so the rate at which energy is delivered to the surface per unit time must be

$$\frac{dU}{dt} = \frac{u_{EM} Ac\,dt}{dt} = Ac\varepsilon_0 E_0^2 \sin^2(k_w x - \omega t) \tag{E16.12}$$

if dt is small enough so that $\sin^2(k_w x - \omega t)$ doesn't vary much within the box.

Definition of the intensity of an electromagnetic wave

The **intensity** of an electromagnetic wave is defined to be the total power per unit area that it would deposit on a surface perpendicular to the wave. By equation E16.12, the intensity of an electromagnetic sinusoidal wave is

$$\text{intensity of EM wave} = \frac{1}{A}\frac{dU}{dt} = c\varepsilon_0 E_0^2 \left|\sin(k_w x - \omega t)\right|^2 \tag{E16.13}$$

Note that the intensity is proportional to the *square* of the electric field amplitude. Now, the average of $\sin^2\theta$ (which oscillates between 0 and 1) over many oscillations is simply $1/2$, so the average intensity is:

$$\text{average intensity of an EM wave} = c\varepsilon_0\left[E^2\right]_{\text{avg}} = \tfrac{1}{2}c\varepsilon_0 E_0^2 \qquad \text{(E16.14)}$$

Purpose: This equation the energy per unit time per unit area deposited on a surface that absorbs a sinusoidal electromagnetic wave.
Symbols: E_0 is the amplitude of the wave's oscillating electric field, c is the speed of light, $\varepsilon_0 = 1/4\pi k$ is the permittivity constant,
Limitations: This equation applies only to sinusoidal waves.

Self-Test E16X.4

Show that the units of the final expression are W/m^2 (the appropriate SI units for a power per unit area). Show also that the constant $1/(c\varepsilon_0) = 4\pi k/c$ has a value of about 377 Ω.

Self-Test E16X.5

Sunlight has an intensity of roughly 1 kW/m^2. Estimate the amplitude of the electric field involved in such light.

E16.4 The Power Radiated by a Charge

Our goal here is to find the power radiated by an accelerating charge

We have seen that we can find wavelike solutions to Maxwell's equations and we have seen that these waves carry energy. But how can we *create* electromagnetic waves? In this section, I will argue that *accelerating* charges create electromagnetic waves and we will estimate the rate at which energy is radiated by an accelerating charge.

A charge must accelerate to radiate EM waves

We might think that any *moving* charge would create electromagnetic wake like that of a boat moving through water. But the theory of relativity precludes this. Consider a charge moving at a constant velocity. We can find an inertial frame where this charge is at rest, and we *know* that a charge at rest does not radiate electromagnetic waves. But electromagnetic waves, since they carry energy and have distinctive physical effects, cannot exist in one inertial frame and not in others. So a charge cannot generate an electromagnetic waves in a frame where it moves at a constant velocity: it must *accelerate*.

We will use the method of *dimensional analysis*

We could work through a complicated derivation of the power radiated by an accelerating charge, but we can use unit consistency to arrive at essentially the same result much more quickly. What could this power depend on? It must depend on the charge q of the particle being accelerated, and as we've seen, it is plausible that it depends on the magnitude of the particle's acceleration a. The Coulomb constant k (or its equivalent $\varepsilon_0 = 1/4\pi k$) appears in nearly every formula having to do with electricity and magnetism. Finally, our formula should plausibly involve the speed of light c, since we are talking about electromagnetic waves. The particle's mass, however, is likely to be irrelevant for this electromagnetic problem, and though the formula might depend on the particle's velocity, we will consider this later and find that it leads to physically unreasonable results. There are no other quantities associated with the particle that could reasonably involved. So let us assume that our formula depends on q, a, k, and c, and nothing else.

Note that if either the charge q or the particle's acceleration a are zero, then the radiated power will be zero: a neutral particle will not radiate no matter how violently it is accelerated, and a charged particle moving at a constant velocity will not radiate, no matter how large its charge is. This suggests that the power must depend on the product of these quantities raised to positive powers. Let's see if we can find a reasonable equation of the form:

$$P = bk^i c^j q^m a^n \tag{E16.15}$$

where b is an unknown unitless constant of proportionality (like 8π or $4/3$ or something) and i, j, m and n are unknown numbers (note that m and n should be positive).

Now, in order for a formula like this to work, its *units* must be consistent. The units of power are watts $= \text{J/s} = \text{kg}\cdot\text{m}^2/\text{s}^3$. The units of q are coulombs, and the units a of are m/s^2. The units of the Coulomb constant k are

$$\frac{\text{N}\cdot\text{m}^2}{\text{C}^2} = \frac{(\text{kg}\cdot\text{m/s}^2)\text{m}^2}{\text{C}^2} = \frac{\text{kg}\cdot\text{m}^3}{\text{C}^2\text{s}^2} \tag{E16.16}$$

So if equation E16.15 is to have self-consistent units, we must have

$$\frac{\text{kg}\cdot\text{m}^2}{\text{s}^3} = \left(\frac{\text{kg}\cdot\text{m}^3}{\text{C}^2\text{s}^2}\right)^i \left(\frac{\text{m}}{\text{s}}\right)^j \text{C}^m \left(\frac{\text{m}}{\text{s}^2}\right)^n = \frac{\text{kg}^i\,\text{m}^{(3i+j+n)}\text{C}^{(m-2)}}{\text{s}^{(2i+j+2n)}} \tag{E16.17}$$

There is only one power of kilograms on the left, so there can be only one power of kilograms on the right: thus $i = 1$. There are no units of coulombs on the left, so we can't have any on the right, so $m = 2$. If we use $i = 1$, we also find that consistency requires

$$2 = 3 + j + n \quad \text{(to make the distance units consistent)} \tag{E16.18a}$$

$$3 = 2 + j + 2n \quad \text{(to make the time units consistent)} \tag{E16.18b}$$

If you subtract equation E16.18a from E16.18b, you can solve for n, and then plug this result back into either equation to find j. If you then plug the resulting values back into equation E16.15, you should find that:

$$P = \frac{bkq^2a^2}{c^3} \tag{E16.19}$$

Self-Test E16X.6

Verify equation E16.19.

Note that the powers of q and a did come out positive, as hoped. We see that this technique (which is called **dimensional analysis**) allows us to determine virtually everything about the formula without a detailed derivation. It does not really matter what a "correct" derivation would look like: if the formula has the form given in equation E16.15 (which was *plausible* in this case) and depends only on q, a, k, and c, then it *must* be as given by equation E16.19.

Unfortunately, this method does not determine the value of b, the possible "unitless constant" in this equation. Our only comfort is that in many of the equations that we have seen before of this type, such constants are rarely an order of magnitude bigger or smaller than one, so substituting $b = 1$ will likely be correct to within an order of magnitude. A genuine derivation in this case shows that $b = 2/3$, implying that:

$$P = \frac{2}{3}\frac{kq^2a^2}{c^3} = \frac{q^2a^2}{6\pi\varepsilon_0 c^3} \quad \text{(E16.20)}$$

The Larmor formula

Purpose: This is the **Larmor formula** for the power P that an accelerating charge q radiates in the form of electromagnetic waves.

Symbols: c is the speed of light, a the particle's acceleration, k is the Coulomb constant, and $\varepsilon_0 = 1/4\pi k$ is the permittivity constant.

Limitations: This applies only to nonrelativistic point particles.

Self-Test E16X.7

Rework the argument to include the possibility that P depends on the particle's speed v, and argue that the result is physically absurd.

Self-Test E16X.8

Imagine that you whirl a ball with a charge of 10 nC at the end of a 1.0-m string around your head at a speed of 5 m/s. At roughly what rate would the ball radiate energy in the form of electromagnetic waves?

The method of *dimensional analysis* used in this section is one of the standard tools of the practicing physicist! It is *very* useful when you know enough physics to choose the right *variables* but not enough to do the detailed derivation. Here is an outline of the method:

An outline of the method of dimensional analysis

1. Determine the variables on which the quantity of interest depends,
2. Invent a plausible equation for the quantity of interest that involves products of powers of those variables,
3. Determine unknown powers in the equation by unit consistency,
4. Assume any unitless constants to be of order of magnitude of 1.

While it is by no means foolproof, the method can provide a useful first guess if thoughtfully applied. Even when a formula is actually a more complicated function of the variables than the simple products of powers assumed here, the product of powers is often a good approximation. Unitless constants rarely differ from 1 by more than a factor of 10.

E16.5 Why the Sky is Blue

It turns out that the Larmor formula provides the key to understanding a simple, everyday mystery: why is the sky blue? The answer has nothing much to do with any of the particulars about our atmosphere, but rather with some very basic physics.

A description of the Rayleigh scattering process

We have seen that light is an electromagnetic wave that causes the electric and magnetic field vectors at a given location to oscillate as the wave passes, so when sunlight hits an atom in the air, it causes the electric field vector at the atom's location to oscillate back and forth. Any electric field at the atom's location will push the atom's positively-charged nucleus one way and its negatively-charged electron cloud the other (as we discussed in chapter E2). Light will therefore cause an atom's nucleus and electron clouds to oscillate in opposite directions (if the nucleus goes right, the electron cloud goes left and vice versa) at same frequency as the light.

Now, the charged nucleus and electron cloud accelerate as they oscillate, so they will radiate electromagnetic waves in all directions that carry away some of the energy received from the initial light. So the light you see from the sky is simply sunlight that has been reradiated by oscillating air atoms. This physical process is called **Rayleigh scattering**.

You may already know that the *color* of light depends on its frequency. Light from the sun is a mixture of waves with various frequencies. It might seem that since the light scattered by an atom must have the same frequency that striking it, the light we see scattered from the sky should have the same color mix as sunlight. So why is the sky blue, not yellow like the sun?

Why some colors are more effectively radiated than others

It turns out that some frequencies get reradiated much more *effectively* than others. The position (in some suitable reference frame) of the center of an electron cloud oscillating in response to a light wave is something like

$$x(t) = x_0 \sin \omega t \tag{E16.21}$$

where ω is the angular frequency of the incident light and x_0 is the amplitude of the cloud's oscillation. If so, the magnitude of the acceleration of the electron cloud's center is

$$a = \left|\frac{d^2x}{dt^2}\right| = \omega^2 x_0 |\sin \omega t| \tag{E16.22}$$

Self-Test E16X.9

Verify that equation E16.22 is correct.

The sky is blue because blue light and violet light are preferentially scattered

According to the Larmor formula, the energy per unit time that an atom reradiates in the form of scattered light waves is proportional to a^2 and thus to ω^4 ! Since light at the violet end of the visible spectrum has nearly twice the frequency of light at the red end, violet light is scattered very roughly 16 times more effectively than red light! Thus colors at the violet end of the spectrum are strongly emphasized over those at the red end in the scattered light.

So why doesn't the sky look violet instead of blue? One reason is that sunlight itself contains much less violet light than blue light, so even though violet light is scattered very effectively, there isn't as much to begin with. Another reason is that human eyes are much less sensitive to violet light than they are to blue light, so we do not see the violet light that is there well.

This also explains the red of the setting sun

This also explains why the sun looks red while setting. When the sun is near the horizon, its light has to travel through much more air to get to our eyes than when it is overhead. This air scatters away most of the energy associated with the higher-frequency portions of the sunlight as it passes. Only the lower-frequency colors (such as red and orange) in the sunlight therefore survive the journey to reach our eyes.

E16.6 Maxwell's Rainbow

While Maxwell's equations require that electromagnetic waves move with the speed of light, they do not put any constraints on the *frequency* that such waves can have, which is usually determined by the frequency of the oscillating charges that create it. There are many kinds of physical situations where charged particles accelerate or oscillate for different reasons. Hertz created the first artificial electromagnetic waves using a circuit that was the electric analogy of a mass on a spring to accelerate electrons back and forth about a billion times per second: the electromagnetic waves he created thus had a frequency of roughly 1 GHz (corresponding to a wavelength $\lambda = c/f \approx 33$ cm).

Different physical processes produce waves with characteristic frequencies

In general, the electromagnetic waves created by the bulk motion of many charges have frequencies that are classified as being either in the **radio** range (very roughly 300 MHz or lower) or the **microwave** range (300 MHz to about 10^{12} Hz). For example, the electromagnetic waves that carry information to your FM radio have frequencies of about 100 MHz and are created by electrons sloshing back and forth in the radio station's antenna (driven by the transmitter). One of the reason that wireless devices have proliferated in the past decade is that modern electronics has made it easier to exploit previously unused frequencies in the microwave region. "Bluetooth" wireless devices communicate using electromagnetic wave with frequencies of roughly 2.45 GHz.

There are other kinds of physical systems where charges accelerate even more rapidly. For example, the atoms in any object that has internal thermal energy vibrate and/or move randomly about. The resulting atomic oscillations and collisions cause electron clouds to accelerate and radiate electromagnetic waves. This becomes obvious when the object is *very* hot: your hand gets warm near a hot coal gets because of the energy it receives from electromagnetic waves radiated by the coal. The electromagnetic waves radiated by thermal processes typically have frequencies of roughly 10^{12} to 10^{14} Hz ($\lambda \approx 100\ \mu$m to 1 μm), which we call the **infrared** range.

Electromagnetic waves in the **ultraviolet** range ($f \approx 10^{16}$ Hz, $\lambda \approx 100$ nm) are usually created by atomic electrons changing energy levels. When electrons are accelerated using an electron gun and then crashed into a metal plate, their sudden deceleration produces **X-rays** with frequencies of very roughly 10^{18} Hz ($\lambda \approx 1$ nm). Transformations inside an atomic nucleus can cause charged protons to shift position suddenly and energetically, radiating **gamma rays** with frequencies of very roughly 10^{22} Hz ($\lambda \approx 0.1$ pm).

The range of possible frequencies is, of course, continuous, but physicists have chosen to break this continuous distribution of frequencies into ranges that roughly reflect the different physical processes that produce such waves (see figure E16.3).

Visible light is only a small part of this range

You can see that visible light, which has frequencies ranging from about 4.3×10^{14} Hz ($\lambda = 700$ nm) to about 7.5×10^{14} Hz ($\lambda = 400$ nm) constitutes only a very narrow part of this range (although, not coincidentally, it is a range where the sun radiates most of its energy). Figure E16.4 on the next page shows various common objects that emit non-visible electromagnetic waves in various frequency ranges.

The creation and detection of electromagnetic waves across this spectrum are so much a part of 21st-century technology that it is hard to imagine that before Maxwell's work in the 1860s, most of "Maxwell's rainbow" outside of the

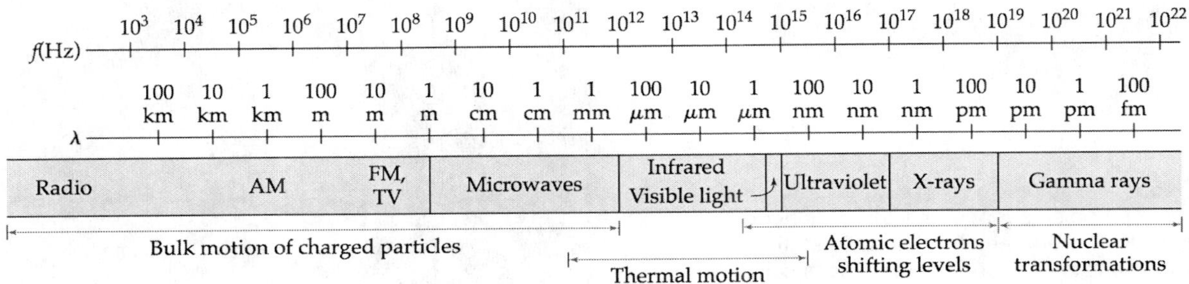

Figure E16.3
Maxwell's rainbow.

visible range was completely unknown. Maxwell's efforts to express Faraday's ideas mathematically was not merely an astonishing intellectual triumph, it also opened up a vast new territory for humankind to explore. As a result, Maxwell's achievement has profoundly shaped history in the past century, and currently affects our daily lives in countless ways. Maxwell's equations are thus among the most important of the great ideas that shaped physics.

(a)

(b)

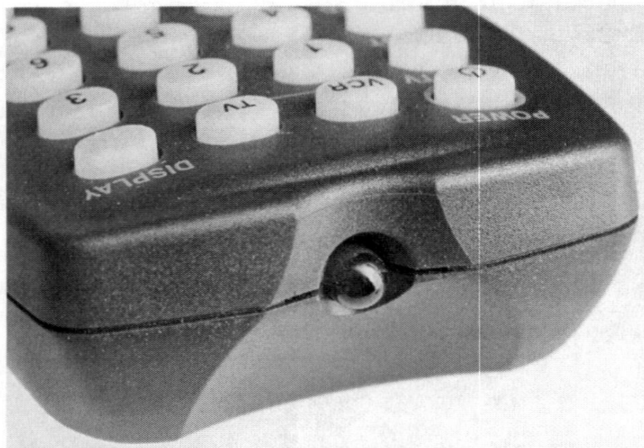

(c)

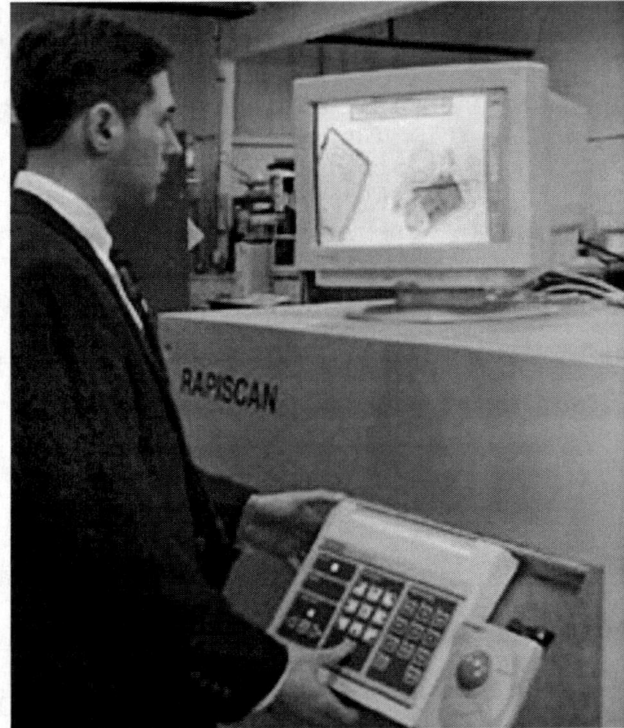

(d)

Figure E16.4
Various common objects that emit invisible electromagnetic waves. (a) The antenna for this radio station emits radio waves at a rate of about 10 W. (b) This cell phone emits waves in the microwave region. (c) The light-emitting diode at the front of a remote control emits infrared waves. (d) This airport security scanner uses X-rays.

TWO-MINUTE PROBLEMS

E16T.1 An electromagnetic wave moving in the $+x$ direction is best described as being

A. A transverse wave
B. A longitudinal wave
C. Either a transverse or longitudinal wave (depending on how it was created)
C. A wave that fits neither category well

E16T.2 It is possible in principle to create a traveling electromagnetic wave in empty space that is purely electric ($\vec{B} = 0$), T or F?

E16T.3 In an electromagnetic wave, $\vec{E} \times \vec{B}$ points in the direction that the wave is moving, T or F?

E16T.4 Imagine that the electric field part of an electromagnetic wave moving in the $+z$ direction is given by $E_x = A\sin(kz - \omega t)$, $E_y = E_z = 0$. The x and z components of the magnetic field part are both zero, T or F? The y-component of the magnetic field part is

A. $B_y = +A\sin(kz - \omega t)$
B. $B_y = -A\sin(kz - \omega t)$
C. $B_y = B_0 \sin(kz - \omega t)$, with B_0 not necessarily equal to A.
D. $B_y = 0$
E. Given by some other expression (specify).

E16T.5 Without Maxwell's correction to Ampere's law, electromagnetic disturbances could not move in empty space, T or F?

E16T.6 The energy carried by a sinusoidal electromagnetic wave is nonnegative everywhere at all times, T or F?

E16T.7 Imagine that when you switch on your study lamp, you increase the intensity of light shining on your textbook by a factor of 16. By what factor does the average electric field strength in this light increase?

A. 256
B. 16
C. 8
D. 4
E. 2
F. 1 (the field remains unchanged)
T. < 1 (the electric field strength gets smaller)

E16T.8 A charge moving at a constant speed cannot radiate electromagnetic waves, T or F?

E16T.9 A charged atom oscillating in a certain molecule has a period of oscillation of about 10 ps. What kind of electromagnetic radiation will it produce?

A. Radio
B. Microwave
C. Infrared
D. Visible
E. Ultraviolet
F. Some other kind (specify)

HOMEWORK PROBLEMS

Basic Skills

E16B.1 Argue that sinusoidal waves of the type described by equations E16.9 satisfy Gauss's law for the magnetic field.

E16B.2 Use equation E13.3 to argue that if the ratio $E/\boldsymbol{B} = 1$ for an electromagnetic wave in any inertial reference frame, it has the same ratio in all reference frames moving parallel to the wave's motion. (*Hint:* Orient your axes so that the x direction is the direction that the wave is moving and the electric and magnetic fields point in the $+y$ and $+z$ directions respectively.)

E16B.3 In a fairly brightly-lit room, the intensity of light is about 200 W/m^2. What is the amplitude of the electric field of the light waves in this room? If the room is 5 m long by 4 m wide by 2.5 m high and the light intensity is fairly uniform throughout the room, about how much energy is stored in the room in the form of light waves?

E16B.4 Near a certain source of light, the amplitude of the electric field in the light waves is about 25 N/C. What is the intensity of this light?

E16B.5 Imagine that a certain light beam has an energy density 1.0 μJ per cubic meter. What is the intensity of this light? How does this compare to the intensity of sunlight?

E16B.6 Electric field strengths in excess of 10^9 N/C can tear electrons out of atoms. What intensity of light will do this? How does this compare to the intensity of sunlight?

E16B.7 Imagine that an object with a charge of 0.1 μC traveling at 30 m/s hits a wall and comes to rest within about 10 ms. How much total energy is radiated in the form of electromagnetic waves in this situation?

Synthetic

E16S.1 Imagine a disturbance in the electric field of the form $\vec{E} = [0, E_y(x,t), 0]$. Go through steps analogous to those in section E16.1 to show that this disturbance must satisfy a wave equation.

E16S.2 Consider the electric field of a charged particle at rest at the origin in a certain reference frame. If the field of such a particle is radial, the field components $[E_x, E_y, E_z]$ at a certain point P will be proportional to that point's position coordinates $[x_P, y_P, z_P]$ (i.e. $[E_x, E_y, E_z] = a[x_P, y_P, z_P]$ for some a: this is what it means to say that $\vec{E}$ has the same direction as $\vec{r}_P$). Now consider the same field at the same point P when viewed in a reference frame moving in the $+x$ direction at speed v relative to the first frame. Use equation E13.3 to find the electric field $\vec{E}'$ in this frame, argue from Lorentz contraction that $x'_P = x_P/\gamma$, and then argue that $[E'_x, E'_y, E'_z] = a'[x'_P, y'_P, z'_P]$ in this frame also, though the value of a' is not the same as the original value of a.

E16S.3 Consider a step wave, where we assume that $\vec{E} = E_0\hat{y}$ and $\vec{\boldsymbol{B}} = \boldsymbol{B}_0\hat{z}$ behind and $\vec{E} = 0$ and $\vec{\boldsymbol{B}} = 0$ in front of a planar wave front that is perpendicular that to the x direction and moves in the $+x$ direction with speed v through empty space. Consider two Amperian loops, each of which has a leg at an x position we will define to be $x = 0$ and another at $x = L$, but which lie in the xy and xz planes respectively. Do *not* assume that L is small or that the values of the flux over a surface bounded by a loop is equal to the field's value in the middle multiplied surface's area; instead, calculate the time derivatives of these fluxes *exactly* at an instant when the wave front's x-position is between 0 and L. Assume that we have defined $t = 0$ to be the instant when the wave front passes $x = 0$: then the position of the wave front will be $x = vt$.

(a) Show that the integral form of Faraday's law implies in this case that $E_{y0} = (v/c)\,\boldsymbol{B}_{z0}$.

(b) Show that the integral form of the Ampere-Maxwell relation for empty space implies that $\boldsymbol{B}_{z0} = (v/c)E_{y0}$.

(c) Prove that this means that this step wave has to move at the speed of light and that $E_0 = \boldsymbol{B}_0$.

E16S.4 Express Maxwell's equations in empty space in terms of completely traditional units (that is, use $\vec{B}$, ε_0, and μ_0 instead of $\vec{\boldsymbol{B}}$, k, and c). Then go through the process illustrated in section E16.1 and show that you end up with wave equations where $1/\varepsilon_0\mu_0$ appears instead of c^2.

E16S.5 Use equation E13.3 to prove that the value of $\vec{E}\cdot\vec{\boldsymbol{B}}$ is frame-independent, and use this result to argue that if the electric and magnetic fields in an electromagnetic traveling wave are perpendicular in one inertial reference frame, they are perpendicular in *all* inertial reference frames (even frames not moving parallel to the electromagnetic wave).

E16S.6 What is the approximate electric field strength of the electromagnetic waves radiated by 100-W light bulb, measured 3.0 m from the bulb?

E16S.7 The Poynting vector $\vec{S}$ for an electromagnetic wave has a direction equal to the wave's direction of motion and a magnitude equal to the wave's intensity in W/m^2. Show that for both polarizations described by equations E16.9a and E16.9b

$$\vec{S} = \frac{c}{4\pi k}(\vec{E} \times \vec{B}) = \frac{1}{\mu_0}(\vec{E} \times \vec{B}) \qquad \text{(E16.23)}$$

E16S.8 An electron moves at a speed of $0.01c$ in a magnetic field of $\boldsymbol{B} = 600$ MN/C perpendicular to its direction of motion. (Remember that this magnetic field will cause the electron to move in a circular orbit: see chapter E7.) How much energy does the electron lose each second? Express your answer in eV ($1 \text{ eV} = 1.602 \times 10^{-19}$ J).

E16S.9 What electrical charge would the moon have to have so that it would radiate away 1% of its current orbital kinetic energy in the form of electromagnetic waves over the course of 1 billion years?

E16S.10 Imagine that I place a charge of 10 nC on one prong of a tuning fork that vibrates at 440 Hz with an amplitude of about 0.4 mm. What is the average power radiated by such a charge in the form of electromagnetic waves?

E16S.11 In the Rutherford model of the hydrogen atom (proposed by Ernst Rutherford in roughly 1910), an electron is imagined to orbit the proton in a circle whose radius is about $r_0 \approx 0.053$ nm.

(a) Use Newton's second law, Coulomb's law, and what you know about acceleration in circular motion to show that the electron's acceleration in a circular orbit of radius r is $a = ke^2/mr^2$ and its kinetic energy is $K = ke^2/2r$, where e = charge on a proton = | charge on an electron | and m is the mass of the electron.

(b) Show that the total orbital energy of the electron in such an orbit is $E = -ke^2/2r$.

(c) Because the electron is accelerating, it will radiate energy in the form of electromagnetic waves. Assuming that it does so slowly enough so that its orbit remains essentially circular, show that the Larmor formula predicts that the rate at which it radiates energy is

$$P = \frac{2ke^2c}{3r^4}\left(\frac{ke^2}{mc^2}\right)^2 \qquad \text{(E16.24)}$$

(d) This has to come at the expense of the electron's orbital energy E, so (since E decreases with time) $P = -dE/dt$. Show using the result of part (b) that we also have

$$\frac{dE}{dt} = \frac{ke^2}{2r^2}\frac{dr}{dt} \qquad \text{(E16.25)}$$

(e) Set P given by equation E16.24 equal to $-dE/dt$ given by equation E16.25 and rearrange to show that

$$r^2 dr = -\frac{4}{3}\left(\frac{ke^2}{mc^2}\right)^2 c\,dt \qquad \text{(E16.26)}$$

(f) Define $t = 0$ to be when $r = r_0$. As it radiates energy, the electron will spiral inward until it reaches $r = 0$ at a time we will define to be $t = T$. By integrating the left side from $r = r_0$ to $r = 0$ and the right side from $t = 0$ to $t = T$ and solving for T, show that

$$T = \frac{r_0^3}{4c}\left(\frac{mc^2}{ke^2}\right)^2 \qquad \text{(E16.27)}$$

(g) Show that $ke^2/mc^2 = 2.8 \times 10^{-15}$ m and then calculate T. Is the Rutherford model plausible?

Rich-Context

E16R.1 How long would it take an object like the Sun to collapse to a black hole if the forces holding it up against its own gravity size were suddenly to disappear? Estimate the time roughly using dimensional analysis. (*Answer:* tens of minutes.)

E16R.2 Imagine that some electrons moving at a speed of $0.001c$ in a magnetic field that keeps them in an circular orbit 20 cm in radius. Assume that the electrons are moving in a vacuum. About how much time will pass before the radius of the electrons' orbit has decreased to 10 cm?

Advanced

E16A.1 A radio transmitter creates a time-dependent current $|I(t)| = I_0 |\sin \omega| t$ in a radio antenna, where $I_0 = 20$ A and $\omega = 6.3 \times 10^6$ /s (corresponding to about the middle of the AM band). What is the average power radiated by this antenna if it is 160 m long? [*Hint:* The EM radiation is produced by charge sloshing back and forth in the antenna. Argue that at any given instant, $|I(t)| = Qv/L$, where Q is the total charge involved in the sloshing, v is the drift speed of the charges and L is the antenna's length.]

ANSWERS TO SELF-TESTS

E16X.1 This is easy: the other components of the curl of $\vec{B}$ and the time derivative of $\vec{E}$ are zero.

E16X.2 You should find that

$$\frac{\partial}{\partial t}\left(\frac{\partial}{\partial x} bx^2 t\right) = \frac{\partial}{\partial x}\left(\frac{\partial}{\partial t} bx^2 t\right) = 2bx \qquad \text{(E16.28)}$$

$$\frac{\partial}{\partial t}\left(\frac{\partial}{\partial x}\frac{x}{x+bt}\right) = \frac{\partial}{\partial x}\left(\frac{\partial}{\partial t}\frac{x}{x+bt}\right) = \frac{2b}{(x+bt)^3} - \frac{b}{(x+bt)^2} \qquad \text{(E16.29)}$$

E16X.3 The quantity $\text{div}(\vec{E}) = \partial E_x/\partial x + \partial E_y/\partial y + \partial E_z/\partial z$ is supposed to be zero in empty space, but while $E_y = E_z = 0$, $\partial E_x/\partial x$ will not be zero if $E_x = E_x(x,t)$.

E16X.4 k/c has units of $(\text{N}\cdot\text{m}^2/\text{C}^2)(\text{s}/\text{m}) = \text{N}\cdot\text{m}\cdot\text{s}/\text{C}^2$. Multiplying the reciprocal of this by the square of the electric field units N/C yields $(\text{N/C})^2(\text{C}^2\text{N}^{-1}\text{m}^{-1}\text{s}^{-1}) = \text{N}\cdot\text{m}^{-1}\text{s}^{-1} = \text{N}\cdot\text{m}\cdot\text{m}^{-2}\text{s}^{-1} = \text{J}/(\text{m}^2\text{s}) = \text{W}/\text{m}^2$. We can convert the units of k/c to ohms as follows: $\text{N}\cdot\text{m}\cdot\text{s}/\text{C}^2 = \text{J}\cdot\text{s}/\text{C}^2 = (\text{J}/\text{C})/(\text{C}/\text{s}) = \text{V}/\text{A} = \Omega$. Finding the numerical result is simply a matter of plugging in numbers.

E16X.5 Solving equation E16.13 for E_0, we get

$$E_0^2 = \frac{2}{c\varepsilon_0}(\text{Intensity}) = 2\left(377\frac{\text{N}\cdot\text{m}\cdot\text{s}}{\text{C}^2}\right)\left(1000\frac{\text{J}}{\text{m}^2\text{s}}\right)$$

$$= 754{,}000\left(\frac{\text{N}\cdot\cancel{\text{m}}\cdot\cancel{\text{s}}}{\text{C}^2}\right)\left(\frac{\cancel{\text{J}}}{\cancel{\text{m}}^2\cancel{\text{s}}}\right)\left(\frac{1\,\text{N}\cdot\cancel{\text{m}}}{1\,\cancel{\text{J}}}\right) = 754{,}000\,\frac{\text{N}^2}{\text{C}^2}$$

$$\Rightarrow\; E_0 = \sqrt{754{,}000\,\frac{\text{N}^2}{\text{C}^2}} = 870\,\frac{\text{N}}{\text{C}} \qquad \text{(E16.30)}$$

E16X.6 Subtracting equation E16.18a from equation E16.18b, we find that:

$$1 = -1+0+n \;\;\Rightarrow\;\; n = 2 \qquad \text{(E16.31)}$$

Plugging this back into equation E16.18a yields

$$2 = 3+j+2 \;\;\Rightarrow\;\; j = -3 \qquad \text{(E16.32)}$$

Plugging these exponents (and $i = 1$) back into equation E16.14 yields equation E16.19.

E16X.7 If we put a factor of speed in the numerator, the power would be zero when the speed is zero, even though the charge might be accelerating violently from positive to negative velocity or vice versa. This contradicts relativity, because in a different frame, the particle's speed would not be zero, and so we would have the relativistically impossible situation where a charge radiates energy in one inertial frame but not another. If we put a factor of speed in the denominator, radiated power would go to infinity when the particle comes to rest. The bottom line is that neither of these predictions seems very realistic.

E16X.8 This is simply a matter of plugging in the numbers (using $a = v^2/r$). The result is 1.4×10^{-29} W.

E16X.9 Taking the first derivative yields

$$\frac{dx}{dt} = \frac{d}{dt}x_0 \sin\omega t = \omega x_0 \cos\omega t \qquad \text{(E16.33)}$$

Taking the second derivative yields

$$\frac{d^2x}{dt^2} = \frac{d}{dt}\omega x_0 \cos\omega t = -\omega^2 x_0 \sin\omega t \qquad \text{(E16.34)}$$

Glossary

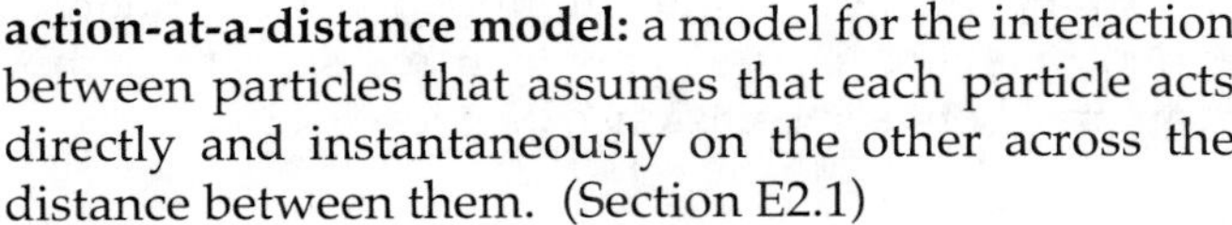

action-at-a-distance model: a model for the interaction between particles that assumes that each particle acts directly and instantaneously on the other across the distance between them. (Section E2.1)

alternating current (AC): a flow of electrical current that varies sinusoidally with time: $I(t) = I_0\sin(\omega t)$, where ω is the angular frequency of the variation in radians/s and I_0 is the maximum current that flows during the cycle. (Section E14.6)

ampere (A): The SI unit of current, corresponding to 1 coulomb per second (C/s) of charge flowing through a specified surface oriented perpendicular to the moving charge, (Section E5.1)

Ampere-Maxwell law: the equation

$$\vec{\text{curl}}(\vec{\boldsymbol{B}}) - \frac{1}{c}\frac{\partial \vec{E}}{\partial x} = \frac{1}{\varepsilon_0}\left(\frac{\vec{J}}{c}\right)$$

This is the differential form of Ampere's law with an additional time-derivative term that makes it possible for the law work for time-dependent fields. (Section E13.5)

Ampere's law: a local field equation that states that $\vec{\text{curl}}(\vec{\boldsymbol{B}}) = \vec{J}/\varepsilon_0 c$. This law links the curl of the magnetic field at a point with the local presence of charge (Section E11.4)

Ampere's law for the Electric Field: a local field equation that states that $\vec{\text{curl}}(\vec{E}) = 0$. This law expresses the consequences of energy conservation for a static electric field. (Section E11.5)

Ampere's law in Integral Form: a form of Ampere's law that has been integrated to make it easier to calculate the magnetic field of a current-carrying object. (Section E12.4)

amperian loop: a closed loop chosen so that it is easy to calculate the sum of $\vec{\boldsymbol{B}} \cdot d\vec{S}$ or $\vec{E} \cdot d\vec{S}$ for step vectors along that loop. (Section E12.5)

amplitude: the magnitude of the maximum displacement of the medium in a sinusoidal wave. (Section E15.2)

angular frequency or **phase rate** ω: the number of radians of oscillation that a sinusoidal traveling wave goes through per unit time at a fixed point in space. (Section E15.2)

anode: see **electron gun**.

anticommutative: the property that a product of two quantitites has if reversing the order of the quantities in the product changes the sign of the result. The cross product of two vectors is anticommutative. (Section E7.4)

aurora: (also called the "northern lights") a phenomenon that looks like glowing curtains in the air, caused by energetic charged particles from the sun that, because they must spiral along the direction of the earth's magnetic field, are directed by the field into the upper atmosphere near the earth's magnetic poles. (Section E7.6)

battery: one or more cells wired together. For example, a standard flashlight battery is a *cell*, but a 12-V car battery is a *battery* consisting of 6 cells wired in series. (Section E6.1)

Biot-Savart law (pronounced "Bee-o Sahvahr"): the law that describes how to compute the magnetic field of an arbitrarily-shaped wire by summing the field's created by short wire segments (see equation E8.10). (Section E9.2)

brushes: sliding contacts that connect the rotating coil of an electric motor or generator to the outside world. (Section E8.3)

capacitance C: the ratio of the charge on a capacitor's positive plate to the magnitude of the potential difference between its plates. A capacitor's capacitance depends only on the size, shape, and arrangement of its plates and the material in which the plates are embedded. (Section E4.5)

capacitor: a pair of conductors that always have opposite charges and that interact electrostatically with each other much more strongly than with anything else. We call the two conductors the capacitor's **plates**. (Section E4.5)

cathode: see **electron gun.**

cathode ray tube (**CRT**): a vacuum tube having an electron gun at one end and a phosphor-coated screen at the other, and (usually) magnetic coils or electric plates that modify the path of the electron beam created by the gun. The screen glows where the electron beam hits it. CRTs are used in TV sets, computer monitors, etc. (Section E7.3)

cell: an electrical device consisting of two conducting plates (**electrodes**) and some kind of charge-transport mechanism (commonly chemical) that gives each charge carrier transported a characteristic energy. (Section E6.1)

charge carriers: the particles that actually transport the charge in an electrical current. In metals, the charge carriers are electrons, but in batteries and in conducting fluids, the charge carriers are often ionized atoms. (Section E5.1)

charge: see **electric charge.**

charge distribution: a huge number of charged particles (usually electrons or positive ions) distributed over the surface or throughout the interior of a macroscopic object. We can calculate the electric field of such a distribution by dividing it into infinitesimal point-like. (Section E3.1)

circuit diagram: a schematic diagram that helps us describe and visualize the structure of an electrical circuit, using stylized symbols to represent circuit elements, and straight lines to represent connections between elements. (Section E6.4)

circuit element: any object or device (such as wires, light bulbs, batteries, electric motors, and so on) that appears in an electrical circuit. (Section E6.4)

closed surface: a surface that completely encloses a certain volume in space. (Section E12.1)

commutator: an arrangement of contacts on a motor's axle that, as the commutator turns under the brushes, feeds an alternating current to that motor's coil. This enables the coil to turn ceaselessly in a static magnetic field. (Section E8.3)

compass: a magnet suspended so that it can rotate freely in the earth's magnetic field. (Section E8.1)

conduction electrons: the electrons in a metal that are free to move and thus carry charge through the metal. Usually, each atom in a metal contributes one electron to the pool of conduction electrons. (Section E5.1)

conductivity σ_c: a scalar quantity (having SI units of $\mathrm{C^2s \cdot kg^{-1}m^{-3}} = (\Omega\cdot\mathrm{m})^{-1}$) that represents the constant of proportionality between the current density in a substance and the electric field driving that current: $\vec{J} = \sigma_c \vec{E}$. Under ordinary conditions, the conductivity depends only on the characteristics of the substance: if Drude's model accurately describes the substance, $\sigma_c = nq^2\tau/m$, where n is the number density of charge carriers, q is their charge, m is their mass, and τ is the mean time between collisions. (Section E5.2)

conductor: A conductor is a material through which charges can easily move. Salty water and most metals are good conductors. In metals, it is electrons that are free to move, but this is not always the case: in salty water, charge is carried by ionized atoms. (Section E1.6)

conventional current: refers to a long-established convention that considers the direction of any current flow to be the direction that *positive* particles would flow if they were the charge carriers in the current. If negative particles (such as electrons) actually carry the charge, the direction of the conventional current is opposite to the direction of the actual motion of the negative carriers. (Section E5.2)

coulomb: the SI unit of electrical charge, defined so that $1\ \mathrm{C} = 6.242 \times 10^{18}$ proton charges. (Section E1.3)
Coulomb constant k: a constant, whose numerical value is $8.99 \times 10^9\ \mathrm{N{\cdot}m^2/C^2}$, that essentially specifies the strength of the electromagnetic interaction. See the **permittivity of free space.** (Section E1.5)

Coulomb's law: the law that expresses the force that one point charge exerts on another in terms of the values q_1 and q_2 of the charges, the distance r between them and the **Coulomb constant** k. The law states that the magnitude of the force on either charge is given by $F_e = |kq_1q_2/r^2|$, and that its direction is toward the other charge if the charges have unlike signs, and away from the other charge if the charges have like signs. (Section E1.5)

crests and **troughs**: the extreme values of the displacement of the medium in a sinusoidal wave. A crest is where the medium is displaced the maximum amount in the positive direction, while a trough is where the medium is displaced maximally in the negative direction (however these directions are defined). (Section E15.2)

cross product rule: the right hand rule that specifies that the direction of the cross product $\vec{u} \times \vec{w}$ is given by your right thumb if you point your index finger in the direction of $\vec{u}$ and your second finger in the direction of $\vec{w}$. (Section E8.4)

curl $\vec{\text{curl}}(\vec{\boldsymbol{B}})$ or $\vec{\text{curl}}(\vec{E})$: a vector quantity that expresses the degree to which a field in the neighborhood of a point is "twisting" around that point. The curl of the magnetic field is nonzero at a point only if there is a nonzero current density at that point. (Section E11.1)

curl-meter: a device that measures curl. One visualization is a square that is free to rotate around an axis going through its center and which has magnetic north poles (or test charges) affixed to the centers of its sides. The component of the curl in a given direction is proportional to the counterclockwise torque that the field exerts on a curl-meter when the curl-meter's axis is aligned in that direction. (Section E11.1)

current density $\vec{J}$: a vector (having SI units of A/m^2) that quantifies the local flow of current near a point in a conductor: $\vec{J} = nq\vec{v}_d = \rho\vec{v}_d$, where n is the number density of charge carriers, q is the charge of the charge carrier, ρ is the density of charge carriers, and $\vec{v}_d$ is the local drift velocity of carriers at the point in question. (Section E5.2)

current vector $\vec{I}$: a vector (having units of A) that describes the magnitude and direction of current flow through a thin and straight segment of wire. (Section 5.2)

cyclotron frequency: the number of times per second that an otherwise free charged particle in a magnetic field moves around in its circular orbit. This frequency is interesting because it is independent of the particle's velocity (as long as $v << c$). (Section E7.6)

cylindrically symmetric (charge distribution): a charge distribution that is unchanged by rotating it *around* some central axis or sliding it an arbitrary distance *along* that axis. A uniformly charged infinite wire or pipe displays this symmetry. (Section E3.2)

dimensional analysis: an approach to guessing the formula for a quantity by deciding what variables are relevant and then making the units come out correctly. (Section E16.4)

dipole: see **electric dipole**.

dipole moment $\vec{p}_e$: a quantity that expresses the strength of an electric dipole's ability to create an electric field or respond to an electric field. This vector has a magnitude equal to *qd*, where q is the magnitude of the dipole's positive charge and d is the separation between the dipole's charges. The direction of $\vec{p}_e$ is the same as the displacement vector from the dipole's negative charge to its positive charge. (Section E2.6)

divergence $\text{div}(\vec{E})$ or $\text{div}(\vec{\boldsymbol{B}})$: a quantity that expresses the extent to which the field at a point is spreading out from or drawing in to that point. The electric divergence is nonzero only if there is a nonzero charge density at that point. (Section E10.2)

div-meter: A device that measures divergence. One visualization of such a device is a cube with positive test charges (or magnetic north poles) affixed to the centers of its faces. The divergence is positive if the cube puffs out or negative if it is drawn in by whatever field acts in its vicinity. (Section E10.2)

domain: a (typically) tiny region inside a ferromagnetic material where atomic current-loops are all aligned. When an external magnetic field is applied, the domains aligned with the field grow by "recruiting" at their edges, causing the material to develop its own magnetic field reinforcing the external field. (Section E9.5)

drift velocity $\vec{v}_d$: the average velocity of charge carriers in a conductor. (Section E5.1)

Drude model: a model that explains how electrons flow through metals by imagining electrons to be particles that move freely in the metal between collisions with metal atoms. The thermal velocities of these particles are imagined to be large and random. If an electric field is applied to the metal, electrons pick up a small amount of momentum opposite to the direction of electric field between collisions. This causes the electrons (on the average) to slowly drift in the direction opposite to the applied field. (Section E5.1)

dynamic (field): A field that changes with time. (Section E1.1)

dynamic equilibrium: A term describing the state of a circuit when it is conducting a steady current. As in the case of static equilbrium, charges arrange themselves on the surface of a conductor, but do so not to make the electric field in the conductor zero but rather to maintain a steady flow of current at all points in the circuit.

***e*:** the magnitude of the charge of a proton or electron: $e = 1.602 \times 10^{-19}$ C. Unfortunately, this symbol is easy to confuse with the base of the natural logarithms e = 2.718: the meaning of an italic e must be determined from context. (Section E1.3)

edge vector: a unit vector that points parallel to a tile's edge in the counterclockwise direction when the tile's nose vector points toward us. (Section E11.1)

electric charge: a fundamental property of matter that acts as the source of an electromagnetic field. There are two kinds of charge, which are arbitrarily designated "positive" and "negative". (Section E1.2)

electric current: any flow of charged particles from one place to another. Current is quantified by determining the rate at which charge flows through a specified surface oriented perpendicular to the flow. One *ampere* of current corresponds to a flow rate through the surface of one coulomb of charge per second. (Section E5.1)

electric dipole: an object consisting of point charges with equal absolute values but opposite signs separated by a distance. (Section E2.5)

electric field: the entire electric field of a charge distribution at a given time t is described by a vector function $\vec{E}(x,y,z)$ that specifies the electric field vector at every point in space at that instant of time. (Section E2.2)

electric field vector $\vec{E}$: the vector that describes the quantitative value of an electric field at a certain point. This vector is defined to be the *electric force per unit charge* experienced by a small positive test charge at rest at the point in question. $\vec{E}$ is measured in units of N/C. (Section E2.2)

electric motor: a device that converts electrical power to mechanical power (most often first in the form of rotational kinetic energy). (Section E8.3)

electric potential (or just **potential**) $\phi(x,y,z)$: the electrostatic potential energy per unit charge that a test particle at $[x, y, z]$ would have compared to what it has at infinity. The potential provides an alternative to representing the field around a charge distribution using the electric field $\vec{E}(x,y,x)$ that has some useful advantages. (Section E3.1)

electricity: a general term for the phenomena associated with electrostatics and current flow. (Section E1.1)

electrodes: the charged plates of a cell or battery where the chemical reactions take place that maintain a certain potential difference between the two electrodes. (Section E6.1) Also calledthe battery's **terminals**.

electrolyte: the part of a battery through which ions move between the electrodes. (E6.1)

electromagnetic field: the concept that physicists use to describe the unity that lies behind electric and magnetic phenomena. An electromagnetic field is created by an object involving unbalanced, separated, and/or moving charges, and mediates the electromagnetic interaction between two objects such objects. The electromagnetic field generally has an electric part $\vec{E}$ and a magnetic part $\vec{\mathbb{B}}$ (the total electromagnetic field in a given reference frame is therefore represented by *six* components). The electromagnetic field field has a frame-independent reality, but the way that it divides into electric and magnetic parts depends on one's choice of inertial reference frame. (Section E13.1)

electromagnetic wave: a traveling-wave disturbance in the electromagnetic field. In empty space, such waves travel with speed c, and have perpendicular electric and magnetic field components such that $E = \mathbb{B}$ and $\vec{E} \times \vec{\mathbb{B}}$ points in the direction the wave is moving. (Section E16.1).

electron: a negatively-charged subatomic particle that is an important constituent of all atoms. Fairly mobile electrons are the typical charge carriers in metals. See also **proton, neutron, electron.** (Section E1.3)

electron cloud: the probability distribution of electrons orbiting an atomic nucleus. Quantum mechanics asserts that the positions of individual electrons orbiting an atom are not well defined: treating the electrons as a cloud-like dispersed charge is a better model. (Section E1.3)

electron gun: a device that creates a beam of electrons with a fairly well-defined velocity. Electrons boil off a heated, negatively-charged plate (the **cathode**) and accelerate toward a positively charged plate (the **anode**). A small hole in the positive plate allows some electrons to escape to form a narrow beam. (Section E7.3)

electrostatic interaction: that aspect of the electromagnetic interaction that operates between charges at rest. (Section E1.1)

electrostatic polarization: see **polarization**.

emf $\mathscr{E}$: the energy per unit charge transferred by *non*-electrical forces *to* electrons or ions as they are transported against the electric field in a battery. A battery generally has a characteristic and fixed emf. Also called the **electromotive force** (even though it is not a force). (Section E6.1)

equipotential curve (or just **equipotential**): a curve on a two-dimensional diagram that connects points having the same potential. (Section E4.1)

equipotential diagram: a diagram showing the equipotential curves on a two-dimensional slice of three-dimensional space. The equipotential curves actually show where the equipotential surfaces intersect the plane of the drawing. (Section E4.1)

equipotential surface: a surface that connects points in a three-dimensional space that have the same potential. (Section E4.1)

farad F: The SI unit of capacitance: 1 F = 1 C/V. (Section E4.5)

Faraday's law: the equation

$$\text{c\"{u}rl}(\vec{E}) + \frac{1}{c}\frac{\partial \vec{\mathbb{B}}}{\partial t} = 0$$

This is a corrected version of Ampere's law for the electric field with an additional time-derivative term that makes it possible for the law to work for time-dependent fields. (Section E13.4)

Faraday's law of induction: the equation

$$\mathcal{E}_{\text{loop}} = -\frac{1}{c}\frac{d\Phi_{\mathbb{B}}}{dt} \quad \text{or} \quad \mathcal{E}_{\text{loop}} = -\frac{d\Phi_B}{dt} \qquad \text{(E14.2)}$$

This equation describes how the induced emf in a conducting loop depends on rate-of-change of magnetic flux through the loop. This equation turns out to be quite general, useful in all nonrelativistic frames and situations. (Section E14.1)

ferromagnetic: any type of material that (when initially unmagnetized) is attracted strongly and equally by both poles of a magnet. Only a few kinds of metals and alloys (notably iron and certain iron oxides) are ferromagnetic: most materials respond only weakly (if at all) to magnets. (Section E7.1); a type of material in which it is energetically favorable for atoms to *align* their magnetic moments. Iron, cobalt, and nickel are common ferromagnetic materials. (Section E9.5)

field diagram: a depiction of the total field created by an object that shows the field vectors at a large number of positions in the space surrounding the object. (Section E2.3)

field model: a model for the interaction between particles that assumes that each particle creates a *field* at all points in the space surrounding it. The other particle interacts with the field created by the first particle, not directly with the particle itself. (Section E2.1)

(net) **flux** Φ (of a field through a surface): the dot product of a field vector and a tile vectors for all tiles on a bounded or closed surface. (We conventionally indicate the field whose flux we are calculating by attaching a subscript to Φ.) For example:

$$\Phi_{\mathbb{B}} \equiv \int \vec{\mathbb{B}} \cdot d\vec{A} \quad \text{over a surface}$$

(Used in Section E14.1)

Fourier's theorem: a mathematical theorem asserting that *any* wave can be treated as a superposition of sinusoidal waves. Thus if one understands the behavior of sinusoidal waves, one really understands the behavior of all waves. (Section E15.2)

frequency *f*: the number of complete oscillations that an observer at a fixed position would measure a sinusoidal wave to go through per unit time. (Section E15.2)

gamma rays: electromagnetic waves with wavelengths shorter than about 30 pm (frequencies in excess of 10^{19} Hz). Such waves are generated primarily by protons and/or neutrons shifting energy levels in an atomic nucleus. (Section E16.6)

gauss (G): a unit of magnetic field strength equal to 10^{-4} T or 30 kN/C. (Section E7.5)

Gauss's Law: the local field equation that says that $\text{div}(\vec{E}) = \rho / \varepsilon_0$, linking the divergence of the electric field to the local presence of charge density. (Section E10.5)

Gauss's Law for the magnetic field: the local field equation that says that $\text{div}(\vec{\mathbb{B}}) = 0$. This equation puts restrictions on the kinds of magnetic fields that can exist. (Section E10.6)

Gauss's Law, the Integral Form: a version of Gauss's law that has been integrated to make the calculation of the electric fields of objects easier. (Section E12.1)

generator: a device that converts energy (usually mechanical energy of rotation) into electrical energy. (Section E8.4)

gradient: the vector $[\partial\phi/\partial x, \partial\phi/\partial y, \partial\phi/\partial z]$, where ϕ is a scalar function of *x*, *y*, and *z*. The electric field vector at a point is the negative gradient of the electric potential at that point. (Section E4.3)

gravitational field vector $\vec{g}$: the vector that (in the newtonian gravity) represents the gravitational field at a point in space in the same way that the vector $\vec{E}$ represents the electric field. This vector is defined to be the *gravitational force per unit mass* experienced by an infinitesimal test mass placed at the given position: $\vec{g} \equiv \vec{F}_g / m_{\text{test}}$. (Section E2.2)

gravitational potential ϕ_g: the potential energy per unit mass associated with a test particle placed in a gravitational field. This is the gravitational analogue to the electrostatic potential. (Section E4.1)

henry (H): The SI unit of inductance. 1 H = 1 Ω·s. (Section 14.3)

ideal battery approximation: assumes that energy losses to thermal energy during charge transport in a battery are zero. If this is true, then *all* of the energy given to the transported charge is converted to electrostatic potential energy, and the potential difference between the battery's electrodes will be equal to the battery's emf, irrespective of the current flowing in the battery. (Section E6.1)

inductance L: a quantity that expresses the degree to which a coil or loop induces an emf in *itself* in response to a given change in the current flowing through the coil. The inductance of a given coil is defined implicitly by the equation $|\mathcal{E}| = L|dI/dt|$. The SI unit of inductance is the *henry,* where 1 H = 1 Ω·s. (Section E14.3)

induction: the process by which an emf in a loop or coil is created as a result of its interaction with a magnetic field. (Section E8.2); the phenomenon whereby a *changing* magnetic flux through a conducting loop induces a current to flow in that loop. (Section E14.1)

infrared (light): electromagnetic waves with frequencies ranging from about 1×10^{12} Hz to a bit over 3×10^{14} Hz (wavelengths from 0.3 mm to 0.7 μm). Such waves are created mostly by thermal vibrations and processes. (Section E16.6)

insulator: In electrical contexts, an insulator is a material through which charges cannot easily move. Air, rubber, plastic, glass and amber are good insulators. (Section E1.6)

intensity I: the energy per time that an electromagnetic wave delivers per unit area to a surface directly perpendicular to the wave. (Section E16.3)

kilowatt-hour: a unit of electrical energy equal to the energy used during one hour at a rate of 1 kilowatt. This unit is the same as 3,600,000 J. (Section 5.5)

Larmor formula: The formula $P = \frac{2}{3}kq^2a^2/c^3$ that expresses the power radiated in the form of electromagnetic waves by an accelerating charge. (Section E16.4)

Lenz's law: asserts that the emf and/or current induced in a loop or coil seeks to *oppose* the change in magnetic field that induces it. (Section E14.2)

light: the common term for waves traveling through an electromagnetic field. (Section E1.1)

local field equation: An equation that links some characteristic of a field at a point to the presence of charge or current at that same point, ignoring the contributions to the field made by distant charges or currents. Such equations sidestep the problems that make action-at-a-distance equations incompatible with the theory of relativity. (Section E10.1).

longitudinal wave: a mechanical wave where the passing wave displaces the medium in a direction parallel to the wave's direction of motion. (Section E15.1)

loop rule: a rule stating that if you curl your right fingers in the direction of the current flowing in a loop, then your right thumb (1) indicates the direction of the magnetic field created at the loop's center, and (2) the south-to-north direction of the magnet equivalent to the loop. When applied to an Amperian loop this rule says that if you curl your right fingers in the direction of the circulation direction defined by the loop's segment vectors, your thumb indicates the direction of tile vectors on the surface bounded by the loop. (Section E8.2)

Lorentz force law: $\vec{F}_{\text{em}} = q[\vec{E} + (\vec{v}/c)\times \vec{\mathbb{B}}]$, which specifies the total electromagnetic force on a particle with charge q moving with speed v in a frame where the electric and magnetic fields are $\vec{E}$ and $\vec{\mathbb{B}}$. Even though the relative mix of $\vec{E}$ and $\vec{\mathbb{B}}$ varies from frame to frame, this equation gives the correct physical force measured in any given reference frame. (This equation also implicitly *defines* the electric and magnetic fields.) (Section E13.1)

LR circuit: a circuit consisting of a coil with significant inductance, a resistor, and possibly a power supply or battery. (Section E14.4)

magnet: any object able to exert magnetic forces on another magnet *and* on a ferromagnetic substance. (Section E7.1)

magnetic force law: $\vec{F}_m = q(\vec{v}/c)\times \vec{\mathbb{B}}$. This law summarizes empirical observations of the effect of magnetic fields on moving charged particles and defines the magnitude and units of $\vec{\mathbb{B}}$. (Section E7.5)

magnetic moment μ: a quantity that characterizes how strongly a current-carrying loop or a dipole magnet responds to a magnetic field. For example, the energy needed to turn either from having its axis aligned with the field to having it anti-aligned with the field is $2\mu B$. (Problem E8R.3)

magnetic monopole: a hypothetical particle or object having a single, isolated, magnetic pole. To the best of our current knowledge, magnetic monopoles do not exist. (Section E7.2)

magnetic permeability constant μ_0 : see **permeability constant**.

magnetic poles: the parts of a magnet that seem to be the source of the magnetic forces, analogous to the charges on an electrical dipole. A magnet always has exactly two unlike poles (breaking a magnet in two yields not two isolated poles but two magnets each with two poles). (Section E7.1)

magnetism: a general term for the phenomena associated with magnets and the non-electrostatic effects of moving charges on each other. (Section E1.1)

Maxwell's equations: The set of four equations that describe the behavior of dynamic electromagnetic fields. These equations are Gauss's law, Gauss's law for the magnetic field, the Ampere-Maxwell relation, and Faraday's law. See section E13.6 for a list of these equations. Together, these four equations provide a complete and relativistically self-consistent description of the electromagnetic field in all known (macroscopic) circumstances. (Section E13.6)

mechanical wave: any kind of wave where the medium carrying the wave is physically displaced by the wave. (Section E15.1)

microwaves: electromagnetic wave with frequencies above about 330 MHz and below about 1×10^{12} Hz (wavelengths from 1 m to 0.3 mm). (Section E16.6)

net charge: the sum of an object's total positive charge and its total negative charge, expressing the latter as a negative number. Thus an object having equal magnitudes of positive and negative charge has zero net charge. (Section E1.3)

negative: one of the two types of electric charge, specifically the type of charge carried by an electron. This type of charge is represented mathematically by a negative number. (Section E1.2)

neutron: see **proton, neutron, electron**.

normal vector: a vector perpendicular to a surface. See "nose vector."

north and south (magnetic poles): the conventional names for the two kinds of magnetic poles. A magnet's north pole is the pole that ends up pointing geographically northward when the magnet is suspended so that it can rotate freely in the earth's magnetic field. (Section E7.1)

nose vector: a unit vector attached to a tile that points in a direction perpendicular to the tile's surface, marking which way the tile faces. (Section E10.2)

number density n: the number of a specified type of particle per cubic meter in a given medium. In this chapter, n usually describes the number density of charge carriers. (Section E5.2)

ohm Ω: the SI unit of resistance: $1\ \Omega = 1\ \text{V}/\text{A}$. (Section E5.4)

Ohm's law: the assertion that the resistance of a conductor is generally independent of the current it conducts (for reasonably small currents). (Section E5.4)

ohmic: a conducting object or device that has an essentially constant resistance and thus obeys Ohm's law. Many simple kinds of conductors are at least approximately ohmic. (Section E5.4)

one-dimensional wave: a wave that depends on only x and t (as opposed to x,y,z and t). (Section E15.2)

(circuit elements in) **parallel:** We describe a set of circuit elements as connected in parallel if (1) a given electron flowing through the set will flow through exactly one element, and (2) if the elements are connected so that the voltage across each element is the same as the voltage across the set. (Section E6.5)

parallel-plate capacitor: a capacitor consisting of two parallel flat conducting plates whose separation is very small compared to the size of each plate. If its plates have area A and are separated by a distance s, the capacitance of such a capacitor is $C = \varepsilon_0 A/s$. This is useful as a simple model for many kinds of real capacitors. (Section E4.6)

partial derivative $\partial f/\partial x$: a derivative evaluated by treating as constant all variables a function $f(x,y,z)$ might depend on except the variable with respect to which one is taking the derivative. (Section E4.3)

period T: the time that an observer at a fixed position measures between successive crests of a sinusoidal wave. (Section E15.2)

permeability constant μ_0 : a constant equal to $1/\varepsilon_0 c^2 = 4\pi k/c^2$, where ε_0 is the permittivity constant, k is the Coulomb constant, and c is the speed of light. This constant is conventionally used in equations that link the magnetic field to the currents that create the field. (Section E9.1)

permittivity of free space or **permittivity constant** ε_0 : a constant equal to $1/4\pi k$, where k is the Coulomb constant. Like the Coulomb constant, this constant expresses the strength of the electromagnetic interaction. (Section E1.5)

permittivity (of a material). See problem E4S.12.

plates (of a capacitor): see **capacitor.**

phase velocity: the velocity of a given feature (such as the crest) of a sinusoidal wave. The magnitude of a wave's phase velocity is its **phase speed.** (Section E15.3)

plane wave: A wave in a three-dimensional space whose value depends on only one of the three spatial coordinates, meaning that the disturbance has the same value on the plane spanned by the other two coordinates. (Section E16.1)

polarization (of a substance): the degree to which the atoms or molecules of a substance have been converted to aligned dipoles by an external electric field. (Section E2.6)

positive: one of the two types of electric charge, specifically, the type of charge carried by the proton. This type of charge is represented mathematically by a positive number (Section E1.2)

positron: the antiparticle corresponding to the electron. It has the same mass and other characteristics as the electron, but is oppositely charged. (Section E1.4)

principle of relativity: the principle that states that the laws of physics are the same in all inertial reference frames. (Section E13.1)

principle of superposition: see **superposition.**

proton, neutron, electron: subatomic particles that are the basic building blocks of the atom. The nucleus of an atom is constructed of protons and neutrons, which have almost equal masses of 1.67×10^{-27} kg (Avogadro's number of either has a mass of about 1.0 g). The proton has a positive charge, while the neutron has no charge. Electrons have a mass roughly 1800 times smaller, and have negative electrical charge whose absolute value is the same as the positive charge of the proton. A normal atom contains an equal number of protons and electrons. An atom's electrons form an **electron cloud** that surrounds the nucleus and is bound to it by electrostatic attraction. (Section E1.3)

radio waves: electromagnetic waves with frequencies below about 330 MHz. Such waves are primarily created by the bulk motion of charges (Section E16.6)

Rayleigh scattering: A process where incident light causes the charged parts of an atom or molecule to oscillate and thus re-radiate the light in all directions with the same frequency. Higher-frequency light is more effectively scattered than lower-frequency light by a factor of ω^4. (Section E16.5)

resistance R**:** the ratio of the potential difference V between a conductor's ends to the current I driven through the conductor by that potential difference: $R \equiv V/I$. The resistance so defined usually depends on temperature and may also be a function of current, but for many conductors, R is essentially independent of I. (Section E5.4)

resistor: technically, a circuit element specifically manufactured to have a certain fixed resistance. More generally, we can use this word to describe to any circuit element that is at least approximately ohmic. (Section E6.4)

(magnetic) **right-hand rule:** a rule stating that when a particle with charge q moves with velocity v in a magnetic field $\vec{B}$, pointing your right index finger in the direction of $q\vec{v}$ and your longest finger in the direction of $\vec{B}$ aligns your thumb with the direction of the magnetic force $\vec{F}_m$ on the particle. The same rule yields the direction of the cross product of two vectors: if you point your right index finger in the direction of $\vec{u}$ and your second finger in the direction of $\vec{w}$, your thumb indicates the direction of $\vec{u} \times \vec{w}$ (see the **cross product rule**). (Section E7.3)

segment vector $d\vec{S}$ **:** see **step vector**.

seismic wave: a wave created by an earthquake that causes the earth's crust to displace as the wave passes. (Section E15.1)

(circuit elements in) **series:** we say that two batteries are *in series* if the positive terminal of one is connected to the negative terminal of the other. The potential difference across two batteries in series is the sum of the voltage differences across each battery alone. (Section E6.2) We say that a general set of circuit elements is *in series* if every charge carrier that goes through one element goes through each other element in the set in sequence. (Section E6.3)

shell theorem: a theorem stating that (1) the potential or electric field outside a spherical shell with a uniformly distributed charge is exactly as if that charge had been concentrated at a point at the shell's center, and (2) the potential in the empty space inside the shell is a constant, implying that the electric field there is zero. (Section E3.3)

sinusoidal wave: a wave where the disturbance of the medium as a function of time can be described by the function $f(t,x) = A\sin(kx-\omega t)$. (Section E15.2)

solenoid: a coil of wire consisting of a number of turns of wire wrapped around some cylindrical form. (Section E11.4)

sound waves: a wave traveling through a medium that compresses or stretches the medium as the wave passes. (Section E15.1)

spherically symmetric charge distribution: a distribution that is unchanged by rotation around any axis. (Section E3.2)

static (field): A field that does not change with time. (Section E1.1)

static equilibrium charge distribution: the distribution of charges on the surface of a conducting object after charges have redistributed themselves so that they can remain at rest. (Section E4.4)

step vector $d\vec{S}$: an infinitesimal step along the boundary of a surface. The magnitude of this vectors is the distance stepped. This is closely related to a side vector, but is used to refer to a small step along a given path instead of specifically describing the side of a tile. (Section E12.4)

superposition principle: states that the force vector or field vector or potential created at a given point by a collection of charged particles is the sum of the force vectors or field vectors or potentials that each individual charged particle produces at that point. (Sections E1.5, E2.4, E3.1)

symmetry argument: a technique for determining useful characteristics of an electromagnetic field created by a charge or current distribution that is not changed by an operation like a rotation around an axis, translation along an axis, or mirror reflection across a plane. (Section E3.2)

terminals: the charged plates of a cell or battery where the chemical reactions take place that maintain a certain potential difference between the two electrodes. (Section E6.1) Also calledthe battery's **electrodes**.

tension wave: a wave traveling along a flexible line (like a string or rope) under tension that causes displacements perpendicular to the line as the wave passes. (Section E15.1)

tesla (T): the official unit of magnetic field strength defines to be 1 $(\text{N/C})(\text{m/s})^{-1}$.

test charge: a point particle with a tiny charge that we use (at least in our imagination) to measure the electric field around a charge distribution. The electric field at a point in space at a given instant of time is defined to be the force experienced by such a test charge at rest divided by the charge of the test charge: $\vec{E} \equiv \vec{F}_e / q_{\text{test}}$. (The test charge is assumed to be tiny so that it doesn't disturb the charge distribution whose field is being measured.) (Section E2.2)

tile: an infinitesimal patch of area, visualized as being a tiny square with a nose vector pointing perpendicular to its surface and (possibly) edge vectors pointing counterclockwise around its edges. (Sections E10.2 and E11.1)

tile vector $d\vec{A}$ **:** a vector that points perpendicular to a tile and has a magnitude equal to the tile's area. (Section E10.2)

transformer: a device that uses induction to transfer electrical power from one circuit to another while changing the emf at which that power is delivered. (Section E14.6)

transverse wave: a mechanical wave where the passing wave displaces the medium in a direction perpendicular to the wave's direction of motion. (Section E15.1)

traveling wave: a wave whose basic shape is preserved in time and whose shape moves through the medium as time progresses. (Section E15.3)

triboelectric series: a list of materials arranged in such an order that if two matterials on the list are rubbed against each other, the one higher on the list loses electrons to the one lower on the list. (Section E1.3)

uniform (field): a field whose field vectors have the same magnitude and direction at all points.

ultraviolet (light): electromagnetic waves whose wavlengths range from about 400 nm to 3 nm. Such waves are primarily produced by electrons changing energy levels in atoms.

vector function $\vec{f}(x,y,z)$: a function that implicitly assigns a vector to every point [x, y, z] in space by specifying how we can calculate the vector $\vec{f}$ given the coordinate values x, y, and z of that point. (Section E2.2)

velocity selector: a device that uses crossed electric and magnetic fields to permit only those charged particles having a certain specific velocity to pass

volt: the SI unit of electric potential. 1 V = 1 J/C. (Section E4.1)

voltage (at a point in a circuit): another name for potential ("voltage" is commonly used in circuit contexts). (Section E6.3)

voltage drop V (across a conductor): the absolute value of the potential difference between the conductor's ends.

water wave: a wave traveling along the surface of a body of water that causes water near the surface to displace both horizontally and vertically as the wave passes. (Section E15.1)

wave: a disturbance that moves through a medium, while the medium itself remains basically at rest. (Section E15.1)

(one-dimensional) **wave equation:** an equation of the form shown in equation E15.14. If such an equation follows from the basic physics of a certain medium, then disturbances in the form of one-dimensional traveling waves can exist in the medium. (Section E15.4)

wavelength λ: the distance between successive crests in a sinusoidal wave at any given instant of time. (Section E15.2)

wavenumber k: the number of radians of oscillation that a sinusoidal wave goes through per unit length. (Section E15.2)

wire rule: The rule stating that if you point your thumb in the direction of the conventional current carried by a wire, the magnetic field will curl around the wire in the same direction as your right fingers. (Section E8.2)

X-rays: electromagnetic waves with frequencies ranging from roughly 10^{17} Hz to 10^{19} Hz (wavelengths from 3 nm down to 30 pm). Such waves are created technologically primarily by crashing electron beams into metal targets.

Index

Note: Page numbers followed by *f* indicate figures.
Page numbers followed by *t* indicate tables.

Legend: 1 — Atomic number; **H** — Symbol; 1.008 — Atomic mass

1 1A	2 2A	3 3B	4 4B	5 5B	6 6B	7 7B	8	9 8B	10	11 1B	12 2B	13 3A	14 4A	15 5A	16 6A	17 7A	18 8A
1 **H** 1.008																	2 **He** 4.003
3 **Li** 6.941	4 **Be** 9.012											5 **B** 10.81	6 **C** 12.01	7 **N** 14.01	8 **O** 16.00	9 **F** 19.00	10 **Ne** 20.18
11 **Na** 22.99	12 **Mg** 24.31											13 **Al** 26.98	14 **Si** 28.09	15 **P** 30.97	16 **S** 32.07	17 **Cl** 35.45	18 **Ar** 39.95
19 **K** 39.10	20 **Ca** 40.08	21 **Sc** 44.96	22 **Ti** 47.88	23 **V** 50.94	24 **Cr** 52.00	25 **Mn** 54.94	26 **Fe** 55.85	27 **Co** 58.93	28 **Ni** 58.69	29 **Cu** 63.55	30 **Zn** 65.39	31 **Ga** 69.72	32 **Ge** 72.59	33 **As** 74.92	34 **Se** 78.96	35 **Br** 79.90	36 **Kr** 83.80
37 **Rb** 85.47	38 **Sr** 87.62	39 **Y** 88.91	40 **Zr** 91.22	41 **Nb** 92.91	42 **Mo** 95.94	43 **Tc** (98)	44 **Ru** 101.1	45 **Rh** 102.9	46 **Pd** 106.4	47 **Ag** 107.9	48 **Cd** 112.4	49 **In** 114.8	50 **Sn** 118.7	51 **Sb** 121.8	52 **Te** 127.6	53 **I** 126.9	54 **Xe** 131.3
55 **Cs** 132.9	56 **Ba** 137.3	57 **La** 138.9	72 **Hf** 178.5	73 **Ta** 180.9	74 **W** 183.9	75 **Re** 186.2	76 **Os** 190.2	77 **Ir** 192.2	78 **Pt** 195.1	79 **Au** 197.0	80 **Hg** 200.6	81 **Tl** 204.4	82 **Pb** 207.2	83 **Bi** 209.0	84 **Po** (210)	85 **At** (210)	86 **Rn** (222)
87 **Fr** (223)	88 **Ra** (226)	89 **Ac** (227)	104 **Rf** (257)	105 **Db** (260)	106 **Sg** (263)	107 **Bh** (262)	108 **Hs** (265)	109 **Mt** (266)	110	111	112	(113)	114	(115)	116	(117)	

58 **Ce** 140.1	59 **Pr** 140.9	60 **Nd** 144.2	61 **Pm** (147)	62 **Sm** 150.4	63 **Eu** 152.0	64 **Gd** 157.3	65 **Tb** 158.9	66 **Dy** 162.5	67 **Ho** 164.9	68 **Er** 167.3	69 **Tm** 168.9	70 **Yb** 173.0	71 **Lu** 175.0
90 **Th** 232.0	91 **Pa** (231)	92 **U** 238.0	93 **Np** (237)	94 **Pu** (242)	95 **Am** (243)	96 **Cm** (247)	97 **Bk** (247)	98 **Cf** (249)	99 **Es** (254)	100 **Fm** (253)	101 **Md** (256)	102 **No** (254)	103 **Lr** (257)